INDIAN ESTUARIES

INDIAN ESTUARIES

S. Z. Qasim

ALLIED PUBLISHERS PVT. LIMITED

NEW DELHI • MUMBAI • KOLKATA • LUCKNOW • CHENNAI
NAGPUR • BANGALORE • HYDERABAD • AHMEDABAD

ALLIED PUBLISHERS PVT. LIMITED

Regd. Off.: 15. J.N. Heredia Marg, Ballard Estate, Mumbai—400038
Prarthna Flats (2nd Floor), Navrangpura, Ahmedabad—380009
3-2-844/6&7, Kachiguda Station Road, Hyderabad—500027
16A Ashok Marg, Patiala House, Lucknow —226001
5th Main Road, Gandhinagar, Bangalore —560009
17 Chittaranjan Avenue, Kolkata —700072
81 Hill Road, Ramnagar, Nagpur —440010
1/13-14, Asaf Ali Road, New Delhi —110002
751 Anna Salai, Chennai —600002

ISBN: 81-7764-369-X

Sponsoring Editor	:	Jyoti Mehrotra
Photograph	:	Dr. V.V. Sugunan

Published by Sunil Sachdev and printed by Ravi Sachdev at Allied Publishers Pvt. Limited (Printing Division), A-104 Mayapuri, Phase II, New Delhi-110 064. Laser Typeset by Printek India, C1 Block, Local Shopping Centre, Janakpuri, New Delhi-110058. Phone: 5554775

Dedicated to

all my former colleagues
who have helped me in conducting researches
on estuaries

Preface

During the last four decades, considerable amount of work has been done on the estuaries of India, and as a result of this, several estuaries, both on the east and west coasts of India, are better known today than nearly a decade ago. Proximity of research establishments and university departments of marine sciences has accelerated researches on a wide variety of problems selected for postgraduate degree courses. For example, the Department of Marine Biology of Annamalai University — now known as the Centre of Advanced Study (CAS) in Marine Biology — established at Porto Novo (renamed as Parangipettai) in the fifties in Tamil Nadu State along the banks of Vellar Estuary, had planned and executed enormous amount of work on hydrography, faunistic survey, phytoplankton and zooplankton ecology, intertidal fauna, benthic studies, ecology of Pichavaram mangroves, microbiology, etc., of the estuary. Collaboration of the CAS with the University of Southampton and Marine Laboratory, Aberdeen (UK), encouraged the visits of well known scientists like K.R. Dyer, J.D. Burton, A.D. McIntyre and several others to Porto Novo, and this stimulated new lines of investigations. Similarly, during the period 1960-65, when the programme entitled "International Indian Ocean Expedition" (IIOE) was going on, a new project called the "International Biological Programme" (IBP) started functioning at Cochin (renamed as Kochi) on the "Productivity and Food Chains of Specialised Environments" which included Cochin Backwaters, sandy beaches and coral reefs. The visit of Dr. J.H. Steele, FRS, from the Marine Laboratory, Aberdeen to Cochin in mid-sixties promoted a joint project between Cochin and Aberdeen on the ecology and food chain of tropical sandy beaches. This brought A.D. Ansell, A. Trevellion, J.H. Blaxter and several others from Aberdeen to Cochin and also resulted in reciprocal visits of Indian scientists to Aberdeen. The author of the book, being fully involved in the IBP, started studies on Cochin Backwaters in 1964, which continued till he joined the National Institute of Oceanography (NIO) at Goa in 1974. Several related institutions at Cochin such as the Indian Ocean Biological Centre (IOBC), the Department of Marine Sciences of Cochin University, Fisheries Institutes and Indo-Norwegian Fishery Project collaborated in the work on estuaries in many ways by providing shipboard and manpower facilities for the collection of data and samples. The IOBC, in particular, stimulated the work on estuarine zooplankton considerably. Thus, the foundation of an organised estuarine research in India laid on the backwaters has resulted in continuing some of the lines of investigations even today. At Karwar, the presence of a Post-Graduate Centre in the Department of Marine Biology of Karnataka University has led to several investigations on Kali Estuary. Likewise, the establishment of the main laboratory, National Institute of Oceanography (NIO), at Goa on a hilly terrain, bordering the Mandovi-Zuari Estuarine System, promoted considerable work in different fields on these estuaries. The Regional Centre of NIO at Bombay (Mumbai) stimulated environmental investigations on the estuaries of Bombay and southern Gujarat. Many of these were carried out as projects sponsored by the industries on pollution control. Dr. M.D. Zingde, the Scientist-in-Charge of the Bombay Centre was the key person heading the various projects.

The work on different estuaries, backwaters and mangroves of the southern-most west coast including the Asthamudi Estuary has largely been carried out by the Department of Aquatic Biology, Kerala University at Trivandrum (renamed as Thiruvananthapuram). The leader of the scientific team was Prof. N.B. Nair, and his association benefitted the estuarine researches a great deal.

Similarly, besides CAS at Vellar, if we look at the genesis of estuarine research along the other regions of the east coast of India, we find a similar situation. The presence of the Department of Marine Biology of Calcutta University was responsible for several detailed studies on the Hooghly Estuary; the Department of Marine Sciences of Berhampur University for the work on Rushikulya Estuary and the Centres of Marine Biology of Andhra and Karnataka Universities for Godavari and Cauvery estuaries. Several research institutions located at Chennai (previously known as Madras) contributed towards the study on pollution problems in the three estuaries (Adyar, Cooum and Ennore) of the Madras region.

The emphasis and totality of the problems investigated in different estuaries were often diverse and varied, and these were worked out as the situation demanded. In some estuaries, where long-term researches lasting for several decades were conducted, the total emerging picture was comprehensive, and these have been described under separate themes and sub-titles. In others, whatever useful and authenic information was available, has been taken into consideration in specific terms.

So far, no book has been written on Indian Estuaries. A collection of brief accounts of the works carried out for 10 years, between 1985 and 1995, on many estuaries of both the coasts of India has appeared in the form of a report in 1997. This has been compiled by the Environmental Information System Centre

(ENVIS) and has proved to be useful while writing the present book. Another report (mimeo), listing the fauna recorded from different estuaries, has been prepared by the Zoological Survey of India in 1985. Of the many seminars, symposia and workshops on estuaries held from time to time in India, two are worth mentioning. One was held in February 1975 at Cochin and the proceedings of which were published under the title "Contributions to Estuarine Biology" in 1977 edited by Prof. C. V. Kurian. The other was held at Trivandrum in June 1985 and its proceedings entitled "Estuarine Management" were brought out in 1987 edited by Prof. N.B. Nair. Many papers appearing in these two volumes have been cited in the present book under relevant sections dealing with different estuaries.

The basic idea behind brining out this book is to provide as much information as possible on each estuary and to indicate how a particular estuary behaved in terms of its richness of flora and fauna and how the tidal regime and seasonal cycle of considerable freshwater discharge during the monsoon season drastically changed its hydrobiological conditions during the year. It is also intended to evaluate the extent the estuary has been polluted and what are the sources of pollution. In providing the different types of information, lack of uniformity became inevitable, because all types of information were not available uniformly on each estuary. Hence, the emphasis on certain features changed from one estuary to the other. Some shortcomings may be noticed by the reader because he may find some searching references omitted, while some casual observations included. The author offers no excuse for this, except to say that a cut-off of earlier works had to be fixed so that the book could be completed within a reasonable time period. Some estuaries on which the available information was too fragmentary have not been included. Contrarily, on several estuarine system, extensive information was available on mangroves. This information has been included on some in a highly abbreviated form because there are so many books and monographs already available on mangrove ecosystems of India and south-east Asia. Even though, the literature on mangroves has been expanding so fast, there is a need for separate books to be written on this topic, even today.

Lack of adequate library facilities on marine and estuarine biology in New Delhi, where the book has been written, was the main constraint. However, this has largely been compensated by Dr. M.P. Tapaswi, the Documentation Officer of NIO, Goa by his prompt and speedy response using the electronic mail and other forms of communication in providing information required from time to time. His labour-intensive efforts in sending the list of relevant references on each estuary and voluminous photocopies of reprints under the auspices of the National Information Centre for Marine Sciences (NICMAS), which he is running so efficiently, became the most valuable source of sharing information for me. I would like to thank him and his colleagues for unhesitantly yielding to my demands and questioning throughout the process of writing. Similarly, Dr. M.D. Zingde and Dr. K.K.C. Nair, the Scientists-in-Charge of the two Regional Centres at Mumbai and Kochi helped me in giving an access to the publications of their centres on estuaries. The overall interest of Dr. E. Desa, Director, NIO, Goa in my writing this book has been inspiring and the freedom that he gave to all his colleagues to interact with me, as and when required, has proved to be most productive and rewarding.

I must express my gratefulness to several of my former colleagues at the NIO, Goa, who have helped me a great deal in revising the draft of the book, Dr. P. M.A. Bhattathiri has gone through the manuscript from cover to cover and the corrections he made on phytoplankton organisms have been very valuable. Similarly, Dr. M. Madhupratap and Dr. S.C. Goswami have carefully checked the portions on zooplankton. Dr. S. R. Shetye has seen the part relevant to his work on tidal propagation. Dr. S. N. Harkantra and Dr. Z. A. Ansari have gone through the sections on bottom communities and intertidal fauna. Dr. (Mrs) Shanta Achuthankutty has read the portions on microbiology. Dr. Anil Chatterji and Dr. B.S. Ingole have seen the sections related to fish and fisheries. Dr. (Mrs). S. Wafar has taken pains to revise the Table 12.4 (Section II) and has checked the portions on mangroves. Dr. M.D. Zingde has seen the sections on estuaries of Mumbai region and southern Gujarat. The overall supervision of Dr. M.V.M. Wafar in the revision of the book is indeed greatly appreciated.

The writing of the book would not have been possible without the support rendered by the Society for Indian Ocean Studies and I must express my gratitude to Prof. Satish Chandra, the Secretary-General of the Society for his interest in the book; to Dr. Kishore Kumar, the Joint Secretary of the Society for his efforts in many matters and to Dr. S.A.I. Rizvi of the Society for going through the entire manuscript of the book in its early stages and making improvements. His advice has been extremely helpful. Shri K.J. Sajy supervised the incorporation of corrections in figures and Ms. Rekha T.K. did the entire data entry in tables and computerisation work skillfully in a highly commendable manner. Mr. Shibu Verghese has spent a great deal of time and efforts in computer drawing of the figures. I would like to express my appreciation and admiration to all of them individually.

New Delhi
March 2001

S.Z. Qasim

Contents

Dedication v
Preface vii
Introduction 1

Section I

Climatic features of the east coast **19**

Chapter 1. Hooghly (Hugli) 27
Chapter 2. Rushikulya 56
Chapter 3. Godavari 67
Chapter 4. Ennore 95
Chapter 5. Cooum 105
Chapter 6. Adyar 114
Chapter 7. Vellar 123
Chapter 8. Cauvery (Kaveri) 168

Section II

Climatic features of the west coast **183**

Chapter 9. Ashtamudi 189
Chapter 10. Cochin Backwaters and Vembanad 201
Chapter 11. Kali 264

Chapter 12.	Mandovi-Zuari System	277
Chapter 13.	Estuaries of Mumbai (Bombay) region	318
	a. Bombay Harbour/Thana Creek	326
	b. Mahim	332
	c. Amba	336
Chapter 14.	Estuaries of Southern Gujarat	345
	a. Mahi	349
	b. Narmada (Narbada)	354
	c. Tapi (Tapti)	356
	d. Mindhola	358
	e. Purna	362
	f. Ambika	365
	g. Auranga	368
	h. Par	371
	i. Kolak	375
	j. Damanganga	378
Conclusion		382
Subject Index		391
Author Index		411

Introduction

Since ancient times, estuaries in India have been a focal point of activities – for human settlement, for development of ports and harbours to be used for transportation of men and material and for trade and commerce. One of the earliest archaeological evidences of maritime activity in India is from a tidal dockyard built in 2300 BC by the Harappans at Lothal (Gujarat coast). Located in the Sabarmati Estuary at the head of the Gulf of Cambay (Khambhat), the Bhogava – a tributary of the Sabarmati River – was used to navigate sizeable ships at high water to reach Lothal Port (Panikkar & Srinivasan, 1971; Rao, 1979), where they could dock along the basin. Figure 1 shows the location of the ancient town of Lothal in relation to the river Sabarmati at the head of Gulf of Cambay. The excavated structure is a trapezoidal or sub-rectangular embankment or basin on the eastern flank of Lothal, excavated, lined and closed by masonry walls of kiln-burnt bricks (Plate 1A). The length of the basin is 212.4 m on the west, 209.3 m on the east, 34.7 m on the south and 36.6m on the north (Nigam, 1988). The foundation of the embankment walls of the basin was 1.78 m wide which decreased to 1.04 m at the ground level. This embankment was connected with the open marine environment with a tidal range of about 5.5 m through the Sabarmati Estuary. The connection was lost due to shoaling of the Gulf of Cambay probably during Holocene. The Harappan's seals, stone weight and anchors (Plate 1B), terracotta boat models, beads of gemstones and many other objects retrieved from the adjoining areas of the dock indicate the existence of extensive overseas trade from Lothal. The occurrence of Indus seals (Harappan's) and other nonperishable objects from Bahrain, Oman, Mesopotamia and ivory pieces of Indian origin in Ugarit (Syria) suggest far-flung trade with India. Lothal was known for its pure copper and this was an important commodity for trade.

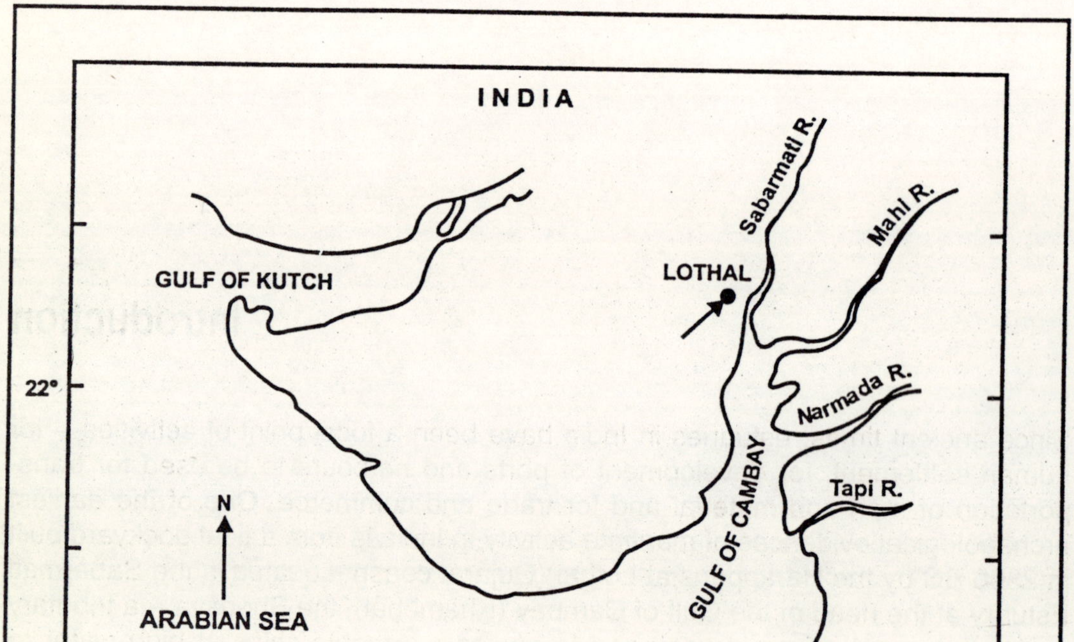

Fig. 1 Map of Gujarat State showing the location of Lothal where the Harappans built a dockyard in 2,300 BC (From Nigam, 1988)

The Peninsular India, comprising Tamil Nadu and Kerala, has also been exposed to international trade since sixth century BC and much activity occurred between 3rd century BC and 3rd century AD from the ancient ports (small or big) located at almost all river mouths. Authentic evidences reveal voluminous commercial activity carried out from the ports of Arikamedu, Kaveripattinam, Alangkulam and Korkai located at the mouths of the rivers Aryyankuppam, Kaveri, Vaigal and Tambraparani (Fig. 2.). Korkai was the capital and an important port of the Pandyans in the centuries preceding the Christian Era. Recent archaeological excavations at Korkai and carbon dating of the retrieved objects provide evidence that the merchants trading from several ports of Peninsular India to Babylon were mostly Dravidians. Babylon at that time was a great mercantile emporium and some of the Indian names of the goods imported and adopted in the west were the adaptations of Tamil words (found in the Hebrew text of the Old Testament). The submerged port of Kaveripattinam, at the mouth of the river Cauvery (Kaveri) had a colony exclusively for Greeks which is a testimony of their well-established contact with India in the 3rd century BC (Rajan, 1988).

In India, the combined length of 113 major and minor rivers is 45,000 km (Envis, 1997) and several metropolitan cities like Bombay (Mumbai), Calcutta (Kolkata), Madras (Chennai), Cochin (Kochi), and major towns of Goa have developed around estuaries. In fact, most of the great cities of the world like London, New York, Tokyo, Shanghai, Buenos Aires, Osaka, Los Angeles, etc., are situated along the estuaries.

Prof. K.R. Dyer of Southhampton University, while writing a preface to his book entitled *Estuaries: a Physical Introduction* states "I think that one of the interesting things about estuaries is that they are so complicated". If I were to add another phrase to this statement, it would be that *no two days in any estuary are ever alike*. Estuaries form the meeting places of freshwater and seawater and share the common features of both the regimes and their interactions. Tides, and their action vary from day to day and their penetration upstream further makes the estuarine environment more complex. Tidal action, river flow and distribution of suspended matter and sediment are continuously changing and therefore no two estuaries will ever be alike and they will never be in a steady-state to attain a balance. Evidently, all these interactions are interlinked and it would not be easy to take them into account into a single classification.

Attempts have been made from time to time to provide a realistic definition of an estuary. Pritchard (1952) classified the estuaries, based on their topographic differences into (1) coastal plain estuaries, (2) fjords and (3) bar-built estuaries.

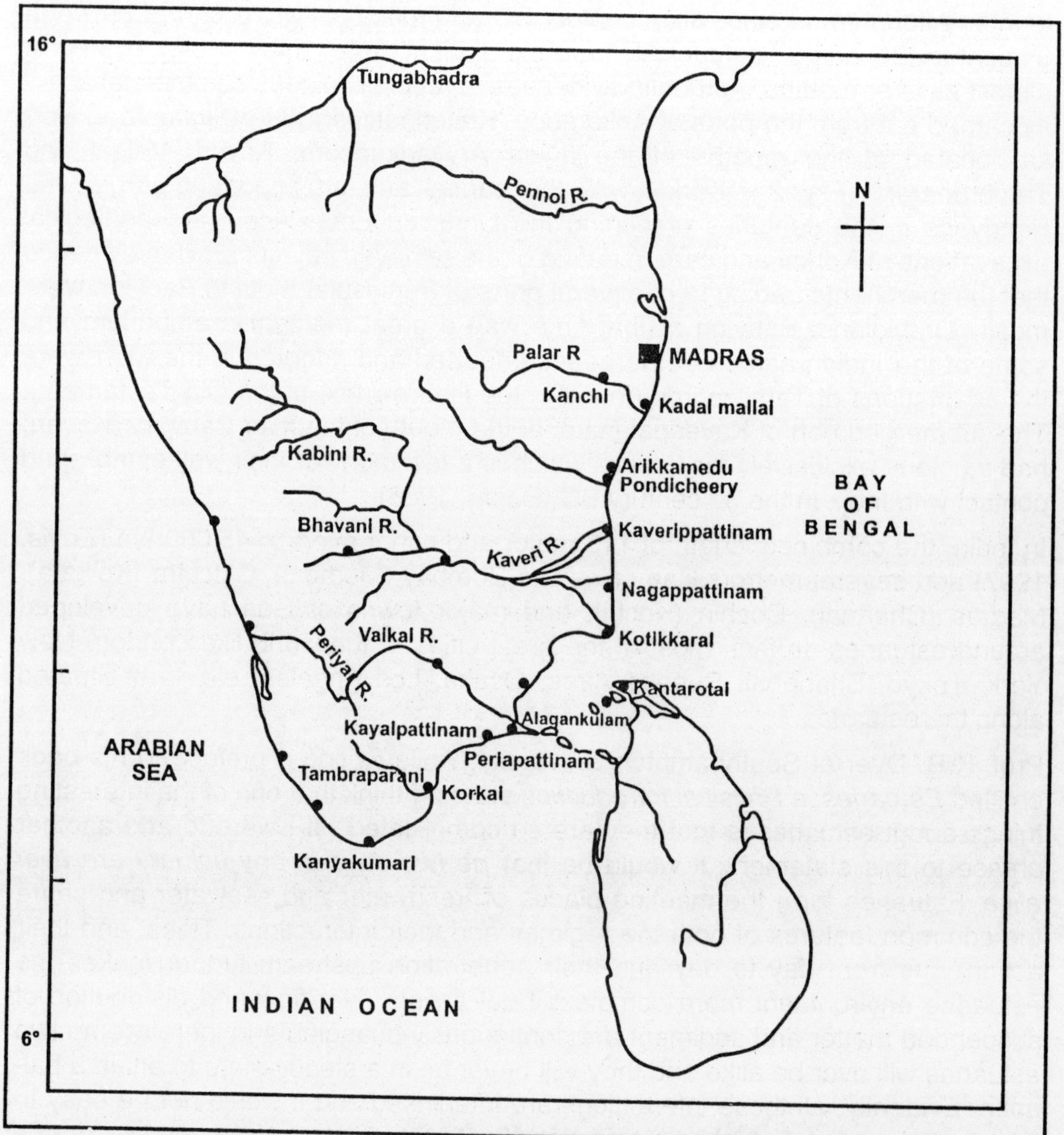

Fig. 2 Map of southern India showing the ancient ports of Tamil Nadu coast which were used for trade with outside world (From Rajan, 1988)

Coastal plain estuaries are generally restricted to coastal regions of temperate latitudes where the river flow is relatively small as compared to the volume of tidal prism (the volume between high and low water levels) and the amount of sediment discharged by them is also small. Fjords are the areas occurring in the mountainous regions of northern Europe, particularly Scandinavia, in the form of coastal indentation. They have rocky floors of very thin sediment and the river enters at the head of fjords with a small discharge as compared to the total volume of the fjord. Their depths range from 40 to 800 m and their outline is rectangular and sharp. Bar-built estuaries are generally shallow with extensive waterways and reservoirs of brackishwater. These are generally associated with large volumes of river water and sediment and are found in tropical latitudes where large deposition of sediment occurs. Bars are formed when there is a considerable flow of river water and these get swept when the flow decreases and are re-established when the flow increases. The definition given by Pritchard (1952) also allows for positive and negative estuaries. In the former, the freshwater inflow from river discharge, precipitation and runoff exceed the losses occurring by evaporation and in the latter, evaporation exceeds the freshwater inputs, resulting in hypersaline conditions.

The definition most widely and commonly adopted is that of Cameron & Pritchard (1965) which states "An estuary is a semi-enclosed coastal body of water which has a free connection with the open sea and within which seawater is measurably diluted with freshwater derived from land drainage". An important source of information is the volume on estuaries (Lauff, 1967) which gives a collection of papers contributed to a conference on "Estuaries" held in Georgia from March 31st to April 3, 1964. The main purpose of this conference was the exchange of ideas between experts in different disciplines and individuals interested in estuarine research, and to summarize the knowledge on estuaries and delineate the direction of research. The volume is undoubtedly a valuable addition to our knowledge on estuaries, as many of the papers deal with the definition and characteristics of the estuaries, and outline the physical, chemical and biological processes. It also includes papers on geology and physics. Unfortunately, it provides very little information on tropical estuaries except on "Estuarine fisheries of the Indian Ocean coastal zone" by T.V.R Pillay. This may be because very little information was available from different regions of lower latitudes at that time and the number of scientists attending the Conference from regions, other than Europe and North America, was limited.

As noted earlier, it is not easy to define an estuary. Nevertheless, an analysis of some of the classical definitions and criteria given earlier would be an useful exercise before attempting to summarize the works done on Indian estuaries. Emery & Stevenson (1957) define an estuary as "wide mouth of a river or an arm of the sea where the tide meets the river currents". Emery (1967) indicates the regional distribution of estuaries corresponds to the regional characteristics of the continental shelves and their continuation with the land (coastal plain). Large estuaries occur where the shelves and coastal plains are wide and nearly flat. Small estuaries, on the other hand, are found where shelves and coastal plains are narrow. Backwaters can be caused by marine deposition of offshore bars and large areas covered by sedimentation. Once formed, estuaries tend to get destroyed by the aggregation of freshwater or brackishwater marshes at their heads or by the deposition of marine marshes and sand islands. Most estuaries are drowned lower ends of the river system. Coastal plain estuaries commonly originate or become modified by the depositional land forms. Advancing deltas are the most formidable natural enemies of estuaries (Russell, 1967).

While giving the biological characteristics of estuaries, Day (1951) remarks that distribution of animals in estuaries can not be based on a single factor. Some animals become adapted to the environmental fluctuations in estuaries and these represent a relatively stable group but do not contain a large variety of animals (Caspers, 1967). Lack of diversity (monotony) of estuarine population has been pointed out by Hedgpeth (1957). Estuarine organisms are mainly euryhaline marine forms which are able to penetrate and exist in an unstable biotope. Such specialized organisms are non-existent in upper reaches of the estuary. Estuaries can be invaded more easily in warm, tropical waters because of the richness of fauna of tropical and subropical regions as compared to those of higher latitudes. The difference has been attributed to an osmoregulatory adaptation (ability) at higher temperatures. There are no flora and fauna which can be designated as strict brackishwater community. The assemblage consists of not only brackish-water organisms which are adapted to a range of brackishwater fluctuations but should be able to adapt greater environmental changes such as found in monsoonal conditions (Hedgpeth, 1957).

The features common to all estuaries are those defined by Barnes (1974). These include a body of water of mixed origin, with a freshwater component supplied by appropriate river system and a marine component derived from the adjacent sea. The body of water of mixed origin does not occupy a constant position. It may move with the state of the tide and with changes in the volume of water dis-charged. The zone of mixing is only static if the freshwater discharge is constant throughout the year and if the tidal amplitude is negligible — the region being partially enclosed by a land mass. Hence, an estuary is primarily a hydrographical phenomenon. Knox (1986), while giving some special features of estuarine ecosystems, has stated that estuaries do differ from one to the other in their basic characteristics. They undoubtedly share a number of essential features on the basis of which generalizations could be made on their structure and function. Some of the unique properties of the estuaries such as retaining both freshwater and saltwater characteristics and high productivity are common to all estuaries. Other features are determined by local conditions, which make each estuary to own its individual and special characteristics (Ketchum, 1983).

Following Pritchard's (1967) classification, there can be the following three distinct types of the origin of estuaries in the Indian conditions:

1. Drowned river valleys – formed by a rise is sea level relative to land.
2. Rise in sea level due to land subsidence and invasion by the sea through the faultline extending to the coast.
3. Bar-built estuaries or semi-enclosed bays formed parallel to the coastline. The extensive development of these occurs in the form of a chain of islands enclosing a large shallow body of water receiving discharge from a number of rivers.

Formation of sand bars or shoals at the river mouth is another common feature to a large number of Indian estuaries which make navigation difficult and demand constant dredging. The bars are generally formed during the postmonsoon season while in others a gradual accumulation of sand continues.

Bowden (1980), while describing the main features of estuarine circulation and mixing has distinguished the following three broad categories:

1. Salt wedge estuaries, in which the saline water extends as a wedge in the river upstream.
2. Two-layered flow estuaries, in which no significant entrapment of freshwater occurs and the salinity at deeper layer remains unchanged.
3 Partially mixed estuaries, in which vertical mixing due to tidal currents extends throughout the depth and there is a gradual increase in salinity from surface to bottom.

One of the important aspects to note in the Indian estuaries is that salinity zonations such as saltwater zone, tidal gradient or mixed water zone and freshwater zones are not clearly defined. Instead, the regimes of three seasons in a year largely regulate the hydrography of the estuaries, viz.,

(a) the monsoon season from June to September (it may vary by a few months along the southeast coast) when the flow of a large volume of freshwater from the rivers and land runoff into the sea nullifies the effect of flood tides and there is a pronounced effect of the ebb tides;
(b) the postmonsoon season from October to January when there is a balance between flood and ebb tides (ebb gradually decreasing from October onwards and flood increasing); and
(c) the premonsoon season from February to May when the effect of flood is considerably stronger and widespread than that of the ebb.

Thus, salinity, phytoplankton production and zooplankton abundance and their distribution in most of the Indian estuaries are controlled by the three seasonal cycles noted above. In estuaries, phytoplankton flora, specifically adapted to the prevailing conditions in the habitat, have evolved (Smayda, 1983). Phytoplankton production is generally low during the monsoon period but the postmonsoon season is followed by blooms of diatoms and dinoflagellates leading to a high organic productivity. Zooplankton diversity and biomass are low during the monsoon season and high during the dry premonsoon season. Generally copepods form the dominant group. Fluctuations in zooplankton are directly related to changes in salinity. Carnivores such as hydromedusae, ctnophores, chaetognaths and several other forms appear in the estuary when the salinity is high during the dry season (premonsoon) increasing the biomass and diversity of zooplankton considerably.

In India, the largest esturaine area is the Ganges-Brahamputra Delta region along the east coast of India in West Bengal, commonly known as the Sunderbans area. Hooghly River Estuary, which has been studied fairly well, forms one of the main distributaries of this region.

Food chains in the estuaries differ from the open sea in several aspects. A greater part of the organic production in estuaries is controlled by larger plants (macroalgae, mangroves, etc.) rather than phytoplankton. As consumers of the organic matter, zooplankton become less important than the suspension and deposit feeders. These groups largely include benthic animals which are non-selective in the type of material they ingest. Organic detritus forms a major sources of food of the estuarine communities. Detritus has no strict definition and it has been identified in various forms. For example, suspended detritus includes floating particles of plant and animal remains, organic aggregates, bacterial collections around inert material, faecal pellets, etc. Settled detritus at the bottom consists of dead and decaying materials of larger plants, sediments rich in organic matter with dead planktonic and benthic microflora and fauna, etc. Thus, it seems that the trophic pathway from detritus, as a source of food, branches off towards micro and macroinvertebrates, nekton, benthic and sessile communities including bottom living fishes and prawns. Caloric value of detritus in one estuarine system of India has been found to range from 173 to 6057 cal/g dry wt (average 1463). In the other estuarine system, the range was smaller, 200-500 cal/g dry wt. In the former case, the detritus was from autochthonous sources which include besides phytoplankton, marginal submerged vegetation, filamentous algae, decaying mangrove leaves, periphyton, etc. (Kumari *et al.*, 1978) whereas in the latter case it was largely composed of swamp vegetation, riverborne material, marginal marshes, etc. (Qasim & Sankaranarayanan, 1972), and the contribution from mangrove vegetation was very limited. Hence, the range in caloric value was smaller. The sources of such detritus are probably allochthonous. In a mangrove ecosystem adjoining the Goa estuaries, the litter yield has been estimated to be 10.2 to 17.0 tonnes/ha/yr and thus contributing enormously to the carbon budget of the estuaries (Wafar *et al.*, 1997).

Estuaries all over the world have been used for land reclamation, developments of engineering works (coastal structures), harbours, shipping, sewage discharge, effluent discharge from industrial complexes, recreation and fisheries. Reclamation takes many years to develop housing colonies, new docks and industrial complexes. A small change in the geomorphology of estuaries may cause localised change in the current pattern and sediment distribution. But large harbour works such as the development of a sizeable container terminal may modify the environment considerably resulting in changes in the current pattern and substrata leading to drastic changes in fauna and flora. Such terminals are associated with dredging in the estuaries to maintain access to shipping. This disturbs the substrata making the water more turbid, and destroys the resident benthic fauna. Shipping further brings about changes in the estuaries by oil pollution and spillage of powdered cargoes during loading and unloading operations.

Sewage (treated, partially-treated and untreated), discharged from urban areas often creates serious situations if the estuary has a low flushing rate. Large volumes of organic matter with low dissolved oxygen, increase the microbial load and create anoxic conditions, often with the production of hydrogen sulphide. Such conditions deplete the normal pelagic and benthic flora and fauna and encourage the large abundance of polychaetes and nematodes which flourish in such anoxic conditions.

Similar conditions are provided by the industrial wastes which are discharged untreated along with domestic wastes through public sewers, specially constructed channels and rainwater drains. The impact of industrial pollutants could be short-lived if the toxicity is not high and the flushing rate is good. Lethal or sublethal concentrations of phenols, acids and alkalis may create heavy mortality if the dilution factor and flushing rate are limited. The discharge of non-degradable wastes such as heavy metals (zinc, copper, lead, mercury, cobalt, cadmium, etc.) or insecticides and pesticides used for agricultural operations and disease-control (DDT, PCB, Dieldrin) stay in the environment for a long time, get accumulated in fishes, crustaceans and molluscs and enter the human food chain, often with disastrous consequences.

The effect of wastes from the oil industry (refinery and petrochemical) or large spillage from ships may lead to diminshing quality of the environment and adverse effect on the estuarine bird, fish, crustacean and molluscan fauna. The residual hydrocarbon in the form of tar balls settles to the bottom and exerts ill-effect on commercial prawns, clams and other molluscan fisheries. All types of pollutants seriously affect the aesthetic value of the estuarine beaches and destroy their recreational use. The sheltered estuarine beaches provide excellent locations for swimming, diving and sailing and contamination of water often provides serious health problems.

From some estuarine complexes such as the Sunderbans, more than 120 species of fish, prawns and crabs are caught in commercial catches. Of these, some are occasional migrants. Major groups include clupeoids, mullets, milk fish, threadfins, pearl spots, catfishes, sciaenids, *Tilapia*, prawns and crabs. Molluscan forms include oysters, clams, mussels, etc. (Pillay, 1967). Fishing methods vary from place to place and the fisheries are of scattered type. Nevertheless, from the larger estuaries such as Hooghly, backwaters of Kerala, Vellar and Mandovi-Zuari, several thousand tonnes of edible varieties are caught annually. Fisheries in most of the estuarine systems are sustainable and continue throughout the year. During the monsoon season when coastal fishing gets suspended, estuaries form the mainstay and contribute to fish production significantly.

Many estuarine areas and mangrove swamps are being reclaimed as ponds for aquaculture of fish, prawns, etc. Different types of designs and layout have been adopted for brackishwater fish and prawn farms. Some are used with dikes to allow the tidal water with mullets, catfish, prawns, snapper, etc. to enter the farm and thus contributing to increased productivity of the pond, while others are specially prepared and heavily stocked with postlarvae of fish or prawns and fed on chemically-defined artificial feeds. In both cases, the farms are drained for harvesting. In this way, semi-intensive and intensive aquaculture practices, usually associated with the application of animal husbandry techniques (hatcheries, etc.), give astonishingly high yields. Thus, the socioeconomic benefits of estuaries are enormous. However, the large-scale man-made changes are definitely going to effect the multiple-use of the estuaries and an appraisal of the various forces and their consequences is urgently needed to make the estuaries fulfil our various economic needs.

The order in which the accounts on different estuaries has been presented in the book needs clarification and this is given below.

FORM OF PRESENTATION

The book has been divided into two Sections, I and II. Section I begins with the climatic conditions of the east coast of India. This is followed by the accounts on eight estuaries of this coast one after the other belonging to different littoral states, and all ending in the Bay of Bengal. The account begins with the northern-most estuary – the Hooghly (Hugli) – located in West Bengal. Thereafter, the estuaries have been described in descending order pertaining to different states — Rushikulya in Orissa and Godavari in Andhra Pradesh. Of the remaining five, three estuaries — Ennore, Cooum and Adyar — are in the Chennai region of Tamil Nadu and the fourth — Vellar — in southern Tamil Nadu. The fifth — Cauvery (Kaveri) — originates in Karnataka but ends in Tamil Nadu.

Section II begins with meteorological features of the west coast of India, followed by the description of estuaries in ascending order, and all ending in the Arabian Sea. The two southern-most estuaries of the west coast — Ashtamudi and Cochin Backwaters with its Vembanad Lake — are located in Kerala; Kali Estuary in Karnataka; Mandovi and Zuari Estuarine System in Goa; estuaries of Mumbai region (Bombay Harbour / Thane Creek, Mahim Creek and Amba) in Maharashtra. Finally, the account ends with ten estuaries of southern Gujarat, starting with Mahi which terminates in the northern-most part of the Gulf of Khambhat (Cambay), followed by nine others of this state in descending order. This form of presentation has been selected for the sake of convenience, and it is greatly hoped that it will not make the book difficult to read and follow.

Figure 3 shows diagrammatic representation of the 25 estuaries described in the book in the map of India. The map indicates 8 estuaries along the east and 17 estuaries on the west coast including 3 from the Mumbai region and 10 from southern Gujarat.

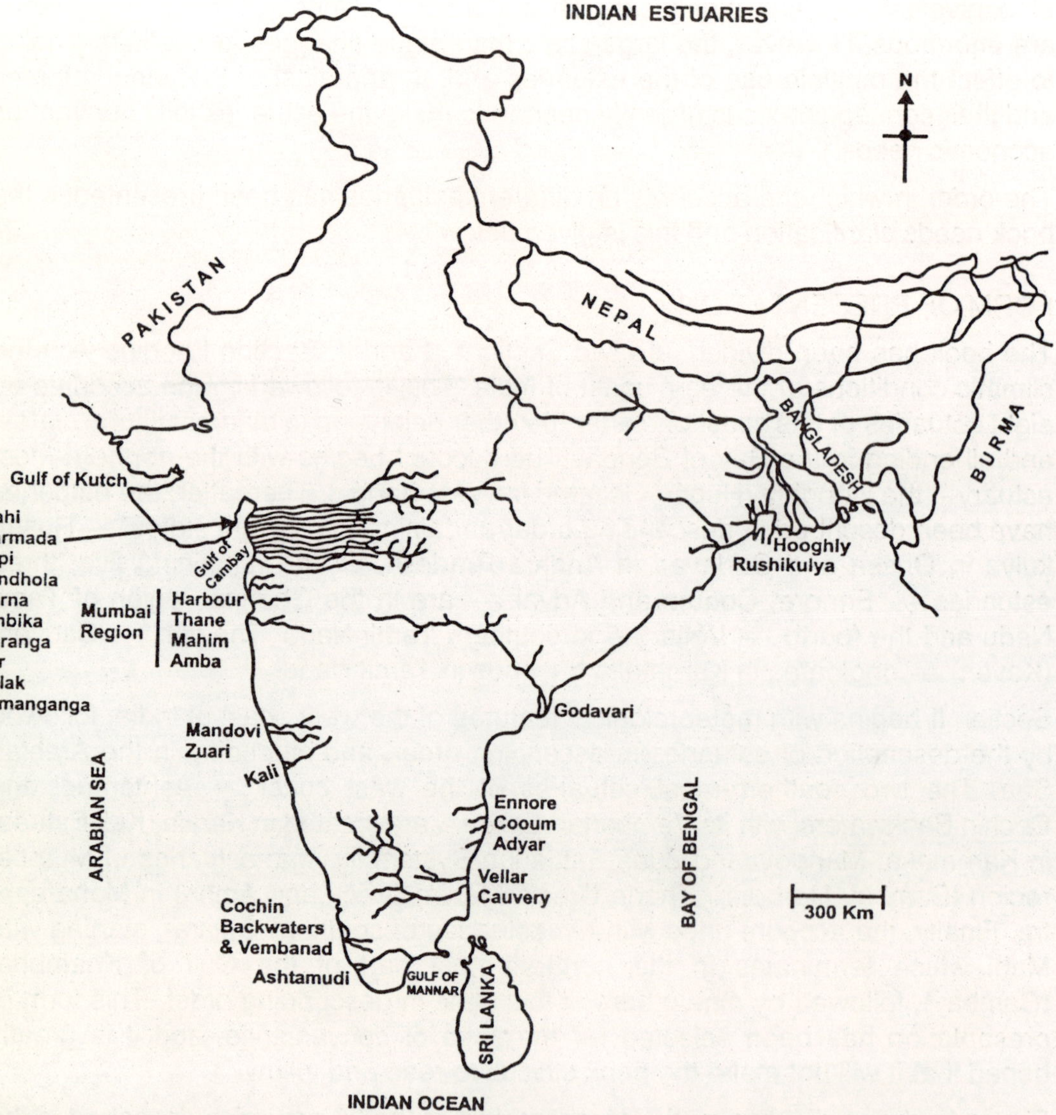

Fig. 3 Map of India showing the locations of the 25 estuaries described in the book. Of these, 8 are located along the east coast starting from the Hooghly in West Bengal and 17 are on the west coast.

A Dockyard at Lothal built by the Harappans using masonry walls of kiln-burnt bricks

B Dr. S.R. Rao, a well-known archaeologist of India showing a single-holed stone anchor found near the dockyard at Lothal

PLATE I

References

1. Barnes, R.S.K., 1974. *Esturaine Biology: The Institute of Biology's Studies in Biology, No. 49*, Edward Arnold, London, 76 pp.
2. Bowden, K.F., 1980. Physical factors: Salinity, temperature, circulation and mixing processes. In: *Chemistry and Biochemistry of Estuaries* (eds.) E. Olausson and I. Cato, John Wiley & Sons Ltd., pp 37-43.
3. Caspers, H., 1967. Estuaries: Analysis of definitions and biological consideration. In: *Estuaries* (ed.) G.H. Lauff, pp. 6-8. American Association for the Advancement of Science, Washington, D.C., 575 pp.
4. Cameron, W.M. & Pritchard, D.W., 1965. Estuaries. In: *The Sea*, Vol. 2, pp. 306-324 (ed.) M.N. Hill, . John Wiley, New York
5. Day, J.H., 1951. The ecology of South African estuaries I. A review of estuarine conditions in general. *Transaction of the Royal Society of South Africa*, Vol 33, pp. 53-91.
6. Emery, K.O., 1967. Estuaries and lagoons in relation to continental shelves. In: *Estuaries* (ed.) G.H. Lauff, pp. 9-11. American Association for the Advancement of Science, Washington, D.C., 575 pp.
7. Emery, K.O. & Stevenson R.E., 1957. Estuaries and lagoons. I. Physical and chemical characteristics. In: *Treatise of Marine Ecology and Paleoecology* (ed.) J.W. Hedgpeth. Gelogical Society American Memoirs, Vol. 67, pp. 673-693.
8. ENVIS., 1997. *Estuaries of India: State-of-the-art Report*, Envis Publication Series 2/97. Environmental Information System Centre. Centre of Advanced Study in Marine Biology, Annamalai University, Parangipettai, Tamil Nadu, 52 pp.
9. Hedgpeth, J.W., 1957. Estuaries and Lagoons. II. Biological aspects. In: *Treatise on Marine Ecology and Paleoecology* (ed.) J.W. Hedgpeth. Geological Society, American Memoirs, Vol. 67, pp. 694-729.
10. Ketchum, B.H., 1983. Estuarine characteristics. In: *Estuaries and enclosed seas – Ecosystem of the world,* Series 26 (ed.) B.H., Ketchum, pp. 1-14, Elsevier Scientific Publishing Company, Amsterdam, Oxford, N.Y., 500 pp.
11. Knox, G.A., 1986. *Estuarine ecosystems: A systems approach.* CRC Press Inc., Florida, Vol. 1, 289 pp.
12. Kumari, L.K., Sumitra-Vijayaraghavan, Wafar, M.V.M., Rajan, J.P. & Rajendran. A., 1978. Studies on detritus in a tropical estuary. *Indian Journal of Marine Sciences*, Vol. 7, pp. 263-266.
13. Lauff, G.H. (ed.), 1967. *Estuaries.* American Association for the Advancement of Science, Washington D.C., 575 pp.
14. Nigam, R., 1988. Was the large rectangular structure at Lothal (Harappan settlement) a 'dockyard' or an 'irrigation tank'? In: *Marine Archeology of Indian Ocean Countries* (ed.) S. R. Rao, pp. 20-21. National Institute of Ocenaography, Goa, 192 pp.
15. Panikkar, N.K. & Srinivasan, T.M 1971. The concept of tides in ancient India. *Indian Journal of History of Science,* Vol. 6, pp. 36-50.
16. Pillay, T.V.R., 1967. Estuarine fisheries of the Indian Ocean coastal zone. In: *Estuaries* (ed.) G.H. Lauff. American Association for the Advancement of Science, Washington, D.C., pp. 647-657.

17. Pritchard, D.W., 1952. Estuarine hydrography. *Advances in Geophysics.* Vol. 1, pp. 243.-280.
18. Pritchard, D.W., 1967. What is an estuary: Physical viewpoint. In: *Estuaries* (ed.) G.H. Lauff. American Association for the Advancement of Science, Washington, D.C., pp. 3-5.
19. Qasim, S. Z. & Sankaranarayanan, V.N., 1972. Organic detritus of a tropical estuary. *Marine Biology*, Vol. 15, pp. 193-199.
20. Rajan, K., 1988. Seafaring activities of Tamil Nadu coast. In: *Marine Archeology of Indian Ocean Countries* (ed.) S. R. Rao. pp. 22-24. National Institute of Oceanography, Goa, 192 pp.
21. Rao, S.R., 1979. Lothal - A Harappan Port town. *Memoirs of the Archeological Survey of India,* No. 78. Vols I & II, New Delhi.
22. Russell, R.J., 1967. Origin of estuaries. In: *Estuaries* (ed.) G.H. Lauff. American Association for the Advancement of Science, Washington, D.C., pp. 93-99.
23. Smayda, T.J., 1983. The phytoplankton of estuaries. In: *Estuaries and enclosed seas – Ecosystems of the world*, 26 (ed.) B.H. Ketchum, pp. 65-102. Elsevier Scientific Publishing Company, Amsterdam, Oxford, N.Y., 500 pp.
24. Wafar, S., Untawale, A.G. & Wafar, M.V.M, 1997. Litter fall and energy flux in a mangrove ecosystem. *Estuarine, Coastal and Shelf Science*, Vol. 44, pp. 111-124.

SECTION – I

Climatic Features of the East Coast

The unique geography of India produces a range of climatic conditions over the landmass offering it a wealth of metereological, biological and cultural diversity. Practically every conceiveable climatic feature is found in the country. From snow-clad peaks of the Himalayas to the dry desert of Rajasthan; from Cherrapunji and Mawsynram which have the highest rainfalls in the world (1080-1141 cm) to practically rainless Thar Desert (rainfall less than 13 cm) are found in the country. Coastal regions have moderate, unvarying warm climate with heavy rains during the monsoon and postmonsoon seasons. The diversity is perhaps greater than any area of similar size in the world. The seasonal changes in the climatic features are discussed in the following sections.

THE COOL SEASON

From December to February, the east coast faces winter and the season has clear skies, fine weather with moderate northerly winds and low humidity. Mean winter temperature increases from north to south and has a range of 14 to 27 °C. During this season, the northern, and on some occasions, even the central parts are influenced by a weather system called *Western disturbances.* These disturbances originate in the west near the Mediterranean and bring in cold air from the Eurasian region over the northern parts causing a cold spell called *cold waves.* During this period, temperature in the north (excluding Kashmir) drops below the normal (6-12 °C), often falling to 4-8 °C, and this cold wave extends towards the east upto West Bengal and towards the south up to Orissa and Andhra Pradesh. Rains during this season occur along the coastline with a maximum in Tamil Nadu and tapering towards the west coast (Kerala).

THE PREMONSOON (SUMMER) SEASON

The period March-May is marked with rising temperature throughout the country with a mean daily temperature of 30-35 °C. Along the coast, land and sea breezes predominate due to strong temperature in contrast to between land and the sea. Tropical cyclones in the form of intense circulation of 200-300 km diameter with wind velocities blowing close to 150 km/h get formed in the Bay of Bengal. The storms generally move first in a northwesterly direction and later take northerly and northeasterly course. Storms are more frequent in the Bay of Bengal than in the Arabian Sea, and 2-3 cyclones with varying frequencies occur during the year. May is the warmest month in the country but March becomes the warmest month in the south (Tamil Nadu). Thunder storms, associated with rain or hail, are predominant during this season. In the central parts of northern India, duststorms occur frequently. Often violent thunder storms with strong wind and rain lasting for short durations occur in the region. These are called *Norwesters* or *Kal Baishakhi.*

THE SOUTHWEST MONSOON SEASON

Southwest (SW) monsoon or the summer monsoon season is generally taken to be of four months over the country (June-September). However, its actual period at a specific place differs and depends upon the dates of the onset and withdrawl of SW monsoon. In Calcutta, the monsoon rains coming from the Chittagong Hill tracts begin in June and last till September with an average rainfall of 1580 mm. Orissa gets maximum rains in July and August whereas Andhra Pradesh gets maximum rainfall in September and October, and Tamil Nadu in November and December. The Bay of Bengal during this season is a source of low pressure called *monsoon depression.* Towards the later half of September, the SW monsoon currents get feeble and start withdrawing.

THE POSTMONSOON OR NOTHEAST MONSOON SEASON

This is a transitional season when northeasterly winds cause periodic showers along the east coast of Andhra Pradesh and Tamil Nadu which decrease towards the interior. Tropical cyclones which form in the Bay of Bengal move, during this season, towards the coast causing heavy rainfall, and Orissa, Andhra Pradesh and Tamil Nadu often receive rainfall solely due to these storms. From September to November, cyclones are very common along this coast. The number of cyclones / severe cyclones in the three states (Orissa, Andhra Pradesh and Tamil Nadu) during the last 104 years (1877-1980) in the four months (September to December) was as follows:

	Orissa/West Bengal	Andhra Pradesh	Tamil Nadu	Total
September	29/8	5/3	0/0	34/11
October	27/7	27/7	6/1	53/17
November	9/5	20/12	27/17	56/34
December	0/0	2/0	12/7	14/7

Note: Number after the slash denotes severe cyclone

Mean day temperature over the coast falls from about 38˚C in September / October to 28˚C in November.

RAINFALL OVER THE COUNTRY

Figure 4 gives the annual (average) rainfall throughout the country from which it can be seen that except for certain parts of Orissa and Andhra Pradesh, the rest of the coastline gets 100-250 cm of rainfall. Figure 5(a) shows the normal dates of the onset, and the withdrawl of SW monsoon over India is shown in Fig. 5(b). In West Bengal and parts of Orissa, the onset is 5th and 10th June respectively, whereas Andhra Pradesh and Tamil Nadu get rain in November and December during the withdrawl of SW monsoon.

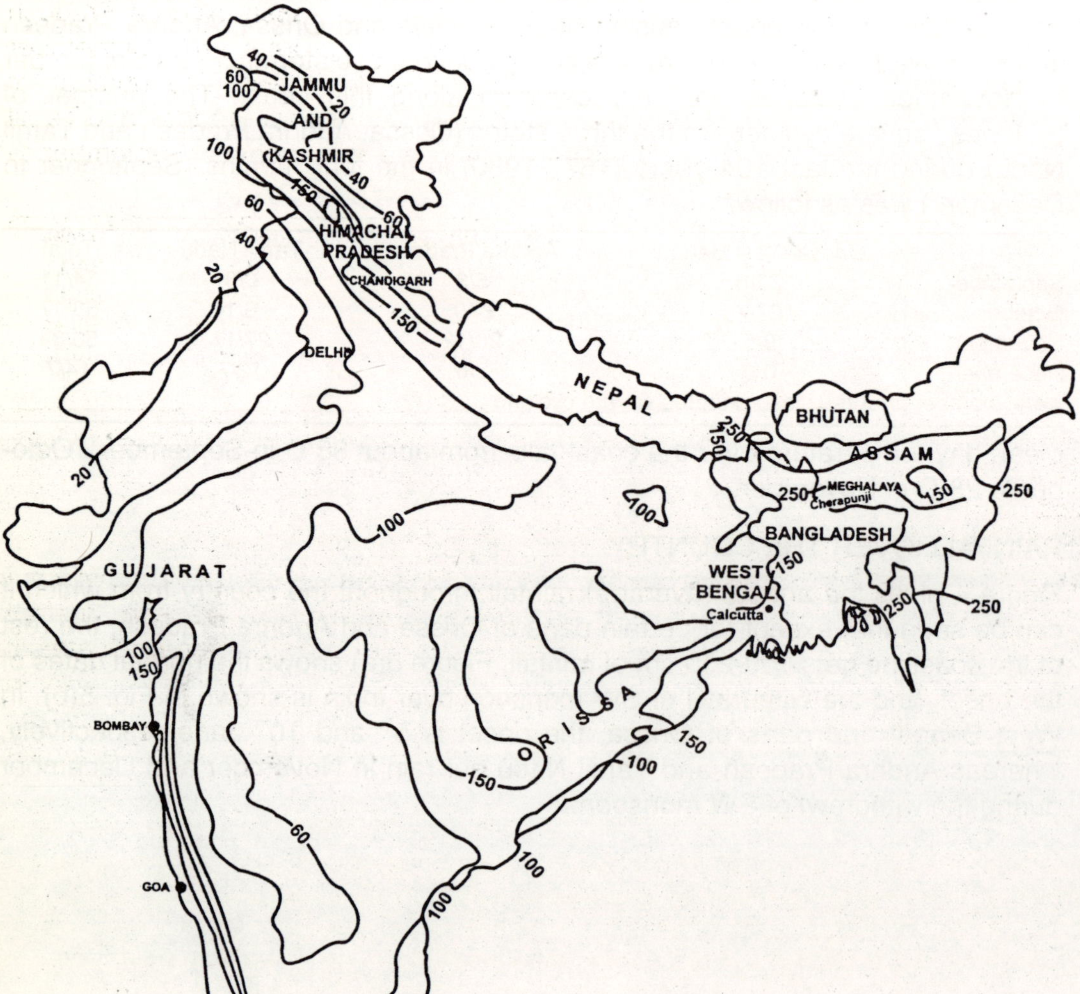

Fig. 4 Average annual rainfall in cm throughout the country.

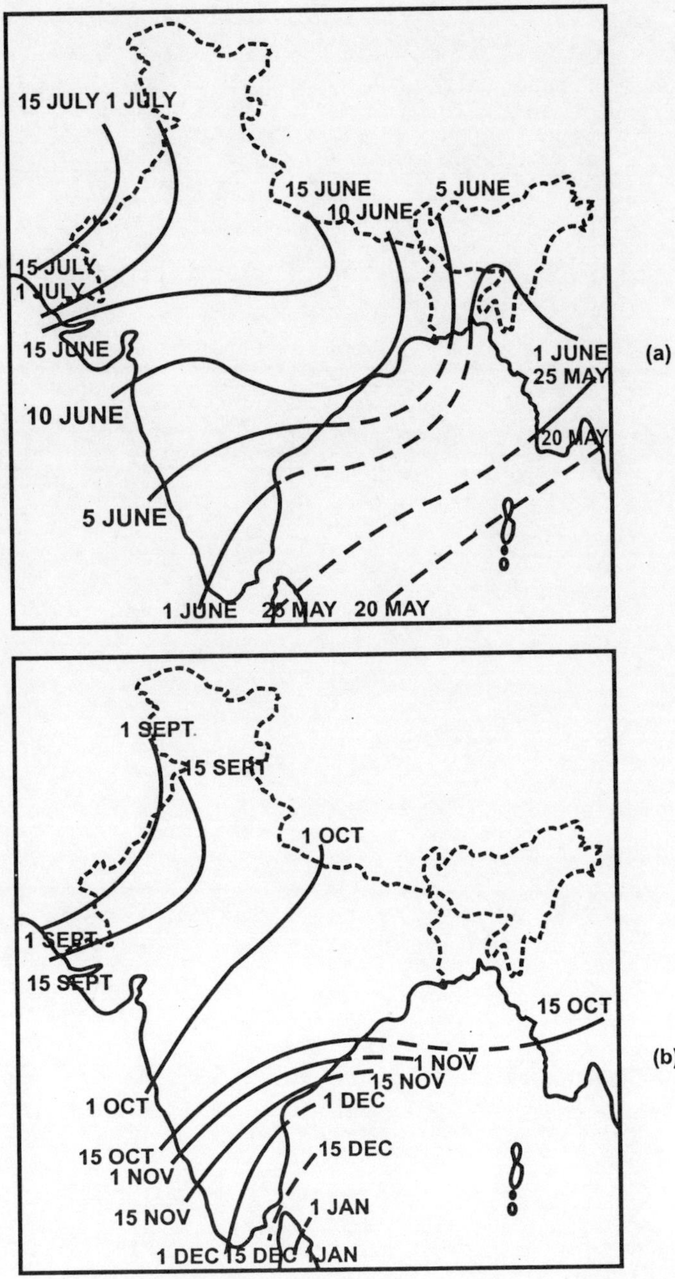

Fig. 5 Normal dates of (a) the coast of southwest (SW) monsoon; and (b) its withdrawl over India

Estuaries of the East Coast of India

Chapter 1

Hooghly (Hugli)

Two major rivers of India namely the Ganga and the Brahmaputra join the Bay of Bengal forming an extensive triangular delta called the Gangetic Basin spread over an area of 40,000 km^2. The Hooghly Estuary, located along Lat. 21 °40 ′N and Long. 87 °47 ′E, is one of the most important estuaries of India and the foremost along the east coast. It is also known as the Hooghly–Matlah Estuarine System and lies in the state of West Bengal. It covers several rivers including the Ganga, Hooghly, Rupnarain and Matlah which are the main feeders to the estuary. There are three other rivers namely the Bagirathi, the Jalangi and the Churni which form a confluence with the Ganga River. The Hooghly River, after traversing a considerable distance inland, passes through the city of Calcutta (renamed Kolkata) which has a port located on its banks (Figure 1.1). Further down, the estuary meets the river Brahmaputra and passes through Diamond Harbour from where it fans out to about 4 km into a funnel-shaped water body which spreads out to more than 20 km before merging into the Bay of Bengal. Within the estuary lies a newly established deep dock system at Haldia. The navigational passage through the estuary and the river has been reported to be difficult, as the

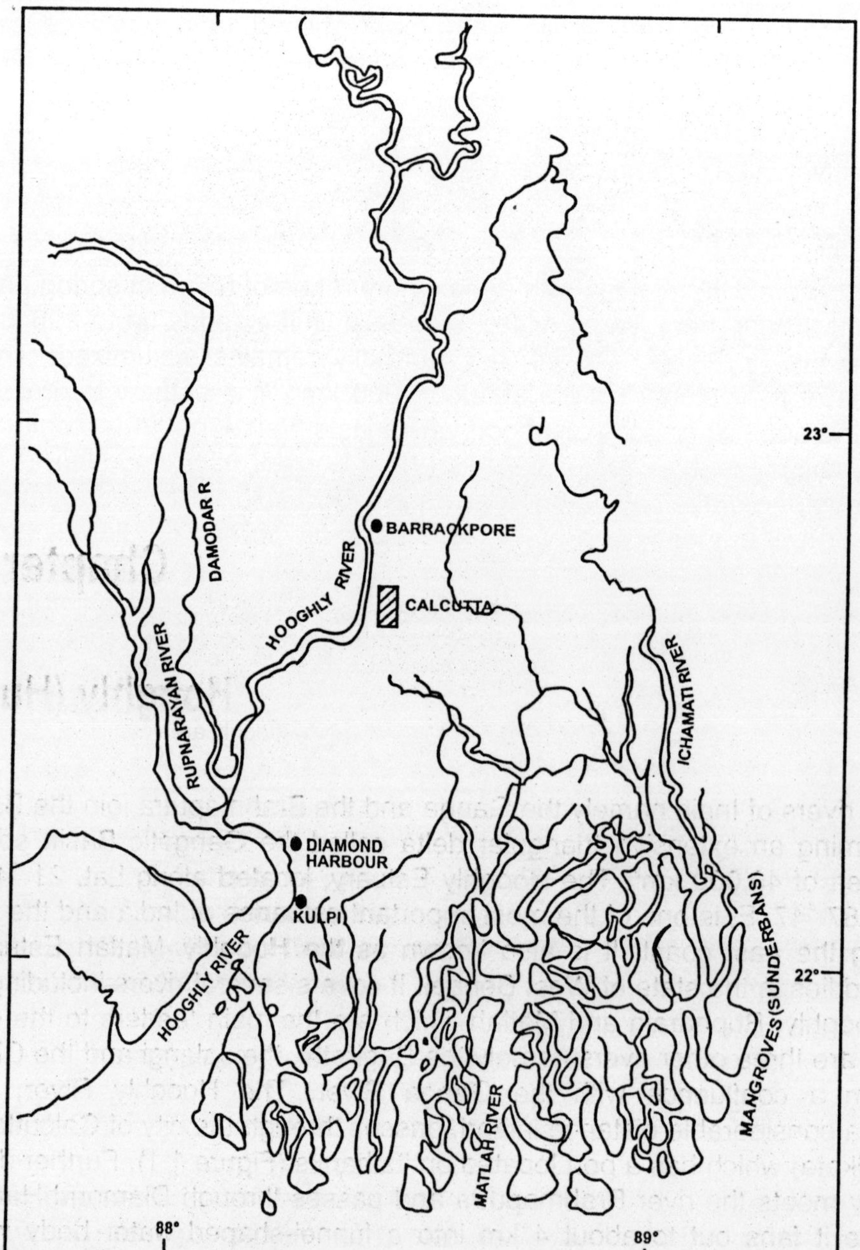

Fig. 1.1 Map of Hooghly Estuarine System with its riverine connections and the associated mangrove forests of Sunderbans

channel leading to Calcutta Port provides a number of sand bars, crossings and islands. Sagar Island which is the largest and well known has a light house. Regular dredging is required to bring the ships of 6 m draught to Kolkata and 9 m draught to Haldia, as the navigational channels are to be maintained at 10.67 and 12.28 m respectively at a high annual cost (Bose, 1956; Chatterjee, 1987).

HYDROGRAPHY

The estuary gets semidiurmal tides with a maximum range of 5.5 m at spring and minimum 1.8 m at neap near Sagar Island. The tidal limit extends up to 296 km upstream from the north and the estuary normally remains well-mixed. The catchment area of the estuary covers about 19,000 km^2. The estuary is greatly influenced by the southwest (SW) monsoon which lasts from June to September. The annual rainfall in the three states of India (West Bengal, Bihar and Uttar Pradesh) which cover the entire catchment area is given in Table 1.1 for three years. The data are old but authentic and are valid even today barring the fluctuations from year to year. As can be seen from Table 1.1, the maximum rainfall (about 80%), occurs from June to September. Normal freshwater discharge into the estuary is of the order of 3000 m^3 /s during the monsoon period and 1000 m^3 /s during the dry season.

Table 1.1— Average rainfall in mm for 3 years in Hooghly area (From Shetty *et al.*, 1963)

Month	1956	1957	1958
January	14.43	67.89	14.54
February	16.65	10.86	14.83
March	35.47	19.94	12.67
April	17.86	7.36	23.27
May	115.56	15.18	36.52
June	290.23	149.94	112.84
July	294.38	378.81	302.79
August	359.97	284.01	393.32
September	411.48	224.42	383.76
October	173.82	30.05	104.10
November	55.07	1.34	3.95
December	35.51	11.22	6.25

Water temperature at the surface in the estuary during the year normally ranges between 18 ˚C and 33 ˚C without any appreciable difference from one region to the other and with a maximum variation of 1.5 ˚C between surface and bottom. Seasonal changes in salinity are large, ranging from 30‰ during the premonsoon season (Feb-May) to almost freshwater conditions – 1.6‰ during the SW monsoon. There is also a marked difference in salinity in the estuary from one region to the other. The water in the upper reaches of the river Hooghly largely remains freshwater practically throughout the year. At the farthest point in the river from the mouth beyond Kolkata, the salinity rises to 2‰ in May/June. The other interesting feature worth noting in this estuary is that there is practically no difference in salinity between the surface and subsurface waters including the bottom except in the riverine part at Kolkata. This is unlike the other estuaries of the Tamil Nadu coast. In Tamil Nadu, the rainfall regime is different and occurs during the NE monsoon when it is not as heavy in the West Bengal region. Moreover, the tidal range in the Hooghly Estuary is large and the currents both at the bottom and surface are strong resulting in obliteration of the vertical gradient which is seen in other estuaries (Bose, 1956; Shetty *et al.*, 1963). Such vertical gradients only exist when the tidal range is small and the currents at the bottom are stronger than at the surface but during the ebb the reverse seems to be true, keeping the two layers in the water column quite distinct, during most parts of the year except in the monsoon when the surface flow of freshwater runoff is continuously large and strong making the tidal flow at the bottom insignificant.

A similar situation exists in the turbidity of the estuary which is reported to be influenced by the seasonal and climatic changes and the tidal flow. During the monsoon period, the finer clay particles coming from the rivers into the estuary make the water highly turbid. During the postmonsoon period, in December/January (winter), the transparency of water increases but from February onwards, stirring up of sediments with a strong incoming tidal flow make the water well-mixed and turbid. The range in *p*H of water in the estuary was found to be between 7.9 and 8.4 during the year, while the alkalinity comes down to minimum during the monsoon (Bose, 1956).

To illustrate the circulation in the estuary, a depth-averaged numerical model has been developed. The model is run with north-easterly winds of 5 m/s and a freshwater discharge of 1000 m^3/s for the dry season. The hydrodynamic model predicts steady state in 8 tidal cycles. Maximum salinity is found to be 28.4‰ at Sagar Island which falls to 13‰ in the first 10 km. The computed results from the model are in agreement with the observed data. By introducing a constant freshwater discharge of 300 m^3/s, the salinity conditions for the wet season are simulated. The computed salinity falls as low as 13‰ at Sagar Island and gradually decreases upward. The estuary becomes salt-free after about 50 km from the mouth upstream. Both computed and observed values are in agreement (Rao *et al.*, 1998).

NUTRIENTS

The concentration of PO_4-P was high during the premonsoon season (summer) and low during the monsoon. The upper reaches of the estuary were richer in phosphate as compared to lower reaches.

Nitrate concentrations in the estuary have been reported to be high from June to October (monsoon) and low from March to May. The fluctuations were less pronounced in the lower reaches (marine zone) as compared to the upper reaches (freshwater zone).

Silicates were uniformly distributed throughout the water-column and no significant difference was seen between surface and bottom. Their values were low during the premonsoon period and high during the monsoon and postmonsoon seasons. Upper reaches showed high values practically throughout the year (Bose, 1956).

PHYTOPLANKTON

For the study of distribution and density of phytoplankton organisms, the estuary was divided into 5 zones. The zone 1 was in the freshwater region and the zone 5 was predominantly marine and the other three zones showed transition between the two extremes. The study was extended for a period of 3 years (1956, 1957 and 1958). Diatoms were the most predominant group in all the zones, followed by bluegreen algae, green algae and miscellaneous organisms consisting of dinoflagellates, euglenoids and other holophytic flagellates (Shetty *et al.*, 1963). Two peaks of diatom abundance could be identified clearly – one during June to August and the other from November to January. Lowest values of phytoplankton counts were in September and October. Figures. 1.2 to 1.5 show the seasonal changes in phytoplankton and zooplankton biomass in relation to temperature and salinity in the 4 zones. Variations in temperature were similar in all the 4 zones while salinity was almost zero throughout the year in zone 1. In zones 2 and 3, there was an increase during the premonsoon period (March-June). This was even more clear in zone 4. Two peaks in phytoplankton counts were seen during November to February and April to July (Shetty *et al.*, 1963). The results of investigations conducted on a seasonal cycle of plankton from January 1959 to December 1962 showed two peaks of phytoplankton abundance with diatoms as dominant group (Saha *et al.*, 1975).

In another study on phytoplankton extended over a period of 3 years (1984 to 1987) in the lower reaches of the estuary, 91 species were recorded. Of these, 49 belonged to the family Bacillariophyceae, 18 to Cyanophyceae, 12 to Dinophyceae, 7 to Chlorophyceae and 5 to Euglenophyceae (Santra & Pal, 1989). During

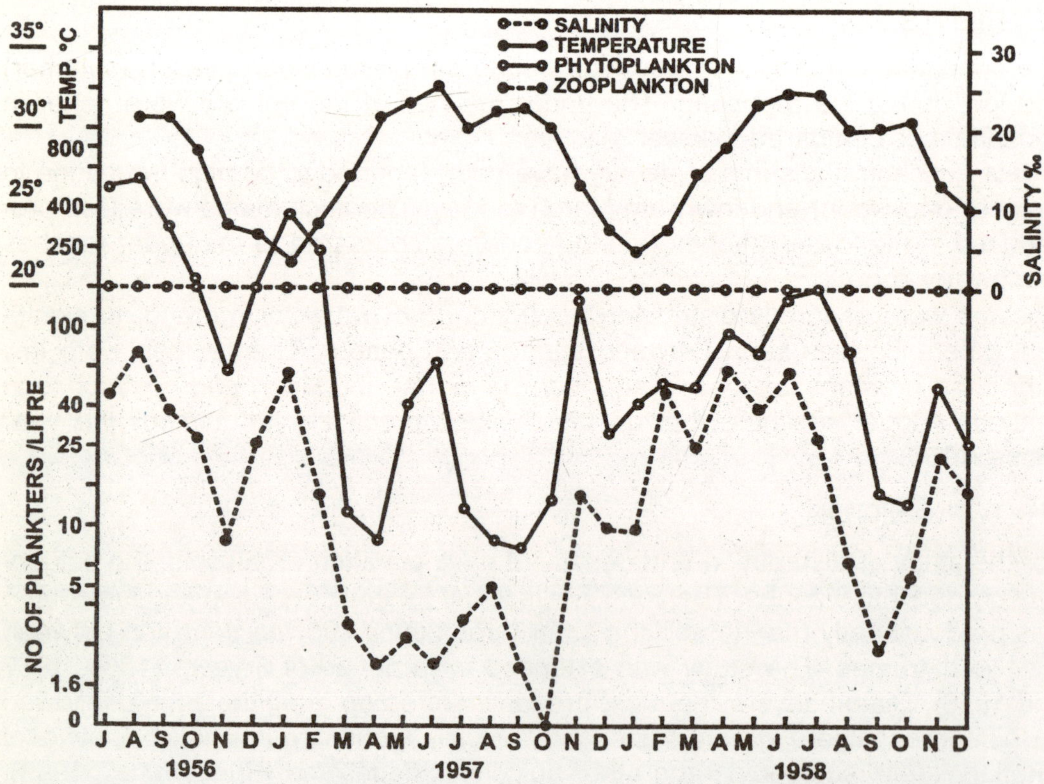

Fig. 1.2 Seasonal cycles of phytoplankton and zooplankton biomass in relation to temperature and salinity in the upper zone (zone 1) of Hooghly Estuary. Salinity in this zone is almost nil throughout the year (From Shetty *et al.*, 1963)

the year 1988, blooms of diatoms were reported during the postmonsoon and early premonsoon seasons (November to April) when the salinity was rising, nutrients were abundant and the turbidity was low. The total cell counts varied from 1720 to 7080 cells/l (De *et al.*, 1991a) From March 1988 to February 1990, phytoplankton organisms were collected from four different stations of the estuary. Station 1 was in the marine zone while station 4 was near the Diamond Harbour (riverine). Total number of cells varied between 12.5×10^5/l and 77×10^5/l with maximum numbers during postmonsoon and early premonsoon. In all, 29 species were observed. Dominance index showed high values during premonsoon period which indicated that the community was dominated by fewer species. Shannon-Weaver's diversity index (H) showed a sharp decline in February when the population was dominated by only two species of diatoms, namely

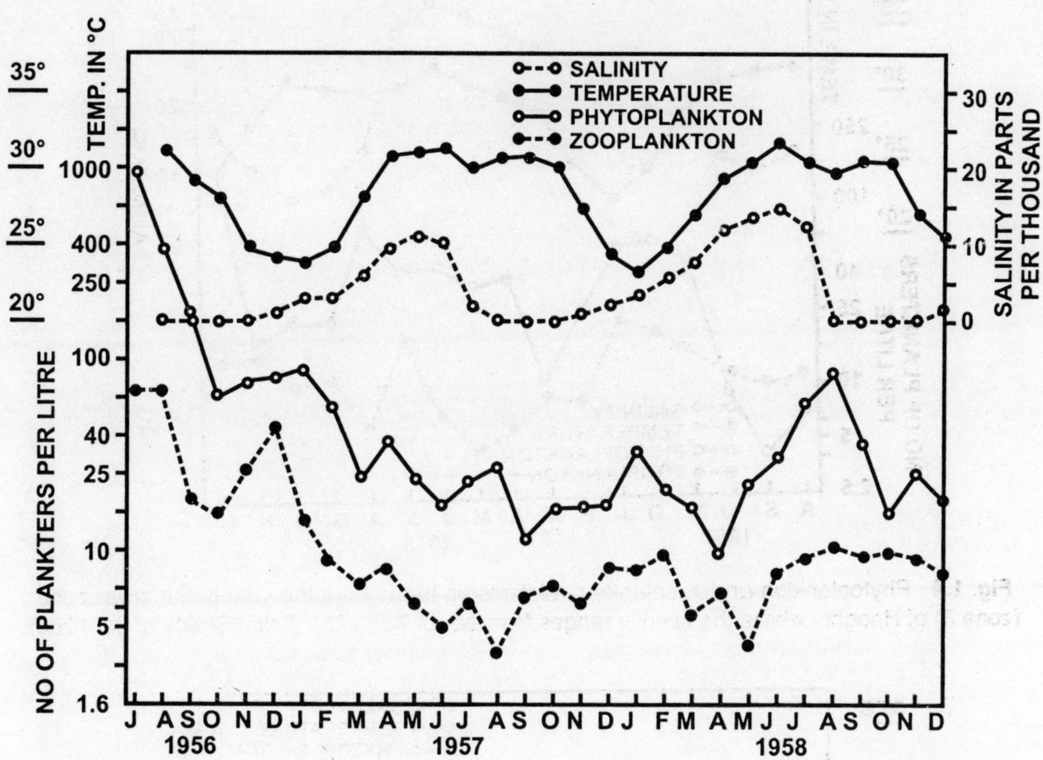

Fig. 1.3 Seasonal cycles of phytoplankton and zooplankton in the middle zone (zone 2) of Hooghly Estuary where salinity rises from almost 0 to about 15‰ . Note the greater regularity of both phytoplankton and zooplankton while there is hardly any change in temperature (From Shetty *et al.*, 1963)

Coscinodiscus radiatus and *C. excentricus*. These two contributed to >50% of the population. Table 1.2 shows some environmental features of the estuary. There is not much difference in temperature, *p*H and dissolved oxygen at the 4 stations while the chlorinity was high at the station 1 and low at station 4. Nutrients (PO_4-P, NO_3-N and SiO_4-Si) were high at all the four stations with maximum values at the station 4. Average values of gross production were always less than the community respiration (Table 1.2). This probably indicates high pollution in the estuary. The ratio between community respiration and chlorophyll *a* can be used as a pollution index. Its high values indicate high organic load (De *et al.*, 1994). Organic production in the estuary is largely contributed by nannoplankton. It

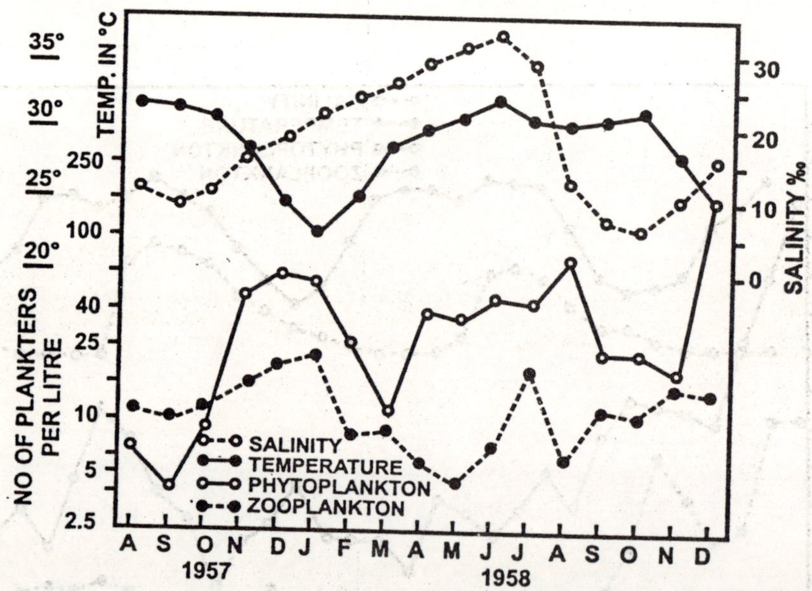

Fig. 1.4 Phytoplankton and zooplankton relationship throughout the year in the lower zone (zone 3) of Hooghly where the salinity ranges from about 7 to 32‰ (From Shetty *et al.*, 1963)

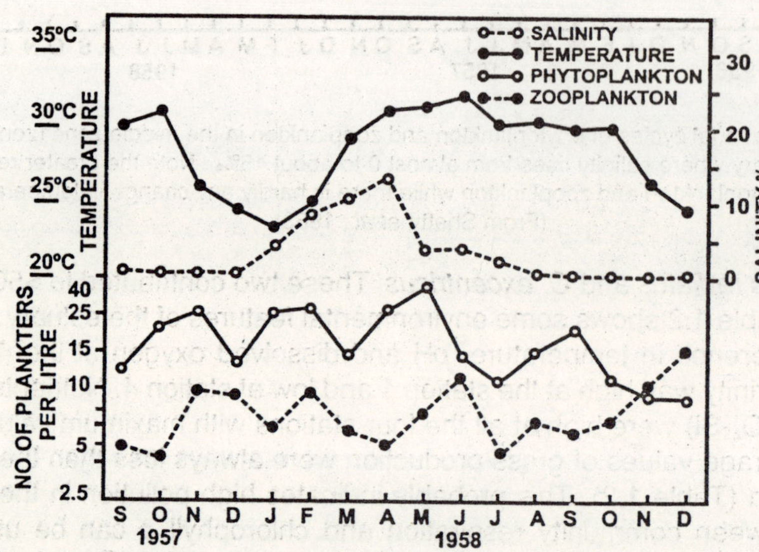

Fig. 1.5 Seasonal relationship between phytoplankton and zooplankton in a typically estuarine zone (zone 4) where salinity remains over a greater part of the year between the range ~0 to 13.5‰ (From Shetty *et al.*, 1963)

ranges between 38 to 73.6% of the total primary production and these small organisms seem to ulilize ammonia–nitrogen more efficiently than nitrate-nitrogen (De *et al.*, 1991 a). Several species of phytoplankton have been reported to bloom in the Hooghly Estuary during the postmonsoon and early premonsoon seasons when the salinity of water is low and transparency is relatively high (De *et al.*, 1991 b).

Table 1.2— Mean variations (1988-90) of some physicochemical properties of surface water in Hooghly Estuary (Mean ± SD) (From De *et al.*, 1994)

Parameters	Station 1	Station 2	Station 3	Station 4
Temp. (^{0}C)	27.5 ± 3.8	27.4 ± 3.6	27.6 ± 3.5	28.2 ± 3.0
Chlor (× 10^{-3})	9.40 ± 3.10	8.27 ± 3.25	5.82 ± 3.24	0.39 ± 0.33
*p*H	8.16 ± 0.23	8.13 ± 0.20	8.11 ± 0.21	8.05 ± 0.21
Diss.Oxy. (ml. l^{-1})	4.81 ± 0.72	4.79 ± 0.47	4.88 ± 0.33	4.92 ± 0.48
PO_4^{-3} -P(μg-at.l^{-1})	1.61 ± 0.71	1.48 ± 0.48	1.55 ± 0.62	1.83 ± 0.67
NO_3-N (μg-at.l^{-1})	15.75 ± 4.57	15.72 ± 4.28	20.44 ± 5.75	25.96± 8.73
SiO_4^{-4} -Si (μg-at.l^{-1})	75.38 ± 20.03	79.86 ± 22.47	91.50 ± 28.28	120.87 ± 25.95
Gross Pr. Prod. (mg C.m^{-3}.h^{-1})	24.9 ± 5.4	26.7 ± 4.04	27.5 ± 5.6	38.3 ± 11.9
Respiration (mg C.m^{-3}.h^{-1})	30.51 ± 5.75	28.24 ± 4.04	30.07 ± 6.47	38.45 ± 8.16
Chlorophyll (mg m^{-3})	3.024 ± 0.598	3.158 ± 0.667	2.67 ± 0.84	2.547 ± 0.789

Seasonal variation of chlorinity, dissolved O_2 and total CO_2 were studied from January to December 1989 at the 4 stations in the estuary. Water was undersaturated in dissolved O_2 throughout the year (Fig. 1.6), indicating high load of organic pollution. Increasing trend of saturation was found towards the mouth of the estuary. Figure 1.6 shows a direct correlation between salinity, dissolved O_2 and total CO_2 (Ghosh *et al.*, 1991 b).

According to Nandy *et al.* (1983) and Lal (1990), there has been a change in the ecology of this estuary after the construction of Farakka Barrage in 1975. Increased discharge of freshwater from the river Ganga into the estuary has resulted into an extension of the freshwater zone downstream, as far as Ulberia which is closer to the mouth. Before the construction of the barrage, the freshwater intrusion was limited only up to Konnagar. Measurement of primary production, based on ^{14}C assimilation, showed an increase in the rate of production because of greater release of nutrients into the estuary.

ZOOPLANKTON

Zooplankton organisms show an assortment of freshwater, brackishwater and marine forms depending upon the site of observation. In the upper stretches,

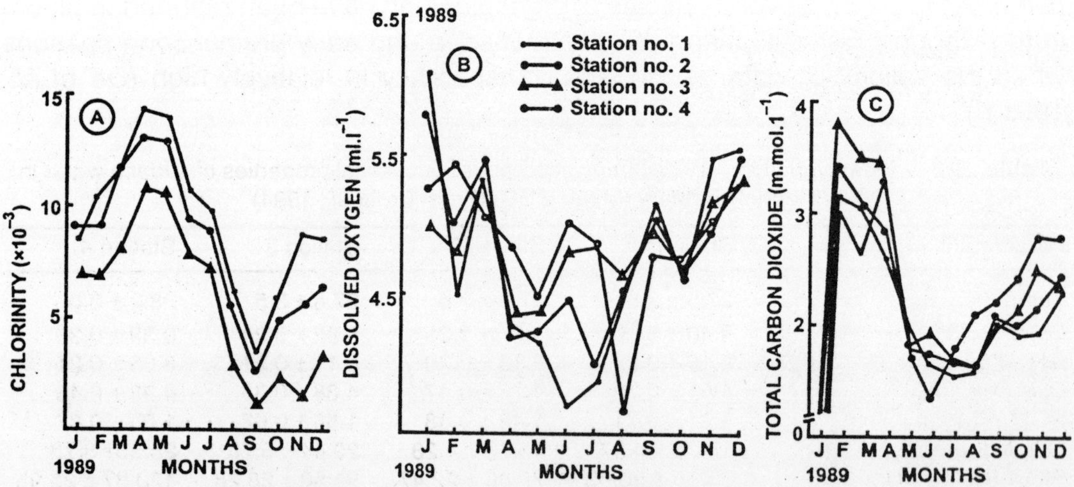

Fig. 1.6 Monthly variation in chlorinity (A), dissolved oxygen (B) and total carbon dioxide (C) at 4 stations in Hooghly during the year 1989 (From Ghosh *et al.*, 1991b)

rotifers, protozoans and cladocerans were found in large numbers. In the middle zone, copepods, mysids, ostracods, cladocerans, etc. were abundant and in the marine zone, many species of crustaceans including lucifers, gammarids, cumaceans, amphipods, hydromedusae and chaetognaths were present. Larval forms of many invertebrates, notably those of crustaceans were abdundantly found in all the zones. (Shetty *et al.,* 1963; Sarkar *et al.* 1984; Sarkar *et al.* 1986a). Copepods formed the most dominant group of the zooplankton community throughout the year, constituting 73.0-96.4% of the total biomass. Figure 1.7 shows seasonal changes in the abundance of organisms at 3 stations in the estuary. During the premonsoon months, the biomass values were high both in total zooplankton and copepods. The latter can be grouped into three categories. The euryhaline species (1st group) were present throughout the year. The second category belonged to those which were present for a limited period in different zones depending upon the rise and fall in salinity, and the third category included those which were casual migrants and were observed occasionally (Sarkar *et al.,* 1985 a &b). Among the three sub-orders of copepods, calanoids were the most abundant group followed by cyclopoids and herpacticoids (Kundu *et al.,* 1987). These authors divided the copepods into three groups

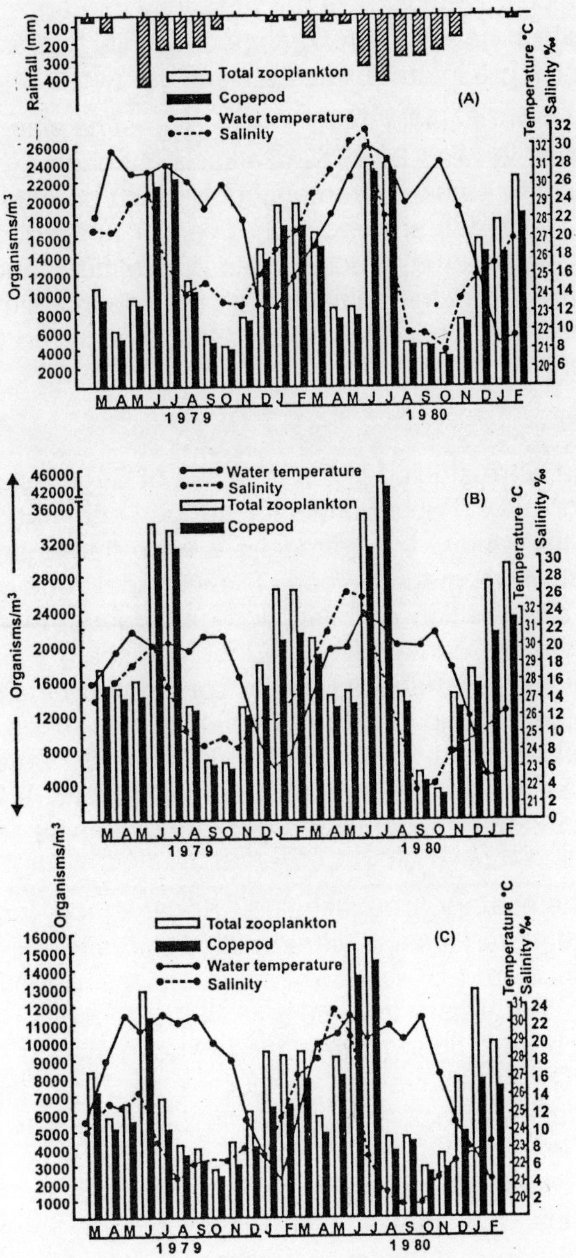

Fig. 1.7 Seasonal changes in total zooplankton density and copepod biomass in relation to rainfall (in mm), temperature and salinity at 3 stations A, B & C of Hooghly Estuary (From Sarkar *et al.*,1986a)

(a) euryhaline, which have a wide range of salinity tolerance,
(b) stenohaline, which have a narrow range of salinity tolerance, and
(c) oligohaline which are intermediate between the two.

In June 1980, a swarm of cladoceran, *Evade tergestina* was seen (185 organisms/m^3) when the salinity was 24.97‰ (Sarkar & Choudhury, 1987). During the high saline period in the estuary (premonsoon), which generally lasts from March to early June, the copepods showed high diversity and abundance. During the monsoon months, their biomass declined to a minimum and many species of copepods disappeared from the estuary. With the rise in salinity from November, repopulation and proliferation in the copepod fauna occurred (Sarkar *et al.,* 1985 a &b; 1986 a &b).

INTERTIDAL FAUNA

Benthic macrofauna were studied in the mudflats of Sagar Island in the Hooghly-Matlah estuarine complex. Two mudflats – Harmbari and Mandirtala – 9 km apart were selected for the study. The former is a wide flat whereas the latter is a narrow and long flat with a gradual slope. The intertidal zone of both the mudflats had similar faunal composition and included gastropods, bivalves, polychaetes, decapods, coelenterates, nemertines and gobiod-fishes. Eels were occasional visitors of the mudflats. Gastropods, largely contributed by *Cerithidea cingulata*, were the most dominant group followed by bivalves, decapods, actinarians, fishes and nemertines at Harimbari. In Mandirtala, gastropods were followed by actinarians, polychaetes, decapods, nemertines, pisces and bivalves. The faunal density ranged from 82.8/m^2 in April to 113.3/m^2 in June at Mandirtala (Nandi & Choudhury, 1983).

In a tidal creek of the estuary (Beguakhali) at Sagar Island, larval and pupal populations of benthic dipteran insects were studied at 5 sites. Two species namely *Culicoides pelilouensis* and *C. oxystoma* were the most dominant among the 4 species and constituted greater than 50% in all the seasons. Highest and lowest indices of dominance were during premonsoon and monsoon respectively (Ray & Choudhury, 1987). In another study conducted at Sagar Island and Chuksar Island, insect population, specially of staphylinid beetles was recorded from the intertidal zone (Poddar & Choudhury, 1992). Abundance of the larvae of rove-beetle (coleoptera) was studied in the intertidal zone of Sagar Island. Two families of marine Coleoptera (Carabidae and Staphylinidae) were common in the intertidal and littoral zones. Maximum number of larvae were recorded in the month of October (Poddar *et al.,* 1989).

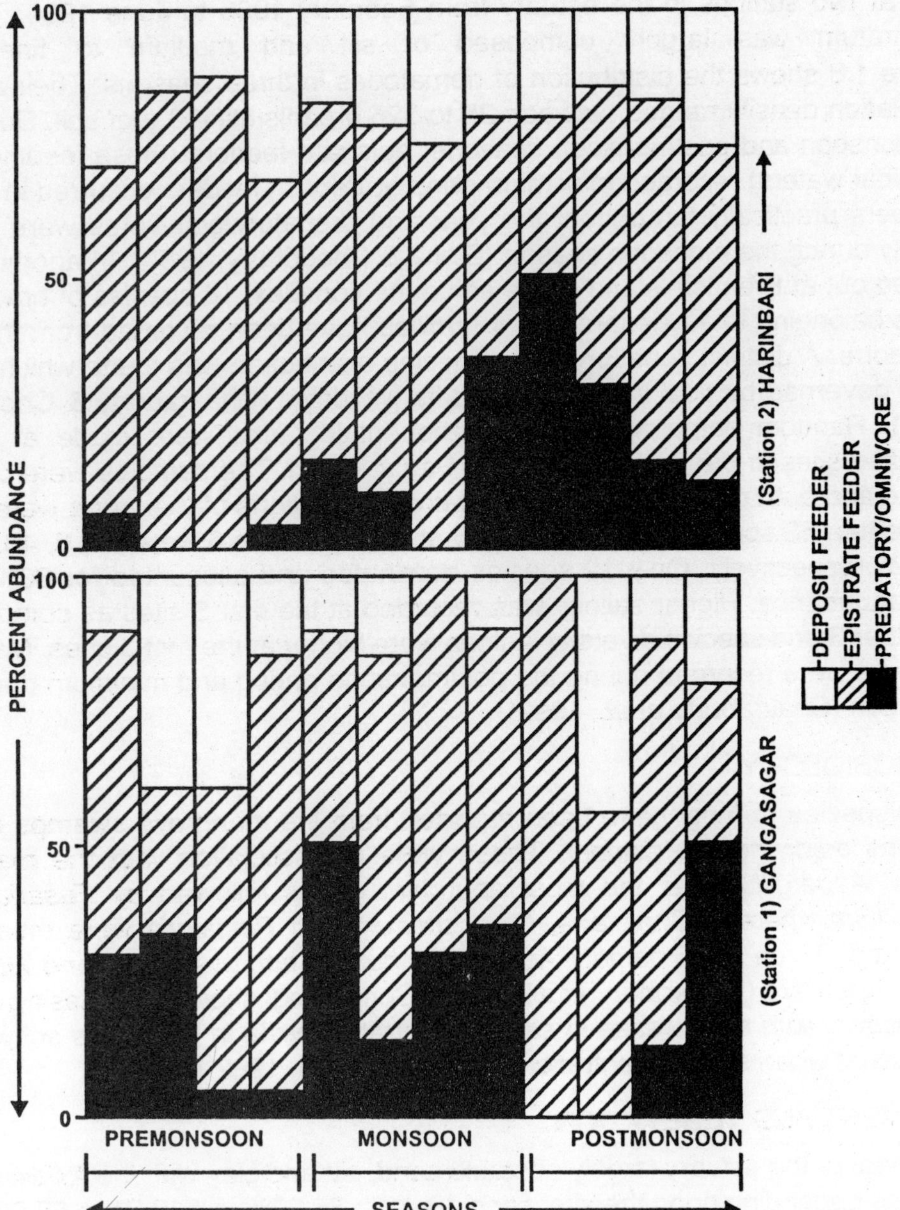

Fig. 1.8 Seasonal distribution of benthic nematodes grouped according to their feeding habits at 2 stations of Hooghly Estuary (From Sinha & Choudhury, 1987)

Intertidal distribution and abundance of benthic nematodes (meiofauna) were studied at two stations in the estuary from February 1985 to June 1986. The soil substratum was largely composed of silt and medium to fine sand. Figure 1.8 shows the distribution of nematodes in three seasons. Their average population density ranged between 25 to 525 organisms/400 g of soil. During the premonsoon and postmonsoon seasons, epistrate feeders (those feeding in the intertidal waters) recorded maximum density; deposit feeders occurred in smaller numbers practically throughout the year and predatory/omnivores were present largely during the monsoon season (Sinha & Choudhury, 1987). In another study carried out at Prentice Island of the estuarine complex, 18 species of brachyuran crabs belonging to 11 genera and 4 families have been recorded from the intertidal zone. A distinct zonation in the species distribution was found which seems to be governed by tidal inundation and its withdrawl (Chakraborty & Choudhury, 1992). Random samplings of macrozoobenthic fauna were made at 6 well-specified sites in the intertidal zone of Sagar Island. The samples were carefully sieved and both qualitative and quantitative evaluations of the fauna were made. Altogether, 53 species identified from 6 study sites, 1 to 6 were 43, 9, 40, 26, 22 and 25 respectively. Only 12 species dominated and accounted for 80% of the total abundance. Higher salinity was recorded at the first 3 sites as compared to the other 3 and species diversity indices were higher at the first 3 sites. Maximum numbers were recorded during the postmonsoon period and minimum during the monsoon (Chakraborty *et al.*, 1992).

MICROBIOLOGY

Many species of fungi have been reported from the mangrove swamps of Sunderbans adjoining the estuary. These were in association with the mangrove plants. *Aspergillus* was the most abundant genus followed by *Fusarium* and *Penicillium* whereas *Curvularia, Cladosporium* and *Pestalotia* were moderately abundant. Three fungi namely *Acrophialophora, Cephalosporium* and *Hamicola* were rather rare (Chowdhery *et al.*, 1982). Some fungi showed increasing cellulolytic activity with an increase in salt concentration while in many this activity was decreased when salt concentration increased (Garg, 1982 & 1983).

SEDIMENT AND VEGETATION

Sediment of the estuary largely contains sand, silt and clay with the following proportions depending upon the site: sand 10.41 to 85.29%; silt 12.21 to 69.09% and clay 0.5 to 20.9%. The estuarine sediments have large fractions of silt and clay, while the nearshore sediments have even greater proportions of silt than the estuarine sediments. In the latter, sand and clay are almost in equal proportions. Organic matter in the estuarine sediments ranged between 1.02-4.48 mg/g and that in the nearshore sediments the range was 4.64-7.10 mg/g. The ranges between total nitrogen and total phosphorus were 0.62-2.4 mg/g and 0.8-1.97 mg/g (Sasamal *et al.*, 1986).

During one of the cruises of the Research Vessel *Gaveshani*, sediment samples were collected from 6 stations. Three of these were from the estuary covering a strech of 70 km and other three were in the coastal waters (Sandhead, New Moore Island and off Paradeep). Humic acid was found to be the major fraction in the riverine and estuarine areas. Fulvic acid comprised the major fraction of the humic acid. Carbon to nitrogen ratio ranged between 13 to 16.5. Humic acid accounted for 66 to 82% of the organic matter present in the sediment. The sediments in the estuary were sandy whereas in the inshore water these contained fine clay (Sardessai, 1989). Surface layers of the bottom sediments in the estuary were found to contain significant amounts of $CaCO_3$, the saturation degree of which is a function of calcium and carbonate. Saturation rate was found to increase from the river end to the sea and the sediments contained 0.75 to 3.3% $CaCO_3$. The average concentration of organic carbon in the sediment was 0.34% which seems to be largely contributed by phytoplankton present in the overlying water (Ghosh *et al., 1992).*

A survey of mangrove vegetation was conducted on 7 islands of the Sundarbans and from the islands of eastern and western sectors. Table 1.3 gives the density of mangroves and dominant species on each island (Matilal *et al.*, 1986; Matilal & Mukherjee, 1989). Much of the organic matter in the estuary is contributed by the adjoining mangrove forests. The average litter fall beneath a plant, *Avicennia marina* in a tidal creek of Sunderbans has been estimated to be 1603 $g/m^2/y$. Leaves of the plant contribute to about 72.2% of the litter and the rest by twigs, flowers, fruits, etc. Maximum litter production (average 553 g/m^2) occurs during the postmonsoon season. From this it has been deduced that the litter forms an important source of detritus on which large communities of fishes, prawns and crabs are able to sustain. The decomposed litter also forms one of the major sources of nutrients (Ghosh *et al.*, 1990a).

In the intertidal zones of the estuarine areas, grasslands of the species *Porteresia coaretata* play an important role in coastal stability, nutrient cycling, sewage filtration and as feed for domestic animals. It is very common in Chermaguri Creek of Sagar Island. Average biomass production of the grass was estimated as 260g/m^2/y (dry wt). Maximum production was obtained during the monsoon and minimum during the postmonsoon months (Ghosh *et al.*, 1991a). The grass has been reported to contain sterols and terpenoids (Misra *et al.*,1987)

Table 1.3— Species density of dominant communities of mangrove plants on different islands of Sunderbans (From Matilal *et al.*, 1986)

Island	Dominant species	Density (No.hectare $^{-1}$)
	Aegiceras majus	16400
H	*Ceriops roxburghiana*	3900
	Sonneratia apetala	0.02
	Ceriops roxburghiana	6100
K	*Aegiceras majus*	1800
	Excoecaria agallocha	1400
	Excoecaria agallocha	1300
J	*Ceriops roxburghiana*	1700
	Xylocarpus mollucensis	0.002
	Ceriops roxburghiana	3600
N	*Phoenix paludosa*	2600
	Excoecaria agallocha	1100
	Ceriops roxburghiana	3000
C	*Excoecaria agallocha*	1600
	Bruguiera gymnorhiza	1100
	Avicennia alba	2100
T	*Phoenix paludosa*	0.08
	Ceriops roxburghiana	0.03
	Acanthus ilicifolius	23500
P	*Avicennia alba*	3500
	Aegiceras majus	0.03

H = Harinbhanga; K = Khatojhora; J = Jhilla; N = Natidhopani; C = Chitori; T = Thakuran; P = Prentice

FISHERY

Among the estuaries of India, the Hooghly-Matlah Estuarine System provides one of the richest grounds for fishery in the country. Nearly 16,000 fishermen live in different zones of the estuary and fishing activity goes on intensively throughout the year and the total annual catch amounts to 8-10 thousand tonnes. Table 1.4 shows the total fish landings during the period 1964-65 to 1969 and also from the lower zone. (Jhingran & Gopalakrishanan, 1973). The biology of many species found in the estuary has been worked out. According to Pillay (1967), more than 120 species of fish, prawns and crabs are found in commercial catches obtained form the Sunderbans area.

Table 1.4— Estimated annual fish landings from Hooghly-Matlah Estuarine System (From Jhingran & Gopalakrishnan, 1973)

Year	Total fish landing in tonnes	Landings from the lower zone in tonnes	% of lower zone landing in total
1964-65	10,413	9,492	91
1965-66	6,513	5,290	81
1966-67	6,766	5,308	78
1968	8,054	5,823	72
1969	8,343	6,156	74

An account on the abundance and distribution of fish larvae of five commercially important species namely *Hilsa ilisha, Setipinna phasa, Pama pama, Polynemus paradiseus* and *Eleutheronema tetradactylum* has appeared. On the basis of their abundance, the probable breeding seasons of these five species have been deduced. *Hilsa ilisha* breeds practically throughout the year with peak during August to October. *S.phasa* breeds in all the months of year with two peaks during October-November and February-March. There is an additional peak reported in August. *P.pampa* also breeds throughout the year with three peaks during February-March, July-August and October-November. *P. paradiseus* breeds round the year with a peak during July-August. *E.tetradactylum* has an extended breeding season and probably breeds throughout the year (Chandra, 1962).

Larvae and juveniles of the "Bhekti" *Lates calcarifer*, ranging between 6 and 69 mm, collected in 'hapas' have been described. They are caught at several places in the estuary. Since neither the eggs nor the very young larvae were caught, it seems that the fish breeds in the sea or in the marine zone of the estuary during the summer and monsoon months and the postlarvae and juveniles enter the estuary (Ghosh, 1973).

The well-liked fish *Hilsa ilisha*, popularly known as 'hilsa' by the common name has been reported to breed in the tidal stretches of the rivers. The eggs are hatched and the larvae grow to about 28 mm in the first month, 16 mm in the second month, 15 mm in the third month and 10 mm in the fourth month and fifth months. At the end of the first year, it attains a growth range of 163 to 171 mm (Sujansingani, 1957). The Gangetic anchovy, *Setipinna phasa*, known in Bengal as 'phasa' migrates into the rivers and has been recorded as far as Allahabad in the river Ganga in totally freshwater conditions. In fact there is a regular fishery of this species along with other migratory forms including the hilsa at Allahabad. It attains maturity at 150 mm in length and spawns several times during the year. The male:female ratio is 1:2.30 (Jhingran, 1961). Similarly another clupeoid, *Coilia borneenis* locally known as 'Amadi' is more abundant in the brackish water areas of the estuarine regions than either in marine or freshwater zones. It grows at the rate of about 10 mm per month and the maximum recorded size of the adult is 145 mm. It largely feeds on small crustaceans and attains maturity at 68 mm in length. It breeds several times during the year. The male:female ratio was found to be 1:1.1 (Varghese, 1961). Experiments on the artificial propagation of hilsa were carried out by Sen *et al.* (1990).

Studies on the biology and fishery of the Gangetic whiting, *Sillago panijus* commonly known as 'tool maach' showed that it forms a commercially important fishery in the Hooghly Estuary. Attempts were made to determine its age from the otoliths and it was deduced that probably two zones on the otoliths are formed during the course of one year. From the investigations on its growth, the fish seems to have a longevity of 5 y or more with the annual growth rate of 60 mm in the first year, 135 mm in the second year, 209 mm in the third year and so on. The maximum recorded size of the fish was 377 mm which was possibly 5.5 y old. It spawns at least twice during the year and the individuals, during the first year of their life (O group fishes), migrate into the upper reaches probably for feeding and after a few months, the young fishes migrate towards the sea. In the Sundarbans, it is caught in bagnets (beejals) and longlines. The catches predominantly belong to first three year classes (Krishnayya, 1963).

Studies on the fecundity of the anchovy, *Setipinna taty* and the ribbon fish *Trichiurus pantulii* showed that the former species produces eggs in the range of 805-3668 and the latter in the range of 1672-9435 depending upon their size (De & Mitra, 1981). The occurrence of the penaeid prawn, *Penaeus japonicus* has been recorded from the Sundarbans probably for the first time (Nandi, 1983).

Mullets form an important fishery of the estuarine system and of the 5 species recorded from the area, two species, namely *Mugil parsia* and *M. tade* are of much commercial importance. They are caught from at least 6 centres using set barriers (pata jal), bagnets (been jal) and shore-siene (ber jal) throughout the year. Table 1.5 gives the landing of the 2 species from 1960-61 to 1965-66. The size range of *M. parsia* fell between 15.5 and 295 mm and that of *M. tade* between 65.5 to 545.5 mm (Thakur, 1970).

Table 1.5— Mullet landings from Hooghly Estuarine System from 1960-61 to 1965-66 in metric tonnes and their percentages in total catch (From Thakur, 1970)

Years (Mar. - Feb.)	*Mugil parsia*	*Mugil tade*
1960-61	26.75	10.93
	(1.4 %)	(0.4 %)
1961-62	22.44	4.39
	(.5%)	(0.1%)
1962-63	54.49	8.19
	(1.1%)	(0.2%)
1963-64	38.87	12.31
	(0.6%)	(0.2%)
1964-65	43.82	8.27
	(0.4%)	(0.1%)
1965-66	59.75	7.88
	(0.9%)	(0.1%)

Among the various species of penaeid prawns which ascend into the Hooghly estuarine system, *Metapenaeus brevicornis* is one of them. It is the commonest prawn and invades shallow estuarine areas and paddy fields and is caught in bagnets. Length frequency distribution of the species shows the first mode at 24-26 mm. Since it is a continuous breeder with two peaks – one in March-April and the other in July-August, the species grows to 24-26 mm in 3-4 months. The rate of growth in females is faster than in males. Maximum longevity appears to be 2 y, as 0, 1 and 2 year groups are represented in the catches. It contributes to more than 30% of the total prawn landings from the estuary. The male:female ratio is 1:1.2 (Rajyalakshmi, 1963).

Experiments were conducted on the culture of the prawn, *Penaeus monodon* in a rain-fed coastal pond of the Sunderbans along with freshwater carps, mullets and milk fish. In two consecutive experiments during 1978 and 1979, the prawns showed relatively faster growth rate attaining 196.0 mm in length and 60.0 g in weight during the 4 months of 1978 and 194.5 mm and 65.0 g during the same period in 1979. The respective daily increments in weight in the two ponds were 0.464 g and 0.59 g. The initial faster rate of growth indicates the ability of the prawn to adapt well to low saline conditions and to grow to marketable size within 4 months. However, when the culture was continued to more than 7 months, the growth rate slowed down. The survival rate in the first experiment was 34.6% and in the second it was less than 1% (Pillai *et al.,* 1987). Prawn landings in the seaward reaches of the estuary during the years 1967, 1968 and 1969 were 619, 555 and 515 tonnes respectively and comprised mostly of the species *Parapenaeopsis sculptilis, Palaemon tenuipes, Metapenaeus brevicornis, Acetes indicus, Palaemon styliferus* and *Penaeus indicus.* These species contribute almost 50% of the total prawn landings from the Hooghly-Matlah Estuarine System (Gopalakrishnan, 1973). Growth of the juveniles of *Penaeus monodon* of the size range 18-26 mm in length, when stocked in nursery ponds of Sunderbans having 0.16-0.18‰ salinity-range, was very rapid. When these prawns were stocked with the mullet, *Mugil cephalus* with an overall density of 8,000 per ha, and repeated harvesting was done, the yield obtained was even higher. Prawns grew with a daily increment of 2.94 mm/1.703 g (Rao *et al.,* 1986).

FISHING GEARS

A variety of gears is used in the estuary for fishing. Of these, the bagnets are the most common and these are particularly designed for their operation in tidal areas. They are known locally by various names (Bin jal, Tor jal, Behundi jal, etc). Bagnets of different sizes are operated in various zones throughout the year. Their *modus operandi* varies but they are operated in such a way as to strain the tidal water. Nearly 4000 bagnets of different mesh sizes are operated in the estuary. Winter season yields the best results and the highest average yield per-unit-effort in this season is about 367 kg. Prawns and Bombay duck form more than half of the bagnet catches. Of the total landings, the bagnet fishery contributes about 70% from the estuarine areas (Pillay & Ghosh, 1962).

The other gear commonly used is nylon drift gill net. Fishing trials using this net of 3 sizes in the lower Sunderbans showed that the captured fishes of commercial importance were sharks in larger mesh sizes whereas hilsa and several other fishes are in smaller mesh size (Banerjee & Chakrabarty, 1969).

Trawling is another common method of fishing in the coastal areas of West Bengal including the deeper parts of the estuary and about 176 trawlers of different sizes are operating in the area. Good catches of prawns are obtained by trawling and the total yield from Pentakota and Sunderbans is 5424 tonnes. Of this, 129 tonnes are obtained by indigeneous crafts from the West Bengal coast (Rao, 1987).

POLLUTION

Since 1949, considerable amount of work has been done to illustrate the problems of pollution in the estuary. A review of the literature is beyond the scope of the present account. However, the basic idea to include this heading is to indicate to the readers the magnitude of the problem of pollution that exists in the estuary. Despite the fact that it is a turbulent estuary with a large tidal range and considerable mixing, dilution and flushing, a gradual accumulation of toxic wastes and progressive reduction of the flow of freshwater over a period of years have resulted in the destruction of benthic habitats leading to progressive reduction in the availability of many species of fish, prawns and their seeds.

A survey conducted by Ghosh *et al.* (1973) in a stretch of 92 km revealed 40 major industries, 55 jute mills and several municipalities discharging their wastes. A more recent survey (Dhan, 1995) indicates 96 units with the following distribution: Pulp and paper 6; Textile 5; Distillaries 3; Tannery 1; Rubber 1; Miscellaneous (Paint and Varnish, Metal Steel, Matches, Shell, etc) 15; Petroleum refineries 4; Thermal power plants 6; Jute mills 55; Domestic and municipal waste – unspecified number; Total – 96 .

These industries discharge their wastewater into the estuary either directly of through specially-built drains or through municipal drainage canals. In addition to these industries, several municipalities also discharge their wastage (largely sewage) into the estuary.

The survey on which the above figures of industries is based was carried out more than 25 years ago. Recent surveys give much larger figures which include many small-scale industries whose number exceeds more than one hundred. The total quantity of wastes discharged (industrial and municipal) has been estimated by Ghosh *et al.* (1973) and Khan (1995) as 1153.80 million litres per day (mld). This generates a B.O.D. load of 106.27 tonnes and solid load of 2318.41 tonnes/day (suspended solid 1057 t/d and dissolved solid 1260.87 t/d). Table 1.6 gives the break-up figures of the pollution load by different industries. The wastes given in Table 1.6 were classified into 3 categories

(a) Organic wastes of biological origin which included effluents of pulp and paper mills, cotton textiles and tannery;
(b) Organic wastes of non-biological origin which contained wastewater from rubber industry, paints and varnishes, oil storage and refinery and hydrogenated oil; and
(c) Wastewater of chiefly inorganic (mineral) origin coming from rayon, metal and steel factories.

Table 1.6— Pollution load in Hooghly Estuary caused by different industries in terms of volume of wastewater, BOD, total solids and suspended solids (From Khan, 1995)

Source	Vol. of wastewater mld	B.O.D t/day	Total solids t/day	Suspended solid t/day
Pulp & Paper	178.6123	28.59	547.40	299.20
Textile	20.3661	7.26	71.80	41.82
Tannery	11.3650	4.54	86.70	13.50
Distillery & Yeast	0.6751	10.29	5.24	0.40
Rubber	10.9104	0.43	8.70	1.70
Hydrogenated oil	14.1835	0.56	18.40	4.80
Miscellaneous				
Paint & Varnish	11.5778	1.49	9.20	2.40
Metal & Steel	11.4468	0.20	11.73	3.30
Matches	1.0911	0.04	2.60	0.20
Shellac	0.4091	0.39	3.70	2.10
Combined wastes of Rishra	90.9200	12.24	128.60	42.50
Petroleum refinery	6.6000	0.16	9.98	0.21
Domestic and Municipal wastewater	795.5500	40.08	1424.36	645.4
TOTAL	1153.7072	106.2700	2318.4130	1057.542

Table 1.7 shows the total volumes of each type, their B.O.D and solid load. The impact of enormous loads of pollutants on the ecology of estuary is particularly severe during the late premonsoon months (May-June) when the freshwater discharge from various points is reduced to minimum leading to very low dilution ratio and high temperature. The conditions near the outfall and up to certain distance away, were not conducive to survival and growth of all types of biota (phytoplankton, zooplankton and fish). Farther from the outfall, about 1 km away, conditions improved and both phytoplankton and zooplankton began to become abundant, probably because of the increase in nutrients liberated by the decomposition of huge quantities of organic matter. However, only a few species could utilize the nutrient enrichment. While the recovery of planktonic organism began

to be noticed at about 500 m below the outfall, the benthic fauna did not show much abundance. This probably indicates the high sensitivity of benthos to pollution. Probably the decomposition of organic matter produces CO_2 and H_2S, reduces the dissolved O_2 and results in anaerobic conditions at the sediment-water interface. Maximum impact of pollution in the estuary was felt during the neap tide phase of premonsoon season when the dilution ratio was minimum and the pollutants remained in the estuary for longer periods.

Table 1.7— Classification of various industrial and domestic wastes discharged into Hooghly Estuary (From Khan, 1995)

Type of wastewater	Volume mld	B.O.D. t/day	Suspended Solid t/day	Dissolved solid t/day
Organic wastes of biological origin	196.4713	45.91	346.522	334.12
Organic wastes of non-biological origin	43.6808	3.028	11.22	38.76
Wastewater largely containing inorganic substanes	27.185	5.010	11.90	32.93

During the monsoon season, because of high dilution factor, the impact of pollution was not so severe. Although the effects were clearly visible near the outfall, the recovery was rapid and conditions begin to improve a short distance below the outfall. However, the season as such was characterized by a low primary productivity and low diversity and abundance of fauna and flora. Phytoplankton largely included 2 species of diatoms, 3 species of bluegreen algae and euglenoids. Zooplankton were characterized by lower density and similar set of species were present as during the premonsoon season. Benthic fauna during this season largely included oligochaetes and dipteran larvae.

During the postmonsoon season, the impact of pollution was reduced quickly and although like the other two seasons, the outfall region was affected, the conditions improved as was evident from 86.5% of primary productivity, 54.3% phytoplankton, 65.1% of zooplankton and 86.6% of benthos in the upper reaches (Khan, 1995).

Concentrations of 5 metals namely Fe, Cd, Ni, Pb and Co in zooplankton from the estuary were measured for one year from January to December 1989. Of the metals, Pb and Co were not detected in any sample throughout the year. The concentration of Fe was the highest and ranged from 1470 to 12051 ppm (average 5102 ppm). The range in Cd was between 6 and 96 ppm (average 33.92 ppm) while Ni recorded the lowest levels 4 to 29 ppm (average 12.41 ppm). Both Fe and Cd showed highest values during the monsoon period (July-October) when the salinity was low indicating their source from land-runoff. Ni values were lowest during the monsoon and postmonsoon seasons and slightly higher during the premonsoon period (Kundu & Choudhury, 1993).

Levels of 5 metals (Cu, Fe, Mn, Zn and Pb) were measured in the tissues of a marine bivalve *Grassostrea cuculata* taken from 2 stations of the estuary. At both the stations, the bivalves had accumulated significant concentrations of metals in their tissues. Among the 5 metals, Fe and Zn were found to be relatively in higher concentrations (Mitra *et al.,* 1987). Sediment samples from marine, estuarine and freshwater zones of the estuary contained hydrocarbons ranging from 4.38 to 7.98% of the organic carbon. Microorganisms present in the estuary were probably responsible for breaking the hydrocarbons into fatty acids and *n*-alkanes (Ghosh *et al.,* 1990b).

Using several species of phytoplankton organisms as monitors, the pollution levels in the estuary were evaluated. Some species were found to be pollution-tolerant while others were sensitive. Diversity index was taken as an index of pollution. In most cases, the diversity index was found to be less than 3 and this was attributed to pollution factor (Pal *et al.,* 1992).

A non-linear, vertically integrated, two-dimensional, depth-averaged numerical, hydrodynamic model has been developed to study pollutant dispersal in the estuary (Sinha *et al.,* 1998). The model demonstrates the utility of simpler numerical schemes in simulating many observed features in a well-mixed estuary and can be used to make realistic estimate of residual circulation and pollutant transport. The effect of wind and the horizontal salinity gradient on the residual circulation were found to be very significant. The computed magnitude and direction of the residual velocities were in reasonable agreement with the available observations of the dry season. The results obtained from the model showed that the pollutants discharged from the upper part of the estuary do not effect the Haldia Channel. The strong ebb flow in the channel flushes off the pollutants out of the estuary. The pollutants released near Haldia have a tendency to remain for a longer time due to weak ebb flow. The problem gets accentuated during the low water conditions. The situation can be improved by controlling the release of pollutants during certain phases of the tidal cycles.

References

1. Banerjee, M.K. & Chakarbarty, R.D., 1969. Drift gill-netting in lower Sunderbans, West Bengal. *Indian Journal of Fisheries*, Vol. 16, pp. 75-81.
2. Bose, B.B., 1956. Observations on the hydrology of the Hooghly estuary. *Indian Journal of Fisheries*, Vol. 3, 101-118.
3. Chakraborty, S.K. & Choudhury, A., 1992. Ecological studies on the zonation of brachyuran crabs in a virgin mangrove island of Sunderbans, India. *Journal of Marine Biological Association of India,* Vol. 34, pp. 189-194.
4. Chakraborty, S.K., Poddar, T.K. & Choudhuary, A., 1992. Species diversity of macrozoobenthos of Sagar Islands, Sunderbans, India. *Proceedings of the Zoological Society Calcutta*, Vol. 45, (supplement A), pp. 435-444.
5. Chandra, R., 1962. A preliminary account of the distribution and abundance of fish larvae in the Hooghly estuary. *Indian Journal of Fisheries*, Vol. 9, pp. 48-70.
6. Chatterjee, A.K., 1987. Estuarine improvement - Numerical simulation. *In: Proceedings of the National Seminar on Estuarine Management*, 4-5 June 1987, Trivandrum. (ed.) N.B. Nair, *National Seminar on Estuarine Management*, Trivandrum, India, 4-5 June 1987. pp. 93-97. State Committee on Science, Technology and Environment, Trivandrum, India. 1987.
7. Chowdhery, H.J., Garg, K.L. & Jaitly, A.K., 1982. Occurrence of fungi in rhizosphere, rhizoplane and non-rhizosphere zones of some mangroves. *Indian Journal of Marine Sciences*, Vol. 11, pp. 138-142.
8. Dasgupta, D. & Sircar, A.K., 1987. Estimation of glycogen level in ovary, liver and muscles of the estuarine gangetic anchovy, *Setipinna phasa* (Hamilton) during the breeding season. *Journal of Marine Biological Association of India*, Vol. 29, pp. 380-383.
9. De, T.K. & Mitra, P.M.., 1981. Studies on the fecundily of *Setipinna taty* (Valenciennes) and *Trichiurus pantulii* Gupta, of the Hooghly estuarine system. *Indian Journal of Fisheries*, Vol. 28, pp. 272-275.
10. De, T.K., & Datta, N.C., 1990. Age, growth, length-weight relationship and relative condition in hilsa, *Tenualosa ilisha* (Hamilton) from the Hooghly estuarine system. *Indian Journal of Fisheries*, Vol. 37, pp. 199-209.
11. De, T.K., Ghosh, S.K., Jana, T.K. & Choudhury, A., 1991a. Extinction coefficient and primary productivity in the mixing zone of Hooghly Estuary. *Journal of Aquaculture in Tropics*, Vol. 6, pp. 201-206.
12. De, T.K., Ghosh, S.K., Jana, T.K. & Choudhury, A., 1991b. Phytoplankton bloom in the Hooghly Estuary. *Indian Journal of Marine Sciences*, Vol. 20, pp. 134-137.
13. De, T.K., Ghosh, S.K., Jana, T.K., 1994. Phytoplankton community organization and species diversity in the Hooghly Estuary, north east coast of India. *Indian Journal of Marine Sciences*, Vol. 23, pp. 152-156.
14. Garg, L.K., 1982. Effect of salinity on cellulolytic activity of some pneumatophore-inhabiting fungi of Sunderban mangrove swamps. *Indian Journal of Marine Sciences*, Vol. 11, pp. 339-340.
15. Garg, K.L., 1983. Vertical distribution of fungi in Sunderban mangrove mud. *Indian Journal of Marine Sciences*, Vol. 12, pp. 48-51.

16. Ghosh, B.B., Ray, P. & Gopalakrishnan, V., 1973. Survey and characterisation of waste-waters discharged into the Hugli Estuary. *Journal of Inland Fishery Society of India*, Vol. 4, pp. 82-101.
17. Ghosh, A., 1973. Observations on the larvae and juveniles of the 'Bhekti', *Lates calcarifer* (Bloch) from the Hooghly-Matlah estuarine system. *Indian Journal of Fisheries*, Vol. 20, pp. 372-379.
18. Ghosh, P.B., Singh, B.N., Chakrabarty, C., Saha, A., Das, R.L. & Choudhury, A., 1990a. Mangrove litter production in a tidal creek of Lothian Island of Sunderbans, India. *Indian Journal of Marine Sciences*, Vol. 19, pp. 292-293.
19. Ghosh, P.B., Misra, S., Choudhury, A. & Ghosh, A., 1990b. Possible sources of aliphatic hydrocarbons in sediments of Hooghly estuary, northeast coast of India. *Indian Journal of Marine Sciences*, Vol. 19, pp. 145-147.
20. Ghosh, P.B., Chakraborty, C., Saha, A., Singh, B.N. & Choudhury, A., 1991a. Productivity of the grass, *Porteresia coaretata* in mangrove forest of Sunderbans. *Indian Journal of Marine Sciences*, Vol. 20, pp.280-282.
21. Ghosh, S.K., De, T.K., Choudhury, A. & Jena, T.K., 1991b. Oxygen deficiency in Hooghly Estuary, east coast of India. *Indian Journal of Marine Sciences*, Vol. 20, pp. 216-217.
22. Ghosh, S.K., Mahapatra, B. De, T.K., Choudhury, A. & Jena T.K., 1992. Calcite and orogonite satuartion in Hooghly Estuary (Bay of Bengal). *Indian Journal of Marine Sciences*, Vol. 21, pp. 207-209.
23. Gopalakrishnan, V., 1973. An assessment of the prawn fishery of the sea-ward reaches of the Hooghly Estuary. *Journal of Marine Biological Association of India,* Vol. 15, pp. 406-410.
24. Jhingran, V.G., 1961. Studies on the maturity and fecundity of the Gangetic anchovy *Setipinna phasa* (Hamilton). *Indian Journal of Fisheries*, Vol. 8, pp. 291-311.
25. Jhingran, C.G. & Gopalakrishnan, V., 1973. Estuarine fisheries resources of India in relation to adjacent seas. *Journal of Marine Biological Association of India*, Vol. 15, pp. 323-334.
26. Krishnyya, C.G., 1963. On the use of otoliths in the determination of age and growth of the gengetic whiting, *Sillago panijus* (Ham. Buch), with notes on its fishery in Hooghly Estuary. *Indian Journal of Fisheries*, Vol. 10, pp. 391-412.
27. Khan, R.A., 1995. The pollution problem of Hughli Estuarine System. *Estuarine Ecosystem Series, Zoological Survey of India*, Part 2, pp. 497-542.
28. Kundu, S.K. & Choudhury, A., 1993. Studies on epipilagic zooplankton from Hooghly Estuary, India. *Current Science*, Vol. 64, pp. 110-112.
29. Kundu, S.K., Sarkar, S.K. & Choudhury, A., 1987. Studies on epipelagic zooplankton with special reference to copepods in Hooghly and Saptamukhi river waters, West Bengal, India. In: *Proceedings of the National Seminar on Estuarine Management, 4-5 June 1987. Trivandrum* (ed.) N.B. Nair, National Seminar on Estuarine Management. Trivandrum, India, 4-5 June 1987. State Commission on Science, Technology and Environment, Trivandrum, India. 1987, pp. 323-326.
30. Lal, B., 1990. Impact of Frakka Barrage on the hydrographical changes and productivity potential of Hooghly Estuary. *Journal of Inland Fishery Society of India*. Vol. 22, pp. 38-42.

31. Matilal, S., Mukherjee, B.B., Chatterjee, N. & Gupta, M.D., 1986. Studies on soil and vegetation of mangrove forests of Sunderbans, *Indian Journal of Marine Sciences*, Vol. 15, pp. 181-184.
32. Matilal, S. & Mukherjee, B.B., 1989. Distribution of mangroves in relation to topography and selection of ecotonal communities for reclaimed areas of Sunderbans. Indian *Journal of Marine Sciences*, Vol. 18, pp. 91-94.
33. Mitra, A., Bhushan, G.P. & Choudhury, A., 1987. A marine bivalve, *Crassostrea acculata* can be used as an indicator species of marine pollution in: *Proceedings of National Seminar on Estuarine Management* (ed.) N.B. Nair. State Commission on Science on Science and Technology and Environment. Trivandrum, pp. 177-180.
34. Misra, S., Choudhury, A., Chattopadhyay, S. & Ghosh, A., 1987. Sterols and terpenoids of the segrass porteresia coarctata grown in two different mangrove habitats of Sunderbans. *Journal of Marine Biological Association of India,* Vol. 29, pp. 365-366.
35. Nandi, N.C., 1983. On the occurrence of the penaeid prawn *Penaeus japonicus* Bate in Hooghly Estuary. *Indian Journal of Fisheries*, Vol. 30, pp. 343-344.
36. Nandi, S. & Choudhury, A., 1983. Quantitative studies on the benthic macrofauna of Sagar Island, intertidal zones. Sunderbans, India. *Mahasagar — Bulletin of National Institute of Oceanography,* Vol. 16, pp. 209-220.
37. Nandy, A.C., Bagchi, M.M. & Majumdar, S.K., 1983. Ecological changes in the Hooghly Estuary due to water release from Farakka Barrage. *Mahasagar—Bulletin of National Institute of Oceanography*, Vol. 16, pp. 209-220.
38. Pal, A.K. & Purakayastha, R.P., 1992. New parasitic fungi from Indian mangrove. *Journal of Mycopathology Research,* Vol. 30, pp. 173-176.
39. Pal, R., Chatterjee, P. & Das, T.M. 1992. Algological evaluation of organic pollution level of Hughli Estuary, West Bengal, India. *Phykos*, Vol. 31, pp. 69-75.
40. Pillai, S.M., Ghosh, P.K., Rajyalakshmi, T., Halder, D.D., Roy, A.K & Chakraborti, R.K., 1987. A note on the growth of *Penaeus monodon* Fabricius in a rainfed coastal pond in Sunderbans. *Indian Journal of Fisheries*, Vol. 34, pp. 108-111.
41. Pillay, T.V.R.& Ghosh, K.K., 1962. The bag net fishery of the Hooghly-matlah estuarine system (West Bengal). *Indian Journal of Fisheries,* Vol. 9, pp. 71-99.
42. Pillay, T.V.R., 1967. Estuarine fisheries of the Indian Ocean coastal areas. In *Estuaries* (ed.) G.h. Lauff. Association for the Advancement of Science, Washington, D.C.,pp. 647-657.
43. Poddar, T.K, Roy, S. & Choudhury, A., 1989. Population structure analysis of larval rove-beetle in the intertidal zone of Sagar Island, Sunderbans, India. *Indian Journal of Marine Sciences,* Vol. 18, pp. 100-102.
44. Poddar, T.K & Choudhury, A., 1992. Arthropod fauna of littoral zone in two islands of Hooghly Estuarine Complex, West Bengal, India. *Journal of Marine Biological Association of India*, Vol. 34, pp. 258-268.
45. Rajyalakshmi, T., 1963. Observations on the biology and fishery of *Metapenaeus brevicornis* (M. Edw.) in the Hooghly estuarine system. *Indian Journal of Fisheries,* Vol. 8, pp. 383-402.

46. Rao, A.V.P., Ghosh, A.N., Verghese, P.U. & Ghosh, P.K., 1986. Observations on the growth of *Penaeus monodon* (Fabricius) in the less saline ponds of Sunderbans with notes on acclimatisation and transport of their seed. *Journal of Marine Biological Association of India*, Vol. 28, pp. 136-140.
47. Rao, G.S., 1987. A preliminary study on the prawn fishery of big trawlers along the northeast coast of India. *Indian Journal of Fisheries*, Vol. 34, pp. 312-328.
48. Rao, Y.R., Sinha, P.C. & Dube, S.K.,1998. Circulation and salinity in Hooghly Estuary: A numerical study. *Indian Journal of Marine Sciences,* Vol. 27, Special issue: Satellite Oceanography and Modelling (ed.) P.C. Pandey, pp. 121-128.
49. Ray, S. & Choudhury, A, 1987. Community organization of benthic dipterans in a tidal creek of Hooghly estuary, Sagar Island, India. In: *Proceedings of the National seminar on* Estuarine Management. 4-5 June 1987. Trivandrum. (ed.) N.B. Nair, National Seminar on Estuarine Management, Trivandrum, India. State Committee on Science, Technology and Environment, Trivandrum, India. pp. 406-409.
50. Saha, S.B., Ghosh, B.B. & Gopalakrishnan, V., 1975. Plankton of the Hooghly estuary with special reference to salinity and temperature. *Journal of Marine Biological Association of India,* Vol. 17, pp. 107-120.
51. Sardessai, S. 1989. Humic and fulvic acids in sediments of the Hooghly Estuary and some coastal areas in the northern Bay of Bengal. *Indian Journal of Marine Sciences*, Vol. 18, pp. 16-20.
52. Santra, S.C. & Pal, U.C., 1989. Phytoplankton of Bhagirathi - Hooghly Estuary: An illustrative accounts. *Indian Biology*, Vol. 29, pp. 1-27.
53. Sarkar, S., Baidya , A., Bhunia, A. & Choudhury, A., 1984. Zooplankton studies in the Hooghly estuary around Sagar Island, Sunderbans, India. In: *Proceedings of the Asian Sysmposium on Mangrove Environment research and Management.* (eds.) by E. Soepadmo & A. N. Rao, The Asian Symposium. On Mangrove Environment Research and Management. Kuala Lumpur, Malaysia, 25-29 Aug. 1980 . Percetaken Ardyos. Kuala Lumpur, Malaysia. pp. 286-297.
54. Sarkar,S.K., Singh, B.N. & Choudhury, A., 1985a. Copepod components of inshore zooplankton of the Bay of Bengal off Sagar Island, West Bengal, India. *Current Science*, Vol. 54, pp. 1217-122.
55. Sarkar,S.K., Singh,.B.N. & Choudhury, A., 1985b. Ecology of chaetognaths in the Hooghly Estuary, Bay of Bengal. *Indian Journal of Marine Sciences*, Vol. 14, pp. 98-101.
56. Sarkar,S.K., Singh,.B.N. & Choudhury, A., 1986a. Composition and variation in abundance of zooplankton in the Hooghly Estuary, West Bengal, India. *Proceedings of the Indian Academy of Sciences*, Vol. 95, pp. 125-134.
57. Sarkar,S.K., Singh,.B.N. & Choudhury, A., 1986b. The ecology of copepods from Hooghly Estuary, West Bengal, India. *Mahasagar – Bulletin of National Institute of Oceanography* , Vol. 19, pp. 103-112.
58. Sarkar,S.K., Choudhury, A., 1986. On the occurrence and abundance *of Mesopodopsis orientalis* (W.M. tattersall) (Crstacea: Mysisdacea) from Hooghly Estuary. *Mahasagar – Bulletin of National Institute of Oceanography,* Vol. 19, pp. 203-207.
59. Sarkar,S.K. & Choudhury, A., 1987. Occurrence of a cladoceran swarm in the lower stretch of Hooghly Estuary, West Bengal, India. *Current Science*, Vol. 56, pp. 431.

60. Sasamal, S.K., Sahu, B.K. & Panigrahy, R.C., 1986. Texture and composition of sediments of Hooghly Estuary and nearshore environment. *Indian Journal of Marine Sciences,* Vol. 15, pp. 201-202.
61. Sen, P.R., De, D.K. & Nath, D., 1990. Experiments on artifical propagation of hilsa, *Tenualosa ilisha* (Hamilton). *Indian Journal of Fisheries, Vol.* 37, pp. 159-162.
62. Shetty, H.P.C., Saha, S.B. & Ghosh, B.B., 1963. Observations on the distribution and fluctuations of plankton in the Hooghly-Matlah estuarine system, with notes on their relation to commercial fish landings. *Indian Journal of Fisheries,* Vol. 8, pp. 326-363.
63. Sinha, B. & Choudhuary, A. 1987. Observations on the ecology of nematodes inhabiting littoral sands of the Hugli Estuary. *Journal of Marine Biological Association of India*, Vol. 29, pp. 124-133.
64. Sinha, M., 1981. Length-weight relationship and relative condition factor of the canine catfish-eel *Plotosus canius* Hamilton. *Journal of Marine Biological Association of India*, Vol. 23, pp. 39-43.
65. Sinha, P.C., Ray, Y.R., Dube, S.K. & Murthy, C.R. 1998. A numerical circulation and pollution transport in a tidal estuary (Hooghly) of NE coast of model for residual India. *Indian Journal of Marine sciences.* Vol. 27, Special issue on Satellite and Modelling Oceanography, (ed) P.C. Pandey, pp 129-139.
66. Sujansingani, K.H., 1957. Growth of the Indian Shad, *Hilsa ilisha* (Hamilton), in the tidal stretch of the Hooghly. *Indian Journal of Fisheries*, Vol. 4, pp. 315-335.
67. Thakur, N.K., 1970. Observations on the mullet fishery in the Hooghly and Mahanadi estuarine systems. *Indian Journal of Fisheries,* Vol. 17, pp. 1-12.
68. Varghese, T.J., 1961. Some observation on the biology of *Coilia borneenis* (Blkr). *Indian Journal of Fisheries*, Vol. 8. pp. 312-325.

Chapter 2

Rushikulya

A shallow tidal estuary, named as Rushikulya Estuary formed by the river Rushikulya, is one of the major estuaries of Orissa State. It is located along Lat. 19°22′ - 19°24′N and Long. 85°02′ - 85°05′E (Fig. 2.1) near Ganjam town. It has a maximum depth of 3.2 m. Its earlier opening (mouth) into the Bay of Bengal had severe siltation problems. Therefore, a new (second) mouth had to be opened on 20 September 1988 (Fig. 2.1). Because of this, the course and flow of the river have undergone modification and several physiographic changes have occurred in the estuary including the tidal flow of seawater which has a greater influx upstream. The tides in the estuary are of semidiurnal type with two floods and two ebbs during 24 h with a range of 1.5-2.5 m. The estuary becomes saltwater-dominated during the premonsoon season and freshwater-dominated during the monsoon period. During the postmonsoon season, transitory conditions prevail when perceptible horizontal and vertical salinity gradients become well-marked.

HYDROGRAPHY

Reliable data from the estuary, for a period of two years (1988 and 1989) were collected at fortnightly intervals on temperature, salinity, *p*H, transparency of

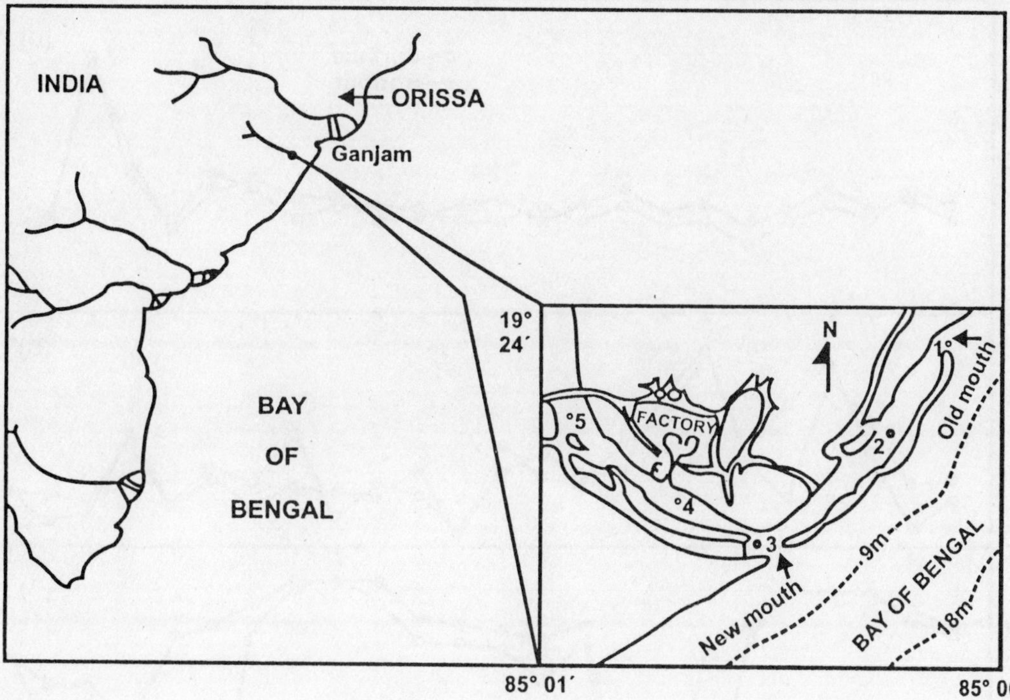

Fig. 2.1 Map of Rushikulya Estuary showing its relation to Ganjam town in Orissa State (From Gouda & Panigrahy, 1993)

water, dissolved oxygen, nutrients, phytoplankton and zooplankton at several stations in the estuary (Gouda & Panigrahy, 1989, 1991, 1992a, 1993, 1995a & 1995b, 1995c). Figure 2.2 shows the seasonal changes in temperature, salinity, dissolved oxygen and *p*H at the surface and bottom. As a typical example, the data shown in Fig. 2.2, refer to the mouth of the estuary. This is because, being a shallow estuary, the changes in the environmental features of the other stations were almost similar.

With minor fluctuations, the temperature of surface water followed the air temperature and varied in the range 25.8 - 32.0 ˚C in 1988 and 23.5 - 33.2 ˚C in 1989. The lowest temperature was recorded in December. There was no significant difference between surface and bottom temperatures. Surface salinity was lowest during August/September (0.05‰) and highest in April/May (34.7‰). Seasonal range at the bottom was 0.3 - 35.7‰. Dissolved oxygen showed random fluctuation from 3.00 to 8.4 ml/l at the surface and 3.00 to 8.4l ml/l at the bottom. Transparency in the estuary was minimum during the monsoon season (July to

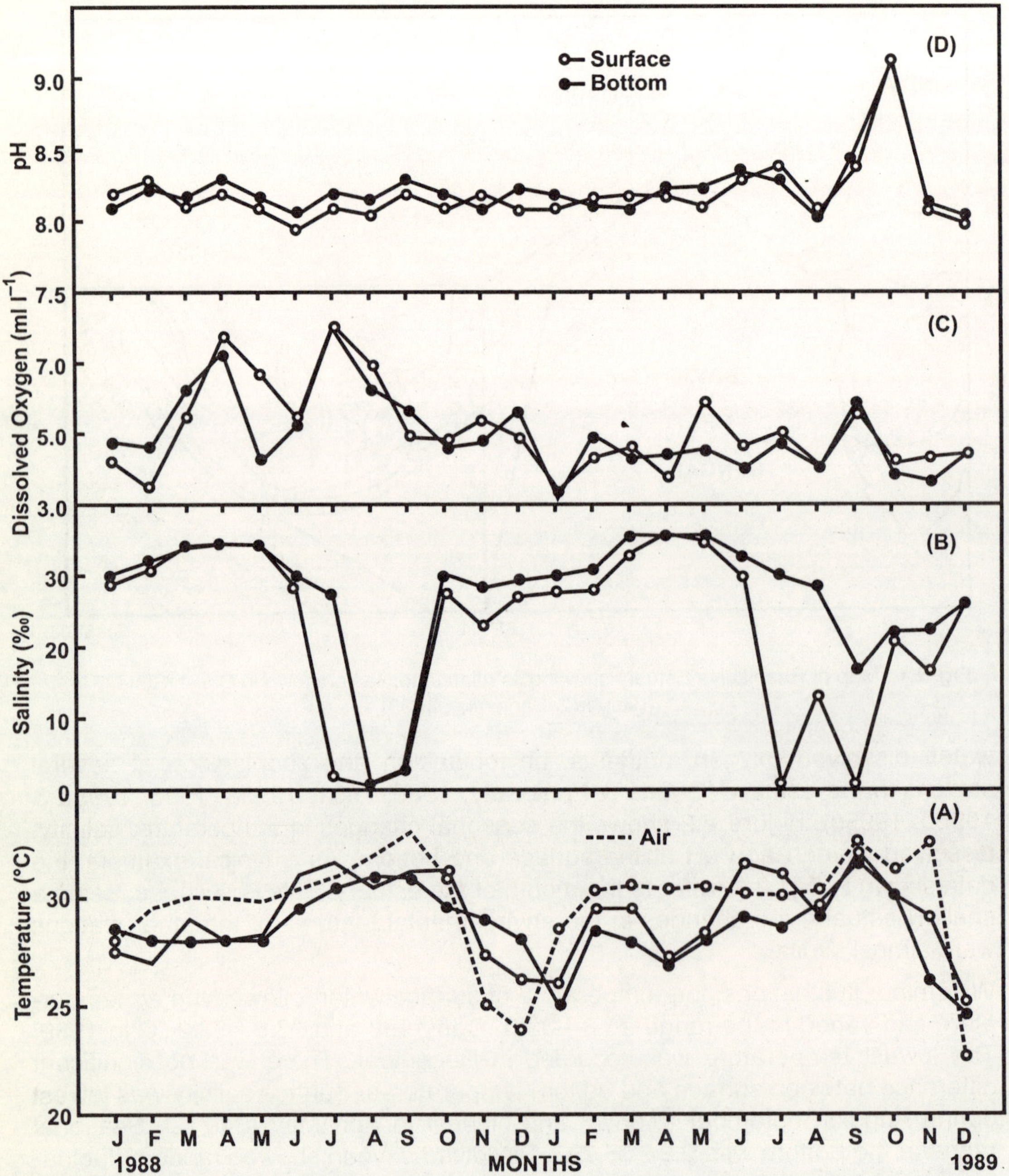

Fig. 2.2 Seasonal changes in temperature, salinity, dissolved oxygen and *p*H at the surface and bottom of the mouth of Rushikulya Estuary (From Gouda & Panigrahy, 1993)

October) and maximum from April to June. Turbidity was largely caused by silt-laden land runoff and clarity by the intrusion of clearer seawater (Gouda & Panigrahy, 1993).

Table 2.1 gives nitrate and phosphate values at the surface and bottom in the 3 seasons along with salinity and N:P ratios for two years. Seasonal cycles of the two nutrients are shown in Fig. 2.3 (A) & (B). Nitrate-nitrogen shows peak values during the monsoon period (July-October) both at the surface and bottom. There is an inverse relationship between nitrate and salinity which signifies that the main source of nitrogen in the estuary is land runoff. Phosphate-phosphorous shows consistency both at the surface and bottom and seasonally there is a random fluctuation except for a well-defined peak which appeared from July to September in 1989 at all the stations. N:P ratios show a wide range (Table 2.1) and such an inconsistency in the ratios is seen in most of the estuaries of India. This is probably because the availability of nitrogen far exceeds its utilization by the phytoplankters (Gouda & Panigrahy, 1992a).

Table 2.1—Seasonal distribution of salinity, nitrate, phosphate and N:P ratios in Rushikulya Estuary (ranges are given in parentheses) (From Gouda & Panigrahy, 1995a)

Parameters		1998			1989		
		Pre-monsoon (Feb-June)	Monsoon (July-Sept.)	Post-monsoon (Oct.-Jan)	Pre-monsoon (Feb-June)	Monsoon (July-Sept.)	Post-monsoon (Oct.-Jan)
Salinity ($\times 10^{-3}$)	S	29.4 (15.3-34.7)	3.2 (0.5-28.0)	22.2 (2.9-31.0)	31.8 (24.1-35.7)	6.2 (0.1-22.4)	23.3 (9.7-33.00)
	B	32.1 (23.0-34.7)	8.5 (0.7-30.82)	24.6 (9.5-32.0)	33.7 (30.4-35.7)	20.1 (0.3-30.6)	24.1 (17.7-33.8)
Nitrate (μg-at.1^{-1})	S	3.46 (0.37-11.16)	8.51 (1.80-18.48)	3.12 (0.87-10.58)	1.6 (0.04-4.41)	9.2 (0.9-22.27)	24.1 (0.08-4.50)
	B	3.13 (9.05-8.26)	7.06 (2.15-13.14)	2.45 (1.05-4.34)	1.82 (0.49-4.00)	3.56 (0.55-10.44)	1.75 (0.28-6.21)
Phosphate (μg-at.1^{-1})	S	0.54 (0.09-0.93)	0.81 (0.19-1.86)	0.44 (0.08-1.4)	0.4 (0.12-1.00)	1.69 (0.42-3.30)	0.56 (0.05-1.19)
	B	0.47 (0.14-1.07)	0.93 (0.19-1.33)	0.46 (0.08-2.0)	0.47 (0.19-1.88)	0.94 (0.23-2.14)	0.57 (0.09-1.59)
Nitrate: Phosphate ratio	S	7.82 (0.7:1-48.5:1)	17.04 (3:1-65.1)	7.4 (0.1:1-17:3:1)	5.84 (1.6:1-13.6:1)	5.4 (1:1-11.9:1)	7.54 (0.6:1-62.5:1)
	B	5.7 (0.9:1-26.1:1)	8.75 (23:1-24.2:1)	5.2 (0.6:1-9.6:1)	4.95 (1.1:1-13.3:1)	6.57 (0.5:1-19.2:1)	6.12 (2:1-17.7:1)

S = Surface; B = Bottom

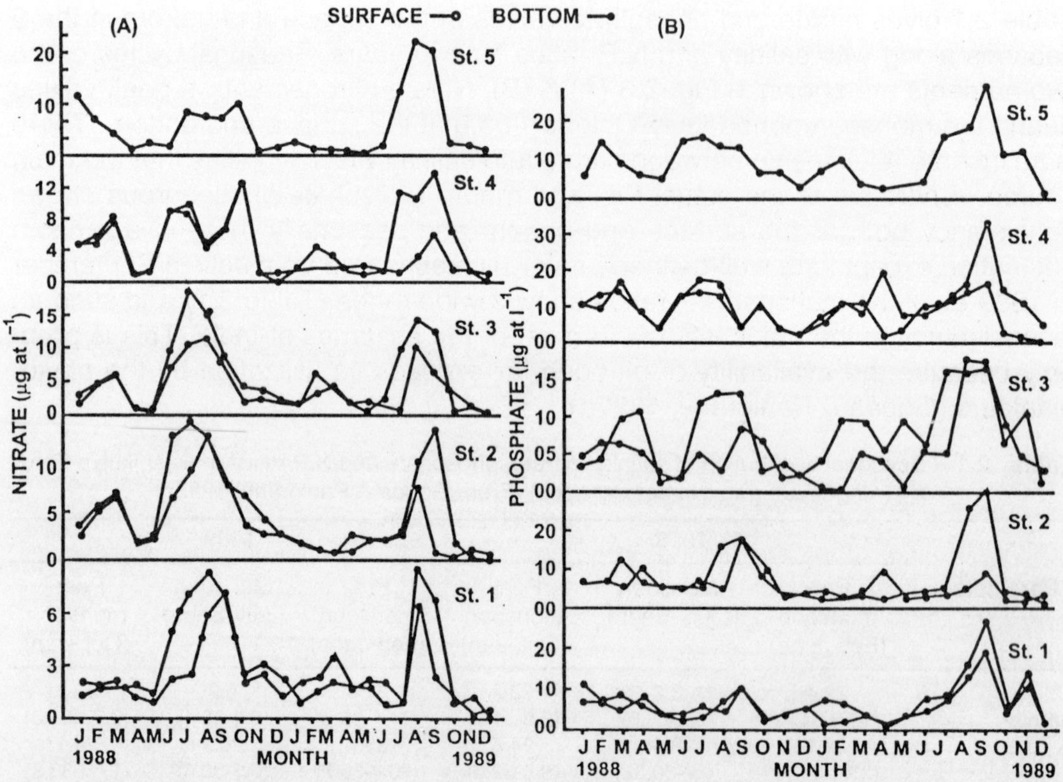

Fig. 2.3 Seasonal changes in nitrate (A) and phosphate (B) at the surface and bottom of 5 stations in Rushikulya Estuary (From Gouda & Panigrahy, 1992a). The data presented in this figure refer to two depths – surface as open circles and bottom as closed circles. In this figure given above by the authors, the open circles have disappeared and are seen as closed circles. However, being a shallow estuary, the differences between surface and bottom do not seem significant (see Table 2.1)

The distribution of calcium (Ca) and magnesium (Mg) in the estuary has also been studied. The average values in surface waters during the premonsoon season were: Ca-322.19 mg/l and Mg-816.42 mg/l. During the monsoon season, the values of both the elements declined : Ca-61.39; Mg-112.87 mg/l. There was a direct relationship between these two cations and salinity, and the same feature was reflected from their spatial distribution in the estuary. The values of both the elements increased with salinity (Tripathy *et al.*, 1990).

PHYTOPLANKTON

The estuary has been found to be rich in phytoplankton population. In all, 89 species were recorded and identified from December 1987 to May 1988. Of these, 72 were diatoms, 10 dinoflagellates, 5 bluegreen algae and 2 green algae. Among the diatoms, the following 7 genera belong to centrales and 9 genera to pennales:

Centrales	**Pennales**
Biddulphia	*Amphora*
Chaetoceros	*Bacillaria*
Coscinodiscus	*Cocceneis*
Guinardia	*Diploneis*
Rhizosolenia	*Nitzschia*
Triceratium	*Pinnularia*
Pyxidicula	*Pleurosigma*
	Navicula
	Surirella

The most common dinoflagellates were *Ceratium furca, C. lineatum* and *Gonyaulax polyedra*. Among the bluegreen algae, *Oscillatoria* sp. and *Trichodesmium* sp. were common – the latter blooms between February and May. The green alga, *Enteromorpha compressa,* was also frequently seen (Gouda & Panigrahy, 1991). Numerical abundance of phytoplankton in terms of cell numbers showed a marked diurnal variation. Maximum abundance (25.23×10^3 /l) was obtained at 0905 hours and minimum (9.50×10^3 /l) at 2105 hours. In general, phytoplankton cells recorded low density during the ebb periods and with the rise of water their number increased. Similar cycle was observed in the values of plant pigments. Among the nutrients, silicate and nitrate values increased markedly during the ebb tides showing inverse relationship with salinity (Gouda & Panigrahy, 1989).

On 4th April 1988, a bloom of the diatom, *Asterionella glacialis* was recorded in the estuary. The bloom lasted for about 5 weeks. Phytoplankton counts during the bloom period ranged from 3.98×10^4 cells to 9.42×10^4 /l. In this bloom, *A. glacialis* alone contributed 72-86.2% of the total density. The bloom declined towards the later part of May. Nutrient levels, particularly silicate and phosphate, were reduced to a minimum towards the end of the bloom. Salinity and dissolved oxygen remained high during the bloom period (Panigrahy & Gouda, 1990).

ZOOPLANKTON

Like phytoplankton, the estuary is reported to be rich in zooplankton fauna. Samples of zooplankton were collected at fortnightly intervals using a conical net from two zones of the estuary. Zone 1 was in the lower reaches while zone 2 in the upper reaches. The study was conducted over a period of two years 1988 and 1989. Sixty three zooplankton species were identified. Among the crustaceans, copepods, mysids, lucifers, amphipods, cladocerans, ostracods, cumaceans and euphausids formed the main components of the zooplankton community. Other groups of frequent occurrence included tintinnids, chaetognaths and siphonophores, while ctenophores, hydromedusae, thaleaceans and appendicularians did not occur regularly. Young forms identified were polychaete larvae, crustacean larvae and fish eggs and larvae in the plankton. The characteristics of some of the groups were as follows:

Copepods were represented by 37 species: Calanoida – 24; Cyclopoida – 12; Harpacticoida – 1. Quantitatively they constituted 51.82 to 86.0% in zone 1 and 53.46 to 91.25% in zone 2 of the total zooplankton. Purely marine forms included 10 species, brackish water 18 species and the rest were freshwater forms.

Other crustaceans shared 0.99 to 7.24% of the total volume in zone 1 and 1.51 to 7.40% in zone 2. Tintinnids included 5 species and their contribution ranged from 0.86 to 18.95% of the total zooplankton. Chaetognath population was represented by *Sagitta bedoti* and *S. enflata* and their contribution ranged from 0.97 to 14.91%. Other groups, namely siphonophores, hydromedusae, ctenophores, appendicularians, dolliloides and salps, were irregular visitors of the estuary. Siphonophores were found during January to June; hydromedusae during October/November and ctenophores (*Pleurobrachia globosa*) occurred in high numbers twice a year during February to May and November to December.

Larvae of crustaceans, polychaetes, fish eggs and larvae showed marked seasonal variations. These together shared between 3.8 to 30.8% of the total zooplankton counts. Larvae of crustaceans were recorded throughout the year. Among these, the larvae of *Penaeus monodon. P. indicus, Metapenaeus dobsoni* and *M. monoceros* occurred in large numbers during June-July and November-December.

Figure 2.4 shows the displacement volume and density (in terms of counts) in each month for the year 1988 and 1989 in the two zones. In the year 1988, the volume in zone 1 ranged from 9 to 131 ml/100 m^3 and from 18 to 104 ml/100 m^3 in zone 2. In the year 1989, the ranges in volumes in zones 1 and 2 were 7 to 142 and 8 to 104 ml/100 m^3 respectively. Seasonal cycle showed two maxima – the primary peak in June and the secondary peak in December in both the years. Zooplankton density closely followed the plankton volume (Fig. 2.4) and there was a linear relationship between the two. In 1988, the range in the density was from 788 to 22897 counts/m^3, and in 1989, it was from 1113 to 17975 counts/m^3 in

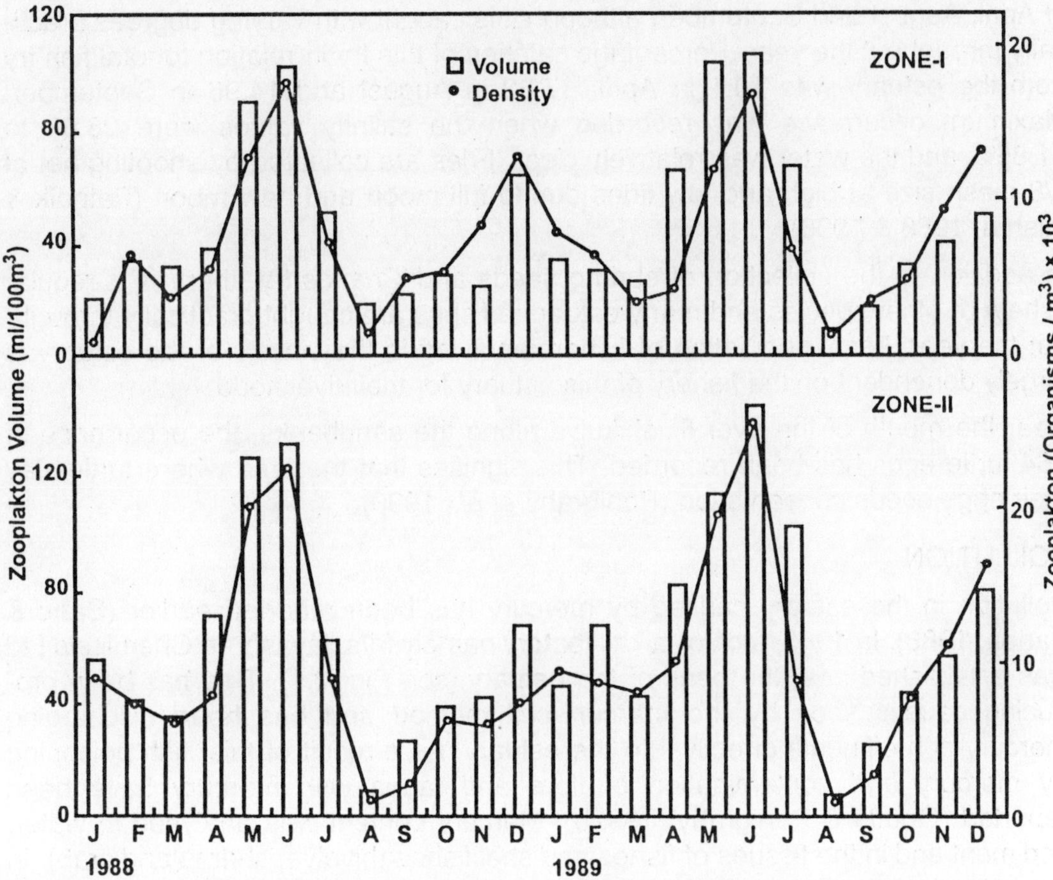

Fig. 2.4 Seasonal changes in the volume and density of zooplankton in Rushikulya Estuary (From Gouda & Panigrahy, 1995b)

zone 1 and from 709 to 25621 and 905 to 16915 counts/m^3 in zone 2 during the two years (Gouda & Panigrahy, 1995b).

FISHERY

The estuary is known for its fishery and, of late, because of the expanding activities of aquaculture in Orissa, it is being used for the collection of penaeid prawn seeds. It also serves as a suitable ground for the collection of the fry of milkfish, *Chanos chanos*. Peak occurrence of *Chanos* fry has been reported in the months of April, August and September, although it is caught with varying degrees practically throughout the year. Percentage catches of this fry in relation to total fish fry from the estuary was 10.1 in April, 17.52 in August and 14.96 in September. Maximum occurrence was recorded when the salinity values were 28.85 to 31.85‰ and the water was relatively clear. Fries are collected by shooting net of 1/8 mesh size at high and low tides during full moon and new moon (Patnaik & Mishra, 1988 & 1990).

In addition to the collection of shrimp seeds and *Chanos* fry, there is a regular fishery of other species and many estuarine fishes are caught practically throughout the year. Local population of fisherman living in the vicinity of the estuary is largely dependent on the fishery of this estuary for their livelihood.

Near the mouth of the river Rushikulya along the sandbanks, the occurrence of 664 turtle eggs has been recorded. This signifies that the area where turtles lay their eggs needs conservation (Panigrahy *et al.,* 1990).

POLLUTION

Pollution in the estuary caused by mercury has been reported earlier (Sahu & Panda, 1988). In 1965, a chlor-alkali factory namely M/s Jayashree Chemicals Ltd was established near the bank of the estuary (see Fig. 2.1). This has been producing caustic soda by the mercury-cell method and has been discharging mercury-rich effluents directly into the estuary. As a result of this, fish poisoning by mercury and contamination of flora and fauna with mercury have been reported (Gouda & Panigrahy, 1992b). Mercury content was analysed in water, sediment and in the tissues of fishes and shellfishes (bivalve, shrimp and crab). In the estuarine water, it showed seasonal and spatial variations. High values were observed at the station close to the effluent fallout from the factory. From this point, there was a progressive decrease in the mercury in the water both upstream and downstream. In the sediments of the effluent channel, high values ranging from 148-2020 μg/g of sediment were recorded (average 669). From January to May, the values were high. Sediments of the estuary had lower values and at the mouth, with the range 0.25 to 1.87 μg/g. Table 2.2 gives the mercury contents in the tissues of fish and shellfish. Among the fishes, *Therapon jarbua* accumulated the highest amount. Bottom dwelling animals generally showed higher level probably because of their proximity with the sediments. As compared to the biota of other bodies of water in which mercury has been reported, the Rushikulya Estuary seems to have a greater contamination of mercury (Gouda & Panigrahy, 1995c).

Table 2.2—Residual mercury contents in some fish and shellfish fauna of Rushikulya Estuary (From Gouda & Panigrahy, 1992b)

Species	No. of Specimens examined	Mean length (cm)	Mercury concentreation (mg/kg wet wt)
Fish			
Gobius giuris	5	10.72 ± 0.57	1.27 ± 0.02
Liza macrolepis	5	12.30 ± 0.57	0.23 ± 0.02
Mugil cephalus	5	10.70 ±0.57	0.62 ± 0.03
Mystus gulio	5	11.30 ± 0.27	1.32 ± 0.03
Sillago sihama	5	08.70 ± 0.57	0.98 ± 0.02
Tachysurus arius	6	22.50 ± 1.30	0.17 ± 0.01
Therapon jarbua	8	08.20 ± 0.57	2.14 ± 0.03
Shellfish			
Donax sp.	8	–	1.16 ± 0.05
Metapenaeus monoceros	8	6.95 ± 0.39	0.52 ± 0.03
Penaeus monodon	8	7.81 ± 0.53	0.32 ± 0.02
Scylla serrata	5	–	2.02 ± 0.04

References

1. Gouda, R. & Panigrahy, R. C., 1989. Diurnal variation of phytoplankton in Rushikulya Estuary, east coast of India. *Indian Journal of Marine Sciences*, Vol. 18, pp. 246-250.
2. Gouda, R. & Panigrahy, R. C., 1991. Studies on the phytoplankton of the Rushikulya Estuary. In: *Aquatic Sciences in India*, pp. 173-187, (eds.) B. Gopal & V. Asthana. Indian Association for Limnology and Ocenography, New Delhi.
3. Gouda, R. & Panigrahy, R. C., 1992a. Seasonal distribution and behaviour of silicate in the Rushikulya Estuary, east coast of India. *Indian Journal of Marine Sciences*, Vol. 21, pp. 111-115.
4. Gouda, R. & Panigrahy, R. C., 1992b. Mercury pollution in the Rushikulya Estuary – A status appraisal. In : *Proceedings of National Symposium on Environment: Scientific approach to Environmental Issues,* February 3-5, Bhaba Atomic Research Centre, Bombay, India, pp. 71-73.
5. Gouda, R. & Panigrahy, R. C., 1993. Monthly variation of some hydrographic parameters in the Rushikulya Estuary, east coast of India. *Mahasagar – Bulletin of National Institute of Oceanography,* Vol. 26, pp. 73-85.

6. Gouda, R. & Panigrahy, R. C., 1995a. Seasonal distribution and behaviour of nitrate and phosphate in Rushikulya Estuary. *Indian Journal of Marine Sciences*, Vol. 24, pp. 233-235.
7. Gouda, R. & Panigrahy, R. C., 1995b. Zooplankton ecology of the Rushikulya Estuary, east coast of India. *Journal of Aquaculture in the Tropics*, Vol. 4, pp. 95-105.
8. Gouda, R. & Panigrahy, R. C., 1995c. Distribution of mercury in a tropical estuary (India), situated near chlor-alkali plant. *Pakistan Journal of Marine Sciences*, Vol. 4, pp. 95-105.
9. Patnaik, K.C. & Misra, P.M., 1988. Distribution of milk fish, *Chanos chanos* (Pisces: Chanidae) fry in Rushikulya Estuary. *Mahasagar – Bulletin of National Institute of Oceanography,* Vol. 21, pp. 239-243.
10. Patnaik, K.C. & Misra, P. M., 1990. Seasonal variation in the physico-chemical properties of Rushikulya Estuary and its effect on the occurrence of *Chanos* fry. *Journal of Indian Fisheries Association*, Vol. 20, pp. 69-71.
11. Panigrahy, R.C., Gouda, R., Misra, S. & Nayak, L. 1990. Availability of marine turtle eggs near Rushikulya river mouth, east coast of India. *The Indian Forester*, Vol. 116, pp. 515-516.
12. Panigrahy, R.C. & Gouda, R., 1990. Occurrence of a bloom of the diatom, *Asterionella glacialis* (Castracane) in the Rushikulya Estuary, east coast of India. *Mahasagar – Bulletin of National Institute of Oceanography*, Vol. 23, pp. 179-182.
13. Sahu, K. C. & Gouda, D.K., 1988. Mercury contamination in Rushikulya Estuary near Ganjam, Orissa. *Pollution Research*, Vol. 7, pp. 145-152.
14. Tripathy, S. K., Panigrahy, R. C., Gouda, R. & Panda, D., 1990. Distribution of calcium and magnesium in the Rushikulya Estuary (Orissa), east coast of India. *Indian Journal of Marine Sciences,* Vol. 19, pp. 212-214.

Chapter 3

Godavari

The Godavari Estuarine System, formed by several rivers of the east coast of India, is located along Lat. 16 °15′N and Long. 82 °5′ and covers an area of 330 km^2 in the state of Andhra Pradesh. Of the various rivers, Godavari is the main river. It originates in the Western Ghats, and after traversing across the Indian Peninsular Shield covering an area of 3×10^5 km^2, forms a delta and drains into the Bay of Bengal at a point near Kakinada. It has a discharge of 3,330 m^3/s. During its course, it divides into two major distributaries — one flowing towards the east called Gautami-Godavari Estuary and the other flowing towards the south termed as Vasista-Godavari Estuary. Both these estuaries are the offshoots of the Godavari River which gets further subdivided into smaller tributaries named as Neelarevu, Vrudha and Vainateyam. Two more rivers — Coringa and Gaderu — which are about 21 km and 11 km long respectively, form prominent channels through which freshwater is drained through the Gautami-Godavari into the Kakinada Bay (Fig. 3.1) during the monsoon period (Sarma & Ganapati, 1971).

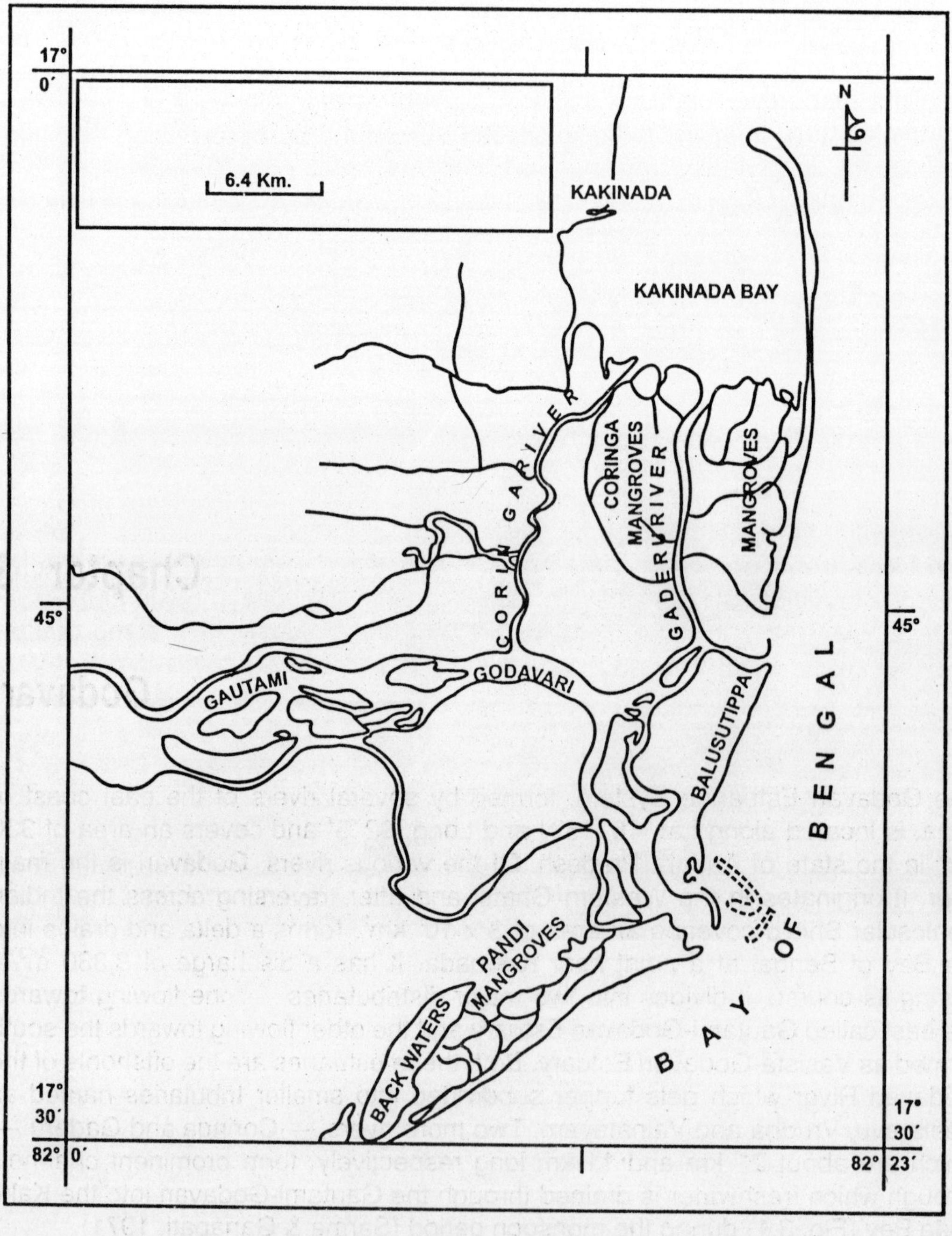

Fig. 3.1 Map of Godavari-Goutami Estuary showing Coringa River and the 3 sectors of mangroves (Pandi, Balusutippa and Coringa) (From Sarma & Ganapati, 1971)

VEGETATION

During the early part of this century, the Godavari Estuary was known to have excellent mangrove forests with dense growth of many species. Unfortunately what is left now, after the overexploitation of mangroves as fuel wood by way of auctions by the State Forest Department and other agencies since 1920, is described below. A lot of destruction of many mangrove forests has also occurred in recent years because of the phenomenal expansion of brackishwater aquaculture. There are three zones of mangrove forest-cover namely Coringa, Balusutippa and Pandi in the estuarine system. According to an estimate of the Andhra Pradesh Forest Department, the total mangrove cover in the three zones amounts to 316.21 km^2 (Table 3.1). Of these, the Coringa zone with its extension is the largest with a total area of 237.09 km^2 (Rao & Rao, 1988; Venkanna, 1991). From the three zones, 17 species of mangroves have been recorded along with their densities and total population. These are given in Table 3.2, and their variations in density in the three zones are shown in Table 3.3. The abundance of mangrove plants varied from one zone to the other and the total number of plants estimated was about 999×10^6 (Table 3.2). Several developmental activities such as a fertilizer plant near Kakinada Bay, oil exploitation in the Godavari Basin and shrimp farming have degraded the mangrove habitat considerably, and some authors have called the mangroves of the Godavari Delta as "vanishing mangroves" (Rao & Rao, 1988). One species (*Scyphiphora hydrophyllacea*) of mangrove recorded from the estuary, is reported to be rare for the Indian mainland (Venkanna, 1991).

Table 3.1— Total area covered by mangrove forests in 3 zones of Godavari Delta *
(From Rao & Rao, 1988)

Zone	Forest area	Total forest area (km^2)
Coringa	Coringa	42.423
	Coringa extention	194.672
Balusutippa	Masanitippa	10.891
	Balusutippa	4.759
	Rathikalva	20.493
	Kothapalem	0.503
Pandi	Kandikuppa	38.022
	Matlatippa	4.451
		316.214

* Data from Andhra Pradesh Forest Department

Table 3.2— Plant population estimated from mangrove forests of Godavari Delta (From Rao & Rao, 1988)

Plant name	Density (no./km^2)	Total population (no. × 10^6)
Suaeda maritima	736400	232.86
Excoecaria agallocha	689500	218.03
Avicennia officinalis	352000	111.30
Suaeda monoica	335400	106.05
Acanthus ilicifolius	291600	92.2
Myiostychya wightiana	193700	61.25
Sonneratia apetala	114500	36.20
Clerodendron inerme	97900	30.95
Acicennia marina f.typica	87400	27.63
Derris trifoliata	86200	27.25
Aegiceras corniculatum	77200	24.41
Lumnitzera racemosa	54800	17.32
Ceriops decandra	39400	12.45
Dalbergia spinosa	2200	0.69
Rhizophora apiculata	1000	0.31
Ipomoea tuba	200	0.06
Bruguiera gymnorhiza	100	0.003
	3159500	998.99

Table 3.3— Variation in density of exclusive mangrove plants in 3 zones of Godavari Delta (From Rao & Rao, 1988)

Species	Density (no./km^2)		
	Coringa zone	Balusutippa zone	Pandi zone
Excoecaria agallocha	643700	581200	843700
Acanthus ilicifolius	250000	387500	237500
Avicennia officinalis	137500	331200	587500
A.marina	0	81200	181200
Aegiceras corniculatum	600	37500	193700
Lumnitzera racemosa	7000	1300	156200
Sonneratia apetaia	75000	268700	0
Ceriops decandra	2500	112500	3200
Rhizophora apiculata	0	1200	1900
Bruguiera gymnorhiza	0	300	0

Sediment characteristics of the mangrove environment include mud, sandy mud and clayey mud. Sand content in the sediments varies from 1-18%, silt 7-63% and clay 15-90%. There was a direct correlation between the plant frequency and fine particles. High density of mangrove population was found where silt was high in the sediment (Rao *et al.*, 1992).

HYDROGRAPHY

The average rainfall in the area is about 1000 mm/y. It largely occurs during the southwest monsoon season which lasts from July to October. The rainfall reaches its maximum in October. Frequently, violent cyclonic weather hits the east coast of India bringing in torrential rain, often exceeding 200 mm in few hours. Maximum surface temperature of about 30 °C is found in the estuary in May, and minimum of approximately 26 °C during December/January (winter). Similar temperature regime is seen in the bottom waters and the annual range in temperature from surface to bottom is about 4 °C depending upon the site of measurement. In general, the bottom waters are cooler than the surface. During the period of maximum freshwater discharge (July to October), the temperature difference from surface to bottom is maximum. When the temperature is high during the dry season, the vertical gradient is small probably because of intense tidal mixing. Large quantities of fresh water discharge from the river Godavari influences the process of upwelling on the east coast of India (John *et al.*, 1993).

Annual variation in salinity is large practically throughout the estuary. Highest values are recorded during the dry premonsoon period (March to June) and lowest during the monsoon season. Unlike the temperature, the salinity values show marked variation from one part of the estuary to the other. For example, within a stretch of 22 km, surface salinity at the mouth was 30‰ , and in the upstream region it was 26.4‰ during the dry season. During the monsoon period, it was 12‰ at the mouth and almost zero at 22 km upstream. At the bottom, maximum recorded salinity was 31‰. The difference in salinity from surface to bottom increases as one moves upstream even when the freshwater discharge is negligible. This suggests that the tidal mixing in the upstream regions is far less than that at the mouth (Reddy & Rao, 1994).

The tides in the estuary are of mixed, semidiurnal type with two highs and two lows in a 24 h period with a range of about 1 m. At the lowermost region, before opening into the sea the estuary has an average width of about 1 km and a depth of approximately 12 m. It gets wider upstream. Diurnal fluctuations in the water temperature are negligible whereas in the salinity both diurnal and tidal fluctuations at the bottom are minimum and maximum upstream, increasing with the flood and decreasing with the ebb (Sai-Sastry & Chandramohan, 1990a &1990b). Estuarine waters are reported to be stratified up to a depth of 6 m in September. Mixing process in the estuary has been studied, based on computed flushing periods and longitudinal diffusion coefficients. In September, the flushing period of the estuary is about 4 tidal cycles (48 h) while in December it is about 46 tidal cycles (552 h). The longitudinal diffusion coefficient varies with the freshwater discharge (Reddy & Rao, 1993). Ionic distribution in the estuarine waters was studied for 4 months (May, June, November and December) in 1976, Electrical conductivity of water samples increased with depth. Analysis of 3 cations namely calcium (Ca), magnesium (Mg) and sodium (Na) and anions – chloride (Cl), bicarbonate (HCO_3) and sulphate (SO_4) indicated that among the anions and cations, chloride, calcium, magnesium and sodium showed considerable variations with depth up to 2 m. Thereafter, there was an increase showing the influence of tide at deeper layers and freshwater runoff in the surface layers (Sarma *et al.*,1985).

Measurements of salinity and currents in the Vasishta branch of Godavari Estuary were made in relation to freshwater discharge and tidal action in 3 representative months (July, September and February). In July, when the river discharge was maximum, the estuary exhibits some characteristics of a salt-wedge type. In September, when the river discharge is declining, the estuary becomes a partially-mixed-type and during February when the discharge is minimum, the estuary becomes well-mixed (Ramana *et al.*,1989).

A multi-level numerical model has been applied to the data of varying degrees of freshwater flow during the year and fluctuating seawater intrusion caused by tidal action (Ramana *et al.*,1989). Flow characterisitcs and salinity structures have been applied to obtain theoretical results from the model. There was a good agreement between the observed and calculated results indicating that the deductions, made for the estuary exhibiting the characteristics of a salt-wedge type in July and becoming well-mixed in February, are valid (Rao *et al.*,1994).

Turbidity of water was found to be maximum at the mouth. It gets reduced upstream. However, high turbidity is recorded during the monsoon months almost throughout the estuary because of land drainage. Transparency of water improves during the postmonsoon season and becomes maximum during the premonsoon months.

Dissolved oxygen in water showed a large variation in shallow areas as compared to deeper regions. Percentage saturation was greater at the surface than at the bottom and it did not show much variation between day and night. However, there was a total absence of anoxic conditions in most parts of the estuary and often oxygen concentrations reached supersaturation levels.

In the Godavari Estuary, inorganic phosphate has been reported to be low in comparison to those found in other Indian estuaries. However, the estuary was moderately rich in nitrite and adequately rich in silicate. Their values at the surface and bottom at the three stations are given in Table 3.4. Station 1 was at the mouth whereas the other two stations were upstream. Seasonal variations in the three nutrients were more pronounced during the monsoon season as compared to other months (Sai-Sastry & Chandramohan, 1990 a & 1990 b).

Table 3.4— Spatial distribution of selected inorganic nutrients in Vasishta-Godavari estuary (October 1981 - June1983) (From Rao & Rao, 1988)

Nutrient	St 1		St2		St3	
(μ g.at.l^{-1})	Min	Max	Min	Max	Min	Max
NO_2-N	S	ND	1.0	ND	10.0	3.3
	B	ND	1.2	ND	3.8	2.5
PO_4-P*	S	0.1	0.1	0.1	0.2	0.1
	B	0.1	0.1	0.1	0.2	0.1
SiO_3-Si	S	13.0	50.0	10.0	338.9	416.7
	B	10.0	41.6	10.0	208.3	454.5

S. Surface; B. Bottom; ND. Not detectable
* Values <0.1µg-at/l rounded to 0.1.

Concentrations of toxic and non-toxic metals such as Cu, Zn Mn, Fe, Co, Ni and Pb were measured both in soluble and particulate forms in the coastal waters of Godavari and Krishna estuaries (western Bay of Bengal) during one of the cruises of *R V Gaveshani* (21st cruise) in August 1979. Primary productivity was also measured along with these using ^{14}C method. Chlorophyll *a* concentrations were also estimated. Carbon assimilation ranged between 2 to 9.4 mg C/m^2/day and chlorophyll *a* from 0.03 to 0.095 mg/m^3. Total suspended matter (TSM) ranged from 0.896 to 3.35 mg/l.

Off Godavari Estuary at the continental edge, the TSM value varied between 0.89 and 7.97 mg/l. Except Mn, all the elements showed higher values in the offshore waters than the average (normal) values reported for the oceanic waters. This has been attributed to the effect of pollution coming from the industrial complex at Visakhapatnam (Rajendran *et al.*, 1982).

In another study on the distribution of suspended particulate matter, in the coastal waters off Godavari, Krishna and adjoining regions, the TSM showed high concentrations ranging from 5 to 231mg/l off Godavari and the range in combustible organic matter was from 5 to 25% which was considered lower from the other regions in the neighbourhood. This is probably because the suspended matter coming from the estuarine areas largely includes inert material (silt, clay, etc.) with little organic matter (Rao, 1985). In the deltaic sediments of Krishna River, the concentration of boron ranges from 52 to 130 ppm (average 78.2 ppm). This range is higher than what was recorded from the freshwater sediments of the same river and it seems unlikely that the distribution of boron is related to variation in the clay minerals. A direct relationship of boron was found with the organic matter (Rao, 1985). In the deltaic sediments, a higher range in boron values is probably because of the greater organic matter (Swamy & Rao, 1974). Seasonal changes in the concentration of both fluoride and dissolved silicon have been measured in the Gautami-Godavari Estuary as a function of chlorinity. Fluoride is considered a pollutant because it gets accumulated in plants and animals and is detrimental to their metabolism. Removal of about 16% fluoride and 41% dissolved silicon occurs during the premonsoon season when there is a greater mixing of sea and river water into the estuary. There is no significant removal of these elements in other seasons. The net flux of silicon from the Godavari into the Bay of Bengal has been estimated to be 4.70×10^5 tonnes/y (Sarma *et al.*, 1993).

Geochemical studies on the Godavari waters showed that the dissolved oxygen in the estuary ranges from 4.26 to 6.76 ml/l. It decreases with increasing chlorinity. Dissolved organic carbon (DOC) varies from 0.2 to 1.0 mg/l and the levels are found to be higher than those reported from other estuaries. Measurements of particulate organic matter (POC), Fe and the concentrations of 23 elements in the suspended matter have been carried out from the estuary (Somayajulu *et al.*, 1993).

Occurrence of native sulphur has been reported in the sediments of Godavari at a depth of about 15 cm from the surface while the topmost layer was free from sulphur. It is preceptible to the naked eye as a yellow layer below. The source of this sulphur is probably the reduction of sulphate or oxidation of H_2S by bacteria (Naidu & Rao, 1963).

In September 1980, during one of the cruises of the Research Vessel *Gaveshani*, currents and temperature structure and their short-term variations were recorded off Godavari using moored Aanderaa current meters at three depths, 15, 115 and 240 m (near bottom). The surface drift was of the order of 2 to 3 knots and was directed towards NE to E. Currents at different depths had a speed of < 1 knot and showed variation in time and a velocity shear. They do not seem to be influenced by the tides. Temperature of the surface waters was about 30 °C and that of the near bottom 11.5 °C. There was no well-defined mixed layer and the temperature decreased with depth (Sarma & Rao, 1986).

Sedimentological studies of the inshore waters in the vicinity of the estuary showed that the bottom sediments include silty sand, sandy silt, silt, clayey silt and silty clay. At the river mouth, the sediment is largely silt due to the influx of silty sediment by the river (Murty & Murty, 1993). Several coastal areas of Andhra Pradesh are known to have black sand on the beaches and at the river mouth extending into the shallow parts of the sea. Magnetic content of the black sand is high (Rao & Kshirasagar, 1991). These are known as placers and contain ilmenite, garnet, zircon, rutile, etc. At several places, both on the east and west coasts, these are being exploited as rare earth.

Seabed morphology of the coastal waters off Krishna-Godavari Delta indicates 3 defined physiographic domains namely continental shelf, continental slope and abyssal plain between the depths of 100 and 3200 m. The first break is recorded at an average depth of about 100 m and the shelf widens up to 40 km. Tributaries of Krishna and Godavari seem to continue offshore between 300 and 300 m depth in the form of shallow channels. The 75 km wide continental slope is characterized by an undulating surface with a number of breaks. Gradation from slope to abyssal plain is rather gradual marked by a total absence of any topographical expression (Bandyopadhyay *et al.*, 1994).

PHYTOPLANKTON

During one of the cruises of *R.V. Gaveshani* (cruise 121), the distribution of phytoplankton and fungi was studied in the coastal waters adjoining the rivers Krishna and Godavari from 9 stations in July 1983. Sixty two species of phytoplankton were recorded form 25, 50, 75 and 100-150 m depths along three transects. Four genera of fungi were also recorded in the water samples. Of the phytoplankters, 50 belonged to the family Bacillarophyceae, 8 to Dinophyceae, 2 to Chrysophyceae and 1 each to Euglenophyceae and Cynophyceae. Table 3.5 gives 19 predominant species of phytoplankters and 4 genera of fungi. Maximum density was recorded at the surface (3000 cells/l). It declined rapidly from 25 to 100 m depth. Vertical cell densities of 6 dominant species along the three transects are shown in Table 3.6. Of the 4 genera of fungi shown in Table 3.5, the distribution of the

Table 3.5— Relative abundance (%) of phytoplankton and fungi along 3 transects of Krishna and Godavari river mouths (From Rao & Sarojini, 1992)

Transect I		Transect II		Transect III	
Phytoplankton/Fungi	RA	Phytoplankton/Fungi	RA		RA
Nitzschia seriata	15.60	*Nitzschia longissima*	13.0	*Thalassiothrix frauenfeldii*	12.00
N. longissima	12.30	*Skeletonema costatum*	12.6	*Thalassionema nitzschiodes*	8.90
Thalassiothrix frauenfeldii	12.20	*Cyclotella meneghiniana*	7.6	*Synedra sp.*	8.80
Thalassionema nitzschiodes	11.70	*Synedra sp.*	7.6	*Thalassiothrix longissima*	8.40
Skeletonema costatum	8.80	*Nitzschia seriata*	5.3	*Ditylum brighwellii*	7.30
Thalassiothrix longissima	3.70	*Thalassiothrix longissima*	4.6	*Cyclotella meneghiniana*	7.10
Cyclotella meneghiniana	3.10	*Thalassiothrix frauenfeldii*	4.1	*Coscinodiscus marginatus*	4.00
Chaetoceros lauderi	2.70	*Thalassionema nitzschiodes*	4.0	*Nitzschia seriata*	3.10
Trichodesmium theibauti	2.40	*Pleurosigma aestuarii*	3.7	*Peridinium ovatum*	3.00
Navicula longa	2.30	*Bacillaria paradoxa*	3.0	*Dinobryon sp.*	2.50
Chaetoceros laciniosus	2.30	*Coscinodisus centralis*	2.7	*Coscinodiscus centralis*	2.70
Coscinodiscus marginatus	2.10	*C. magrinatus*	2.6	*Skeletonema costatum*	2.30
C. centralis	1.80	*Navicula longa*	2.3	*Nitzschia longissima*	2.10
Chaetoceros crinitum	1.70	*Euglena sp.*	2.1	*Prorocentrum micans*	2.10
Prorocentrum micans	1.70	*Peridinium ovatum*	1.9	*Ceratium fusus*	1.40
Asterionella japonica	1.40	*Ditylum brightwellii*	1.8	*Pleurosigma aestuarii*	1.40
Chaetoceros sp.	1.10	*Chactoceros lorenziamus*	1.6	*Ceratium furca*	1.40
Peridinium ovatum	1.10	*Pleurosigma delicatula*	1.6	*Distephanus speculus*	1.30
Chatetoceros gracile	1.00	*Ceratium fusus*	1.5	*Rhizosolenia alata*	1.10
Other Species(39)	11.00	*Other Species (28)*	16.4	*Other species (30)*	9.20
Aspergillus	34.40	*Fumago*	35.8	*Fumago*	53.90
Monilia	30.90	*Aspergillus*	34.3	*Aspergillus*	23.50
Fumago	29.20	*Monilia*	21.9	*Monilia*	19.10
Derechslera	5.50	*Derechslera*	8.0	*Dreschslera*	3.50

RA = Relative abundance

genus *Dreschslera* was scanty. Fungi, particularly, occurred opposite to the estuarine habitats off Krishna and Godavari rivers. This and the occurrence of *Euglena* signify that the water is rich in organic matter coming from the mangrove habitats (Rao & Sarojini, 1992).

Measurements of primary production using light and dark bottle technique were made in the impounded waters of Godavari River during the years 1967, 1968 and 1969. Gross production was maximum in June, November and May with values of 1058 mg C/m^3/day, 743 mg C/m^3/day and 705 mg C/m^3/day respectively were recorded. The values were high in the well-illuminated zone and decreased substantially with depth probably because of turbidity. The ratio between gross and net production ranged from 0.34 to 0.85. Respiration formed 13 to 41% of gross production (Rajyalakshmi & Premswarup, 1975).

Table 3.6— Mean densities of 6 phytoplankters at different depths along three transects at the mouth of Godavari Estuary (cells/l) (From Rao & Sarojini, 1992)

Depth (m)	*Nitzschia seriata*			*Nitzschia longissima*			*Thalassiothrix frauenfeldii*		
	I	II	III	I	II	III	I	II	III
0	715	18	8	365	43	5	277	30	57
25	379	60	18	193	50	13	397	23	53
50	123	65	47	330	132	12	185	45	89
75	118	50	15	298	160	20	47	10	35
100	65	–	–	165	–	–	10	–	–
150	–	0	0	–	15	–	–	15	–
	Thalassionema nitzschiodes			*Skeletonema costatum*			*Thalassiothrix longissima*		
	I	II	III	I	II	III	I	II	III
0	390	30	27	1150	103	12	25	28	40
25	260	30	48	295	58	10	130	28	50
50	210	30	64	237	112	16	118	38	41
75	65	45	80	72	115	0	38	30	45
100	35	–	–	145	–	–	25	–	–
150	–	0	–	–	40	–	–	15	–

ZOOPLANKTON

Copepods formed the bulk of zooplankton in the estuary. During the day time and particularly at the high tide, neritic organisms like coelenterates, chaetognaths and decapod larvae were common in the collections. At night, copepods, adult crustaceans and invertebrate larvae (mostly veligers) and oikopleurans formed

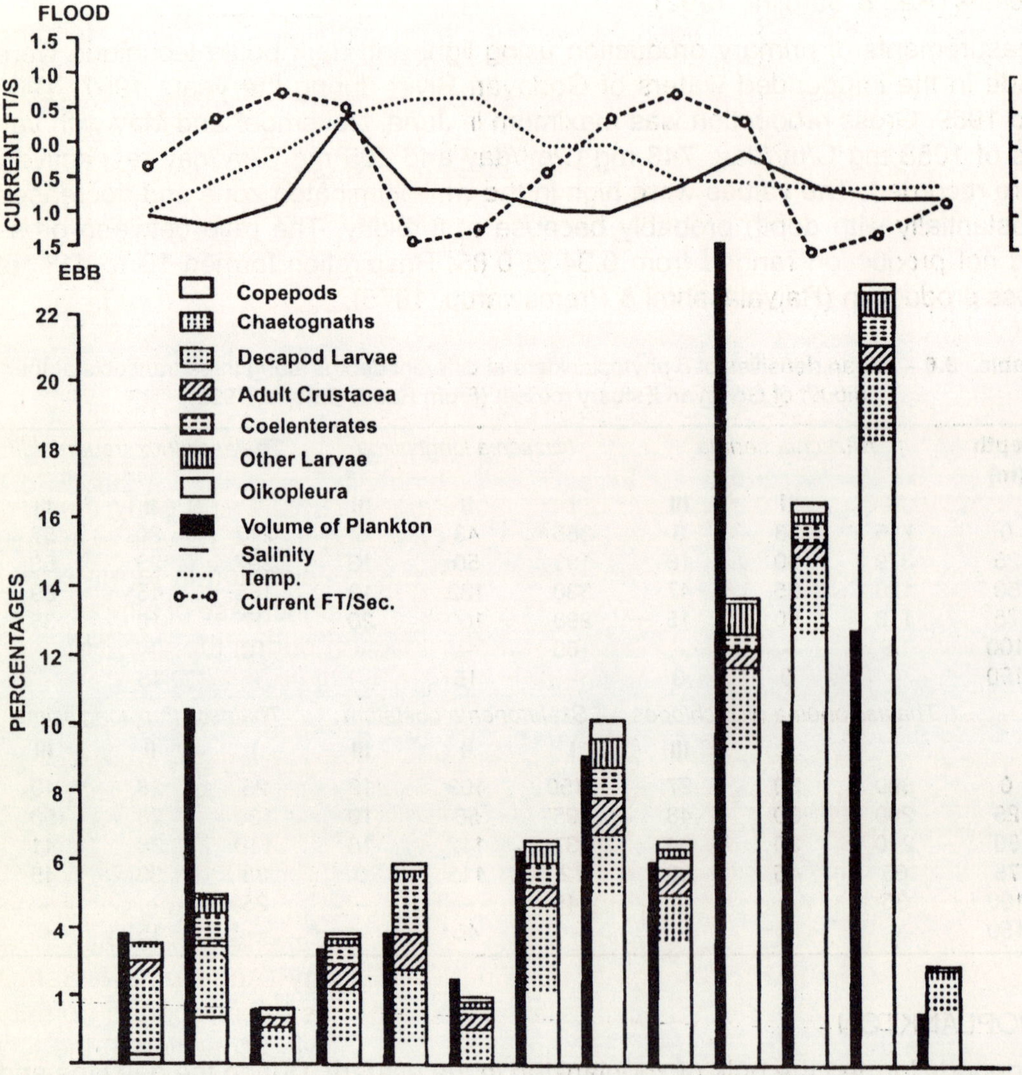

Fig. 3.2 Percentage composition in Godavari Estuary of zooplankton volume and their composition at one station during a tidal cycle (day and night) in February 1961. Curves at the top show changes in currents, temperature and salinity (From Chandramohan & Rao, 1972).

the main bulk. The distribution of copepods in a 24 h period was particularly interesting. The samples collected in the morning at high water contained 25% copepods. At noon, their numbers decreased and in the evening their numbers went on increasing and late in the night their proportion was maximum (80%) irrespective of the state of tide and hydrographical conditions indicating their photonegative diurnal migration. Figure 3.2 shows their cycle of abundance in relation to day and night hours and the state of tides. The species commonly represented are *Tortanus forcipatus, Pseudodiaptomous binghami, Eucalanus elongatus, Acartia erythraca and Paracalanus* sp. Infrequent appreance was recorded of *Centropages dorsispinatus, Macrosetella gracilis* and a few cyclopoids. Next in abundance were decapod larvae (zoea and brachyuran larvae) in the samples collected in the evening and morning during the ebb tide.

Among the coelenterates, hydromedusae were abundant while siphonophores and ctenophores were few. These appeared particularly during the day time. Chaetognaths occurred predominantly at high water. *Sagitta* species were the most common. Fish eggs and larvae and the pelegic tunicate, *Oikopleura* were generally present in the samples collected at high tide, while molluscan larvae were collected in large numbers during the low tide at night and early morning. Thus, the fluctuation in zooplankton abundance during the 24 h cycle was quite pronounced. Figure 3.2 also shows the volume of zooplankton in terms of percentage and composition of 7 groups. There was a clear increase of almost all the groups during the night hours and a marked reduction during the day. No direct relation became apparent with the state of tides (Chandramohan & Rao, 1972).

In 1978, during the 21st cruise of *R V Gaveshani*, a dense swarm of the neritic pteropod, *Creseis acicula*, has been reported from the Bay of Bengal off Krishna Estuary. The abundance of this species reached 4,7380/100 m^3 which is 3.7 times higher than the records ever reported earlier by an organism in the Bay of Bengal. The swarming of this species appears to be seasonal and is often associated with high zooplankton production (Peter & Paulinose, 1978). In 1979, the occurrence of a new species of podocopan benthic ostracod, *Tanella indica,* has been reported from the lower reaches of the Godavari Estuary (Annapurna & Sarma, 1979). An assemblage of 90 species of foraminifera has been reported from the Godavari and Krishna estuaries. Of these, 57 were in living condition at the time of collection. The most abundant species were 23, of which 14 were recorded from the Godavari and 9 from the Krishna. The forminiferan fauna was more diversified in the Godavari than in Krishna, which has been attributed to a greater abundance of food and more favourable substrate in the former (Narrappa *et al.,*

1982). From the zooplankton samples, 19 forms of polychaete larvae were identified. The entire larval assemblage can be divided into two categories. One belonging to those from the neritic waters into the estuarine system and the other, purely endemic species living in the estuary throughout the year. Tidal currents, (flood and ebb) and food supply seem to control their abundance in the estuary (Chandramohan & Chetty, 1988).

Planktonic coelenterates occur commonly in the Vasishta-Godavari Estuary. In all, 28 species were recorded from the estuary with the following composition:

Hydromedusae	19
Scyphomedusae	3
Siphonophores	3
Ctenophores	3

Of these, 23 were from the lower reaches and five from the upper reaches. Diversity in the occurrence of coelenterates increased with higher salinity. Out of the total 28, 15 species form the first record from this estuarine system (Sai-Sastry & Chandramohan, 1989). Species composition of chaetognaths from the Godavari Estuary has been reported by Srinivasan (1994).

INTERTIDAL FAUNA

The occurrence of the polychaete, *Poecilochaetus johnsoni* was recorded at the mean low tide level from the estuary by Rao & Sarma (1978). Its habitat included fine mud mixed with fine sand rich in organic matter. At the collection site, temperature, salinity and dissolved oxygen were 33 °C, 22.2‰ and 4.704 ml/l, respectively. Another polychaete, *Nephthys oligobranchia*, was recorded from the intertidal area of the estuary on 26 December 1977. It inhabits clean and sandy substratum. An examination of its gut contents suggested that it is carnivorous in its feeding habit (Rao & Sarma, 1980). A more intensive study, extended for more than 15 months on the ecology and distribution of fauna in the intertidal habitat, by the same authors showed that of the 270 samples collected from different tidal levels from October 1976 to January 1978, *N. oligobranchia*, was present in 80% of the samples. Its maximum density was recorded at mean mid water mark (MMWM), where the substrata was muddy or included sandy mud. It was absent in coarse sandy subtratum. Its occurrence in high density during the summer months (March to June) suggests that its maximum breeding takes place when both temperature and salinity of the environment are high (Rao & Sarma, 1980). In December 1976, from the intertidal zone of the estuary, another species of polychaete namely *Megalona cinta* was reported. Its quantitative distribution at different tidal levels showed its maximum abundance at MMWM and mean low tide mark (MLTM). It probably enters the estuary in larval form during the period when the salinity is increasing and prefers to settle in silty clay substrata (Rao & Sarma, 1979). Distribution and abundance of the polychaete, *Dendronereis arborifera,* were also studied at different tidal levels of the estuary. It occurred in 55% of the samples at mean high water mark (MHWM), in 88% of the samples at MMWM, and in 51% of the samples from MLTM. Although it seems to prefer MMWM, tidal level provides no barrier for its distribution. It was totally absent in coarse, sandy substrata and abundant in sediments containing high silt-clay fractions (Sarma & Rao, 1982).

A mangrove mudsnail, *Terebralia palustus,* has been reported from the Krishna Estuarine System. It seems to avoid substrata having sand content greater than 50% and prefers the substrata with plants (Rambabu *et al.*, 1987).

A survey of meiofauna in the Gautami-Godavari estuary yielded 12 groups, with nematodes 90.5% and harpacticoid-copepods 3.7%. Maximum and minimum densities (2292 and 267/10 cm^2) were recorded in the lower and upper regions respectively of the estuary (Murty & Kondalarao, 1987).

The ecology of intertidal meiofauna of the Kakinada Bay adjoining the Gautami-Godavari Estuarine System, has been studied in the mid-littoral zone from February 1978 to January 1980 covering a distance of 300m by taking core samples. Meiofauna comprised the following 13 groups:

Nematodes, harpacticoid-copepods, ostracods, kinorhynchs, turbellarians, molluscs, polychaetes, *Halacarida*, oligochaetes, tardigrades, crustacean larvae, insect larvae and amphipods.

Nematodes constituted the most dominant group and governed the rise and fall of the total meiofauna. Ostracods came next with peak abundance in February. Harpacticoid copepods were composed of 9 genera and 6 families. These showed irregular seasonal abundance. Kinorhynchs showed two peaks during the year whereas polychaetes larval forms and turbellarians appeared sporadically. The total meiofauna ranged between 302 and 5924 in 10 cm^2, generally recording high densities in mangroves biotope (Kondalarao & Murty, 1988).

Meiobenthic harpacticoid copepod fauna included 32 species belonging to 25 genera. Maximum density was recorded in the clayey-silt sediments of mangrove biotope. The diversity in the copepod communities was high in the lower reaches and low in the upper reaches (Kondalarao, 1984).

BENTHIC FAUNA

Both macro and meiobenthos of the Godavari Estuary were studied along with three other estuaries namely Krishna, Mahanadi and Hooghly. The sites of observation in all the three were their mouth regions (openings) into the Bay of Bengal. For macrobenthos, samples from the bottom were collected during one of the cruises (94th) of *R V Gaveshani* using Petersen-type grab of 0.1 m^2 (penetration 25 cm) from which subsampling was done by a 170 cm^2 plexiglass quadrant. The contents (sediment) were sieved through a 500 µm mesh screen and the fauna retained were analysed.

For meiofauna, subsamples were drawn from the undisturbed bottom deposits using plexiglass core tube (10 cm in length and 4.5 cm in diameter). The core was divided into 0-5 cm and 5-10 cm sections and the contents were preserved and analysed.

Table 3.7— Macrofauna density/m^2 and biomass g/m^2 wet weight from different stations outside 4 estuaries (From Ansari *et al.*, 1982)

Faunal group	Stations			
	K	G	M	H
Polychaeta	50	1189	708	59
Bivalvia	10	87	118	118
Scaphopoda	0	1480	0	0
Euphausiaceae	10	0	0	0
Tanaidacea	0	116	0	0
Gammaridea	0	1856	0	0
Penaeidea	0	58	0	0
Cumacea	0	0	59	0
Sipunculida	0	0	0	0
Hydrozoa	0	0	59	0
Ophiuroidea	10	0	118	0
Echiuroida	0	29	0	0
Total population/m^2	90	4785	1062	177
Total biomass (g/m^2)	0.11	3.64	16.04	2.48

K = Krishna; G = Godavari; M = Mahanadi; H = Hooghly.

Table 3.7 gives the composition density and biomass of macrofauna in the 4 estuaries. Generally polychaetes and bivalves were the most dominant groups, with polychaetes comprising 24.8 to 66.7% of the total macrofauna. Other groups, which were not found regularly in all the 4 estuaries, included euphausids, amphipods, decapods, cumaceans, sipunculids, hydrozoans, ophiuroids and echiuroids. A close examination of Table 3.7 will reveal that of the four estuaries.

Table 3.8— Distribution of meiofauna in pentriplicate core samples taken along 4 estuarine stations (From Ansari *et al.*, 1982)

	Core Sample											Total% composition
	1		2		3		4		5			
	0-5	5-10	0-5	5-10	0-5	5-10	0-5	5-10	0-5	5-10		
St Krishna												
Nematoda	176	83	196	34	144	42	204	72	92	52	1095	69.7
Polychaeta	25	9	20	6	18	0	28	9	26	2	143	9.1
Harpacticoida	25	6	14	0	31	2	39	0	25	5	147	9.3
Ostracoda	12	0	3	0	0	0	4	0	7	0	26	1.6
Turbellaria	13	0	19	0	12	0	22	0	8	2	76	4.8
Others	7	2	12	4	15	5	21	9	6	1	82	5.2
Total	258	100	264	44	220	49	318	90	164	62	1569	99.7
St Godavari												
Nematoda	584	76	381	52	560	125	506	218	414	163	3079	86
Polychaeta	25	7	18	2	30	12	39	1	17	0	151	4.2
Harpacticoida	51	3	16	0	32	10	26	0	22	0	160	4.5
Turbellaria	25	3	32	3	10	0	12	0	9	2	96	2.6
Lamellibranchiata	19	0	12	0	4	2	9	0	8	2	56	1.5
Others	4	3	6	2	3	1	9	2	3	3	36	1
Total	708	92	465	59	639	150	601	221	473	170	3578	
St Mahanadi												
Nematoda	435	120	360	55	700	95	498	41	521	64	2889	81.7
Polychaeta	45	13	22	2	62	15	42	2	17	0	220	6.2
Harpacticoida	41	2	51	0	48	5	32	0	33	0	212	6
Turbellaria	22	8	19	0	42	4	9	0	14	2	120	3.4
Kinorhyncha	7	0	0	0	4	0	6	2	2	0	21	0.6
Lamellibranchiata	15	3	7	2	9	0	0	0	12	0	48	1.3
Others	2	0	6	2	3	0	0	2	4	4	23	0.6
Total	567	146	465	61	868	119	587	47	603	70	3533	
St Hooghly												
Nematoda	240	39	182	30	296	29	313	34	262	55	1480	68.7
Polychaeta	20	8	24	6	35	12	41	20	34	2	202	9.3
Harpacticoida	60	0	48	0	36	0	89	0	52	3	288	13.3
Ostracoda	19	0	9	0	13	0	18	0	8	0	67	3.1
Turbellaria	15	0	3	0	19	6	6	0	9	0	58	2.6
Others	14	11	7	3	2	3	16	4	6	3	69	3.2
Total	368	58	273	39	401	50	483	58	371	63	2164	

Godavari Estuary has the richest macrofauna. It has the maximum population of animals. Macrofaunal density in the 4 estuaries ranged from 90 to 4785 animals/m^2 and biomass from 0.11 to 16.04 g/m^2 (Ansari *et al.,* 1982). The ratios of biomass and density between macrofauna and meiofauna in the four estuaries are given in Table 3.9. The biomass ratio of 2:01 and density ratio of 1:94 were found in the Godavari Estuary.

Table 3.8 shows the composition of meiofauna in the 4 estuaries. In terms of the overall numbers, Godavari Estuary had the richest meiofauna. Nematodes were the most important group followed by harpacticoids and polychaetes. Turbellarians, ostracods, lamellibranchs and kinorhynchs were present in lesser numbers and had a patchy distribution. Other taxa including gastrotrichs, tardigrades, rotifers and crustacean nauplii were inconspicuous. Table 3.9 shows the ratios between macro to meiofauna in terms of biomass and density. The biomass ratio of 2:01 and density ratio of 1:94 were found in the Godavari Estuary. Meiofauna was numerically 94 to 2193 times greater than macrofauna. Richest meiofauna came from the sediment having median grain diameters. In soft muddy deposits, the nematodes were most dominant in all the four estuaries with a maximum in Godavari. Vertically the bulk of the meiofauna (>70%) was concentrated in the top 5 cm layer of the substratum. Probably a greater availability of food and oxygen governed their distribution in the top layer (Ansari *et al.,* 1982).

Table 3.9— Ratios of biomass and density between macrofauna and meiofauna/m^2 along 4 stations (From Ansari *et al.*, 1982)

St	Area	
	Biomass (macro:meio)	Density (macro:meio)
K	1:2.7	1:2193
G	2:1	1:94
M	3:1	1:417
H	1:1.7	1:1531

K = Krishna; G = Godavari; M = Mahanadi; H = Hooghly.

Another survey of meiofauna conducted in the Gautami-Godavari Estuary at 4 stations yielded 12 groups of meiobenthic organisms. These were nematodes, harpacticoid-copepods, ostracods, kinorhynchs, turbellarians, halacaridans, oligochaetes, tradigrades, crustacean larvae, insect larvae and amphipods. Nematodes were the most dominant group (90.5%), followed by benthic copepods (3.7%) and ostracods (3.6%). Twenty seven species of harpacticoid copepods, belonging to 11 families and 22 genera, were recorded from the estuary. Maximum occurrence of meiofauna was from February to May (dry season). Kinorhynchs were present in the lower and middle reaches and were absent in the upper reaches (Murty & Kondalarao, 1987).

BIOFOULING

Investigations on biofouling were carried out at selected stations in the Kakinada Bay (Kakinada Port) which forms a part of the Godavari Estuary. Test panels of mango timber (*Mangifera indica*) and glass (window pane) were kept suspended just below the low water mark (0.3 m). The sizes of the panels were 15 × 8 × 2 cm for wood and 15 cm × 8 cm × 2 mm for glass. The period of study was one year, from December 1983 to November 1984. Replicated 12 wooden and 12 glass panels were exposed and all were retrieved after one month for examination and counting. These were short-term experiments. Long-term experiments included the retrieval of one out of the 12 panels of each kind every month so that the last set of panels remained in water for 12 months.
Fouling organisms which settled on the panels were as follows:

Coelenterates

The contribution of this group was not appreciable because they settled only occasionally in small numbers. Two species of hydroids and one species of anemone were identified on the panels.

Bryozoans

These formed important components of the fouling community. Both encrusting and stolonate species were identified. In all, there were 8 species. Both web-like delicate colonies and luxuriant growths of encrusting types often dominated the fouling community and settled throughout the year.

Polychaetes

The calcareous tube-dwelling surpulid was the most important organism which formed dense, intertwined masses several centimetres high. They settled throughout the year.

Barnacles

Balanus amphitrite was the most abundant organism which dominated the fouling community frequently on some panels during most of the year. On older panels, the barnacle contribution exceeded 70%. Occasionally, heavy mortality of barnacles was noticed possibly due to overcrowding and interspecific competition.

Other organisms

Several species of free-living crustaceans (isopods, amphipods, tanaids, decapods) were seen among the fouling complex, but their contribution was not significant. Six species of bivalves were collected from the panels. Of these, the most important was the oyster, *Crassostrea madrasensis.* The ascidians were represented by a single species.

At station 1, the biomass values on the timber panels ranged from 0.5 to 3.15 kg/m^2 (wet weight) and 0.28 to 1.87 kg/m^2 (dry weight). On glass panels, the values were 0.535 to 3.2 kg/m^2 (wet weight) and 0.31 to 1.9 kg/m^2 (dry weight). Highest values recorded on the timber panels were 8.26 (wet weight) and 4.71 kg/m^2 (dry weight). At station 2, the biomass values both on timber and glass panels were much higher. Bryozoans settled more on smooth glass plates whereas barnacles more on timber (Rao & Balaji, 1988).

FISH AND FISHERY

Earlier studies on fish from this estuary were confined to faunistic reports. Rao (1965) gave an account on the occurrence of *Anchovilla commersonii* (whitebait) along the Andhra coast including the Godavari Estuarine System. The estuarine stocks of this fish occurred from February to June when the salinity was high and these were absent during the flood period when the salinity was low. He studied the meristic characters to determine whether the estuarine stocks were different from those of the Waltair Coast and concluded that they constituted two different populations and did not constitute distinct stocks because the heterogeneity in morphometric characters was not significant statistically.

From the genus *Setipinna,* a species forming notable fishery in the Godavari Estuary has been named as *S. godavariensis* (a new species) because it differed significantly in its meristic characters from the 3 other species of this genus (Rao & Joglekar, 1967). Another species of this genus, *S. taty,* was also found in the estuary. Investigations on the biology of the former species revealed that it spawns at least twice during the year.

Five species of blennies namely *Omobranchus bhattacharyae, O. japonícus, O. bipunctatus, Cruantus smithi* and *C. dealmeida* occur in the estuary (Rao, 1970a). The breeding account and the early development of *O. bipunctatus* and occurrence of a new species of anchovy from the estuary have been given by Dutt & Rao (1961a & 1961b). Breeding habits and early developments of *O. japonicus* and *C. smithi* have been described by Rao (1970a). Both the species breed successively, the eggs are attached to substrata, and the parents guard the eggs till they are hatched. Development in captivity goes on well till the larvae are hatched. Those have been figured by Rao (1970a). A new species from the genus *Incara* from the estuary has been described and it has been named as *I. muilts-quamatus* (Rao, 1969). Another new species from the genus *Chiramenu* (goby) and named as *C.fluviatilis* has been reported by Rao (1970b).

Along the Andhra Coast in a village in East Godavari District, a bumper catch of fish has been reported. The gear used was shore-seine and the estimated catch on 15 February, 1968 was 40 tonnes. It was sold for Rs. 23,000. The sciaenid *Pseudosciaena axillaris* formed about 90% of the catch (Sastry, 1968).

Migratory behaviour of commercial prawns in the estuary is well known. From the estuary, continuous inward and outward migration of penaeid prawns was recorded from November 1961 to July 1962. The prawns were *Metapenaeus monoceros, M. brevicornis, M. dobsoni, M. affinis, Penaeus indicus* and *P. monodon.* The observations were based on the catches obtained from the stake nets operated near the mouth of the estuary. Prawns of all sizes seem to undertake such a migration from November to July. More prawns migrated at dawn than at dusk. During the new moon, their numbers were higher than during the full moon. Catches were heavier during the darker fortnight of the month than those at the high tides, and particularly during the nocturnal low tides than during the day low tides (Subramanyam, 1965). Another observation on the landings of *P. monodon* is worth-mentioning. When the catch per net per day was taken as an index, it showed higher landings during the new moon phase than those during the full moon phase. Generally, larger size groups were available during the new moon period (Subramanyam, 1967a). During this study, it could not be ascertained whether the same populations of prawns moved in and out of the estuary or these were different populations. Hence, a method of marking of prawns using different stains was tried and Trypan blue stain lasted for 55 days (Subramanyam, 1967b). However, the marked prawns could not be identified as these were neither released nor recovered.

Studies on the recruitment pattern of the larval and post-larval stages of 2 species of penaeid prawns namely *Penaeus monodon* and *Metapenaeus monoceros* in the estuary for a period of 3 years from 1959-60 to 1961-62 showed that post-larvae of both the species occur in the estuary throughout the year, but their numbers are maximum during the periods, November to January and April to

June (dry months). Their rate of incursion was maximum during the full moon and new moon periods and greater at night than during the day (Subramanyam & Ganapati, 1971).

Experiments on prawn culture in salt pans were conducted in East Godavari District. The first experiment was conducted from June to December 1974 (7 months) and the two salt pans used measured 0.61 ha and 0.48 ha. These were stocked with juveniles of *P. monodon* and *P. indicus* with and average length of 65 mm. In these ponds, the temperature and salinity varied from 29.2 to 35.0˚C, and from 21.97‰ to 47.39‰ respectively. At the harvest in December, the average size of *P. mondon* was 165.4 mm and that of *P. indicus* 140.7 mm. The rates of production for a 6 month period was 164 kg/ha and 189 kg/ha, respectively in the two pans and the net profit was Rs 980/ha and Rs. 1113/ha in the two pans. In the second experiments, 9470 juveniles of *P. monodon* with and average length of 54.2 mm were stocked in a salt pan of 0.26 ha. The pond temperature varied between 25.5˚C and 31.0˚C and salinity from 21.27‰ to 45.39‰. Rice bran was provided as supplementary feed. After 168 days, the prawns had a mean length of 123.4 mm with a survival rate of 79.3% and the yield was 259 kg/ha with a net profit of Rs 1388/ha (Rao *et al.*, 1988).

The estuary is well known for its rich prawn fishery throughout the country. Prawns are brought at 3 main landing centres in all the months of the year and the annual catch of penaeid prawns is more than 4,000 tonnes. Peak catches are obtained from September to December. The total number of species of penaeid prawns contributing to the fishery is 23. Of these, 8 species (*M. monoceros, P. indicus, M. dobsoni, P. monodon, M. brevicornis, P. semisulcatus, P. marguiensis* and *P. japonicus*) contribute to the maximum. Prawns in the length range of 40-100 mm (2-4 months old) formed the bulk of the catches. *M. monoceros* grew at the rate of 16-18 mm/month, *P. indicus*, 27.5-32.5 mm/month and *P. mondon* 32.5-37.5mm/month. At the 3 landing centres, the annual yield of *M. monoceros* amounted to 2,693 tonnes contributing to about 59.7% of the penaeid prawns yield. Females dominated the catches, *M. brevicornis* with a catch of 167 tonnes formed 3.7% of the yield, *M. dobsoni* yielded 374 tonnes (8.3%) of the total, *P. indicus* 466 tonnes (10.34%), *P. mondon* 365 tonnes (8.1%), *P. semisulcatus* 126 tonnes (2.8%), *P. merguiensis* 79 tonnes (1.8%), and *P. japonicus* 46 tonnes (1.0%) (Devi, 1988).

The estuary and the adjoining areas provide excellent sources of prawn seeds. These are caught in push nets, drag nets and stake nets from 2-3 centres. Seasonal distribution of the seed catches was studied for a period of two years (1969-71) based on the three types of nets at two main centres. They were caught with varying frequencies practically throughout the year. The seeds of 7 species in their order of abundance were *M. monoceros, P. indicus, M. dobsoni, P. monodon, M. affinis, P. marguiensis*. It has been estimated that from the entire estuarine system, based on the gear census of 21 villages, about 2,030 thousand million seeds are caught during the year. This number has been reported to be enough to stock 21,800 hectares of prawn farms. The penaeid prawns namely *P. monodon, P.indicus,* and *P. marguiensis* are known to be the prime species for aquaculture. Seed resources of these three alone from the estuary can meet the stocking of 3,770 hectares (Rao, 1990).

OTHER STUDIES

The Krishna-Godavari Basin, covering an area of 45,000 km^2, is rich in hydrocarbon resources. The potential of the basin has been estimated using a probablistic model and the results indicated that the hydrocarbon resources are sizeable (Sikka, 1990). Another study on the geology and hydrocarbon prospects of the sedimentary basin showed that the region is promising for hydrocarbon exploration (Rao, 1993).

The sediments in the Godavari area are finer than those of Krishna while the riverine sediments contain predominantly sand. Muddy sand is widespread in the tidal channels. Placer deposits containing garnet and several other important elements are found in transitional sequences from freshwater to marine environment (Rao & Swamy, 1991).

In the Godavari Delta System (east Godavari District in Andhra Pradesh), Kakinada is a well known coastal town or port city. A survey of the groundwater quality of the town was made by making observations on 29 wells spread all over the town by monitoring the quality of water during the year 1995. It was concluded that because of the unconfined nature of the shallow watertable, the water quality gets affected easily. Analysis of the groundwater samples showed that the wells near Kakinada Lock and Salt Creek (areas of the town) are not satisfactory when compared with the permissible limits of salt and impurities contents of ISI drinking water standards (Rao *et al.,* 1997). The Godavari Estuary is flanked by several kinds of industries. In addition, there are natural gas wells, aquaculture farms, and these collectively are changing the landscape, topography, soil salinity, seawater seepage, saline water intrusion and are causing soil erosion. Contamination of well water is just one symptom of man-made changes which has been investigated.

References

1. Annapurna, C. & Sarma, D.V.R., 1979 Occurrence of podocopan ostracod, *Tanella indica* sp. nov. in the marginal water bodies. *Indian Journal of Marine Sciences*, Vol. 8, pp. 117-118.
2. Ansari, Z.A., Rodrigues, C.L., Chatterji, A. & Parulekar, A.H., 1982. Distribution of meiobenthos and macrobenthos at the mouth of some rivers of the east coast of India. *Indian Journal of Marine Sciences*, Vol. 11, pp. 341-343.
3. Bandyopadhyay, A., Raha, B.N. & Das, S., 1994. Seabed morphology off Krishna-Godavari delta with special reference to paralongitudinal channel in abyssal plain. *Indian Journal of Marine Sciences*, Vol. 23, pp. 143-146.
4. Chandramohan, P. & Chetty, P.M., 1988. Polychaete larvae of the Vasishta-Godavari Estuary, east coast of India. *Indian Journal of Marine Sciences*, Vol. 17, pp. 81-82.
5. Chandramohan, P. & Rao, T.S.S., 1972. Tidal cycle studies in relation to zooplankton distribution in the Godavari Estuary. *Proceeding of the Indian Academy of Sciences* (B), Vol. 75, pp. 23-31.
6. Devi, S.L., 1988. Observation on the fishery and biology of penaeid prawns from Godavari Estuary. *Indian Journal of Fisheries*, Vol. 35, pp. 52-63.
7. Dutt, S. & Rao, V.V., 1961a. On the breeding habits and early development stages of *Petroscirtes bipunctatus* (Day). *Journal of Zoological Society of India*, Vol. 12, pp. 158-161.
8. Dutt, S. & Rao, B.V.S., 1961b. On a new species of anchovy of the genus *Coilia* Gray, *Journal of Bombay National History Society*, Vol. 69, pp. 136-138.
9. Johns, B., Rao, A.D., Dube, S.K. & Sinha, P.C., 1993. The effect of freshwater discharge from the Godavari River on the occurrence of local upwelling off the east coast of India. *Estuarine, Coastal* and *Shelf Sciences*, Vol. 37, pp. 299-312.
10. Kondalarao, B. & Murty, K.V.R., 1988. Ecology of intertidal meiofauna of the Kakinada Bay (Gautami-Godavari Estuarine System), east coast of India. *Indian Journal of Marine Sciences*, Vol. 17, pp. 40-47.
11. Kondalarao, B., 1984. Distribution of meiobenthic harpacticoid copepods in Gautami-Godavari Estuarine System. *Indian Journal of Marine Sciences*, Vol. 13, pp. 80-84.
12. Murty, K.V.R, & Kondalarao, B., 1987. Survey of meiofauna in the Gautami-Godavari Estuary. *Journal of Marine Biological Association of India*, Vol. 29, pp. 37-44. (Issued in June 1988)
13. Murty, M.R. & Murty, P.S., 1993. Sedimentological studies off Vasistha-Vainateyam Godavari Delta sediments, central east coast of India. *Indian Journal of Marine Sciences*, Vol. 22, pp. 119-122.
14. Naidu, A.S. & Rao, C.B., 1963. Native sulphur in recent sediments from the Godavari Delta Basin. *Current Science*, Vol. 32, pp. 264-266.
15. Narappa, K.V., Rao, M.S. & Rao, M.P., 1982. Comparison of foraminiferal assemblages from Godavari and Krishna River Estuaries. *Indian Journal of Marine Sciences*, Vol. 11, pp. 220-224.
16. Peter, K.J. & Paulinose, V.T., 1978. Swarming of *Creseis acicula* rang (Pteropoda) in the Bay of Bengal, *Indian Journal of Marine Sciences*, Vol. 7, pp. 126-127.

17. Rajendran, A., DeSousa, S.N. & Reddy, C.V.G., 1982. Dissolved and particulate trace metals in the Western Bay of Bengal. *Indian Journal of Marine Sciences*, Vol. 11, pp. 43-50.
18. Rajyalakshmi, T. & Premswarup, T.V., 1975. Primary productivity in river Godavari, *Indian Journal of Fisheries*, Vol. 22, pp. 205-214.
19. Ramana, Y.U., Rao, V.R. & Reddy, B.S.R., 1989. Diurnal variation in salinity and currents in Vasishta-Godavari Estuary, east coast of India. *Indian Journal of Marine Sciences*, Vol. 18, pp. 54-.
20. Rambabu, A.V.S., Prasad, B.V. & Rao, M.B., 1987. Response of the mangrove mudsnail *Terebralia palustris* (Sinnaeus) (Prosobranchia: Potamididae) to different substrata. *Journal of Marine Biological Association of India*, Vol. 29 pp. 140-143.
21. Rao, A.D., Chamarthi, S. & Sinha, P.C., 1994. The modelling study of flow in Vasistha-Godavari Estuary. *Mausam*, Vol. 45, pp. 1-6.
22. Rao, M.U. & Rao, G.M.N., 1988. Mangrove population of the Godavari Delta complex. *Indian Journal of Marine Sciences*, Vol. 17, pp. 326-329.
23. Rao, B.K., Rao, P.S. & Swamy, A.S.R., 1988. Granulometric studies on modern barrier system of the right bank of Krishna Delta, east coast of India. *Indian Journal of Marine Sciences*, Vol. 17, pp. 283-286.
24. Rao, B.N. & Kshirasagar, T.V.S.R., 1991. Magnetic susceptibility of black sand concentrates of Krishna District, east coast of India. *Indian Journal of Marine Sciences*, Vol. 20, pp. 292-293.
25. Rao, Ch.M., 1985. Distribution of suspended particulate matter in the waters of eastern continental margin of India. *Indian Journal of Marine Sciences*, Vol. 14, pp. 15-19.
26. Rao, D.S. & Sarma, D.V.R., 1978. On the occurrence of *Poecilochaetus jhonsoni* Hartman 1939 (Polychaeta: Trochochaetidae) in the Indian waters. *Indian Journal of Marine Sciences*, Vol. 7, pp. 127-128.
27. Rao, D.S. & Sarma, D.V.R., 1979. Ecology of *Magelona cincta* Ehlers, 1908 (Polychaeta: Magelonidae) in the Vasishta Godavari Estuary, east coast of India. *Indian Journal of Marine Sciences*, Vol. 8, pp. 182-183.
28. Rao, D.S. & Sarma, D.V.R., 1980. Ecology of *Nephtys oligobranchia* Southern, from the Vasista Godavari Estuary. *Indian Journal of Marine Sciences*, Vol. 9, pp. 218-220.
29. Rao, B.K. & Swamy, A.S.R., 1991. Sediment characteristics of environments in the modern Krishna-Godavari Deltas. *Memoirs Geological Society of India*, No. 22, pp. 121-138.
30. Rao, G.N., 1993. Geology and hydrocarbon prospects of east coast sedimentary basins of India with special reference to Krishna Godavari Basin. *Journal of Geological Society of India*, Vol. 41, pp. 444-454.
31. Rao, G.N., 1994. Sedimentation and strati-structural control for hydrocarbon accumulation in Krishna-Godavari Basin. *Indian Journal of Marine Sciences*, Vol. 23, pp. 153-163.
32. Rao, G.S., 1990. An assessment of the penaeid prawn seed resource of the Godavari Estuary and the adjacent backwaters. *Indian Journal of Fisheries*, Vol. 37, pp. 99-108.

33. Rao, K.S. & Balaji, M., 1988. Biological fouling at Port Kakinada, Godavari Estuary, India. In: *Marine Biodeterioration: Advanced techniques applicable to the Indian Ocean.* (eds.) M.F. Thompson, R. Sarojini & R. Nagabhushanam. International Conference on Marine Biodeterioration, Goa, India, Jan 1986. Oxford & IBH. New Delhi, India. pp. 551-574.
34. Rao, M.B., 1965. Biomass studies on *Anchovilla commersoni* (Lecepedes) (Euqraulidae; Pisces) from Andhra Coast. *Journal of Marine Biological Association of India*, Vol. 7, pp. 369-376.
35. Rao, M.B., 1969. Some observations on the juveniles of *Hilsa ilisha* (Hamilton) (Pisces: Clupeidae) from Godavari Estuary. *Journal of Bombay Natural History Society*, Vol. 66, pp. 116-131.
36. Rao, V.V., 1969. *Incara multisquamatus* gen. et sp. nov. (family eleotridae) from Godavari Estuary. *Journal of Marine Biological Association of India*, Vol. 11, pp. 329-332.
37. Rao, V.V., 1970a. Breeding habits and early development of two blenniid fishes *Omobrranchus japonicus* (Bleeker) and *Cruantus smith* (Visweswara Rao) from Godavari Estuary. *Journal of Marine Biological Association of India*, Vol. 12, pp. 175-182.
38. Rao, V.V., 1970b. *Chiramenu fluviatilis* gen. et sp. nov. (Pisces: Gobiidae) from Godavari Estuary. *Journal of Marine Biological Association of India*, Vol. 12, pp. 183-186.
39. Rao, D.S. & Sarma, D.V.R., 1980. Ecology of *Nephtys oligobranchia* from the Vasishta Godavari Estuary. *Indian Journal of Marine Sciences,* Vol. 9, pp. 218-220.
40. Rao, M.U. & Sarojini, Y., 1992. Composition, abundance and vertical distribution of phytoplankton and fungi off Krishna and Godavari river mouths, east coast of India. *Indian Journal of Marine Sciences,* Vol. 21, pp. 128-132.
41. Rao, V.B., Rao, G.M.N., Sarma, G.V.S. & Rao, B.K., 1992. Mangrove environment and its sediment characters in Godavari Estuary, east coast of India. *Indian Journal of Marine Sciences,* Vol. 21, pp. 64-66.
42. Rao, M.B. & Joglekar, A., 1967. Comparative studies on *Setipinna godavariensis* Rao (Pisces: Engaraulidae) from Godavari and Hooghly estuaries. *Journal of Marine Biological Association of India,* Vol. 9, pp. 38-60.
43. Rao, G.S., Narasimham, K.A. & Murty, V.S., 1988. Prawn culture in salt-pans in east Godavari District, Andhra Pradesh. *Journal of Marine Biological Association of India,* Vol. 30, pp. 151-156.
44. Rao, Y.R.S., Vijay, T., Jain, C.K. & Seethapathi, P.V., 1997. Groundwater quality monitoring and evaluation in Kakinada coastal aquifer, Andhra Pradesh. *Proceedings of 8th National Symposium on Hydrography (Theme: Coastal Hydrography),* Calcutta, pp. 22-26.
45. Reddy, B.S.R. & Rao, V.R., 1993. Flushing and dispersion characteristics of Godavari Estuary under different river discharge conditions. *Indian Journal of Marine Sciences,* Vol. 22, pp. 111-114.
46. Reddy, B.S.R. & Rao, V.R., 1994. Seasonal variation in temperature and salinity in the Gautami-Godavari Estuary. *Proceedings of Indian Academy of Sciences, (Earth & Planetary Science),* Vol. 103, pp. 47-55.
47. Sai-Sastry, A.G.R. & Chandramohan, P., 1989. Planktonic coelenterates of Vasistha-Godavari Estuary, east coast of India. *Indian Journal of Marine Sciences,* Vol. 18, pp. 160-164.

48. Sai-Sastry, A.G.R. & Chandramohan, P., 1990a. Physicochemical characteristics of Vasishta-Godavari Estuary, east coast of India: Pre-pollution status. *Indian Journal of Marine Sciences,* Vol. 19, pp. 42-46.
49. Sai-Sastry, A.G.R. & Chandramohan, P., 1990b. Diel and tidal fluctuations in the water quality of Vasista-Godavari Estuary. *Indian Journal of Marine Sciences,* Vol. 19, pp. 133-136.
50. Sarma, D.V.R. & Ganapati, P.N., 1971. Hydrography of the Coringa River of the Gautami-Godavari Estuarine System. *Journal of Marine Biological Association of India,* Vol. 13, pp. 234-248.
51. Sarma, D.V.R., & Rao, D.S., 1982. Abundance and distribution of *Dendronereis arborifera* Peters, 1834 (Nereidae: Polychaeta) in the Vasishta-Godavari Estuary. *Indian Journal of Marine Sciences,* Vol. 11, pp. 90-92.
52. Sarma, M.S.S. & Rao, L.V.G., 1986. Currents and temperature structure off Godavari (east coast of India) during September 1980. *Indian Journal of Marine Sciences,* Vol. 15, pp. 88-91.
53. Sarma, V.V., Sudhakar, U. & Varaprasad, S.J.D., 1993. Behaviour of flouride and dissolved silicon in Gouthami-Godavari Estuarine environment. *Mahasagar — Bulletin of National Institute of Oceanography,* Vol. 26, pp. 105-113.
54. Sarma, V.V.J., Ramakrishna, A., Sharma, V.S. Prasad, P.R. & Prasad, N.V. B.S.S., 1985. A note on ionic distribution in the estuary of Vasista Godavary. *Mahasagar— Bulletin of National Institute of Oceanography,* Vol. 18, pp. 377-380.
55. Sastry, A.G.R.S. & Chandramohan, P., 1995. Zooplankton of Vasishta-Godavari Estuary: A pre-pollution status survey. *Journal of Marine Biological Association of India,* Vol. 37, pp. 249-258.
56. Sastry, Y.A., 1968. A note on an unusually heavy catch of fish in a shore-seine on the Andhra Coast. *Journal of Marine Biological Association of India,* Vol. 10, pp. 169-170.
57. Somayajulu, B.L.K., Martin, J.M., Eisma, D., Thomas, A.J., Borole, D.V. & Rao, K.S., 1993. Geochemical studies in the Godavari Estuary, India. *Marine Chemistry,* Vol. 43, pp. 83-93.
58. Sikka, S.N., 1990. Quantitative hydrocarbon resources assessment of Krishna-Godavari Basin, India. *Journal of Geological Society of India,* Vol. 35, pp. 661-669.
59. Srinivasan, M., 1994. Chaetognatha from the estuaries of India — A review. *Journal of Marine Biological Association of India,* Vol. 36, pp. 221-225.
60. Subrahmanyam, M., 1965. Lunar, diurnal and tidal periodicity in relation to the prawn abundance and migration in the Godavari Estuarine System. *Fisheries Technology,* Vol. 2, pp. 26-41.
61. Subrahmanyam, M., 1967a. Further observations on lunar periodicity in relation to the prawn abundance in the Godavari Estuarine System. *Journal of Marine Biological Association of India,* Vol. 9, pp. 111-115.
62. Subrahmanyam, M., 1967b. Observations on marking prawns with vital stains. *Journal of Marine Biological Association of India,* Vol. 9, pp. 202-203.
63. Subrahamanyam, M. & Ganapati, P.N., 1971. Observations on post larval prawns from the Godavari Estuarine System with a note on their role in capture and culture fisheries. *Journal of Marine Biological Association of India,* Vol. 13, pp. 195-202.

64. Swamy, A.S.R. & Rao, Ch.M., 1974. Boron in the modern deltaic sediments of the Krishna River and its offshore region, east coast of India. *Mahasagar — Bulletin of National Institute of Oceanography,* Vol. 7, pp. 187-191.
65. Venkanna, P., 1991, Present status of the estuarine flora of the Godavari and the Krishna. *Journal of Bombay Natural History Society,* Vol. 88, pp. 47-54.

Chapter 4

Ennore

The river Ennore passes through Chennai City and carries fairly large volumes of freshwater during the monsoon months (Jul-Aug and Nov-Dec). It joins the Bay of Bengal at Ennore which is located on the northern side of Madras Harbour. At one time, the estuary formed a good source for the collection of zoological specimens. At present there are a number of industries located along the banks of the river which discharge a lot of untreated and partially-treated wastes into the river and estuary. A thermal power plant draws coolant water from a point about 4 km upstream from the mouth of the estuary and discharges hot water and fly ash into the sea. There are two fertilizer factories and a refinery which discharge their partially-treated wastes upstream into the estuary. The Ennore Estuary has another peculiarity. At its mouth a sand bar gets formed continuously because the direction of the longshore currents is towards the mouth resulting into partly closing the connection between the estuary and the sea. Therefore, continuous dredging operations are required to keep the mouth fully open (Sridhar, 1982).

From January to December 1985 (except in Feb. and March), water samples were collected by Sivaswamy (1990) from three stations of the Ennore River and estuary for the study of physical and chemical features. Station 1 was in the estuary, station 2 at a point called Ennore Spout and station 3 near the mouth called Santhome. Table 4.1 shows the environmental features at the three stations. Temperature of water generally followed the air temperature except at station 2, where coolant water from the Ennore Thermal Power Plant (ETPS) raises the temperature of water. There is hardly any seasonal change in the *p*H at the three stations.

Table 4.1— Analysis of water samples at different stations of Ennore River (From Sivaswamy, 1990)

Parameters	Jan.	April	May	June	July	Aug.	Sept.	Oct.	Nov.	Dec.
					Ennore estuary (St. 1)					
Temp (°C)	33.5	31.5	32.0	29.0	32.0	35.0	33.0	32.5	33.0	29.5
Atm. Temp (°C)	34.5	34.0	35.0	31.0	33.0	33.0	35.0	33.0	32.0	28.5
*p*H	8.23	8.03	8.16	8.10	8.10	7.80	7.98	8.19	5.02	8.00
Salinity (× 10^{-3})	34	36	35	34	33	35	35	29	4	29
DO (mg.l^{-1})	6.40	6.00	6.40	–	2.00	7.60	7.20	7.60	8.40	7.60
Phosphate (mg.l^{-1})	1.75	0.50	0.77	0.15	0.15	1.30	0.23	0.15	0.46	1.84
Nitrate (mg.l^{-1})	1.77	1.77	2.26	2.99	–	–	–	–	–	–
Nitrite (mg.l^{-1})	0.066	0.099	0.025	0.200	0.103	0.099	0.069	0.165	0.314	0.685
					Ennore spout (St. 2)					
Temp (°C)	33.0	36.0	37.0	32.5	36.0	37.0	37.0	31.0	30.0	35.5
Atm. Temp (°C)	29.0	33.0	34.5	31.5	33.5	34.0	34.5	34.0	32.0	30.5
*p*H	7.65	8.00	7.79	7.91	7.90	7.72	7.91	8.09	7.87	7.80
Salinity (× 10^{-3})	17	35	35	35	32	34	33	30	27	26
DO (mg.l^{-1})	4.45	8.00	5.20	6.00	2.00	6.40	5.12	6.40	7.60	6.40
Phosphate (mg.l^{-1})	–	1.125	0.770	0.077	0.613	1.300	0.123	0.153	1.226	0.153
Nitrate (mg.l^{-1})	–	2.304	3.145	3.449	–	–	–	–	–	–
Nitrite (mg.l^{-1})	–	0.087	0.058	0.240	0.124	0.116	0.041	0.043	0.041	0.900
					Santhome (St. 3)					
Temp (°C)	28.0	30.0	31.5	30.0	30.0	27.0	29.5	30.0	28.2	27.0
Atm. Temp (°C)	32.0	34.0	33.5	37.5	32.5	30.5	32.0	31.0	29.0	27.5
*p*H	8.19	8017	8.06	8.05	8.14	7.95	8.08	8.09	7.81	8.00
Salinity (× 10^{-3})	32	34	35	35	33	34	33	32	29	32
DO (mg.l^{-1})	4.45	7.60	5.60	6.00	2.80	6.80	6.24	6.00	6.80	6.80
Phosphate (mg.l^{-1})	–	BDL	0.230	0.077	0.077	1.150	BDL	0.230	BDL	0.153
Nitrate (mg.l^{-1})	–	1.106	2.702	11.87	–	–	–	–	–	–
Nitrite (mg.l^{-1})	–	0.050	0.016	0.021	0.041	0.041	0.008	0.029	0.338	0.297

February and March samples were not estimated
BDL = Below Detectable Level

Salinity, on the other hand, showed a sudden decline from October to December (during NE monsoon) in the Ennore Estuary (station 1). The decrease was not so

Table 4.2— Concentration of organochlorine pesticides at different stations of Ennore (From Sivaswamy, 1990)

Pesticide*	Station 1		Station 2		Station 3	
	W (mg/l)	S (mg/g)	W (mg/l)	S (mg/g)	W (mg/l)	S (mg/g)
DDT	–	Feb. 1.326	March 0.224	–	Feb. 0.101	–
Endosulfan	Jan. 0.093	Jan. 0.002	Jan. 0.489	–	–	Jan. 0.0014
	July 0.568	July 519.212	–	–		July 432.40
Heptachlor	Jan. 0.017	Feb. 7.399	Jan. 0.059	Feb. 6.604	Feb. 0.438	Feb. 3.369
	–	–	Feb. 0.441	–	–	–
Lindane	Jan. 0.006	Feb. 1.719	Jan. 0.018	Feb. 2.212	Feb. 0.108	–
	–	–	Feb. 0.692	–		–

W = water; S = sediment
* Pesticides were not detected in samples of other months

Table 4.3— Concentration of metals at different stations of Ennore (From Sivaswamy, 1990)

	Cadmium		Copper		Nickel		Lead		Zinc	
	W	S	W	S	W	S	W	S	W	S
					St I					
March	BDL	BDL	0.740	BDL	0.008	1.875	0.162	7.575	1.670	BDL
April	0.002	BDL	0.604	BDL	BDL	6.250	0.045	21.730	0.271	6.30
					St 2					
Jan.	BDL	BDL	0.171	BDL	BDL	BDL	0.013	0.143	0.208	1.75
Feb.	BDL	0.003	0.640	0.041	0.020	1.775	0.084	BDL	0.180	1.2
March	BDL	–	0.750	–	0.018	–	0.113	–	0.180	–
April	0.002	BDL	0.608	BDL	0.006	BDL	0.026	18.300	0.302	3.25
					St 3					
Jan.	BDL	BDL	BDL	BDL	0.056	0.182	BDL	0.286	0.528	2.64
Feb.	0.100	BDL	0.700	BDL	0.013	0.318	0.336	0.429	0.260	2.06
March	BDL	BDL	0.760	0.800	0.010	2.050	0.085	BDL	0.370	BDL
April	0.009	BDL	0.704	BDL	BDL	8.675	BDL	31.700	0.270	2.25

W = water; conc: mg/l; S = sediment; conc: μg/g; BDL = Below Detectable Level

well-pronounced at the stations 2 and 3. Dissolved oxygen declined in July at all the three stations, otherwise it remained stable. Phosphate was relatively high at station 1 as compared to the other two stations (showing a decline in April and May), while the data for nitrate were meagre, nitrite seems to remain uniform at all the stations. Concentrations of pesticides and heavy metals are shown in Tables 4.2 and 4.3. These are of much ecological importance as the values of both are high and exceed the levels prescribed by the Bureau of Indian Standards (Sivaswamy, 1990). The two contaminants are harmful to both plant and animal life.

In another study, the characteristics of water at different sampling points of the estuary were evaluated (Sridhar, 1982). These are given in Table 4.4. As can be seen from the table, from the entry point to the sea up to about 4 km upstream, the river and estuary are intensely polluted. Both 4 hour P.V. and water soluble P decrease considerably even beyond 4 km upstream.

Table 4.4— Characteristics of water in Ennore Estuary at different sampling points (samples collected between 0900h and 1100h) (from Sridhar, 1982)

Sampling point and distance	4h P.V (mg l^{-1})	Water-soluble P (mg l^{-1})
Close to entry into sea	5.5	23.3
0.5 km upstream	9.5	21.0
1.0 km upstream	10.5	17.0
1.5 km upstream	8.5	14.5
3.0 km upstream	10.5	4.5
4.0 km upstream	8.5	1.5
4.5 km upstream	6.5	0.7
5.0 km upstream	5.5	1.0
5.5 km upstream	2.5	1.0
6.0 km upstream	7.0	0.5

Values for ammonia, nitrite and nitrate nitrogen nil.
P.V indicated permanganate value

Table 4.5— Dominant phytoplankton species in water samples collected at different stations of Ennore Estuary (From Sivaswamy, 1990)

St 1

Nitzschia longissima, Thallasiothrix frauenfeldii, Asterionella japonica, Navicula species, *Biddulphia mobiliensis, Ceratium furca, Melosira sulcata, Pleurosigma normanii*

St 2

Pleurosigma elongatum, Skeletonema costatum, Tabellaria fenestrata, Asterionella japonica, Navicula species, *Thallasionema nitzschioides, Thallosiothrix frauenfeldii*

St 3

Asterionella japonica, Thallasiothrix frauenfeldii, Biddulphia mobiliensis, Melosira sulcata, Navicula species, *Ceratium furca, Thallasionema nitzschioides*

Table 4.5 shows the dominant species of phytoplankton recorded at the three stations and Table 4.6 gives the values of chlorophyll a, b and c at the three stations from March to May. Seasonal cycle of abundance of phytoplankton is

Table 4.6— Chlorophyll (mg/m^3) in water samples* of Ennore Estuary (From Sivaswamy, 1990)

February			March			April			May		
Chl: a	b	c	a	b	c	a	b	c	a	b	c
St 1											
0.0018	0.0093	0.0124	0.0049	0.0094	0.0362	0.0108	0.0075	0.0566	0.009	0.003	0.0457
St 2											
–	–	–	0.0096	0.0052	0.0253	0.0095	0.0208	0.0314	1.0314	0.02	0.0296
St 3											
0.0659	0.0366	–	–	–	0.0019	0.0086	0.0048	0.001	0.0048	0.014	0.0137

* Samples collected during other months were not estimated for chlorophyll

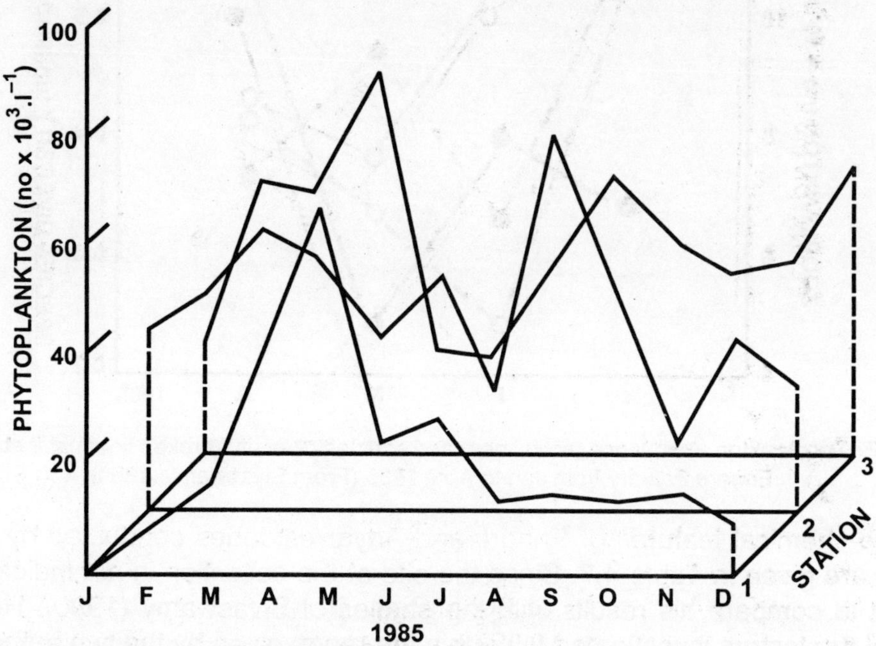

Fig. 4.1 Seasonal changes in abundance of phytoplankton at three stations of Ennore Estuary during the year 1985 (From Sivaswamy, 1990)

shown in Fig. 4.1. Their density does not seem to be affected significantly by sewage and other pollutants. Two peaks – one during April to July and the other from September to November in the phytoplankton production are clearly seen. Chlorophyll values, during the 4 months of observations did not vary much (Table 4.6).

Zooplankton population was studied at stations 2 and 3 for 4 months from January to April and their species diversity was also recorded. This is shown in Fig. 4.2. Their population declined in March as compared to the other months and the diversity showed an inverse relationship with their abundance. Evidently there was no serious influence of pollution on their population (Sivaswamy, 1990).

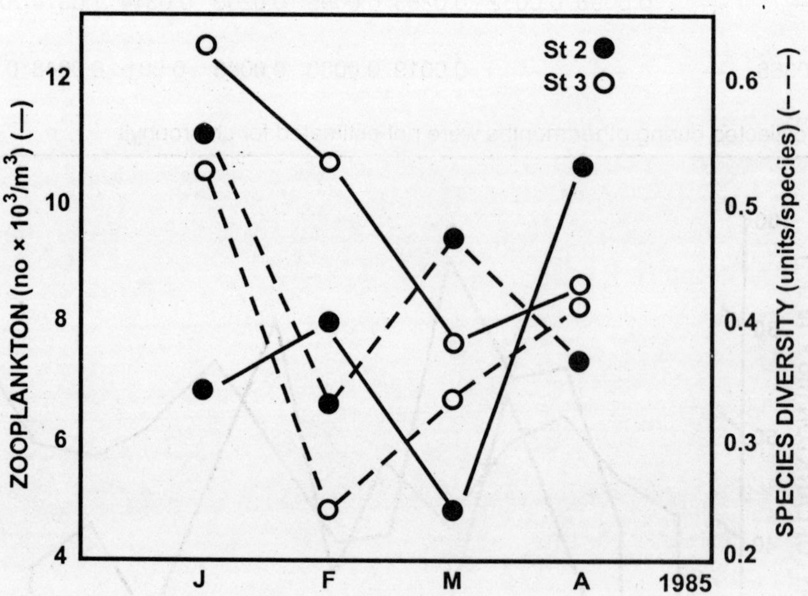

Fig. 4.2 Zooplankton abundance (solid lines) and species diversity (broken lines) at 2 stations of Ennore Estuary from Jan to April 1985 (From Sivaswamy, 1990)

Physico-chemical features of Ennore and Adyar estuaries conducted by Joseph (1989) are given in Table 4.7. Since the site of the collection is not indicated it is difficult to compare his results with the studies of Sivaswamy (1990). However, most of the factors investigated fall within the range given by the two authors.

Table 4.7— Physicochemical characteristics of water of two estuaries in Chennai (From Joseph, 1989)

Parameters	Estuaries	
	Adyar	Ennore
Water Temperature in ˚C	29.5 - 32.0	29.5 - 33.2
Dissolved oxygen (ppm)	2.2 - 5.2	2.4 - 5.8
*p*H	6.2 - 7.1	7.6 - 8.1
Salinity (ppt)	8.8 - 38.1	10.0 - 37.5
C.O.D (ppm)	6.8 - 35.0	5.8 - 22.0

Table 4.8— Concentrations* of heavy metals in water, sediment and fish (*Mystus gulio*) samples** collected from Ennore Estuary (From Joseph, 1989)

Samples	Metals	Ennore Estuary
Water ($\mu g.ml^{-1}$)	Zn	0.12
	Pb	0.1
	Cu	0.09
	Cr	0.18
	Ni	0.06
	Cd	0.001
Sediment ($\mu g.g^{-1}$ DW)	Zn	145
	Pb	46
	Cu	15
	Cr	2.9
	Ni	3
	Cd	0.09
Fish ($\mu g.g^{-1}$ DW)	Zn	280
	Pb	4
	Cu	32
	Cr	1.8
	Ni	4
	Cd	0.02

DW = Dry Weight
* Average of 4 samples
** Triplicate metal determination

Table 4.8 shows the concentrations of 6 heavy metals in water, sediment and fish collected from the Ennore Estuary. The values fall within the range shown in the Adyar Estuary indicating that all the three (Ennore, Cooum and Adyar) are equally polluted with heavy metals. Concentrations of the 6 heavy metals in three different tissues of the mullet, *Liza macrolepis* from the Ennore Estuary are given in Table 4.9 and their sequential listing as indicated by Nammalwar (1987) is given below:

Gill : Fe > Zn > Ni > Pb > Cu > Cd > Hg
Liver : Fe > Zn > Cu > Ni > Pb > Cd > Hg
Muscle : Zn > Fe > Ni > Cu > Cd > Pb > Hg

Bioaccumulation of these metals seems to fall within the reported safe level concentrations of the heavy metals (Nammalwar, 1987).

It has been reported that in the seventies, a large number of different species of fishes, prawns and crabs used to be caught from the Ennore Estuary and it provided a rich fishing ground. Table 4.10, compiled by Sridhar (1982), gives a list of the species identified by him. He further states that in 1982, only 7 species were found. Since a large number of industries have come up along the banks, pollution has intensified and the estuary emits a foul odour and is unable to support much flora and fauna.

Table 4.9— Distribution and concentrations of heavy metals in gill, liver and muscle tissues of mullet *Liza macrolepis* from Ennore Estuary (From Nammalwar, 1987)

Heavy metals	Gill (ppm/dry wt)	Liver (ppm/dry wt)	Muscle (ppm/dry wt)
Cd	0.82	0.68	1.70
Cu	2.83	6.76	2.50
Zn	45.20	86.65	67.28
Ni	15.62	4.50	8.62
Pb	2.90	1.62	1.34
Fe	148.21	160.25	13.80
Percentage of water content	80.50	78.65	79.42
Heavy metal	Gill (ppm/dry wt)	Liver (ppm/dry wt)	Muscle (ppm/dry wt)
Hg	0.08	0.14	0.1

Flow characteristics of the estuary were determined by measuring current velocities and direction during the flood and ebb tides using a current meter. In addition, fluorescein dye solution was released at one point and the distance travelled by the dye was measured to determine the current speed. This was confirmed by the

Table 4.10— Fish recorded in Ennore Estuary in 1972 (From Sridhar, 1982)

Common name	Scientific name
Mullet	*Mugil cephalus*
	Mugil dussumieri
	Mugil occur
Others	*Macrones vittatus*
	Therapon jarona
	Chaetoessus chaneda
	Tilapia mossambica
	Engraulis purava
	Tuthis sp.
Half beak	*Hemirhamphus sp.*
White bait	*Stolephorus sp.*
	Sillago sihama
Cock-up	*Lates calcarifer*
Jew fish	*Sciaena sp.*
Silver bellies	*Equnea sp.*
	Gerres filamentosus
	Saccobranchus sp.
	Platycephalus sp.
	Chrysophris suba

In addition, the prawn (*Penaeus indicus*) and green crab (*Scylla serrata*) were also found in large numbers.

release of floats. All these studies indicated that pollutants after entering the Bay of Bengal do not go deep into the sea. This is because the tidal flow is weak and there are strong longshore currents in the northern direction. Because of these features, whatever wastes are discharged either in the estuary or directly into the sea are brought back to the mouth of the estuary and get accumulated. Ennore Estuary has a fairly large flow of freshwater but in spite of this, it has limitations in assimilating large amounts of pollutants. As a result, the sand bar which is continuously formed prevents any flushing out into the sea. Figure 4.3 shows the direction of the river flow and also the directions in which the flood and ebb tides flow and the direction of the longshore current. The result is that a triangular area gets demarcated. Any discharge of waste within this triangle or inside the estuary will remain within the triangular region and will not be flushed out. The ideal discharge zone would be beyond this triangle (Sridhar, 1982).

Thus it is possible to save the estuaries around Chennai if a scientific approach to the discharge of treated effluents is made by conducting studies on flow characteristics and determining a proper discharge point through submarine pipelines. This will result in better environmental conditions of the estuaries and will increase

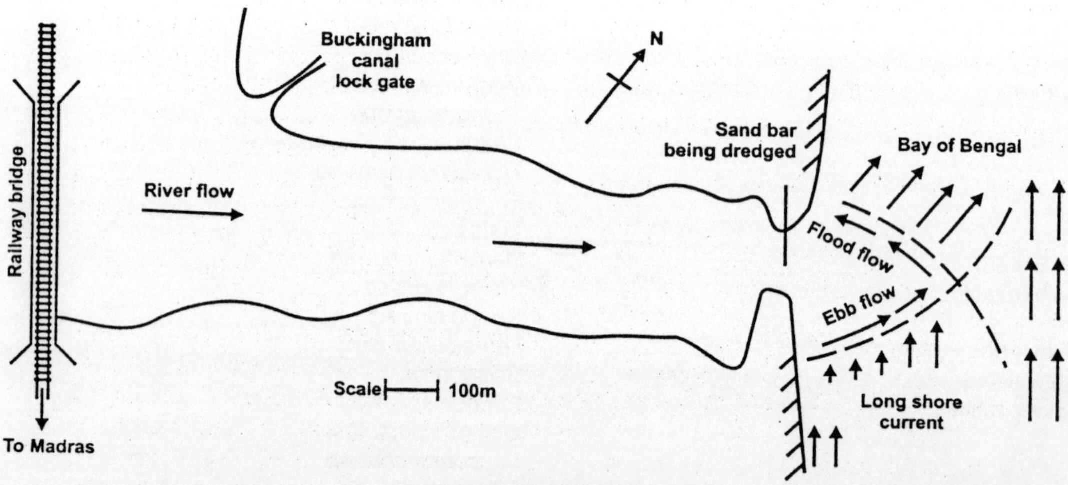

Fig. 4.3 A sketch of Ennore Estuary showing the direction of the river flow and also the direction of the flow of flood and ebb tides and the long shore current (From Sridhar, 1982)

fish production once again. Pollution in the Buckingham Canal (see Cooum) has become practically out of control because of the lack of flushing and siltation. Nevertheless, it is still possible to save Adyar, Cooum and Ennore estuaries by conducting diffusion and dispersion studies.

References

1. Joseph, K.O., 1989. Heavy metal contamination of fish of the estuarine environment in Madras region. *Proceedings of the National Academy of Sciences, India,* Vol. 59 (B), pp. 45-50.
2. Nammalwar, P., 1987. Pollution impact and management of the coastal estuaries around Madras, India. *Proceedings National Seminar on Estuarine Management* (ed.) N. B. Nair, State Committee on Sciences, Technology and Environment, Government of Kerala, Trivandrum, pp. 190-193.
3. Sivaswamy, S.N., 1990. Plankton in relation to coastal pollution of Ennore, Madras coast, *Indian Journal of Marine Sciences,* Vol. 19, pp. 115-119.
4. Sridhar, M. K.C., 1982. A field study of estuarine pollution in Madras, India. *Marine Pollution Bulletin,* Vol. 12, pp. 233-236.

Chapter 5

Cooum

The river Cooum Starts from Saltair village in Chinglepett District and flows up to a distance of 65 km. It passes through the city of Chennai (Fig. 5.1), and before opening into the Bay of Bengal, it forms a narrow estuary (13°10 ′ N-80°16′ E). The river begins as a channel for the collection of surplus flow of water from about 80 small tanks and carries with it untreated sewage of the Chennai City and industrial wastes. Slums have developed along the bank of this estuary and their wastes also enter the estuary (Sridhar, 1982). At several places, the water is blackish and emits unpleasant odour. Near the mouth of the estuary, a boating club functions as a source of recreation.

The Buckingham Canal, (see Fig. 5.2) connects this estuary with Adyar (Rao & Valsaraj, 1984). This canal was used earlier for inland transport. However, as it enters the Chennai City, it receives enormous quantities of wastes and becomes like a slurry, with animals walking on solid wastes and garbage on either side used as landfill. Because of restriction in its flow probably due to heavy load of organic matter which it contains, anaerobic decomposition occurs leading to the production of hydrogen sulphide at several places.

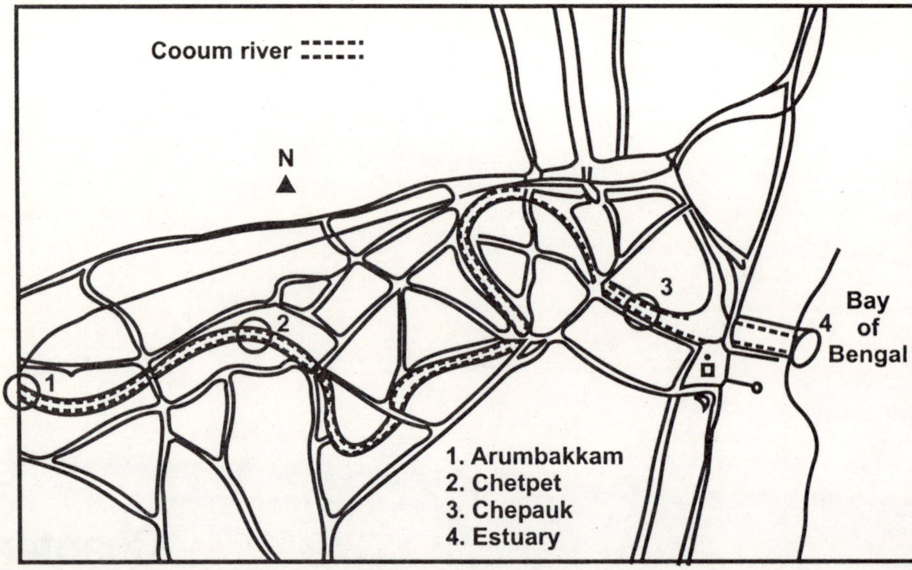

Fig. 5.1 Map of river Cooum showing stations 1-4 within Chennai City where studies were conducted (From Rao & Valsaraj, 1984)

Rao & Valsaraj (1984) and Anantharaj *et al.* (1987) have made detailed studies on hydrobiological conditions of the river Cooum and its estuary and some of their findings would be very relevant even today. Temperature of water at the surface follows the air temperature and because of restriction in depth, there is little difference in temperature between surface and bottom . The *p*H values range between 6.5 - 8.0, increasing slightly during the day in summer months. There was no significant change in carbonate alkalinity in the river up to the mouth of the estuary but bicarbonate alkalinity increased towards the mouth because of the intense pollution by sewage. Dissolved oxygen in the water was very low and ranged between nil to 8 mg/l. Depletion of oxygen was recorded at all the stations worked in the river and estuary. It was largely due to decomposition of organic matter present in the sewage by the heterotrophic bacteria using the available dissolved oxygen. Concentration of free carbon dioxide was linked with the seasons, showing high values during the monsoon and low values during the summer. Sporadic fluctuation was probably associated with the release of free CO_2 during the breakdown of organic matter in the sediments.

Total phosphate ranged 0.10 - 7.94 mg/l and showed no seasonal pattern. Random high and low values were probably due to eutrophication of water with sewage at different points of entry. Nitrate – nitrogen values ranged between 0.77 to

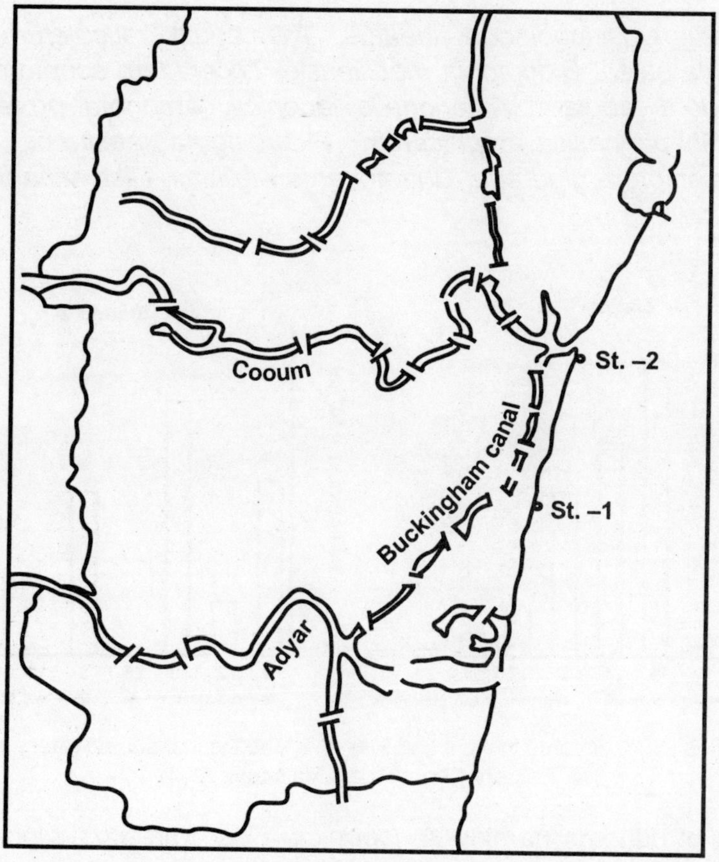

Fig. 5.2 Location of the stations 1 and 2 near the mouth of Cooum and inshore waters and the Buckingham Canal connecting the two estuaries (From Rao & Valsaraj, 1984)

11.76 mg/l. Slicate-silicon showed an inverse relationship with salinity – the values being high in freshwater-dominated areas and there was no relationship (either direct or inverse) with the abundance of diatoms.

Phytoplankton abundance at the two stations in the inshore waters close to the estuary (see Fig. 5.1 for position of stations) is shown in Fig. 5.3 during April and May. Station 1 (see Fig. 5.2) which was away from the estuarine outfall (station 2) showed a much greater density of organisms than the other station (Rao & Valsaraj, 1984). This is because of the effect of pollutants coming from the city into the estuary and entering into the inshore waters. Some of the diatoms and silicoflagellates identified from the collections were:

Paralia sulcata, Coscinodiseus lineatus, Triceratium reticulatum, Triceratium favus, Nitzschia palea, Biddulphia mobiliensis, Triceratium scuptum, Triceratium dubium, Syndera tabulata, Asterionella japonica, Amphora proteus, Navicula cancellate, Rhaphonesis amphiceros, Pleurosigma aestuarii, Chaetoceros perpusilla, Amphiprora gigantea, Chaetoveros wighami, Dictyocha fibula and Silicoflagellate sp.

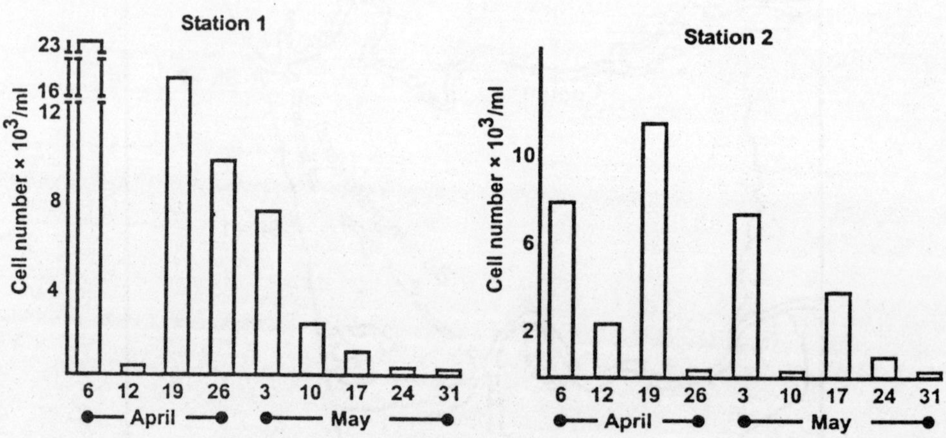

Fig. 5.3 Abundance of diatoms in April and May at 2 stations in inshore waters close to Cooum Estuary (From Rao & Valsaraj, 1984)

Four species of diatoms namely *A. japonica, Coscinodiscus wighami, Coscinodiscus lineatus* and *Melosira sp.* were dominant and occurred on all dates of the collection and in large numbers (Rao & Valsaraj, 1984). Table 5.1 shows their abundance at two stations. At station 1, which had uniformly marine hydrographical conditions, their density was much greater than that of station 2 which was influenced by the water coming from the river.

Anantharaj *et al.* (1987) recorded 14 species of zooplankton from 4 stations of the river Cooum and its estuary. These belonged to the groups protozoan, rotifers, copepods, cladocerans and larvae of others crustaceans. Cladocerans and copepods were present in large numbers and rotifers occupied numerically the last place in the order of abundance. Figure 5.4 shows the seasonal abundance of 5 categories of zooplankton. At station 1, copepods were present with varying abundance throughout the year. Otherwise, their distribution was patchy at almost all other stations. Cladocerans were present at all the stations but not uniformly in all the months. A decrease in zooplankton number was noticed during the north-east monsoon (October-December). Low density of zooplankton probably

Table 5.1— Abundance of four dominant diatoms in the collections of inshore waters off Chennai. Values given are numbers/ml (From Rao & Valsaraj, 1984)

Station 1									
	April 1984				May 1984				
Diatom	6	12	19	26	3	10	17	24	31
Asterionella japonica	3477	125	4057	331	752	657		63	28
Chaetoceros wighami	266	80	685	102	300	85	220	25	–
Coscinodicus lineatus	144	38	970	215	605	852	400	50	39
Melosira sp.	17700	142	8701	–	4187	170	–	–	28
Station 2									
	April 1984				May 1984				
Diatom	6	12	19	26	3	10	17	24	31
Asterionella japonica	1650	653	4328	237	886	156	525	381	32
Chaetoceros wighami	230	–	285	134	57	12	2125	64	–
Coscinodicus lineatus	66	–	2284	86	–	50	320	150	23
Melosira sp.	5906	1579	1915	–	3209	23	–	–	10

indicates the effect of pollution which makes their survival difficult.

POLLUTION

Characteristics of water in the Cooum estuary from its outfall to the sea and at 5 other sampling stations, 1 km apart upstream, are given in Table 5.2. An analysis of the data indicates that Cooum Estuary carries considerable amounts of organic matter (as shown by 4 h. P.V.), ammonia-nitrogen and water soluble phosphorus. These pollutants get considerably diluted as the water reaches the sea. It is also of interest to note that as the estuary approaches the sea, the mineral content of the water increases because of the tidal effect (Sridhar, 1982). Further observations on the dilution characteristics of the water of the estuary are presented in Table 5.3. As can be seen from this table, because of dilution, the quality of water changes. Total bacterial counts including the coliform groups show a considerable decline in numbers.

HEAVY METALS

Observation at 4 sampling stations shown in Fig. 5.1 for a period of one year showed that the iron (Fe) content was high at stations 1 and 2 reaching about 900 mg/l during the rainy season. In the month of January, it was very low approach-

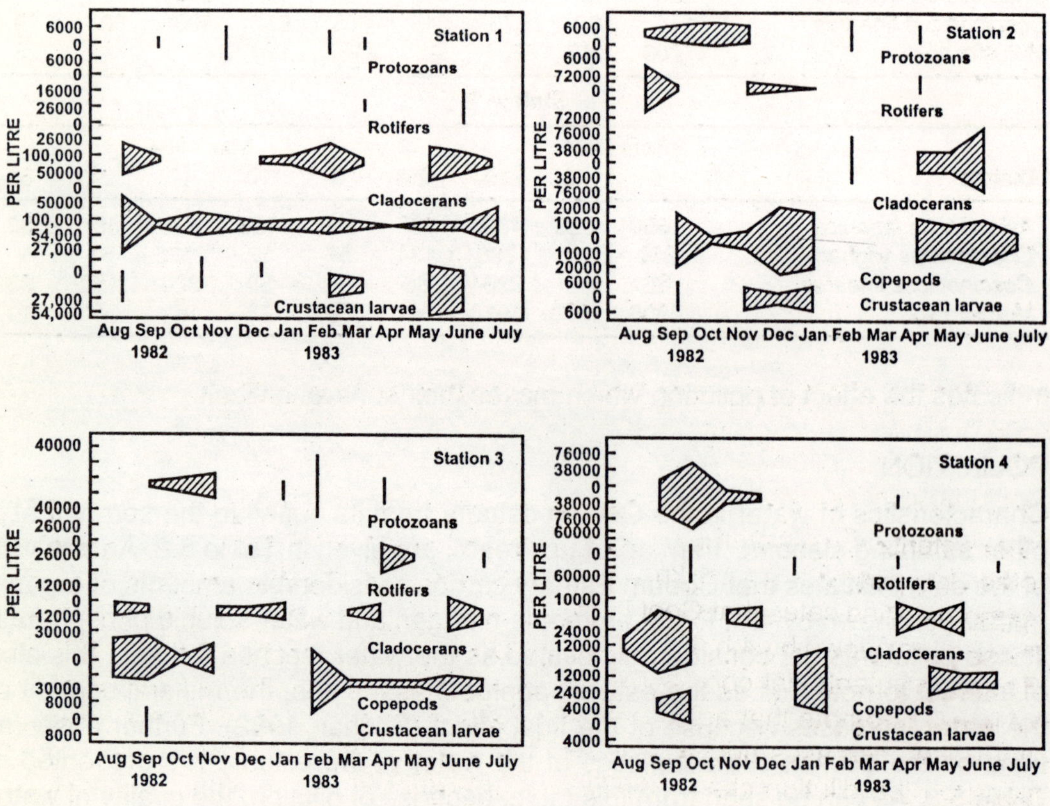

Fig. 5.4 Distribution of 5 groups of zooplankton at 4 stations of Cooum River Estuary shown in Fig. 5.1 (From Anantharaj *et al.*, 1987)

ing beyond the detection limits. Probably the sources of excess iron were sewage and industrial wastes heavily brought down by land run-off. Similarly, lead (Pb) and nickel (Ni) were maximum at station 1 – the two ranging between 275 mg/l and 1312.5 mg/l respectively during the rainy season. Zinc concentration was also

Table 5.2— Characteristics of water in Cooum Estuary at different sampling points. P.V. indicates permanganate value. (From Sridhar, 1982)

Sampling point	Time	Depth (cm)	4 h P.V. (mg/l)	NH_3-N (mg/l)	NO_2-N (mg/l)	Water soluble (P mg/l)	Total hardness (mg/l)	Ca (mg/l)	Mg (mg/l)
At outlet to sea*	0845 h	170	4.0	7.0	Nil	0.5	6996	531	1379
1.0 km upstream	0928 h	230	10.0	12.0	Nil	0.2	6524	529	1200
2.0 km upstream	0930 h	130	11.0	15.0	Nil	0.7	4452	311	894
3.0 km upstream↑	0940 h	207	18.5	20.0	Nil	1.5	3392	181	715
4.0 km upstream↑	0955 h	185	20.0	23.0	Nil	1.0	3021	243	587
6.0 km upstream↑	1010 h	170	25.0	30.0	Nil	2.0	1325	27	306

The chloride concentration ranged between 12000 and 24000 mg/l at different periods of the day

* Fish were found

↑ Black colour, offensive odour

Table 5.3— Chemical and bacteriological analysis of water samples from Cooum Estuary and the sea at the mouth of the estuary (From Sridhar, 1982)

Characteristic	Cooum estuary	Seawater
Turbidity (Klett scale reading)	20	Nil
3 min permanganate value (mg/l)	5.0	2.0
Ammonia nitrogen (mg/l)	9.5	Nil
Nitrite nitrogen (mg/l)	0.5	Nil
Nitrate nitrogen (mg/l)	Trace	Trace
Water-soluble phosphorus (mg/l)	0.9	Nil
Chloride (mg/l)	13000	14980
Total bacterial count (per ml)	80000	20000
Total coliforms (MPN/100ml)	6800	600

high at station 1 (32.5 mg/l) and its value varied widely at all the 4 stations and with seasons. This may be because of the low speed of flow of the river (Anantharaj *et al.*, 1987).

Bioaccumulation and distribution of seven heavy metals in 3 different tissues of the mullet (*Liza macrolepis*) are given in Table 5.4. In almost all the tissues, the values of the metals in this estuary were higher than those of the Ennore Estuary. Arrangements of the sequential listing of the metals in the 3 tissues as indicated by Nammalwar (1987) were as follows:

Gill : Fe > Ni > Zn > Pb > Cd > Cu > Hg
Liver : Fe > Zn > Ni > Cu > Cd > Pb > Hg
Muscle : Zn > Ni > Fe > Pb > Cd > Cu > Hg

Table 5.4— Distribution and concentration of heavy metals in gill, liver and muscle tissues of mullet, *Liza macrolepis* from Cooum Estuary (From Nammalwar, 1987)

Heavy metals	Gill (ppm/dry wt)	Liver (ppm/dry wt)	Muscle (ppm/dry wt)
Cd	1.84	2.85	1.40
Cu	1.52	5.28	1.10
Zn	38.34	46.40	32.00
Ni	62.25	41.00	22.64
Pb	4.84	2.56	1.80
Fe	196.40	165.48	18.65
Percentage of water content	73.64	80.20	79.65
Hg	0.88	0.64	0.45

Because of large volumes of sewage and effluents coming from the city and industries, pollution load in Cooum Estuary is higher than in Ennore. Roughly 15.4 million gallons / day pollutants flow into the Cooum Estuary. Field bioassay tests carried out in this estuary, based on the survival rates of two grey mullets (*Mugil cephalus*, and *Liza macrolepis*) indicate that Cooum Estuary in its present stage is totally unsuitable for the culture of fishes even on an experimental basis. This is because of oxygen deficit reaching up to nil values as a result of heavy sewage pollution and its high degree of fluctuation (Nammalwar, 1992). Although some improvement in the oxygen values occurs during the high tide because the incoming seawater is rich in oxygen, the flushing rate in the estuary is slow and feeble. The asphyxication levels of the two grey mullets were found to be in range of 0.78 to 0.89 ml/l. Therefore, if the sewage discharge in the estuary gets controlled and the oxygen concentration is maintained at above 2 ml/l, the prospects of fish culture in the estuary can be improved.

WATER CHARACTERISTICS IN BUCKINGHAM CANAL

Table 5.5 shows the quality of water in Buckingham Canal from which it is clear that the canal is intensely polluted and there is hardly any flow or tidal incursion to promote flushing of the canal or renewal of water. The canal remains stagnant with a gentle flow except during the rainy season when it gets flushed. It can thus be concluded that Cooum Estuary is one of the highly polluted estuaries in the country and that there are no proper studies carried out on this estuary.

Table 5.5— Characteristics of water in Buckingham Canal (From Sridhar, 1982).

Characteristic	Value
Turbidity (Klett scale reading)	81
3 min permanganate value (mg l^{-1})	13
Ammonia nitrogen (mg l^{-1})	8.2
Nitrite nitrogen (mg l^{-1})	Trace
Nitrate nitrogen (mg l^{-1})	Nil
Water-soluble phosphorus (mg l^{-1})	1.98
Chloride (mg l^{-1})	380
Total plate count at 25 °C (per ml water)	40 000 000
Total plate count at 37 °C (per ml water)	20 000 000
Total coliforms (MPN/100ml)	240 000 000
Coliform type	Intermediate type I *Aerobacter acrogenes* var. I

References

1. Anantharaj, B., Bagyalakshmi, V. & Lakshmi, R., 1987. Limnology of the river Cooum with special reference to sewage and heavy metal pollution. *Proceedings of the Indian Academy of Sciences,* Vol. 96, pp. 141-149.
2. Nammalwar, P., 1987. Pollution impact and management of the coastal estuaries around Madras, India. *In: Proceedings of the National Seminar on Estuarine Management* (ed.) N. B. Nair, State Committee on Science, Technology and Environment, Government of Kerala, Trivandrum, pp. 190-193.
3. Nammalwar, P., 1992. Field bioassay in Cooum and Adyar estuaries for environmental management. *In: Tropical Ecosystem: Ecology and Management* (eds.) K.P. Singh and J.S. Singh, pp. 359-370. Wiley Eastern Ltd., New Delhi.
4. Rao, V.N. R. & Valsaraj, C.P., 1984. Hydrobiological studies in the inshore waters of the Bay of Bengal. *Journal of Marine Biological Association of India*, Vol. 26. pp. 58-65.
5. Sridhar, M.K.C., 1982. A field study of estuarine pollution in Madras, India. *Marine Pollution Bulletin*, Vol. 13, pp. 233-236.

Chapter 6

Adyar

There are three main rivers Ennore, Cooum and Adyar running in the city of Chennai (Madras). Each of these flows into the Bay of Bengal forming estuaries close to the outfall. The Adyar Estuary (13˚8′N - 80˚16′E), like the other two, is intensely polluted and carries about 2 million gallons of domestic sewage per day (Nammalwar, 1987). Figure 6.1 shows the location of the estuary. Hydrographical conditions of coastal waters around Adyar and Cooum estuaries are given in Figs. 6.2, 6.3 and 6.4. Maximum rainfall in this region occurs during the north-east (NE) monsoon from September to December when the salinity of water goes down to about 24‰ (Fig. 6.4). But in the estuary it is much lower upstream (8‰). Maximum salinity of about 34‰ is recorded from April to August particularly at the outfall. Hydrogen ion concentration (*p*H) shows no marked fluctuation and ranges between 8.42 and 8.65. Fluctuation in dissolved oxygen is small and maximum values are recorded from November to February (Fig. 6.2). Both phosphate and nitrate concentrations are high in the months of July and August before the onset of north-east monsoon, but peak values of both the nutrients are recorded during the rainfall when salinity goes down (Thirupad & Reddy, 1959).

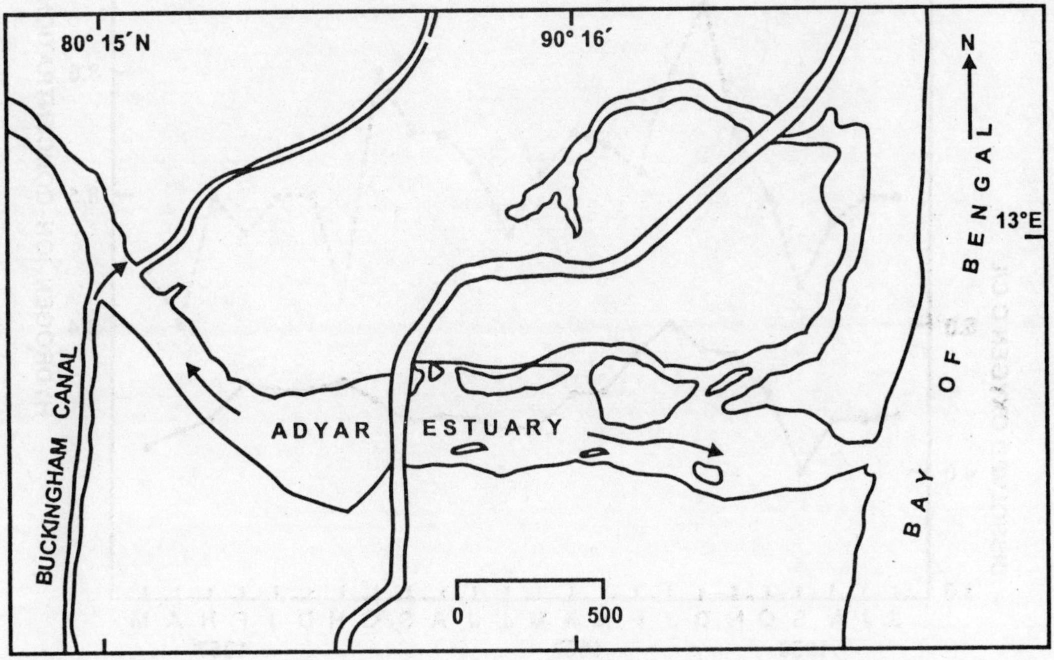

Fig. 6.1 Map showing the location of Adyar Estuary and its connection with Buckingham Canal.

Phytoplankton blooms in the estuary as well as in the nearshore waters occur when the salinity of water is low. This is attributed to the dilution caused by precipitation, and the nutrients brought by land runoff which occurs along both the coasts of India (Subramanyan, 1959). In fact the estuary gets an influx of euryhaline diatoms from October to December. Predominant species found are *Skeletonema costatum, Cyclotella meneghiniana, Amphora coffeaeformis, Navicula halophila, Nitzschia closterium, Asterionella japonica, Achnanthes stomii, Pleurosignma nomanii* and *Pinnularia viridis* (Ragothaman & Rao, 1977a). In the inshore waters, sites of low salinity coincide with dense diatom population (Rao & Valsaraj, 1984). One of the dominant diatoms namely *A. coeffeaeformis* shows maximum abundance in the estuary when the salinities range between 8 and 20‰, as recorded during a two year period of investigation. Laboratory studies on several isolates of this species from the estuary confirmed that it prefers to grow in a medium of low salinity. The diatom does not grow well either in freshwater or when the salt content of the medium is high (Ragothaman & Rao, 1977b).

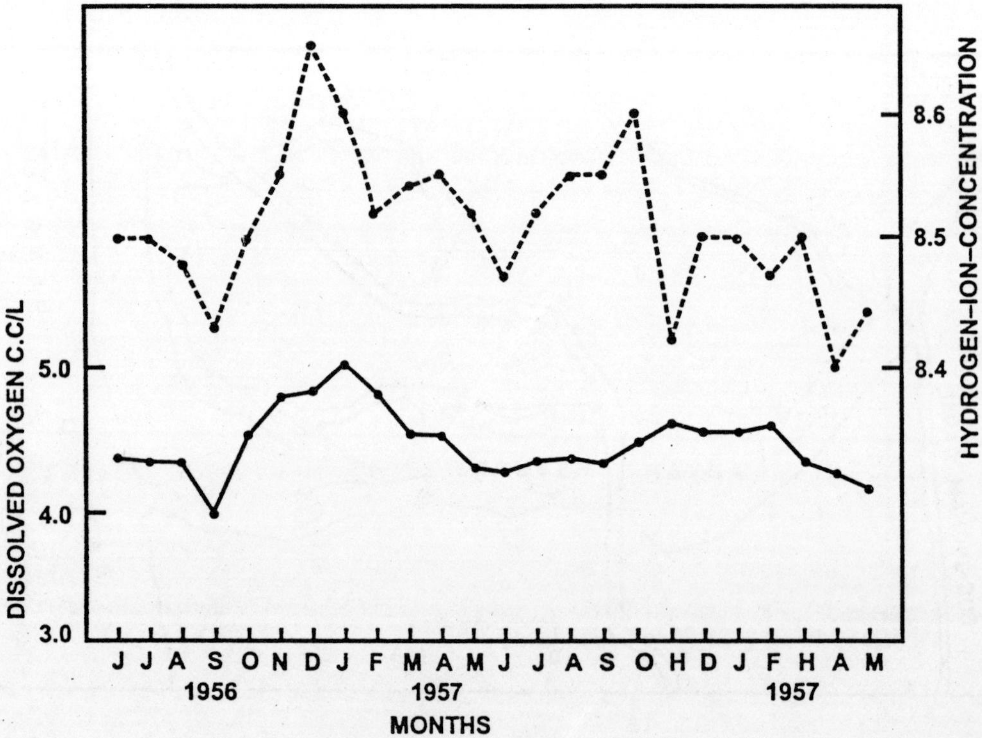

Fig. 6.2 Seasonal change in hydrogen-ion-concentration and dissolved oxygen in the inshore waters off Chennai (From Thirupad & Reddy, 1959)

From the information available on zooplankton from Adyar, Cooum and Ennore estuaries, it seems that the zooplankton population largely consists of protozoans, rotifers, copepods, cladocerans and larvae of other crustaceans. Their density is sparse in the regions dominated by freshwater but increases downstream.

According to Daniel (1987), there are authentic records available to show that in the forties, there was an abundance of fauna in the Adyar Estuary representing lamellibranchs, gastropods, polychaetes and crabs. Four decades later, because of dense human settlement along with small-scale industries around the settlement, the mudflats around the Adyar River and a stretch of about 20 kilometres of the Chennai coast have become dumping grounds of garbage, solid waste and untreated sewage, etc., for landfill,. Thus, after reclamation and filling of the low-line areas, only a few crabs, which are extremely hardy, are now surviving. Rotifers of the species *Branchionus rubens* and *B. plicatilis* are found in abundance showing their relationship with suspended matter and salinity. In the

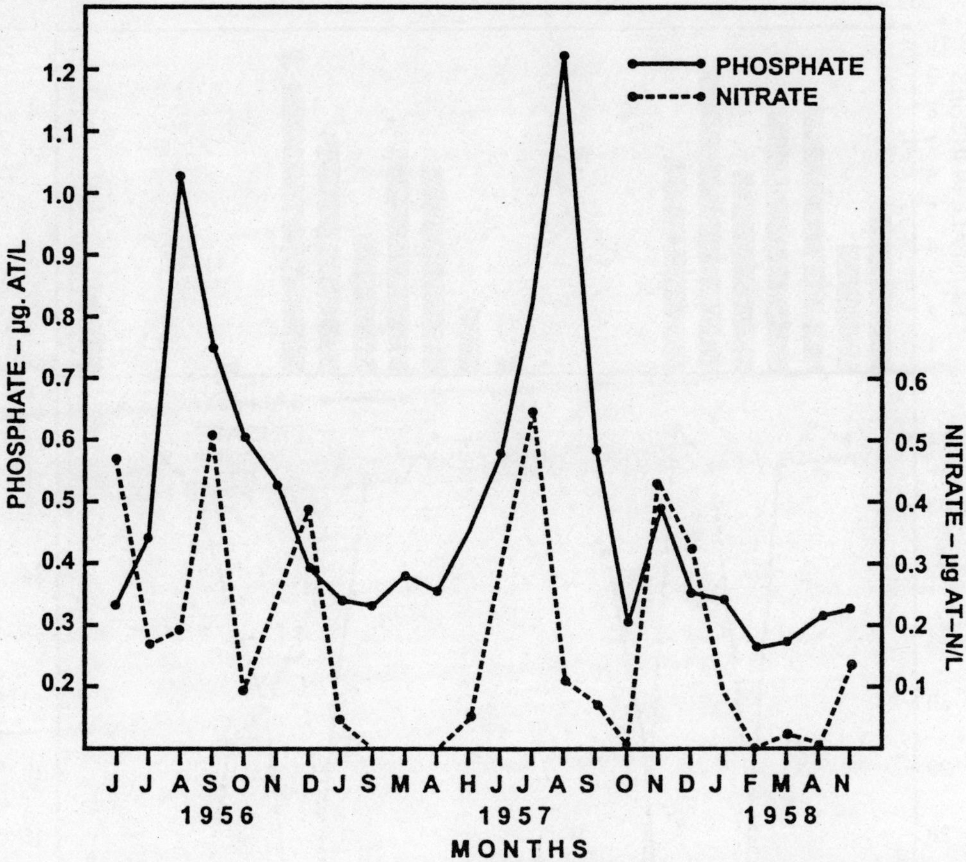

Fig. 6.3 Seasonal change in phosphate and nitrate concentration in the inshore waters off Chennai (From Thirupad & Reddy, 1959)

upper reaches of the estuary, where high suspended matter and low salinity prevail, the biomass of rotifers is high (Konnur and Azariah, 1987).

POLLUTION

Besides the untreated domestic sewage, garbage and other types of wastes, the Adyar River and its estuary carry a considerable load of heavy metals. Water, sediments and biota including fish show contamination with zinc, lead, copper, chromium, nickel and cadmium (Joseph, 1989). Table 6.1 shows the concentrations of heavy metals in water, sediment and fish collected from the Adyar Estuary. Concentrations of zinc and chromium indicate the influence of industrial effluents coming probably from petrochemical complex, Madras refine-

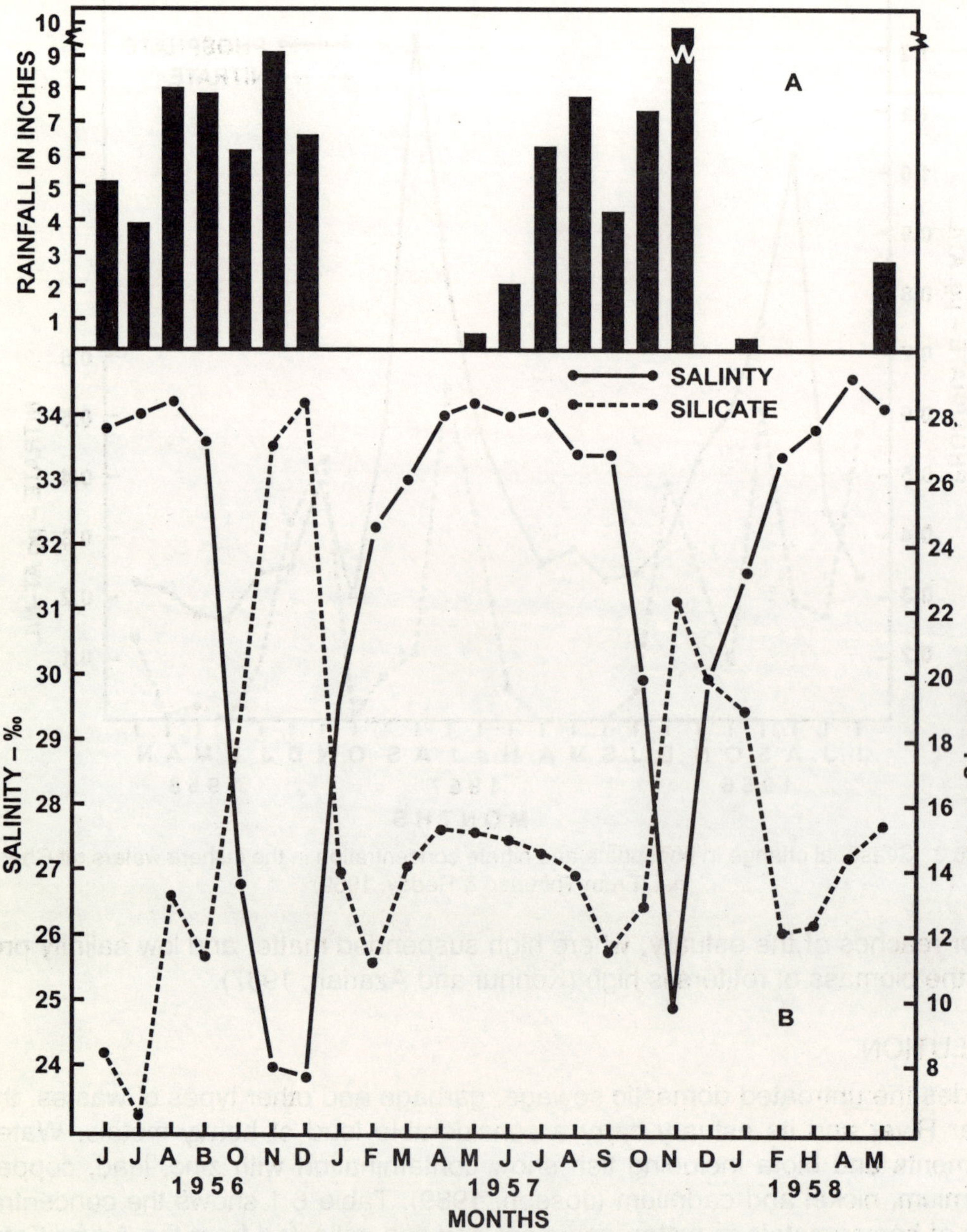

Fig. 6.4 Seasonal change in salinity and silicate in relation to rainfall from June 1956 to May 1958 in the inshore waters off Chennai (From Thirupad & Reddy, 1959)

Table 6.1— Concentrations* of heavy metals in water, sediment and fish (*Mystus gulio*) samples** collected from Adyar Estuary (From Nammalwar, 1987)

Samples	Metals	Concentration
Water (µg/ml)	Zn	0.1
	Pb	0.2
	Cu	0.16
	Cr	0.16
	Ni	0.08
	Cd	0.03
Sediment (µg/ml)	Zn	120.0
	Pb	68.0
	Cu	10.0
	Cr	1.6
	Ni	5.6
	Cd	0.5
Fish (µg/ml)	Zn	160.0
	Pb	7.6
	Cu	42.0
	Cr	2.1
	Ni	7.0
	Cd	0.1

* Average of 4 samples
** Triplicate metal determination of all samples

Table 6.2— Distribution and concentration of heavy metals in gill, liver and muscle tissues of mullet, *Liza macrolepis* from Adyar Estuary (From Nammalwar, 1985 & 1987)

Heavy metals	Gill (ppm/dry wt)	Liver (ppm/dry wt)	Muscle (ppm/dry wt)
Cd	0.74	0.78	1.55
Cu	1.63	8.19	0.6
Zn	55.21	76.68	47.15
Ni	19.89	3.61	2.45
Pb	2.83	1.51	1.25
Fe	163.72	170.18	12.75
Percentage of water content	80.31	79.78	78.94
Heavy metals	**Gill (ppm/dry wt)**	**Liver (ppm/dry wt)**	**Muscle (ppm/dry wt)**
Hg	0.1	0.09	0.12
Cd	0.74	0.78	1.55

ries and fertilizer industries. Zinc and chromium concentrations in the outfall area of Madras refineries were 2.90 and 0.72 μg/ml (Joseph, 1989). Levels of bioaccumulation of cadium, copper, zinc, nickel, lead and iron in gills, liver and muscle tissues of the grey mullet (*Liza microlepis*) are given in Table 6.2. There seems to be a difference in the levels of concentration of various metals. Iron and zinc seem to be most dominant bioaccumulants while mercury was found to be appreciably low. Gills and liver have the maximum levels as compared to muscle tissues (Nammalwar, 1985 & 1987). Sequential listing of the seven different heavy metals, when arranged according to their concentrations in three different tissues as given by Nammalwar (1987), was as follows:

Gill	:	Fe > Zn > Ni > Pb > Cu > Cd > Hg
Liver	:	Fe > Zn > Cu > Ni > Pb > Cd > Hg
Muscle tissues	:	Zn > Fe > Ni > Cd > Pb > Cu > Hg

The reported safe level concentrations of heavy metals are: mercury 0.04 - 0.10 ppm; cadmium, 0.31 - 0.70 ppm; copper 0.5-0.95 ppm; zinc 5.80 - 14.6 ppm; nickel 0.02 - 10 ppm; lead 0.2 - 9.5 ppm; and iron 2.2 - 9.2 ppm (Nammalwar,1987).

Maximum flow of water in the Adyar River occurs during the northeast monsoon (October to December). In other months, the flow is not continuous and the estuary gets cut off from the sea by the formation of a sand bar. As noted earlier, the estuary receives a heavy load of untreated city sewage through Adyar River and a canal known as Buckingham Canal which connects the Adyar with Cooum Estuary (see Cooum).

Both Adyar River and Buckingham Canal pass through the main city areas of Chennai collecting washings from the slums, cattle yards, wastes from automobile workshops, electroplating units, leather tanneries, foundries, ferrous and non-ferrous industries. It has been estimated that about 7,75,000 l/day of industrial wastes are released into the estuary.

All the investigations carried out on heavy metal pollution of Adyar and other estuaries of the Chennai region indicate pollution of the highest form and call for the introduction of immediate remedial measures. The synergistic effect of some of the metals at low *p*H, low dissolved oxygen, high temperature and variable salinities can kill practically all living organisms and the ill-effects of metal contamination can be long lasting. The industries must be asked to take preventive measures to treating their wastes properly. They must develop their own monitoring systems to bring the effluents to the prescribed levels of standard. The State Pollution Control Board of Tamil Nadu should take appropriate steps to ensure that the health of the Adyar Estuary progressively improves.

Bioassay tests in the Adyar Estuary were conducted on *Mugil cephalus* and *Liza macrolepis* in experimental floating net cages erected in the estuary. Survival and growth rate of both the species under field culture conditions were quite satisfactory. In fact no mortality occurred for four months, from January to April 1980 and their growth rate under captive conditions was better than those coming from the natural population. However, by mid July the survival rate decreased to 50% and by the end of July all fishes died when the mouth of the estuary was closed. Since the two species of mullets are detritus feeder, the estuarine effect containing domestic sewage produced short-term beneficial effect on the young fishes (fingerlings), but the long-term effect of collective pollutants proved to be disastrous. This experiment, however, proves that if the quality of water in the estuary is reasonably improved by controlling pollution, the estuary can serve a useful purpose for developing cage culture of several omnivorous species of fish (Nammalwar, 1992).

References

1. Daniel, A., 1987. Estuarine animals and their adaptations. *Journal of Marine Biological Association of India*, Vol. 29, pp. 351-353.
2. Joseph, K.O., 1989. Heavy metal contamination of fish of the estuarine environment in Madras region. *Proceedings of National Academy of Sciences of India*, Vol. 59 (B), pp. 46-50.
3. Konnur, R. & Azariah, J., 1987. Distribution of rotifer biomass in the estuarine region of river Adyar with reference to suspended particulate matter. *Journal of Marine Biological Association of India*, Vol. 29, pp. 286-290.
4. Nammalwar, P., 1985. Heavy metal pollution in Adyar Estuary, Madras, India. *Proceedings of the Assessment of Environmental Pollutions.* The Academy of Environmental Biology, India. pp. 235-238.
5. Nammalwar, P., 1987. Pollution impact and management of the coastal estuaries around Madras, India. *In: Proceedings of National Seminar on Estuarine Management* (ed.) N.B. Nair, State committee on Science, Technology and Environment, Government of Kerala, Trivandrum, pp. 190-193.
6. Nammalwar, P., 1992. Field bioassay in Cooum and Adyar estuaries for environmental management. *In: Tropical Ecosystem: Ecology and Management* (eds.) K.P. Singh and J.S. Singh, pp. 359-370, Wiley Eastern Ltd., New Delhi.
7. Ragothaman, G. & Rao, V.N.R., 1977 a. Studies on the diatom *Amphora coffeaeformis.* Agardh: Salinity changes on growth and auxopore formation. *Indian Journal of Marine Sciences*, Vol. 6, pp. 62-65.

8. Ragothaman, G. & Rao, V.N.R., 1977 b. Diatom abundance in the near shores of the Bay of Bengal, off Madras. *Indian Journal of Marine Sciences*, Vol. 6, pp. 65-66.
9. Rao, V.N.R. & Valsaraj, C.P., 1974. Hydrobiological studies in the inshore waters of the Bay of Bengal. *Journal of Marine Biological Association of India*, Vol. 26, pp. 58-65.
10. Subramanyan, R., 1959. Studies on the phytoplankton of the west coast of India: Parts I & II. *Proceedings of the Indian Academy of Sciences*, Vol. 50, pp. 113-252.
11. Thirupad, P.U.V. & Reddy, C.V.G., 1959. Seasonal variations of the hydrological factors of the Madras coastal waters. *Indian Journal of Fisheries*, Vol. 6, pp. 298-305.

Chapter 7

Vellar

The Vellar Estuary is situated along Lat. 11°29′N and Long. 79°49′E, near Parangipettai (Fig. 7.1 a & c), a small town (formerly known as Porto Novo) on the southeast coast of India, about 75 km from Pondichery. A well known Marine Biological Station of the Annamalai University, presently named as the Centre of Advanced Study in Marine Biology, is located at Parangipettai, about 1.5 km from the estuary (Fig. 7.1 b). This Centre has carried out extensive studies on the hydrography and biology of this estuary for more than four decades and as a result of these investigations, the Vellar Estuary is one of the best-studied estuaries of the east coast of India. It has a permanent connection with the Bay of Bengal and near its mouth it gets connected with a complex system of backwaters extending southwards to the Coleroon Estuary, about 15 km away. The river Coleroon is a tributary of the river Cauvery. It ends up in creeks, mudflats and canals merging with the Pichavaram mangroves, which occupy an area of about 800 hectares (Fig. 7.1 a).

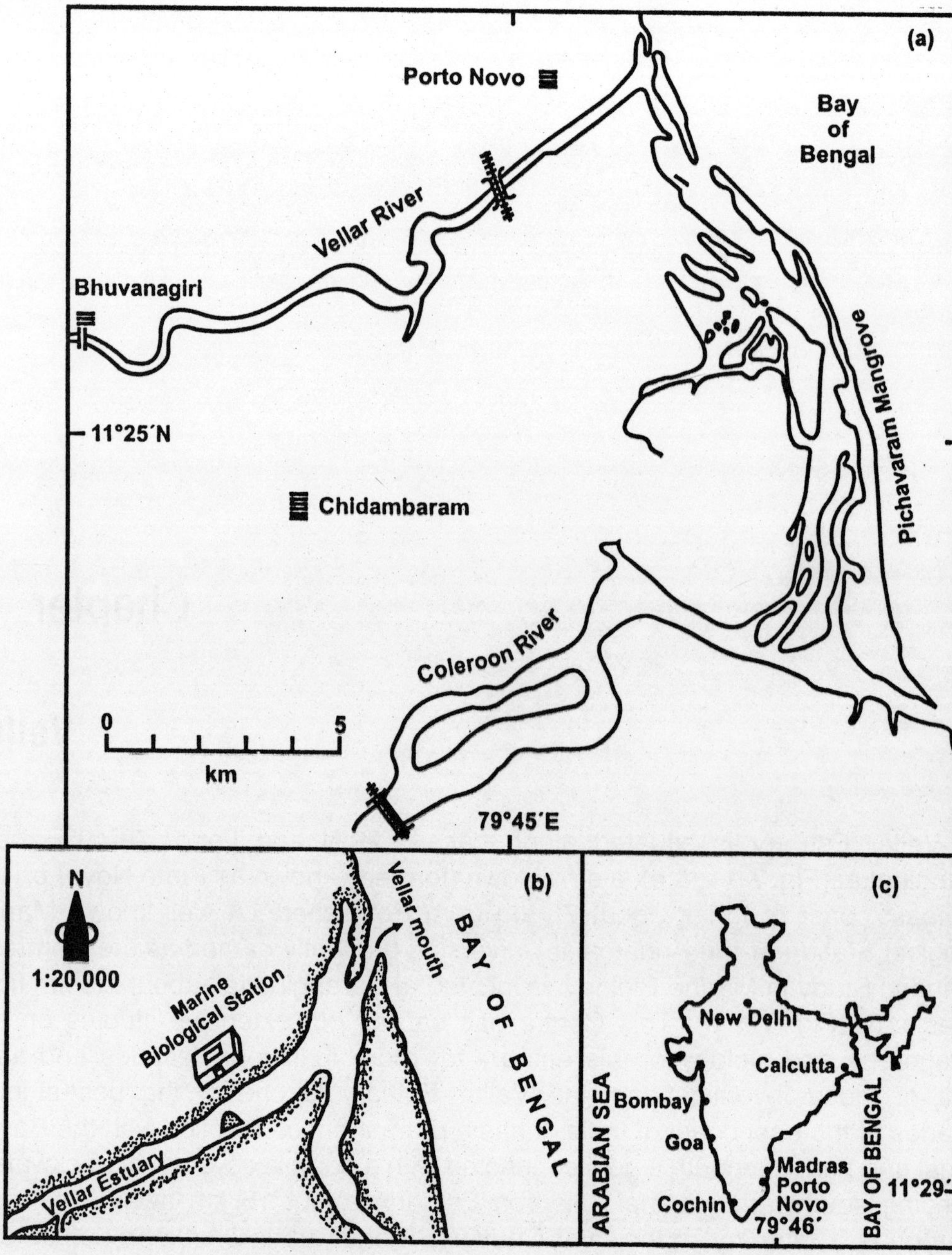

Fig. 7.1 Map of Vellar-Coleroon Estuarine System and its connection with Pichavaram mangrove (a); Vellar Estuary with its opening in the Bay of Bengal and the location of the Marine Biological Station (b); location of Porto Novo (renamed Parangipettai) (c).

HYDROGRAPHICAL FEATURES

Physical

Vellar is a shallow estuary with an average depth of 2.5 m and a maximum depth of 5.2 m during the high tide. The river Vellar originates in the hills of Salem District (Tamil Nadu), and after travelling a distance of 480 km, it forms an estuary before opening into the Bay of Bengal. The tidal range in the estuary is about 1 m and its influence extends up to a distance of 16 km upstream. The tides in the estuary are semidiurnal, with two high and two low water every 24 h. On the basis of salinity gradient in the estuary in relation to flow and ebb tides, the estuary has been divided into 4 zones.

(a) Marine zone extending upstream from the mouth up to 1.6 km with an average salinity of 33.72‰ and no difference between bottom and surface waters (homogeneous),

(b) A tidal zone with higher salinity at the bottom and lower salinity at the surface, and the difference between the two progressively increasing upstream,

(c) A gradient zone with the difference in the salinities at the bottom (salt-wedge) and surface progressively decreasing and merging into, and

(d) Freshwater zone (homogeneous)

These findings have been reported by Rangarajan (1958) and Seshaiya (1959). Further studies on the distribution of salinity, temperature and currents were made by conducting three surveys in the months of January and February 1967 at 17 stations in a part of the estuary up to a distance of 5 km from the mouth (Dyer & Ramamoorthy, 1969). The distribution of salinity during the flood and ebb tides showed that at the flood, there was an intrusion of saline-wedge formed within 0.5 m depth where the salinity was 20‰ from the surface. This layer was occupied by freshwater coming from the river. The wedge acted as a barrier and impounded the river water from mixing. At high tide, the water was moderately stratified at the mouth but the bottom salinity was increasing. Only a short distance from the mouth, freshwater was present at the surface but the depth of penetration of the salt-wedge increased as the river discharge decreased. At about high water, the impounded water was released which quickly established a homogeneous surface layer with horizontal halocline throughout the estuary. The halocline was rapidly pushed downwards until it reached the sill between the basins. The saline waters were isolated within the basin and the freshwater flowed over the sills.

At the beginning of the ebb, the surface flow of the river water decreased and the saline water began to move landward at the bottom of the mouth causing an

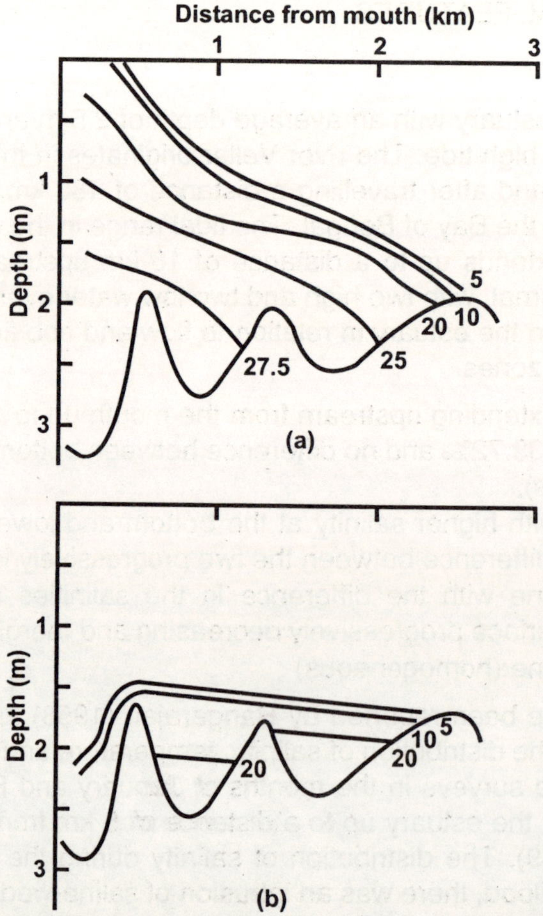

Fig. 7.2 Longitudinal distribution of salinity on 20 Jan. 1967 in Vellar. High water (a); Low water (b) contours in ‰ (From Dyer & Ramamoorthy, 1969).

abrupt increase in salinity at the bottom. The sequence of events described above is shown in Figs. 7.2, 7.3 and 7.4 (Dyer & Ramamoorthy, 1969). Thus the Vellar Estuary is a typically bar-built estuary and the mixing process in the estuary showed a period of drought from May to July when the estuary becomes seawater-dominated, and during the period of northeast monsoon from October to November when it becomes freshwater-dominated. Transitions occurred between these two extreme periods (Ramamoorthi, 1971).

In the Vellar Estuary, the river runoff during the year varies from season to season. During the dry season (May to July), the influx from the river and other

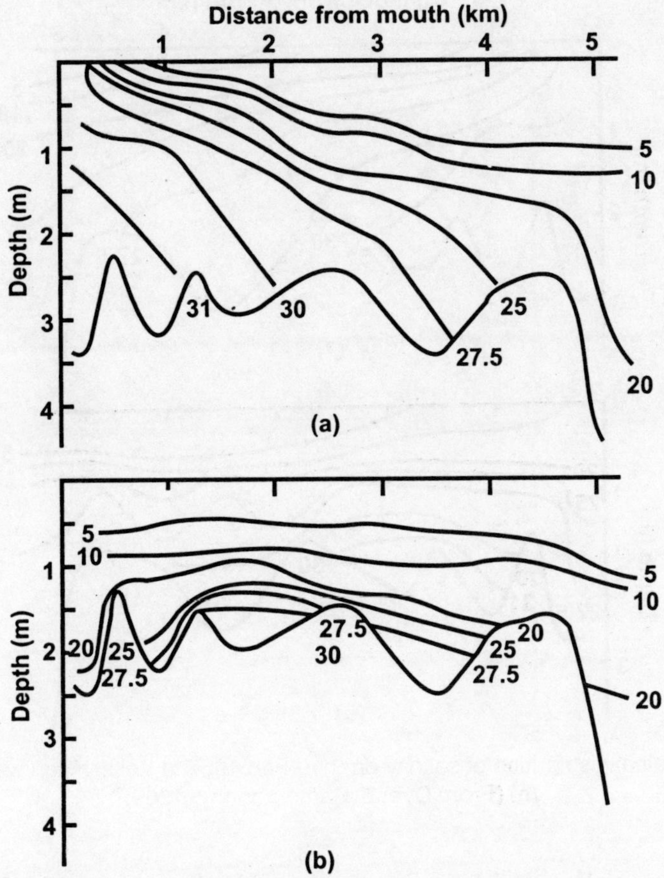

Fig. 7.3 Longitudinal distribution of salinity on 27-28 Jan. 1967 in Vellar. High water (a); Low water (b) (From Dyer & Ramamoorthy, 1969).

feeding channels gets limited and almost the entire estuary is occupied by salt water and salinity at the mouth rises to above 30‰. Mixing is nearly complete except at the head (5 km from the mouth) where a distinct halocline exists. Here, the difference between the surface and bottom salinity is 20‰. During August, some rainfall changes the distribution of salinity and at the head a difference of 20‰ is seen. With the onset of northeast monsoon (September, large scale runoff occurs which persists throughout October. The salinity of the water in the estuary at almost all depths in the upper reaches comes down to 1.0‰. In late November, when the river discharge decreases and neritic penetration gains prominence, a

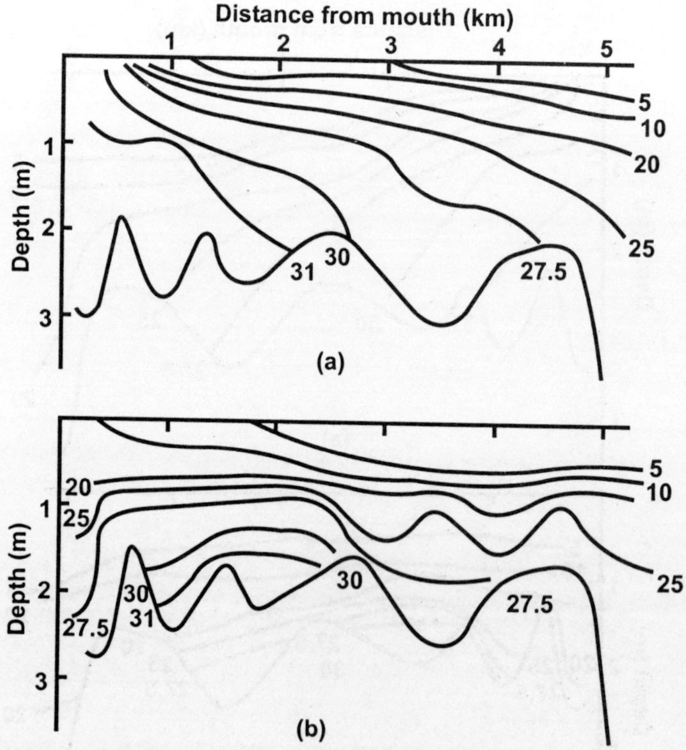

Fig. 7.4 Longitudinal distribution of salinity on 9-10 Feb 1967 in Vellar. High water (a); Low water (b) (From Dyer & Ramamoorthy, 1969).

vertical gradient gets established once again (Ramamoorthi & Venugopalan, 1976). In another survey on environmental features conducted in a section of the Vellar-Coleroon Estuarine System by Krishnamurthy & Sundararaj (1973) in November 1970, the following ranges in values were recorded: temperature 29.50 to 30.50°C, salinity 10.40 to 30.50‰, pH 7.50 to 8.30, dissolved oxygen 3.69 to 5.44 ml/l.

Vellar estuary provides a turbid environment because a lot of suspended inert material constantly flows from the river into the estuary. Observations on light penetration were made using a luxmeter and Secchi Disk from January to April when the turbidity was not so high because of decreased inflow from the river. More than 35% of the solar radiation falling on the surface gets absorbed within 1 m depth. Blue and yellow regions of the spectrum, as measured using cut-off filters, have been reported to reach 4m depth (Bhatnagar & Purushothaman, 1974).

Diurnal variation in temperature of water at the surface closely followed the tidal rhythm with low values occurring during the flood and high values during the ebb. Salinity was maximum during the two phases of the high tide and minimum at the ebb. Dissolved oxygen, on the other hand, showed an inverse relationship with salinity and in turn with the tidal flow. Nutrients (PO_4-P, NO_3-N, NO_2-N, and SiO_4-Si) showed high values with the low tide and low values with the high tide. Silicate values at the surface were significantly higher than at the bottom. Phytoplankton in terms of numbers were high at the second tidal flow while zooplankton abundance followed the tidal rhythm, being high at the high water and low during the ebb. The distribution of plant pigment was closely related to phytoplankton abundance during the tidal rhythm (Vijayalakshmi & Venugopalan, 1973).

In another study, daily variations in particulate organic carbon (POC), nitrogen (PON), phosphorus (POP), carbohydrate (PCHO) and clorophyll were studied in relation to 24 h tidal cycle and it was concluded that flood and ebb tides have no direct influence on these constituents. Increase in the POC, PCHO and clorophyll during the day time was probably due to zooplankton grazing (Subramanian & Venugopalan, 1980). In another study, fractions of dissolved, particulate and mud phosphorus were studied at different stations of the Vellar Estuary in 1970-71. High values of organic phosphorus were recorded when the estuary becomes salt-water-dominated during the dry months (premonsoon). Blooms of phytoplankton occur during the postmonsoon months . Low concentrations of total and reactive phosphorus are recorded during this period. Due to shallowness of the estuary, stirring up of the bottom sediments takes place and this helps in the release and transport of phosphorus from the bottom to the overlying water. Important sources of particulate organic phosphorus seem to be the unconsumed phytoplankton and river-borne detritus (Rajendran & Venugopalan, 1973). In the Vellar Estuary, long lines of slicks and patches of foam are commonly seen. The foam often persists for a few minutes to few hours. Microscopic examination of the foam revelaed diatoms, blue-green algae, *Trichodesmium* and detrital material. Chemical analysis of the foam showed high values of nitrate, phosphate, silicate, iron, copper and manganese. Slicks contained large amounts of organic matter. However, their chemical compositions varied considerably at different sites of the collection (Pandian & Venugopalan, 1975).

Seasonal changes in temperature, salinity, dissolved oxygen, *p*H and light extinction coefficient (*k*) were studied for a period of full two years during 1977 and 1978 by Chandran & Ramamoorthi (1984a). These are shown in Figs. 7.5, 7.6, and 7.7 in relation to high and low tide marks. The site of the collection was in front of the Marine Biological Station, about 1.6 km upstream from the mouth of the estuary

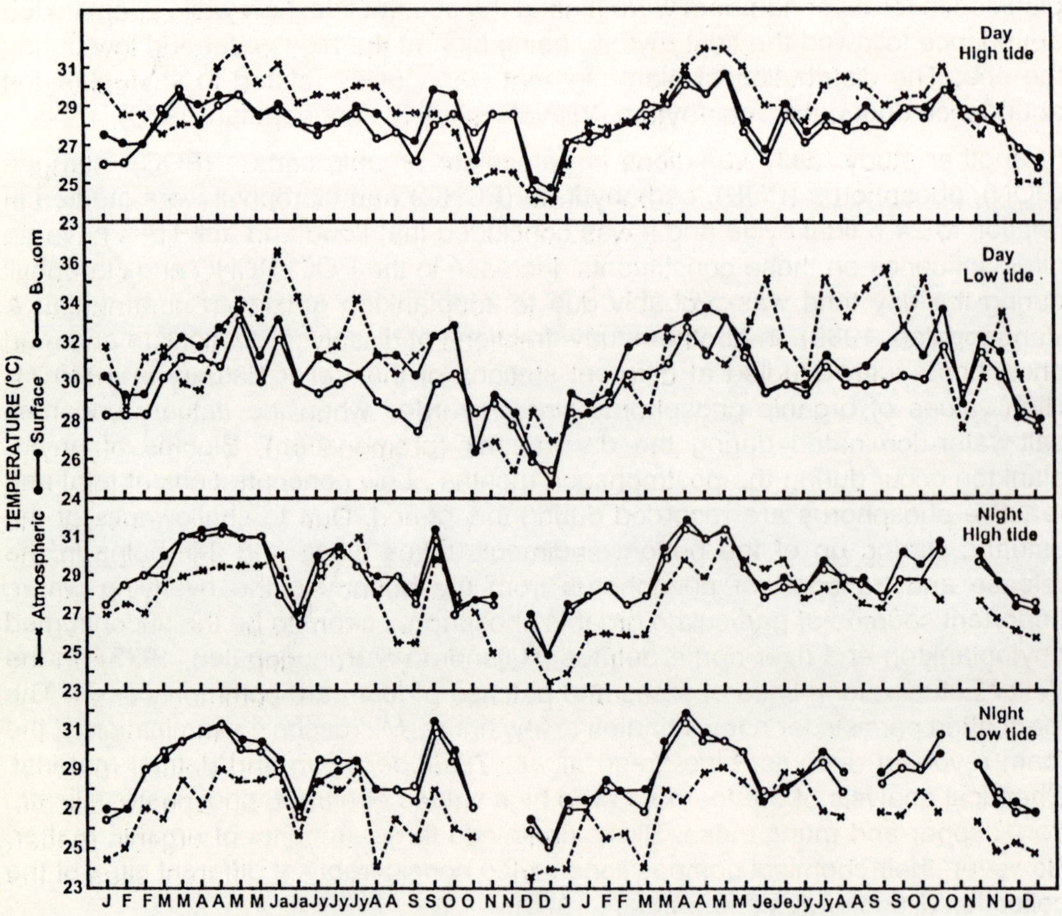

Fig. 7.5 Seasonal changes in atmospheric and water temperatures (surface and bottom) at fortnightly intervals for two years in relation to tidal cycle in Vellar Estuary (From Chandran & Ramamoorthi, 1984a).

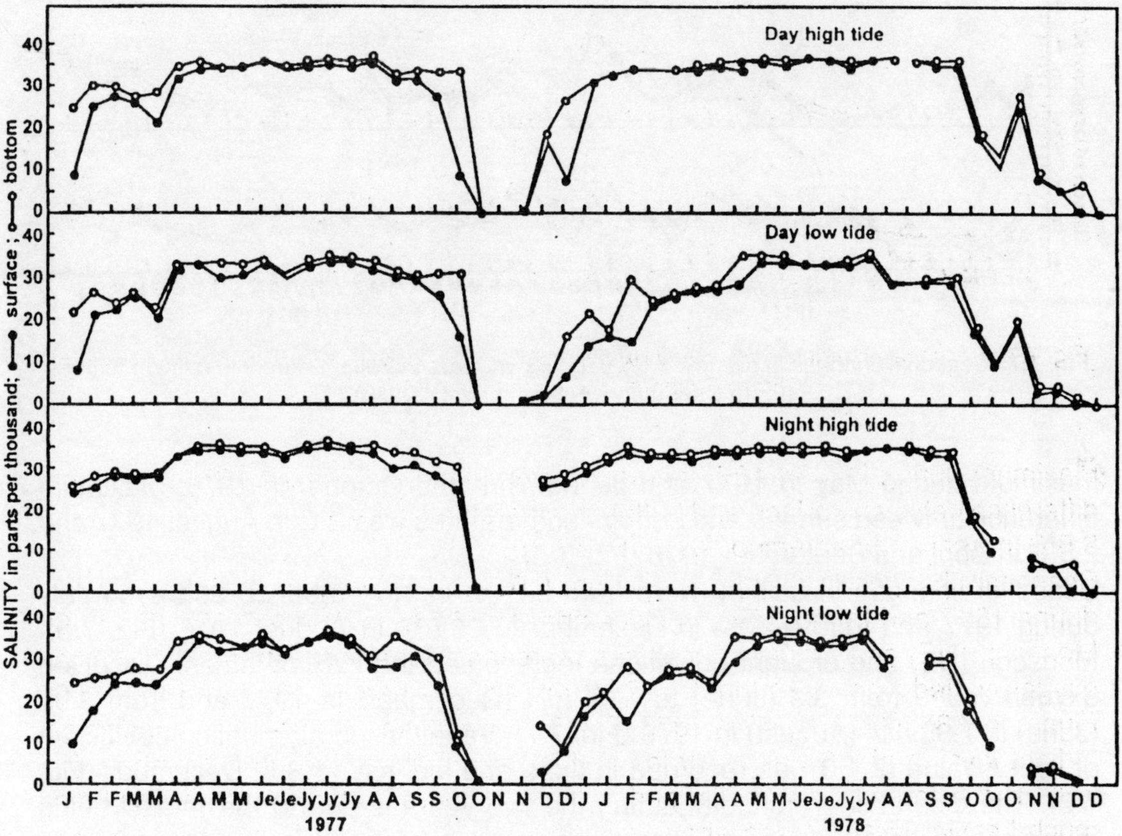

Fig. 7.6 Seasonal changes in surface and bottom salinity for two years in relation to tides in Vellar Estuary (From Chandran & Ramamoorthi, 1984a).

where the average water depth was 2.25 m and collections were made on every full and new moon days during both high and low tides. Maximum rainfall at Parangipettai occurs during NE monsoon (October-December). In 1977, the rainfall was much heavier than in 1978 because of a cyclonic storm which occurred in November – the average rainfall in November 1977 was 160.1 mm and in 1978 during the same month it was 129.9 mm.

Atmospheric temperature ranged between 23.5 to 36.5˚C whereas water temperature varied between 24 and 33.5˚C in 1977 and between 26.5 and 33.5˚C in 1978. Minimum values were recorded in December during both the years and

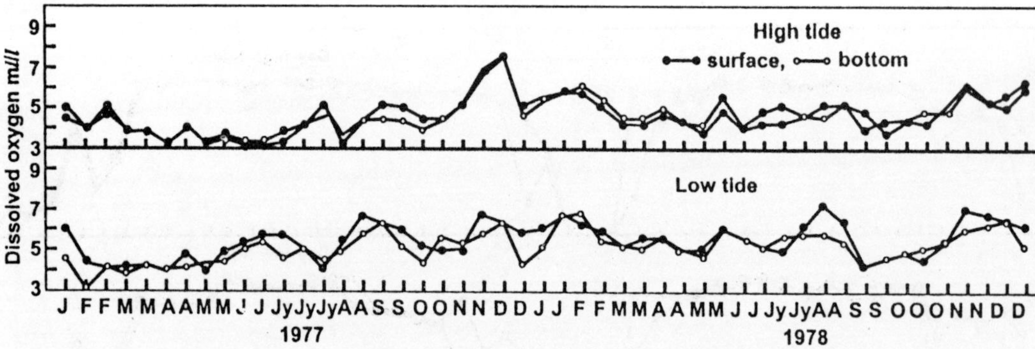

Fig. 7.7 Seasonal changes in dissolved oxygen for two years in Vellar Estuary in relation to tides (From Chandran & Ramamoorthi, 1984a).

maximum during May in 1977 and during April and October in 1978. Maximum difference between surface and bottom temperatures was 3°C in August 1977 and 2.5°C in April and September 1978 (Fig. 7.5).

Seasonal changes in salinity were from 0.01‰ in November to 36.3‰ in July during 1977 and from 0.27‰ in December to 36.5‰ in August 1978 (Fig. 7.6). Monsoon (NE) and drought conditions represented the two extremes. Dissolved oxygen varied from 3.9 (June) to 7.62 ml/l (December) in 1977 and from 3.95 (June) to 7.35 ml/l (August) in 1978 (Fig. 7.7). Variations in attenuation coefficient of light *k* value of 1.3 was recorded in June and highest 11.3 in December (Fig. 7.8). The difference in turbidity during the two years is due to the rainfall being much heavier in 1977 (see above). Changes in *p*H ranged from 7.75 to 8.25 in 1977 and from 7.70 to 8.35 in 1978 (Fig. 7.9). There was no marked tidal or seasonal variation in *p*H except that during the months of rainfall the values were generally low.

Chemical

Nutrients

Seasonal variations in the concentrations of nutrients (PO_4-P, NO_2-N, NO_3-N, SiO_3-S) for the years 1977 and 1978 are shown in Figs. 7.10, 7.11, 7.12 and 7.13 in relation to high and low tidal marks (2 values for each month) for both surface and bottom waters. High values were regularly recorded during the premonsoon months (Jan to June). A sudden pulse of high PO_4-P during the early part of April 1977 may be because of the instantaneous entry of phosphorus-rich water into

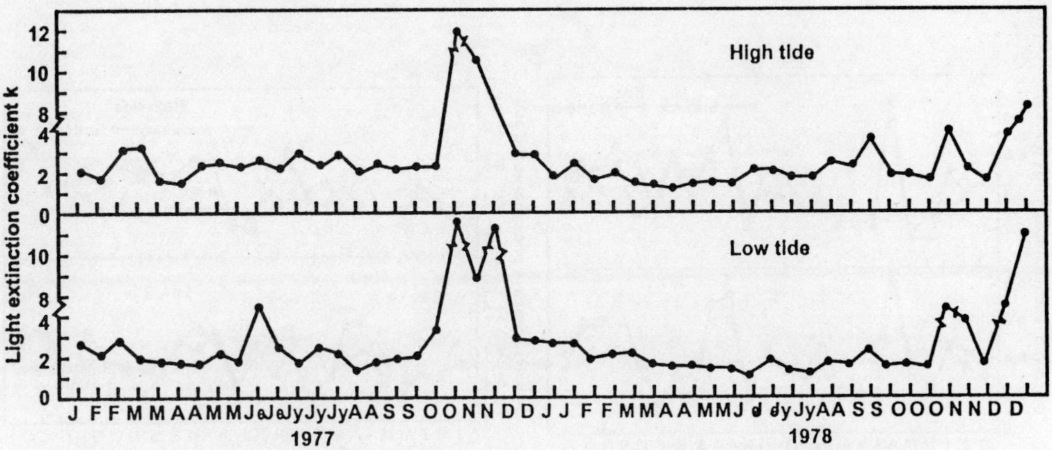

Fig. 7.8 Seasonal changes in light extinction coefficient (*k*) for two years in relation to tides in Vellar (From Chandran & Ramamoorthi, 1984a).

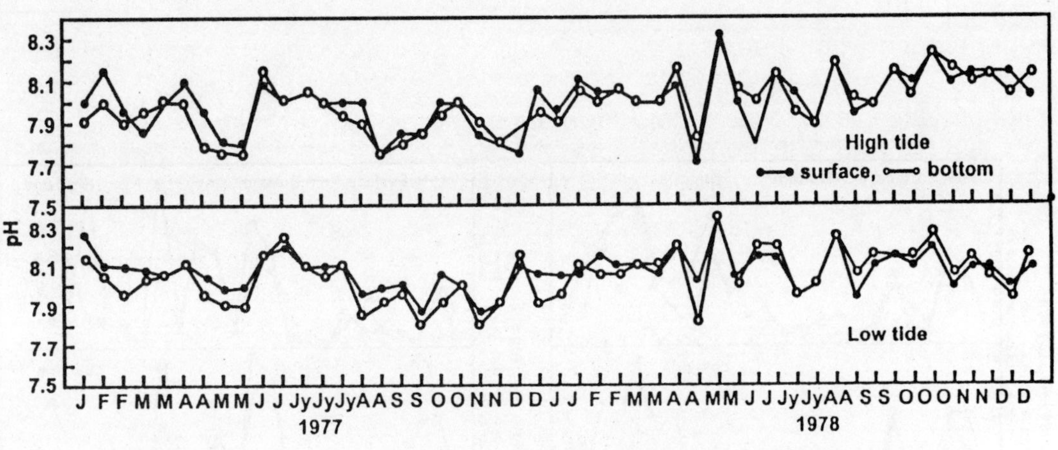

Fig. 7.9 Seasonal changes in *p*H for two years in Vellar in relation to tides (From Chandran & Ramamoorthi, 1984a).

the estuary through land runoff. This was not repeated during the following year. The tidal influence on the phosphorus was not well-marked except for some increase at low water. The trend in fluctuation between surface and bottom was

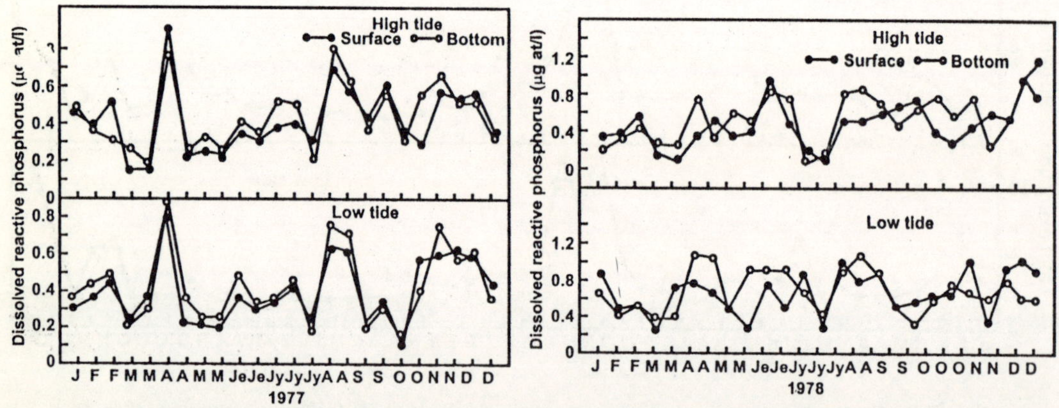

Fig. 7.10 Seasonal changes in dissolved reactive phosphorus in Vellar Estuary in relation to tides during the years 1977 and 1978. Measurements were made at fortnightly intervals (From Chandran & Ramamoorthi, 1984b).

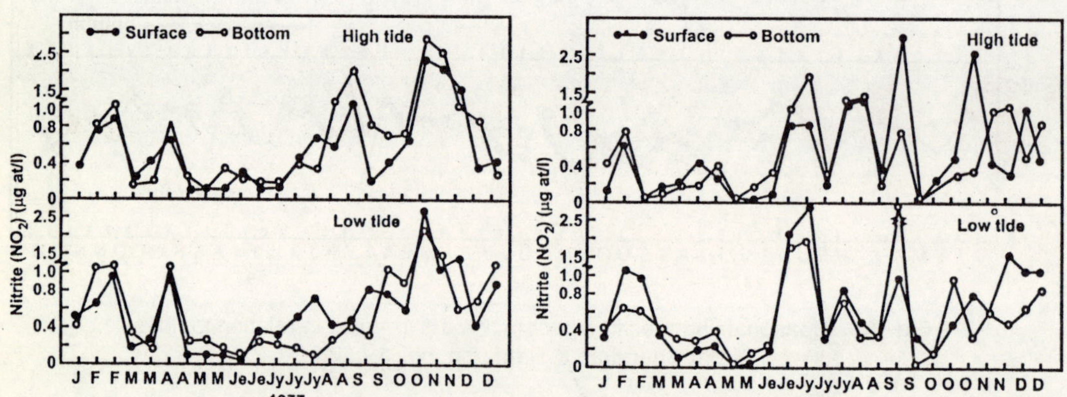

Fig. 7.11 Seasonal changes in nitrite concentration in Vellar Estuary in relation to tides during the years 1977 and 1978 (From Chandran & Ramamoorthi, 1984b).

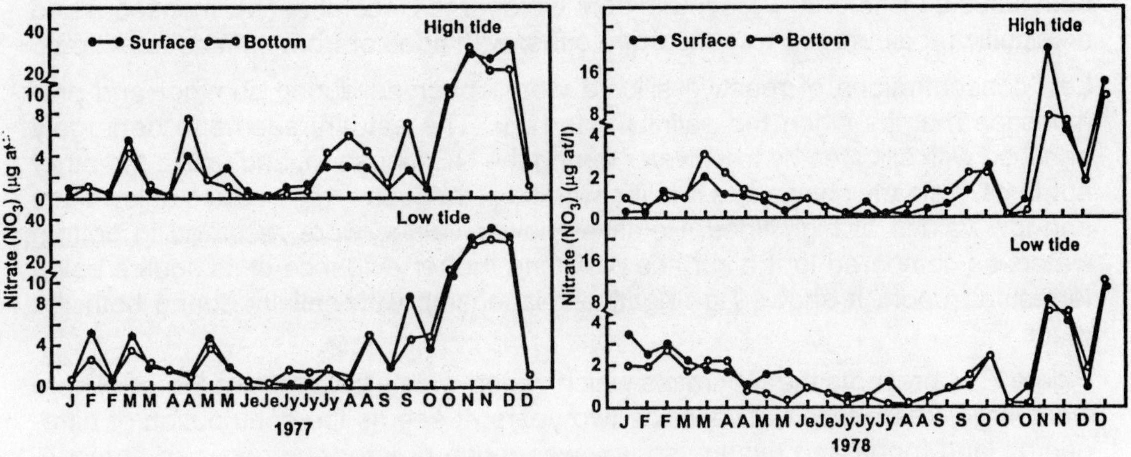

Fig. 7.12 Seasonal changes in nitrate concentration in Vellar Estuary in relation to tides during the years 1977 and 1978 (From Chandran & Ramamoorthi, 1984b).

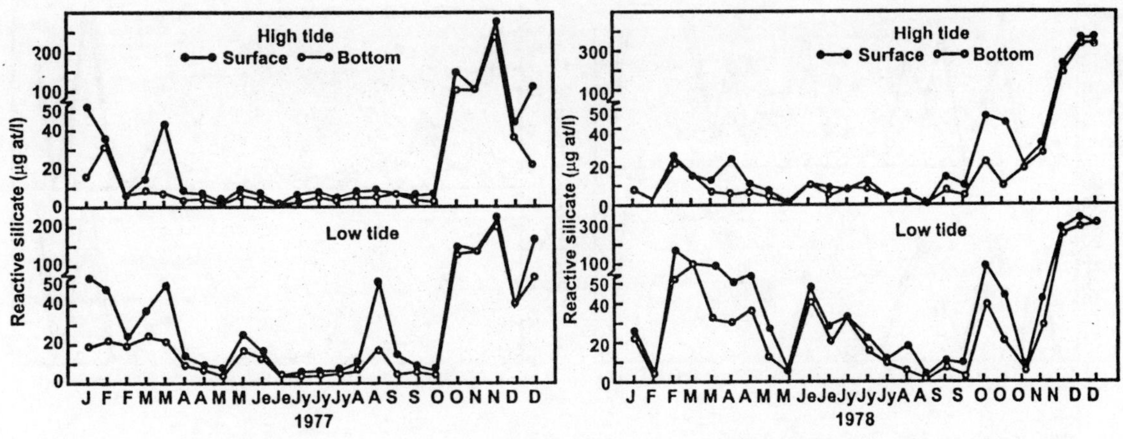

Fig. 7.13 Seasonal changes in silicate concentration in Vellar Estuary in relation to tides during the years 1977 and 1978 (From Chandran & Ramamoorthi, 1984b).

also not pronounced. A comparison with seasonal changes in salinity indicated an inverse relationship with reactive phosphorus.

The source of nitrogenous nutrients largely seems to be freshwater and terrestrial runoff. Nitrite-nitrogen was much lower than nitrate-nitrogen and higher values of both these constituents were found from October to December (NE monsoon) and no significant difference was recorded either with tides or from surface to bottom.

Low concentrations of reactive silicate were observed during summer and pre-monsoon months when the salinity was high. The estuary seems to be largely enriched with silicates by freshwater during the NE monsoon, and unlike the other nutrients, it clearly showed its relation with tidal variation – high values at low tides and low values at high tides. Relatively lower values were recorded in bottom waters as compared to the surface providing further evidence of its source being terrestrial runoff. It showed a negative relationship with salinity during both the years.

Figure 7.14 presents the N:P ratios which varied widely from 15:1 to 59.5:1. There were large differences between the two years. It seems the contribution of nitrogen by land runoff and riverine source was much greater and occurred at incon-

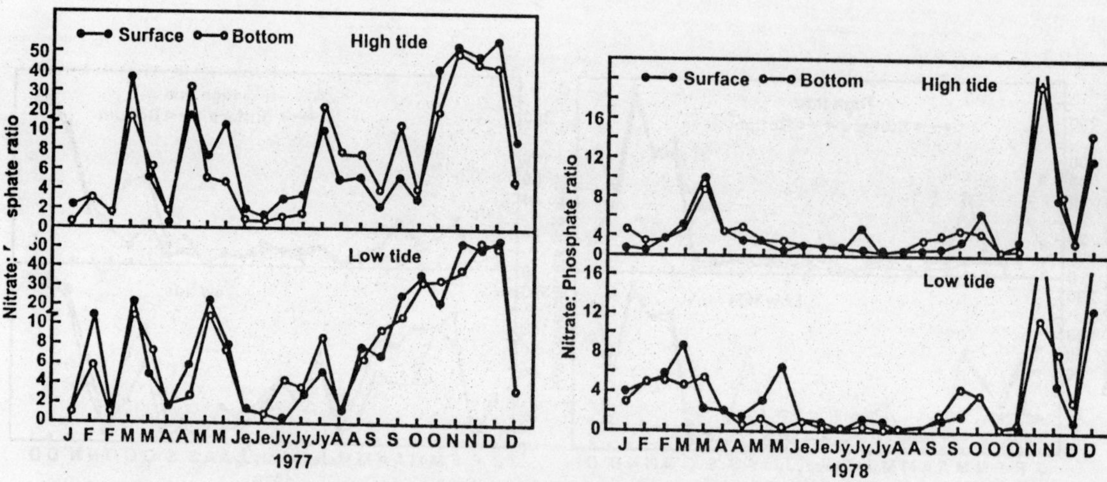

Fig. 7.14 Seasonal changes in the ratios between nitrogen and phosphorus in Vellar Estuary in relation to tides during the years 1977 and 1978 (From Chandran & Ramamoorthi, 1984b).

sistent rates than phosphorus. During the postmonsoon period, the ratios were high and attained low values during summer and early premonsoon. Probably low rate of inflow by the river water and a greater utilization of nitrogen by the phytoplankton may give rise to low ratios (Chandran & Ramammoorthi, 1984b). In an earlier study, considerable temporal and spatial variations in the N:P ratio were recorded in the estuary. The ratios were high in the marine zone and low upstream. Similarly, a lot of variation in the ratios occurred during the premonsoon, monsoon and postmonsoon seasons (Venugopalan *et al.,* 1981).

During February 1968, a study was undertaken on the relationship between the concentration of dissolved silicon and chlorosity in the Vellar Estuary. In the samples of water collected from the Vellar River, the concentration of dissolved silicon was higher by about two orders of magnitude than in the samples of seawater at the mouth of the estuary. Dilution with freshwater was a dominant influence on the distribution of dissolved silicon in the estuary. In a simple mixing of these two components, there was an inverse linear relationship but in the samples of intermediate chlorosity, there was considerable divergence from this relationship indicating that freshwater of lower dissolved silicon concentration enters the estuary through irrigation canals and this disturbs the inverse relationship (Burton, 1970). In another study, highest values of dissolved silicon were obtained in the upstream regions because the dissolved content of silicon was very high in the river water. A linear inverse relationship was observed between silicon and salinity. However, the observed deviation from linearity is attributed to the removal of silicon by biological processes. In the upper reaches, the removal was about 12% but in the lower reaches it is greater because of mixing of the river water with seawater (Purushothaman & Venugopalan, 1972).

In the Vellar-Coleroon estuarine complex, the range in nutrient values was as follows:

Total phosphorus 0.72 to 3.34 μg-at/l; inorganic phosphate 0.19 to 1.59 μg-at/l; ammonia 0.34 to 0.36 μg-at/l; nitrite 0.11 to 10.25 μg-at/l; nitrate 2.85 to 6.94 μg-at/l; silicate 18.49 to 134.92 μg-at/l (Krishnamurthy & Sundararaj, 1973).

Investigations were carried out from August 1970 to July 1972 on ammonia, nitrite, nitrate, dissolved organic nitrogen (DON) and particulate organic nitrogen (PON) at 4 stations in the Vellar Estuary. The cycles of nutrient consumption and regeneration were not clearly defined as the turn over in the estuary was high. However, the appearance of ammonia, nitrite and nitrate in sequence was observed at the surface at all the 4 stations (Venugopalan & Rajendran, 1975).

Maximum concentration of ammonia was first found in April after the phytoplankton bloom. Subsequently, nitrite and nitrate maxima were observed. During May to August, ammonia was reduced to a low level and it seems that it formed the main nitrogen source. This was followed by the depletion of nitrate from February to May. The increase in the levels of ammonia and dissolved organic nitrogen (DON) during the northeast monsoon (September and October) suggests that rainfall and terrestrial runoff are the major sources of their addition. The constant influx of seawater by the tides and the monsoonal floods seem to be the major abiogenic factors controlling the distribution of inorganic and organic nitrogenous fractions in the Vellar Estuary. A rise from October till December occurs when the estuary remains freshwater-dominated but in dry summer months neritic waters coming from the sea probably form the other source of nitrogeneous fractions. Particulate matter in the estuary is largely composed of detritus as shown by the relationship between organic carbon, chlorophyll and particulate phosphorus (Venugopalan, 1971).

Biological

Phytoplankton

Phytoplankton population and their density were studied in the estuary for three years from January 1966 to December 1968 (Joseph, 1975). During this period, 47 species of diatoms belonging to 36 genera were recorded at the mouth of the estuary. Table 7.1 gives a list of diatoms identified during a period of 36 months. Of these, several species belonging to the 3 genera *Chaetoceros, Rhizosolenia* and *Coscinodiscus* occurred almost throughout the year. Their seasonal abundance is shown in Figs. 7.15, 7.16 and 7.17. Four species of *Chaetocoros* were found in greater abundance than the rest. They were absent only in November 1966 and October 1967. Two species of *Rhizosolenia* were dominant during the three years except in few months whereas 3 species of *Coscinodiscus* were recorded practically throughout 1967 except in the month of October, when only 2 species of this genus were present during 1966 and 1968 (Fig. 7.17). In another study carried out during 1977-78, among the 155 species recorded, 102 were diatoms, 35 dinoflagellates and the rest were miscellaneous forms. Their density was found to be greater during the day than at night (Chandran, 1985).

Dinoflagellates were represented by *Noctiluca miliaris, Ceratium tripos* and *Peridinium depressum.* Apart from these three, several other species of dinoflagellates occurred sporadically. The only blue-green alga appearing in the surface samples in March was *Trichodesimium erythraeum* in all the three years.

Table 7.1— List of diatoms collected during 1966-1968 from Vellar Estuary (From Joseph, 1975)

Centric Diatoms	Pennate Diatoms
Chaetoceros affinis	*Fragilaria oceanica*
C.didymum	*Thalassionthrix longissima*
C.lauderi	*T. frauenfeldii*
C.lascinosum	*Asterionella japonica*
Rhizosolenia alata	*Gyrosigma balticum*
R. robusta	*Pleurosigma elongatum*
Coscinodiscus excentricus	*Navicula longa*
C. consinnus	*N. clavata*
C. marginatus	*Diploneis smithii*
Melosira sulcata	*Pinnularia alpina*
M. granulata	*Amphora lineolata*
Skeletonema costatum	*Cymbella marina*
Thalassiosira cormandeliana	*Bacillaria paradoxa*
Cyclotella striata	*Nitzschia closterium*
Corethron hystrix	*N. seriata*
Guinardia flaccida	*Surirella eximia*
Bacteriastrum varians	*Campylodiscus iyengarii*
B. hyalinum	
Eucampia zodiacus	
Bellerochea malleus	
Ditylum brightwellii	
Triceratium reticulum	
Biddulphia sinensis	
Hemidiscus hardmannianus	
Hemiaulus sinensis	

Seasonal variation in total phytoplankton for the 3 years is shown in Fig. 7.18. Two peaks of maximum density were seen every year. In 1966, the primary peak was during March (44120 cells/10 ml) and the secondary peak in August (38800 cells/10 ml). Lowest density (1530 cells/10 ml) was seen during November (NE monsoon). With little modifications, similar cycles were repeated during the next two years. The double mode of phytoplankton distribution seems a characteristic feature of Indian estuaries. During March 1966, *Trichodesmium erytheraeum* contributed as a major component (32400 cells/10 ml) to the peak. Maximum plant pigments (chlorophyll a, b, c and carotenoids) showed peak values during the morning and late evening hours (Krishnamurthy & Purushothaman, 1971).

Diurnal variation in net and nannoplankton production in November 1975 showed that a larger portion of primary production during the day was largely contributed by nannoplankton as compared to net (larger) phytoplankton organisms both at the surface and bottom (Subramanian & Venugopalan, 1978).

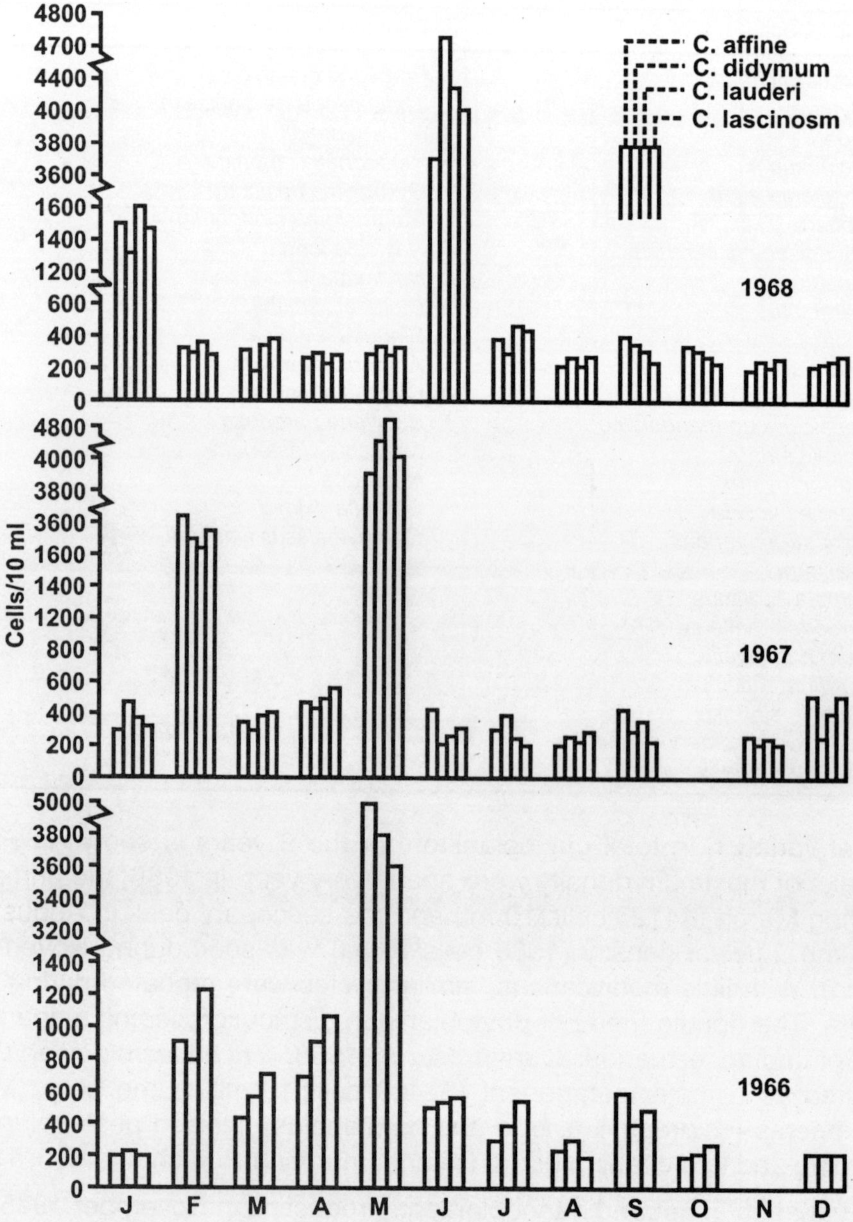

Fig. 7.15 Seasonal variations of 4 species of *Chaetoceros* in Vellar Estuary during the years 1966 to 1968 (From Joseph, 1975).

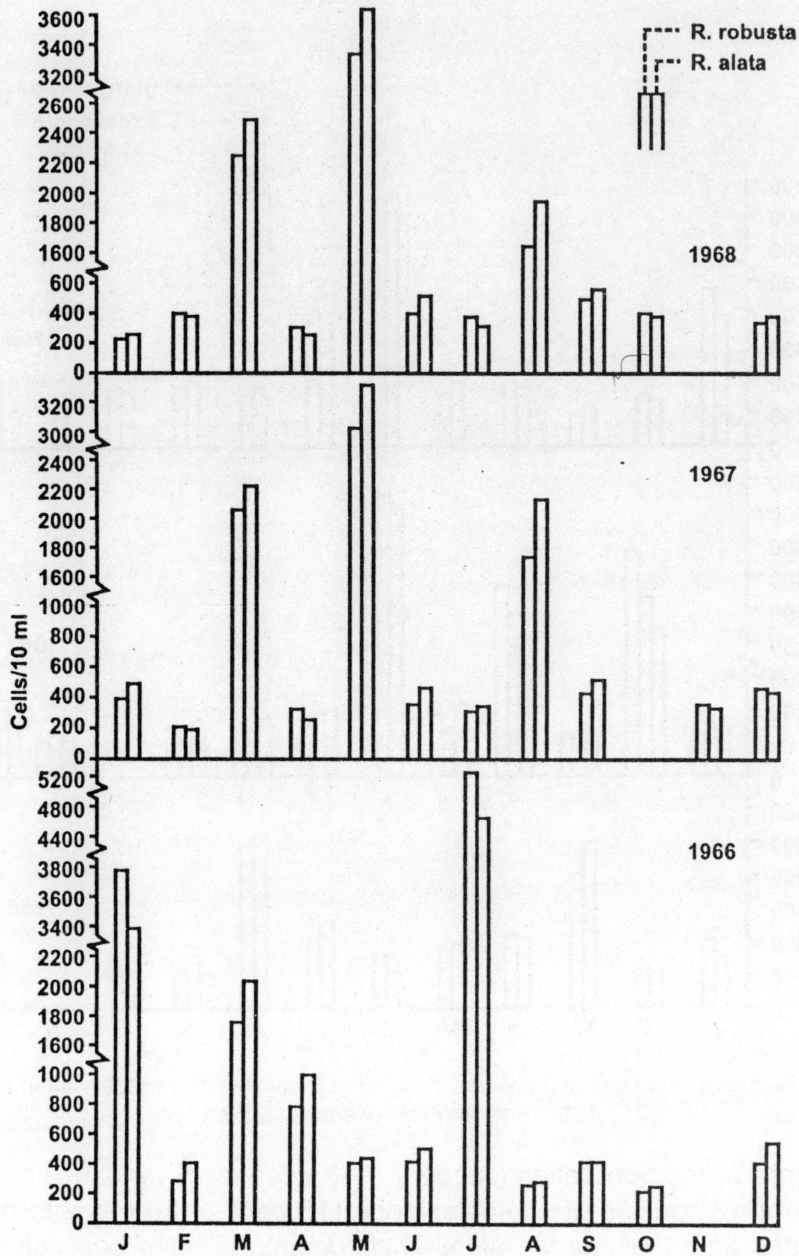

Fig. 7.16 Seasonal variations of 2 species of *Rhizosolenia* in Vellar Estuary during the years 1966 to 1968 (From Joseph, 1975).

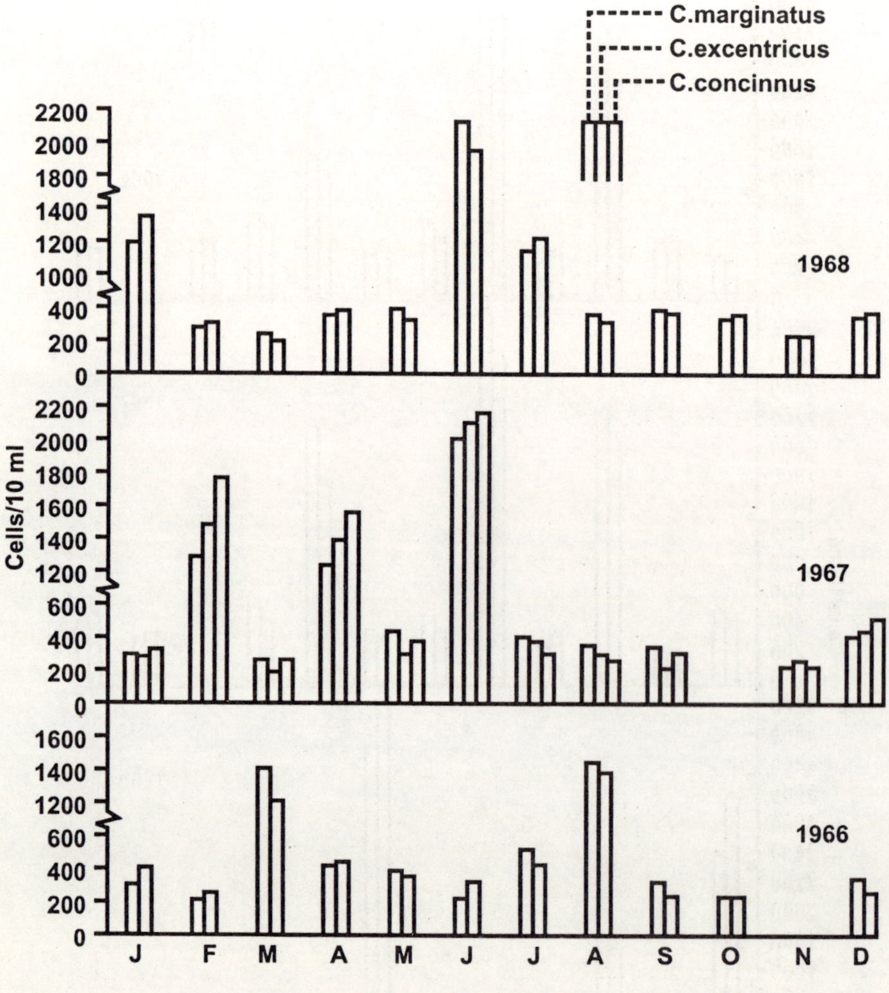

Fig. 7.17 Seasonal variations of 3 species of *Coscinodiscus* in Vellar Estuary during the years 1966 to 1968 (From Joseph, 1975).

In another interesting publication (Joseph, 1982), seasonal variations in numerical abundance of 42 species of phytoplanktons (18 centric, 20 pennate diatoms, 3 dinoflagellates and 1 bluegreen alga, *Trichodesmium*) have been studied for 3 years, 1966, 1967 and 1968. A trimodal variation was seen in the density of these diatoms and a negative correlation was recorded between the diatom-density and blooms of dinoflagellates and *Trichodesmium*. Correlation matrix of 10 major

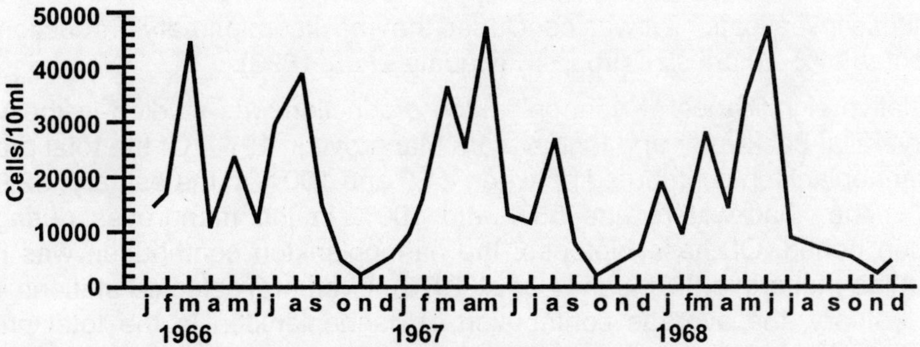

Fig. 7.18 Seasonal variations in total phytoplankton in Vellar Estuary during the years 1966 to 1968 (From Joseph, 1975).

groups of organisms showed both positive and negative variability indicating that the estuary is a natural habitat for their coexistence and most of the genera are typically estuarine (endemic) forms extremely well-adapted to salinity changes. There are, however, several exceptions to this rule suggesting that there are coastal representatives which appear in the estuary when in gets saltwater-dominated (see Joseph, 1982).

Krishnamurthy (1967) studied both phytoplankton and zooplankton for 3 years in Parangipettai waters at two stations – one was in the inshore waters of Bay of Bengal at 60 m depth and the second at the mouth of the estuary. He recorded 3 peaks in the inshore waters contributed by diatoms, dinoflagellates and *Trichodesmium* which appeared in June-July after the peak in the estuary. The latter preceded in May-July. The other two minor peaks were from January to March and in August. Investigations on the succession of species, their diversity, distribution and the ecology of dinoflagellates (family Dinophyceae) were carried out for two years from 1978 to 1980 in the estuary and in the inshore waters outside the estuary. The total number of species recorded was 103. Of these, about 20 species were oceanic. Some from them have been reported to be the indicators of upwelling, richness and uneveness. From this study, it was concluded that maximum density occurs during the dry summer months when salinity in the estuary is lower than seawater (intermediate). Some dinoflagellate taxa belonging to other geographical regions were also recorded in the inshore waters (Ilangovan, 1987). Phytoplankton biomass and productivity of different size-fractions were estimated in the estuary and Pichavaram mangrove from chlorophyll concentration and gross production in July 1988. Maximum quantity of chlorophyll was found in the fraction 5-10 μm at both the sites (3.6 μg-at/l ~ 33% of the total chlorophyll). This agreed well with the measurement of gross production of the same size-fraction.

From these investigations it was concluded that maximum primary production was contributed by 5-10 μm size group (Kawabata *et al.,* 1993).

The relative significance of nannoplankton production was studied in the Vellar Estuary, Killai Backwater and Pichavaram Mangrove in 1974. Of the total production, nannoplankton contributed between 44.8 and 100% in the estuary, 32.9 and 100% in the backwaters and 55.4 and 100% in the mangroves during the monsoon period. Of these biotopes, the nannoplankton contribution was maximum in the mangrove (Ramadhas *et al.*,1976). Even at 3 selected stations in the Vellar Estuary, the average contribution of nannoplankton in the total primary production during the premonsoon and monsoon months of 1974 was about 71.1%, irrespective of the surface or bottom waters. The salinity at these stations was lower than the normal seawater (Subramanian *et al.*, 1977).

In addition to larger (net) phytoplankton and nannoplankton, the bluegreen algae play an important role in the ecology of Vellar Estuary. In all, 13 species of bluegreen algae belonging to 11 genera namely *Anabaena, Anabaenopsis, Aphanocapsa, Ulothrix, Lyngbya, Nodularia, Oscillatoria, Phormidium, Spirulina, Stigonema and Trichodesmium* were recorded. The occurrence, distribution and seasonal variation of these showed an interesting pattern in the three environments namely estuary, coastal water and mangroves. The study was extended over a period of two years from January 1978 to December 1979. Each year was divided into 4 seasons of 2-4 months – postmonsoon (January-February), summer (March-May), premonsoon (June-August), monsoon (September-December). Table 7.2 shows their population and their contribution in total phytoplankton abundance during the 4 seasons in the three different study areas has been noted in Table 7.2 along with some relevant environmental features. Their seasonal cycle is shown in Fig. 7.19. Maximum population of bluegreen algae was observed during the summer when these constituted 20-30%, 10% and 15% of the total phytoplankton by cell counts in the estuary, coastal waters and mangroves respectively. The general pattern of distribution of bluegreen was almost similar to the other groups. However, the abundance of a single planktonic species *Trichodesmium* which forms blooms in March and April outnumbered all other organisms. High temperature, high salinity, maximum solar radiation and stability of water column appears to favour the summer abundance of bluegreen algae in all the three biotopes. Similar observations have been made in other regions of the Indian Ocean on *Trichodesmium* (Qasim, 1970, 1972, 1979). The distribution pattern in different seasons followed the order summer > postmonsoon > monsoon > premonsoon. The nitrogen fixation ability of the planktonic

Table 7.2— Seasonal variation of planktonic bluegreen algae and related environmental parameters in 3 environments (From Ramachandran & Venugopalan, 1987)

Season	Rainfall mm	Study Area	Surface Temp. ˚C	Surface Salinity ‰	Population Nos/l	Percent in TPP
1978						
Postmonsoon (January & February)	nil	Estuary	26.1	18.4	70	5.46
		Coastal Waters	25.5	33.9	44	0.65
		Manrgrove waters	25.5	30.7	114	7.25
Summer (March & May)	3.48	Estuary	32.7	24.0	2313	28.85
		Coastal Waters	31.3	34.3	2576	11.40
		Manrgrove waters	29.8	29.3	1162	15.15
Premonsoon (June & August)	47.77	Estuary	29.6	20.6	144	0.50
		Coastal Waters	29.6	32.6	22	0.15
		Manrgrove waters	29.8	29.3	151	0.50
Monsoon (September & December)	351.02	Estuary	26.7	7.1	39	4.45
		Coastal Waters	25.6	29.2	35	0.50
		Manrgrove waters	24.9	19.3	79	24.4
1979						
Postmonsoon (January & February)	3.25	Estuary	27.5	17.1	253	5.0
		Coastal Waters	26.5	33.7	105	3.70
		Manrgrove waters	26.7	28.2	186	11.65
Summer (March & May)	4.00	Estuary	32.3	22.3	1940	31.14
		Coastal Waters	31.2	34.4	1033	4.25
		Manrgrove waters	31.5	31.3	1002	7.35
Premonsoon (June & August)	15.83	Estuary	31.6	20.3	202	5.30
		Coastal Waters	29.6	33.1	11	0.22
		Manrgrove waters	29.0	29.7	34	0.85
Monsoon (September & December)	375.57	Estuary	26.9	5	110	13.5
		Coastal Waters	25.6	29.3	24	0.4
		Manrgrove waters	25.1	19.6	109	3.8

bluegreen algae was also estimated. This is shown in Table 7.3. The estimated rates were 36μ moles N_2/m^3/day (or 0.184g N_2/m^3/y for the estuary; 17μ moles N_2/m^3/day or 0.87g N_2/m^3/day) for coastal rates and 24μ moles/m^3/day (or 0.132g N_2/m^3/y for mangroves (Ramachandran & Venugopalan, 1987). Thus their

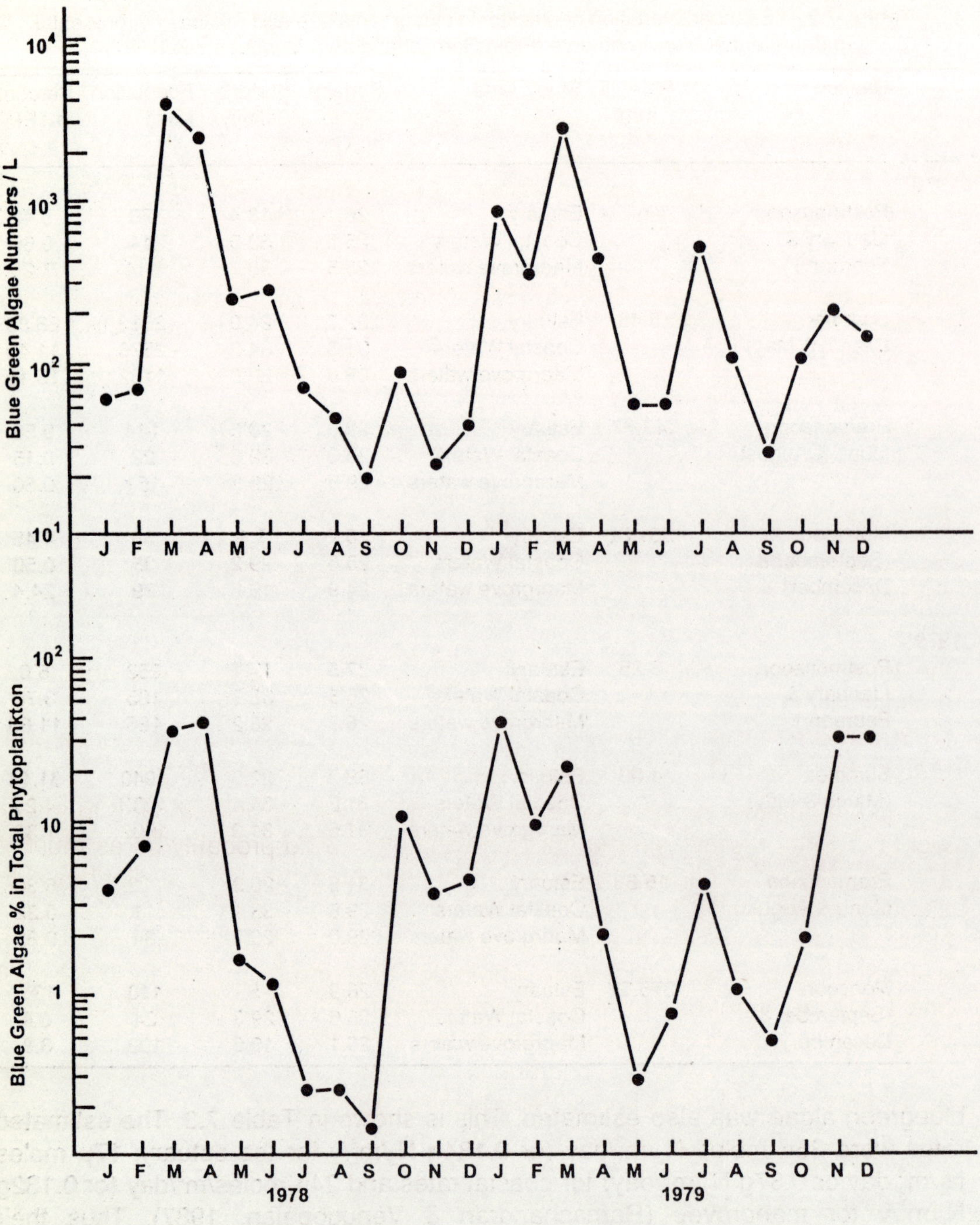

Fig. 7.19 Seasonal variations of bluegreen algae in Vellar Estuary during 1978 and 1979 (From Ramachandran & Venugopalan, 1987).

Table 7.3— Nitrogen fixation estimates for planktonic bluegreen algae and their contribution to nitrogen requirements in 3 environments (From Ramachandran & Venugopalan, 1987)

I. *Estuarine environment:*

Ethylene reduced for samples	9 n moles/h/l
Hence nitrogen fixed/l/hr	3 n moles
" /m^3/h	3 μ moles
" /m^3/d	36 μ moles
	= 0.504 mg

Assuming the average daily production rate of 100 mg C per day per m^3 and a C : N ratio of 6, the nitrogen requirement will be 15.2 mg/day and the contribution will be @ 3.5%

II. *Coastal waters:*

Similarly for the coastal waters wherein the estimated rates of nitrogen fixation was 17 μ moles/m^3/d (0.238 mg), the contribution will be @ 1.6%

III. *Mangrove waters:*

The estimated rate of nitrogen fixation was 24 m moles per m^3 per day (0.336 mg) for mangrove waters and hence the contribution will be @ 2.25%.

the total nitrogen requirement of phytoplankton were 3.5%, 1.6% and 2.25% respectively (Table 7.3). Since these estimates were made for the month of July (1980) when their populations were not high, the values may not represent the real contribution to the total nitrogen budget in the other seasons.

During the summer months, the density of bluegreen algae is about 5 to 8 times higher. Therefore, the nitrogen fixation estimates could probably be as much as 10-20% of the total nitrogen requirement of phytoplankton. On a similar basis, the nitrogen fixation rates associated with benthic algae were 3.22 and 3.32 mg N_2/m^2/day for the estuarine and mangrove environments respectively and the estimated rates of epiphytic algae would be 0.968 mg N_2/m^2/day for the estuary and 1.347 mg N_2/m^2/day for the mangrove waters. The importance of submerged vegetation in aquatic productivity especially in shallow waters has been recognized. However, in Vellar, the contribution of benthic and epithytic algae would be less than 1% (Ramachandran & Venugopalan, 1987).

Zooplankton

Collections of zooplankton were made for 2 years (1974-76) from 4 stations – one was in the inshore waters and three were in the estuary, by filtering 100 litres of

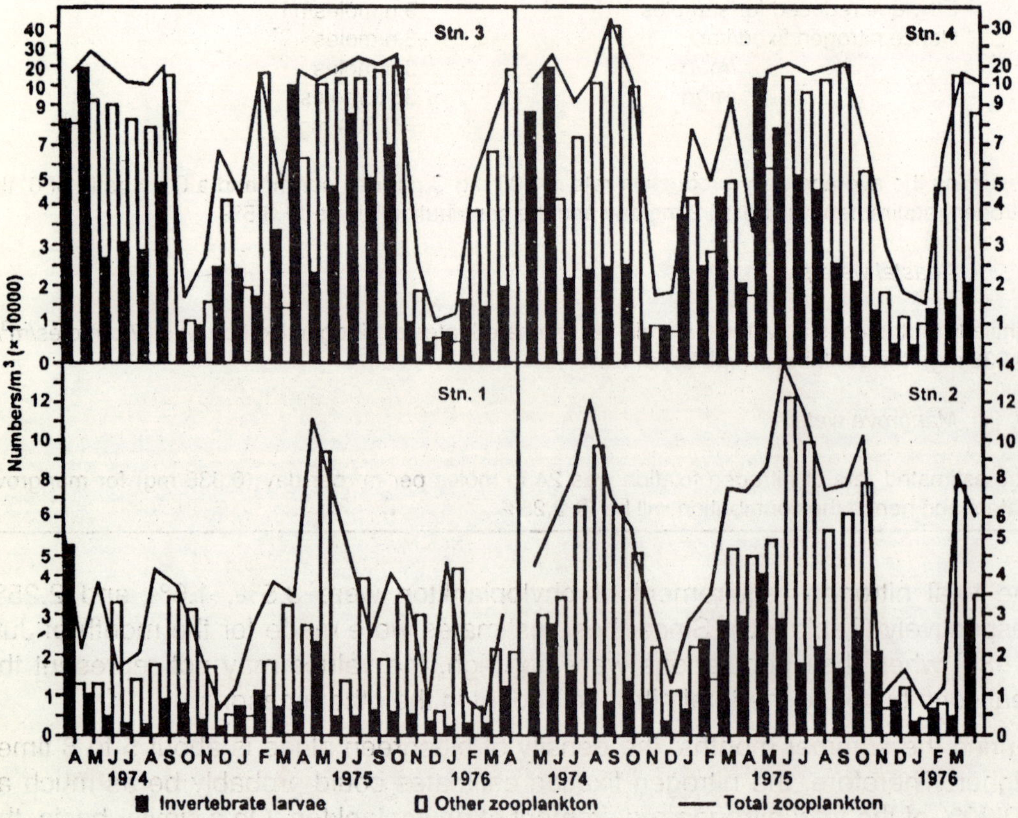

Fig. 7.20 Seasonal variations in numbers of invertebrate larvae, other zooplankton and total zooplankton at 4 stations of Vellar Estuary during the years 1974, 1975 and 1976 (From Shrikrishnadhas, *et al.*, 1993).

water from the surface. The total zooplankton population was greater in the estuary than in the coastal waters and increased at the stations upstream within the estuarine-marine zone. The population largely included invertebrate larvae. Figure 7.20 gives the quantitative distribution of 2 categories of organisms and their total numbers. The contribution of invertebrate larvae to the zooplankton in the nearshore waters was 23.84% in contrast to 37.23% in the different zones

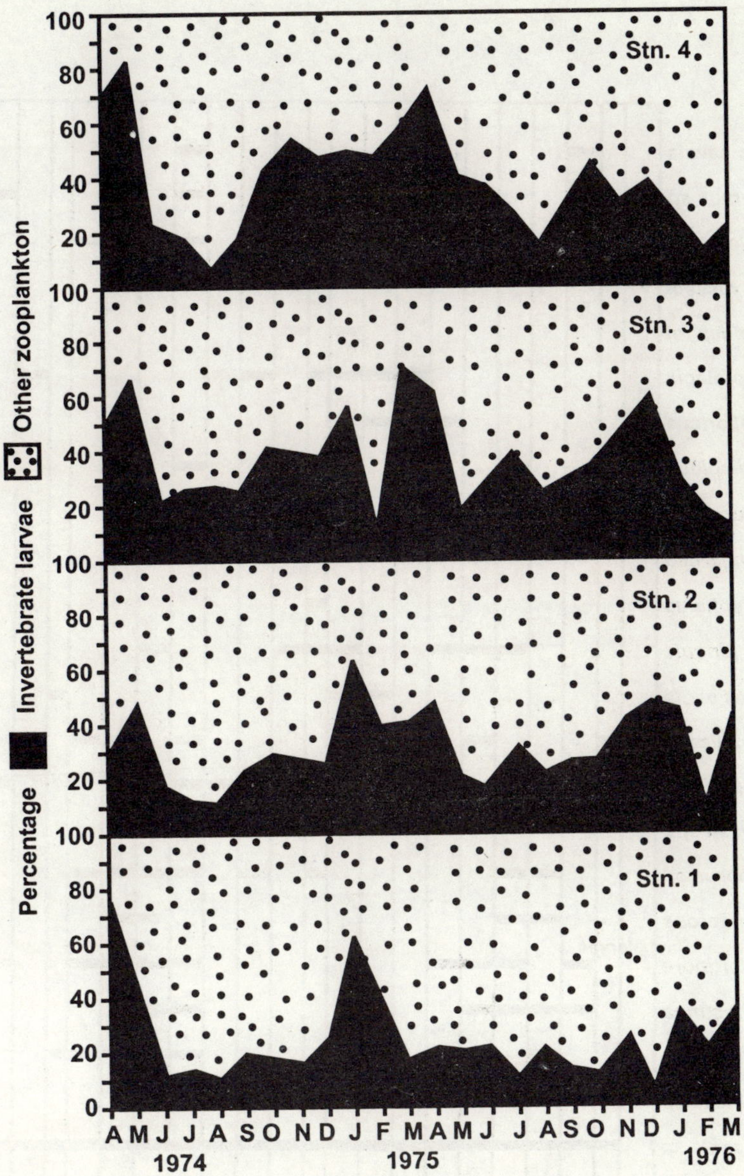

Fig. 7.21 Seasonal variations of invertebrate larvae (mean in %) and other zooplankton organism in total zooplankton at 4 stations of Vellar Estuary from 1974 to 1976 (From Shrikrishnadhas *et al.*, 1993).

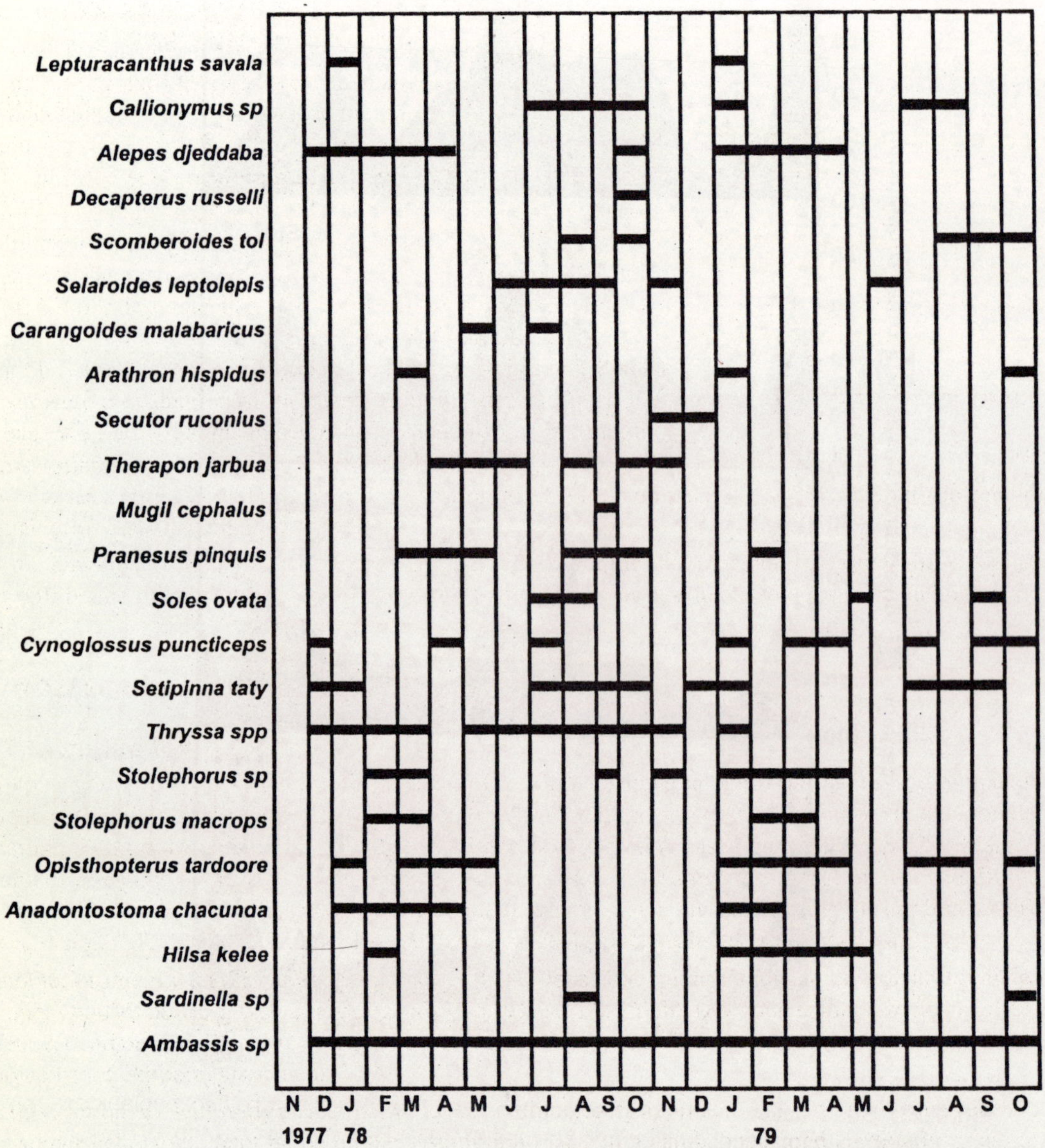

Fig. 7.22 Seasonal occurrence of fish eggs in Vellar Estuary from 1977 to 1979 (From Thangaraja, 1995).

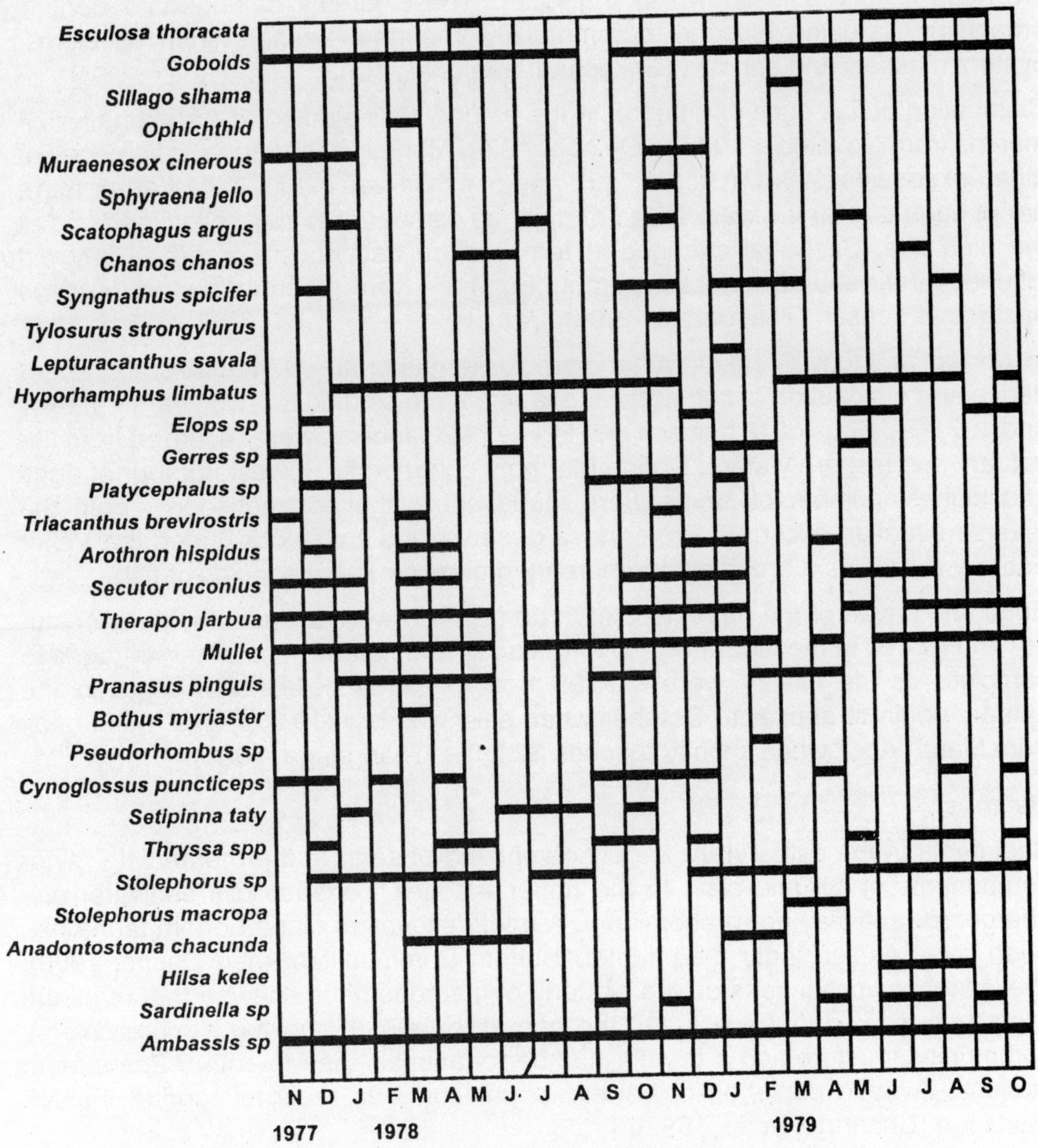

Fig. 7.23 Seasonal occurrence of fish larvae in Vellar Estuary from 1977 to 1979 (From Thangaraja, 1995).

of the estuary. Premonsoon period recorded the highest number in all the zones and the lowest were during the monsoon period. Quantitative contribution of invertebarte larvae is shown in Fig. 7.21. These largely belonged to benthic organisms including those of commercially important animals such as clams, oysters mussels and shrimps (Srikrishnadhas *et al.,* 1993).

Distribution of fish eggs and larvae in the estuary was studied at 4 stations for 24 months from November 1977 to October 1979. Monthly occurrence of fish eggs of different species is shown in Fig. 7.22 and of fish larvae in Fig. 7.23. Larger number of eggs and larvae were found at night as compared to day collections and at the high tide. Seasonal changes in temperature had no effect but salinity did influence their abundance as maximum numbers were recorded during the days of summer season (Thangaraja, 1995).

In an earlier study (Venkataramanujam & Ramamorthi, 1974), seasonal abundance and distribution of fish eggs and larvae were studied for two years 1970-71 and 1971-72. Eggs of 18 species and larvae of 28 species were recorded from the estuary and inshore waters. During the monsoon months, lowest number of eggs and highest number of larvae were found but in the postmonsoon month the reverse situation occurred. From these observations it was concluded the Vellar Estuary serves as a breeding and nursery ground for many species of fish.

Eggs and larvae of the pufferfish, *Anthron hispidus* were collected from the estuary and reared in the laboratory up to 6 stages and figured. The other 4 stages to complete its life history were studied from plankton collections. Eggs in the estuary begin to appear to October when salinity is low (19.8‰) and attain peak from March/April, when salinity reaches 32.34‰ (Thangaraja, 1984).

Benthos

Sediments in the estuary are largely composed of sand at the mouth with minor components of silt and clay. In the upper reaches, because of freshwater discharge, silt and clay are predominant. A brief description of the bottom fauna has been given earlier under the chapter "Bottom Communities" (see Qasim, 1999). Preliminary investigations on the ecology of macrobenthos showed that of all the 3 stations worked in the estuary, the one at the mouth showed a more diverse community structure and a greater number of animals than the other 2 upstream stations. A rapid depletion of benthic population was recorded during the NE monsoon (Chandran *et al.,* 1982).

A systematic study of macrobenthos was conducted for a period of two years from January 1977 to December 1978 at one station (Chandran, 1987). Along with macrobenthic fauna, total organic carbon, total nitrogen and total phosphorus in the sediment samples were also studied. Seasonal variations in the sediment composition (sand, silt and clay fractions) were also determined. Benthic fauna included ploychaetes, crustaceans, bivalves, gastropods and other groups such as anemones, planarians, polyclads and phoronids. In all, 47 species belonging to the groups noted above were identified. Of these, there were 21 species of polychaetes, 4 species of gastropods, 7 species of bivalves, 9 species of crustaceans and 6 species belonging to other groups as indicated in Table 7.4. Among these,

Table 7.4— Check list of benthic fauna encountered in the gradient zone of Vellar estuary (From Chandran, 1987)

Polychaetes :		Bivalves:	
	Ancistrosyllis constricta		*Anadara grenosa*
	Axiotella sp.		*Katelysia opima*
	Ceratoneries costae		*Meretrix meretrix*
	Capitellid (unidentified)		*M. casta*
	Cossura delta		*Solen* sp.
	Glycera alba		*Tellina* sp.
	Glycinde sp.		*Grandidievella* sp.
	Hesionid (unidentified)	Crustaceans:	
	Heteromastus similis		Isopod (unidentified)
	Laoneme indica		*Eriopisa chilkensis*
	Lumbriconeries sp.		*Apseudes gymnophobia*
	Nephthys polybranchia		*A. killaiyenesis*
	Pectinaria crassa		*Idunella chilkensis*
	Poecilochaetus serpens		*Matuta victor*
	Prionospio cirrobranchiata		*Clibanarius longitarsus*
	P. malmgreni		*C. olivaceus*
	P. pinnata		*Alpheus malabaricus*
	Pseudopolydora kempi	Miscellaneous:	
	Spiochaetopterus costatum		Sea anemone (unidentified)
	Megelona sp.		Polyclad (unidentified)
	Terrbellidus stromi		*Virgularia* sp.
			Phoronis architeca
Gastropods:	*Cerithidea (Cerithideopsilla) fluviatilis*		Namatode worm (unidentified)
	Nassa sp.		Ostracod (unidentified)
	Natica macrochinensis		
	Nudibranch (unidentified)		

polychaetes dominated both in species composition and abundance. The total benthic population varied from 0 to 900 organism/m^2. Tides had no significant influence on the population density. Among the different environmental features, salinity and sediment composition appear to play an important role in the abundance of animals. A lot of difference was noticed in the composition of sediment between 1977 and 1978. Blood and muscle proteins of the crabs from the estuary were studied by Kannupandi & Paulandian (1975). Several glyco-and lipoprotein fractions were recorded.

In an extensive study spread over several years, from 1973 to 1978, polychaete fauna from the inshore waters of Parangipettai-Vellar estuary, backwaters and mangroves have been reported (Srikrishnadhas *et al.,* 1987). Polychaetes were collected from the plankton, sediments of the intertidal and subtidal regions and from the shells of bivalves and gastropods and other hard structures. The total number of polychaetes identified was 123. These belonged to 94 genera and 44 families. The authors give an impressive list of nomenclature indicating the habitat, niche and maximum density of each species.

Depending upon their distribution and salinity preferences, they were sub-divided into the following 4 groups:

(a) those which are purely marine
(b) those which are marine but enter into saltwater-dominated
(c) those which are estuarine but are often found in seawater
(d) those which are purely estuarine

Some of the common species in the estuary falling under the third group were found in large numbers in the nearshore waters during the monsoon season. This shows temporary shifting of the population into the sea to avoid monsoon effects. The populations of polychaetes in the estuary, backwaters and mangroves become very thin during the monsoon months because of low salinity.

Age and growth of the estuarine clam, *Meretrix meretrix* from the Vellar Estuary were studied by Jayabal & Kalyani (1986). The clam attained 24.5, 47 and 61.5 mm shell length during 0, 1st and 2nd years respectively and its life span appears to be 2-3 years. Biochemical composition of the two bivalves, *Meretrix casta* and *Sanguinolaria diphos* found in Vellar Estuary showed 81.9% and 80.32% water; 10.7% and 10.8% protein, 2.12% and 2.0% fat; 0.38% and 0.35% carbohydrate and 2.19%, 3.6% ash in the two species respectively. Seventeen amino acids in the free form and 15 in the bound form in the meat of *M.casta* and 16 free forms and 16 bound forms in *S. diphos* were recorded (Wafar, 1974). The distribution of *M. casta* was studied in the marine and estuarine zones of the estuary for one year. The bivalve seems to prefer marine-dominated estuarine areas where the sediment was largely composed of silt and clay (Balasubrhamanyan & Natarajan, 1987). The oyster (*Saccostrea cucullata*) occurs in Parangipettai waters and forms natural beds. It was induced to spawn in the laboratory by increasing the temperature of water and by the addition of sperm extract. Fertilised eggs underwent metamorphosis and developed into adults after 28 days (Kalyanasundaram & Ramamoorthi, 1987). Studies on protein, lipid and carbohydrate in the hard clam, *M. meretrix* showed that during the spawning period the biochemical constituents were low in the bivalve and high during the maturation period. The former phase, occurs during the summer and premonsoon seasons and the latter during the monsoon and postmonsoon (Jayabal & Kalyani, 1987). Seasonal variations in protein, carbohydrate, lipid, and water in the clam, *M. meretrix* followed the gonodial cycle, being high when the clams were ripe (Jayabal & Kalyani, 1987). Biochemical studies on another clam *Katelysia opima* showed similar results and seasonal variations were largely due to reproductive cycle (Jayabal, 1994). These surveys conducted on the occurrence of bivalves in the estuary showed 38 species belonging to 3 orders and 15 families. Bivalve resources as oyster beds are found in all types of habitats – marine, estuarine and backwaters. Shellfish landing constitute 64.4% of the total landings, of which 55.2% are clams (Jayabal & Kalyani, 1989).

INTERTIDAL FAUNA

Intertidal fauna of two beaches namely the estuarine beach and *Dotilla* beach of the Vellar Estuary have been described by Qasim (1999). Macrofauna of the former included the ghost crab, *Ocypoda macrocera*, the amphipod, *Talorchestia spinipalma*, fiddler crab, *Uca* sp., smaller brachyuran decapod, *Dotilla myctiroides* and several other species of amphipods, bivalves, gastropods and cumaceans. Meiofauna comprised nematodes at all levels, harpacticoids, nauplii, isopods, ostracods, amphipods and kynorhynchs.

The intertidal zone of the latter (*Dotilla* beach) has dense concentrations of *Dotilla myctiroides*. Other species present were *Uca* sp., gastropods, *Potomides cingulatus* and *Neritina oualaniensis*, 4 species of bivalves, nemertines and *Nepthys* sp. The meiofauna of this beach was richer than that of the former and included all the groups noted above (McIntyre, 1968).

Reproductive cycle of three species of barnacles namely *Balanus variegatus, Balanus amphitritbe amphitrite* and *Balanus pallidus* were studied from the estuary. The last two species breed throughout the year whereas the maximum breeding of *B. variegatus* is restricted to postmonsoon months although it also breeds throughout the year. Decrease in salinity seems to control its spawning activity (Fernando, 1987). The estuarine crab, *Macropthalmus (Venitus) latreilli* occurs readily in muddy substrata. It freely breeds in captivity and full metamorphosis takes place in the laboratory. Five zoeal stages and one megalopa stage have been observed during its development which takes 20 days (Selvakumar *et al.,* 1988). The hermit crab, *Coenobila cavipes* takes shelter in empty gastropod (snail) to escape predation. It has been found in 16 different species of gastropod shells to escape predation. These shells belong to marine, estuarine and freshwater snails. The choice of the number of shells is restricted to 16 whereas several other species of hermit crabs inhabit in 72 species of gastropods. Shell volume seems to be the main criterion of its selection. (Sripathi *et al.,*1977; Khan *et al.,* 1980). Intertidal hermit crabs occur abundantly in the marine zone of the estuary close to the mouth. Their numbers decrease further upstream. Besides the availability of certain types of molluscan shells, high salinity of water favours habitat selection (Khan & Natarajan, 1981). The hermit crab, *Clibanarius longitarsus* has been reported to breed over an extended period of the year with two peaks — one from Feb. to April and the other from July to September (Khan & Natarajan, 1977). Among the 5 species of hermit crabs studied, the breeding season of *C. padavensus* was the shortest with a single peak in April. *C. olivaceus* breeds throughout the year with two distinct peaks, when the salinity of water is high. *Diogenes avarus,* like the former species, is also a continuous breeder. *C. carpes* has two distinct breeding periods during the year. These occur during premonsoon and monsoon seasons (Khan & Natarajan, 1981). *C. longitarsus* has been bred successfully in the laboratory. Four zoeal stages and a galaucothoe stage (post-larval) were found to intervene the development. These have been figured and their identification characters were noted (Khan & Natarajan, 1981). In the Pitchavaram mangrove, the crab, *Sesaram brockii,* known as the mangrove crab is very common. There are several other species of the genus *Sesarma* which are also found in the mangroves. Berried females of *S. Brockii* spawned in the laboratory and 4 zoeal stages and one megalopa stage were obtained and figured. These were compared with the two other species of the mangrove crabs. Ovigerous females of an edible crab, *Thalamiter danae* from the estuary spawned in the laboratory and zoea larvae were reared up to stage 4 and megalopa stage turned to first instar crab in 25‰ salinity. Zoea stage took 6 months to reach the crab stage (Krishnan & Kannupandi, 1988).

It has been reported that the meiofauna of the intertidal zone perform distinct vertical and horizontal migration within the top 10 cm of the sediment. Vertical migration downwards occurs in response to light and desiccation and horizontal during the receding tides in search of favorable sites for food (Fernando & Natarajan, 1987). Community structure of benthic diatoms along the intertidal zone showed maximum species diversity at the station close to the mouth as compared to the station in the estuarine zone. The life span of the oyster (*Crassostrea madrasensis*) based on age and growth studies was found to be 3-4 y. A linear relationship was found between length and weight (Somasekar *et al.,* 1982). In the two intertidal bivalves, *C. madrasensis* and *Anadara rhombea* feeding and digestive rhythms have been shown to follow tidal rhythm. Active feeding occurs during the low tides and digestion and absorption during the high tides (Hameed & Paulpandian, 1987). Unidentified larvae of a barnacle were collected from the estuary which were reared in the laboratory successfully and its nearest classification has been given (Karande *et al.,* 1997). Seasonal distribution of both macro and meiofauna in the estuary was studied at different zones namely marine, gradient and tidal. Dominant macrofauna was found to be different in each zone and their maximum occurrence was at low tides, while the meiofauna was similar at the three zones dominated by nematodes followed by harpacticoids (Fernando, 1987). Five species of bryozoans were recorded from the estuary and 16 species from the mangroves. Their population increased during the summer and premonsoon seasons while during monsoon it decreased (Nair, 1991).

FISHERY

The estuary provides a productive environment for fishery. There are 5 villages around the estuary in which the total population of fishermen is about 640. Fishing is normally carried out between 5 am and 6 pm, although night fishing is not uncommon. During the monsoon months, the activity slows down. The catches include mullets, sciaenids, catfishes, prawns, crabs, clams and miscellaneous fishes, as major categories. The total fish landing estimated during the period Dec. 1973 to Nov. 1974 (12 months) was 3,801,51 kg and their composition (weight in kg) was as follows:

Mullets	*Arius*	*Thrissocles*	*Sardinella*	*Leiognathus*	Sciaenids
89391	11410	2734	2370	5219	6843
Pomadasys	*Polynemus*	*Sillago*	*Scatophagus argus*		
1684	2781	860	215		
Serranus	Rays	Miscellaneous	Prawns	Crabs	Clams
248	1897	9333	21920	13246	210000

Main gears employed for fishing are different types of cast nets with varying mesh sizes. Fishing by a hollow cone-shaped basket is also employed. According to Natarajan *et al.* (1979), who have collected the above fishing data, the period for which the data refers was not a good fishing year. Otherwise, the total annual landing normally is higher than that noted above. Peak fishing seasons are summer and premonsoon months, although intensive fishing starts soon after the rains. Mullets constitute 23.5% of the total fish landings. Good catches of mullets are obtained from the mangrove areas even during the monsoon months. During the period of the study noted above 1,34,785 kg of finfishes and 35,166 kg of crustaceans were landed. Prawns constituted 13% of the total landings, while crabs formed about 7.8%. The contribution of molluscan fishery was very substantial (64.40%) in the total although these are sold at a cheap rate and their shells are utilized for the production of lime.

From the estuary, eggs and larvae of the flatfish, *Cynoglossus puncticeps* were collected and reared in the laboratory up to 4 stages while the rest of the 7 stages (6 stages and 1 juvenile) were collected from the plankton samples. In this way the entire life history of the fish was studied and the stages figured (Thangaraja, 1984).

Eggs and larvae of the fish *Stolephorus* sp. from the estuary were also studied by rearing 5 early stages in the laboratory and by obtaining 6 stages from the plankton collections. The eggs commonly occur in the marine zone (Thangaraja, 1986). Length-weight relationship of the clam, *Katelysia opima* from the estuary showed allometric relationship (Kalyanasundaram & Kasinathan, 1983). Green mussel (*Perna viridis*) was cultured in the estuary on ropes suspended from rafts. It adapted to this situation well and its early growth was fast. However, fouling organisms and epifauna caused disturbance leading to their dropping from the ropes into the water (Jayabal & Subramaniam, 1988).

The Indian white prawn, *Penaeus indicus* grew fast in cages kept in the estuary when fed on pelleted food at the rate of 10% of their body weight in the first month and 15% for the next two months. Water temperature in the cage varied between 25.6 to 30.3°C, salinity 1.2 to 34.1‰ (because of heavy rainfall from 15 October to 5 November, there was a sudden drop in salinity), pH 7.8 to 9.1; dissolved oxygen 3.2 to 5.0 ml/l. The rate of growth was 1.76 mm/day in length and 0.279 g/day in weight. Production rate of the stocked prawns after 90 days was worked out as 1975 kg/ha (Shanmugam *et al.,* 1995).

POLLUTION

The foregoing account on the richness of flora and fauna provides evidence that so far the Vellar Estuary has largely remained free from the kind of pollution we have seen in other estuaries of Tamil Nadu. It is perhaps the only estuary of Tamil Nadu which is least polluted and probably this is one of the reasons that it has attracted the visits of many scientists from different parts of India and abroad. However, there have been some useful laboratory studies to evaluate the toxicity of copper and cadmium on the pistol prawn and hermit crab from the estuary and of the organochlorine pesticides on zooplankton. The influence of salinity and copper on the larvae of pistol prawn, *Alpheus malabaricus* from the estuary was studied. The 72 h LC_{50} showed that the optimum salinity for them was 28‰, as they were stenohaline. Copper in the form of $CuSO_4$ was insoluble and affected the respiratory system (Perumal & Subramanian, 1985). Larvae (zoea) of *Calibanarius longitarsus,* hatched in the laboratory, were exposed to a sublethal concentrations of cadmium and the 96 h LC_{50} value was found to be 270 ppb. There was some evidence of the larvae developing resistance to low concentrations of cadmium (Lyla *et al.,* 1988). Similarly, when 4 species of zooplankton (*Acartia* sp., *Eucalanust* sp., *Lucifer* sp., and *Sagitta* sp.) collected from the estuary, were exposed to organochlorine pesticides (DDT, lindane and endosulfane), their 24 h LC_{50} values with their confidence limits showed that DDT was far more toxic followed by lindane and endosulfane. *Sagitta* sp., was more tolerant to DDT and endosulphane than the other three organisms (Rajendran & Venugopalan, 1988).

Other studies conducted were on the distribution of dissolved and particulate forms of iron in relation to phytoplankton population at 4 stations of estuary and seasonal variation in the organochlorine residues. Samples of organisms collected from the bottom showed higher values of dissolved and particulate iron than the surface samples. Dissolved iron showed no relation with phytoplankton population and an inverse relationship was found between particulate iron concentration and phytoplankton. However, iron in either form was not a limiting factor on phytoplankton production (Ramadhas *et al.,* 1972).

Seasonal variations in the occurrence of organochlorine insecticides such as HCH (BHC) and DDT were studied throughout the year in the Vellar River and Pichavaram Mangroves. Both these insecticides showed higher levels from October to February. In the HCH, this trend was more pronounced than in DDT. This shows that larger quantities of HCH are being used on rice crop than DDT. The different isomers of HCH and DDT were higher in the river water except during the dry season. These chemicals were found to be in the water phase. In the urban areas of India, both HCH and DDT are still being used for vector control while

HCH is largely being used in agriculture. The contamination with organochlorine insecticides in India is higher than in many other countries of the world (Ramesh *et al.,* 1990).

MICROBIOLOGY

The occurrence of black ascosporogenous yeasts has been recorded from Parangipettai waters earlier (Iyer & Pillai, 1970). In the regeneration of phosphorus from the decaying phytoplankton, both bacteria and ciliates played an important role in the estuary (Rajendran & Venugopalan, 1977). Pure cultures of bacteria (*Micrococus* sp.) and yeast (*Candida tropicalis*), isolated from the Vellar Estuary, were developed and maintained in the laboratory. In addition, a pure culture of the centric diatom (*Melosira sulcata*) was already present at the Centre. These three were used for feeding 3 species of bivalves namely *Arca granosa, A. inaequivalvis* and *Donax cuneatus* in the laboratory under controlled conditions. All the three bivalves fed on the yeast showed a greater increase in weight than on other diets. *D. cuneatus* showed a greater increase than the others (Krishnamurthy *et al.,* 1966). Marine *Thiobacilli*, isolated from the sediments of the estuary, grew well when the source of energy for their growth was thiosulphate. The cells were identified as Gram-negative, motile rods, requiring seawater for their optimum growth. The ability to utilize thiosulphate differed among the 8 cultures tested. Concentrations of thiosulphate higher than 5% inhibited their growth (Devendran *et al.,* 1975). Three strains of marine silicate-dissolving bacteria (*Pseudomonas* sp.), isolated from the sediments of the estuary, showed that when exposed to synthetic silicates (magnesium trisilicate), they were able to synthesize silicate from the medium (Purushothaman *et al.,* 1975).

Both ammonia-oxidizing bacteria and nitrite-oxiding bacteria were estimated from the sediments and overlying water of different zones of the estuary. Generally the nitrification process was greater in the sediments than in the water column. Salinity seemed to be the controlling factor in the distribution of marine and limnetic form of nitrifying bacteria. Total heterotrophic bacteria in the marine and freshwater zones of the estuary were also estimated (Rajendran & Venugopalan, 1977). To study the nitrification process in the estuary, *in situ* experiments were conducted by collecting sterile samples from 5 m depth and incubating them in the estuary at that depth (26-28°C). A second batch was incubated at a lower temperature range (10-14°C) in the laboratory. In the first week, both ammonification and nitrite formation took place but it could also be due to the reduction of nitrite (denitrification) in the presence of low oxygen. Total inorganic nitrogen increased steadily up to 8th week and then declined. It was thus concluded that ammonia

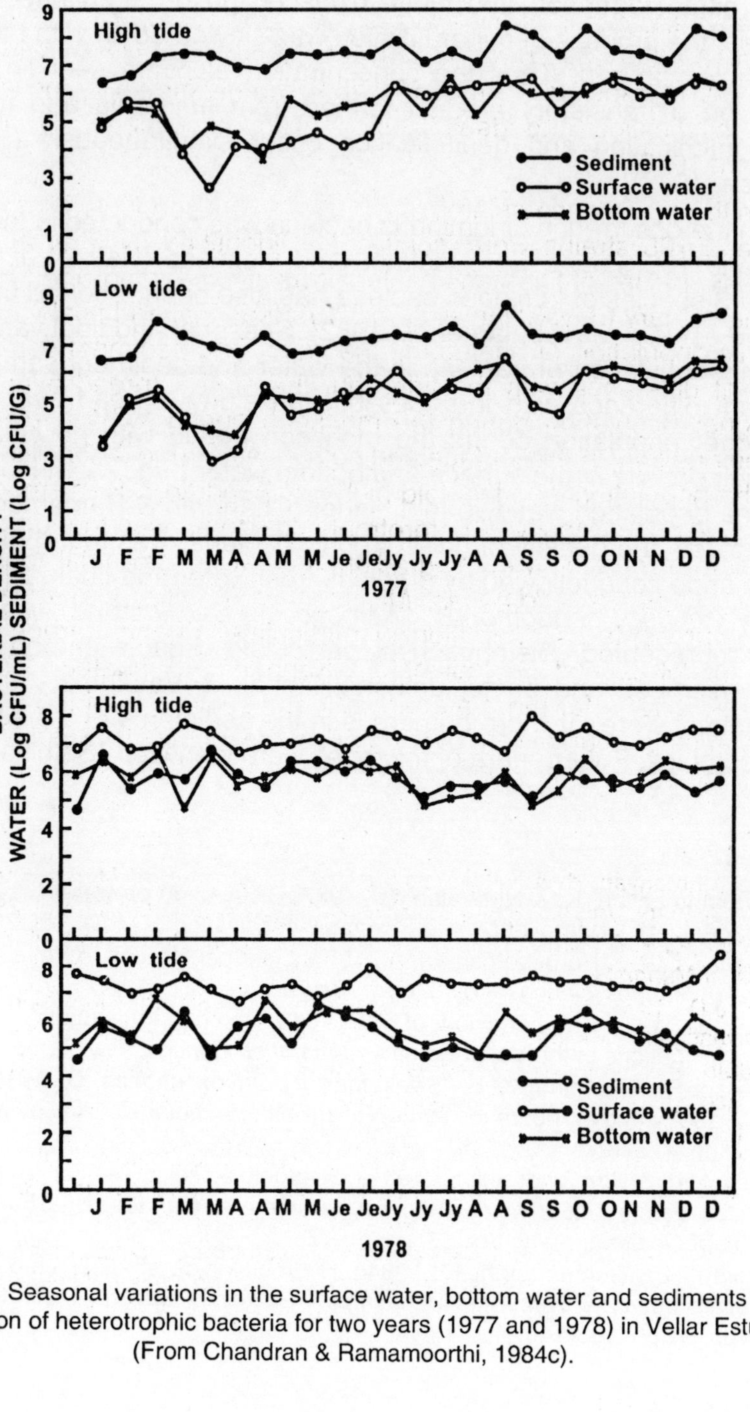

Fig. 7.24 Seasonal variations in the surface water, bottom water and sediments of the population of heterotrophic bacteria for two years (1977 and 1978) in Vellar Estuary (From Chandran & Ramamoorthi, 1984c).

production, nitrite formation and nitrite oxidation go on simultaneously. At low temperatures, the process of mineralization was slowed down with the accumulation of organic nitrogen. Thus the concentration of nitrite seen in the system appears to be a transistory product formed from ammonia and nitrite as the process of nitrification and denitrification occur simultaneously (Rajendran & Venugopalan, 1977).

A survey on the occurrence of luminous bacteria was conducted in the estuary for 4 months and 105 strains were isolated and identified (Nair *et al.,* 1979). The presence of 3 species of luminous bacteria has also been reported from the sediments of the estuary (Jayabalan *et al.,* 1982). Seasonal and tidal variations in the heterotrophic population of bacteria in the water and sediment samples showed no significant difference with the tides but the study, spread over for 2 years, showed higher population during the monsoon period with no clear difference between their density in the surface and bottom water (Fig. 7.24). However, in the sediment the population was two fold higher (Chandran & Ramamoorthi, 1984c). In another study, the density of heterotrophic bacteria was found to be the highest in the marine zone followed by gradient, freshwater and tidal zones. Five genera namely, *Vibrio, Pseudomonas, Micrococcus, Bacillus* and *Alcaligenes* were commonly represented. Distribution of particulate organic carbon followed the density of microbes and phytoplankton (Kannan & Vasantha, 1986). Copper-tolerant bacteria were far more numerous in the sediments of the estuary than in the water samples. Four genera of microbes were identified (Sathiyamurthy *et al.*, 1992).

References

1. Balasubrahmanyan, K. & Natarajan, R., 1987. Distribution of *Meretrix casta* (Chemniiz) in Vellar estuary. *Journal of Marine Biological Association of India*, Vol. 29, pp. 144-147.
2. Bhatnagar, G.P. & Purushothaman, A., 1974. Light penetration in Vellar Estuary. *Indian Journal of Marine Sciences*, Vol. 3, pp. 178-179.
3. Burton, J.D., 1970. The behaviour of dissolved silicon during estuarine mixing II, Preliminary investigations in the Vellar Estuary. *Journal du Conceil.* Vol. 33, pp. 141-148.
4. Chandran, R., Thangaraj, G.S., Sivakumar, V., Srikrishnadhas, B. & Ramamoorthi, K., 1982. Ecology of macrobenthos in the Vellar Estuary. *Indian Journal of Marine Sciences*, Vol. 11, pp. 122-127.
5. Chandran, R. & Ramamoorthi, K., 1984a. Hydrobiological studies in the gradient zone of the Vellar Estuary: 1. Physico-chemical parameters. *Mahasagar – Bulletin of National Institute of Oceanography*, Vol. 17, pp. 69-77.
6. Chandran, R. & Ramamoorthi, K., 1984b. Hydrobiological studies in the gradient zone of the Vellar Estuary: 2. Nutrients. *Mahasagar – Bulletin of National Institute of Oceanography*, Vol. 17, pp. 133-140.

7. Chandran, R. & Ramamoorthi, K., 1984c. Hydrobiological studies in the gradient zone of the Vellar Estuary: 3. Heterotrophic bacteria. *Mahasagar – Bulletin of National Institute of Oceanography*, Vol. 17, pp. 197-201.
8. Chandran, R., 1985. Seasonal and tidal variation of phytoplankton in the gradient zone of the Vellar Estuary. *Mahasagar – Bulletin of National Institute of Oceanography*, Vol. 18, pp. 37-48.
9. Chandran, R., 1987. Hydrobiological studies in the gradient zone of the Vellar Estuary: 4. Benthic fauna. *Mahasagar – Bulletin of National Institute of Oceanography*, Vol. 20, pp. 1-13.
10. Devendran, K., Chandramohan, D. & Natarajan, R., 1975. Studies on marine Thiobacilli: 3. All India Symposium on Estuarine Biology. Cochin, India, Feb 1975. *Bulletin of Department of Marine Science, University of Cochin,* Vol. 7 pp. 91-102. Special issue: Contribution to Estuarine Biology, (ed.) C.V. Kurian.
11. Dyer, K.R. & Ramamoorthy, K., 1969. Salinity and water circulation in the Vellar Estuary. *Limnology and Oceanography*, Vol. 14, pp. 4-15.
12. Fernando, O.J. 1987. Studies on the intertidal fauna of the Vellar estuary. *Journal of Marine Biological Association of India*, Vol. 29, pp. 86-103.
13. Fernando, O.J., & Natarajan, R., 1987. Diurnal migration of estuarine intertidal meiofauna. *Mahasagar – Bulletin of National Institute of Oceanography*, Vol. 20, pp. 255-262.
14. Hameed, P.S. & Paulpandian, A.L., 1987. Feeding and digestive rhythms in intertidal bivalve mollusc, *Anadara rhombea* (Born) and *Crassostrea madrasensis* (Preston). *Indian Journal of Marine Sciences,* Vol. 16, pp. 151-154.
15. Ilangovan, G., 1987. A comparative study on species diversity, distribution and ecology of the Dinophyceae from Vellar estuary and nearby Bay of Bengal. *Journal of Marine Biological Association of India*, Vol. 29, pp. 280-285.
16. Iyer, K.M. & Pillai, V.K., 1976. Microbiological investigations in Indian coastal waters and the Indian Ocean. *Journal of Marine Biological Association of India*, Vol. 18, pp. 266-271.
17. Jayabal, R. & Kalyani, M., 1986. Age and growth of the estuarine clam *Meretrix meretrix* (L) inhabiting the Vellar estuary. *Mahasagar – Bulletin of National Institute of Oceanography*, Vol. 19, pp. 141-146.
18. Jayabal, R. & Kalyani, M., 1989. Check-list of estuarine and marine bivalves of Porto Novo waters. *Mahasagar – Bulletin of National Institute of Oceanography*, Vol. 22, pp. 147-150.
19. Jayabal, R. & Kalyani, M., 1987. Reproductive cycle of the estuarine bivalve *Meretrix meretrix* (Linn) of the Vellar estuary. *Indian Journal of Fisheries*, Vol. 34, pp. 229-232.
20. Jayabal, R. & Subramaniam, P., 1988. Raft culture of green mussel, *Perna viridis* (L) in estuarine environment from the east coast of India. *Indian Journal of Fisheries*, Vol. 35, pp. 113-114.
21. Jayabal, R., 1994. Biochemical studies in the estuarine clam *Katelsia opima* from Vellar estuary. *Journal of Marine Biological Association of India*, Vol. 36, pp. 303-305.
22. Jayabalan, N., Chandran, R., Sivakumar, V. & Ramamoorthi, K., 1982. Occurrence of luminescent bacteria in sediments. *Current Science,* Vol. 51, pp. 710-711.
23. Joseph, P.S., 1975. Seasonal distribution of phytoplankton in the Vellar Estuary, east coast of India. *Indian Journal of Marine Sciences*, Vol. 4, pp. 198-200.

24. Joseph, P.S., 1982. Temporal variability of phytoplankters in Vellar Estuary. *Indian Journal of Marine Sciences*, Vol. 11, pp. 63-69.
25. Kalyanasundram, M. & Kasinathan, R., 1983. Age and growth in the estuarine clam, *Katelysia optima* (Gmelin) from the Vellar Estuary. *Indian Journal of Marine Sciences*, Vol. 12, pp. 247-248.
26. Kalyanasundaram, M. & Ramamoorthi, K., 1987. Larval development of the clam *Meretrix meretrix* (Linnaeus). *Mahasagar — Bulletin of National Institute of Oceanography*, Vol. 20, pp. 115-120.
27. Kannan, L. & Vasantha, K., 1986. Distribution of heterotrophic bacteria in Vellar Estuary, east coast of India. *Indian Journal of Marine Sciences*, Vol. 15, pp. 267-268.
28. Kannupandi, T. & Paulpandian, A.L., 1975. Studies on the blood and muscle proteins of crabs of Porto Novo: 3, All India Symposium on Estuarine Biology. Cochin, India, Feb 1975. *Bulletin of Department of Marine Science, University of Cochin*, Vol. 7, pp. 609-622. Special issue: Contributions to Estuarine Biology, (ed.) C.V. Kurian.
29. Karande, A.A., Udhayakumar, M. & Chavan, J.B., 1997. Development of planktonic larvae of unidentified barnacle species from Vellar Estuary (south east coast of India). *Indian Journal of Marine Sciences*, Vol. 26, pp. 297-301.
30. Kawabata, Z., Magendran, A., Palanichamy, S., Venugopalan, V.K. & Tatsukawa, R., 1993. Phytoplankton biomass and productivity of different size fractions in the Vellar estuarine system, southeast coast of India. *Indian Journal of Marine Sciences*, Vol. 22, pp. 294-296.
31. Khan, S.A. & Natarajan, R., 1977. Annual reproductive cycle of the hermit crab, *Clibanarius longitarsus* (De Haan) and factors influencing breeding. *Indian Journal of Marine Sciences*, Vol. 6, pp. 102-104.
32. Khan, S.A. & Natarajan, R., 1981. Reproductive strategy in hermit crabs of Vellar Estuary. *Indian Journal of Marine Sciences*, Vol. 10, pp. 70-73.
33. Khan, S.A., Thomas, M. & Natarajan, R., 1980. Principal component analysis in shell selection behaviour of the land hermit crab *Coenobita cavipes* Stimpson. *Indian Journal of Marine Sciences*, Vol. 9, pp. 293-294.
34. Krishnamurthy, S., Seshadri, R. & Ramamurthy, V.D., 1966. Role of microbes in the nutrition of some estuarine and marine bivalves. *Journal of Marine Biological Association of India*, Vol. 8, pp. 231-235.
35. Krishnamurthy, K., 1967. Seasonal variation in the plankton of Porto Novo waters (India). *Hydrobiologia*, Vol. 29, pp. 226-238.
36. Krishnamurthy, K. & Purushothaman, A., 1971. Diurnal variations in phytoplankton pigments in the Vellar Estuary. *Journal of Marine Biological Association of India*, Vol. 13, pp. 271-274.
37. Krishnamurthy, K. Sundararaj, V., 1973. A survey of environmental features in a section of the Vellar Coleroon estuarine system, south India. *Marine Biology*, Vol. 23, pp. 229-237.
38. Krishnan, T., & Kannupandi, T., 1988. Morphology of the larvae and first crab of an edible estuarine crab, *Thalamita danae* Stimpson, 1858 (Portinidae) from Indian waters. *Indian Journal of Fisheries*, Vol. 35, pp. 118-120.

39. Lyla, P.S., Khan, S.A. & Natarajan, R., 1988. Toxicity of heavy metal cadmium on the ontogeny of the estuarine hermit crab, *Clibanarius longitarsus* (De Haan). *Journal of Marine Biological Association of India*, Vol. 30, pp. 224-229.
40. McIntyre, A.D., 1968. The meiofauna and macrofauna of some tropical beaches. *Journal of Zoology*, London, Vol. 156, pp. 377-392.
41. Nair, G.B., Abraham, M. & Natarajan, R., 1979. Isolation and identification of luminous bacteria from Porto Novo estuarine environs. *Indian Journal of Marine Sciences*, Vol. 8, pp. 46-48.
42. Nair, P.S.R., 1991. Occurrence of bryozoa in Vellar Estuarine Region, South East Coast of India. *Indian Journal of Marine Sciences*, Vol. 20, pp. 277-279.
43. Natarajan, P., Devadoss, P. & Muniyandi, K., 1979. Fisheries of Vellar estuary, Porto Novo. *Indian Journal of Fisheries*, Vol. 26, pp. 201-206.
44. Pandian, A. P. & Venugopalan, V.K., 1975. Studies on foam. *Journal of Marine Biological Association of India*, Vol. 17, pp. 175-180.
45. Perumal, P. & Subramanian, P., 1985. Effects of salinity and copper on larval development in pistol prawn, *Alpheus malabaricus malabaricus* Fabricius. *Indian Journal of Marine Sciences*, Vol. 14, pp. 35-37.
46. Purushothaman, A. & Venugopalan, V.K., 1972. Distribution of dissolved silicon in the Vellar Estuary. *Indian Journal of Marine Sciences*, Vol. 1, pp. 103-105.
47. Purushothaman, A., Chandramohan, D. & Natarajan, R., 1975. Studies on certain aspects of marine silicate dissolving bacteria: 3. All India Symposium on Estuarine Biology, Cochin, India, Feb 1975. *Bulletin of Department of Marine Science, University of Cochin,* Vol. 7, pp. 57-67. Special issue: Contribution to Estuarine Biology, (ed.) C.V. Kurian.
48. Qasim, S.Z., 1970. Some characteristics of *Trichodesmium* bloom in the Laccadives. *Deep-Sea Reserach,* Vol. 17, pp. 655-660.
49. Qasim, S. Z., 1972. Some observations on *Trichodesmium* blooms. In: *Taxonomy and Biology of blue-green algae.* pp. 433-438, (ed.) T.V. Desikachary, University of Madras.
50. Qasim, S.Z., 1979. Occurrence of *Trichodesmium* phenomenon in the Strait of Malacca. *Mahasagar — Bulletin of National Institute of Oceanography,* Vol. 12, pp. 191-193.
51. Qasim, S.Z., 1999. *The Indian Ocean: Images and Realities.*. Oxford and IBH Publishing House Co. Pvt. Ltd. New Delhi, 340 pp.
52. Rajendran, A. & Venugopalan, V.K., 1973. Distribution of dissolved, particulate and mud phosphorus in Vellar estuary. *Indian Journal of Marine Sciences*, Vol. 2, pp. 13-18.
53. Rajendran, A. & Venugopalan, V.K., 1977. Microbiology of nutrient regeneration. Part 3. Experimental studies on marine nitrification. *Indian Journal of Marine Sciences*, Vol. 6, pp. 10-14.
54. Rajendran, A. & Venugopalan, V.K., 1988. Toxicity of organochlorine pesticides to zooplankton of Vellar Estuary. *Indian Journal of Marine Sciences*, Vol. 17, pp. 168-169.
55. Ramachandran, S. & Venugopalan, V.K., 1987. Bluegreen algae from Vellar estuarine environment. In: *Proceedings of National Seminar on Estuarine Environment,* (ed.) N. B. Nair, pp. 285-295. State Committee on Science, Technology and Environment, Government of Kerala, Trivandrum.

56. Ramadhas, V., Rajendran, A. & Venugopalan, V.K., 1972. Distribution of iron in Vellar Estuary. *Journal of Annamalai University of Science*, Vol. 30, pp. 179-186.
57. Ramadhas, V., Subramanian, B.R. & Venugopalan, V.K., 1976. The significance of nannoplankton in primary production in Porto Novo waters. *Mahasagar — Bulletin of National Institute of Oceanography,* Vol. 8, pp. 171-181.
58. Ramesh, A., Tanabe, S., Iwata, H., Tatsukawa, R., Subramanian, A. N., Mohan, D. & Venugopalan, V. K., 1990. Seasonal variation of persistent organochlorine insecticide residue in Vellar River waters in Tamilnadu, South India. *Environmenteal Pollution,* Vol. 67, pp. 289-304.
59. Ramamoorthi, K., 1971. Some aspects of mixing processes of the Vellar Estuary. *Journal of Marine Biological Association of India*, Vol. 13, pp. 261.
60. Ramamoorthi, K. & Venugopalan, V.K. 1976. Distribution of salinity and mixing patterns in the Vellar estuary. *Journal of Marine Biological Association of India*, Vol. 18, pp. 461-468.
61. Rangarajan, K., 1958. Diurnal tidal cycle in Vellar Estuary. *Journal of Zoological Society of India*, Vol. 10, pp. 54-67.
62. Sathiyamurthy, K., Purushothaman, A. & Ramaiyan, V., 1992. Heavy metal and drug resistant bacteria in the Vellar Estuary, southeast coast of India. *Mahasagar — Bulletin of National Institute of Oceanography,* Vol. 25, pp. 119-122.
63. Selvakumar, S., Ajmalkhan, S. & Natarajan, R., 1988. Laboratory reared larval stages of ocypodid crab, *Macropthalmus* (Venitus) *latreilli* (Desmarest).*Mahasagar — Bulletin of National Institute of Oceanography,* Vol. 21, pp. 161-172.
64. Seshaiya, R.V., 1959. Some aspects of estuarine hydrology and biology. *Current Science,* Vol. 28, p. 54.
65. Shanmugam, A., Rajamanickam, S. & Kannupandi, T., 1995. Cage culture of *Penaeus indicus* in Vellar estuary. *Journal of Marine Biological Association of India*, Vol. 37, pp. 166-170.
66. Sripathi, K., Khan, S. A. & Natarajan, R., 1977. Shell selection by the land hermit crab *Coenobita cavipes* Slimpson. *Indian Journal of Marine Sciences*, Vol. 6, pp. 163-165.
67. Somasekar, M., Sriraman, K. & Kasinathan, R., 1982. Age, growth and length-weight relationship in the backwater oyster, *Crassostrea madrasensis* (Preston). *Indian Journal of Marine Sciences*, Vol. 11, pp. 190-192.
68. Srikrishnadhas, B., Ramamoorthi, K. & Balasubrahmanyan, K., 1987. Polychaetes of Porto Novo waters. *Journal of Marine Biological Association of India*, Vol. 29, pp. 134-139.
69. Srikrishnadhas, B., Sundararaj, V. & Ramamoorthi, K., 1993. Zooplankton of Porto Novo coastal zone with special reference to invertebrate larvae: Symposium on Tropical Marine Living Resources, Cochin, India, 12-16 Jan 1988. *Journal of Marine Biological Association of India*, Vol. 35, pp. 141-144.
70. Subramanian, B.R., Ramadhas, V. & Venugopalan, V.K., 1977. Nannoplankton production in Vellar estuary. *Current Science,* Vol. 46, pp. 212-215.
71. Subramanian, B.R. & Venugopalan, V.K., 1978. Diurnal variation in net phytoplankton and nannoplankton primary production and chlorophyll *a* in the Vellar estuary. *Indian Journal of Marine Sciences*, Vol. 7, pp. 191-193.

72. Subramanian, B.R. & Venugopalan, V.K., 1980. Diel variation in some organic constituents of particulate matter in the Vellar estuary. *Indian Journal of Marine Sciences*, Vol. 9, pp. 246-249.

73. Thangaraja, M., 1984. Laboratory reared fish eggs and larvae and subsequent stages from plankton of Vellar Estuary, Porto Novo: 2. The flatfish, *Cynoglossus puncticeps* (Richardson). *Mahasagar — Bulletin of National Institute of Oceanography,* Vol. 17, pp. 103-111.

74. Thangaraja, M., 1986. Report on two types of leptocephalus eel from Vellar estuary (Bay of Bengal). *Journal of Indian Fisheries Association*, Vol. 16-17, pp. 11-15.

75. Thangaraja, M., 1995. Certain ecological impacts on the distribution and abundance of fish eggs and larvae of Vellar estuary, Porto Novo (Bay of Bengal). *Journal of Marine Biological Association of India*, Vol. 37, pp. 56-73.

76. Venkataramanujam, K. & Ramamoorthi, K., 1994. Studies on the seasonal abundance of the fish eggs and larvae of Porto Novo waters. *Indian Journal of Fisheries*, Vol. 21, pp. 454-462.

77. Venugopalan, V.K., 1971. The particulate matter of the Vellar estuary. *Journal of Marine Biological Association of India*, Vol. 13, pp. 258.

78. Venugopalan, V.K. & Rajendran, A., 1975. Dissolved and particulate nitrogen in Vellar Estuary: 3. All India Symposium on Estuarine Biology. Cochin, India, Feb 1975. *Bulletin of Department of Marine Sciences, University of Cochin,* Vol. 7, pp. 885-897. Special issue: Contributions to Estuarine Biology, (ed.) C. V. Kurian.

79. Venugopalan, V. K. & Ramdhas, 1975. Distribution of dissolved, particulate and sedimentary iron in Vellar Estuary. *Bulletin Department of Marine Science, University of Cochin*, Vol. 7, pp. 106-108.

80. Venugopalan, V.K., Vijayalakshmi, G.S. & Rajendran, A., 1981. Nitrate-phosphate relationship in a tropical estuarine environment. *Indian Journal of Marine Sciences*, Vol. 10, pp. 379-381.

81. Vijaylakshmi, G.S. & Venugopalan, V.K., 1973. Diurnal variation in the physico-chemical and biological properties in Vellar estuary. *Indian Journal of Marine Sciences*, Vol. 2, pp. 19-22.

82. Wafar, M.V.M., 1974. Biochemical composition of the lamellibranches *Meretrix casta* (Chemnitz) and *Sanguinolaria diphos* (Gmelin). *Indian Journal of Fisheries*, Vol. 21, pp. 289-292.

Chapter 8

Cauvery (Kaveri)

The Cauvery Estuary of the east coast of India is formed by the Cauvery River and includes a part of the river basin which occupies an area of approximately 800 km^2 (Ramanathan *et al.,* 1988). The Cauvery River originates in Karnataka, travels about 800 km inland and at Grand Anicut, where a dam is located, it bifurcates into two large branches, the Cooleroon and Cauvery (Ramanathan *et al.,* 1993). Figure 8.1 shows the location of the estuary with its delta along Lat. 11°07′N and Long. 79°50′E. The upper reaches of the estuary start from Anicut and below it, the river flows almost in a flat plain with a gentle slope from west to east. The estuary occupies a land area that seems to have emerged from the sea forming a delta which drains into the Bay of Bengal. Geographically, the Cauvery Estuarine Delta lies between Pondicherry and Vedaraniyam. It consists of several distributaries of the Cauvery River (Fig. 8.1) with a shallow average depth of less than 1 m, minimum width of about 50 m and maximum width of about 1500 m. At Grand Anicut, the Cauvery River has an average discharge of 602 m^3/s flowing into the estuary. The estuarine delta is fringed with discontinuous patchy belts of mangrove forests (Rahaman, 1987).

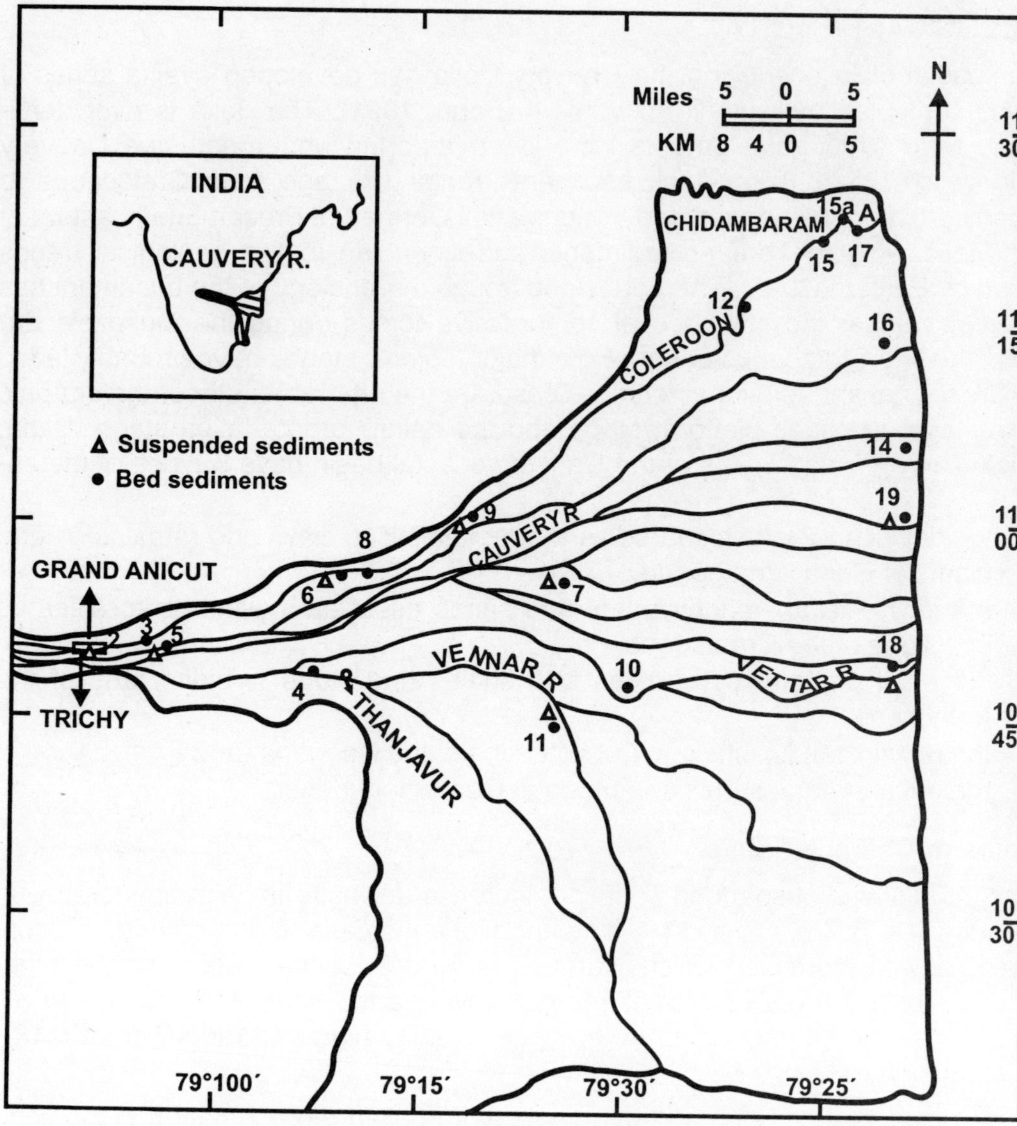

Fig. 8.1 Map showing Cauvery Estuarine System with its distributaries. At Grand Anicut it bifurcates into two and leads to several riverine branches. The positions of stations where suspended and bed sediments were collected are shown. The inset shows the location of Cauvery in the country (From Seralathan & Seetaramaswamy, 1979b).

GEOLOGICAL HISTORY

The coastal plain occupying the Cauvery Delta has developed over a series of basins controlled by tectonic movement (Babu, 1991). The delta is river dominated. Nine structural elements have been reported underneath the Cauvery Delta which has 6-8 km thick sediments ranging in age from Cretaceous to Recent. The floor has ridges and troughs and is formed of Precambrian basement with Mesozoic and Tertiary sediments corresponding to the geological trends shown by Eastern Ghats. The ridges and trough morphology of the basement has developed under the influence of compressive forces during the Mesozoic Era and in the late Cretaceous period. Four major tectonic stages have probably led to compressional and tensional forces. These are the rift-graben stage, the cratonic basin stage, the shelf platform stage and the deltaic progradation stage (Babu, 1991). Thus, the sediments of the Cauvery coastal basin have 5 types of materials.

(a) the fluvial and deltaic coarse sand with kaolinised clays and remains of land plants of Gondwana period,
(b) the fluvial-deltaic-marine muds and sands associated with rich fossilferous limestone of the Cretaceous,
(c) the shelf platform carbonates and shales and slope turbidite fans of the Paleocene,
(d) the deltaic sands, silts and trubidite fans of the Neogene, and
(e) the deltaic littoral sands and muds of Quaternary period.

Sediment Characteristics

Concentrations of suspended sediment increase downstream with an increase in chlorinity. Na, K, Zn, Ca and Hg concentrations increase as the chloride content increases with the mixing of seawater. Dissolved Si concentration, on the other hand, decreases from the upper reaches towards the sea (Ramanathan *et al.*, 1988). The level of phosphate in the water is fairly high and ranges from 0.12 - 0.82 mg/l.

Palynological analysis of mangrove vegetation (pollen representation in the sediments) was made by taking core samples from two sites in the Cauvery Delta (Muthupet – southern part and, Pichavaram – northen part). Two cores, 1.50 m and 6 m deep, were taken at Muthupet whereas at Pichavaram, the two cores taken were 3.90 m and 6.90 m long. From such an analysis it was estimated that mangrove vegetation in the Cauvery Delta is about 2000 years old (Tissot, 1987). Four periods of mangrove vegetation corresponding to the sedimentation process of the estuary could be recognised at Muthupet while at Pichavaram only three periods could be identified. In the two older periods, the evolution of mangrove vegetation at both the sites is similar but in the recent periods because of human activities of selective wood cutting and grazing in the mangrove forest, pollen representation is very disturbed.

Size analysis of the bed sediments shows a decrease in the size of particles from the upper reaches to the lower reaches indicating a decrease in river discharge in the estuarine part. Coarse sand dominates the upper reaches followed by fine and silt in the lower reaches.

X-ray diffraction of the < μm fraction of the sediment samples showed that smectite forms the dominant clay mineral. The other clay minerals in the order of decreasing relative abundance are kaolinite, illite and chlorite. Smectite content decreases downstream whereas the percentages of the other 3 clay minerals increase. Clay minerals seem to be detrital in origin (Seralathan & Seetaramaswamy, 1982 a & b). The mean size of the sediment varies from 4.7 to 8.3 phi (mean; fine-silt) with moderate to poor sorting textural characteristics (Ramanathan & Subramanian, 1998).

Phosphorus in the sediments showed lowest concentrations in the freshwater side of the river channel (0.152%) and goes on increasing with the marine influence reaching 0.194% close to the mouth (Seralathan & Seetaramaswamy, 1979a). High concentration towards the marine side of the environment is because of cumulative effect of detrital phosphate and high organic productivity. In general, the phosphorus content shows a positive relationship with organic matter and total iron content (Fig. 8.2). Clay fractions of the marine sediments have the highest organic matter (av. 3.51%) and the river clay has the lowest (av. 1.44%). Organic matter in the bulk sediments generally follows the distribution pattern of the sediments, finer the texture greater the organic matter (range in clay fraction 0.7 - 5.97%). Mangrove sediments and situations of planktonic bloom favour the richness of organic matter. The average organic matter of clay fraction in the sediments of Cauvery Delta has been found to be the highest as compared to other deltas of the east coast (Seralathan & Seetaramaswamy, 1979 b).

Geochemistry

Studies on the concentration of various elements such as Mn, Ti and $CaCO_3$, some alkali (Na, K, Li) and alkaline earth (Ca, Mg, Sr) showed a general increase of Mn, Ti, $CaCO_3$, Na, K, Li, Mg and Sr. Ca and Sr contents, on the other hand, decreased steadily downstream and similar was the case with Mn and Ti while

$CaCO_3$ increased seaward. In the deltaic sediments, geology of the rocks seems to influence the concentrations of Mn, Ti and Ca, while the clay minerals seem to control the distribution of Na, K, Li, Mg and Sr (Seralathan, 1987).

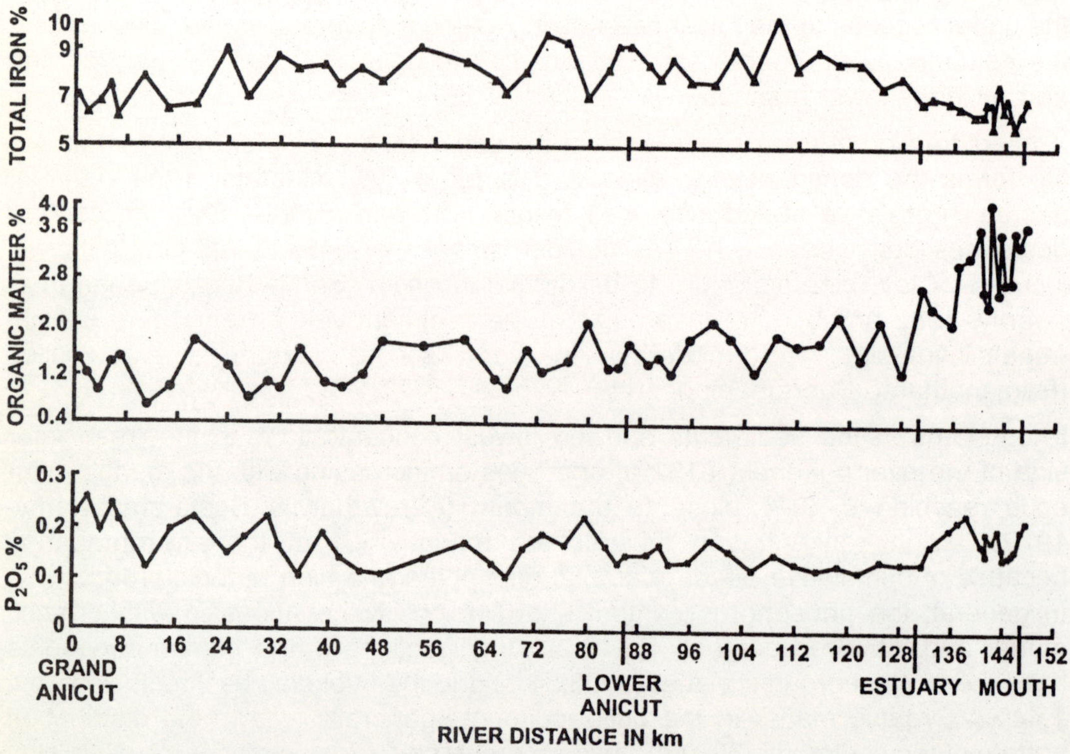

Fig. 8.2 Variations of phosphorus, organic matter and total iron downstream from Grand Anicut up to the outfall in Cauvery River and Estuary (From Seralathan & Seetaramaswamy, 1979b).

Further investigations on trace elements such as Cu, Co, Ni, Zn, Pb, Ga, V and Cr indicated that concentrations of these elements increase downstream but at the mouth of the estuary Cu, Co, Zn and Pb concentrations decrease considerably. Figure 8.3 shows the concentration variation of 10 trace elements with distance downstream. The reduction in the amounts of 4 trace elements may be because of the adsorption of these minerals in the clay coming from freshwater into the saline environment. Fe and Mn oxides show somewhat inverse relationship downstream (Seralathan, 1986 & 1987). The concentrations of Fe, Zn, Cu, Co and Hg are higher in the suspended sediments than in the bed sediments due to

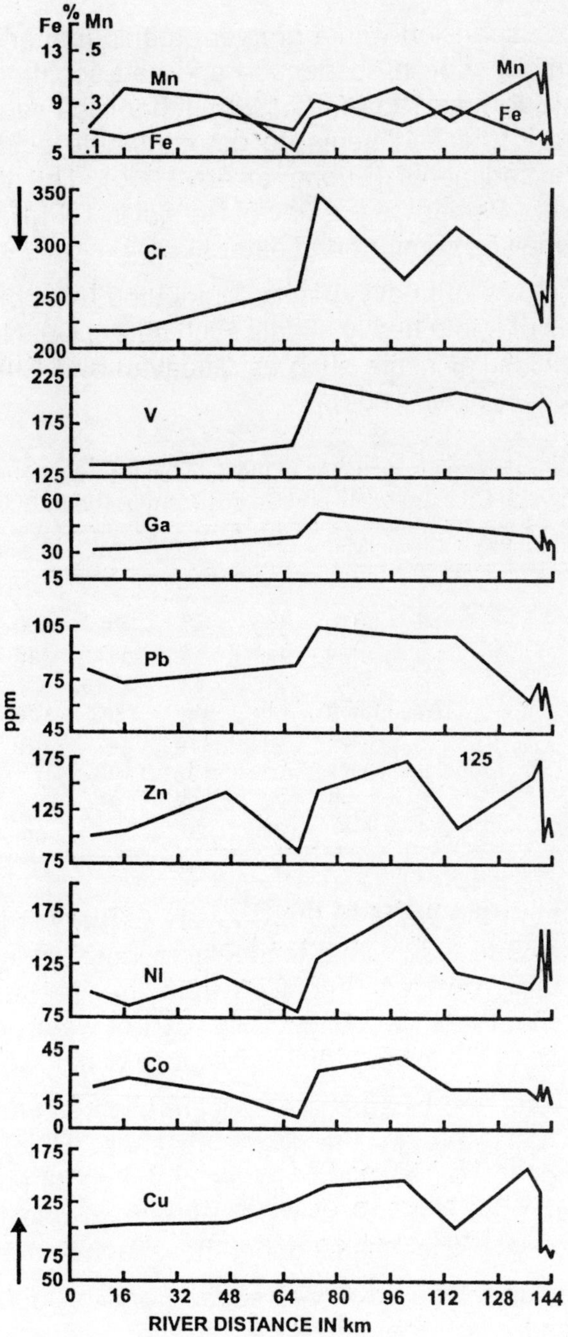

Fig. 8.3 Variations of trace metals downstream in Cauvery River (From Seralathan, 1987).

finer particle size in suspension with a greater organic matter in them. The average values of organic matter in suspended and bed sediments are 1.31% and 0.05% respectively (Subramanian *et al.,* 1989). It has also suggested that detrital components present in the sediments do not contribute significant amounts of heavy metals to the sediments (Subramanian, 1980). The total sediment load contributed by Cauvery Estuary to the Bay of Bengal is 1.4 MT/y (Subramanian *et al.,* 1987) which is small as compared to other rivers.

Table 8.1 gives the fluxes of heavy metals contributed by some rivers to the Bay of Bengal. The fluxes of some heavy metals such as Zn, Cu, Ni and Cr to the Bay of Bengal by the peninsular rivers such as Godavari and Krishna appear to be significant (Subramanian *et al.,* 1989).

Table 8.1— Heavy metals in various estuaries of India and in the sediments of Bay of Bengal. Fe in %, all others except Hg and Cd in μg/g (Hg and Cd in 10^{-3} μg/g) (From Subramanian *et al.,* 1989)

Source of sediments (reference)	Fe	Mn	Ni	Cd	Zn	Cr	Pb	Cu	Hg
Cauvery Estuary									
Bed	3.4	1310	379	33	75	229	38	1850	118
Suspended	4.0	1968	379	55	347	246	38	3410	165
Ganges Estuary	4.2	732	49	44	151	98	32	–	1400
Krishna Estuary	10.0	6978	149	69	1482	174	4 (4)	–	–
Godavari Estuary	7.6	1294	91	119	–	128	5 (4)	–	–
Narmada Estuary	8.9	1077	81	136	140	–	–	–	–
Tapti Estuary	7.6	1125	70	128	125	–	–	–	–
Bay of Bengal sediments	3.9	529	64	26		84	–	–	2000

Chemical composition of the water of the Cauvery Estuary is given in Table 8.2. The *p*H varies from 7.56 to 8.30 with a tendency to increase inconsistently in the lower reaches indicating no clear transition from the freshwater-dominated to marine-dominated zone. Electrical conductivity (EC) of water, on the other hand, shows a clear increase in the lower reaches because of salt water dominance.

Among the major anions, the bicarbonate concentration, because of the influx of saltwater shows a decrease in the lower reaches. Chloride concentration increases from 76 mg/l to 10,000 mg/l because of the dominance of salt water in the lower reaches and the process of mixing in the middle reaches. Sulphate concentration also shows higher values under the influence of seawater mixing.

Among the nutrients, dissolved silica decreases from the upper reaches to the lower reaches, because of the influence of river water upstream draining

Table 8.2— Chemical composition of the water of Cauvery Estuary. All values in μg/l except *p*H and conductivity (μS/cm.). TDS = Total dissolved solids. TSM = Total suspended matter (From Ramanathan *et al.*, 1993)

Location	*p*H	EC	HCO_3^-	Cl^-	H_4SiO_4	PO_4^{-3}	F^-	SO_4^{2-}	K^+	Na^+	Mg^{2+}	Ca^{2+}	TDS	TSM
1	7.65	518	191	76	18	0.25	0.10	15	2	34	12	28	375	2
2	8.30	818	140	140	95	0.82	1.01	30	21	123	27	53	520	97
3	8.00	852	213	176	25	0.33	0.44	21	35	85	21	52	629	10
4	7.93	926	201	490	18	0.22	0.11	15	3	91	11	52	881	28
5	7.73	996	205	550	24	0.18	0.12	24	4	80	3	62	953	18
6	7.91	940	202	352	27	0.28	0.39	26	20	128	26	80	863	8
7	7.56	915	174	752	18	0.17	0.13	26	6	118	11	44	1,150	25
8	7.63	1,630	166	900	22	0.18	0.12	25	8	200	12	36	1,369	7
9	7.64	1,981	183	100	23	0.19	0.08	144	12	310	52	22	1,716	45
10	8.00	1,614	164	1,123	31	0.02	0.62	60	15	97	35	30	1,605	90
11	8.20	1,582	226	1,123	31	0.12	0.89	20	9	281	29	49	1,756	52
12	8.10	1,614	195	1,101	27	0.06	1.16	74	14	300	39	70	1,821	121
13	8.10	1,730	200	1,120	30	0.02	0.62	60	15	747	35	30	2,239	90
14	8.30	1,725	166	1,127	31	0.02	0.82	135	23	290	81	140	1,994	150
15	8.30	1,805	320	1,185	33	0.22	0.87	125	14	630	37	46	2,391	76
16	7.96	12,990	217	1,748	16	0.16	0.39	256	97	1,080	39	152	3,381	26
17	8.10	11,800	204	2,740	14	0.18	0.65	440	106	1,330	49	209	5,092	26

(*Contd.*)

Table 8.2— (Contd.)

Location	*p*H	EC	HCO_3^-	Cl^-	H_4SiO_4	PO_4^{-3}	F^-	SO_4^{2-}	K^+	Na^+	Mg^{2+}	Ca^{2+}	TDS	TSM
18	7.83	19,230	198	3,800	24	0.18	0.11	133	112	2,978	27	116	7,385	12
19	8.00	17,800	182	3,960	8	0.33	0.75	700	140	3,830	46	284	9,150	82
20	7.93	18,103	142	4,635	12	0.13	0.17	647	302	3,910	61	250	9,377	107
21	8.10	18,600	156	4,950	5	0.36	0.61	790	358	4,179	47	261	10,747	29
22	7.93	26,642	155	6,785	11	0.31	0.40	702	203	4,488	56	301	12,701	128
22a	7.86	29,110	156	6,935	11	0.15	0.39	598	226	5,020	61	341	13,347	274
23	7.96	30,392	148	8,325	12	0.20	0.38	539	203	6,542	71	370	16,121	32
24	8.20	30,400	150	9,010	4	0.33	0.79	1,220	336	6,672	47	390	17,830	430
25	7.96	30,560	139	10,040	3	0.32	0.78	765	367	7,010	46	402	18,773	690

through crystalline rocks. In the lower reaches, a minimum value of 3 mg/l of dissolved silica has been recorded. The concentration of phosphate in the Cauvery Estuary is generally high. It shows an increasing tendency downstream with irregular variations (Table 8.1).

Major cations such as Na^+, K^+, Ca^{2+}, Mg^{2+} showed increase in their concentrations downstream indicating an interesting correlation with the chloride ions. Similar feature in the behaviour of cations has been recorded from other estuaries indicating their contribution from seawater (Ramanathan *et al.,* 1993).

Total dissolved solids (TDS) increase from about 0.4% in the upper estuary to 18.8% in the lower estuary (Table 8.2). Total suspended matter (TSM) largely follows an increase towards the lower reaches, although there is no regular pattern. Particulate organic carbon (POC) and particulate organic nitrogen (PON) show a decrease in the estuary towards the sea (Ramanathan *et al.,* 1996). ·Rate of deposition of phosphorus (P) in the Cauvery Estuary is less as compared to other major rivers of India and almost negligible in comparison to the accumulation rates in the Bay of Bengal. However, the levels of phosphorus in the sediments of Cauvery Estuary are higher than in many other Indian rivers. It seems that the bulk of P-rich sediments transported by the Cauvery River does not get deposited in the estuary because of their extreme fine size, and escapes into the Bay of Bengal thus contributing to the total phosphorus budget of the coastal waters (Subramanian *et al.,* 1993).

The river Cauvery flows through two states of India, namely Karnataka and Tamil Nadu. On sharing the water of this river, there has been a dispute between the two states since centuries. How old is this dispute can be ascertained from the historical record (*Thankkaga-p-parani* and *Rajarajan ula*). According to Prof. G. Venkataram, Head, Department of History, Madras University, as reported in the media, it goes back to the erstwhile presidencies of Mysore and Madras when the irrigation policies, from the year 1800 till about 1950, were being evolved and framed. When the two states questioned the sharing of water, tribunals were formed to settle the dispute. Earlier than 12th Century AD, Tamil Nadu enjoyed the right to the Cauvery water. Between 1146 AD and 1163 AD, when Rajaraja II was ruling the Chola Kingdom and King Narasimhan I was the ruler of Mysore, the latter put up artificial blockades on the bed of Cauvery and diverted the river flow with the result that the irrigation channels in the Chola Kingdom got dried up and there was a threat of famine. Rajaraja used force to get the blockades removed and brought the flow of the river back to Tamil Nadu. The king also constructed new channels called Pudukaverikal, and to meet the cost of this development, a new tax called "Kaverikarai Viniyokam" was levied.

A similar situation arose in the 17th century when Chikkadevaraya ruled Mysore, the Naik Queen Rani Mangammal of Madurai and the King Sakasi of Thanjavur ensured that the Cauvery flowed freely into Tamil Nadu, despite their differences. During the medieval period, state-support for irrigational development was made available, and significant works connected with irrigation were undertaken during this period. The early Chola ruler, Karikala Chola, constructed the Grand Anicut, a dam-like structure across the Cauvery in the first century AD to provide perennial irrigation from the river.

The account given above has been included to enlighten the readers that the dispute over sharing the water of the river Cauvery is not just political but there are historical records to suggest how important this river is for the economy and livelihood of millions of people in the states of Karnataka and Tamil Nadu.

References

1. Babu, P.V.L., 1991. Cauvery Delta – its past and present. *Memoirs of the Gelogical Society of India*, No. 22, pp. 91-101.
2. Rahaman, A.A., 1987. Ecosystem studies and management in coastal belt of Cauvery Delta at Muthupet, Tamil Nadu, *Proceedings on the National Seminar on Estuarine Management*, pp. 168-171, (ed.) N.B. Nair, State Committee on Science, Technology & Environment, Government of Kerala, Trivandrum.
3. Ramanathan, A.L., Subramanian, V. & Vaithyanathan, P., 1988. Chemical and sediment characteristics of the upper reaches of Cauvery Estuary, east coast of India. *Indian Journal of Marine Sciences*, Vol. 17, pp. 114-120.
4. Ramathan, A.L., Vaithyanathan, P., Subramanian, V. & Das, B.K., 1993. Geochemistry of the Cauvery Estuary, east coast of India. *Estuaries*, Vol. 16, pp. 459-474.
5. Ramanathan, A.L., Subramanian, V. & Das, B.K., 1996. Biogeochemical studies in the Cauvery Estuary, east coast of India. *Indian Journal of Marine Sciences*, Vol. 25, pp. 71-73.
6. Ramanathan, A.L., & Subramanian, V., 1998. Textural characteristic and mineralogy of the suspended sediments of the Cauvery River basin, India. *Journal of Geological Society of India*, Vol. 52, pp. 111-114.
7. Seralathan, P., 1986. Use of textural (cm) pattern for identification of depositional processes and environments of sediments of the Cauvery Delta. *Bulletin of the Department of Marine Sciences, University of Cochin*, Vol. 14, pp. 17-26.
8. Seralathan, P., 1987. Trace element geochemistry of modern deltaic sediments of the Cauvery River, east coast of India. *Indian Journal of Marine Sciences*, Vol. 16, pp. 235-239.
9. Seralathan, P., & Seetaramaswamy. A., 1979a. Phosphorus distribution in the modern deltaic sediments of the Cauvery River. *Indian Journal of Marine Sciences*, Vol. 8, pp. 130-136.
10. Seralathan, P., & Seetaramaswamy. A., 1979b. Organic matter in the modern deltaic sediments of the Cauvery River. *Indian Journal of Marine Sciences*, Vol. 8, pp. 137-140.

11. Seralathan, P., & Seetaramaswamy. A., 1982. Clay mineral in the modern deltaic sediments of the Cauvery River. *Indian Journal of Marine Sciences*, Vol. 11, pp. 167-169.
12. Subramanian, V., 1980. Mineralogical input of suspended matter by rivers of India. *Marine Geology*, Vol. 36, pp. 29-34.
13. Subramanian, V., Bikshan, G. & Ramesh, R., 1987. Environmental geology of peninsular river basins of India. *Journal of Geological Society of India*, Vol. 30, pp. 393-401.
14. Subramanian, V., Ramanathan, A.L., & Vaithyanathan, P., 1989. Distribution and fractionation of heavy metals in the Cauvery Estuary, India. *Marine Pollution Bulletin*, Vol. 20, pp. 286-290.
15. Subramanian, V., Ramanathan, A.L., & Ramesh, R, 1993. Nature of phosphorus distribution in the Cauvery Estuary. In: *Sustainable management of coastal ecosystems* (eds.) M.S. Swaminathan & R. Ramesh, M.S. Swaminathan Foundation, Madras, India, pp. 135-151.
16. Tissot, C., 1987. Recent evolution of mangrove vegetation in the Cauvery Delta: A palynological study. *Journal of Marine Biological Association of India*, Vol. 29, pp. 16-22.

SECTION – II

Climatic Features of the West Coast

Practically every aspect of life along the west coast of India gets dominated by the phenomenon of monsoon and this coast really gets the full fury of southwest (SW) monsoon. The cool season (winter) is followed by hot dry season from March to early June. The popular image of the monsoon can be fitted with the coastal regions of Maharashtra, Goa, Karnataka and Kerala.

During April-June, due to high temperature caused by sun's direct radiation, the vast plains of the northern subcontinent get intensely heated and the air above this region also gets hot and expands, causing a low pressure belt all over. At this time, the Arabian Sea is relatively cooler and the air above is also cool and highly moist. Because of the low pressure above the landmass, the sea winds are driven towards land. On reaching the land, the Himalayas form a barrier and prevent the winds from escaping. Blowing from the south, these get turned in a westerly direction because of the rotation of the earth known as the 'Coriolis Effect'. The winds thus blowing from the Arabian Sea reach the Himalayas and get condensed resulting in heavy rainfall. The increase in temperature leads to what is known as *sensible heat* which can be sensed and is driven towards the subcontinent in a southwesterly direction.

The west coast of India has some special feature: the coastline of Kerala is faced with a great extension of long bars with backwaters and lagoons and provides great contrast with the regions of northern Karnataka, Goa and Maharashtra which have a succession of inlets, faults and folds. These have rocks of different nature. Limestone, sandstone, basalt, granite, laterite, etc., constitute the edge of the sea, as a sea eating into them accentuates the details. Most parts of the coastline have complicated geological history. Relatively to the sea level, it has either submerged, emerged and parts of it submerged again, each time retaining some features left behind from its previous geological history.

By about the end of May and early June, Kerala gets the monsoon rain which attains full force by the middle of June. As can be seen from Figure 4 the west coast up to Goa and northern Maharashtra, get heavy rainfall ranging from 200 cm to more than 250 cm from June to September. Figure 5 (a), indicates the dates of the onset of monsoon. As can be seen from this figure, from 1st June to 15th June the monsoon spreads all along the west coast, except the Gujarat coast where the effect of monsoon is very little. The arid coastline of this region is aluvival and the Gulfs of Kachchh (Kutch) and Khambhat (Cambay) get little rain during June and July. The region is associated with east-west faulting. It is flat with marshland and sand dunes while the remaining region is lush green with dense vegetation and mangroves with extensive swamps and soft mud. The northern Gujarat (Kuchchh region) is fringed with small islands which are provided with fringing coral reefs, most of them spoilt and destroyed by human activities. The Kachchh region has extensive mangrove forests and is the second largest on the mainland of India, measuring about 954 km^2, next only to the Sunderbans which are in West Bengal.

Southwest monsoon ends in September along this coast and there is little effect of NE monsoon or the withdrawl of SW monsoon. In October and November, the rains in Kerala are accompanied with lightning and thunder and unlike the Bay of Bengal, the Arabian Sea is far less vulnerable to cyclones. During the 104 years, from 1877 to 1980, the data on cyclones/severe cyclones pertaining to three regions of the west coast — Kerala-Karnataka, Maharashtra and Gujarat-Saurashtra are as follows:-

Month		Regions		Total
	Kerala-Karnataka	Maharashtra	Gujarat-Saurashtra	
April	0/0	0/0	1/0	1/0
May	2/2	1/1	1/0	4/3
June	0/0	0/0	4/3	4/3
July	0/0	0/0	2/0	2/0
August	0/0	0/0	0/0	0/0
September	0/0	0/0	4/1	4/1
October	0/0	1/1	4/1	5/1
November	2/1	4/2	3/3	9/6
December	0/0	0/0	0/0	0/0
January	0/0	0/0	1/0	1/0

Figures after the slash denote severe cyclones

As can be seen from the data given above, the Gujarat-Saurashtra region is most vulnerable along the west coast. The cyclone seasons for this area are April to July and September to January. Then comes Maharashtra where the cyclones have occurred in May and from October to November. The Kerala-Karanataka region including Goa is the least vulnerable and records show that only in the months of May and November cyclones have occurred in this region.

Taking the overall picture of both the coasts, one can conclude that the east coast is eight times more vulnerable to cyclones than the west coast.

Estuaries of the West Coast of India

Chapter 9

Ashtamudi

Located in between the Lat. 8° 53′-9° 02′ N and Long. 76° 31′-76° 41′ E in the southern part of Kerala State, and covering an area of 32 km^2, the Ashtamudi Estuary is the second largest estuary, after Cochin Backwaters along the west coast of India. On its northern region the Kallada River, originating in the Western Ghats, enters the estuary (Fig. 9.1) after traversing 120 km into the state. It has a catchment basin of 960 km^2 and $75 \times 10\ m^3$ of freshwater flows into the estuary. In addition to Kallada River, there are a number of smaller rivers flowing into the estuary. The estuary branches off into eight zones as the name implies (Ashta-eight; Mudi-zones in Malayalam). Ashtamudi forms the central portion of the large backwater system and constitutes an important fishing zone. The estuary opens into the Arabian Sea through a 200 m wide mouth which forms a permanent connection. It has an average depth of 2.14 m at Neendakra — the town in which the estuary has a fishing harbour and forms one of the biggest fish-landing centres of the southwest coast in the country (Nair *et al.,* 1983a). The estuary on the whole is shallow with an average depth ranging 2-3 m. Table 9.1 gives both minimum and maximum depths along with the average depths in all the 8 zones. Because of extensive siltation, a number of islands have appeared in the estuary (Fig. 9.1).

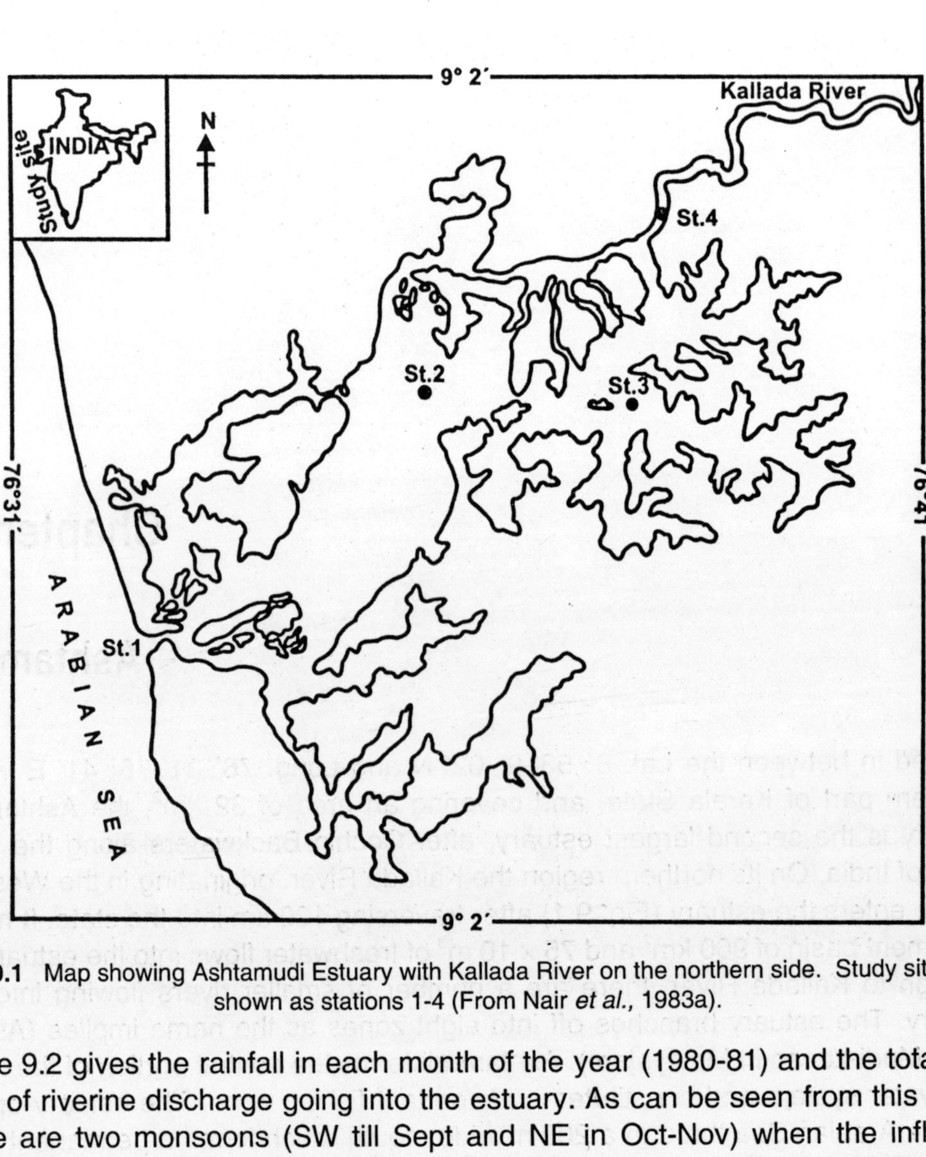

Fig. 9.1 Map showing Ashtamudi Estuary with Kallada River on the northern side. Study sites are shown as stations 1-4 (From Nair *et al.*, 1983a).

Table 9.2 gives the rainfall in each month of the year (1980-81) and the total volume of riverine discharge going into the estuary. As can be seen from this table, there are two monsoons (SW till Sept and NE in Oct-Nov) when the inflow is maximum and January is the only dry month when there is no freshwater flow into the estuary. The tides in the estuary are semidiurnal with a range of about 1 m, similar to what is experienced in Cochin Backwaters and saline water permeates practically throughout the estuary. Thus the sources of sedimentation in the estuary are enormous quantities of silt-laden freshwater inflow from the rivers and the stirred-up sediments coming into the estuary with the flood tides (Nair & Azis, 1987).

Table 9.1— Depth profile of different zones in Ashtamudi Estuary during March 1981 (From Nair & Azis, 1987)

Sl. No	Name of zone	Depth (cm) minimum	Depth (cm) maximum	Average
1	River zone	188.00	598.00	294.00
2	Confluence zone	75.00	634.00	255.00
3	Kanjirakode zone	193.00	330.00	271.30
4	Ashtamudi zone	183.00	314.00	244.50
5	Chavara zone	106.00	307.00	221.00
6	Thoppikadavu zone	219.00	372.00	302.83
7	Kandachira zone	155.00	320.00	233.20
8	Marine zone	129.00	360.00	214.33

Table 9.2— Monthly variations in rainfall at Kallada River basin and monthly river discharge into Ashtamudi Estuary during 1980-81 (From Nair & Azis, 1987)

Month		Rainfall (mm)	River discharge (Mm^3)
Feb. '80	Premonsoon	2.38	18.40
Mar. '80		53.39	25.20
Apr. '80		125.45	21.94
May. '80		101.98	25.42
Jun. '80	Monsoon	1025.18	138.87
Jul. '80		446.37	291.95
Aug. '80		281.31	204.92
Sept. '80		168.34	90.95
Oct. '80	Postmonsoon	264.02	146.84
Nov. '80		203.2	144.91
Dec. '80		97.45	73.69
Jan. '81		–	–

HYDROGRAPHY

Minimum temperature recorded in the estuary was 26˚C in June/July and maximum (35.5˚C) in April/May. Because of shallowness, there was not much difference in temperature between the surface and bottom. The range in pH was 7.2 (minimum) to 8.5 (maximum) and seasonal variations were not pronounced either at the surface or at the bottom. Monthly variations in salinity, on the other hand, were large reaching from 0.12 (surface) and 0.3‰ (bottom) in some parts of the estuary during the SW monsoon (July-August) to 35.05‰ in February/March.

Hardly any stratification was noticed in the water column and no salt wedge was present at any station studied. The range in dissolved oxygen was from 7.23 to 9.83 ml/l. Turbidity in the estuary, as can be expected, was high throughout the year and maximum during the two monsoons, particularly in regions nearer to the riverine outfalls. Maximum transparency of water, as indicated by Secchi Disk readings, was recorded during the premonsoon season (Nair *et al.,* 1983a; Nair & Azis, 1987).

NUTRIENTS

Figure 9.2 shows monthly variations in phosphate-phosphorus, nitrite-nitrogen, nitrate-nitrogen and silicate-silicon measured at fortnightly intervals at 4 locations. Apart from a brief increase in PO_4-P at stations 1 and 4 during February, March and April, the values declined till June and then showed an increase during the monsoon and postmonsoon months till November. This indicates that the increase in phosphorus is probably associated with rainfall and river runoff both in surface and bottom waters. Thus it seems that sediments form a source of phosphorus from where it is released to the surface. Enrichment of the estuary with nitrate-nitrogen can be clearly seen from Fig. 9.2; with the rainfall and land runoff, there is progressive increase from premonsoon to monsoon and postmonsoon seasons both at the surface and bottom. A similar seasonal cycle was noticed in nitrite-nitrogen (Fig. 9.2). Silicate-silicon recorded high values throughout the estuary. Monthly variations showed minimum during the premonsoon period and maximum during the monsoon months. A decline was recorded during the postmonsoon period at all the stations. Values at the surface were higher than at the bottom (Fig. 9.2). Sediments in the estuary varied from coarse sand to fine silt and clay. Much of the organic matter present in the estuary was associated with fine silt and clay and similar was the relationship with total phosphorus and total nitrogen (Nair *et al.,* 1983a; Nair & Azis, 1987; Shoba & Miranda, 1987).

PHYTOPLANKTON

In the estuary, phytoplankton community included 52 species belonging to 38 genera. Dominant groups were Cynophyceae (42.9%), Chlorophyceae (30.06%), Bacillariophyceae (25.56%), Dinophyceae (0.04%) and miscellaneous forms (0.82%). Two peaks—the first primary and short-lived was in February/March caused by the bloom of *Trichodesmium* sp. as was seen in the Vellar Estuary practically every year during the same period and the second was of longer

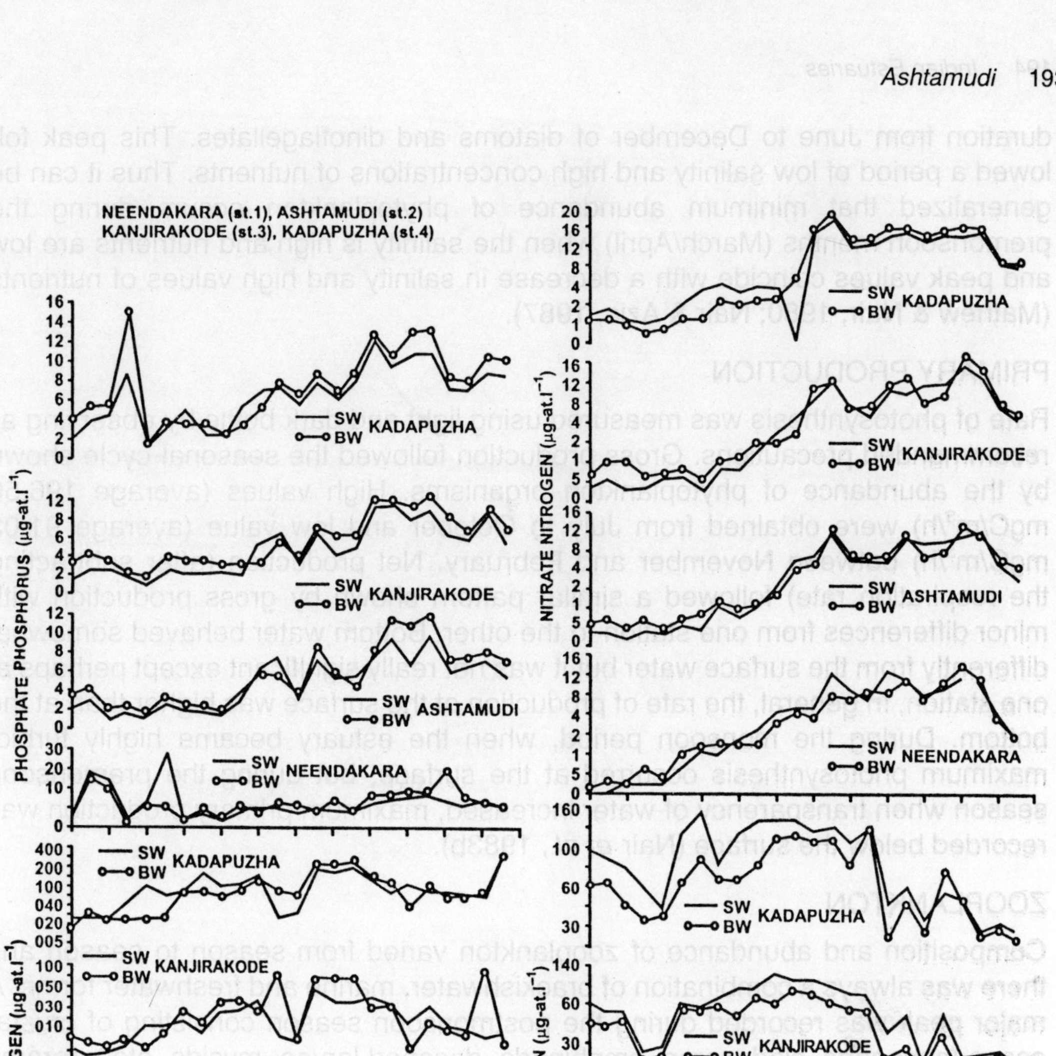

Fig. 9.2 Seasonal variations in phosphate-phosphorus, nitrate-nitrogen, nitrite-nitrogen and silicate-silicon at fortnightly intervals at 4 stations marked in Fig. 9.1 in Ashtamudi Estuary during 1980-81;SW- surface water; BW- bottom water (From Nair *et al.,* 1983a).

duration from June to December of diatoms and dinoflagellates. This peak followed a period of low salinity and high concentrations of nutrients. Thus it can be generalized that minimum abundance of phytoplankton occurs during the premonsoon months (March/April) when the salinity is high and nutrients are low and peak values coincide with a decrease in salinity and high values of nutrients (Mathew & Nair, 1980; Nair & Azis, 1987).

PRIMARY PRODUCTION

Rate of photosynthesis was measured using light and dark bottle by observing all recommended precautions. Gross production followed the seasonal cycle shown by the abundance of phytoplankton organisms. High values (average 196.56 $mgC/m^3/h$) were obtained from July to October and low value (average 91.03 $mgC/m^3/h$) between November and February. Net production (after subtracting the respiration rate) followed a similar pattern shown by gross production with minor differences from one station to the other. Bottom water behaved somewhat differently from the surface water but it was not really significant except perhaps at one station. In general, the rate of production at the surface was higher than at the bottom. During the monsoon period, when the estuary became highly turbid, maximum photosynthesis occurred at the surface, but during the premonsoon season when transparency of water increased, maximum primary production was recorded below the surface (Nair *et al.,* 1983b).

ZOOPLANKTON

Composition and abundance of zooplankton varied from season to season and there was always a combination of brackishwater, marine and freshwater forms. A major peak was recorded during the postmonsoon season consisting of crustaceans (copepods, cladoceran, amphipods, decapod larvae, mysids, etc.), foraminiferans, polychaetes hydromedusae, nematodes, chaetognaths, tunicates, fish eggs and larvae, etc. Hydromedusae and chaetognaths were present from March to early May and their distribution was restricted up to the brackishwater zone. Two species of chaetognaths (*Sagitta bipunctata* and *S. pulchra*) were frequently recorded and these were completely absent in the freshwater zone. Polychaetes were represented by larval forms belonging to the families Nereidae and Eunicidae and these formed a very small component of the total abundance of organisms.

Copepods were the most important component of the zooplankton community throughout the year with their peak abundance representing 13 genera and 11 families. Marine forms like *Paracalanus* sp. and *Acrocalanus* sp., *Undinula* sp., *Euchaeta* sp., *Centropages* sp., *Euterpina* sp., were very commom near the mouth. In the brackishwater zone, *Acartia* sp., *Pseudodiaptomus* sp., *Oithona* sp. were abundant while *Cyclops, Mesocyclops* and *Diaptomus* sp. were recorded nearer to the freshwater zone. Cladocerans were represented by *Evadne* sp., *Leydgia* sp. and *Diaphanosoma* sp.

Other crustaceans such as ostracods, mysids, cumaceans, amphipods, tanaidaceans and decapods were not very abundant but crustacean larvae formed a significant part of the zooplankton community practically throughtout the year (Divakaran, *et al.,* 1985; Nair & Azis, 1987). Figure 9.3 shows the biomass and numerical counts of the zooplankton organisms at one station in the estuary.

SEDIMENTS

A study of clay mineralogy of 21 samples of sediments taken from the estuary showed that the clay minerals were composed of kaolinite, montmorillonite and illite. The former two were the most abundant clay minerals. Kaolinite was dominant in the eastern part and montmorillonite in the western part. In the central part, both kaolinite and montmorillonite share in equal proportions, but the amount of kaolinite progressively decreases towards the central portion (Sajan & Damodaran, 1986).

In the sediments, organic carbon content varied from 0.06 to 4.95%. For the study of organic carbon, 52 samples were collected from 8 zones mentioned earlier. Organic carbon was lowest in the marine zone and highest in the riverine zone. In the other zones, the values were intermediate between the two, and in the two sheltered zones particularly, the values were high (Nair *et al.,* 1983a).

BENTHIC FAUNA

Both qualitatively and quantitatively the benthic fauna of the estuary was not rich as compared to other estuaries and backwater systems. It was composed of polychaetes, gastropods, bivalves, nemertines, gastrotrichs, sipunculids, isopods, amphipods, etc. Six to nine groups were represented at all the stations studied. Polychaetes and bivalves were present at all the stations. Among the 14 taxa of polychaetes, *Nereis, Diopatra* and *Prionospio, Gylcera, Polydora* and *Nephthys* species were the commonest. These were well-represented during the pre-and postmonsoon months and became fewer in numbers during the monsoon. *Polydora* sp., however, was in abundance during the monsoon. Molluscs (gastropods and bivalves) formed the second largest component of the benthic fauna. Bivalves

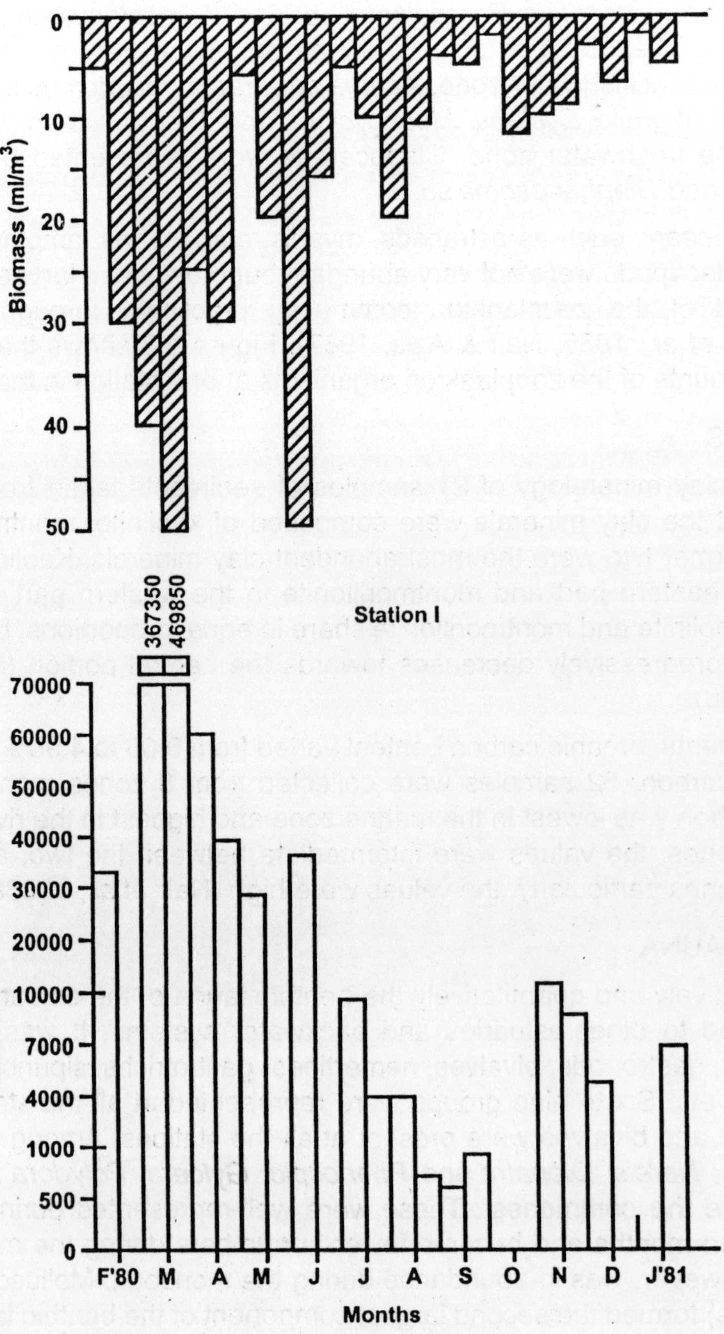

Fig. 9.3 Seasonal variations in numerical abundance and biomass of zooplankton at fortnightly intervals at station 1 in Ashtamudi Estuary during 1980-81 (From Nair *et al.*, 1985).

were represented by *Meretrix casta, Donax* sp., *Katelysia* sp., *Villorita* sp., *Musculista* sp. and *Modiolus* sp. Of these, several species are exploited commercially as there are extensive beds on several of the small islands located in the estuary (Divakaran *et al.,* 1981; Nair & Azis, 1987).

Meiofauna of the two backwaters close to the estuary (Edava-Nadayara and Paravur) were studied in relation to pollution caused by retting of coconut husk (Azis & Nair, 1983). Nematodes, polychaetes, harpacticoids and amphipods were present in both the biotopes. Foraminiferans were absent in one backwater but present in the other in small numbers. Nematode population ranged from 32.84 to 49.39% of the total meiofauna in the two backwaters. Ten species of namatodes could be identified. In the Edava-Nadayara backwaters, because of retting activity of coconut husk, H_2S formation occurs in the sediment with the total exclusion of oxygen. In such a polluted zone, 12 species of meiofauna were identified. In the paravur backwaters, which is free from retting and provides a healthier environment, 28 species of organisms were present (Azis & Nair, 1983).

FISHERY

There is sizeable fishery in the estuary which provides a source of livelihood to thousands of people living in the adjoining areas. Ninety seven species belonging to 39 families of fishes, prawns, crabs and clams, etc. have been identified. Most of the species are marine and estuarine forms and a few are also freshwater forms. Of the 39 families, 12 contribute to the fishery substantially. Mullets and the pearl spot are the most abundant forms having a good market value. Anchovies form a seasonal fishery from July to October. The estuary has rich prawn resources and the peak prawn fishery season lasts from August to October (Nair *et al.,* 1983b; Nair & Azis, 1987).

Fishing crafts used in the estuary are the traditional dug-out canoes and four types of fishing gears namely seine nets, cast nets, Chinese dipnets and drag nets are commonly used for fishing in the estuary. One of the interesting methods employed is "lure fishing", in which heaps of branches of trees are immersed in the water using a stone weight and allowed to stay underwater for 5 to 10 days. It serves as an artificial shelter for the fish to gather by offering protection. Finally, the lure is covered by a fishing net and the gathered fishes are caught. The other method used is 'scare-line fishing' in which a long rope with tender leaves of coconut palm are attached at intervals. When it is dragged in water, it creates a noise and the fishes swim away from it and are caught by a drag or cast net towed along with the scare-line. Lots of mullets and pearl spot are caught using this method. Besides the capture fishery, the estuary provides a good scope for fish and prawn culture (Nair *et al.,* 1983b).

BIOFOULING

In the estuary, the edible oyster, *Crassostrea madrasensis* is exploited both for food and lime industry. Intense biofouling occurs on both living and dead shells of this oyster throughout the year. Oysters, collected from the estuary, were examined and the organisms settled on the right valves of both living and dead oysters were counted and the intensity of fouling was calculated as fouled space. Major fouling organisms were barnacles, serpulids, bryozoan, and modiolids (mussels). Minor groups included sponges, hydroids, crustaceans, algae, etc. Barnacles were represented by one species (*Balanus amphitrite communis*), serpulid consisted of 3 species of tube worms, bryozoan by 4 species and mussels by 3 species. Miscellaneous fouling by groups included sea anemones and sponges. Fouling intensity varied from 73 to 179% on the valves of living oysters and 65 to 172% on dead valves. Barnacles were the most dominant fouling organisms and contributed 26% of infestation, serpulids 22%, bryozoan 15% modiolids 12% and miscellaneous about 25%.

Figure 9.4 shows the fouling intensity of both living and dead valves. Assemblage of fouling organisms has an adverse effect on the growth of oysters as it has to spend more energy than otherwise to open the valves for feeding. Most of the fouling organisms compete with the oysters themselves for food at the same trophic level. Pathogenic organisms associated with mud contaminate the flesh of the oysters (Nair *et al.,* 1984b).

POLLUTION

Several major factories namely the Punalar Paper Mills, the Lakshmi Starch Factory and the Alind and Ceramic Factory, located along the shores of this estuary, release effluents which form the major sources of pollution. Retting of coconut husk in some parts, sewage disposal from the adjoining human habitations, organic wastes from fish-landing centres and oil spillage from fishing boats operating in large numbers from Neendakara, contribute substantially to the pollution of this estuarine system. Depletion of oxygen often leading to anoxic conditions has been reported from different regions.

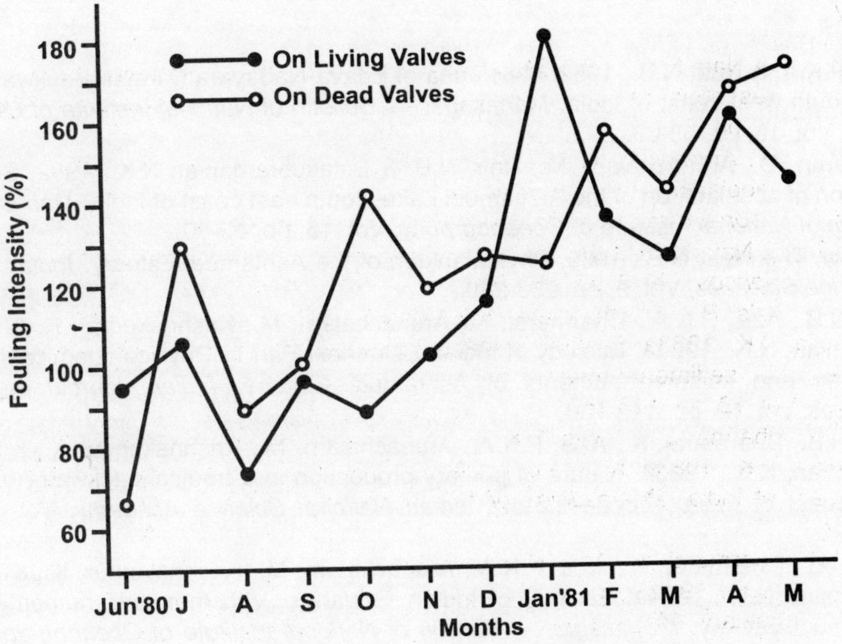

Fig. 9.4 Monthly variations in the intensity of biofouling on living and dead shells in Ashtamudi Estuary (From Nair *et al.*, 1984b).

HEAVY METALS IN SEDIMENTS

Concentration of mercury in the sediments ranged 0.01 to 0.037 µg/g, that of lead from 67 to 92 µg/g, iron from 1200 to 3900 µg/g, copper from 15 to 154 µg/g, nickel from 9 to 18 µg/g and zinc from 38.20 to 115.20 µg/g. The concentration of iron (annual mean value) was the highest followed by copper, zinc, lead, nickel and mercury.

The data on heavy metals in the sediments, indicate that although these are not very high, should be viewed with alarm because sediments are known to act as sink for most of the trace metals. They remain biologically active for a long time. These, along with the other pollutants, harm the benthic fauna, as has been demonstrated with meiofauna in regions where retting of coconut husk is being practised. The most important redeeming feature that has emerged from the study of this estuary is that this water body has displayed amazing degree of resistance against pollution by registering a reasonably high degree of flora and fauna (Nair & Azis, 1987).

References

1. Azis, P.K.A. & Nair, N.B., 1983. Meiofauna of Edava-Nadayara Paravur Backwater System, south west coast of India. *Mahasagar — Bulletin of National Institute of Oceanography*, Vol. 16, pp. 55-65.
2. Divakaran, O., Arunachalam, M., Nair, N.B. & Balasubramanian N.K., 1982. Seasonal variation of zooplankton of the Ashtamudi Lake, south east coast of India. *Mahasagar — Bulletin of National Institute of Oceanography*, Vol. 15, pp. 43-50.
3. Mathew, T. & Nair, N.B., 1980. Phytoplankton of the Ashtamudi Estuary. *Indian Journal of Marine Sciences*, Vol. 9, pp. 253-259.
4. Nair, N.B., Azis, P.K.A., Dharmaraj, K., Arunachalam, M., Krishnakumar, K. & Balasubramanian, N.K., 1983a. Ecology of Indian Estuaries. Part I - Physico-chemical features of water and sediment-nutrients of Ashtamudi Estuary. *Indian Journal of Marine Sciences*, Vol. 12, pp. 143-150.
5. Nair, N.B., Dharmaraj, K., Azis, P.K.A., Arunachalam, M., Krishnakumar, K. & Balasubramanian, N.K., 1983b. Nature of primary production in a tropical backwater of south-west coast of India. *Proceedings of Indian National Science Academy*, Vol. 49, pp. 581-597.
6. Nair, N.B., Dharmaraj, K., Azis, P.K.A., Arunachalam, M., Krishnakumar, K. & Balasubramanian, N.K., 1984a. Ecology of Indian Estuaries. VIII. Inorganic nutrients in the Ashtamudi Estuary. *Mahasagar — Bulletin of National Institute of Oceanography*, Vol. 17, pp. 19-32.
7. Nair N.B., Dharmaraj, K., Azis P.K.A., Arunachalam, M. & Krishnakumar, K., 1984b. Ecology of biofouling on *Crassostrea madrasensis* (Preston) (Mollusca: Bivalvia) in a tropical backwater. *Proceedings of Indian Academy of Sciences (Animal Science)*, Vol. 93, pp. 419-430.
8. Nair, N.B., Arunachalam, M., Azis, P.K.A., Krishnakumar, K. & Dharmaraj, K., 1985. Ecology of Indian estuaries: Distribution and seasonal variation of zooplankton in the Ashtamudi Estuary. *Proceedings of National Academy of Sciences India*, Vol. 55, pp. 271-289.
9. Nair, N.B. & Azis, P.K.A., 1987. Hydrobiology of Ashtamudi Estuary - a tropical backwater system in Kerala. *Proceedings of National Seminar on Estuarine Management* (ed.) N.B. Nair, National Committee on Science, Technology & Environment, Government of Kerala, Trivandrum, pp. 268-280.
10. Sajan, K. & Damodaran, K.T., 1986. Clay mineralogy of the sediments of the Ashtamudi Estuary, west coast of India. *Bulletin of the Department of Marine Science, University of Cochin,* Vol. 14, pp. 67-74.
11. Shoba, V. & Miranda, P.I., 1987. Nature of plankton production in Kadinamukulan Lake and Ashtarnudi Estuary of Kerala. *Proceedings National Seminar on Estuarine Management* (ed.) N.B. Nair, National Committee on Science, Technology & Environment, Government of Kerala, Trivandrum, pp. 307-317.

Chapter 10

Cochin Backwaters and Vembanad

The backwaters of Kerala are located along Lat. 9°30′-10°10 ′N and Long. 76°15′-76°25 ′E and extend from Azhikode in the north to Alleppy in the south. They form a complex system of shallow estuarine network spread over more than 325 km, running parallel to the coastline of Kerala. They occupy an area of about 260 km^2. Closely embraced by the mainland and several thickly populated islands, the backwaters also receive a complex system of canals, rainwater and sewage drains and perennial, semi-perennial and seasonal rivers. Four important rivers (Periyar, Pamba, Meenachil and Muvattupuzha) open into the backwaters discharging large quantities of freshwater during the monsoon season. The back-water system has two permanent openings to the Arabian sea — one at Cochin (renamed as Kochi) and the other at Azhikode. The Cochin connection is about 450 m wide which forms the main entrance to the Cochin Harbour. At the northern end of the backwater, the other connection at Azhikode is much smaller in width. (Fig. 10.1)

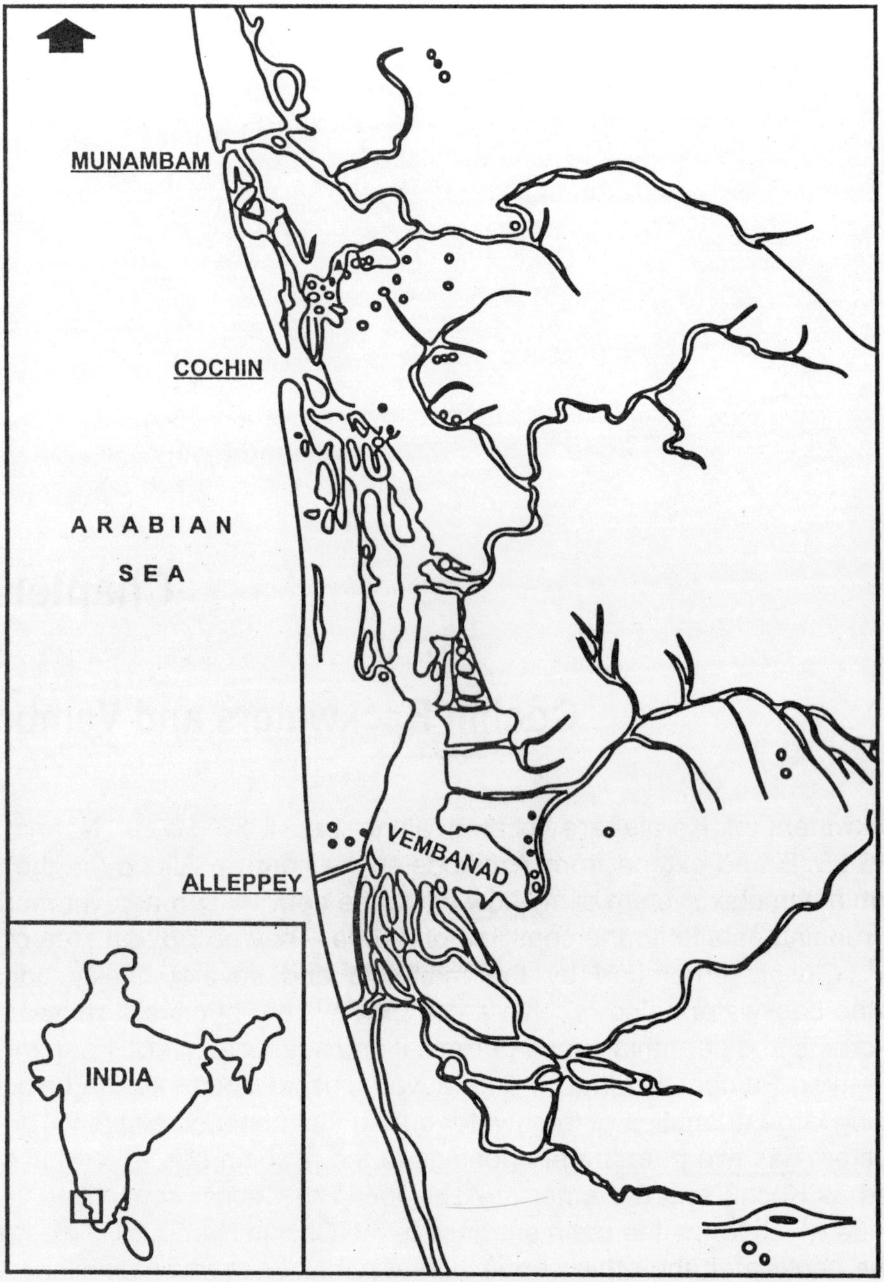

Fig. 10.1 Diagrammatic layout of Cochin Backwaters with their associated rivers ending in Vembanad Lake. The two connections with the Arabian Sea are also indicated. Inset shows the location of backwaters in the country.

Embracing the beautiful lush-green coastline, fringed with coconut palms and mangroves, the estuarine system around Cochin and neighbouring areas is known as Cochin Backwaters (Fig. 10.1). It is the largest water body of its kind on the west coast of India and one of the very well-studied estuarine systems, perhaps the most-intensively investigated area in the country during the last four decades. The entrance channel provides an access to all types of boats, country-crafts, ferries, etc., including ocean-going vessels and oil tankers to the harbour which is situated near the channel on one of the islands called the Willingdon Island (see inset in Fig. 10.2A). The harbour area, with its entrance is relatively deeper with depth ranging 5-15 m maintained by regular dredging. The rest of the backwaters are shallower (2-5 m deep).

The total amount of rainfall at Cochin is about 3200 mm, of which nearly 75% occurs during the period June to September. During July/August, 40-50 mm of rainfall can occur within a few hours. The onset of SW monsoon and its duration may, however, vary from year to year. Normally, it lasts from June to September with premonsoon showers beginning in May. In the estuary, salinity variations from place to place and from surface to bottom are very wide. The deeper areas (entrance channel and harbour) are marked with flushing of the estuary with flood and ebb tides having a maximum range of about 1 m. The other reaches of the estuary, which are shallower, get little or no tidal influence and have a markedly low salinity. Because of considerable influence of land, dense population and harbour, the Cochin Backwaters become intensely polluted.

The backwaters terminate at their southern end and spread out into a lake called the "Vembanad Lake". It is the largest water body on the west coast of India, located between Lat. 9°28′ and 10°10 ′N and Long. 76°13′ and 76°3 ′E. The lake is 115 km long, 500 m to 12 km wide and covers an area of 135 km^2. It has no other permanent connection with the sea except the main entrance to the Cochin Harbour noted above. Six rivers with their tributaries (Periyar, Pamba, Achancoil, Manimala, Meenachil and Moovattupuzha) flow into the lake. In addition, it receives freshwater from several canals and drains during the monsoon months. Thus, the inflow of freshwater into the Vembanad is considerable and varies from season to season. It also gets a regular flow of salt water through the tidal incursion which diminishes considerably towards the end of the lake. The Cochin Backwater system is believed to have attained its present configuration in the 4th century AD. It was primarily a marine environment with an alluvial bar boundary running parallel to the coast and interrupted at places by the Arabian Sea. In 1341 AD, a catastrophic cyclone occurred which made the river Periyar change its course resulting into the formation of a number of islands and separating a distinct

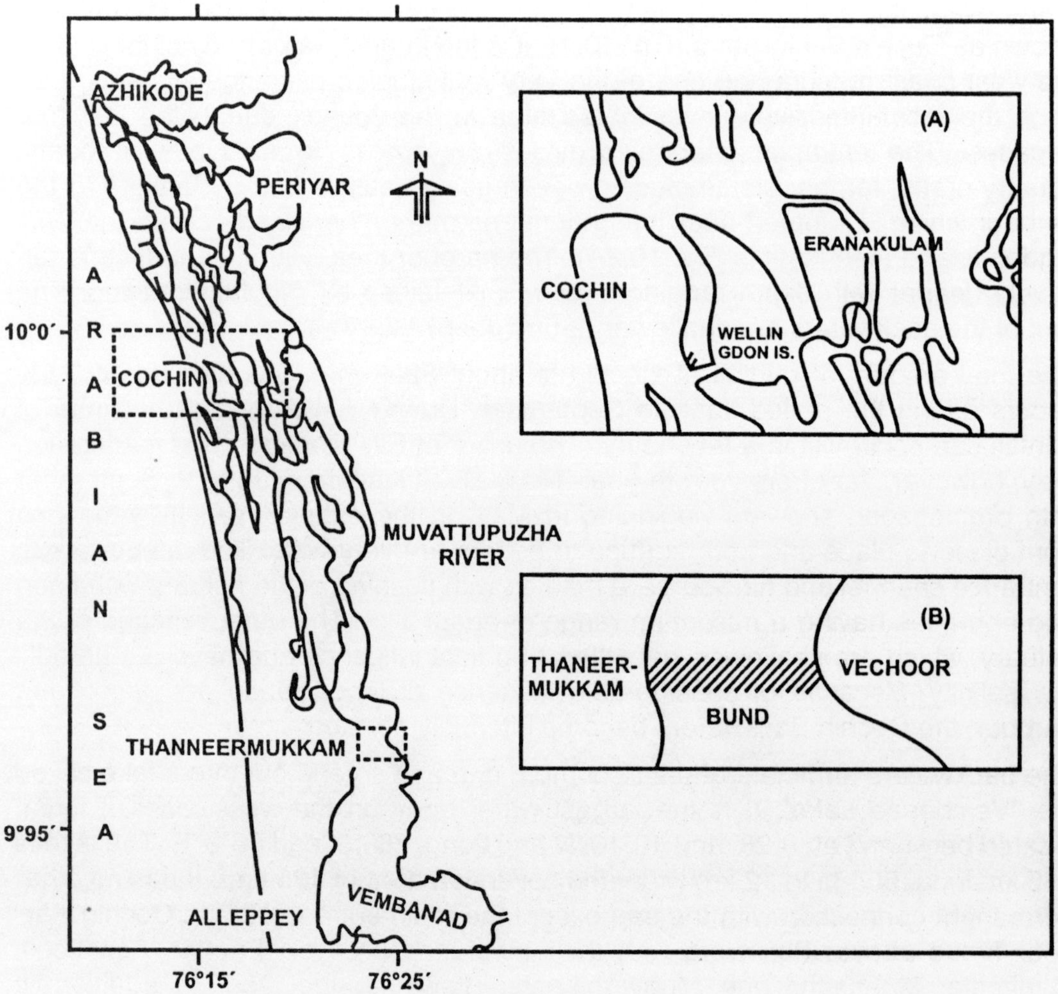

Fig. 10.2 Map of Cochin Backwaters from Azhikode to Alleppy. Inset (A) shows the backwater system at Cochin with its main connection with the sea. This area has been intensively studied for more than four decades. Inset (B) shows the site where Thanneermukkam Bund has been built (From Qasim & Madhupratap, 1979).

waterbody from the sea and yet maintaining its connection with the sea (Menon, 1913). Thus arose a brackish water system called the 'backwaters'. According to the definition of estuaries given by Pritchard (1967), the backwaters conform to 'bar-built estuary'.

DEVELOPMENT OF COCHIN PORT

The idea that Cochin can be developed into a major port on the west coast of India was conceived by the eminent British harbour engineer Sir Robert Bristow. It took shape into a project and work commenced in 1920 under the direct supervision of Sir Robert. The work involved removing the material at a position of the coastal belt to create a mouth and cutting an approach channel 120 m wide, 3300 m long and 10 m deep. The project in its first phase was completed in 1936 (Bristow, 1959). During this period, as a result of constant dredging, an island came into existence which was named as Willingdon Island (Fig. 10.1A). This man-made island and its surroundings are the present location of the Cochin Port. Its original reclaimed area was 365 ha. Subsequently, two more areas of about 142 ha each, were reclaimed and added as extensions to the Willingdon Island. Provision for annual dredging had to be made to remove the semisolid silt deposited in the approach channels, 1-1.5 m thick. During dredging, sharp changes in the nutrients are recorded when the sediments are stored up, but no deterioration in the water quality was found after the sediments get settled (Joseph *et al.,* 1998).

The opening of Cochin Port for shipping ushered in a new era in the life and economic prosperity of the state of Kerala and the people of Kerala have always remained grateful for that. The Cochin Port Trust celebrates the event annually in remembrance of the great humanitarian work that Bristow has accomplished for them.

MODIFICATIONS AND MAN-MADE CHANGES

The backwaters have played an important role in the socioeconomic and cultural history of Kerala. They provide an inland water transport system for carrying men and material practically throughout the coastal belt, as far as the waterways extend and astonishingly they can reach far off villages and small towns where no other transport system can. They provide rich fishing grounds and the total fish landings at Cochin constitute about 8% of the landings of the State. A series of majestic Chinese dipnets, picturesquely installed along the entrance of the harbour, form a delightful sight for any person entering the harbour by boat. They are operated practically throughout the year. Many of these nets are also fixed inland along the waterways.

The backwaters provide ideal breeding grounds for many fishes and shellfishes and for completing the life histories of several commercially important species, specially prawns. The tidal influence in the backwater reaches inside all over the system up to 60 km southwards where the range of the spring tide is about 20 cm. The configuration of the land is such that all the drains and rivers flow in one direction. The land bordering the area is low-lying, densely populated and highly fertile. Therefore, any interference with the environment is likely to make it sensitive to change.

Continuous reclamation of backwaters has been going on for the past 150 years and the land thus obtained is being used for human habitation, expansion of agriculture, aquaculture, harbour development and construction of engineering works. Thus, these environmental changes have led to an alarming decrease of the total water area by about 35%. Siltation caused by the river discharge and tidal influx has been decreasing the depth of water gradually with the result that the average depth of the backwater has come down from 6.7 m to 4.4 m during the course of 50 years at the rate of 0.2 cm/y. This has further accelerated the rate of reclamation as the cost of land in most of the towns of Kerala has become prohibitive.

Increased human settlement in Kerala from other parts of India has given acceleration to the growth of population from 11.0 millions in 1941 to 25.4 millions in 1981. Today Kerala supports 3.4% of India's population, the density of population being 654/km^2 as against the average of 221/km^2 for the country. The pressure on land in the narrow coastal belt, in and around Cochin, is acute and in this part, the population has reached 1500/km^2. The booming city of Cochin which is the biggest city on the west coast of India after Mumbai has a population of over 1 million. Nearly 70% of the chemical industries of the state are located in the vicinity of this city along the banks of the rivers Periyar and Muvatupuzha for the manufacture of fertilizers, chemicals, insecticides, rare earths, petroleum products, rubber, rayon, paper, alcohols, etc. An estimated 260 million m^3/day of effluents from these industries are released into the backwaters forming the major source of pollution. In addition, the backwaters receive organic wastes from domestic sewage, coconut husk rutting yards, fish processing plants, etc. The effluents from the industries are either discharged directly or only after partial treatment. Lack of appropriate technology for waste treatment, high cost involved for pollution control measures, lack of awareness or total disregard for the environment, are the main reasons for pollution in the backwaters which has escalated in the last decade. Salinity intrusion in the upper reaches of the river Periyar has negatively affected drinking water supply. To control further influx of seawater flow into the river, temporary bunds were constructed which have also restricted the flushing in the river leading to an increase in toxicity and drastic decrease in the *p*H of water to 3 and 4 resulting in massive mortality of fauna and flora of the backwaters. Rich fishing grounds have been seriously affected and the yields of prawns have come down from 500 kg to less than 250 kg in the case of *Penaeus indicus* and from 1500 kg to 400 kg for *Metapenaeus dobsoni* per season (Kumar, 1997; Balakrishnan & Devi, 1982).

DEVELOPMENT OF KUTTANAD

The Kuttanad District situated towards the south of the Vembanad Lake has been known for its high rice production in the state and it is called the rice-bowl of Kerala. The Government of Kerala in its efforts to increase rice production further, implemented the following two programmes for development in the Kuttanad region:

(a) Construction of a 340 m long spillway at Thottapally, 20 km south of Alleppey, to control flooding of rice fields.

(b) Construction of a dam across the backwaters at Thanneermukkam to cut off the Vembanad Lake with spillways from rest of the backwaters for the cultivation of rice. It is known as Thanneermukkam Bund (Fig. 10.2B).

It should be noted that more than 60% of Kuttanad region lies below the sea level making the paddy fields 0.5 to 2 m below the water level in the adjoining canals and rivers. The area remains submerged during the SW monsoon.

The construction of Thattapally spillway started in 1951 and it was completed in 1955. It was designed to control 64,000 m^3/s of floodwater out of 180,000 m^3/s discharged by the rivers into the deltaic region. Thus, only 30% of the total capacity could be handled. However, many factors in the design and construction of the spillway have been ignored. For example, the changes in the flow pattern during the variable rainfall during the monsoon months, the occurrence of high levels of water at the mouth of the spillway defying calculations and the formation of sand bar across the mouth are some of the factors which raise serious questions about the selection of the site of the spillway. If all these are to be corrected, the investment involved would be quite considerable.

The construction of Thanneermukkam barrage began in 1955, but after 18 years only 60% of the work was accomplished. In 1974, a crash programme to block the remaining 40% by sand, gravel, stakes, etc., was undertaken. The water regulators on either side of the barrage are supposed to remain closed from December to May (6 months) when the salinity of the water is high. They are opened when the salinity reaches zero to irrigate the paddy fields. However, the temporary bunds, separating the fields from the waterways, had to be raised and reinforced to carry out effective agricultural operations. With all these manipulations, the cost of production of rice including labour, fertilizer, pesticides increased sharply and the floodwater rich in nutrients and detritus, is being carried into the sea. The latter could hardly be utilised for rice cultivation as a manure. However, the cost of production of rice in the extra land created from the backwaters, after the manipulation of all what is needed becomes so high that it has now become necessary to evaluate whether the economic benefits really outweigh environmental loss of a natural ecosystem.

The Vembanad Lake area was known to be rich in its fishery particularly of the prawn *Macrobrachium* sp. and the pearl spot *Etroplus* sp. The construction of the Thanneermukkam bund across the backwaters as a barrier to the entry of saline water, has prevented the entry of prawns and fishes with the result that there is practically no fishery of these two species left in the Vembanad Lake.

THE AFRICAN PAYAL[1]

The weed *Salvinia* sp., commonly known as the African Payal, is believed to have come from Africa or south or central America and entered the backwaters probably by accident, perhaps through ship ballasts. Within a few years it has become a major menace to the backwaters by its prolific spreading. Prior to the construction of the barrage, salt water used to enter the Vembanad Lake after the monsoon, causing decay of *Salvinia*. At present this area remains freshwater dominated throughout the year resulting in choking of the paddy fields and waterways of Kuttanad with *Salvinia*. Flushing of the lake water with the incoming and outgoing tides has been stopped causing stagnation of water. During the monsoonal outlet of water, when the spillways remain open, enormous quantities of weeds are flushed into the rest of the backwater system. The accumulation of weeds has resulted in preventing light penetration into the water column thus affecting phytoplankton productivity. Choking the waterways with weeds has also affected the movement of boats in the canals of the backwaters.

---

[1] There was no trace of weed *Salvinia* sp. in 1964, when the present author began his studies on the ecology and productivity of Cochin Backwaters. No publication which appeared in the sixties and seventies on this estuarine system mentioned the presence of this weed anywhere. I left Kerala in January 1974 and in the early seventies the weed began to appear in small patches. No scientist took much notice of its existence, let alone investigating where did it come from. If it is left alone, it will become such a menace after a few years. I am not aware, whether a serious thought has been given from where and how it came to Kerala and what is its biological control in its native land which is nonexistent in Kerala. I am not sure if the popular name given to this weed is really correct.

About 1000 tonnes of pesticides are used in the Kuttanad area every year during paddy cultivation (KSSP, 1978). The accumulation of pesticides, because of the stagnation of water, has severely affected the water quality of the area causing problems in the supply of drinking water from the wells which get affected due to seepage and very often leading to health problems.

FISHERY OF VEMBANAD BEFORE MAN MADE CHANGES

According to the report of Kerala Sastra Sahitya Parishat (KSSP, 1978) — a very reliable voluntary agency and a non-governmental organisation (NGO) totally devoted to the cause of environmental protection, conservation of endangered ecosystems, unbiased and impartial in its approach of evaluation and fearless in reporting through the media — prawns alone worth about Rs. 50,000 (1979 price) used to be caught from the Vembanad Lake every day. After the introduction of the engineering works, there is practically no catch from the lake. Many other estuarine fishes, which used to enter the lake with the entry of seawater twice a day with the flood tides, have disappeared completely. The operation of stake nets within the lake or outside the bund has been practically stopped because there is no flow of water. Because of the accumulation of *Salvinia* and another weed *Eichornia* sp. — the two spread over the water surface like a thick carpet — any fishing operations including the use of cast nets have become impossible. The bund and the weeds have severely affected the benthic ecology of the backwaters (Qasim & Madhupratap, 1979).

Clam shell deposits in the seabed largely of *Villorita* sp. and *Meretrix* sp. were exploited and used by some factories such as the Travancore Cements Ltd. and Travancore Electrochemicals Ltd., for the manufacture of cement and chemicals and also for the extraction of lime by the lime manufacturers. These activities have stopped because of stagnation of water and weed accumulation at the bottom which are changing the nature of the substrata affecting clam shell recovery.

Earlier studies on the benthos of backwaters over a period of one decade (Desai & Kutty, 1967; Kurian, 1972; Ansari, 1977) have shown that considerable reduction in the population of bivalves, gastropodes, amphipods, etc., has occurred because of pollution and changing ecology of backwaters.

OTHER ENGINEERING WORKS

In 1975, a large area of the backwaters, near the mouth of the estuary has been used for the construction of a jetty for berthing of oil tankers. This has changed the pattern of water flow causing severe depletion of oyster beds and leading to appreciable reduction in the spatfall and settlement of oysters (Purushan, 1978).

As noted earlier, dredging is done annually to maintain a desired depth of water for shipping. Figure 10.3 shows the three navigational channels of the Cochin Harbour area. These include an approach channel and two inner channels — the Ernakulam Channel and the Mattanchery Channel. These are approximately

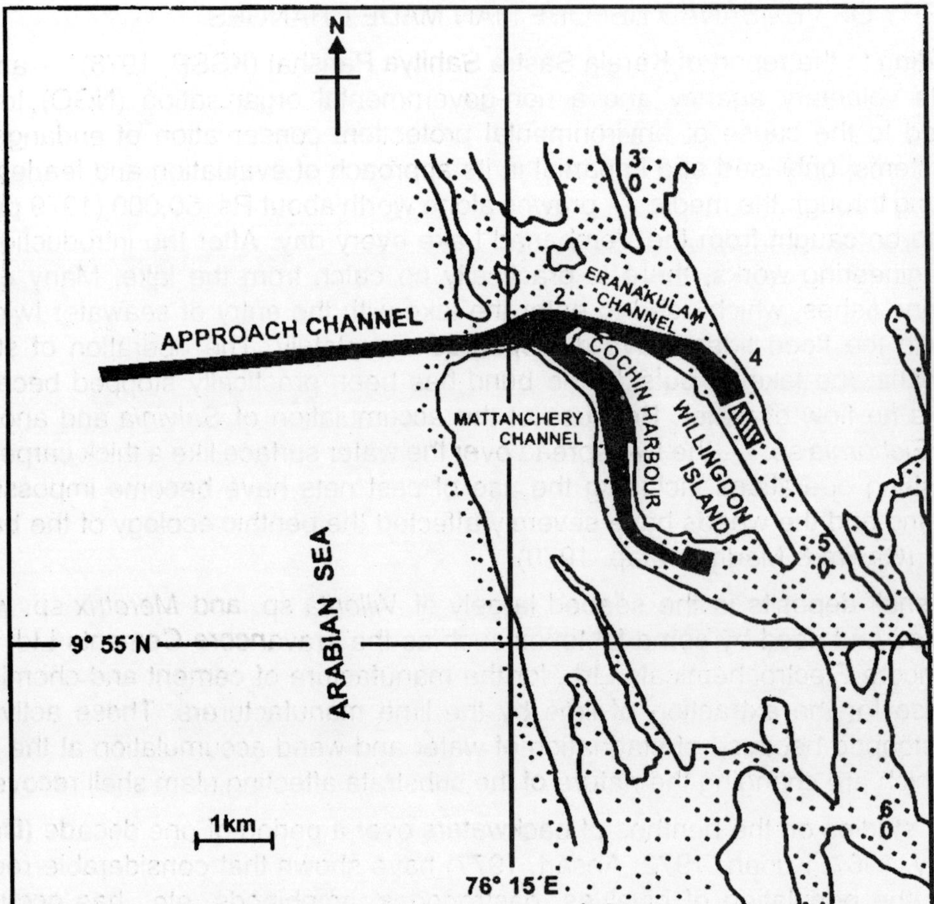

Fig. 10.3 Map showing the backwaters at Cochin with the locations of 6 study sites and the dredged approach channel to Cochin Harbour, the dredged Mattanchery and Ernakulam Channels. The area measuring 0.26 km^2 where seasonal variations in the bed profile were studied has been marked (From Gopinathan & Qasim, 1971).

6 km, 3 km and 4 km long, respectively. A gradual rise in the bed of these channels occurs every year and the quantity of material removed from these channels by dredging is of the order of 2×10^6 m^3/y. Nearly 70% of this material is taken out from the approach channel, 28% from the Mattanchery Channel and the rest from the Ernakulam Channel. Normally, January and February are the months when approach channel is dredged. According to Bristow (1938), the surface currents in the nearshore area off Cochin are southerly from February to September and northerly from October to January. Silting starts in March, soon after dredging is over. It increases considerably from July to September. From October, it decreases and probably no silting occurs in the approach channel in December (Gopinathan & Qasim, 1971). Studies conducted on the silt movement in the area using radioactive tracer technique showed that during the postmonsoon and premonsoon months, the material dumped about 850 m away, either on the southern or northern sides of the approach channel, finds its way into the channel. Material dumped about 2 km south of the approach channel, also finds its way into the channel. However, the material dumped during the monsoon months, 2 km north of the channel and 5 km west of the coast, did not find its way into the channel (see Gopinathan & Qasim, 1971). Heavy siltation occurring in the backwaters and its peculiar circulation pattern have led to the formation of small islands of dredged material close to the harbour area. Water quality in the vicinity of the dredging site did not show any appreciable change. While dissolved nutrients recorded sharp changes in the water column and the conditions at the dredging site appeared to be different from the predredging site, normal conditions in the channels are restored within a short time (Joseph *et al.,* 1998).

Dredging operations invariably cause much physical damage to the benthic communities by their dislocation from the site, clogging and blinding of animals. Therefore, it is desirable that as far as possible, dredging should be avoided during the spawning months because it would seriously affect the population as is evident from the decline of rock oyster (*Crassostrea sp.*) from all the dredging sites.

During the last two decades, an area of about 200 ha has been reclaimed by the Urban Development and Town Planning Department for the construction of a foreshore road and for the expansion of the adjacent shipyard for additional berthing facilities. There are also plans by the Cochin Development Authority to reclaim 270 ha on the northern foreshore of the city. Looking at the fast shrinking backwaters, the need to protect the system is obvious. New strategies must be developed to ensure a healthy future for the backwaters.

HYDROGRAPHY BEFORE THE CHANGES

Systematic investigations on Cochin Backwaters began from the late fifties when George (1958) made his observations on plankton. In the early sixties, the work on hydrographic features of shelf waters around Cochin is worth mentioning (Ramamirtham & Jayaraman, 1963). These authors divided the sequence of events during the year into 4 seasons — period of SW monsoon, period of upwelling (August to October), period of sinking (October to February) and period of stable conditions (March to May). Derbyshire (1967) has also identified four seasons along the Kerala coast, of which the monsoon season is of particular interest with reference to changes in the salinity of surface waters. She has shown that a tongue of low salinity water juts out from the backwaters into the sea. Concurrent with the freshwater discharge from the backwaters, during the monsoon months, there is an incursion of cold, saline and nutrient-rich water from the Arabian Sea into the backwaters. This water becomes particularly noticeable at the bottom and has been recognised as upwelled water which finds its way into the backwaters through the main channel (Ramamirtham & Jayaraman, 1963). The influence of tidal incursion on the surface salinity was shown by George & Kartha (1963). A more detailed study on the tidal cycle and its influence on several environmental features such as temperature, salinity, dissolved oxygen, *p*H, seston, nutrients, alkalinity and chlorophyll was carried out by Qasim & Gopinathan (1969) in which it was established that all these characteristics are greatly influenced by the tidal rhythm. The differences are more marked at the surface than at the bottom. Diurnal changes in dissolved oxygen follow the course of daily sunlight intensity. Gross primary production follows almost a similar course. According to Shynamma & Balakrishnan (1973), tidal incursions and flooding due to freshwater during the monsoon season introduce major changes in the hydrographical conditions.

Estimation of chlorophylls a, b and c and plant carotenoids from the backwaters showed inconsistency in their relationship because the extract contained a lot of dead chlorophylls and their derivatives coming from detritus and stirred-up sediments. Phytoplankton biomass during the monsoon months was largely made up of diatoms and dinoflagelletes (Qasim & Reddy, 1967). The backwaters receive maximum solar radiation from December to March and minimum from June to September. High turbidity affects light penetration which is small throughout the year and least during the monsoon months. The euphotic zone varies from 2 to 6 m and attenuation coefficient (*k*) ranged from 0.60 to 5.54. No relation was found between *k* and suspended matter and transmission of surface light at Secchi depth was 23%. Zone of optimum illumination for maximum photosynthesis lay between 0 and 1.5 m (Qasim *et al.,* 1968). Particulate matter brought into the estuary from extraneous sources seem to affect the attenuation coefficient considerably (Devi, 1989).

PRIMARY PRODUCTION

Primary production using ^{14}C assimilation ranged from 266 to 883 mgC/m^2/d during the year. Both gross (using oxygen method) and net (^{14}C method) gave similar results (Qasim *et al.,* 1969). Figure 10.4 shows seasonal changes in primary production in relation to environmental factors. Annual cycle of production forms three peaks in April, July and October. These peaks are small and hardly exceed twofold. It can thus be concluded that primary production in the backwaters goes on at a uniform level, with little seasonal increase, throughout the year. Solar radiation falling on the sea surface (Fig. 10.4a) is minimum during the cloudy days when the rainfall is maximum (Fig. 10.4b). Peak values in the production are independent of high or low illumination because peaks occur in April, July and October (see Fig. 10.4f) when the values of illumination are very different. This indicates that total radiation is not a limiting factor. Opacity of water, on the other hand, reduces the light penetration considerably which makes primary production non-existent below 4 m. Seasonal changes in temperature at all depths are well marked in Fig. 10.4d although these hardly exceed 5-6°C. Minimum changes in temperature are recorded at the surface and maximum at 9 m depth. Temperature seems to have no direct effect on primary production. Changes in salinity are well-marked during the year (Fig. 10.4d). In July and August almost freshwater occupies the surface but little variations are seen near the bottom (9 m). Except for April, productivity peaks occur during a period a low salinity in the euphotic zone. This indicates that the plant organisms are not only euryhaline but have their optimum range of photosynthesis at low salinities. The predominant organisms in the estuary consist of diatoms and dinoflagellates. Figure 10.4h shows the seasonal changes in the stability of water column 0-4 m where photosynthesis is largely confined. High values of stability from June to November indicate that water layers do not get mixed and the upper zone remains stable whereas for the rest of the year it is well mixed. Stability has an inverse relationship with salinity. Peak value of primary production in April coincides with low stability probably because of a sudden influx of nutrients (see phosphate) curve in Fig. 10.4e. The other two peaks in July and October coincide with a period of greater stability. For the euphotic zone, average values of two important nutrients, nitrate and phosphate, are given in Fig. 10.4e. Silicates in the estuary were always excessive and seem to be associated with freshwater influx and land runoff. The N:P ratios by atoms were found to be highly variable from the normal ratio of 16:1. During

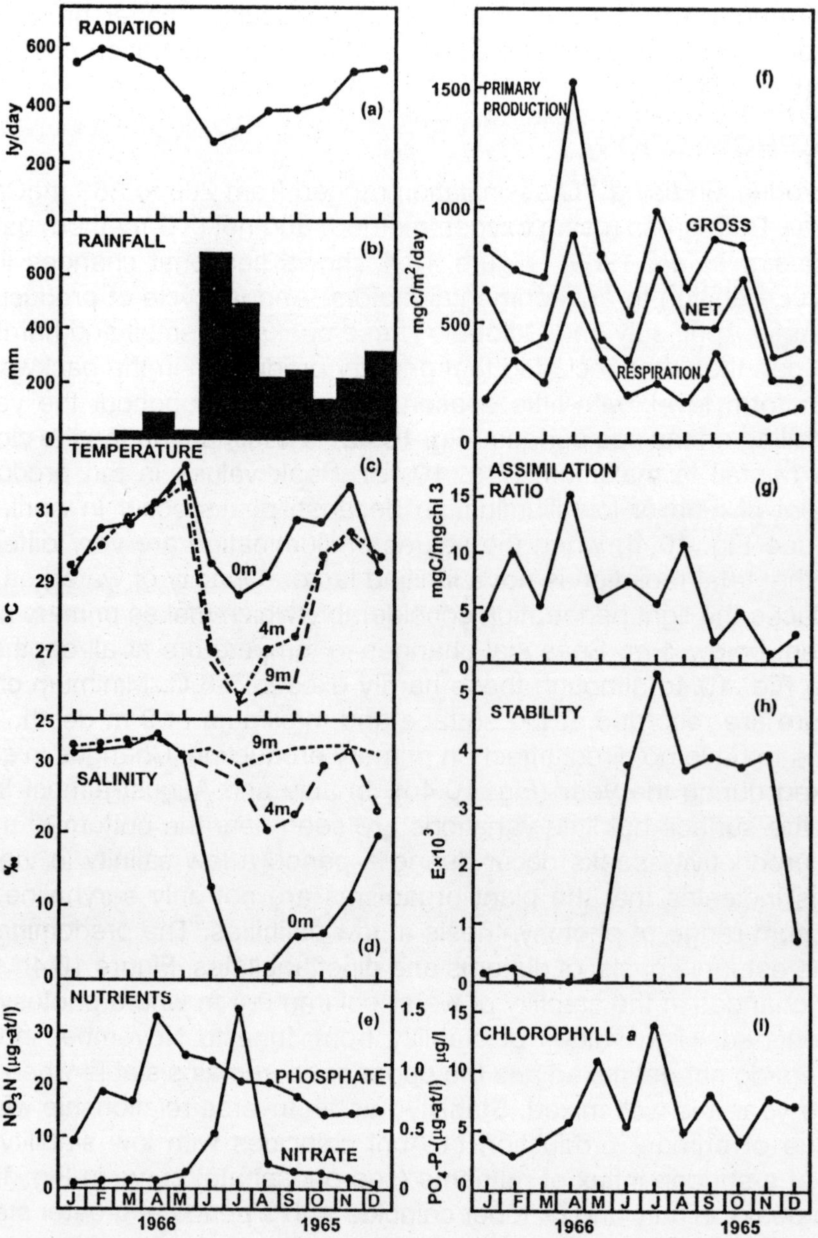

Fig. 10.4 Seasonal changes in various environmental factors (radiation, rainfall, temperature, salinity and nutrients in relation to primary production (gross, net and respiration) in Cochin Backwaters. The values of production, nutrients, assimilation ratio and chlorophyll refer to euphotic zone whereas stability was calculated for 0-4 m (From Qasim *et al.*, 1969).

the monsoon months, the ratios were remarkably high reaching 40:1 in July. In the other months these were extremely low — the minimum being 0.53:1 in December. A close examination of Fig. 10.4e and 10.4f reveals that while there is a close correlation between the cycle of phosphorus and organic production in the backwaters, the nitrogen cycle is completely unconnected with the productivity rhythm, for most of the year there is little or no nitrate-N.

The range in the ratio between carbon assimilation and chlorophyll *a* was considerable, 0.6 - 15. This gives a further evidence that phytoplankton population is highly variable and no consistency in the ratio under highly varying hydrographical conditions is expected. Seasonal fluctuations in the ratio very often fell in accordance with a rise and fall in the production ratio, but in some months these were quite independent of carbon assimilation.

In another study, two seasonal peaks of primary production were noticed at all the four stations worked — a primary peak during the postmonsoon period. Chlorophyll *a* values showed only a single peak which occurred during the monsoon period indicating an inverse relationship with primary production. The error may possibly lie in the estimation of plant pigments coming from living and inert materials. The cell counts, on the other hand, corresponded with the rise and fall in the values of primary production (Gopinathan *et al.,* 1974).

Primary production with depth

Figure 10.5 shows the rate of production with depth after pooling the values for the entire period of observation into three seasons. Nearly 90% of the total production is confined to a narrow zone of 0-1.5 m. During the monsoon and postmonsoon seasons, when the turbidity is very high, maximum production occurs at the surface, but in the premonsoon months it is found slightly below the surface. There was a slight deviation in the picture of gross production which shows a maximum at 0.5 m during the monsoon months (Qasim *et al.,* 1969).

NUTRIENTS

The backwaters remain saltwater-dominated for about 6 months (November to April) and then rather suddenly within a few weeks in May these become freshwater-dominated. The far reaches of the estuary, both at the northern and southern ends remain almost freshwater-dominated throughout the year except for a brief period in April/May when the saltwater by tidal action penetrates practically throughout the backwater system. A detailed study on the nutrients carried out by Sankaranarayanan & Qasim (1969) is summarized below.

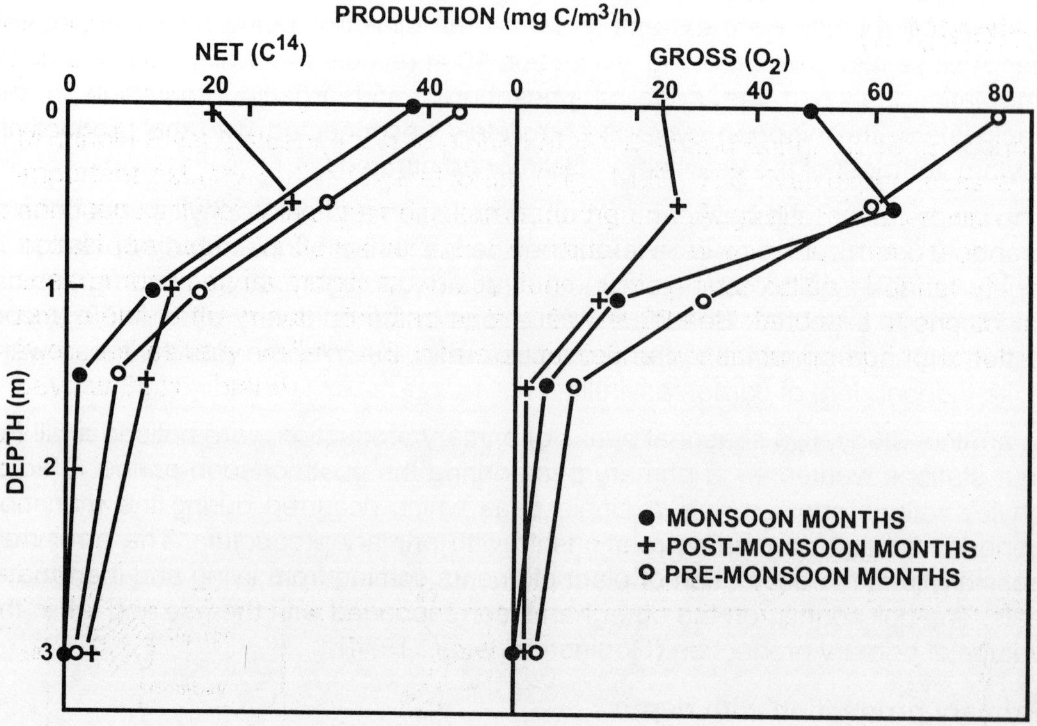

Fig. 10.5 Gross and net primary production in the three seasons in relation to depth in Cochin Backwaters (From Qasim *et al.*, 1969).

Phosphorus

Both inorganic and organic phosphorus remain low, from January to April, when homogeneous conditions prevail, practically throughout the water column. When the rains start in May-June they attain their first peak. The difference in the depth profile also becomes well-marked as the values increase with depth. Figure 10.6a shows monthly values of inorganic phosphorus at three depths at the mouth of the estuary from June 1965-May 1966. The values increased with depth throughout the year. High values occur during the monsoon and postmonsoon periods. Figure 10.6b shows the seasonal changes in organic phosphorus. The values are much higher than those of inorganic phosphorus and there is no well-defined seasonal rhythm. Short pulses of high and low phosphorus occur in different months. In general, organic phosphorus is greater at the bottom than at the surface. Probably it remains adsorbed with the sediment and its uneven distribution

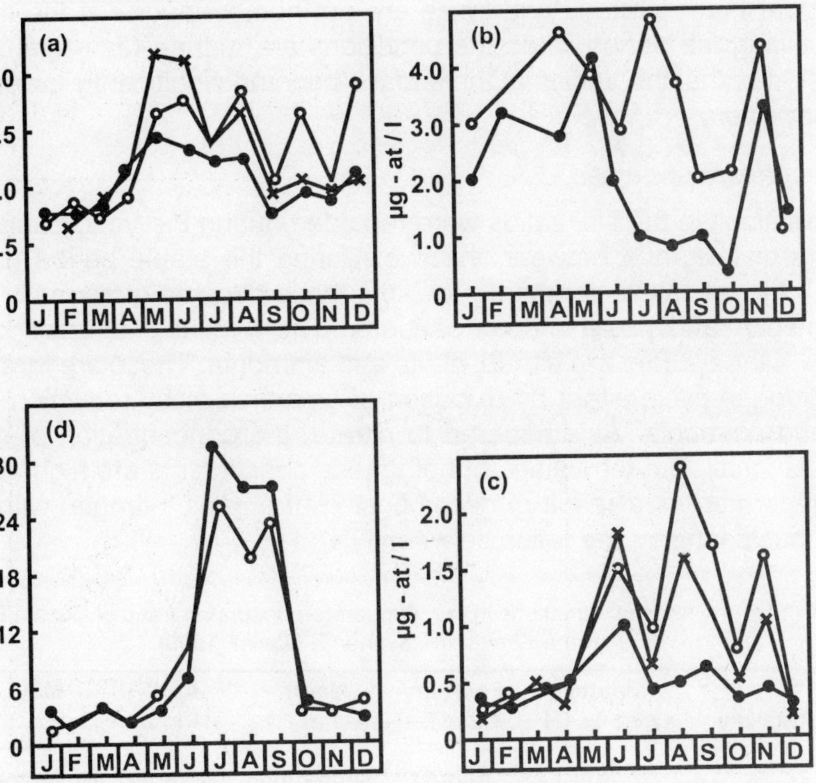

Fig. 10.6 Distribution of nutrients at the mouth of Cochin Backwaters (a) inorganic-phosphorus (b) organic phosphorus (c) nitrite-nitrogen (d) nitrate-nitrogen. Surface: closed circles; mid-depth: crosses; bottom: open circles (From Sankaranarayanan & Qasim, 1969).

during the year may be because it remains bound with suspended matter. Seasonal runoff does not seem to provide a source of phosphorus enrichment.

Nitrogen

Figure 10.6c shows monthly values for nitrate-N. For most of the year there is little or no nitrate-N in the estuary particularly when marine conditions prevail. From May the values increase sharply reaching 25-30 μg-at/l in July-September. This seems to be due to land runoff and freshwater discharge. The distribution of nitrate-N seems homogeneous throughout the water column with little difference between surface, mid-depth and bottom. Enrichment with nitrate-N seems to occur during the early part of the rainfall with no further contribution in subsequent months. Nitrite-N shows a trimodal seasonal cycle (Fig. 10.6d). The values are much lower than nitrate-N and these are not homogeneous at the three depths except during the period when the conditions are marine (Jan-April). During the monsoon months, the values at the surface become significantly lower than those at deeper layers.

Nitrogen:phosphorus ratio

Wide variations in the N:P ratios were recorded during the year. Table 10.1 gives the range in the ratio between the two. During the stable period (premonsoon months), the ratios are constantly low, but these become abnormally high during the monsoon and postmonsoon seasons. The available sources of inorganic nitrogen in the estuary are nitrate, nitrite and ammonia. These are formed as parts of the nitrogen cycle either by oxidation of ammonia or by reduction of nitrate to nitrite and ammonia. As compared to nitrate, the concentration of nitrite in the estuary is small. But the values of both these constituents are high at the bottom probably formed as a result of decomposing of organic nitrogen within the sediments, thus changing the ratios between N and P.

Table 10.1— Seasonal variations in the nitrogen-to-phosphorus ratio of Cochin Backwaters (From Sankaranarayanan & Qasim, 1969).

N:P	**January**	**February**	**March**	**April**	**May**	**June**
Ranges at stations 1 to 6	3:1 to 1:1	1:2 to 2:1	1:1 to 2:1	1:1 to 2:1	1:1 to 3:1	3:1 to 23:1
N:P	**July**	**August**	**September**	**October**	**November**	**December**
Ranges at stations 1 to 6	12:1 to 99:1	9:1 to 80:1	1:1 to 7:1	1:1 to 13:1	1:1 to 7:1	1:4 to 4:1

Silicon

Silicon values remain low from December to April and become very high during the monsoon months. It seems entirely dependent upon the influx of freshwater as the values decrease from surface to bottom showing inverse relationship with salinity. Maximum values in July and August indicate that silicon is associated with heavy silt load (Sankaranarayanan & Qasim, 1969).

Carbon assimilation to Chlorophyll a Ratio

The range in ratio as shown in Fig. 10.6g is very wide during the year and this variability is largely due to the observed chlorophyll values which may not be photosynthetically active due to the presence of a lot of pigments coming from dead and detrital matter. Phytoplankton organisms form only a small fraction of the particulate matter.

Relationship between Zooplankton and Phytoplankton

Zooplankton and phytoplankton biomass in terms of their carbon equivalent is shown in Fig. 10.7a. [For conversion factors see Qasim *et al.,* (1969) and Qasim (1970)]. Zooplankton abundance in the estuary was predominantly associated with changes in salinity and thus could be related to monsoon cycle. Maximum zooplankton occurred from January to April (premonsoon) when salinity in the backwater was high. During this period, the estuary becomes an arm of the adjoining sea. The zooplankton biomass during the monsoon months remains at a low level and does not show any appreciable change until December.

The ratio of gross photosynthesis to carbon of phytoplankton is shown in Fig. 10.7b as production coefficient. The range in the ratio is very large (3.7-119). This probably indicates that the phytoplankton crop sampled by the plankton-net included only a small fraction of the total carbon assimilation (1-28%) as measured by the rate of photosynthesis. During the period when the ratio was large (monsoon and postmonsoon months), the crop was mainly dominated by such "small forms" (nannoplankton) which were not retained by the net. Similarly, the low ratio obtained from November to March signifies that the net sampled one-quarter of the standing crop consisting mainly of larger marine diatoms and dinoflagellates. Fig. 10.7b also includes the ratio of zooplankton to phytoplankton (z/p). Seasonal fluctuations in z/p fall in accordance with a similar increase and decrease in the production coefficient. This probably indicates that the type of phytoplankton production in the estuary is so adjusted that, with the seasonal changes in zooplankton composition, it provides the specific food requirement of the herbivores.

Taking the daily metabolic requirement of tropical zooplankton in terms of carbon as 12% of its dry weight, the seasonal changes in the rate of consumption works out as 10% of the production by plants during the monsoon months, 20% during the postmonsoon months and 40% during the premonsoon months. The estimated gross production in the estuary ranges from 270-295 $gC/m^2/y$ (average 280 gC/m^2) while the net production, for days only, is 180-200 $gC/m^2/y$ (average 195 gC/m^2). The average daily net production (24 h) is approximately 124 $gC/m^2/y$. The estimated annual consumption by the zooplankton herbivores is only about 30 gC/m^2. This indicates that there is a large surplus of basic food in the estuary. A general lack of zooplankton herbivores seems to be main factor responsible for such an inefficient utilisation of primary production, which in turn, may be due to changing environmental features of the estuary. From the general composition of

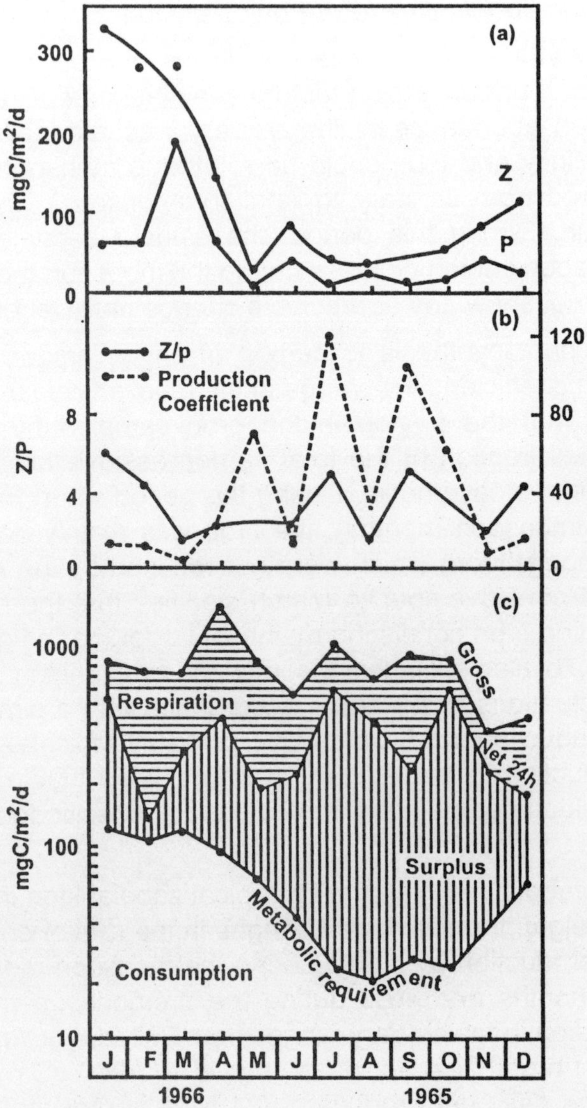

Fig. 10.7 Relation between phytoplankton (p) and zooplankton (z) taken from parallel hauls on the same day in every month of the year 1965-66 (b) Relation between zooplankton : phytoplankton ratio (z/p) and production coefficient (photosynthesis : carbon content of phytoplankton) (c) Relation between metabolic requirement of zooplankton and gross and net (24 h) primary production. The lower portion shows approximate consumption of primary production by zooplankton herbivores; the middle portion shows the approximate surplus and the upper portion shows the average respiration (24 , (From Qasim *et al.*, 1969).

the zooplankton organisms however, there seems to no evidence to suggest that the herbivore population is kept to a minimum because of the presence of a large number of carnivorous forms (Qasim, 1970).

FOOD CHAIN

Surplus primary production does not provide any "wastefulness" of the food produced, because other than planktonic herbivores, the unconsumed basic food is efficiently used by several animal groups of the estuarine community. One such alternate pathway gets directly linked with the herbivorous fishes (mullets, *Chanos*, clupeoids, etc.) and shellfishes (mussels, oysters, etc.) which consume the excess plant food and these are abundantly found in the estuary. Another direct link from the basic food would be with the omnivorous shrimp population through detritus, as the backwaters are well known for their prawn fishery. Finally, a substantial portion of the basic food, which keeps sinking to the bottom would be consumed by the sedentary animal communities. The small depth of the euphotic zone greatly increases the rate of loss from this zone and thus prevents the excessive outburst of phytoplankton bloom at any one time of the year. The unconsumed food, which on reaching the bottom becomes a part of the sediment, may be chemically and biologically altered, but remains in the system to take part in the cycle of events. Two reviews of the works summarized above have appeared earlier (Qasim, 1973 & 1979).

Steele (1965) has suggested that in a typically marine environment, nearly 80% of the primary production is consumed by the zooplankton herbivores, while the remaining 20% is utilised by the demersal animal communities. In the oceanic environment such as the Sargasso Sea which has maximum transparency, the utilisation of basic food by the zooplankton herbivores is even more efficient and works out nearly 100% (Menzel & Ryther, 1961). These figures remain valid in such environments where primary production is spread over a large column of water and has to travel a long distance to reach below the eupotic zone where it is likely to decay and get chemically altered. Therefore, its chances of being grazed are invariably high. In a shallow tropical estuary, an increase in the pelagic and benthic herbivorous forms and detritus feeders, thus compensates for the lack of zooplankton, and probably makes the system just as efficient. It is, therefore, not surprising to find primary production in the estuary, far exceeding the rate of consumption by zooplankton herbivores.

A diagrammatic and rather simplified representation, based on the above discussion, has been constructed in Fig. 10.8. It is based on the generalised scheme enunciated by Steele (1965) to provide an overall picture of the transmission of

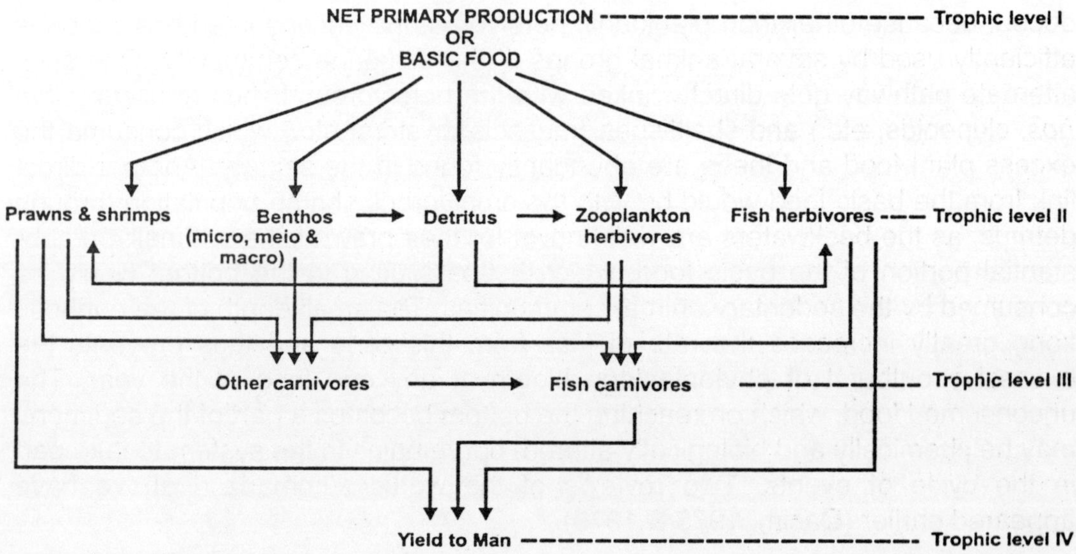

Fig. 10.8 A generalized representation of food web in Cochin Backwaters (From Qasim, 1970).

food to different trophic levels I-IV. The representation, though to a large extent arbitrary, indicates some possible links within each trophic level and from one to the next trophic level.

DETRITUS

Collections of settled detritus were made continuously in the estuary for a period of one year. It was largely composed of fine silt and inert particles around which organic matter adheres to form aggregates. In addition to phytoplankton, which forms a small fraction (0.1-1%) of the settled detritus, significant quantities of benthic algae suspended soft mud and the material brought down by the rivers and land runoff constitute the main sources of detritus. Detritus sedimentation attains its maximum value from April to June in the estuary and forms a major portion of seston. Pigments present in detritus include degraded chlorophyll (phaeophytin), detrital carbon, phosphorus and nitrogen. Degraded chlorophyll has a marked seasonal variation while carbon and phosphorus show little change during the year. Caloric value of detritus does not appear to be high. However, being a readily available material, its entry into the food chain seems to increase the efficiency of energy transfer from one trophic level to the other (Qasim & Sankaranarayanan, 1972).

PHYTOPLANKTON COMPOSITION

Phytoplankton standing crop, as represented by cell numbers, varies from season to season and from one site to the other in the estuary. Two peaks were noticed in their abundance — one in January and February and the other in July and August. During these peaks the phytoplankton crop largely included diatoms. The primary peak was dominated by the diatom *Skeletonema costatum*. During the secondary peak, the dinoflagellates namely *Prorocentrum micans* and *Ceratium furca* formed major components along with *Skeletonema costatum*. Silicoflagellates such *Dichtoyocha fibula* and *Destephamis micans* and *Destephamis speculum* were found during February, May, June and October. Chlorophycean organisms were represented by *Spirogyra* and desmids such as *Euastrum, Cosmarium, Closterium* and *Micrasterias*. These were abundant in August, December and April. Bluegreen algae such as *Trichodesmium, Oscillatoria* and *Meresmopodia* were recorded in abundance during July, September and November. The most abundant organism was the diatom, *Skeletonema costatum* in January.

In the backwaters, 120 species of phytoplankton organisms, excluding nannoplankton were recorded. Of these, 88 species were diatoms — 74 species of diatoms occur regularly while 14 were rare. Their peak abundance was during the monsoon and postmonsoon season (June to December) following a period of low salinity and nutrient enrichment (Gopinathan, 1972). Table 10.2 shows monthly variations in cell counts at four stations in the estuary. Maximum representation and density was in January and minimum in March but the distribution of the organisms was practically uniform at all the stations (Gopinathan *et al.,* 1974). These authors have also indicated the usefulness of the measurement of chlorophyll *a* as an index of phytoplankton productivity although a direct relationship existed between phytoplankton counts and chlorophyll *a* in their study. It was not so between productivity and chlorophyll *a*.

Seasonal composition of 31 genera occurring at 7 stations and covering a large area of the estuary is shown in Fig. 10.9. A considerable variation was found with seasons and at the stations both in their composition and total abundance. During the premonsoon months, the crop was largely composed of diatoms of the genera *Chaetoceros, Cosinodiscus, Skeletonema, Pleurosigma, Nitzschia* and the

Table 10.2— Total number of surface phytoplankton per litre at four stations of Cochin Backwaters (From Gopinathan *et al.*, 1974)

	Month	Station I	Station II	Station III	Station IV
1973	January	521500	863700	898800	780500
	February	454500	367200	340800	319800
	March	109100	90600	100700	142300
	April	204500	191100	191700	229800
1972	May	162500	167500	136100	148900
	June	252000	207400	533800	473400
	July	443500	479400	400400	429900
	August	471500	606400	161200	210300
	September	214100	322800	412800	464000
	October	366200	276600	332200	350900
	November	208100	184800	203000	179900
	December	118900	110300	108000	95700

dinoflagelletes of the genera *Peridinium, Gymnodinium* and *Ceratium*. During the monsoon months, the flora included freshwater forms of the genera *Pledorina, Volvox, Pediastrum* and *Desmids*. During the postmonsoon season, the freshwater forms were gradually replaced by marine forms. The total cell counts indicated in Fig. 10.9 may not reflect the biomass of the total flora but it does indicate the seasonal and spatial variations of different forms (Joseph & Pillai, 1975).

In another seasonal study on phytoplankton distribution at three stations in Cochin Backwaters, statistical analyses were carried out and the mean values and the coefficients of variation of different species were calculated. Intergroup matrix of correlation coefficient was prepared and cluster analyses using dendograms showing grouping at various similarity levels were drawn. This analysis showed that *Skeletonema costatum* was the most abundant species at all the three stations. The distribution of *Nitzschia closterium* was most consistent and that of *Asterionella japonica* was the least consistent. Calculation of diversity indices of the species showed that the degree of abundance of the species varied from station to station but not from season to season (Jayalakshmi *et al.*, 1986).

In another study on the contributions of microplankton and nannoplankton of the backwaters in their production rate, it was found that the contribution of small forms or nannoplankton was much greater than that of microplankton. Nannoplankton were defined as those organisms which passed through the net made of the finest mesh of bolting nylon and microplankton were those which were retained by the net. Thus four different size groups of alge were sampled from

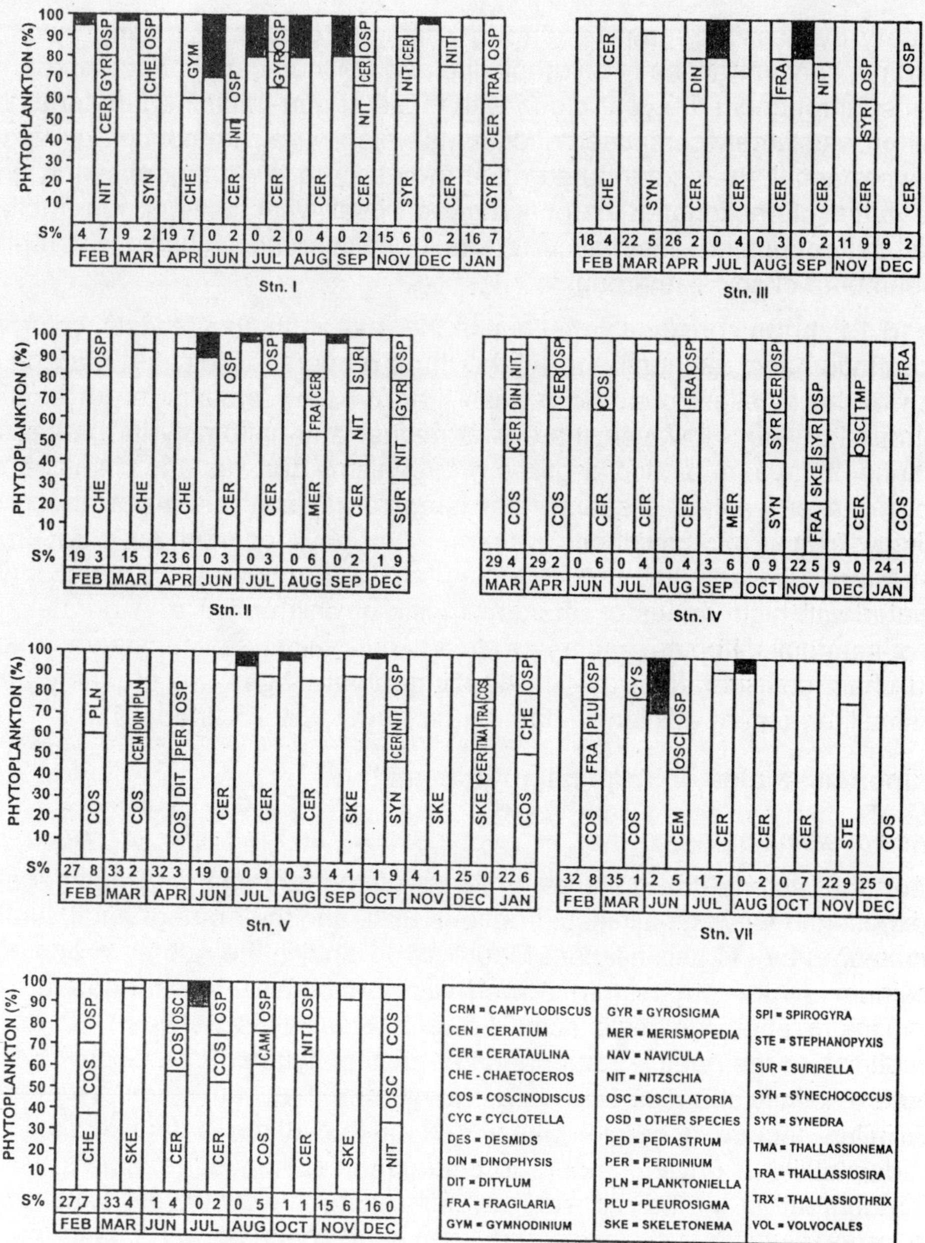

Fig. 10.9 Seasonal variation in species composition of phytoplankters at 7 stations of Cochin Backwaters (From Joseph & Pillai, 1975).

the estuary by passing seawater through different grades of bolting nylon. ^{14}C assimilation, concentrations of chlorophyll *a* and cell numbers of each group were determined throughout the year along with those of non-fractioned material. Nannoplankton was largely composed of diatoms which were common to both groups. If they were small, they contributed most profusely to the nannoplankton group. Pooled values of fractionated material agreed closely with those of non-fractioned material, but no regular seasonal cycle was found in photosynthesis, chlorophyll *a* or cell numbers of any size group.

Figure 10.10 shows seasonal variations in the rate of photosynthesis, chlorophyll *a* concentration and cell numbers. All the three properties indicated that the contribution of the smallest organisms (less than 64 μm) remains large practically throughout the year. However, there was neither any uniformity in the seasonal abundance of any one particular group of organisms nor was any clearly marked rhythm in the properties. It seems that larger organisms need not have correspondingly higher photosynthetic rate or chlorophyll content as compared to smaller forms. Similarly, the high counts of smaller forms may not necessarily be associated with high values of photosynthesis or chlorophyll *a*. A greater dominance of nannoplankton as primary producers over microplankton seems relevant to food chain consideration, as filter-feeding larval stages are probably able to utilise small form more efficiently, than larger forms (Qasim *et al.*, 1974).

Experimental studies on tropical phytoplankton

Influence of salinity

Pure but not bacteria-free cultures of 12 species of diatoms and dinoflagellates were exposed to varying salinities, from 5 to 35‰ and their rate of photosynthesis was measured by ^{14}C assimilation. Figure 10.11 shows the rate as a percentage of maximum. All the organisms showed wide adaptability to changes in salinity and maximum photosynthesis occurred at low salinities between 10 to 20‰. Observations on the relative abundance of phytoplankton in the Cochin Backwaters, where salinity changes were large, confirmed that, within limits, waters with low salinities support a greater density of phytoplankton organisms in nature. Wide adaptability of phytoplankters to changes in salinity corresponds to conditions brought about by the monsoon system along the southwest coast of India where large dilutions are associated with enrichment of water with nutrients (Qasim *et al.*, 1972a).

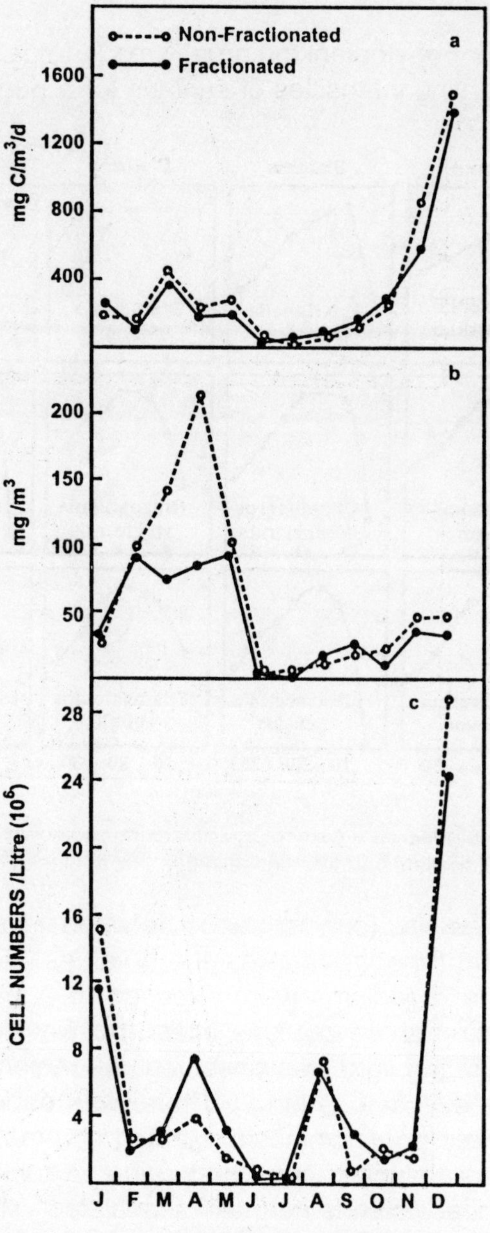

Fig. 10.10 Seasonal cycles of (a) photosynthesis (b) chlorophyll *a* and (c) cell numbers shown by non-fractionated samples and pooled values of fractionated samples taken from the Cochin Backwaters (From Qasim *et al.*, 1974).

Effect of illummation

Intensity effect in different phytoplankton organisms (11 species) was determined by exposing them to varying intensities of sunlight for a period of 2 h. Saturation

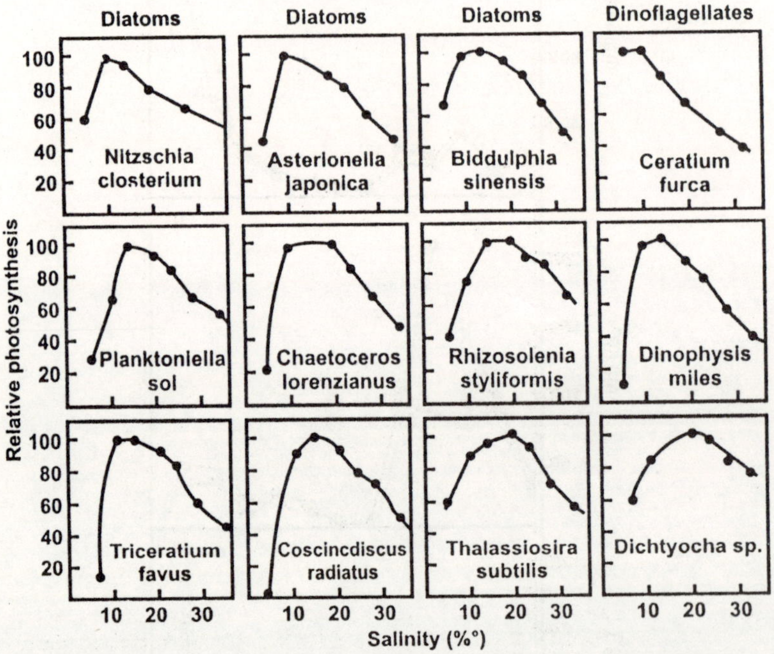

Fig. 10.11 Rate of photosynthesis as a percentage of maximum shown by unialgal cultures of diatoms and dinoflagellates at different salinities (From Qasim et al., 1972a).

point (I_K) in most species was found to range between 11 and 15 kilolux. In *Rhizosolenia styliformis* and *Dinophysis miles*, the I_K values were found to be exceptionally high. When the organisms were exposed to a particular range of the visible spectrum by using sharp cut-type filters, no wavelength dependence of photosynthesis in saturating light was observed. All regions of the visible spectrum were found to be effective as long as there was enough light intensity (radiant energy) to stimulate photosynthesis. Marked chromatic adaption displayed by the organisms seems advantageous to estuarine phytoplankton forms because of their floating existence, which is normally associated with fairly rapid changes in light conditions, because of the turbidity in water. All the organisms tested experimentally showed a similar adaption despite the qualitative dissimilarities which they might possess in their pigment composition (Qasim *et al.*, 1972b).

Nutrient requirement

Nutrient-depleted cells of the diatom, *Biddulphia sinensis* and the dinoflagellate *Ceratium furca*, were grown in different concentrations of phosphate and nitrate either singly or in combination. The relationship in their growth and nutrient concentrations was hyperbolic, and followed the Michaelis-Menten expression. Variations in the half-saturation constants (K_S) for both the species in each nutrient gave an index of their capacity to utilise these nutrients when available either singly or in combination. Maximum growth rate (μ_{max}) of the two species did not follow the trends shown by K_S. Seasonal abundance of the two species in the backwaters showed that, at low concentrations of nutrients, *C. furca* becomes predominant. High concentrations of nutrients present in the estuary during the monsoon months favour the increase in abundance of *B. sinensis*. The differences in the K_S values of the two organisms seem to reflect their observed seasonal abundance in the estuary (Qasim *et al.*, 1973).

APPLICATION OF A MODEL TO ESTUARINE ECOSYSTEM

Margalef (1967) developed a simple analog for an estuarine plankton system in which the density of a population, *N*, is determined by its natural rate of increase, *R*, and the flushing rate of the estuary *F*. In a steady state

$$N = Ne^{R} - FN \qquad \ldots(10.1)$$

Thus, if a planktonic population is to maintain itself in an estuary, its natural rate of increase must compensate for the state at which it is washed out, i.e.

$$R = \log_e(1 + F) \qquad \ldots(10.2)$$

The most important implication of Margalef's model is that the ratio of algal production, *P*, to algal biomass, *B*, must increase as the flushing rate increases. This follows, since $P : B = (N_1 - N_0)/N_0$, where N_1 and N_0 are the standing crop values at time t_1, and t_0. Therefore,

$$P{:}B = [N_0(e^{R} - 1)]/N_0$$

From equation 10.1, $e^{R} - 1 = F.$

Hence, $P{:}B = F \qquad \ldots(10.3)$

Estimates of *P:B* were obtained by dividing the net production by the algal cell counts (see Qasim *et al.,* 1969). These values have been plotted together with the index of flushing rate in Fig. 10.12. As can be seen from Fig. 10.12, the value of *P*:*B* increases sharply between May and July as *F* increases, and *P*:*B* remains high for further two months even when the freshwater discharge declines. Thus, the increased flushing rate of the estuary caused by the southwest monsoon is seen as the main driving force behind the changes which take place. Fish

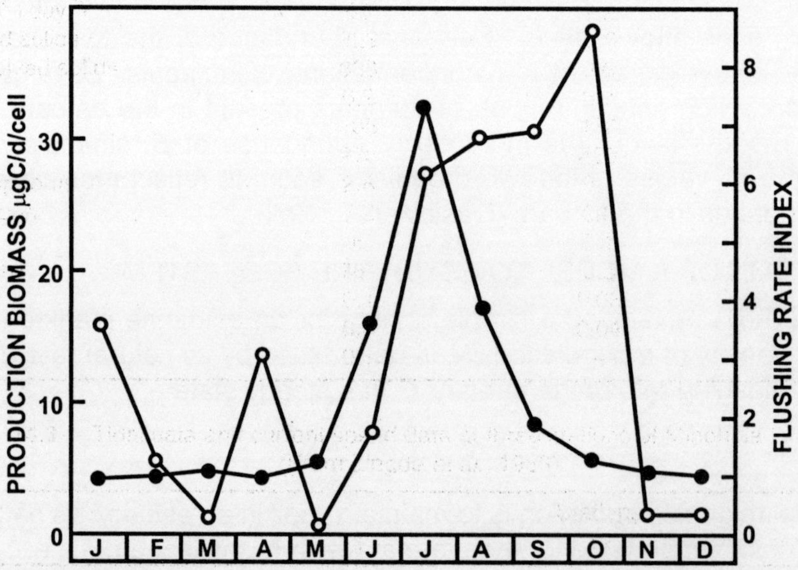

Fig. 10.12 Relative flushing rate of Cochin Backwaters and the P:B ratios for each month of the year. Closed circle - flushing index; open circles - P:B ratio (From Wyatt & Qasim, 1973).

production in the estuary is high as compared to primary production. This is because of the additional source of energy that comes from detritus as an important component of the food web (Wyatt & Qasim, 1973).

ZOOPLANKTON

In an earlier study (George, 1958), seasonal abundance of zooplankton in the backwaters was broadly divided into the following categories:

(a) Organisms occurring throughout the year (Copepods – *Acartia* sp., *Pseudodiaptomus (Schmackeria) tollingeri*: Cirripedes — barnacle nauplii and cyprids: Mysid – *Mesopodiopsis orientalis:* Amphipods – *Corophium trienonyx; Photis longicaudata:* Decapods — post-larvae of *Metapenaeus monoceros,* larvae of Caridae – *Periclimenes* sp., *Palaemon* sp., brychyuran zoea: Oyster larvae and gastropod veligers: Polychaetes — 2 species of pelagic polychaetes).

(b) Organisms occurring during monsoon and postmonsoon months (Cladoceran – *Evadne tergestina:* Ostracods – several species: Copepods – *Apseudes* sp., *Halicyclops* sp., *Acartia gravelyi* : oyster larvae and gastropod veligers).

(c) Organisms occurring during the premonsoon months (Hydromedusae – fairly large numbers: Ctenophores – *Pleurobrachia globosa* : Chaetongnaths – *Sagitta enflata, S. bedoti; S. robusta:* Copepods – *Paracalanus aculeatus; Labidocera pectinata; L. kroyere var gallensis; Acrocalanus monachus; Eucalanus crassus; Canthocalanus pauper; Centropages* sp: Cumacean – *Eocuma* sp.; *Paradiastylis culicoides:* Isopod – *Sphaeroma* sp.: Amphipods – *Perioculodes longimanus; Grandidierella* sp.; *Hyperia* sp.: Decapods – post-larvae of *Metapenaeus dobsoni; Penaeus indicus; P. carinatus;* adults of *Lucifer hanseni*; *Ogyrides striaticauda; Periclimenes indicus* : Stomatopod – larvae of *Alima* sp).

Zooplankton abundance was predominantly associated with changes in salinity and thus could be related to the annual monsoon cycle. Maximum zooplankton both in volume and diversity occurred during the period of high salinity (January to May) when its composition was very similar to that of the inshore waters. This study, though carried out as early as 1958, the categories of the organisms that the author has drawn at that time are valid even today.

Zooplankton biomass was minimum at the stations where salinity was lowest during the monsoon period and increased progressively towards the mouth up to 562 mg/m^3. During the premonsoon season, when the whole system becomes saline with a weak salinity gradient, the biomass and faunal composition at different stations showed remarkable variation ranging from 92 mg/m^3 where the salinity was lowest to 2682 mg/m^3 where the salinity was maximum. Night hauls recorded a greater biomass at most of the stations (Nair & Tranter, 1971).

Silas & Pillai (1975) in a detailed study on a dynamics of zooplankton in the backwaters described the composition of the organisms under the headings (a) holoplankters and (b) meroplankters.

Holoplankters

This group included hydromedusae (32 species), scyphomedusae (1 species), ctnophores (1 species), siphonophores (5 species), polychaetes (1-2 species), cladocerans (2 species), copepods (33 species), cyclopoid copepods (11 species), ostracods (1 species), mysids (2 species), cumaceans (2 species), tanaidaceans (2 species), isopods (1 species), amphipods (6 species), adult decapods (9 species), chaetognaths (5 species), pelagic tunicates (1 species).

Meroplankters

This group was represented by polychaete larvae (several species), cirripede larvae (1 species), bryozoan larvae (several species), [decapod larvae – post larvae of penaeids (4 species), caridean larvae (2 species), brachyuran zoeae (several species)], stomatopod larvae (1 species), molluscan larvae [gastropod (2 species), lamellibranch (several species)], fish eggs and larvae (several species).

Figure 10.13 shows the seasonal variation in total zooplankton biomass in relation to temperature and salinity variations along with copepod biomass. Also included in the figure is the seasonal composition of the 3 main groups – carnivores, herbivores and omnivores. Copepods constitute the main bulk of zooplankton biomass with omnivores dominating as the largest feeding group followed by carnivores during the dry season and herbivores in the wet season (Silas & Pillai, 1975).

Among the copepods, the dominant component belonged to the family Acarticidae. At least 9 species were found to inhabit the backwaters. Large salinity changes associated with monsoonal flooding lead to changes in species composition. Species diversity was highest during the dry season and lowest in the wet season. Catastrophic flooding, it is suggested, keeps a regular check on interspecific competition and leads to maximum diversity of the faunal composition (Tranter & Abraham, 1971). Thus, it has been clearly shown that the ecological distribution of most of the groups and species of zooplankton in the backwaters is controlled by hydrographic changes, the major variable being the salinity (Rao *et al.,* 1975). Figure 10.14 shows the recorded salinity range and the commonest species occurring in the estuary. About 6 species of copepod occur at low salinities. Chaetognaths and hydromedusae are abundant in summer months (dry season), when the salinity is high. The more common species of these two groups are able to withstand fluctuations in salinity (Madhupratap, 1987). An inverse relationship between diversity and biomass of copepods was found. This means that copepod population is heterogeneous when the biomass is low and homogeneous when the biomass is high (Pillai *et al.,* 1973). Among the calanoid copepods, mean diversity indices were high at the stations near the mouth and decreased upstream. Significant variations existed between the months of the year and also between the observation sites (Madhupratap *et al.,* 1975). Of the 69

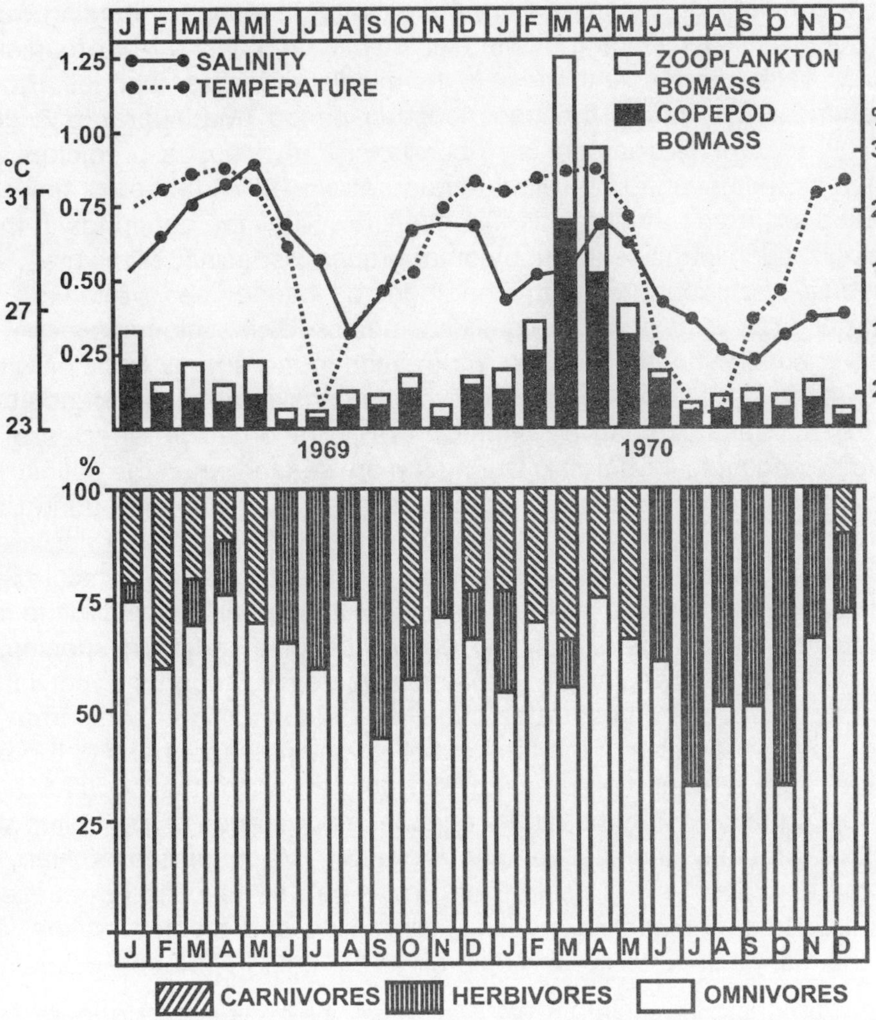

Fig. 10.13 Seasonal variation in the total quantity of zooplankton in Cochin Backwaters in relation to temperature and salinity. In the top figure shaded portions indicate the contribution of copepods in the total zooplankton biomass. The lower figures give the percentage composition of three different categories of copepods (carnivores, herbivores and omnivores) in monthly samples collected during 1969 and 1970 (From Silas & Pillai, 1975).

species of calalnoid copepods recorded from the estuaries of India, 37 species occur in the backwaters. Some are permanent residents while others form transitory visitors (Pillai, 1971). Spatial and seasonal variations are not confined to copepod populations alone, but these are reflected from different groups and species of zooplankton recorded from the estuary. Monsoonal flooding wipes out most of the organisms which thrive in high salinity and only a few organisms, tolerant to low salinity, are able to thrive in the middle and upper reaches. Process of repopulation begins during the postmonsoon period (Madhupratap & Haridas, 1975). This feature of zooplankton abundance can also be predicted using a regression model of variability (Madhupratap *et al.,* 1977). It should, however, be noted that apart from numerical dominance showed by the copepods in the estuary, ecological dominance exerted by other groups, especially carnivores, such as hydromedusae, ctenophores and chaetognaths cannot be overlooked. These being larger organisms form a significant portion of the biomass even though occurring in smaller numbers. Their importance in the energy transfer within the trophic system, since they are carnivores, is of considerable importance (Madhupratap, 1978). Santhakumari & Vannucci (1971) recorded 20 species of hydromedusae belonging to 11 genera. During the dry season when the salinity is high, 18 species are present at almost all the stations. Their absence during the wet season and the presence of only 8 species in the postmonsoon period are attributed to dilution of water. As the tidal variations in the estuary are small (~1 m), the zooplankton organisms are able to maintain their position within the estuary during the tidal exchange. Thus, the population of a common species, which extends over a large area, largely remains stable even though the individuals get shifted. This has been demonstrated by taking gradual oblique hauls from bottom to the surface, irrespective of the time of collection, in deeper parts of the estuary. Patterns of vertical migration showed that only a part of the population moves towards the surface during the night because the presence of low saline water at the surface probably inhibits vertical migration (Madhupratap & Rao, 1979). Among the copepods, three ecological groups can be identified in successional sequences. These include high saline, low saline and medium saline species. Most of the marine species are stragglers into the estuary (Madhupratap, 1979).

Gammarid amphipod population of 11 species, belonging to 9 genera from the estuary was also reported to be controlled by salinity, ranging from 0 to 36.2‰ which affected both their numerical density and species diversity. Highly saline species (3 in number) were recorded in January. All other species, except, two, contributed to the ecosystem. These two failed to establish themselves in the marine environment. *Corophium triaenonyx* was the most dominant species inhabiting all the stations and showing its maximum numerical abundance (Nair *et al.,* 1983).

An examination of sediment samples collected from the estuary showed the occurrence of 78 species of Foraminaifera. The fauna was poor during the monsoon season but rich (living + dead) in other seasons when the salinity is high. Sediments containing muddy-sand are rich in Foraminifera than those which contain only mud or sand. Apparently, seasonal dredging does not seem to have an adverse effect on the foraminiferan fauna (Rao & Balasubramanian, 1996).

INTERTIDAL FAUNA

Macrofauna of the intertidal zone of Cochin beach has been studied by Ansell *et al.* (1972a, 1972b & 1972c). The size of the sand particles along the beach ranges between 290 to 310 μm. Heavy rainfall during the monsoon period brings the temperature of the beach down and a sharp decrease in salinity occurs reaching 5‰ in July and August. During this period, the beach gets completely eroded and the high water mark moves about 50 m landward. The rainfall, land runoff and outflow of the rivers from the backwater system obliterate the beach profile completely. From October onwards, when the monsoon begins to retreat, accretion on the beach starts and by the end of the November the original profile of the beach is almost restored .

The bivalves, *Donax incarnatus, D. spiculum*, the gastropod, *Bullia melanoides*, and among the crustaceans the mole crab, *Emerita holthuisi*, the isopod, *Eurydice* sp. the ghost crab, *Ocypode ceratophthalma* and the polyhaete, *Glycera alba* formed the macrofauna of the intertidal zone. Monsoon reduces the distribution of the fauna and the zonation of the animals. Therefore, all the faunal components noted above do not occur throughout the year. However, the isopod *Eurydice* sp. occurred throughout the year and the mole crab *Emerita holthuisi* from January to June. Maximum density of *Donax spiculum* ($2630m^2$) was found in April. Smaller specimens of *D. incarnatus* and *D. spiculum* are recruited on the beach in May and June. Maximum longevity of the two bivalves seems to be about 2 years. *D. incarnatus* probably reaches maturity within 6 to 8 months.

Four species of bryozoan namely *Electra crustulenta, E. bengalensis, Alderina arabianesis* and *Schizoporella cochinensis* have been reported from the intertidal zones of Cochin Backwaters. Their growth rate was studied from their settlement on glass panels exposed to intertidal waters. In the young colonies, growth was initially slow but gets accelerated after 15 days. *E. crustulenta* seems to be adapted to a wide range of salinity variation (Menon & Nair, 1972).

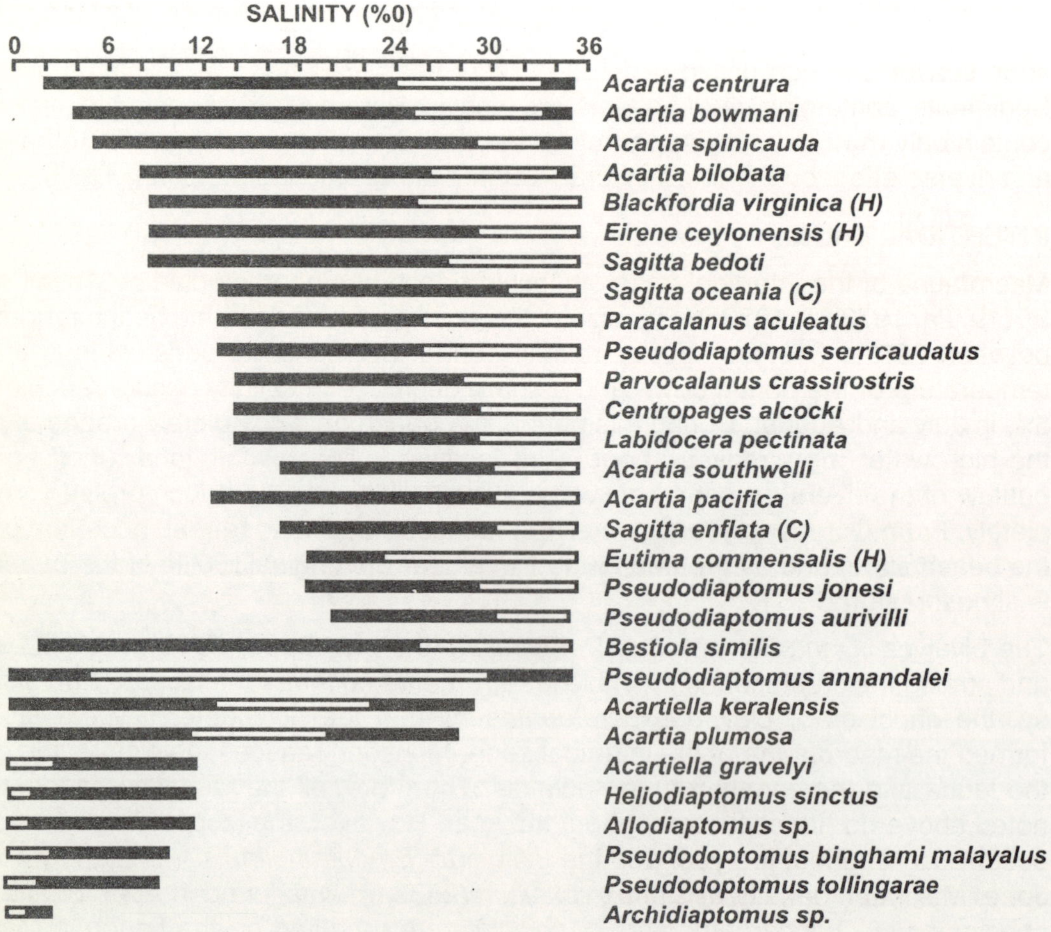

Fig. 10.14 Recorded salinity range (optimum unshaded) and common species occurring in Cochin Backwaters. (H) Hydromedusae, (C) Chaetognaths. The rest are copepods (From Madhupratap, 1976).

An estuarine wood-boring community from the backwaters was identified by Nair (1994). It consists of molluscan 59% and crustaceans 40% organisms. Collections for identifying the organisms were made from 40 localities of the backwaters by sawing a fixed volume of infested wood (1000 cm^3) from stationary piles spread throughout the backwater system. Of the molluscan group, the shipworms constituted 35.3% and the pholads 27.5%. Maximum activity of these organisms was recorded at the mouth connecting the estuary with the sea. The riverine zone was largely free from borers. In the mixed zone, their distribution depended on the prevailing salinity. Pholads needed at least 8.2‰ salinity and attained high density at salinity 11‰. The crustacean community included two species of isopods namely *Spheroma terebrans* and *S. annandelei*. The former occurred from the middle zone up to the mouth while the latter appeared only rarely (Nair, 1994).

BENTHOS

Benthic biomass was found to be greater in regions near the sea than in the brackishwater zones. Bivalves, gastropods and polychaetes were the most dominant benthic groups. The presence of the larger bivalve, *Meretrix ovum* and the polychaete, *Diopatra neapolitana* increased the biomass considerably. Organisms of lesser importance were crabs, fishes, ophiuroids and sea anemones. Meiobenthos in the estuarine zone included a high abundance of foraminiferans and nematodes. Foraminifera were more abundant near the sea than in blackishwater zones showing their preference to marine conditions. Nematodes, on the other hand, were dominant in the estuarine conditions. A substratum of fine and coarse sand seems to support a denser benthic population. Quantitative distribution of benthos seems to be governed by salinity than any other environmental factor. Larvae of bivalves and gastropods of purely marine origin do not seem to settle in estuarine conditions (Desai & Kutty, 1967a).

Two types of bottom samplers namely the van Veen and Peterson grabs were used for sampling the benthic fauna from the substratum. A comparison of the efficiency of the two samplers showed that the van Veen grab, which is heavier among the two and has a larger biting area brought more representative samples of the organisms (Kutty & Desai, 1968).

Desai & Kutty (1967b), while making a comparison of benthic fauna between the nearshore waters, 11.2 km away from the coast in the Arabian Sea, and the backwaters, have reported that while the main faunal groups in both the areas were similar, their composition was different. Foraminiferans, nematodes, polychaetes, bivalves and gastropods were present in both the areas but in the backwaters, the bivalves and polychaetes were represented by a greater number of species. A greater diversity of species in the backwaters may be because of the availability of a greater variety of substrates.

Benthic fauna of the backwaters is dependent upon changing hydrographical conditions associated with the tidal incursion, flushing of the estuary and the seasonal changes induced by the monsoon with heavy rainfall, land runoff and overflowing rivers (Ansari, 1977). Thus the fauna reflects fairly large tolerance of salinity being derived from the sea as well as from the riverine environment. Dominant groups of macrofauna include polychaetes, amphipods, isopods, prawns, bivalves, gastropods, sea-anemones, fishes (gobies) and brittle stars. Polychaetes occur abundantly throughout the year near the entrance (barmouth) and at the stations inside the estuary where the sediment is muddy. Amphipods and isopods are more abundant in late monsoon than in other seasons and occur in the upper reaches. The bivalves, *Meretrix* sp. and *Modiolus* sp. occur almost throughout the year. The former species was abundant at the mouth and the latter is found in muddy deposits. The average number of specimens was 1470/m^2 and the biomass varied from 50 to 150 g/m^2 (wet weight). The bivalve, *Villorita* sp., appeared in low salinity waters. Meiofauna was composed of nematodes, copepods, ostracods, foraminiferans and small bivalves. They largely occurred in silt and clay deposits (Kurian, 1972).

According to Ansari (1977), wide variations were seen in the macrobenthic fauna at the four stations of the backwaters investigated by him. Molluscs, polychaetes and crustaceans formed the main bulk amounting to about 85% of the total number — varying from 481 to 1100/m^2 with average biomass in dry weight from 37.33 to 106.32 g/m^2. Maximum numbers were recorded at the barmouth and minimum in the upper reaches. Polychaetes, specially *Prionospio* sp. showed no marked changes in their density in the estuarine part and this indicates their high tolerance to changes in salinity. Among the crustaceans, amphipods were abundant at the barmouth, while decapods were recorded from all the stations. The crabs, *Viaderiana* sp. and *Halicarnicus* sp. seem to prefer brackishwater. Among the molluscs, *Nuculana* sp. which has been reported earlier to be in abundance was found to be sparse.

As noted earlier, the introduction of African payal, *Salvinia* sp. into the backwater system, probably by accident, has adversely affected the ecology of the entire estuarine complex. It has also disturbed the distribution of benthic fauna. Gopalan *et al.,* (1987) have reported that thick deposits of degraded weeds are found at the bottom, particularly in the areas where salt water intrusion has been restricted because of Thaneermukkam bund. In the regions where flushing occurs, weed deposits have been found to be associated with bivalves and polychaetes.

Benthic communities at 9 stations in the backwaters were studied by Devi *et al.* (1991). Thirty species of polychaetes were the commonest organisms recorded. According to these authors, some of the polychaete species were in high densities where the water was polluted with industrial wastes while other animals avoided pollution and were conspicuous by their absence.

Benthic organisms in relation to substratum characteristics in some areas of the backwaters, where prawn culture is being practised, have been studied by Arvindakshan *et al.* (1992). Areas of high abundance of animals are characterised by sediment comprising fine sand, silt and clay with not less than 20% of fine sand. Sand, clay and silt were found to be important components to control benthic biomass. Generally, benthic organisms showed little coexistence and preferred independent existence. Polychaetes, amphipods and tanaidaceans were positively correlated with sand and clay but negatively with silt. Species diversity and biomass showed a lot of seasonal variation.

MICROBES

A high degree of abundance of coliform group in the backwater was reported by Santhakumary (1965) signifying considerable pollution of backwaters by sewage discharge. From the mud of the backwaters, green photosynthetic bacteria belonging to the genus *Chlorobium* were isolated (Gore, 1972). Two species of thiobacilli were isolated from the mud sample of Cochin Backwaters. These were able to oxidise thiosulphate into sulphate and sulphuric acid. Corrosive action by these bacteria on concrete blocks has been demonstrated after 92 days of incubation at room temperature (Gore & Unnithan, 1977). The magnitude of faecal pollution in the backwater has been estimated by quantitative abundance of the two coliforms (*Escherichia coli* and *Streptococcus faecalis*) in the sediment and water samples. Water samples showed a greater occurrence of *E. coli*, whereas sediment samples had a greater abundance of *S. faecalis*. FC/FS (faecal coliform/faecal streptococci) ratio indicated that the sources of faecal pollution are land discharge, sewage discharge and dumping of organic wastes. Bottom-dwelling fishes, prawns, bivalves, etc., appear to be the potential carriers of these bacteria rendering them unfit for human consumption (Gore *et al.,* 1979). From the decomposing floating weed, *Salvinia* sp., 13 strains of bacteria were isolated. Broths made from 5% weed extract gave accelerated response of growth in 8 bacterial isolates whereas the rest showed slow growth. The activities of these microbes give rise to *Salvinia* detritus which is a seasonal phenomenon because the weed appears profusely during the monsoon months and undergoes decomposition when the salinity of water rises, leaving behind its detritus which appears to be another source of food to bottom-dwelling animals (Radhakrishnan *et al.,* 1979).

FISHERY

The occurrence of hilsa, *Hilsa ilisha* has been reported from the backwaters (Pillay, 1960). During a very successful season of mackerel fishery in 1961, when bumper catches of mackerel were obtained from the west coast of India, George (1965) reported the entry of both mackerel (*Rastelliger kanagurta*) and oil sardine (*Sardinella longicep*) into the backwaters where these fishes were caught.

In August and September 1972, juveniles of oil sardine measuring 35-60 mm were caught at several places in the backwaters. They occurred in the Chinese dipnet operating 5 km inland. The catch included several species of penaeid prawns (*Penaeus indicus* formed the bulk of the catches along with the oil sardine), *Anchoviella, Ambassis, Sciaena, Thrissocles* and *Lieognathus* spp., all in their juvenile stages were landed. Specimens of oil sardine caught from the backwaters were not actively feeding but their partially–filled gut contents included diatoms and remains of copepods. In the regular sardine fishery season of inshore waters, the size group included 55 to 100 mm. The smaller size group seen in the backwaters was absent. The water samples in the areas from where the juveniles were caught had an average salinity of 2.96‰ with a temperature of 28.8°C and depth of about 2 m (Reghu, 1973). Two species of clupeoid fishes namely *Dayella malabaricus* and *Ehirava fluviatilis* were reported from the backwaters. Both the species were caught from the areas where salinity was low (Kurup & Samuel, 1980).

Eggs and larvae of several species of flatfishes belonging to the families Cynoglossidae and Soleidae have been reported from the backwaters. Larvae of five species namely *Cynoglossus puncticeps, C. brevis, C. cynoglossus, C. lida* and *Solea heinii* occur during the premonsoon months when the salinity is high. These, in spite of being euryhaline, do not seem to tolerate low salinity conditions for long durations. From the seasonal occurrence of their eggs and larvae, it can be deduced that *C. puncticeps* is a continuous breeder while others breed during the postmonsoon and premonsoon seasons (Devi, 1993).

Besides the miscellaneous teleosts which are caught from the backwaters regularly, the estuarine system is well-known for its prawn fishery. Postlarvae of penaeid prawns, *P. indicus, M. dobsoni* and *M. monoceros* occur abundantly in the plankton samples collected from the backwaters because prawns breed practically throughout the year. This has been deduced from a study spread over 5 years (1956-60). The early postlarvae enter the backwaters because the estuaries form nursery grounds for the prawns (George, 1962). It seems that the abundance of postlarvae and their recruitment in the plankton of backwaters, prior to the commencement of regular fishing season, can be used for forecasting the prawn fishery season of the area (George, 1963).

In the inshore waters, larvae and postlarvae of practically all commercially important species occur profusely in the plankton samples. Their abundance however, has a wide fluctuation from year to year. Hydrographical conditions of the inshore waters are largely influenced by the adjoining backwaters which empty large volumes of freshwater. Mass migration of postlarvae into the backwaters is induced by the decline in salinity (Rao, 1972).

In the seasonal fields, paddy is grown during the monsoon months (June to September) when the backwaters become freshwater-dominated. Soon after the monsoon, paddy is harvested and when the water becomes brackish, postlarve and juveniles of prawns, which are commercially important, migrate into these fields in large numbers. They are allowed to grow on natural food and are harvested from time to time through suitably located sluice gates. The season ends in April/May. The perennial fields, where prawns are harvested throughout the year, are deeper than the seasonal fields. In the seasonal fields, maximum production (362 kg/ha) is obtained in February and minimum (~40 kg/ha) in December. In the perennial fields of the same area, production goes on intermittently from January to April (60 to 125 kg/ha). In some seasonal fields, because of pollution caused by nearby industries, prawn production has declined (Nair *et al.,* 1988).

Among the commercially important prawns, three species namely *Penaeus indicus, Metapenaeus dobsoni* and *M. monoceros* are the most important. The seeds of these three species are being collected in large numbers from the backwaters for aquaculture. The seeds of *P. indicus* are most abundant during the premonsoon months (April-May). Their numbers decrease during the monsoon months but increase again from September and October (postmonsoon) and continue to do so in subsequent months. Seeds of *M. dobsoni* are collected practically throughout the year with their peak abundance from June to August. In *M. monoceros* also, peak abundance of seed is found during the monsoon months (Easo & Mathew, 1989). Prawn seeds are largely detritivorous and therefore, living food alone does not control their peak abundance because their large-scale migration into the estuaries from the inshore waters is for feeding where enough food (detritus) is available all the time. Salinity, more than any other factor, influences the abundance of postlarvae and juveniles of penaeid prawns (Kuttyamma, 1980).

Juveniles of *P. indicus* and *M. dobsoni* were kept in experimental tanks with a closed seawater circulating system (aquarium) and fed on variable quantities of earthworm and their growth was estimated from length-weight relationship. Different feeding levels showed differences in growth rate. Maximum growth occurred when prawns were fed 5 times a day. However, their coefficient of condition (*K*) was found to remain constant in the two species despite the differences in feeding levels (Nair *et al.,* 1982). In another study of length-weight relationship in specimens of *P. indicus* and *M. dobsoni,* collected from the natural environment (backwaters), similar results were obtained on growth but the condition factor (*K*) varied among the two species indicating that the natural environment was more conducive to their growth and well-being than the experimental tanks (Devi *et al.,* 1983).

Most of the commercially important prawns are known to breed in succession throughout the year and hence the rate of growth is difficult to estimate from samples obtained from natural conditions because of the overlap in length-frequency distribution. Hence cage experiments become reliable for the evaluation of the rate of growth. Experiments on *P. indicus* conducted in cages with densities of 5, 10, 20 and 40 specimens in each cage kept in natural environment showed that maximum growth occurred when the density was 5 and minimum with 40 specimens. Since the prawns are voracious feeders, even a small crowding leads to competition in food and it affects their growth rate (Arvindakshan *et al.*, 1980). Experiments conducted on their food preferences in reasonably controlled conditions on *M. dobsoni* showed that it prefers to eat the tenaidacean, *Apseudes chilkensis*. Amphipods such as *Eriopsa chilkensis* and *Maera othonides* are not eaten so readily and a related species of amphipod, *Apseudes gymnophobia* is avoided as food. Live and freshly killed organisms are preferred to dead and decaying animals. Preying efficiency of prawns decreases with increasing quantity of mud in the substratum while depth of water has no effect on the preying efficiency (Balasubramanian *et al.,* 1979).

To identify the conditions of the substratum that effect the preying efficiency and degree of adaptability, experiments were conducted with two species of prawns (*P. indicus* and *M. dobsoni*) by exposing them to different combinations of sand, silt, clay and mud. Preying efficiency declined with a larger percentage of silt and clay and increased with muddy substratum, particularly with *P. indicus* (Devi et al., 1980). A study of shallow low-lying areas of the backwaters, where prawn culture is being practiced on natural food, showed that these ponds are rich in nutrients with high primary production and a detritus-dominated simple food chain. In these ponds, production far exceeds consumption rates and hence these ponds fulfil culture requirements (Balasubramanian *et al.,* 1995).

POLLUTION

It has been briefly mentioned at several places in the text that the backwaters have a high degree of various types of pollution. Organic pollution is caused by sewage system of Cochin Corporation and other municipal wastes which are emptied into the backwaters through several connecting canals. The wastes largely consist of freshwater, contaminated with dissolved and particulate matters of varying degrees. A part of the sewage of the city is treated in a mechanically aerated and activated sludge treatment plant, run by the State Public Health Engineering Department. It has a capacity of 1 million gallons per day. The rest of the sewage water, mixed with domestic waste, is carried along 6 major canals which drain into the backwaters. These canals vary from 0.5 to 1.5 m in depth. Due to tidal action, there is a homogeneous mixing of sewage water with the estuarine water. The tidal currents regularly sweep with the result that oxygen content in the estuary declines at low water and increases significantly at high water. Similar is the case with biochemical oxygen demand (BOD) which becomes high because of the consumption of oxygen by bacteria during decomposition of sewage largely at the bottom and this is clearly reflected at low tides by the production of hydrogen sulphide (H_2S) with the decomposition of organic wastes, particularly in the estuary near the canals. At several places, H_2S values range between 2.25 and 3.41 mg/l in the estuary at the bottom. Effects of pollution are clearly reflected from the zooplankton biomass and bottom fauna obtained from 'polluted' and 'clean' stations (Unnithan *et al.,* 1975). Production of H_2S has also been reported from the backwaters in areas where retting of coconut husk is carried out during the pre- and postmonsoon months. The decomposition process releases H_2S which dissolves in water replacing oxygen content and thus effects the flora and fauna (Zachariah, 1992).

Seasonal changes in some hydrographic features showed that sewage discharge does not lead in significant changes in salinity. High temperature and rapid decomposition during the premonsoon (summer) season lead to low values of oxygen and high values of BOD and sulphide content. The effect of organic pollution starts getting minimised during the premonsoon season and become negligible in the monsoon months (Vijayan *et al.,* 1976). Quantitative abundance of indicator bacteria (coliforms) in the water and sediment samples provide further evidence of contamination with human waste (see under microbes).

Several animals have been identified which become abundant in regions polluted by sewage discharge or from retting of coconut husk. Nineteen species of polychaetes, molluscs and crustaceans were collected from the retting yards. Of these, two species of polychaetes namely *Paraheteromastus tunuis* and *Prionospio polybranchiata* deserve special mention. These animals favour living in places of intense organic enrichment and could be used as indicator organisms. Two polluted sites in the backwaters, which were not far from each other, had their own characteristic assemblage of indicator organisms (Remani *et al.*, 1983).

Using simple, one dimensional approach, flushing period of a part of the estuarine system, which has a connection with the Arabian Sea at Azihikode, has been estimated. Freshwater discharge in the estuary during the dry seasons varies between 21 m^3/s in January to 10 m^3/s in April. During the wet season (June to September), it varies between 123 m^3/s and 387 m^3/s. Cumulative flushing time of the estuary seems to vary from 4.8 tidal cycles in April to 1.22 tidal cycles in August. Longitudinal eddy diffusion, which is a measure of pollution dispersion, lies between 2×106 cm^2/s and 42×10^6 cm^2/s in January (Revichandran & Pylee, 1998).

Besides sewage and organic wastes, pollution coming into the backwaters from industrial wases is quite considerable. There are a number of industrial establishments located in Eloor (Udyogamandal) and this industrial belt extends up to about 5 km from Varapuzha to Alwaye along the banks of the Periyar River which connects the upper reaches of the estuarine system.

Table 10.3 shows some of the features of the effluents which ultimately reach the backwaters. All the effluents have abnormal polluting properties such as high temperature, high chlorinity, alkalinity, suspended matter, COD, BOD and high ammonia to make them environmentally hazardous (Devi *et al.*, 1979). Several instances of fish mortality because of industrial pollution have been reported. Dead and floating specimens of *Ambassis gymnocephalus* were observed on 27 February 1976 probably because of poisoning with ammonia which had far exceeded the accepted limit and resulted in mass killing due to asphyxiation (Unnithan *et al.*, 1997). Another incidence of fish kill occurred on 5 June 1980 in a small tributary of the backwaters (Chitrapuzha) when a number of species (*Eteroplus, Scatophagus and Belone*) were found dead in large numbers (Venugopal *et al.*, 1980). The report says that mortality has been happening for the last several years when the first few monsoon rains occur but in June 1980 it was much heavier than the previous years.

Table 10.3— Chracteristics of effluents after entering the Periyar River (February 1977) (From Devi *et al.*, 1979)

Source of effluent	Temp. (ppm)	Chlorinity (ppm)	*p*H	Diss. Oxygen (m/l)	Alkalinity (mg $CaCO_3$/l)	Susp. Solids (mg/l)	Permanganate consumed (mg/l)	COD (dichromate; mg/l)	BOD (mg/l)	Ammonia (ppm)	Colour of effluents
Periyar chem.	33.90	200	8	1.8	117	264	51.3	4400	51.3	0.12	Orange
Catalysts & Chem India Ltd.	43.9	310	6	1.4	16.4	184	7.67	20	14.30	2.76	Brown
Cominco Binani Zinc Smelters (1)	35.5	300	2	< 0.05	195.8	8	11.93	50	1.3	0.15	Colourless
Bleach Smelters (2)	32.2	50	2	4.5	157.7	16	6.67	10	–	1.1	do
Indian Rare Earths Ltd	36.0	50	6	4.2	10.8	15	12.67	20	6.3	1.86	do
FACT	30.2	50	6	4.4	16.3	12.5	14	30	5.3	3	Light grey
TCC	31.0	150	7	4.3	16.4	50	14.67	190	–	0.18	Colourless
Water Sample Upstream	29.5	50	6.5	6.9	18	8	5.3	20	9	0.03	do

Pollution not only effects the pelagic fauna but also the benthic fauna as one of the studies carried out from the barmouth to the Periyar River covering 9 stations upstream has indicated. Of the 5 major faunal groups and 26 other (minor) communities found at the entrance, polychaetes and molluses were only two groups present in all the 9 stations. The polychaete, *Capitella capitala* was present in enormous numbers near thè waste discharge points and can be considered as an indicator species (Devi & Venugopal, 1989). Sediments of the estuary also showed the effects of pollution when these came from a coconut husk retting yard in the estuary. These were black in colour in stagnant basins. Piths on fibres of the husk in appreciable quantities were also black. The sediments were rich in organic matter but the effect of retting posed adverse problems to benthic communities resulting in low diversity. In such yards, there is low level of tidal mixing and inadequate monsoonal dilution and flushing (Remani *et al.,* 1981).

Colour and texture of the sediments varied from station to station. At the sites of effluents, the colour of the sediment changed with seasons and occasionally contained sulphur particles. In contrast to this, the colour of the sediment at a clean station (barmouth) was constantly dark with abundance of organic matter (Remani, 1979). Concentrations of trace metals such as Co, Zn, Ni, Fe, Mn and Cu in the water samples (surface and bottom) using auto-correlation technique showed no stability in time in relation to most of the metals indicating that these are not controlled by physico-chemical or biological processes but external forces like pollution are involved in their lack of stability (Jayalakshmy & Sankaranarayanan, 1983). An analysis of heavy metals such as Hg, Pb, Zn, Cr and Cd in the sediments of the estuary showed that high concentrations of Hg, Zn and Cd are reaching the backwaters through industrial wastes. Zn and Cd are the potential contaminants of the estuarine sediments (Ouseph, 1987). The concentrations of dissolved and particulate trace metals in surface and bottom water samples showed high seasonal and spatial variability in respect of Cu, Zn and Cd whereas in the case of Ni and Pb, seasonal variability was negligible. Iron was found to be removed while it is in dissolved state. Ultimately, the Arabian Sea acts as a sink for the heavy metals discharged from the industries (Ouseph, 1992).

The distribution of 6 metals (Ni, Zn, Co, Mn, Fe and Cr) in the surficial sediments of Cochin Backwaters (top 5 cm layer) was analysed. The result showed selective accumulation of Mn and Ni in organic sulphide forms while Co was in exchangeable form in marginal amounts. Fe and Cr occurred largely in residual fractions. Zn was noticed in composite fractions. Most of the metals seem to exceed natural levels and indicate pollution coming from the industries (Nair & Balchand, 1993).

Concentrations of four heavy metals (Cu, Zn, Fe and Mn) were estimated in three different tissues (muscle, alimentary canal and gills) of 14 different species of fishes caught in the Chinese dipnet operating at the entrance to the harbour. Generally, their levels were lower in the muscle, which forms the edible part, than in liver and gills. Fe was found to be the most abundant heavy metal in the tissues of fishes. The observed concentrations, however, were within the acceptable limits (Nair *et al.,* 1997).

Vembanad

Mention has been made earlier that the backwater system which has two connections with the Arabian Sea terminates into a large reservoir, called the Vembanad Lake. Among the numerous estuaries and lagoons present on the west coast, it is the largest brackish water lake extending from Vaikom in the north to Alleppey in the south. It is about 115 km long and has an area of 135 km^2. At its southern end, a part of the area has been reclaimed for agricultural purposes after constructing bunds. On the western side, it is separated by the Arabian Sea by a landmass which forms a vast barrier beach along its periphery. Three major rivers namely Pampa, Manimala and Achankoil join the lake at its southern end and almost midway between Cochin and Alleppey, another river Muvattupuzha with its branch Ittupuzha joins the lake in the north. It is a shallow lake with depth varying between 8-10 m in the central part and 2-5 m near the points of river discharge.

Prior to the construction of a bund at its narrowest point at Thaneermukkam, the lake used to get seawater incursion and it was brackish in nature, being flushed regularly. The description, therefore, which follows gives an account of the conditions, which prevailed before the construction of the bund. After the bund was completed, the ecology of Vembanad has changed.

SEDIMENT CHARCTERISTICS

Seven types of sediments have been identified in the estuarine system including the lake. These are: (1) sand, (2) silty sand, (3) sandy silt, (4) clayey silt, (5) sand-silt clay, (6) silty clay, (7) clayey sand. Their grain size ranges from 4 to 8 phi. In terms of texture, the sediments which spread over a large area come under four categories: (1) sand, (2)silty sand, (3) silty clay and (4) clayey silt. Sand is confined to the western margin of the lake as a narrow band running all along the length. In the northern region also, sand is found above Vaikom. Silty sand occupies a greater area of the southern half of the lake. Silty clay is mostly confined to the dredged channels on either side of the Willingdon Island. The fourth type, clayey silt does not spread out much and occurs in patches.

Organic matter in these sediments ranges from 0.10 to 6.00% (average 2.55%). The break-up figures of each of the four types are 0.10-2.80% for sand; 1.38-4.28% for silty sand; 2.90-6.00% for silty clay and 3.30-6.00% for clayey silt. In general, finer sediments show higher values of organic content than coarser sediments (Murty & Veerayya, 1972a). Phosphorus content of the sediments has a wide range, 37-1679 μg/g (average 416 μg/g). The fine-grained sediments namely silty clays and clayey silt have a higher concentration of phosphorus than those of the normal sands and silty sand. Another feature worth noting is that the fine-grained sediments in the estuarine regions have higher concentrations of phosphorus than the freshwater-dominated regions (Murty & Veerayya, 1972b). Sorting of the coarse and fine-grained sediments is done by the major rivers along with the tidal flow into the lake. Coarser fractions, confined to the western part of the southern region of the lake are brought into the lake by the major rivers Muvattupuzha and Ittupuzha. Similarly, medium sand also occurs in these two rivers. Therefore, both coarse and medium sand largely come from these two rivers. Fine sand, very fine sand, silt and clay are not found in high percentages in the two rivers and therefore these types of sediments seem to be brought into the lake by the tidal incursion as the deposition of these into the regions reflects the areas where the tidal currents are pronounced (Veerayya & Murty, 1974). Distribution of trace elements in the sediments of the lake (Fe, Mn, Ti, Ni, Co and Cu) seem to follow the texture of the sediments. Sands coming from the rivers contain very low concentrations of trace elements. A direct relationship seems to exist between trace elements and grain size. Finer grains have higher contents of trace elements as compared to coarse grains. Some trace elements show a direct relationship with the levels of organic matter present in the sediments (Murty & Veerayya, 1981). In a subsequent study (Malik & Suchindan, 1984), the sediments in the lake, south of Thanneermukkam were found to contain quartz as the main component which is an admixture of clay, silt and sand. According to these authors, two main processes seem to be responsible for the formation of sediments in the lake — the initial tectonic phase followed by natural sedimentation processes affected by waves, currents and tides. The grain size of the sediments of northern region of the lake has been reported to be finer than that of the southern region and a high percentage of organic matter has been found to be associated with finer sediments (Purandra & Dora, 1987).

HYDROGRAPHY

As has been pointed out earlier, hydrographic conditions in the backwaters in any season are highly variable from one region to the other. Most of the earlier studies on environmental feature have been restricted to the backwaters in and around Cochin and only a few investigations have been made on the Vembanad Lake. These studies have also been confined to three seasons only — premonsoon, monsoon and postmonsoon — and not carried out continuously in all the months of the year. Therefore, the account presented here is largely related to the three seasons. Nevertheless, it gives some idea of the hydrographic condition prevailing in the Vembanad Lake.

During the premonsoon (taking March as a typical month) and monsoon seasons (taking August as a typical month), some of the hydrographical conditions are shown in Table 10.4.

Table 10.4— Some environmental features of Vembanad Lake during premonsoon and monsoon season (From Devassy & Gopinathan, 1970), S - Surface; B - Bottom

	Premonsoon				Monsoon			
	Thannermukkom (northern region)		Alleppey (southern region)		Thannermukkom (northern region)		Alleppey (southern region)	
	S	B	S	B	S	B	S	B
Temperature °C	29.80	28.30	29.10	29.80	29.80	28.90	29.90	–
Salinity ‰	8.60	7.00	7.00	6.45	0.5	0.6	0.0	0.0
*p*H	6.7	6.5	6.5	6.2	6.5	6.5	–	–
Dissolved O_2 (ml/l)	5.90	3.93	5.50	5.20	–	–	–	–

During the premonsoon seasons, the intrusion of seawater extends in all parts of the backwaters including the Vembanad Lake. In the monsoon season, some effects of salinity is felt up to the northern parts of the Vembanad Lake but in the southern parts it is all freshwater; *p*H and dissolved oxygen do not seem to vary much in the lake.

PHYTOPLANKTON

In March, the biomass of algae increased in the lake because of the presence of freshwater forms such as *Spirogyra* (70 counts/l). The bluegreen algae, *Oscillatoria* and *Spirulina* were also fairly abundant in the lake. In August, there was a predominance of freshwater green algae (*Spirogyra, Pediastrum, Mougetia, Chlorella, Coelophaerium, Cladophora, Closterium, Sataurastrum, Xanthidium, Pleuritaenium, Kirchenerilla* and *Ulothrix*). Bluegreen algae namely *Microcystis, Oscillatoria, Lyngbia* and *Plormidium* were also abundant (Devassy & Gopinathan, 1970).

ZOOPLANKTON

Only a few forms were seen in the lake in March and these included copepods, crustacean larvae and fish eggs. Total biomass was very low. In August, however, there was an increase in the biomass contributed by common freshwater rotifers (*Keratella* and *Trichocera*), cladocerans (*Bosminopsis* and *Ceriodaphnia*) and *Chironomus* larvae.

BOTTOM FAUNA

Polychaetes and bivalves were abundant in the lake. Their counts were 2229/m^2 in August. Of these, polychaetes alone gave 1625 counts/m^2. Taking the entire backwater system as a whole, the highest biomass was recorded from the lake — in March and August, the values were 14.32 g/m^2 and 18.71 g/m^2 respectively. These were largely contributed by polychaetes and bivalves. Meiofauna largely included nematodes, insect larvae and amphipods. Their counts and biomass were relatively low in March but high (667 animals/m^2) in August (Devassy & Gopinathan, 1970). The polychaete, *Diopatra neapolitana* has been recorded from the Vembanad Lake, particularly from the regions where salinity is as low as 18‰. It occurs in firm substrata of fine sand and mud and is rarely seen in the clay of pure sand (Parameswaran, 1973).

According to Rasalam & Sebastian (1976), the lime-shell deposits of the Vembanad Lake have been known since centuries. Bivalve-species (clams) of the genera *Meretrix* and *Villorita* have settled in the lake finding it a suitable environment. In the northern part of the lake, where salinity is relatively high, the genus *Meretrix* got established whereas in the southern part the more freshwater-tolerant species of the genus *Villorita* occupied a considerable portion at one time. During the monsoon months, catastrophic flooding and silt-laden water from the rivers led to the death of the clams *enmasse* which got buried year after year. This process and probably coupled with others, leading to natural mass mortality, might have contributed over the centuries to the accretion of a wealth of clam shell or lime-shell deposits in the lake. The shells can broadly be classified as "white shells" and "black shells". The former are found as subsoil deposits and are known to extend up to 2.5 m below the surface. Dredgings conducted by the Travancore Cement Factory indicate that these deposits may even go deeper up to 5 m below the surface. These are "sub-fossil" or dead remains which have accumulated through the centuries of the once living populations of clams. These shells got discoloured and bleached. The black or brown shells are obtained from the existing population of living clam *Villorita* sp. Live clams from the bottom of the lake are collected, boiled, their flesh is separated and empty shells are marketed.

The following three large factories were operating in the sixties and seventies and these were depending on the lime shells of Vembanad Lake as a major source of raw material:

(a) The Travancore Cement Ltd., Nattakam, Kottayam.
(b) The Travancore Electrochemical Industries Ltd., Chingavanum.
(c) Pallathra Bricks and Tiles Ltd., Kochuramapuram, Shertallai.

For the manufacture of cement and especially the white cement, lime-shells became an ideal raw material. About 50,000 tonnes of lime-shells were utilised annually. Table 10.5 gives the production of cement for 4 years based on the resources of the lake.

Table 10.5— Production of cement by the factory (Travancore Cement Ltd., Nattakam, Kottayam) from 1965 to 1968 (From Rasalam & Sebastian, 1976)

Year		Production of grey cement (tonnes)	Production of white cement (tonnes)	Total production of cement (tonnes)
1965	..	16,140	28,400	44,540
1966	..	42,060	6,700	48,760
1967	..	39,550	10,000	49,550
1968	..	39,260	11,040	50,300

The second factory used to consume about 15,000 tonnes of lime-shells annually for the production of calcium carbide as shown in Table 10.6.

Table 10.6— Production of calcium carbonate by the factory (Travancore Electrochemical Industries Ltd., Chingavanum) from 1965 to 1968 (From Rasalam & Sebastian, 1976)

Year			**Calcium carbonate (tonnes)**
1965	..	..	3,770
1966	..	..	6,118
1967	..	..	8,815
1968	..	..	7,478

Similarly, the production of bricks per day used to be 21,000 for a shift of 8h or about 3 million bricks annually (Table 10.7).

In addition to these factories, the shells were burnt for lime production and the total lime production from the area around Vembanad Lake comes to about 35 thousand tonnes for the year 1968.

Table 10.7— Production of bricks by the factory (Pallathra Bricks and Tiles Ltd.) from 1965 to 1968 (From Rasalam & Sebastian, 1976)

Year		Number of bricks produced per annum				
		Big	Medium	Small	Medium	Total
1965	..	2,59,160	8,38,450	19,23,450	–	30,21,060
1966	..	10,04,597	12,99,141	–	–	23,03,738
1967	..	1,01,018	–	1,78,500	8,37,552	11,17,070
1968	..	–	–	66,080	30,41,781	31,07,861

A marked depletion of living clams has been reported earlier (Rasalam & Sebastian, 1976). The average size of the fished clams has been going down year after year as the young and undersized live clams are removed indiscriminately. The main source of pollution of the live clam beds is the retting of coconut husk in the shallow areas of the lake. The construction of bund at Thaneermukkam has changed the ecology of the lake completely as a large part of the lake has come under freshwater regime, for this project has resulted into the exclusion of saltwater into the lake. It is, therefore, doubtful whether the clams will be able to exist in the lake and their reproduction and propagation will take place in such a changed situation. There was a proposal earlier on the possibility of conservation of this renewable resources by the establishment of a clam sanctuary in the area. It seems now impractical and far-fetched. This was the opinion expressed by Rasalam & Sebastian in 1976.

Hetrotrophic bacteria isolated from the black clam were found to be resistant to heavy metals such as Hg, Cd and Cu. Most of the isolates showed multiple resistance to heavy metals (Sreekumari & Lakshmanaperumalswamy, 1987).

Gopalan *et al.* (1987) have very rightly emphasised the importance of the weed *Salvinia* sp. which covers practically the entire Vembanad Lake. Before the construction of the bund at Thaneermukkam, as noted earlier, because of the intrusion of salinity after the monsoon season, the weeds used to decay in the lake forming mats of detritus at the bottom, but now because there is no tidal action in the lake, the weed is choking the lake practically in all seasons.

FORAMINIFERA

Extensive studies on Foraminifera of the estuarine system including the Vembanad Lake were carried out by Anthony (1980) which have shown a rich assemblance of 32 living species in the sediments. Of these, 21 were calcareous and 11 chitinous and siliceous forms. Their distribution in the environment showed a clear preference of certain salinity conditions on the basis of which they can be divided into the following four groups:

(a) *Stenohaline marine forms* - These were restricted to the barmouth area where marine conditions prevail and are not transported in living conditions into the estuary. They are truly marine forms and are not seen in the regions where salinity is below 30‰. Eighteen species have been included in this group.

(b) *Marine forms with tolerance of small variations in salinity* - Of the 21 calcareous species, 4 occur at salinity 28‰. These species are found up to 6 km inside the estuary from the barmouth.

(c) *Moderately tolerant euryhaline forms* - Nine calcareous marine forms are included in this category. They occur up to 16 km inside the estuary where salinity is about 26‰.

(d) *Highly tolerant euryhaline forms* - Eight calcareous species are distributed where salinity goes down to 24‰ and occurs up to 28 km inside. All the chitinous and siliceous species are highly euryhaline forms and can tolerate very low salinities and occur even in freshwater conditions. These are found in Vembanand Lake.

Although sediment samples were collected up to 8 m depth, a detailed analysis of the population revealed that a significant percentage of the total fauna was found in the upper few centimetres of the sediment. Their vertical distribution in the sediments seems to be controlled by salinity. In the seasons when salinity falls down, Foramenifera occur deeper but never below the oxygenated layer. As these organisms feed in the topmost layer, they seldom go down below 1 cm (Anthony, 1980).

Besides salinity, the quality of sediment (substrate) also appears to have a considerable effect on the distribution of foraminiferal fauna in the estuary. Highest values of living fauna were found in the areas where the bottom sediment consisted of medium-grain sand, mixed with a low percentage of mud. When the percentage of mud increased to more than 40%, their population decreased. Similarly, wherever there was a high percentage of silt in the sediment, foraminiferal density became low. Areas, with coarse sand deposit also had a thin density. High abundance was found where the sediment was clayey sand or has a mixture of sand, silt and clay. This is because such an admixture makes the substrate loose and not compact. Silt-clay combination leads to compact sediment becoming unfavorable for the existence of Foraminifera. Scarcity of Foraminifera in muddy substrate is probably due to a decline in oxygen content caused by bacterial decomposition of the organic matter. Thus, it is seen that salinity and the type of sediment are the two most important characteristics determining the distribution of living Foraminifera (Anthony, 1981).

FISHERY

The occurrence of hilsa, *Hilsa ilisha* in the estuarine system has been reported by Pillay (1960) and has been noted earlier in the text. Two more species namely *Dayella malabaricus* and *Ehirava fluviatilis* (Family: Clupeidae, Sub-family: Pellonulinae) have been reported and described by Kurup & Samuel (1980). The former species occurs in the Vembanad Lake from February to June when the salinity ranges from 0.1 to 3.7‰. It is caught in shrimp nets and constitutes less than 5% of the total catch. The latter species (*E. fluriatilis*) occurs from October to June in the lake. It constitutes a minor fishery from January to May predominantly in the regions where the salinity range is 7.0 to 26.3‰ and is also caught in the Chinese dipnets. In drag nets, the size range 40.0 to 65.0 mm predominantly occurs and the average catch is 6-10 kg/day/craft (Kurup & Samuel, 1980).

Molluscan fishery of the backwaters including the Vembanad Lake is largely sustained by the black clam *Villorita cyprinoides*. Kurup *et al.* (1990) have given an account of the clam fishery based on the data collected from June 1988 to June 1989. Clam beds are found extensively in the backwaters and the fishing methods employed are hand picking and storing them in collection baskets, combing and heaping at low tides with toothed-iron rakes and rakes fitted with bag nets. The entire area of the backwater was divided into 10 zones, of which the occurrence of clam beds was recorded from 8 zones. The annual production of live calm from the 8 zones during the period July 1988 to July 1989, was estimated to be 7025.86 kg at the rate of 333.72 kg/ha. The total area of live clam is about 1565 ha. Maximum quantity is obtained from the southern part of the Vembanad Lake. Over the years, drastic changes have occurred in the distribution and abundance of clams. Extensive beds of *Meretrix meretrix* and *M. casta* which were reported earlier, in addition to *V. cyprinoides*, are now only confined to narrow belts in the northern parts. Their niches in the lake seem to have been taken by the black clam as the fishery now is largely supported by black clams because this species is known to tolerate extreme variations in salinity from 0 to 29.55‰ (Nair & Shynamma, 1975). According to the observation of Kurup *et al.* (1990), maximum yields have come from the regions where salinity ranged from 0 to 13‰ and the largest size group 30-34 mm came from very low saline areas (0-2‰ regions) of southern Vembanad and lower Kuttanad. A comparison of the existing clam resources with the earlier reports shows declining trends over the years. The annual production of clams from 1979 to 1984 was 21490 tonnes. It reached 13804 tonnes in 1984 and 7203 tonnes in 1990. It seems that commissioning of the Thaneermukkam project had initially no marked effect on the clam beds but it is yet to be evaluated in the long run. Predominance of juveniles, measuring 10-14 mm in the catches, indicates a change in the population structure of clams in the Vembanad Lake. The black clam has been found in abundance in Colvale River (Goa) which is entirely freshwater (Chatterji *et al.*, 1984).

The exploited fish, prawn and clam resources are disposed off in 51 fish markets and 32 landing centres located in and around the lake. The list of exploited fishes, prawns etc., includes 110 species of fishes, 6 species of penaeid prawns, 3 species of palaemonids, 3 species of crabs and large quantities of black clam meat (Kurup *et al.*, 1985). Among the 110 species of fishes, *Etroplus suratensis* constituted the maximum quantity of 459 tonnes (10.68%) between June (1988) and May 1989, followed by *Sarotherodon mossambicus* 201.66 tonnes (4.69%), *Etroplus maculatus* 199.74 tonnes (4.65%), *Ehirava fluviatilis*, 198.27 (4.61%), *Daysciaena albida* 162.62 tonnes (3.79%), *Mystus gulio* 124.39 tonnes (2.89%), *Tachysurus maculatus* 106.59 tonnes (2.47%) and *T. subrostratus* 94.83 tonnes (2.20%).

Among the prawns, *Metapenaeus dobsoni* contributed 693.79 tonnes and *Penaeus indicus* 104.69 tonnes (2.44%). The freshwater prawn, *Macrobrachium idella* contributed 258.5 tonnes (6%) and the yield of edible crab, *Scylla serrata* of 98.89 tonnes came to 2.30% of the total catch. The annual production of fishes, prawns and crabs is 7202 tonnes. In addition to this, 7026 tonnes of live clams are obtained annually (Kurup *et al.*, 1985).

References

1. Ansari, Z.A., 1977. Macrobenthos of the Cochin Backwaters. *Mahasagar — Bulletin of National Institute of Oceanography*, Vol. 10, pp. 169-171.
2. Ansell, A.D., Sivadas, P., Narayanan, B., Sankaranarayanan, V.N. & Trevellion, A., 1972a. The ecology of two sandy beaches in south-west India. I. Seasonal changes in physical and chemical factors and in macrofauna. *Marine Biology*, Vol. 17, pp. 38-62.
3. Ansell, A.D., Sivadas, P., Narayanan, B. & Travellion, A., 1972b. The ecology of two sandy beaches in south-west India. II. Notes on *Emerita holthuisi. Marine Biology*, Vol. 17, pp. 311-317.
4. Ansell, A.D., Sivadas, P., Narayanan, B. & Trevellion, A., 1972c. The ecology of two sandy beaches in south-west India. III. Observations on the population of *Donax incarnatus* and *D. spiculum. Marine Biology*, Vol. 17, pp. 318-332.
5. Anthony, A., 1980. Foraminifera of the Vembanad Estuary. *Bulletin Department of Marine Science, University of Cochin*. Vol. 11, pp. 25-63.

6. Anthony, A., 1981. Foraminifera in relation to substrate in the Vembanad Estuary. *Bulletin Department of Marine Science, University of Cochin.* Vol. 12, pp. 129-137.
7. Aravindakshan, P.N., Balasubramanian, T., Devi, C.B.L., Nair, K.K.C., Gopalakrishnan, T.C., Jayalakshmy, K.V. & Kutty, M.K., 1992. Benthos and substratum characteristics of prawn culture fields in and around Cochin Backwaters. *Journal of Marine Biological Association of India*, Vol. 34, pp. 203-217.
8. Aravindakshan, P.N., Paulinose, V.T., Balasubramanian, T., Menon, P.G. & Krishnankutty, M., 1980. On the growth of *Penaeus indicus* experimented in cages at different densities in a selected nursery ground. Paper presented in *Coastal Aquaculture,* published by *Marine Biological Association of India*, Cochin.
9. Balakrishnan, K.P. & Devi, C.B.L., 1982. Development and ecodisaster: A lesson from Cochin Backwaters system. *Water Science Technology, Rotterdam*, Vol. 16, pp. 707-716.
10. Balasubramanian, T., Devi, C.B.L. & Kutty, M.K. 1979. Feeding behaviour and preying efficiency of *Metapenaeus dobsoni. Indian Journal of Marine Sciences*, Vol. 8, pp. 197-199.
11. Balasubramanian, T., Viswakumar, M. & Venugopal, P., 1995. Ecological evaluation of two prawn culture fields in the Cochin Backwater based of premonsoon diurnal observations. *Journal of Marine Biological Association of India*, Vol. 37, pp. 212-220.
12. Bristow, R.C., 1938. *History of mud banks*, Vols. 1 and 2, Government of India Press Cochin, 174 pp. and 53 pp.
13. Bristow, R.C., 1959. *Cochin Saga*, Cassell & Co. Ltd., London, 264 pp.
14. Chatterji, A., Ansari, Z.A. & Parulekar, A. H., 1984. Growth of the black clam, *Villorita cyprinoides (Grey)* from Colvale River (Goa). *Indian Journal of Marine Sciences,* Vol. 13, pp. 119-120.
15. Derbyshire, M., 1967. The surface waters off the coast of Kerala, south-west India. *Deep- Sea Research,* Vol. 14, pp. 295-320.
16. Desai, B. N. & Kutty, M. K., 1977. Studies on benthic fauna of Cochin Backwaters. *Proceedings of Indian Academy of Sciences,* Vol. 66B, pp. 123-142.
17. Desai, B.N. & Kutty, M.K., 1967b. A comparison of marine and estuarine benthic fauna of the nearshore regions of the Arabian Sea. *Bulletin of the National Institute of Sciences of India,* Vol. 38, pp. 677-683.
18. Devassy, V.P. & Gopinathan, C.K., 1970. Hydrographical features of the Kerala Backwaters during premonsoon and monsoon months. *Fishery Technology*, Vol. 7, pp. 190-194.
19. Devi, C.B.L., 1993. Seasonal fluctuation in the distribution of eggs and larvae of flatfishes (Pleuronectiformes - Pisces) in the Cochin Backwaters. *Journal of Indian Fisheries Association*, Vol. 23, pp. 21-34.
20. Devi C.B.L., Balasubramanian, T., Iyer, H.K. & Krishnankutty, M., 1980. Feeding efficiency of *Penaeus indicus* and *Metapenaeus dobsoni* in different experimental substrata. *Mahasagar — Bulletin of National Institute of Oceanography*, Vol. 13, pp. 353-357.
21. Devi, C.B.L., Nair, K.K.C., Balasubramanian, T., Gopalakrishnan, T.C., Arvindakshan, P.N. & Kutty, M.K., 1983. Length-weight relation and condition factor of *Penaeus indicus* and *Metapenaeus dobsoni* in different experimental substrata. *Mahasagar — Bulletin of National Institute of Oceanography*, Vol. 13, pp. 353-357.

22. Devi, K.S., 1989. Temporal and spatial variations in particulate matter, particulate organic carbon and attenuation coefficient in Cochin Backwaters. *Indian Journal of Marine Sciences*, Vol. 18, pp. 242-245.
23. Devi, K.S., Jayalakshmy, K.V. & Venugopal, P., 1991. Communities and coexistence of benthos in northern limb of Cochin Backwaters. *Indian Journal of Marine Sciences*, Vol. 20, pp. 249-254.
24. Devi, K.S. & Venugopal, P., 1989. Benthos of Cochin Backwaters receiving industrial effluents. *Indian Journal of Marine Sciences*, Vol. 18, pp. 165-169.
25. Devi, K.S., Venugopal, P., Remani, K.N., Lalitha, S. & Unnithan R.V., 1979. Hydrographic features and water quality of Cochin Backwaters in relation to industrial pollution. *Indian Journal of Marine Sciences*, Vol. 8, pp. 141-145.
26. Easo, S. & Mathew, K.J., 1989. Seasonal variations in the abundance of penaeid prawn seeds in relation to environmental parameters in the seed grounds of Cochin Backwaters. *Indian Journal of Fisheries*, Vol. 32, pp. 125-132.
27. George, K.C., 1965. On the unusual fishery for mackerel in the Cochin Backwaters. *Journal of Marine Biological Association of India*, Vol. 7, pp. 219-222.
28. George, M.J., 1958. Observation on the plankton of Cochin Backwaters. *Indian Journal of Fisheries*, Vol. 5, pp. 375-401.
29. George, M.J., 1962. On the breeding of penaeids and recruitment of their post larvae into the backwaters of Cochin. *Indian Journal of Fisheries*, Vol. 9, pp. 110-116.
30. George, M.J., 1963. Postlarval abundance as possible index of fishing success in the prawn, *Metapeaneus dobsoni* Miers. *Indian Journal of Fisheries*, Vol. 10, pp. 135-139.
31. George, M.J.& Kartha, K. N. K., 1963. Surface salinity of Cochin Backwaters with reference to tide. *Journal of Marine Biological Association of India*, Vol. 5, pp. 178-184.
32. Gopalan, U.K., Meenakshikunjamma, P.P. & Vengayil, D. T., 1987. Macrobenthos of Vembanad Estuary in relation to the deposition of degraded water from *Salvinia* and other macrophytes. In: *Proceedings of the National Seminar on Estuarine Management*, (ed.) N. B. Nair, pp. 410-414. State Committee on Science, Technology and Environment, Government of Kerala, Trivandrum.
33. Gopinathan, C.K. & Qasim, S. Z. 1971. Silting in navigatinoal of channels of the Cochin harbour area. *Journal of Marine Biological Association of India*, Vol. 13, pp. 14-26.
34. Gopinathan, C.P., 1972. Seasonal abundance of phytoplankton in the Cochin Backwater. *Journal of Marine Biological Association of India*, Vol. 14, pp. 568-577.
35. Gopinathan, C.P., Nair P.V.R. & Nair, A.K.K., 1974. Studies on the phytoplankton of the Cochin Backwater — a tropical estuary. *Indian Journal of Fisheries*, Vol. 21, pp. 501-513.
36. Gore, P.S. & Unnithan, R.V., 1977. *Thiobacilli* from Cochin Backwaters and their oxidative and corrosive activities. *Indian Journal of Marine Sciences*, Vol. 6, pp. 170-172.
37. Gore, P.S., 1972. Isolation and characterisation of *Chlorobium sp.* from estuarine mud at Cochin. *Current Science*, Vol. 41, pp. 737.
38. Gore, P.S., Raveendran, O. & Unnithan, R.V., 1979. Pollution in Cochin Backwaters with reference to indicator bacteria. *Indian Journal of Marine Science*, Vol. 8, pp. 43-46.
39. Jayalakshmi, K.V., Kumaran, V.S. & Vijayan, M., 1986. Phytoplankton distribution in Cochin Backwaters — a seasonal study. *Mahasagar — Bulletin of National Institute of Oceanography*. Vol. 19, pp. 29-37.

40. Jayalakshmi, K. V. & Sankaranarayanan, V.N., 1983. Auto-correlograms and auto-regressive models of trace metal distribution in Cochin Backwaters. *Indian Journal of Marine Sciences*, Vol. 12, pp. 236-238.
41. Joseph, K.J. & Pillai, V. K., 1975. Seasonal distribution of phytoplankters in Cochin Backwaters. *Bulletin of Departmenrt of Marine Sciences, University of Cochin*, Vol. 7, pp. 171-180.
42. Joseph, T., Balachandran, K.K., Nair, M., Venugopal, P. & Sankarnarayanan, V.N., 1998. Changes in water quality at Cochin harbour dredging site, south west coast of India. *Indian Journal of Marine Sciences*, Vol. 27, pp. 250-252.
43. KSSP (Kerala Sastra Sahitya Parishat), 1978. *Problems of Kuttanad.* A study report in Malayalam, 73 pp.
44. Kumar, P.K.D, 1977. Cochin Backwaters: A sad story of manipulation. *Ambio*, Vol. 26, pp. 249-50.
45. Kurian, C. V., 1972. Ecology of benthos in a tropical estuary. *Proceedings of the Indian Academy of Sciences*, Vol. 38, pp. 156-163.
46. Kurup, B. & Samuel, C. T., 1980. Fishes of the subfamily Pellonulinae (Pisces: Clupeoidae) from Vembanad Lake, Kerala, South India. *Bulletin of the Department of Marine Science, University of Cochin*, Vol. 11, pp. 85-98.
47. Kurup, B.N., Sebastian, M.J., Sankaran, T.M. & Rabindranath, P., 1990. Exploited fishery resources of the Vembanad Lake. Part III. Clam fisheries. *Mahasagar — Bulletin of National Institute of Oceanography*, Vol. 23, pp. 127-137.
48. Kurup, B.N., Sebastian, M.J., Sankaran, T.M. & Rabindranath, P., 1985. Exploited resources of the Vembanad Lake : 4. Estimate of marketable surplus of production. *Journal of Marine Biological Association of India*, Vol. 37, pp. 1-10.
49. Kutty, M. K. & Desai, B. N., 1968. A comparison of the efficiency of the bottom samplers used in benthic studies of Cochin. *Marine Biology*, Vol. 1, pp. 168-171.
50. Kuttyamma, V.J., 1975. Studies on the relative abundance and seasonal variations in the occurrence of penaeid prawns in the Cochin Backwaters. *Bulletin of the Department of Marine Sciences, University of Cochin,* Vol. 7, pp. 213-219.
51. Madhupratap, M., 1976. Studies on the zooplankton of Cochin Backwaters (a tropical estuary). Ph. D. Thesis. University of Cochin, 196 pp.
52. Madhupratap, M., 1987. Status and strategy of zooplankton of tropical Indian estuaries: a review. *Bulletin of Plankton Society of Japan*, Vol. 34, pp. 65-81.
53. Madhupratap, M. & Haridas, P., 1975. Composition and variation in the abundance of zooplankton of backwaters from Cochin to Alleppey. *Indian Journal of Marine Sciences*, Vol. 4, pp. 77-85.
54. Madhupratap, M. & Rao, T. S. S., 1979. Tidal and diurnal influence on estuarine zooplankton. *Indian Journal of Marine Sciences*, Vol. 8, pp. 9-11.
55. Madhupratap, M., 1978. Studies on the ecology of zooplankton of Cochin Backwaters. *Mahasagar — Bulletin of National Institute of Oceanography*, Vol. 11, pp. 45-56.
56. Madhupratap, M., 1979. Distribution, community structure and species succession of copepods from Cochin Backwaters. *Indian Journal of Marine Sciences*, Vol. 8, pp. 1-8.
57. Madhupratap, M., Haridas, P., Rao, T. S. S. & Iyer, H.K., 1975. Species association of calanoid copepods in an estuary. *Indian Journal of Marine Sciences*, Vol. 4, pp. 183-184.

58. Madhupratap, M., Rao, T.S.S. & Iyer, H.K., 1977. A model for the prediction of zooplankton in an estuary. *Indian Journal of Marine Sciences*, Vol. 6, pp. 183-184.
59. Malik, T.K. & Suchindan, G. K., 1984. Some sedimentological aspects of Vembanad Lake, Kerala, west coast of India. *Indian Journal of Marine Sciences*, Vol. 13, pp. 159-163.
60. Margalef, R., 1967. Laboratory analogue of estuarine plankton system, pp. 515-521. In: *Estuaries* (ed.) G. H. Lauff, Publication of American Association of Advancement of Science, Series No. 83.
61. Menon, C.A., 1913. *Cochin state manual.* Mangalodayam Company, Trichur, 688 pp.
62. Menon, N. R. & Nair, N. B., 1972. The growth rate of four species of intertidal bryozoans in Cochin Backwaters. *Proceedings of the Indian Academy of Sciences*, Vol. 38 B, pp. 392-402.
63. Menzel, D.W. & Ryther, J.H., 1961. Annual variations in primary production of the Sargasso Sea off Bermuda. *Deep-sea Research*, Vol. 7, 282-288.
64. Murty, P.S.N. & Veerayya, M., 1972a. Studies on the sediments of Vembanad Lake, Kerala State: Part-I - Distribution of organic matter. *Indian Journal of Marine Sciences*, Vol. 1, pp. 45-51.
65. Murty, P.S.N. & Veerayya, M., 1972b. Studies on the sediments of Vembanad Lake, Kerala State: Part-II - Distribution of phosphorus. *Indian Journal of Marine Sciences*, Vol. 1, pp. 106-115.
66. Murty, P.S.N. & Veerayya, M., 1981. Studies on the sediments of Vembanad Lake, Kerala State: Part-IV - Distribution of trace elements. *Indian Journal of Marine Sciences*, Vol. 10, pp. 165-172.
67. Nair, C.K. & Balachand, A.N., 1993. Speciation of trace metals in sediments of a tropical estuary. *Environmental Geology*, Vol. 21, pp. 96-102.
68. Nair, G. S. & Shynamma, C.S., 1975. Studies on the salinity tolerance of *Villorita cyprinoides var, cochinensis* (Hanley). *All India Symposium on Estuarine Biology, Cochin. Bulletin of the Department of Marine Sciences, University of Cochin.* Vol. 7, pp. 537-542.
69. Nair, K.K.C., & Tranter, D.J., 1971. Zooplankton distribution along salinity gradient in the Cochin Backwaters before and after the monsoon. *Journal of Marine Biological Association of India.* Vol. 13, pp. 203-210.
70. Nair, K.K.C., Gopalakrishnan, T. C., Venugopal, P., Peter, M.G., Jayalakshmi, K.V. & Rao, T. S. S., 1983. Population dynamics of estuarine amphipods in Cochin Backwaters, *Marine Ecology — Progress Series*, Vol. 10, pp. 289-295.
71. Nair, K.K.C., Sankaranarayanan, V. N., Gopalakrishnan, T. C., Balasubramanian, T., Devi, C.B.L., Arvindakshan, P.N.R. & Kutty, M.K., 1988. Environmental conditions of some paddy-cum-prawn culture fields of Cochin Backwaters, southwest coast of India, *Indian Journal of Marine Sciences*, Vol. 17, pp. 24-30.
72. Nair, M., Balachandran, K.K., Sankaranarayanan, V.N. & Joseph, T., 1997. Heavy metals in fishes from coastal waters of Cochin, southwest coast of India. *Indian Journal of Marine Sciences*, Vol. 26, pp. 98-100.
73. Nair, N.B., 1994. Distribution of wood-borers in the Vembanad Backwaters. *Fishery Technology*, Vol. 31, pp. 108-111.

74. Nair, S.R.S., Iyer, H.K., Devi, C.B.L & Kutty, M.K., 1982. Studies on the growth of penaeid prawns: 1. Length-weight relation and condition factor under different levels of feeding. *Mahasagar — Bulletin of National Institute of Oceanography*, Vol. 15, pp. 95-104.
75. Ouseph, P.P., 1987. Heavy metal pollution in the sediments of Cochin estuarine system. *Proceedings of National Seminar or Estuarine Management.* (ed.) N.B. Nair, State Commisssion on Science, Technology and Environment, Government of Kerala, Trivandrum, pp. 123-127.
76. Ouseph, P.P., 1992. Dissolved and particulate trace metals in the Cochin Estuary. *Marine Pollution Bulletin*, Vol. 24, pp. 186-192.
77. Parameswaran, U.S., 1973. Distribution of *Diopatra neapolitana* Delle Chiaje (Polychaeta) in the south-west coast of India. *Indian Journal of Marine Sciences,* Vol. 2, pp. 62-63.
78. Pillai, P.P., 1971. Studies on estuarine copepods of India. *Journal of Marine Biological Association of India*, Vol. 13, pp. 162-172.
79. Pillai, P.P., Qasim, S. Z. Nair, A. K. K., 1973. Copepod component of zooplankton in a tropical estuary. *Indian Journal of Marine Sciences*, Vol. 2, pp. 672-676.
80. Pillay, T.V.R., 1960. On the occurrence of hilsa, *Hilsa ilisha (Hamilton)* in the Vembanad Backwaters (Kerala). *Science and Culture*, Vol. 26, p. 48.
81. Pritchard, D.W., 1967. What is an estuary: Physical viewpoint, pp. 3-5. In: *Estuaries* (ed.) G. H. Lauff, Publication of American Association of Advancement of Science, Series No. 83.
82. Purandra, B.K. & Dora, Y.L., 1987. Studies on texture and organic matter in the sediments of Vembanad Lake nearshore sediments. In: *Proceeidings of the National Seminar on Estuarine Management* (ed.) N.B. Nair. State Commission on Science, Technology and Environment, Government of Kerala, Trivandrum, pp. 449-452.
83. Purushan, K.S., 1978. *The ecological studies of oysters - Crassostrea* species in Cochin Backwaters. M. Sc. thesis, University of Cochin, 207 pp.
84. Qasim, S. Z. & Gopinathan, C.K., 1969. Tidal cycle and environment features of Cochin Backwaters (a tropical estuary). *Proceedings of the Indian Academy of Sciences*, Vol. 59 B, pp. 236-247.
85. Qasim, S. Z. & Reddy, C.V.G., 1967. The estimation of plant pigments of Cochin Backwaters during the monsoon months. *Bulletin of Marine Science*, Vol. 17, pp. 95-110.
86. Qasim, S. Z. & Sankaranarayanan, V. N. 1972. Organic detritus of a tropical estuary. *Marine Biology*, Vol. 15, pp. 193-199.
87. Qasim, S. Z. & Madhupratap, M., 1979. Changing ecology of Cochin Backwaters. Contribution of Marine Sciences, Dedicated to Dr. C. V. Kurian, pp. 137-149. Published by the Department of Marine Sciences, University of Cochin.
88. Qasim, S. Z., 1970. Some problems related to the food chain in a tropical estuary. In: *Marine Food Chains* (ed.) J.H. Steele, Oliver & Boyd, Edinburgh, pp. 45-51.
89. Qasim, S. Z., 1973. Productivity of backwaters and estuaries. In: *The biology of the Indian Ocean.* (ed.) B. Zeitzschel, pp. 143-154. Springer-Verlag, Berlin, New York.
90. Qasim, S. Z., 1979. Primary production in some tropical environments. In: *Marine Production Mechanisms, International Biological Programme* 20, (ed.) M.J. Dubar, Cambidge University Press, Cambridge, New York, pp. 31-69.

91. Qasim, S. Z., Bhattathiri, P.M.A. & Abidi, S.A.H., 1968. Solar radiation and its penetration in a tropical estuary. *Journal of Experimental Biology and Ecology,* Vol. 2, pp. 87-103.

92. Qasim, S. Z., Bhattathiri, P.M.A. & Devassy, V.P., 1972a. The influence of salinity on the rate of photosynthesis and abundance of some tropical phytoplankton. *Marine Biology*, Vol. 12, pp. 200-206.

93. Qasim, S. Z., Bhattathiri, P.M.A. & Devassy, V.P., 1972b. The effect of intensity and quality of illumination on the photosynthesis of some tropical phytoplankton. *Marine Biology*, Vol. 16, pp. 22-27.

94. Qasim, S. Z., Bhattathiri, P.M.A. & Devassy, V.P., 1973. Growth kinetics and nutrient requirements of two tropical phytoplankters. *Marine Biology*, Vol. 21, pp. 299-304.

95. Qasim, S. Z., Sumitra-Vijayaraghavan, Joseph, K.J. & Balachandran, V.K., 1974. Contribution of microplankton and nannoplankters in the water of a tropical estuary. *Indian Journal of Marine Sciences*, Vol. 3, pp. 146-149.

96. Qasim, S. Z., Wallershaus, S., Bhattathiri, P. M. A & Abidi, S.A.H., 1969. Organic production in a tropical estuary. *Proceedings of the Indian Academy of Sciences*, Vol. 59B, 51-94.

97. Radhakrishnan, E.V., Gore, P.S., Raveendran, O. & Unnithan, R.V., 1979. Microbial decomposition of the floating weed, *Salvinia modesta* Aublet in Cochin Backwaters. *Indian Journal of Marine Sciences*, Vol. 8, pp. 170-174.

98. Ramamirtham, C.P. & Jayaraman, R., 1963. Some aspects of hydrobiological conditions of the backwaters around Willingdon Island (Cochin). *Journal of Marine Biological Association of India*, Vol. 5, pp. 178-184.

99. Rao, K.K. & Balasubramanian, T., 1996. Distribtution of Foraminifera in the Cochin Estuary. *Journal of Marine Biological Association of India*, Vol. 38, pp. 50-57.

100. Rao, P.V., 1972. Seasonal abundance of larvae and post-larvae of the commercially important penaeid prawns in the inshore waters of Cochin. *Indian Journal of Fisheries*, Vol. 19, pp. 86-96.

101. Rao, T.S.S., Madhupratap, M. & Haridas, P., 1975. Distribution of zooplankton in space and time in a tropical estuary. *Bulletin of the Department of Marine Science, University of Cochin*, Vol. 7, pp. 695-704.

102. Rasalam, E.J. & Sebastian, M.J., 1976. The lime-shell fisheries of the Vembanad Lake, Kerala. *Journal of Marine Biological Association of India*, Vol. 18, pp. 323-355.

103. Revichandran, C. & Pylee, A., 1998. Mixing and flushing time scales in the Azhikode Estuary, southwest coast of Indian. *Indian Journal of Marine Sciences*, Vol. 27, pp. 163-166.

104. Reghu, R., 1973. Migration of the juvenile oil sardine, *Sardinella longiceps* (Val) into the backwaters of Cochin. *Indian Journal of Fisheries*, Vol. 20, pp. 655-658.

105. Remani, K.N., Devi, K.S., Venugopal, P. & Unnithan, R.V., 1983. Indicator organisms of pollution in Cochin Backwaters. *Mahasagar — Bulletin of National Institute of Oceanography*, Vol. 16, pp. 199-207.

106. Remani K.N., 1979. Studies on the effects of pollution with special reference to benthos in Cochin Backwaters - Ph. D. thesis, University of Cochin.

107. Remani, K.N., Venugopal, P., Devi, K.S. & Unnithan, R.V., 1981. Sediments of a retting yard. *Indian Journal of Marine Sciences*, Vol. 10, pp. 41-44.

108. Sankaranarayanan, V. N. & Qasim, S. Z., 1969. Nutrients of Cochin Backwaters in relation of environmental characteristics. *Marine Biology*, Vol. 2, 236-247.
109. Santhakumari, V. & Vannucci, M., 1971. Monsoonal fluctuations in the distribution of hydromedusae in the Cochin Backwaters 1968-69. *Journal of Marine Biological Association of India*, Vol. 13, pp. 211-219.
110. Santhakumary, N. 1966. Some bacterial characteristics of the Cochin Backwaters. *Current Science*, Vol. 35, pp. 310-311.
111. Shynamma, C.S. & Balakrishnan, K.P., 1973. The diurnal variation of some physicochemical factors in the Cochin Backwaters during south west monsoon. *Journal of Marine Biological Association of India*, Vol. 15, pp. 391-398.
112. Silas, E.G. & Pillai, P.P., 1975. Dynamics of zooplankton in a tropical estuary (Cochin Backwaters), with a review on the plankton fauna of the environment. *Bulletin of the Department of Marine Science, University of Cochin*, Vol. 7, pp. 329-355.
113. Sreekumari, K.R. & Lakshmanaperumalswamy, P. 1987. Antibiotic resistance of heterotropic bacteria isolated from water and black clam in Cochin Backwater. *Journal of Marine Biological Association of India*, Vol. 29, pp. 306-309.
114. Steele, J.H., 1965. Some problems in the study of marine resources. , *Special Publication, International Commission North West Atlantic Fisheries*, Vol. 6, pp. 463-476.
115. Tranter, D.J. & Abraham, S., 1971. Coexistence of species of Acartidae (Copepoda) in the Cochin Backwaters, a monsoonal estuarine lagoon. *Marine Biology*, Vol. 11, pp. 222-241.
116. Unnithan, R.V., Vijayan, M. & Remani, K.N., 1975. Organic pollution in Cochin Backwaters. *Indian Journal of Marine Sciences*, Vol. 4, pp. 39-42.
117. Unnithan, R.V., Vijayan, M., Radhakrishnan, E.V., & Remani, K.N., 1977. Incidence of fish mortality from industrial pollution in Cochin Backwaters. *Indian Journal of Marine Sciences*, Vol. 6, pp. 81-83.
118. Veerayya, M. & Murty, P.S.N., 1974. Studies on sediments of Vembanad Lake, Kerala State: Part III – Distribution and interpretation of bottom sediments. *Indian Journal of Marine Sciences*, Vol. 3, pp. 16-27.
119. Venugopal, P., Remani, K.N., Sarladevi, K. & Unnithan, R.V., 1980. Fish kill in Chitrapuzha. *Seafood Export Journal*, Vol. 12, pp. 1-4.
120. Vijayan, M., Remani, K.N. & Unnithan, R.V., 1976. Effects of organic pollution on some hydrogrphic features of Cochin Backwaters. *Indian Journal of Marine Sciences*, Vol. 5, pp. 196-200.
121. Wyatt, T. & Qasim, S. Z., 1973. Application of a model to an estuarine ecosystem. *Limnology and Oceanography*, Vol. 18, pp. 301-306.
122. Zachariah, T., 1992. Effects of salinity and hydrogen sulphide on the dissolved oxygen in the natural backwaters of Kerala. *Pollution Research*, Vol. 11, pp. 232-233.

Chapter 11

Kali

The river Kali is one of the important rivers of Karnataka. It originates in the Western Ghats and after flowing in southwestern direction, opens into the Arabian Sea at Karwar Bay forming the Kali Estuary along Lat. 14°50′N and Long. 74°07′E (Fig. 11.1). Like others, it is also a mixed estuary because it is influenced by the tidal flow from one side and dilution with freshwater from the other side. From June to September, the area receives heavy rainfall during the southwest monsoon and a sand bar appears at the mouth of the river. The estuary has a considerable impact on the adjoining coastal waters and forms an important source of fishery and fish and prawn seed resources.

Like the other estuaries of the west coast, the physicochemical conditions of the Kali estuary are controlled by the freshwater regime during the monsoon period and the seawater incursion by the tides (Gunaga & Neelakantan, 1987). The tides in the area are semidiurnal with a range of about 2 m. The time and range, however, of the two floods and two ebbs show marked variations.

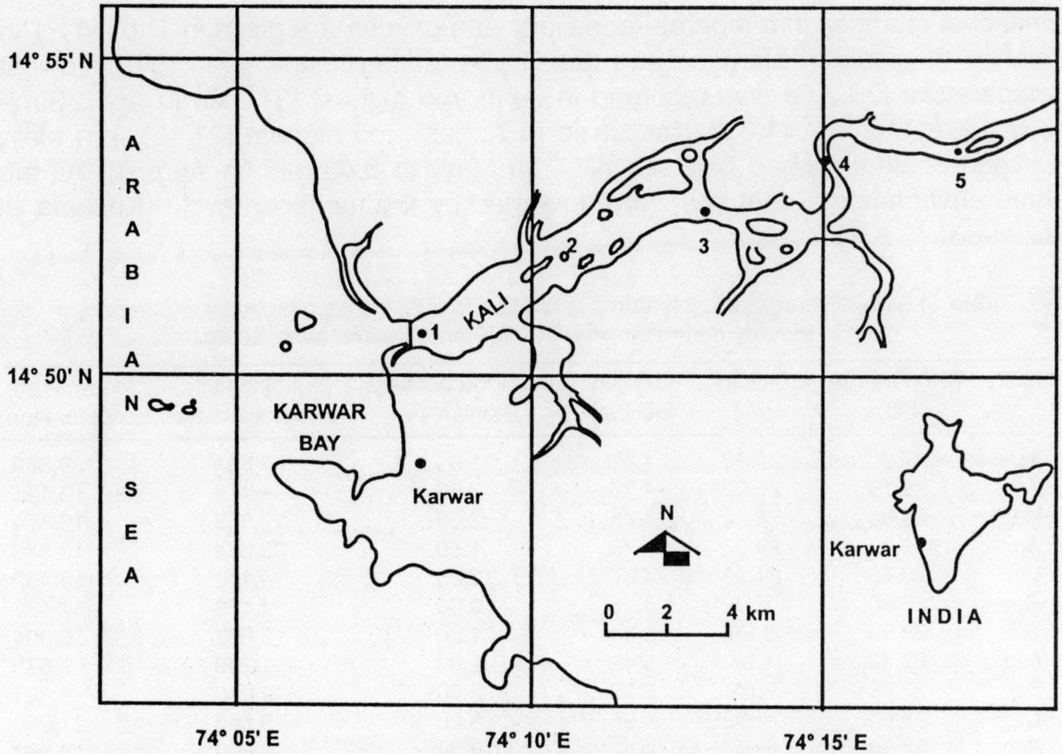

Fig. 11.1 Map showing the location of Kali estuary and the 5 study stations (From Bhat & Neelakantan, 1984-85).

HYDROGRAPHY

Changes in hydrographical features were studied in relation to tides during different lunar phases in the months of August and September 1986 (SW monsoon). Temperature of water was independent of tidal rhythm but some variation in temperature was noticed with the time of the day. Salinity, on the other hand, was greatly influenced by the tides. Higher salinity values were recorded during the high and receding tides and low values during the low and rising tides. A greater fluctuation in salinity was noticed during the full-moon and new-moon (total range

1.46 – 28.87 ‰) and minimum during the half-moon (range 5.75 – 15.31 ‰). In general, the concentration of dissolved oxygen was high during the low tide and low during the high tide (Gunaga & Neelakantan, 1987).

Seasonal changes in temperature, salinity and oxygen are given in Table 11.1 in relation to plankton biomass and density pertaining to the year 1979. Lowest temperature (26.2°C) was recorded in June and highest (31.3°C) in April. Similarly, lowest salinity (1.33‰) occurred in August and highest (31.12‰) in May. Oxygen content ranged between 4.67 (in May) to 5.42 ml/l (in August). All the three environmental features were governed by the monsoon cycle (Kusuma *et al.,* 1988).

Table 11.1— Hydrographical features in relation to total plankton biomass and density in Kali Estuary during the year 1979 (From Kusuma *et al.,* 1988)

Month	Temperature (°C)	Salinity (‰)	Oxygen (ml/litre)	Plankton biomass (ml/m^3)	Plankton density (counts/m^2)	
					Phytoplankton	Zooplankton
Jan	27.90	27.82	4.81	1.60	40,631	9,509
Feb	28.10	27.92	4.77	3.60	54,175	19,451
Mar	29.00	28.22	4.75	2.00	27,953	18,874
Apr	31.30	29.03	4.78	1.50	23,334	13,543
May	28.70	31.12	4.67	2.20	14,120	13,432
Jun	26.20	7.10	5.26	0.90	4,178	4,437
Jul	26.80	3.86	5.34	1.20	2,881	5,904
Aug	27.30	1.33	5.42	2.80	1,229	2,678
Sep	27.50	8.02	5.29	2.00	2,080	9,221
Oct	27.60	14.92	4.96	3.20	13,543	21,900
Nov	27.80	19.06	4.87	2.50	3,602	12,391
Dec	27.50	24.61	4.73	1.30	5,182	9,365

PLANKTON

Biomass and Diversity

Values of total planktonic biomass (phyto and zoo combined) varied between 0.9 and 3.6 ml/m^3 during the year (Table 11.1). Two peaks were recorded — one between August and November and the other between January and April. An increase in the value was found again in May (Table 11.1). Plankton density was not strictly correlated with the biomass. Nevertheless, a bimodal abundance was clearly evident during the year. The peaks obtained in February were the highest on both phyto-and zooplankton. Maximum density of phytoplankton was recorded in February and lowest in August. A reduction in phytoplankton counts during the peak abundance of zooplankton from September to November seems to indicate the effect of grazing (Kusuma *et al.*, 1988).

Composition

Seasonal cycle of the three main families of phytoplankton namely Bacillariophyceae, Dinophyceae and Myxophyceae, recorded from the estuary is shown in Table 11.2. Their maximum abundance was from January to April although they were abundant in the postmonsoon period also.

Major species representing Bacillariophyceae were *Thallassiosira gravida, Nitzschia seriata* and *Asterionella japonica.* Dinophyceae was represented by *Noctiluca miliaris, Peridinium depressum, Ceratium furca* and *C. fusus*. Myxophyceae was represented by *Trichodesmium erythraeum* from January to March.

Zooplankton was represented by 8 groups with copepods and protozoan recording greater abundance than the other forms (Table 11.2). Copepods varied between 12.5 and 32.2% of the total counts whereas chaetognaths, polychaetes, pteropods, etc., occurred in low percentages. Larval forms were represented by bivalves, crustaceans, echinoderms, etc., whereas the miscellaneous group consisted of fish eggs, amphipods, isopods and cladocerans. Major controlling factor in the distribution of zooplankton organisms in the estuary was the monsoon cycle (Kusuma *et al.*, 1988).

Table 11.2— Seasonal variation (%) in the composition of plankton in Kali Estuary during the year 1979 (From Kusuma *et al.*, 1988)

Group	Jan	Feb	Mar	Apr	May	Jun	Jul	Aug	Sep	Oct	Nov	Dec
Phytoplankton												
Total density	73.8	73.9	57.7	62.6	46.2	49.2	35.3	39.5	26.7	34.2	30.7	32.2
Bacillariophyceae	71.3	25.1	38.8	45.6	26.9	33.9	15.2	27.0	15.0	34.2	30.7	32.2
Dinophyceae	2.2	46.4	16.6	17.0	19.3	15.3	20.1	12.5	11.7	–	–	–
Myxophyceae	0.3	2.4	2.3	–	–	–	–	–	–	–	–	–
Zooplankton												
Total density	26.2	26.1	42.3	37.4	53.8	50.8	64.7	60.5	73.3	65.8	69.3	67.8
Protozoa	4.3	3.4	7.0	3.6	11.8	8.6	7.6	–	16.3	22.6	14.9	9.0
Copepoda	12.5	18.0	22.0	16.2	22.4	20.4	28.0	23.8	28.3	13.4	23.0	32.2
Chaetognatha	–	–	0.6	2.3	5.2	–	–	1.7	5.8	6.2	–	–
Polychaeta	0.3	–	0.9	1.0	–	–	–	–	–	–	–	–
Pteropoda	–	0.4	0.3	–	–	–	–	–	–	–	–	–
Protochordata	–	–	–	–	–	–	–	–	–	3.0	2.5	–
Larval forms	3.1	3.6	6.8	7.5	8.4	11.8	13.9	15.8	10.9	10.1	20.6	17.0
Miscellaneous	6.0	0.7	4.7	6.8	6.0	10.0	15.2	19.2	12.0	10.5	8.3	9.6

Mangrove vegetation along the Kali estuarine region varies from sparse to dense growth of forests in which 17 species have been identified. A study on the chlorophyll and light attenuation by the leaves of 12 species of mangrove was conducted (Menon & Neelakantan, 1992). Three types of leaves were selected for this study. These were young, intermediate and old leaves. The leaves selected for pigment analysis were taken from two areas. One was directly exposed to continuous sunlight and the other was under the shade which received diffused light. The study was spread over 7 stations. The leaves in the shaded areas were found to contain more pigments than the leaves under the sun. Mature leaves in the shade had a greater concentration of pigments and these probably absorbed more radiation than the other types of leaves. The differences in pigment content of the leaves probably give a reflection on the photosynthetic activity of the plants (Menon & Neelakantan, 1992).

BENTHIC FAUNA

Larval Development

A small hermit crab, *Diogenes avarus* is very common in sandy areas of the intertidal zone of Kali Estuary. The adults of this species are found in groups. Berried females were collected and brought to the laboratory and hatched larvae were reared through their complete metamorphosis up to the 1st instar crab in the laboratory. The life cycle passed through 4 zoeal and a glaucothae stages. The different larval stages have been described and figured (Sankolli & Shenoy, 1975).

Larval development of the pea crab, *Pinnotheres gracilis* was also studied in the laboratory by obtaining ovigerous crabs from the Kali Estuary in June 1973. The crabs occur infesting the common edible clam, *Katelysia opima*. Its life history comprises 4 zoeal and one megalopa stages which have been described and figured (Kakati & Sankolli, 1975).

A complete larval development of the spider crab, *Elamenopsis demeloi* was studied from the larvae hatched by an ovigerous crab collected from the estuary and reared in the laboratory. Three zoeal and one megalopa stages intervene before the formation of the first stage crab. The life history has been described and the various stages figured (Kakati, 1988).

Biomass and Population Density

A detailed study of the benthic fauna of Kali Estuary was carried out in the year 1974 in which seasonal changes in the biomass and population density were measured in relation to changes in environmental features at 7 stations. There was a decline in the biomass with the onset of monsoon and minimum values were recorded during this period. It began to increase during the postmonsoon season reaching the maximum values during the premonsoon. A similar cycle was shown by their population density. The fauna was mainly composed of bivalves, *Paphia malabarica* and *Meretrix casta*, followed by polychaetes, gastropods, gammarids, isopods, amphipods, mysids, and crabs. Dominance of bivalves was observed at 5 stations which had sandy bottom whereas polychaetes were abundant at two stations where muddy bottom prevailed. Clams contributed to more than 65% of the total biomass which varied from 0.125 in September to 110.52g wet weight / m^2 in March with a corresponding population density in numbers from 25 to 650/m^2 during the year. Salinity showed a wide variation from 6.45 to 33.65‰. Changes in the composition of fauna and their biomass seem to be regulated by differences in the type of substrata and fluctuations in salinity (Harkantra, 1975a).

Large quantities of clams are being collected from the estuary for food and these are also used as a bait for fishing. Their shell is utilized for making lime. Hand picking and scoop net fishing are commonly employed for their collection. Observations on the ecology, growth and spawning of *Meretrix casta* showed that it grew at the rate of 2.9 mm per month. Its growth was faster in some months when the salinity and temperature of water were high. Increase in shell weight was faster than any other linear dimension. The clam is a continuous breeder with a succession of spawnings. It has some break in winter when the temperature is low. It begins to spawn at 10 mm in size and juveniles occur practically throughout the year (Harkantra, 1975b).

Another study on both meio and macrobenthos was undertaken from September 1981 to September 1982 at 5 stations in which 16 meiobenthic and 14 macrobenthic taxa were identified. Both the groups of benthic fauna showed a typical bimodal distribution with a minimum in September and two peaks during the postmonsoon and premonsoon periods. Dominant meiobenthic group was nematodes followed by harpacticoids, Foraminifera, etc. Among the macrobenthic group, no single taxa dominated at all the five stations where the work was carried out. At some stations, polychaetes were maximum while in others bivalves outnumbered the other taxa (Bhat & Neelakantan, 1984-85).

Another study on meiobenthos in relation to environmental factors confirmed the existence of 15 taxa with nematodes as the dominant group. The nature of substrata and salinity were the two important factors contributing to their distribution. Organic carbon in the interstitial water was another factor to influence their density. It was greater in finer substrates (Bhat & Neelakantan, 1991).

Distribution of macrobenthic fauna in the Kali Estuary at 5 stations is shown in Table 11.3. Polychaetes dominated all other groups at all the stations followed by bivalves, gastropods and crustaceans. Seasonal distribution of the total macrobenthic fauna is given in Table 11.4. Maximum abundance is seen from October to May and minimum from June to September (Table 11.4). A greater abundance of the fauna was found at stations 1, 3 and 4 (Table 11.4) where salinity remained higher than at other stations (Bhat & Neelakantan, 1988).

Table 11.3— Percentage frequency of macrobenthos distribution at 5 stations in Kali Estuary (From Bhat & Neelakantan, 1988)

Taxa	Stations				
	1	2	3	4	5
Foraminifera	3.69	2.04	5.36	8.79	1.61
Coelenterata	3.02	–	–	–	–
Polychaeta	46.48	21.93	37.85	51.26	17.74
Gastropoda	4.53	10.20	5.65	3.19	11.29
Bivalvia	15.77	30.61	21.19	4.79	22.58
Harpacticoida	4.53	3.06	3.11	5.46	3.23
Cumacea	5.44	1.53	2.26	3.86	3.23
Tanaidacea	4.87	3.57	3.67	5.73	4.84
Isopoda	2.52	1.02	1.69	3.46	1.61
Amphipoda	2.01	2.55	2.82	5.46	1.61
Mysidacea	–	3.57	3.11	–	–
Shrimps	2.18	6.12	6.50	2.53	22.58
Crabs	4.87	12.24	6.50	3.73	8.06
Pisces	–	–	0.28	0.13	1.61

FISHERY

Karwar is one of the important fish landing centres of the central west coast of India. It forms a stretch of 144 km of the northern Karnataka coastline. The waters of Karwar are rich in important food fishes like mackerel, sardine, sciaenids and prawns and the fishery is supported by both pelagic and demersal fishes. Different types of crafts and gears are used for fishing. A significant share of the landings is contributed by conventional or traditional methods. A detailed account of the types of craft and gear used and the fishing methods employed has been given by Shetty *et al.* (1993). The methods broadly include:

(a) Traditional
  (i) Rampani
  (ii) Boat sienes
  (iii) Gill nets
(b) Mechanised
  (i) Purse-seining
  (ii) Trawling

Table 11.4— Seasonal variation of macrobenthic fauna (no/m^2) at 5 stations in Kali Estuary (From Bhat & Neelakantan, 1988)

Months	Stations 1	2	3	4	5	Mean
1981						
September	76	59	83	103	45	73.20
October	385	36	247	455	54	235.40
November	739	242	484	1114	86	533.00
December	1408	443	869	1790	124	926.80
1982						
January	1274	362	706	1448	90	776.00
February	767	281	530	1057	66	527.00
March	592	186	370	668	41	371.40
April	976	261	519	1156	69	596.20
May	1074	370	628	1374	94	708.00
June	227	146	178	268	28	168.40
July	113	27	62	149	27	75.60
August	54	21	42	82	27	46.00
September	62	64	75	91	41	66.00
Mean	595.92	192.15	368.69	750.31	60.92	

Traditional

Rampani

It is believed that this method of fishing was introduced by a Portuguese priest Rev. Fr. Rampon. It is an exceptionally long net containing several hundred pieces, each about 10-12 m long of varying breadth, laced together. The mesh size of the net decreases from the outer to the central part while the thickness of the twine increases. Basically it has three parts — a central portion joined with wing-like nets on either side. Each part can be increased or decreased by adding or removing the number of pieces. Usually the length of the wings constitutes 85-95% of the total length. The head of the net is kept buoyant with floats and the foot rope is weighed with sinkers. A large float is fixed at the centre of the net to indicate its entire position.

About 80-90 fishermen are required to operate this net depending upon its size. A motor boat 15-16 m long called 'Pandy' and 4-6 dugout canoes locally known as 'Dhoni' are used during its operation. When a shoal of fish is sighted, the pandy boat is steered in a semicircular path paying one end of the net and bringing back the other end surroundings the shoal. The small dhoni boats are used to keep the net in an erect position. The net is then dragged from both ends to bring the catch either ashore or impounded in the water near the shore for several days and the fishes are caught in stages depending upon their demand. Sardines and mackerel are the main fishes caught by rampani operation (Shetty *et al.,* 1993).

Boat seines

These are of different sizes operated up to 30 m depth and are known by different names locally depending upon their length, mesh size and the type of fish to be caught. Their depth of operation also differs and is based on their size. The method of their operation is similar to that of rampani and in each case a shoal is encircled and hauled on to the shore. Different types of boats are used in paying the net in the form of an arc. Most of the time the net is operated by 3-4 persons and at times using a single boat when it is small (Shetty *et al.,* 1993).

Gill nets

These are passive types of nets used for catching moving fishes from different depths. The nets are fixed by anchoring in one position or are allowed to drift at the surface, midwater or bottom along with the wind, tides or currents. Fishes are caught by entangling their gills in the meshes. The nets are hauled twice in 24 h during the day and at night.

Mechanised Fishing

Purse-seining

This method was introduced in 1975 in northern Karnataka and is now dominating the other types of gears. It is an innovation employed to catch pelagic fishes. The net is operated either by a single boat or by 2-3 boats depending upon its size. It encircles a shoal and its bottom is pulled in such a way that an artificial pond is created in the sea and thus the entire catch gets trapped in a purse-like fashion and hence it derives its name.

Trawling

This method was first introduced in 1963 by the Indo-Norwegian Project to modernise fishing. Usually otter trawls are used and their depths of operation range between 20 and 60 m. The length of the trawl ranges between 9 and 13 m and 45 - 65 HP boats are used for laying the trawl and hauling it up on to the boat. The net is made of synthetic fibre and normally it catches demersal fishes at or near the bottom including prawns.

FISHING IN KAḶI ESTUARY

Several diversified methods of traditional fishing are used in the estuary almost throughout the year. These include :

(a) Gill nets of various sizes set in the estuary.
(b) Cast nets operated either from the shore or from the boats. These are either stringless with peripheral pockets or stringed without pockets.
(c) Hook and line – baited hooks tied to a line.
(d) Pole and line – baited hooks mounted on a line attached to a pole.
(e) Drag nets made of nylon cloth of varying dimensions used for catching prawn seeds.
(f) Scoop nets made of nylon material mounted loosely on a rectangular frame.
(g) Light fishing using strong light to attract fishes at night.
(h) Scarce line – coconut leaves tied to a line at intervals and moved to scare the fishes which are driven towards a fixed net.
(i) Crab fishing using bamboo traps with baits and
(j) Clam fishing by hand-picking at low tide or by dragging bagnets of wire meshes.

TOTAL LANDING

At Karwar the total fish landing from 1981-82 to 1986-87 was between 10,000 and 15,000 tonnes from the inshore waters. Catches from the Kali Estuary form the mainstay throughout the year (Shetty *et al.,* 1993).

PRAWN SEEDS

Postlarvae and early juvenile stages are collected at about low tide from the estuary in large numbers for stocking them in prawn farms (Gunaga *et al.,* 1990a). In the year 1986-87, about 1539 seeds of *Penaeus merguiensis*, 4117 of *Metapenaeus dobsoni*, 952 of *M. monoceros* and 138 of *M. affinis* were collected from the estuary. Their size ranged from 6 to 10mm. From the seasonal availability of seeds in the estuary, it can be deduced that all the species noted above breed continuously throughout the year (Gunaga *et al.*, 1989 & 1990b). Along with tides, there is a lunar influence on the availability of prawn seeds. Their maximum abundance occurs during the new moon (Gunaga *et al.*, 1990c).

PRAWN FARMING

The annual prawn production from the 320 km coastline of Karnataka ranged between 2594 and 8440 tonnes (average 5088 tonnes) for the years 1975 to 1984. Along the coast, there are several estuaries. Of these, Kali, Aghashini ad Gangolli provide great potential for prawn culture. The total brackishwater area suitable for prawn farming amounts to 4000 ha. Of these, nearly 2500 ha are being used for traditional trapping and holding a system of culture which gives rise to about 150 tonnes of prawns every year. This can easily be doubled by practising intensive and semi-intensive prawn culture techniques (Krishnamurthy, 1987). A study conducted during 1984-85 on the water quality, soil fertility and biotic components (plankton and benthos) of the Kali Estuary showed that it has a great potential for aquaculture. About 750 acres of the 1217 acres of low-lying areas have been found to be suitable for prawn farming. Bottom soil in most of the areas is composed of silty sand and clayey sand rich in organic carbon, nitrogen and phosphorus (Neelakantan *et al.*, 1987).

SEDIMENT MOVEMENT

Nayak (1996) studied the distribution of grain size parameters along the 11 km stretch of beach sediments between Majali and Karwar. His findings indicate that there is a marked decrease in grain size on either side of the mouth of the Kali River. Continuous supply of material by freshwater discharge into the river, particularly during the monsoon months, leads to the formation a shoal. This shoal along with small islands occurring outside the estuary obstruct the littoral currents and there is a change in the direction of flow resulting in the formation of a bar near the river mouth. Northerly currents along the beach seem to be responsible for the transportation of finer material on either side.

POLLUTION

None of the papers on which the present account on Kali Estuary is based has mentioned about pollution existing in the Kali Estuary. No sizeable industry of a polluting nature seems to exist at Karwar. Therefore, one can assume that Kali is one of the cleanest estuaries of the country. The mere fact that the life histories of several species of crustaceans have been worked out based on the larval forms reared in the laboratory is a testimony that no toxicity is present in the Karwar seawater. The only threat that has been mentioned is the indiscriminate exploitation of molluscan resources, generally clams and the extraction of sand from the beaches for commercial purposes which may alter the profile of the bed and may thus effect the benthic fauna (Bhat & Neelakantan, 1988).

References

1. Bhat, U.G. & Neelakantan, B., 1984-85. Composition and distribution of benthos in Kali Estuary, Karwar. *Journal of Indian Fisheries Association*, Vol. 14-15, pp. 27-35.
2. Bhat, U.G. & Neelakantan, B., 1988. Environmental impact on the macrobenthos distribution of Kali Estuary, Karwar, central west coast of India. *Indian Journal of Marine Sciences*, Vol. 17, pp. 134-142.
3. Bhat, U.G. & Neelakantan, B., 1991. Distribution of meiobenthos in relation to environmental parameters in Kali Estuary, Karwar. *Comparative Physiological Ecology*, Vol. 16, pp. 60-68.
4. Gunaga, V. & Neelakantan, B., 1987. Changes in the hydrological parameters of the Kali Estuary in relation to tides during monsoon period. In: *Proceedings of the National Seminar on Estuarine Managements* (ed.) N.B. Nair. State Committee on Science, Technology and Environment, Government of Kerala, Trivandrum, India, pp. 73-75.
5. Gunaga, V., Neelakantan, K. & Neelakantan, B., 1989. Seasonal abundance of penaeid postlarvae in the Kali Estuary. *Mahasagar — Bulletin of National Institute of Oceanography*, Vol. 22, pp. 193-197.
6. Gunaga, V., Neelakantan, K. & Neelakantan, B., 1990a. Tidal occurrence of penaeid prawn seed in the Kali Estuary, Karwar. *Indian Journal of Fisheries*, Vol. 37, pp. 37, 43.
7. Gunaga, V., Neelakantan, K. & Neelakantan, B., 1990b. Size distribution of penaeid prawn seed in the Kali Estuary, Karwar. *Indian Journal of Fisheries*, Vol. 37, pp. 109-117.
8. Gunaga, V., Neelakantan, K. & Neelakantan, B., 1990c. Tidal and lunar influence on penaeid prawn seed abundance in the Kali Estuary, Karwar. *Mahasagar — Bulletin of National Institute of Oceanography*, Vol. 23, pp. 63-69.
9. Harkantra, S.N., 1975a. Benthos of the Kali Estuary, Karwar. *Mahasagar — Bulletin of National Institute of Oceanography*, Vol. 8, pp. 53-58.
10. Harkantra, S.N., 1975b. Some observations on the clam beds of Kali Estuary, Karwar. *Mahasagar — Bulletin of National Institute of Oceanography*, Vol. 8, pp. 101-108.
11. Kakati, V.S. & Sankolli, K.N., 1975. Larval development of the pea crab, *Pinnotheres gracilis* Burger, under laboratory conditions (Decapoda, Brachyura). In : All India Symposium on Estuarine Biology, Cochin, India. *Bulletin Department of Marine Sciences, University of Cochin*, Vol. 7, pp. 965-979, Special Issue : Contribution to Estuarine Biology (ed.) C. V. Kurian.
12. Kakati, V.S., 1998. Larval development of the Indian spider crab, *Elamenopsis demeloi* (Kemp) (Brachyura, Hymenosomatidae) in the laboratory. *Mahasagar — Bulletin of National Institute of Oceanography*, Vol. 21 pp. 219-227.

13. Krishnamurthy, V., 1987. Present status and prospects of prawn farming in Karnataka. In: *Proceedings of National Seminar on Estuarine Management* (ed.) N.B. Nair. State Committee on Science, Technology and Environment, Government of Kerala, Trivandrum, India. pp. 364-366.
14. Kusuma, M.S., Neelakantan, B. & Konnur, R.G., 1988. Plankton distribution in the Kali Estuary, Karwar, central west coast of India. *Environmental Ecology*. Vol. 6, pp. 115-119.
15. Menon, G.G. & Neelakantan, B., 1992. Chlorophyll and light attenuation from the leaves of mangrove species of Kali Estuary. *Indian Journal of Marine Sciences*, Vol. 21, pp. 13-16.
16. Nayak, G.N., 1996. Grain size parameters as indicator of sediment around river mouth, near Karwar, west coast of India. *Indian Journal of Marine Sciences*, Vol. 25, pp. 346-348.
17. Neelakantan, B., Prasad, P.N., Naik, U.G., Gunaga, V. & Kusuma, M.S., 1987. Culture potentiality of Kali Estuary and adjoining brackishwater systems. In: *Proceedings of National Seminar on Estuarine Management* (ed.) N.B. Nair. State Committee on Science, Technology and Environment, Government of Kerala. Trivandrum, India, pp. 350-358.
18. Sankolli, K.N. & Shenoy, S., 1975. Laboratory culture of the hermit crab, *Diogenes avarus* Heller (Crustacea, Decapoda, Anomura). In: All India Symposium on Estuarine Biology, Cochin, India. *Bulletin Department of Marine Science, University of Cochin*, Special Issue, Vol. 7, pp. 293-308 (ed.) C.V. Kurian.
19. Shetty, D.C., Reddy, C.R., Kusuma, M.S. & Neelakantan, B., 1993. Fishing methods of Karwar waters. *Journal of Marine Biological Association of India*, Vol. 35, pp. 95-104.

Chapter 12

Mandovi-Zuari System

The estuarine system formed by the two rivers, Mandovi and Zuari, is located along Lat. 15°25′ to 15°31 ′N and Long. 73°45′ to 73 °59 ′E in Goa. It is also one of the very well-studied estuarine systems in the country. Both the rivers have their sources in the Western Ghats. The Mandovi and Zuari rivers run about 75 km and 70 km, respectively before meeting the Arabian Sea (Fig. 12.1). The width at the mouth of Mandovi Estuary is about 3.2 km and that of the Zuari is approximately 5.5 km — the former narrows down to less than 0.25 km and the latter to about 0.5 km upstream. The two rivers are influenced by the seawater inflow caused by the tidal action up to a considerable distance inland. During the southwest monsoon season (June to September), the two rivers receive considerable volumes of freshwater, but little during the rest of the years. The average rainfall in Goa is about 3000 mm/y, of which nearly 80% takes place during June, July and August (3 months). Each of these months; records more than 500 mm of rainfall. Monsoon precipitation feeds both the rivers which also receive large volumes of land runoff from the catchment areas of 1150 and 550 km^2 of Mandovi and Zuari basins, respectively. A number of other rivers and rivulets join the

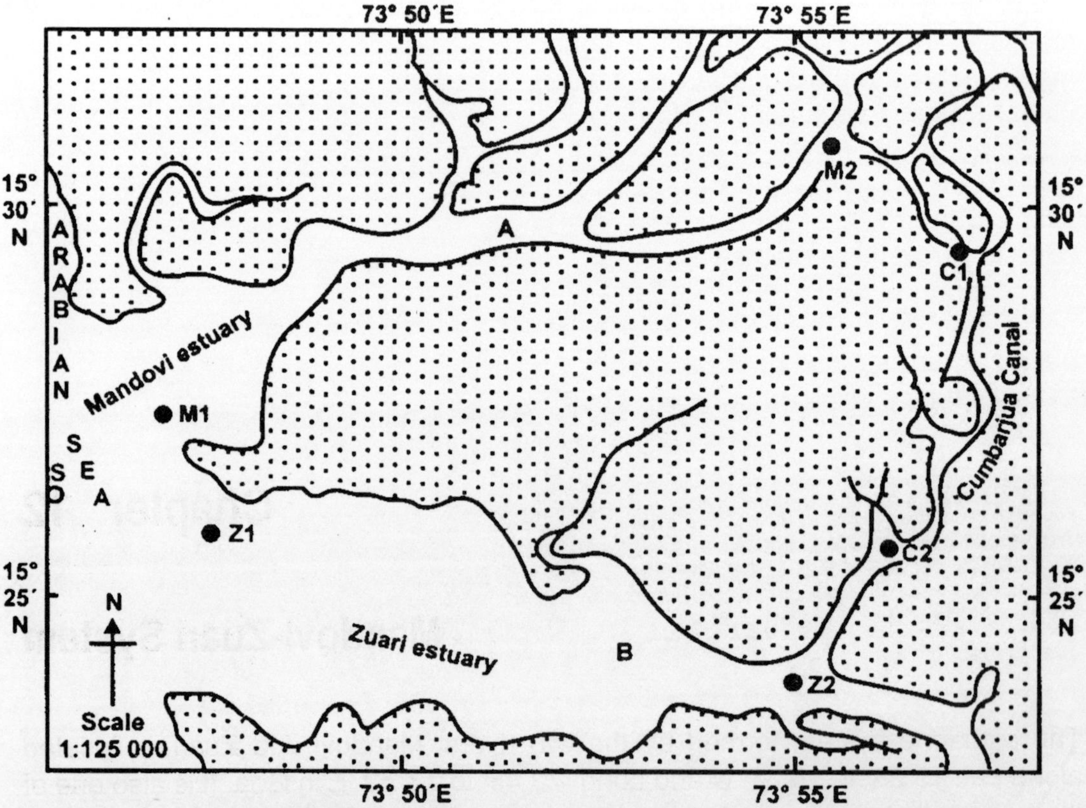

Fig. 12.1 Map of Mandovi-Zuari Estuarine System of Goa with its marine and riverine connections. Closed circles indicate the main stations where seasonal measurements of environmental characteristics were made. Z1 and Z2 refer to Zuari stations while M1 and M2 are Mandovi stations and C1 and C2 are the stations in Cumbarjua Canal. A and B indicate the sites where current measurements were made. Station S (open circle) refers to the source station for computation of dilution factor (From Qasim & Sen Gupta, 1981).

estuarine system. Mandovi has many tributaries and receives a greater runoff than the Zuari which has only a few tributaries.

A canal called the Cumbarjua Canal connects the two rivers inland. This canal is located at a distance of 14 km from Mandovi and 11 km from Zuari. It is about 17 km in length and 0.5-0.7 km in width. Thus, the two rivers with their estuaries and Cumbarjua demarcate the island of Panaji (Panjim) (Fig. 12.1).

All boat traffic gets suspended in the Mandovi during the SW monsoon (June to September) because of the appearance of shoals/bars in this estuary. These shoals are popularly known as the Aguada Bar and the Reis Magos Bar. The former is located in the Aguada Bay which is a part of the Mandovi Estuary and the latter is opposite to an old Portuguese fort (Reis Magos Fort) situated on top of an adjoining hill facing the Mandovi. The details of these shoals/sand bars will be given later. Because of these sand bars, navigation in the Mandovi River is considered hazardous and the port of Panaji is declared closed for all boat traffic from June to August. No such navigational problems arise either in the river Zuari or in the Cumbarjua Canal in which boat and barge traffic, carrying iron and manganese ores goes on uninterrupted, practically throughout the year although becomes less intense during the rainy season (Qasim & Sengupta, 1981).

HYDROGRAPHY

Investigations on the hydrography of this estuarine system began in 1969 and the earlier publications are on the changes in some of the environmental features in relation to tidal cycle (Dehadrai, 1970). Seasonal changes in the rate of primary production and chlorophyll-*a* were found to be regulated with the flood and ebb tides. Pulses of bloom were noticed in both the riverine and neritic areas of the estuary and the production rates in the two estuaries fluctuated with seasons (Dehadrai & Bhargava, 1972). Studies on the flow characteristics in the Cumbarjua Canal showed that during the premonsoon season when the riverine flow of freshwater is minimal, the flow in the canal is regulated by the tides, and the differences observed in salinity between the Mandovi- and Zuari-ends of the canal are regulated by the amount of freshwater present in the upper reaches of the two estuaries. The flow in the canal is from the Zuari side to Mandovi side (Das *et al.*, 1972). In the premonsoon season, higher current speeds were observed during the flood tide than at the ebb. Maximum speeds during the flood and ebb were 160 and 108 cm/s, respectively. During the southwest monsoon, the flow of a large volume of freshwater into the estuaries increases the effect of the ebb and controls the flow of the flood. Salinity in the two estuaries varied with the tides (Murty & Das, 1972). Phytoplankton pigments in Mandovi recorded maximum values during the premonsoon season and minimum during the monsoon. These were also controlled by the tides (Bhargava, 1973). In the Zuari, several environmental features such as temperature, salinity, oxygen and nutrients were studied in relation to tides. All factors were related to tidal rhythm except the nutrients which were independent of tidal variations (Singbal, 1973). Variations in the hydrographic conditions were minimum during the premonsoon season. Suspended matter was greater in the middle and upstream of the Zuari than at the mouth. This was because the tidal currents were stronger in the middle upstream (Cherian *et al.,* 1974). Similar changes were observed in the Mandovi and the estuary gets stratified during the monsoon and well-mixed in other seasons (Varma *et al.,* 1975).

Tidal Propagation

Mormugao Bay, located at the mouth of the Zuari, experiences tides of mixed semidiurnal type with a range between 2 and 2.3 m. During the year 1993, the levels of water and salinity were monitored in April (for the dry season) and in August (for the wet season) for 3 days to determine the characteristics of tidal propagation in the estuarine network. The speed of propagation of both the diurnal and semidiurnal tides through the main channels of the network was found to be about 6 m/s. The amplitude of the semidiurnal band was the largest of all the constituents and it remained almost similar in both dry and wet seasons. In the Zuari, it increased marginally but remained unchanged upto about 40 km from the mouth, and then dropped sharply over the next 10 km (Shetye *et al.,* 1995). Fig. 12.2 (a) shows the variation in the amplitude in relation to distance during both dry and wet seasons. The two estuaries (Zuari and Mandovi) behave in a similar fashion. The lower part of Fig. 12.2 (b) shows the changes of phase (in minutes) of the semidiurnal tide in the main channel of Mandovi with respect to the tides at Marmugao. Momentum balance in the estuarine channels (Mandovi and Zuari) is between the pressure gradient and friction. Both the channels converge strongly and because of frictional dissipation leave the tides unchanged over a distance of 40 km. The balance, however, breaks down at the upstream end of the channel. The cross-section of the channel being small, the mean velocity associated even with a small volume of freshwater influx, as it is in the dry season, seems to be sufficient to prevent the tide from propagating upstream and thus it comes to an abrupt halt. The decay is more rapid during the periods of higher runoff (Shetye *et al.,* 1995; Unnikrishnan *et al.,* 1997; Shetye, 1999). According to these authors, the model presented for the Mandovi-Zuari should be applicable to other shallow and narrow estuarine systems found on the west coast which are influenced by the SW monsoon in a similar fashion.

Temperature

The temperature of water increased from January to May. It was followed by a decline during the monsoon months and again an increase thereafter. Both the

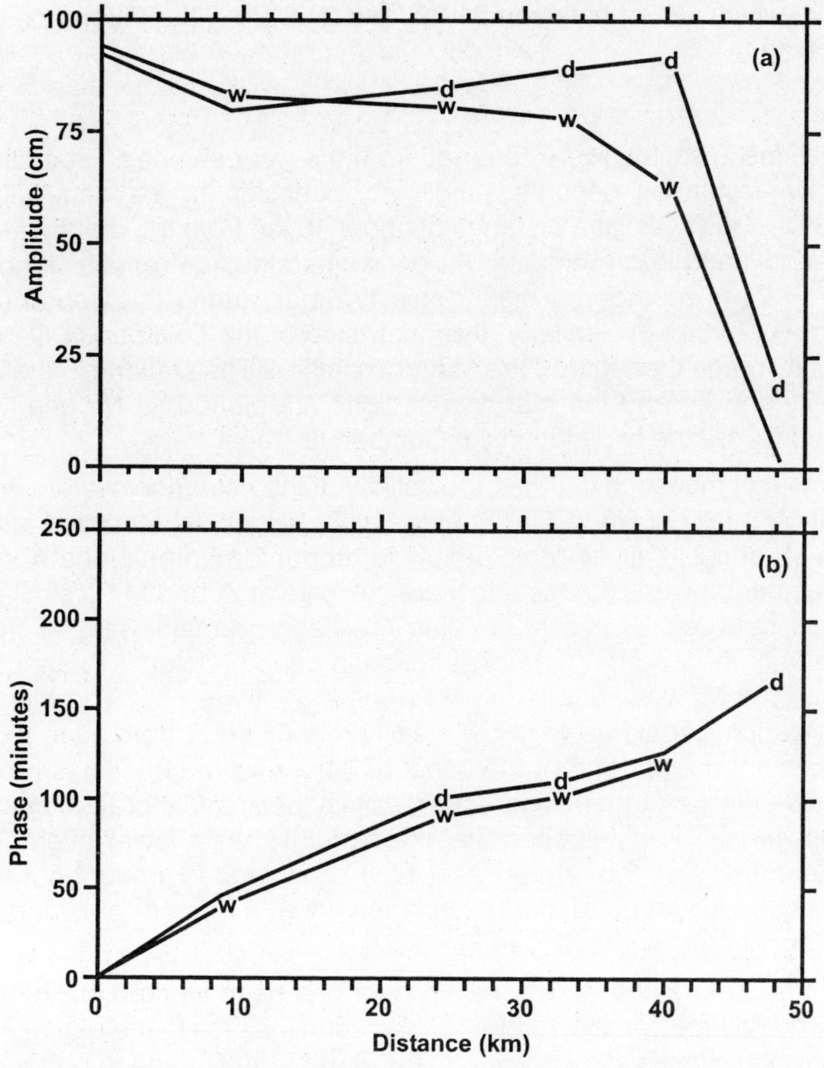

Fig. 12.2 Tidal propagation in Mandovi Estuary (a) shows variations in amplitude (cm) of the semi-diurnal component of the tide with distance (km) along the main channel of Mandovi during the observations in dry season (d) carried out from 7 to 9 April 1993 and observations made during the wet season (w) from 19 to 21 August 1993 (b) change of phase in minutes of the semidiurnal band in the main channel of Mandovi with respect to tide at Marmugao, d-dry season; w-wet season. Horizontal axis gives the distance (km) from the mouth of the channel. During the wet season, the phase at the upstream and beyond 40 km has not been shown because the flow was controlled by freshwater influx and there was no tidal influence (From Shetye, 1999).

estuaries and the Cumbarjua Canal behaved in a similar fashion in changes of temperature which varied between 31.02° and 24.8°C — the difference in annual variation being 5-7°C.

Salinity

Large variations in salinity were reported from the two estuaries. From January to May, the two estuaries become simply an extension of the sea with salinity reaching 35‰. However, at a distance of about 40 km from the mouth, the salinity both in Mandovi and Zuari remains 0‰ even when the tide remains high (Shetye *et al.,* 1975). Zuari recorded a higher salinity range during this period (31-35‰) than Mandovi (29-34‰). Similarly, the Zuari side of the Cumbarjua Canal had a higher salinity range than that of the Mandovi portion. The stations in the Zuari are shown as Z_1 and Z_2 and the Mandovi stations are plotted as M_1 and M_2 in Fig. 12.1. C_1 and C_2 are the two stations in Cumbarjua Canal.

With the onset of monsoon in June, the salinity of the estuarine system decreases sharply. At M_1 it falls down to 5‰ whereas at Z_1 the lowest recorded in July was 10.5‰. At M_1 and Z_1 salinity remains low for about 3 months (June-August), but from September onwards it begins to increase. Like at Z_1 and M_1, a similar feature was noticed between Z_2 and M_2 — the M_2 station remains largely freshwater dominated than the Z_2 during the postmonsoon period (October to January). The lowest salinity at M_2 was zero in July whereas at Z_2 it was 6‰. The Mandovi end of the Cumbarjua Canal has very low salinity (nearly zero) from June to September whereas in the Zuari end of the canal (C_2) freshwater conditions remain only for 3 months (June - August). Thereafter, salinity begins to increase sharply from October onwards. Thus, it is seen that the Mandovi has a lower average salinity than the Zuari because the former receives a considerable amount of runoff from a larger tributary system and along its course it has a number of islands, narrow bends and mangrove swamps (see Fig. 12.1).

For the Zuari Estuary, the annual salt budget has been worked out by Shetye & Murty (1987). Salinity from November to May remains high in the estuary because of the freshwater runoff which is low and the water from surface to bottom remains well-mixed. Heavy runoff, on the other hand, from June to October, creates stratification and the salt-wedge extends up to a distance of about 12 km into the river. The water column clearly demonstrates this feature as shown in Fig. 12.3. The extent of salt water penetration in the river upstream is shown in Fig. 12.4 for both the estuaries. Taking the index of seawater penetration as 1‰ salinity, the distance in Mandovi varies from a maximum of about 65 km in May to a minimum of 11 km in July and more than 65 km in Zuari in May to 20 km in June (Fig. 12.4).

Examining the salinity gradient it becomes evident that at any given time of the year, there is much greater amount of saltwater in Zuari than in Mandovi. Using the same data noted above, Shetye and Murty (1987) prepared curves by

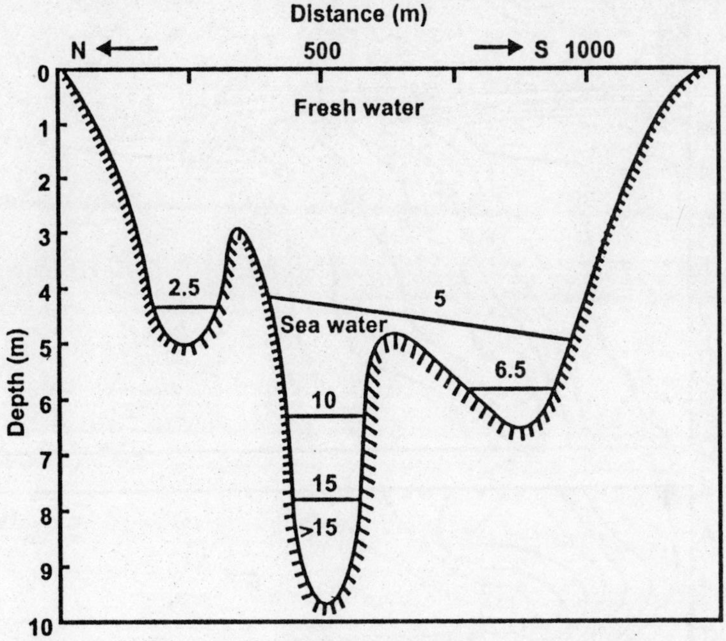

Fig. 12.3 Diagrammatic representation showing the presence of salt wedge at the bottom in a cross section across Mandovi. Values indicate salinity (‰) of water in July 1978 (From Qasim & Sen Gupta, 1981).

fitting polynomial least square to the data. The curves gave for each month, salinity *S* as a continuous function of *x*, the upstream distance from the mouth of Zuari. The total salt in the estuary S_{tot} can be determined from,

$$S_{\text{tot}} = \int_0^x S(x)A(x)dx$$

where *A* is the cross-sectional area. The upper limit of the integral is the far upstream where *S* disappears. From November to May, the estuary is vertically well-mixed and the two processes controlling the transport of salt are the runoff-induced advective transport out of the estuary and the tidally-induced diffusive transport into the estuary. The magnitude of the latter is 20% larger, leading to a salinity rise in the estuary. The diffusion coefficient has been estimated to be

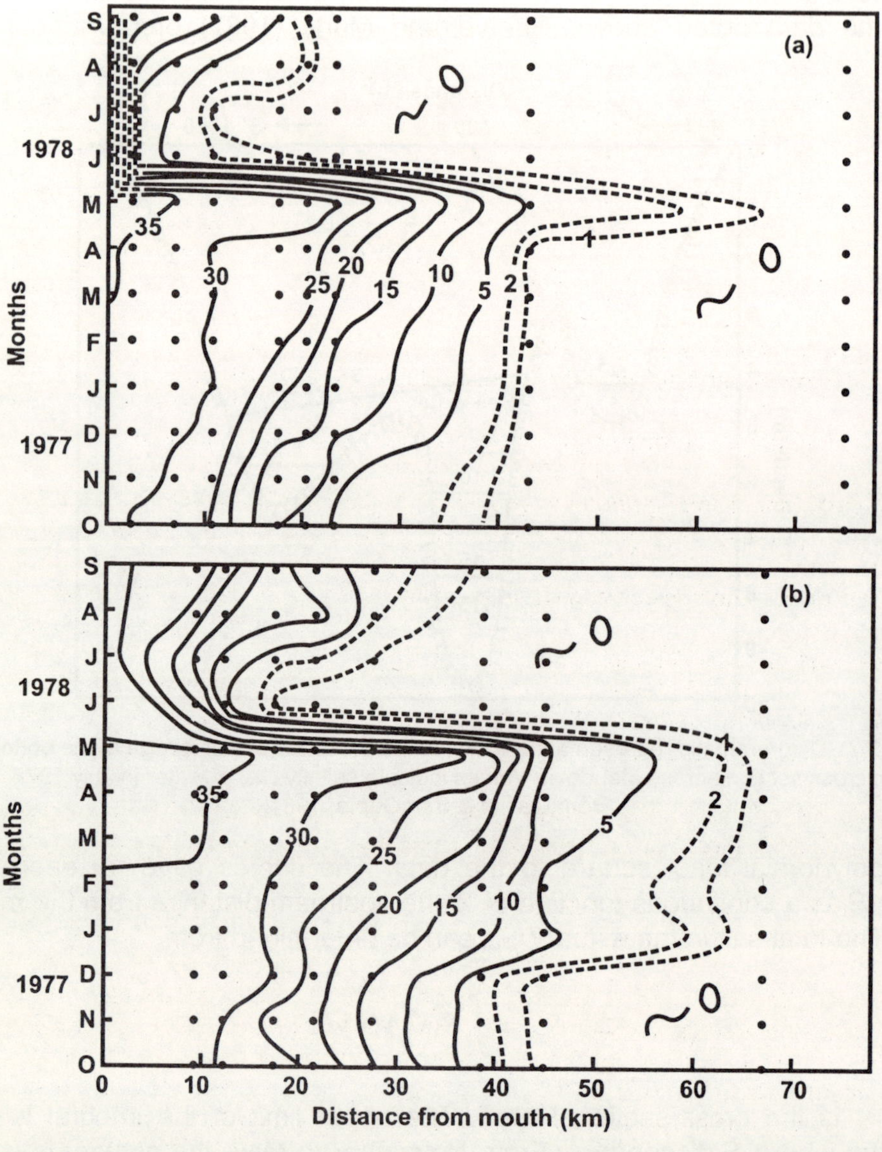

Fig. 12.4 Diagrammatic representation showing the extent of saltwater penetration from the mouth of (a) Mandovi River and (b) Zuari River upstream in different months of the year. Continuous isolines give the salinity at 5‰ intervals. Broken lines indicate salinities of 2 and 1‰ (From Qasim & Sen Gupta, 1981).

233± 101 m^2/s. With the onset of monsoon, the runoff increases dramatically and the estuary loses 75% of its salt during the first 2 months of the season. About 2/3 of this loss is recovered in the next 2 months when the runoff decreases. During the period when the estuary is partially stratified (June-October), gravitational circulation is expected to play a role in addition to tidal diffusion and runoff. The magnitude of the contribution of gravitational circulation has not been determined (Shetye & Murty, 1987).

Flow Pattern

Current measurements at different sites in the two estuaries showed that the maximum current speed during the flood and ebb tides was in the middle region at the points shown as A and B in Fig. 12.1 in the two estuaries and minimum at the mouth (station M_1 and Z_1 in Fig. 12.1). During the postmonsoon and premonsoon seasons, the speed was faster during the flood tides practically everywhere in the estuaries whereas during the monsoon months the currents became stronger during the ebb tides, as the river runoff accelerated the flow (Varma *et al.,* 1975). During the monsoon season, because of the formation of two salt-wedges, the rivers become stratified 2-3 m below the surface depending upon the depth of the estuary. The salt-wedge extends upto 10 km in the Mandovi and 12 km in the Zuari. Beyond these points, during the peak monsoon period, the rest of the estuarine system remains filled with freshwater with practically no salt-water incursion anywhere. Immediately after the monsoon, when the runoff remains still high, mixing of salt water and freshwater begins but some stratifications continue at few places, as pointed out by Murty & Das (1972). No stratification is found anywhere during the premonsoon season and the water remains well-mixed. The tidal influence with salt water incursion is felt far beyond Cumbarjua in the riverine network (Fig. 12.1).

Stability characteristics of the two estuaries were calculated by the dimensionless Richardson's number (R_1). In the Zuari, R_1 ranged from 6 to 39 and in the Mandovi, the range was 0.06 to 48 in different regions and seasons (for the details of calculation, see Qasim & Sen Gupta, 1981). Dilution factors in both the estuaries were found to be of a similar magnitude during the three seasons. Maximum values were obtained during the premonsoon season when the freshwater flow was minimal. Any pollutants, therefore, released during this season will be diluted 6 times by seawater before it finally reaches the sea. During the monsoon season, the dilution with seawater would be minimum. Residence period of the water has been reported to be 5-6 days in the Mandovi during the monsoon season and about 50 days in the dry season. For Zuari, the residence period would be somewhat longer (Qasim & Sen Gupta, 1981).

FORMATION OF SHOALS/SAND BARS

As has been noted earlier, the formation of shoals/sand bars near the entrance of the Mandovi has been known since centuries. These are commonly called in Goa as the Aguada or Reis Magos bars. The map of Goa published in 1610 and known as the Map of Manuel Godinho de Eredias (Bois Penrose, 1960) shows these shoals near the entrance of the Mandovi. Since then, little appears to have changed and even today the shoals/bars have neither grown nor reduced in size. During the dry season, for about 9 months (end of September to early June), the waterway poses no navigational problem, but during the monsoon, the water gets completely closed for boat traffic because of the appearance of a ramp-like structure with a depth gradient of 10 to 4 m. The depth over the shoals ranges from 1.5-2 m.

Figure 12.5 gives the details of the bathymetry of the navigational channel in the Aguada Bay. Because of heavy swells coming from different directions (S, SW, NW and N), the water circulation follows the current directions shown in Fig. 12.5. Waves in the Aguada Bay are small during the fair seasons, but during the monsoon season both significant period and significant height increase dramatically by several folds leading to highly turbulent conditions over the shoals. Large quantities of material from the nearby beaches are removed and are transferred in and around the navigational channel resulting in a ramp-like structure and highly turbulent conditions. After the monsoon season, the lost material from the beaches and shores is brought back to its original position and the former profiles of the beaches are restored. During the fair (dry) season, the shoals get exposed at low water but during the monsoon months, they are not seen even at the lowest spring tides. This may be because the shoals get deepened probably by the removal of material lying above.

DISSOLVED OXYGEN

During all the tidal cycles, the oxygen concentration decreases with rising tide and increases with the falling tide. Uniform oxygen concentrations was found in both the estuaries from surface to bottom during pre- and postmonsoon seasons when the water was well-mixed. During the monsoon season, because of stratified conditions in the water column, high oxygen values were found at the surface and low

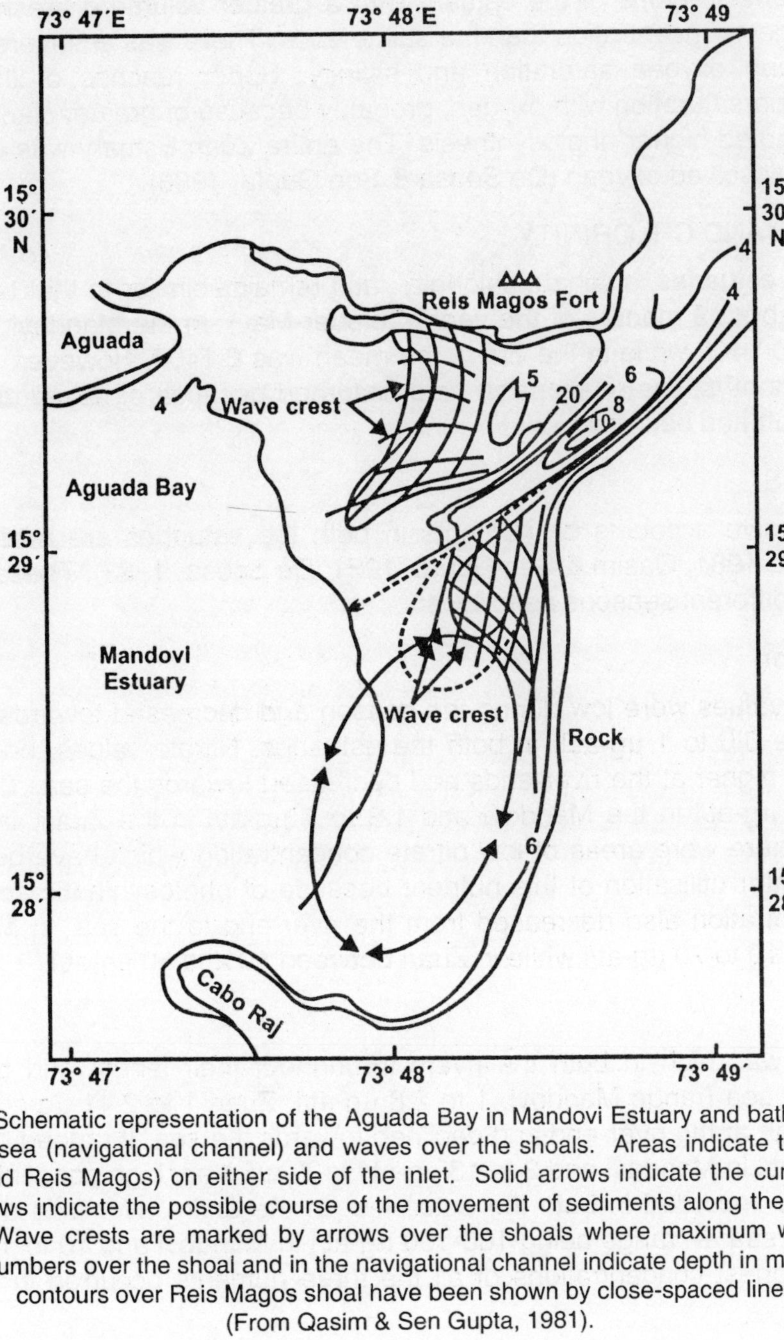

Fig. 12.5 Schematic representation of the Aguada Bay in Mandovi Estuary and bathymetry of the inlet of the sea (navigational channel) and waves over the shoals. Areas indicate the two shoals (Aguada and Reis Magos) on either side of the inlet. Solid arrows indicate the current direction, broken arrows indicate the possible course of the movement of sediments along the shoals and in the inlet. Wave crests are marked by arrows over the shoals where maximum wave breaking occurs. Numbers over the shoal and in the navigational channel indicate depth in metres. Depth contours over Reis Magos shoal have been shown by close-spaced lines (From Qasim & Sen Gupta, 1981).

at the bottom. Regions of the estuary with a greater volume of freshwater had higher oxygen concentration than the saline ends. There was an inverse relationship between oxygen saturation and salinity. Upper reaches of the estuary showed supersaturation with oxygen, probably because of greater clarity of water which promoted higher photosynthesis. The entire Zuari Estuary was undersaturated with dissolved oxygen (De Sousa & Sen Gupta, 1986).

SULPHATE AND CHLORINITY

In both the estuaries, sulphate-chlorinity ratio remains similar to that of the open ocean for about 9 months of the year (October-May). In the Mandovi, the mean value was 0.1409 while in the Zuari, the mean was 0.1404. However, during the monsoon months, this relationship gets disturbed because of heavy dilution due to river runoff and becomes low.

NUTRIENTS

Comprehensive accounts on nutrients in both the estuaries are available. (De Sousa *et al.,* 1981; Qasim & Sen Gupta, 1981; De Sousa, 1983). These are summarized in different seasons as follows:

Premonsoon

Phosphate values were low during the season and decreased towards the river-ends (range 0.6 to 1 µg-at/l) in both the estuaries. Nitrate values, on the other hand, were higher at the river-ends and decreased towards the sea. Their range was 1 to 2 µg-at/l in the Mandovi and 1.3 to 7 µg-at/l in the Zuari. In both the estuaries, there were areas of low nitrate concentration which have been attributed to greater utilisation of this nutrient because of photosynthetic activity. Silicate concentration also decreased from the river-end to the sea. In Mandovi, it varied from 10 to 70 µg-at/l while in Zuari between 10 and 50 µg-at/l.

Monsoon

Phosphate was high in both the rivers throughout their length and decreased towards the sea (range Mandovi, 1 to 2.8 µg-at/l; Zuari 1 to 2.41 µg-at/l). Nitrate was also high at the river-end and declined towards the sea. It ranged between 4 and 20 µg-at/l in Mandovi and 3 to 13 µg-at/l in Zuari. Very high concentrations of silicate were recorded in both the estuaries in the entire river side decreasing towards the sea — range being 100-160 µg-at/l in Mandovi and 10 to 190 µg-at/l in Zuari. Highest concentrations of all the three nutrients occurred in June and

July when rainfall and runoff were maximum. The sources of enrichment seem to be land drainage and large amount of fertilizers being used in agriculture during this season.

Postmonsoon

Phosphate during this season ranged between 0.6 and 2.4 μg-at/l in Mandovi and from 0.5 to 2.0 μg-at/l in Zuari. There was an increase towards the sea and highest concentrations were recorded at the mouth. Nitrate ranged between 1.1 and 12.7 μg-at/l in Mandovi and from 2.3 to 12.7 μg-at/l in Zuari. Highest values were recorded in the middle of both the estuaries which decreased both towards river and sea sides. Silicate ranged from 10 to 80 μg-at/l in Mandovi and 10 to 60 μg-at/l in Zuari. Its concentrations were high at the river-ends and decreased towards the sea-end. Experiments conducted under controlled conditions on the phosphorus retention capacity of the sediments of Mandovi Estuary indicate that the process of adsorption and desorption of phosphorus are *p*H dependent. Adsorption of phosphorus is maximum (58 to 99%) at *p*H 4 (Rajagopal & Reddy, 1984). Concentrations of urea in the estuarine region varied between 0 to 4.6 μg-at-N/l and showed 3 peaks. Maximum phytoplankton production was associated with a decrease in urea from June to October when ammonia and nitrate concentrations were also high. It was thus deduced that urea forms a source of nitrogen during the monsoon season (Verlencar, 1985).

FLUORIDE

Measurements of fluoride concentrations in the estuarine system showed that these are regulated largely by saltwater intrusion. Highest concentrations were observed during the premonsoon season, when the saltwater flow was maximum. There was an increase in flouride from the riverine-end to the sea-end. Lowest concentrations of fluoride were recorded during the monsoon season, except near the bottom where higher values were noted because of salt wedge formation. Postmonsoon season showed intermediate values. Fluoride-chlorinity relationship was linear during the monsoon and postmonsoon periods and exponential during the premonsoon period (De Sousa & Sen Gupta, 1978).

PHYTOPLANKTON

Short-term observations on phytoplankton made in the two estuaries during pre- and postmonsoon seasons showed that the composition of algal population was almost similar in both the estuaries but a greater algal concentration was found in Mandovi than in Zuari (Qasim & Sen Gupta, 1981). This has been attributed to lower salinity and greater transparency in Mandovi as compared to Zuari. (Devassy & Bhargava, 1978). Seasonal studies on phytoplankton were extended over a period of 12 months (November 1979 - October 1980) at 6 stations — 2 in Mandovi, 2 in Zuari, 1 in Cumbarjua and 1 in the inshore waters; the last one forms an entrance channel to both the estuaries. These provide details of the community structure of phytoplankton in the estuarine system. In all, 82 species of phytoplankton were recorded. Of these, 63 were diatoms, 14 dinoflagellates, 3 blue-green and 2-green algae. Considerable predominance of diatoms was an important feature to note, except in the month of September when a dinoflagellate bloom (*Ceratium furca*) contributed 72.5 to 77.6% of the total algal biomass. Similarly, at the coastal station entering the mouth of the two estuaries, massive blooms of *Trichodesmium eryhraeum* accounted for more than 90% of the total crop in March and April (Devassy & Goes, 1988). The bloom of this blue-green algae in the coastal waters of Goa from start to finish including the red colour it imparts to the sea has been studied earlier (Devassy *et al.,* 1978). Another intense bloom of the diatom, *Fragilaria oceanica,* forming 94.4% of the total phytoplankton biomass was recorded in Mandovi during September.

Table 12.1 shows the abundance of the various groups of phytoplankton in 4 locations of the estuarine system, and Fig. 12.6 gives the monthly variations in surface phytoplankton (3 groups). As can be seen from the figure, apart from minor fluctuations in some months largely in the populations of dinoflagellates, all the stations behaved in a similar fashion. Mandovi sustained a higher population as compared to Zuari and Cumbarjua. This is because typically estuarine conditions prevailed in Mandovi during the period of investigation which promoted a greater abundance of algae. Diatoms formed the most successful group in the estuarine complex even at very low salinities (<1‰). The diatom, *Fragilaria oceanica*, tolerated a wide range of salinity (2.5 - 31.5‰) while, dinoflagellate, *Ceratium furca*, formed blooms at salinities between 25.5 and 31.8‰.

With the onset of monsoon there was a spontaneous outburst of phytoplankton. This seems to be triggered by the premonsoon showers during late May and early June. Following heavy rainfall from late June onwards, enormous quantities of freshwater, through land runoff and river discharge, bring about extensive dilution, stratification of the water column and salt-wedge formation in the estuary. During this period, phytoplankton density and composition become lowest, in spite of enormous amount of nutrients present in the water which remain unutilized. Due to high turbidity of water and cloud cover, light penetration gets reduced which may also contribute to low phytoplankton crop. Towards the end of

Table 12.1— Seasonal abundance in the estuarine system of diatoms (DT), dinofalgellates (DF), other algae (OA) and total phytoplankton (TP) (all values expressed as $\times 10^2$ cells) (From Devassy & Goes, 1988)

	Postmonsoon				Premonsoon				Monsoon			
	DT	DF	OA	TP	DT	DF	OA	TP	DT	DF	OA	TP
Mandovi	250.63	1.63	7.22	259.48	69.56	1.41	67.97	138.94	88.75	2.00	2.90	93.65
Cumbarjua	64.25	2.13	2.88	69.26	93.88	3.90	116.75	215.53	86.88	2.75	1.63	91.26
Zuari	95.53	70.15	2.16	104.84	85.56	2.66	5.44	93.66	22.32	19.19	0.76	47.72
Coastal	95.13	13.38	6.00	114.51	40.13	1.18	140.13	181.44	–	–	–	–

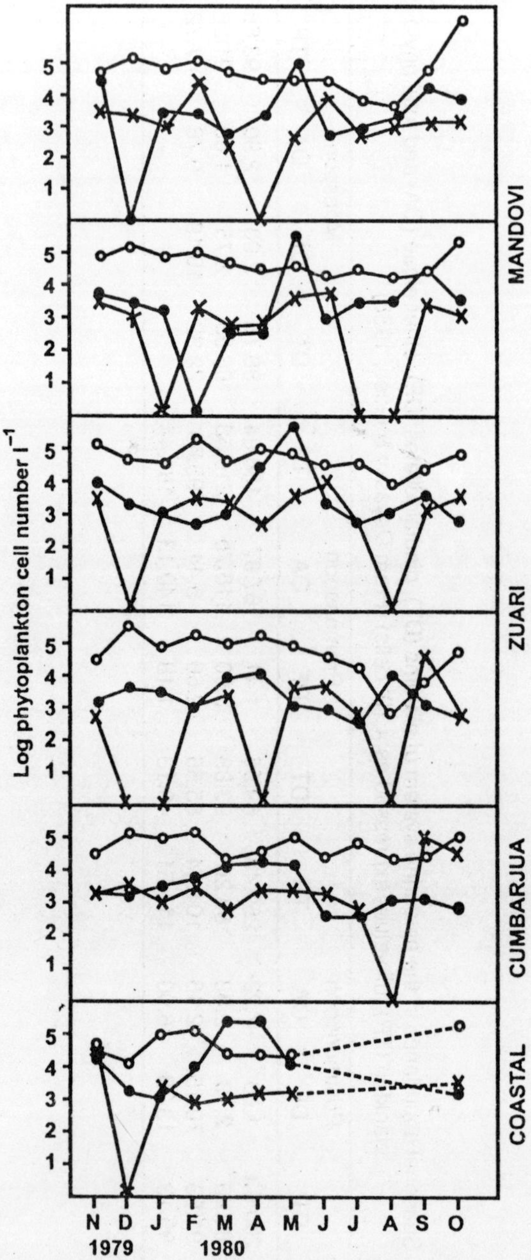

Fig. 12.6 Seasonal changes in three categories of phytoplankton in Goa estuarine system (O) diatom; (X) dinoflagellates; (●) other algae (From Devassy & Goes, 1988).

monsoon, there is progressive increase in salinity and with the return of postmonsoon conditions, massive blooms of *Ceratium furca* begin to appear. Other dominant forms which occur during this period are *Fragilaria oceanica and Nitzschia closterium*. Thus, a gradual repopulation of phytoplantkon crop occurs during the postmonsoon period, which is maintained is subsequent months (Devassy & Goes, 1988).

Primary production in the three sections of the estuarine system — Mandovi, Zuari and Cumbarjua — was measured during the monsoon period (June - September) using carbon assimilation. Maximum average production of 316 mg C/m^2/day was recorded in Cumbarjua, followed by Zuari (249) and Mandovi (247). Chlorophyll- *a* was also maximum in Cumbarjua (Bhattathiri *et al.,* 1976). Nannoplankton organisms, which pass through 60 μm mesh, were found to be responsible for almost 90% of CO_2 fixation in the estuary (Pant *et al.,* 1976). In another study, the contribution of nannoplankton to the chlorophyll-*a* and primary production was found to be just as high. Of the total chlorophyll-*a*, the contribution of nannoplankton was from 32.8 to 100%. The average organic production of nannoplantkon was 271 in Cumbarjua, 215 in Zuari and 209 mg $C/m^2/d$ in Mandovi. Nannoplankton production was greater than 84.8% of the total production in any sector of the estuarine system and nutrients were not found to be a limiting factor in the estuary (Bhargava *et al.,* 1977). Only for 3 months during the premonsoon season, chain-forming net plankton contributed significantly. An inverse relationship was found between phytoplankton abundance and fixation of extracellular products in the *in situ* incubated samples which varied from 0 to 22.1 mg $C/m^2/h$ or 0 to 40% of the particulate fixation. During the premonsoon period (Jan. and Feb. 1976), extracellular release was higher in filtered samples than those of the unfiltered ones (Pant *et al.,* 1977).

Further studies on the fixation and release of organic compounds by phytoplankton during photosynthesis in the estuary showed that the pattern of ^{14}C fixation of both intracellular (particulate) and extracellular compounds was different during premonsoon and monsoon seasons. Figure 12.7 shows the ^{14}C uptake in the form of absorbed as particulate and released as extracellular products during the premonsoon (on 8 May 1984) and monsoon (20 June 1984) seasons as two representative experiments. A large difference in the extracellular release between the two seasons was found, and a proportion of the labelled carbon was incorporated into carbohydrates during the premonsoon period. In June (monsoon) its incorporation into carbohydrates decreased and into proteins increased. Glycolic acid was the major organic acid which incorporated the radioactive carbon during the premonsoon when the days were bright and the sea was calm. During the monsoon, dull days and turbulent sea were probably responsible for reducing the labelling of the glycolic acid fraction (Shailaja & Pant, 1986).

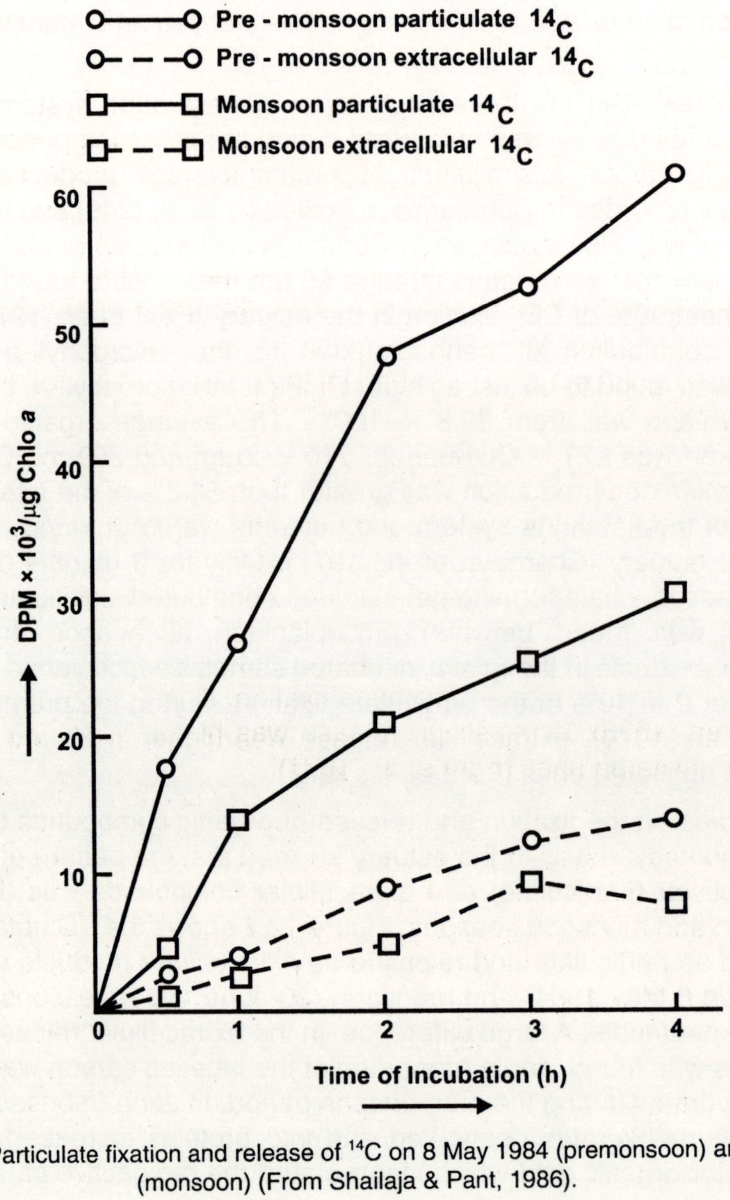

Fig. 12.7 Particulate fixation and release of ^{14}C on 8 May 1984 (premonsoon) and 20 June (monsoon) (From Shailaja & Pant, 1986).

Studies on the effect of some metal ions on the rate of photosynthesis of larger algae (microplankton) and smaller algae (nannoplankton) showed that some metals stimulated the rate while others inhibited the activity. The response in both the groups of phytoplankton varied with different metals. Copper stimulated photosynthesis in both the groups. Zinc was found to be less toxic to nannoplankton than to microplankton. Iron inhibited photosynthesis in both the groups. A marked increase in photosynthesis was noticed with molybdenum, manganese and cobalt at low levels of concentration. Phytoplankton organisms are known to concentrate metals like Mn, Fe, Cu and Zn from seawater and much of the uptake is probably due to passive adsorption rather from through active processes. However, this is possible only up to a certain level. Higher concentrations work as pollutants and become toxic (Rajendran *et al.,* 1978).

ZOOPLANKTON

Like phytoplankton, the estuarine complex has a rich zooplankton fauna. Eighteen taxa of both holo- and merozooplankton were found in the samples. Besides these, some groups such as Cephalochordata (*Amphioxus* sp.), water insects (*Halobates* sp.) and crustacean nauplii were observed. Table 12.2 gives the composition of 18 taxa in the three sectors of the estuarine complex. Crustaceans in general and copepods in particular dominated the zooplankton population. After copepods, decapod larvae were next in the order of abundance followed by cirripede larvae, sergestid, cladocerans, fish eggs, chaetognaths and copelats, gastropod larvae, hydromedusae, fish larvae, cumaceans and amphipods. Apart from minor differences, the composition in the three sectors of the estuarine system was similar.

Hydromedusae, siphonophores, ctenophores and chaetognaths were the carnivores and these usually occurred in Mandovi and Zuari during the high saline periods. Siphonophores were generally stragglers found in small numbers and chaetognaths were abundant during the late postmonsoon and premonsoon seasons. Ctenophores occurred more in the Zuari than in the other sectors with their peak abundance in April (Padmavati & Goswami, 1996).

During the monsoon season (June to September), the total zooplankton biomass with major taxa were greater in Zuari than in Mandovi because the former had greater marine influence than the latter even during the monsoon season. Copepods formed the largest single group but dominance of no single group was noticed during the monsoon season (Goswami & Singbal, 1974). The average rate of secondary production calculated from the total biomass values of zooplankton for one year was found to be highest in Mandovi followed by Zuari and Cumbarjua

(Selvakumar *et al.,* 1980). In the Zuari, surface zooplankton samples were collected during three months (August, February and April, 1972) representing monsoon, postmonsoon and premonsoon periods at day and night and during the entire tidal cycles. Maximum biomass was obtained during August when the salinity was low and at night in all the three months as compared to day hauls. Similarly, at high water the biomass was greater than at low water because many neritic organisms were transported with the tidal current (Goswami *et al.,* 1979). In the Zuari, considerable short-term variability was found in the zooplankton biomass. During February and March 1979, 26 collections of zooplankton were made on alternate days near the mouth of the estuary. Biomass varied from 52 to 1388 mg C/100 m^3. Dry weight of 1 ml of zooplankton ranged between 55 to 70 mg and organic carbon content varied between 26 and 33% of dry weight (mean 29%). Six peaks of zooplankton biomass were obtained and the time lag between the 2 peaks was 7 to 14 days. High values were associated with the high water (Nair *et al.,* 1983).

Table 12.2— Average numerical counts (no/m^3) and percentage composition (in parentheses) of major groups of zooplankton in Mandovi-Zuari Estuarine System of Goa (From Padmavati & Goswami, 1996)

Zooplankton Groups	Mandovi	Zuari	C. canal
Hydromedusa	2.5 (0.15)	1.2 (0.08)	2.3 (0.3)
Siphonophora	0.01 (0.00)	0.5 (0.03)	0.0 (0.0)
Ctenophora	0.1 (0.01)	1.4 (0.09)	0.1 (0.01)
Chaetognatha	10.6 (0.67)	21.1 (1.43)	28.3 (3.31)
Cladocera	4.1 (0.26)	10.4 (0.73)	0.3 (0.03)
Ostracoda	0.0 (0.0)	0.2 (0.01)	0.01 (0.00)
Copepoda	1354 (86.11)	1242 (84.35)	696 (81.39)
Amphipoda	0.2 (0.01)	0.1 (0.01)	0.2 (0.02)
Lucifers	33.3 (2.12)	43.4 (2.95)	13.5 (1.57)
Mysidacea	1.1 (0.06)	2.5 (0.16)	0.7 (0.08)
Cumacea	0.2 (0.01)	0.5 (0.03)	0.3 (0.03)
Invertebr. eggs	0.5 (0.03)	0.9 (0.06)	0.1 (0.01)
Invertebr. larvae	154.3 (9.81)	131.6 (8.93)	109.8 (12.83)
Pteropoda	0.0 (0.0)	0.1 (0.0)	0.0 (0.0)
Copelata	4.5 (0.29)	9.7 (0.65)	0.8 (0.09)
Fish eggs	4.0 (0.25)	4.7 (0.32)	0.04 (0.0)
Fish larvae	2.8 (0.19)	2.0 (0.13)	2.7 (0.31)
Miscellaneous	0.1 (0.01)	0.1 (0.01)	0.1 (0.01)

As noted earlier, copepods formed the most dominant group of zooplankton. Subsequent studies gave a total of 49 species, of which 46 were identified (Goswami & Selvakumar, 1979). Two peaks of biomass were obtained — one during October-November and another in March-April. More species of copepods were added in another study, making the total to 55 species in the surface collections from the estuarine complex. Of these, 43 were calanoid belonging to 18 genera and these formed 97.8% of the total annual copepod counts. The remaining 2.2% included 4 genera and 9 species of cyclopoid copepods (1.8%) and 3 species of harpacticoid copepod (0.4%). These were grouped into high saline species, brackish water forms and low saline (euryhaline) species dominant in Cumbarjua Canal. Depending upon the occurrence and abundance during different months of the year, the species were grouped into 3 main categories—

(a) Species recorded either throughout the year or most part of the year
(b) Species which occurred during certain months of the year
(c) Species which were seen occasionally in the collection

The first category constituted 50-60% of the total copepod counts and the animals were distributed in the entire estuarine system. The copepods of the second category were immigrants from the coastal waters and were abundant from February to May. The third category included mostly limnetic species occurring at <0.5‰ salinity (Goswami, 1982).

The general pattern of copepod succession based on species dominance revealed 3 types of successional sequence. The first two were extremes — high saline species (preferring > 30‰) and low saline species (preferring > 5‰) — and the third medium range salinity (6 - 30‰). The highest species diversity was seen in the high saline forms (premonsoon) and lowest in the low saline forms (monsoon). Succession of copepod species commences in the postmonsoon season when coastal forms begin to invade the estuary with the increase in salinity and go on adding to the succession with time (Goswami, 1983). Figure 12.8 gives a diagrammatic sequence of succession of copepod species in the estuarine system. In this succession, salinity plays the most important role in their seasonal abundance.

Maximum abundance of copepods has been reported from both the estuaries and coastal water when the salinity is high. Monsoon season has a catastrophic effect on the population of copepods as their abundance dwindles when the salinity declines drastically. When the salinity recovers they are repopulated in the estuary. Figure 12.8 shows the range of greater abundance of the 34 most common copepod species. Of the 34, 13 belong to the wide saline category (5-36‰)

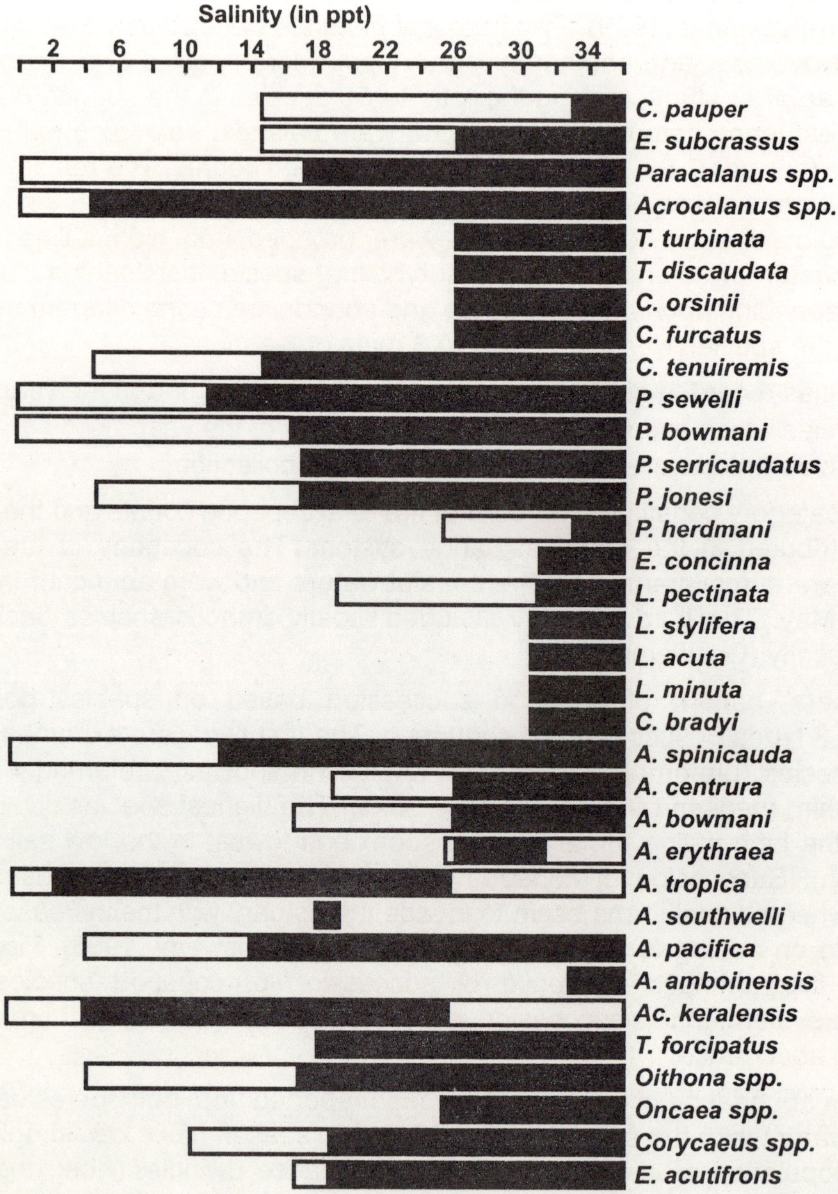

Fig. 12.8 Salinity ranges and the occurrence of different copepod species in Goa estuarine complex. Shaded areas indicate their range of greater abundance (From Achuthankutty *et al.*, 1995).

which live both in estuarine and coastal conditions. Only 3 fall in the medium saline category (5-26‰) and these are all *Acartia* species and could be termed as truly estuarine copepods. The remaining 18 species belong to the high saline category (26-36‰) and can be termed as truly coastal species (Achuthankutty *et al.,* 1995).

Cladocerans form an important group of crustaceans and their occurrence in large numbers, often forming swarns, in the estuarine environment has been reported from many estuaries. They have a high reproductive potential because of parthenogenesis. Females of this group are parthenogenetic and have been observed to carry 7-10 embryos. Under favourable conditions, they reproduce very fast. During adverse conditions, they produce resting eggs (cysts) which settle to the bottom and hatch when conditions return to optimum. Two species, namely *Evadne tergestina* and *Penilia avirostris* represented the cladoceran population in the estuary. The former species was very dominant constituting about 86% of the population. Another species (*Podon*) occurred in Cumbarjua in August in small numbers. Maximum population densities of cladocerans in the Mandovi and Cumbarjua were from September to November. In Zuari, it was from October to December. They were absent from the estuarine complex from January to April (premonsoon) which seems difficult to explain because they are known to tolerate a wide range of salinity and therefore high salinity alone could not be the only factor for their absence. They serve as a favourite food for pelagic fishes and are often addressed as indicator organisms for a successful fishery. The occurrence of caldoceran swarms and the onset mackeral fishery is not just a chance factor but appears to be a real coincidence. Therefore, the grazing effect on them by the pelagic fishes could be one explanation for their absence (Goswami & Devassy, 1991).

In the Mandovi-Zuari estuarine complex, the range in the organic carbon of zooplankton is 24-39.9% in Mandovi and 26.4-38.8% in Zuari based on their dry weight. Maximum organic carbon content in the estuary was obtained in November. Average organic carbon, of the nearshore zooplankton on the other hand, is 34.5% and of oceanic zooplankton is 41% of dry weight. Variations in organic carbon result from the composition of zooplankton. Diversity in zooplankton increases from estuarine to oceanic realm with a concomitant rise in the value of organic carbon. The average dry weight of 1 ml of nearshore and oceanic zooplankton is 61.9 and 81.7 mg, respectively (Nair, 1980a). Two peaks have generally been observed in zooplankton production in the estuarine complex — one in November and the other in March/April. Only one peak of zooplankton biomass normally occurs in the nearshore waters of Goa and that is in April in association with *Trichodesmium* bloom. Average values for Mandovi, Zuari and nearshore waters are 51, 69 and 136 C/m^2/day, respectively. Crustaceans form the main herbivores while chaetognaths and coelenterates are the chief carnivores. Higher diversity of zooplankton is associated with high ratios of predators (Nair, 1980b).

Chaetognaths constitute an immigrant fauna from the sea to the estuary and salinity appears to be the major factor controlling their distribution in the estuarine system. They are found throughout the year at the mouth of the estuary where fluctuations in salinity are not so well-marked. Their abundance was maximum from January to May. In the upper reaches, chaetognaths are absent during the monsoon season. The Zuari Estuary had a greater abundance of chaetognaths because it has more marine conditions than the Mandovi. Of the six species encountered in the estuarine system, *Sagitta bedoti* alone could be considered as a true inhabitant of this estuarine system. *S. enflata* was found during the period of high salinity and *S. pulchra* was caught in the first week of June. Others (*S. ferox, S. robusta* and *Pterosagitta draco*) seem as accidental immigrants to the estuary. From the young ones caught from the estuary, it has been deduced that *S. bedoti* breeds throughout the year in the estuary (Nair & Selvakumar, 1979).

SEDIMENT

The river Zuari enters the Marmugao Bay at its eastern end. The bay is 14 km in length and 6.5 km at its maximum width. Sand and gravel predominate in the inshore region. On the northern, southern and central sides, sand occupies 60 to 90% of the bottom. It becomes less than 10% in the western and eastern portions. Soft mud dominates the central portion. Silt in general represents a pattern similar to that of sand and gravel and increases from the inshore region to the central bay. Clay is almost absent along the northern margin except in isolated pockets (Rao & Rao, 1974). The depth of the bay ranges from 2 to 16 m and from 7-15 m in the navigational channel. Even topography marks the central parts but in the northern and northwestern parts, it becomes uneven. Northern and northeastern areas are covered with sand whereas the southern and southeastern areas have clay cover. Rock outcrops are prominent towards the northern and northwestern sides (Wagle *et al.,* 1988). Sediment load in the water adjoining the harbour is less than 15 mg/l and in the harbour it varies between 20 to 100 mg/l (extinction coefficient of light, $k < 0.85$). Turbidity gradually increases towards the head of the bay where k is > 2.8 (Cherian *et al.,* 1974). Soft mud dominates the central portion.

In the estuarine system, 32 species of Foraminifera were recorded from the sediments. These included both living and dead organisms (Rao, 1974). Alkaline phosphatase activity was found in the sediments of Mandovi Estuary, and it was indicative of the extent and rate of decomposition of organic phosphorus in the sediments (D'silva & Bhosle, 1990).

DETRITUS

Detrital material in an estuary is derived either by autochthonous sources (phytoplankton, submerged vegetation, mudflat algae, filamentous algae, periphyton, etc.) or by allochthonous sources (mangrove leaves, swampy products, organic matter derived from various sources, shore material washed during high water, wind-blown matter, etc.). Caloric value of detritus ranged from 173 to 6057 cal/g dry wt (average, 1463) which is much higher than that found in Cochin Backwaters where the range was 200 - 500 cal/g dry wt. This is because detritus of Zuari is a product of decaying mangrove leaves and the contribution of primary producers to the detritus formation is insignificant and detritus forms a potential source of energy at the secondary producers level (Kumari *et al.,* 1978) and in the estuarine environment instead of a grazing food chain a 'detritus-induced food chain' seems more appropriate (Untawale *et al.,* 1977). The Mandovi-Zuari complex is a mangrove-fringed ecosystem (1600 hectares of mangrove-forest are spread all along the estuarine areas) in which *in situ* decomposition of the litter of 4 species of mangroves has been studied. Litter yield ranged from 10.2 to 17.0 tonnes/ha/y with a maximum fall in pre- and postmonsoon months and minimum during the monsoon season. Thus, mangroves become a very important source for maintaining the carbon budget, sustaining microbal food chain and recycling of nutrients in the estuarine complex (Wafar *et al.,* 1997).

INTERTIDAL FAUNA

In the estuarine system, there are several beaches which are being used for recreational purposes. Of these, Siridao Beach in the Zuari Estuary and Miramar Beach in the Mandovi are quite well known as tourists resorts. During the season, which begins from October and continues till March/April, the two beaches get crowded with holiday-makers. Siridao can be cited as a typical estuarine beach which has been studied for its sand-dwelling macroinvertebrate fauna from January 1981 to May 1982 and meiofauna from July 1991 to August 1992. It has fine sand-grains. Thirty five species belonging to 12 major taxa have been recorded from this beach (Harkantra & Parulekar, 1985). Bivalves (35.83%) and polychaetes (25.65%) formed the dominant groups, although in terms of species, polychaetes exceeded in numbers. This seems a general feature as polychaetes showed a greater dominance in the estuarine beaches than the open sea beaches. As far as the composition in terms of numbers is concerned, the bivalve (*Donax faba*, 34.78%), harpacticoid (*Scottolana* sp. 19.78%), polychaete (*Nerine cirratulus*, 16.90%), brachyuran crab (*Dotilla mycticroides*, 5.84%) and polychaete (*Glycera alba*, 4.56%) formed the main groups. Faunal abundance was minimum during the monsoon period. It increased progressively during the post- and pre-monsoon seasons (Harkantra & Parulekar, 1985; Ingole & Parulekar, 1998). A similar faunal composition and abundance have been reported from other beaches of Goa (Achuthankutty *et al.,* 1978; McLusky *et al.,* 1975). Distribution and abundance of subtidal meiofauna in the Mandovi Estuary were studied from June 1983 to June 1984. Free living nematodes were the dominant group and harpacticoids came next, followed by other groups. More than 60% of the fauna occurred in the top 2 cm of the sediment. Abundance ranged from 491 to 2791/10 cm^2 and biomass from 0.16 to 2.80 mg dry wt/10 cm^2 (Ansari & Parulekar, 1993).

BOTTOM FAUNA

Macrobenthic fauna reported in 1974 showed a predominance of molluscs. In sandy subsrata, the bivalves outnumbered the other faunal groups by at least 10 times, whereas in other types of sediments they accounted for more than 50%. In the Mandovi Estuary, the commercially important clam, *Meretrix casta* dominated the estuarine zone whereas the two other bivalves namely *Perna viridis* and *Vellorita cyprinoides var* dominated the high and low saline zones, respectively. The other major groups were polychaetes and crustaceans (Parulekar & Dwivedi, 1974). There is a regular fishery of *M. casta* in the estuarine regions. At low tides, it is hand- picked largely by women at the early hours of the morning or late in the afternoon before sunset. They are also collected by locally made scoop net. It attains a maximum size of 55 mm. Being a continuous breeder, recruitment of juveniles goes on practically throughout the year (Parulekar *et al.,* 1973).

In the Zuari Estuary, the average benthic biomass was 40.2 g/m^2 wet wt. Polychaetes and bivalves were dominant (Parulekar *et al.,* 1975). Benthic studies carried out in 1971-73 in the Mandovi-Zuari-Cumbarjua estuarine system showed a rich fauna consisting of 111 species. Polychaetes followed by molluscs (largely bivalves) dominated the bottom communities and these two groups constituted > 70% of the total fauna (Parulekar *et al.,* 1980). A similar investigation carried out almost 10 years later showed 69 species altogether in the estuarine complex. Maximum density (2425/m^2) was observed during the high salinity season and minimum (650/m^2) during the monsoon period. Polychaeta formed a dominant group in both the estuaries followed by Crustacea and Mollusca (Ansari *et al.*, 1986). Thus, it is clear that there has been a decline not only in the number of species but the composition of the fauna seems to have changed during the last 12 years. From 111 species reported in 1980, based on the study of 1972-73, the number has come down to 69 in 1986, based on the study carried out in 1982-83. Thus, a reduction of 40% has been recorded in less than 10 years. The clams which dominated the bottom fauna have been replaced by polychaetes and clams came down to second place. In 1994, it was again replaced by crustaceans and it came down to third place. An increase in siltation over the commercial clam-beds appears to be the main cause of their decreasing numbers (Parulekar *et al.*, 1986).

Macrobenthic assemblage has been studied in the soft mud of the central portion of the Marmugao Bay at 18 stations. The faunal composition, represented by 3 major groups, has been shown in Table 12.3. Polychaetes followed by molluscs and crustaceans were the dominant taxa. The less abundant groups were nemerteans and echiuroid worms, bryozoans, sipunculids and fishes. Among the families of animals recorded, Nereidae was the most widespread family followed by Cirratulidae and Ciralonidae (Ansari *et al.*, 1994).

Table 12.3— Percentage (%) of faunal composition, density (no/m^2) and biomass wet weight (g/m^2) at the stations studied in Marmugao Bay (From Ansari *et al.*, 1994)

St. no.	Polychaeta	Mollusca	Crustacea	Others	Density	Biomass
1	34	45	12	9	699	24.6
2	55	14	26	5	707	2.5
3	49	12	29	10	572	3.2
4	56	8	28	8	498	3.3
5	44	11	30	15	908	4.3
6	42	6	38	14	592	6.2
7	60	16	14	10	1107	12.8
8	32	58	6	4	911	4.3
9	48	16	24	12	829	46.2
10	42	40	10	8	615	3.3
11	47	34	12	7	764	5.9
12	48	25	14	13	562	6.1
13	36	47	13	4	1026	44.3
14	40	45	9	6	608	18.2
15	42	38	15	5	515	10.2
16	47	33	12	8	588	14.2
17	31	54	10	5	882	42.4
18	28	52	12	8	907	45.2

Distribution and abundance of subtidal meiofauna in the Mandovi Estuary showed the monthly faunal abundance to range from 491 to 2791/10 cm^2, and dry weight biomass from 0.16 to 2.80 mg/10 cm^2. Free living namatodes were the dominant group contributing over 75% of the total density and 30 to 42% of the total biomass. Harpacticoids came next forming 6.9 to 8.7% of the total meiofauna followed by turbellarians (3.8 to 4.5%), small polychaetes (2.8 to 3.2%) and ostracods (1.6 to 4.5%). The combined contribution of other groups to faunal density was 4.5 - 6.2% (Ansari & Parulekar, 1993).

In another communication, an attempt was made to work out the ecological energetics of microphytobenthos, meiobenthos and microbenthos. The average annual production rates (consisting of detrital pigments coming from decaying mangrove leaves, etc.), was estimated to be 42.68g C/m^2/y. For meiobenthos and macrobenthos, the estimates of annual rates of production were 6.19 and 9.20g C/m^2/y respectively. Meiobenthos were dominated by nematodes, harpacticoids, polychaetes, turbellarian and ostracods. The macorfuanal components included polychaetes followed by crustaceans and molluscs. Most of the organisms were filter feeders and detritivores and their density was maximum in the detrital mud. The available sources of energy produced in the estuary fell considerably short to meet the food requirement of meio-and macrobenthos. Hence, the detritus-rich sediment was the major source of meeting the energy needs of both the benthic groups (Ansari *et al.,* 1994; Verlencar & Qasim, 1984).

MANGROVES

Mangroves are absent at the mouth of the estuary where the shoreline is rocky with laterite. Otherwise, all along the adjoining portions and in the riverine regions, where salinity can penetrate, mangroves are found. Along the Cumbarjua Canal, rich mangrove vegetation occurs. Mangrove flora of the estuarine system include 16 species belonging to 8 families as shown in Table 12.4 (Untawale *et al.,* 1973; 1982). The data published in 1973 indicate 31 species belonging to 18 families which have been revised in 1982 based on satellite imagery. Benthic algae present on the muddy substratum and the detritus derived from mangrove foliage probably formed the food for fish, prawns and other organisms found in the swamp. Polychaetes, crustaceans and a few molluscs constituted the fauna of the substratum (Untawale & Parulekar, 1976).

In the Zuari Estuary, a benthic red alga, *Caloglossa leprieurii*, is reported to form a mat in the intertidal area, on the pneumatophores and on other root systems of *Rhizophora mucronata, Avicennia* sp. and other associated mangroves in the swamp. This alga grows equally well under the shade of trees. Maximum biomass of the alga was recorded in October (Jagtap & Untawale, 1980). Mangrove plants with their associated biota contribute a major portion of the organic matter in the mangrove environment (Jagtap, 1987). In the Zuari Estuary and Cumbarjua Canal, 8 species and in the Mandovi 7 species of mangroves have been reported, neglecting some of the minor species (Jagtap, 1985). Data obtained by remote sensing (aerial photographs) have revealed a total cover of about 2,000 hectares of mangrove forests in all the estuaries of Goa. Of this, approximately 700 ha are found in Mandovi-Zuari estuarine system and about 200 ha in the Cumbarjua Canal (Untawale *et al.*, 1982).

Table 12.4— Dominant species of mangroves recorded from the estuaries of Goa (Untawale *et al.*, 1982)

Family	Species	
Rhizophoraceae	1	*Rhizophora mucronata*
	2	*Rhizophora opiculata*
	3	*Rhizophora conjugata*
	4	*Kandelia candel*
	5	*Bruguiera gymnorhiza*
	6	*Bruguiera parviflora*
Fabaceae	7	*Derris heterophylla*
Sonneratiaceae	8	*Sonneratia alba*
	9	*Sonneratia casiolaris*
Acanthaceae	10	*Acanthus ilicifolius*
Aviceniaceae	11	*Avicennia marina*
	12	*Avicennia officinalis*
	13	*Avicennia alba*
Euphorbiaceae	14	*Excoecaria agallocha*
Myrsinaceae	15	*Aegiceras corniculatum*
Pteridaceae	16	*Acrostichum aureus*

FISHERY

The annual fish catch from the estuarine system varies from 150 to 350 tonnes with an average value of about 200 tonnes. Demersal fish, mainly prawns and finfishes contribute from 50 to 70% of the total catch. The dominant group of the demersal finfishes of the estuaries include catfishes, sciaenids, flatfishes, rock and sand whiting. Besides these, there are extensive beds of the estuarine clam, *Meretrix casta*, the average yield of this clam from different beds is estimated to be about 80 tonnes (Ansari, 1978).

In Goa, there is a considerable scope for cultivation of bivalves on ropes suspended from floating rafts in the estuaries. Experiments in this field began in 1974 and the first publication on the raft culture of green mussel, *Mytilus (Perna) viridis*, appeared a few years later (Qasim *et al.*, 1977). Mussel seeds were transplanted from the natural bed at Velsao to Dona Paula, about 20 km away (close to NIO) and were allowed to grow on nylon ropes suspended from floating rafts. They grew at the rate of 8 mm/month and attained marketable size in about 5 months. Growth on ropes was faster than in their natural bed. Total caloric content of cultured mussel was higher than those of the natural bed. Annual production of mussels was of the order of 23 kg mussel meat per rope or approximately 1150 kg of mussel meat per raft. In terms of yield in area, it works out to be about 480 tonnes of mussel/ha/y. Cost of production was about Rs. 2500/raft and the value of mussel produced was about Rs. 6900. Rope culture thus gave a fairly high rate of return.

Another experiment on the raft culture of weaving mussel (*Modiolus metcalfei*) in the estuary did not give as encouraging result as with the former species (*Mytilis viridis*) because its growth was slower on the raft than in the natural bed which was 5 km away within the estuary. Competition for space and food probably affected their growth. However, their culture possibilities have been clearly demonstrated (Parulekar *et al.*, 1984). In *Mytilis (Perna) viridis*, physiological adaptions because of changed environmental conditions from natural beds to estuarine conditions have been evaluated and it has been pointed out that the raft grown mussels adapt themselves behaviourally, physiologically and biochemically to wide-ranging external conditions and respond appropriately to changing conditions (Parulekar *et al.*, 1982). Seasonal variations of two elements (Ca and Mg) and 4 trace metals (Fe, Cu, Zn and Mn) were determined in the mussel (*Perna viridis*) cultured on raft. The concentrations of most of the elements and trace metals in the mussel tissue were generally lower than in seawater indicating that there is no contamination of mussel from outside source (Rivonkar & Parulekar, 1998). Mass culture of several species of edible bivalves namely *Meretrix casta, Paphia malabarica, Villorita cyprinoides, Donax incarnatus, Modiolus metcalfei* and *Crassostrea gryphoides* using different methods such as ground clutch, floating rafts with suspended ropes, nylon bags, sandwich nets, plastic trays, etc., was demonstrated. The cost for each type of cultivation was determined and the rate of return was found to be high (Parulekar *et al.*, 1984).

Traditional types of fish and prawn farming in Goa is being practised since time immemorial. Normally brackishwater ponds are used to serve other purposes besides fish farming. Some are permanent fish farms while others are used as salt-cum-fish culture or for paddy-cum-fish culture. Most of these are low-lying wetlands along the tidal marshes and are protected from innundation by embankment. Inflow and outflow of water are regulated by sluice gates. The total yields of fish, salt and paddy from these ponds are quite substantial and the rates of return are high (Parulekar & Verlencar, 1984). Details of mullet (*Mugil cephalus*) and pearl spot (*Etroplus suratensis*) culture have given by Matondkar (1978) and the rate of growth of the green mussel (*Perna viridis*) in Zuari from a raft-grown population has been estimated by Rivonakar *et al.* (1993).

The distribution and abundance of the larvae of commercially important penaeid prawns from both Mandovi and Zuari estuaries have been determined. Larvae of all the species were more abundant in Zuari than in Mandovi and their maximum abundance was during the postmonsoon season. Post-larvae, on the other hand, were more abundant in Mandovi (Achuthankutty *et al.,* 1977). Most of the species have their initial growth in mangrove swamp and later stay in the estuary before migrating into the coastal waters (Achuthankutty & Nair, 1983). Larvae of the sergestid shrimp (*Acetes* sp.) also occur in the estuarine system throughout the year and their peak abundance is during the premonsoon period (Achuthankutty & Selvakumar, 1979). Larvae of three species of penaeid prawns (*Metapenaeus dobsoni, M. affinis* and *Penaeus marguiensis*) were generally found to be largely distributed in the lower reaches of the two estuaries (at the mouth). Their abundance in the middle and upper reaches was relatively not well-marked. Probably strong currents prevailing in the middle and upper reaches physically prevent their migration upstream and thus they tend to aggregate as clusters at the mouth (Achuthankutty, 1987). Larvae of the prawn, *M. dobsoni* grow up to 40 mm in length in the mangrove habitat bordering the Mandovi Estuary (7 km^2). Between November and March, peak migration of post-larvae occurs from mangroves to the lower reaches of the estuary. They attain a length of 50-60 mm in the open estuary (Achuthankutty, 1988). Mature specimens of another species of penaeid prawn (*Metapenaeus moyebi*) were recorded in abundance in the Mandovi Estuary throughout the year. These constitute a good share of prawn fishery of the estuary. About 13 species of penaeid prawns are caught in the stake net. Fully mature specimens of both sexes occurring in large numbers suggest that this species attains its first maturity in the estuary and probably breeds in the estuarine habitat (Nair *et al.,* 1993). There is a regular fishery of lobsters in the estuary and the spiny lobster, *Panulirus polyphagus*, is caught at Dona Paula and other nearby places. It was first recorded from the Zuari by Thomas (1975).

MICROBIOLOGY

Soil samples taken from the swamps of Goa, 6 km and 15 km away from the mouth of the river Zuari, have been reported to contain phenolic acids. These acids have antimicrobial properties and also have some role in the degradation of organic matter. They are produced in areas of low productivity with anaerobic conditions. Although their role in the mangrove environment is not properly understood, their presence is of special interest to microbiologists (Karanth *et al.*, 1975). A bacterial strain, capable of fixing CO_2, was isolated from an estuarine beach of Goa. The strain grew well in the laboratory under anaerobic conditions and was found to be Gram-negative. It varied from spiral to Y shapes. It had no sulphur deposit anywhere and produced purple pigments. Based on its characteristics, it was identified as non-sulphur bacteria belonging to the family Athiorhodaceae (Karanth *et al.,* 1977). Some of the estuarine beaches of Goa were found to be rich in heterotrophic bacterial flora with a strong dehydrogenase activity (Lokabharathi *et al.,* 1977). From the tar balls accumulated on the estuarine beaches, a fungus, *Fusarium* sp. was isolated, which grew well in the laboratory in a medium containing hydrocarbons (kerosene and petrol). The concentration of kerosene and petrol for its optimum growth was found to be 4% (Nair & Lokabharathi, 1977).

From one of the beaches of Zuari Estuary (Dona Paula), sulphate-reducing bacteria (SRB), together with the total aerobic and anaerobic microbial flora of the beach, were estimated (Lokabharathi & Chandramohan, 1985). Similarly, the SRB were also recorded from the mangrove swamps of Goa, and their counts were 10^3/g dry sediment which decreased with depth. Lactate utilisers of SRB were higher than acetate utilisers. The strains were all mesophilic and euryhaline. Their physiological characteristics showed that they utilised a greater degree of propionate and butyrate than lactate and acetate (Saxena *et al.,* 1988; Lokabharathi *et al.,* 1991). Seasonal variation of microbial density on an estuarine beach (Dona Paula) was studied for a period of 6 months. Maximum density was noted at 1 cm depth. About 155 isolates were identified which fell into 13 genera. The predominant genus was *Coryneforms* (Lokabharathi *et al.,* 1990).

Shells of the rock oysters, collected from the estuarine beaches of Goa, showed that these were infected by a fungus, *Ostracoblabe implexa.* The fungus grows within the matrix of the shell and causes dark flecks on the inner surface of the valves. The fungus was separated and cultured. Infection can be induced in the shells in the laboratory (Raghukumar & Lande, 1988). Similarly, the calcareous shells of the window-pane oyster, collected from the Zuari Estuary, were found to be heavily infested with shell-boring cynobacteria. Three species of cynobacteria were identified. The chlorophyll content present in the bacteria makes the infested shells lose their calcium and protein and become brittle (Raghukumar *et al.*, 1988).

Fungal parasites occur in the algae found on the beaches of Goa estuaries. These parasites do not grow on healthy specimens because phenolics contained in the algae act as a defence mechanism but during the process of decomposition of algae, populations of 3 groups of organisms namely thraustochytrids, fungi and bacteria grow rapidly in the algal detritus and enhance the nutritive value of detritus (Raghukumar, 1986). This was confirmed by conducting studies on decomposing brown alga, *Sargassum cinereum*, contained in litter-bags at the Dona Paula jetty close to the mouth of the Zuari River. Algal detritus of 0, 7, 14 and 28 days old were obtained from litter-bags and these were inoculated with 3 fungi and 2 thraustochytrids. Most of the organisms grew best on 7 and 14 days old detritus indicating that microbial biomass would increase in later stages of decomposition after phenolic contents of the algae get reduced. With the growth of the microbial biomass, the protein values of detritus increased and amino acid content declined sharply (Sathe-Pathak *et al.*, 1993).

POLLUTION

On the west coast of India or perhaps in the entire country, the Mandovi-Zuari Estuarine System is one of the cleanest and unpolluted water bodies. This is because the people of Goa are extremely sensitive about the environment of their State and would like to maintain it as clean as possible for as long as they can. This can be judged from the uproar and demonstrations which took place in September 1973 when fish mortality occurred for the first time in Velsao Bay where effluents from a fertilizer factory (Zuari Agrochemicals Ltd.) were being discharged. This factory has an annual production capacity of 220,000 tonnes of ammonia, 340,000 tonnes of urea and 150,000 of N-P-K. It went into production in June 1973 and began to discharge about 500 m^3/h of wastewater into the Velsao Bay which is an important fishing area. The bay was virtually uncontaminated prior to the commissioning of the factory. The manufacturing process used by the factory at that time was Vetrocoke which involves the use of arsenous oxide in the gasification of naphtha. The major contaminants in the effluent going into the bay were thought to be arsenic, ammonia and urea.

A team from the NIO commissioned for this investigation collected dead animals washed ashore on the beach for analysis. Investigations of the bay water and dead animals did not give any conclusive proof of the cause of mortality. Although arsenic in the dead animals (crabs and fishes) was found to be high, it did not reach a level to cause mortality. Trace metals such as Mn, Fe, Ni, Cu, Zn and Pb did not indicate high values either in the water or in dead animals. Probably the mortality was caused by high concentration of ammonia which was released into the water and this probably replaced dissolved oxygen. Subsequently, the manufacturing process was changed from Vetrocoke to Benfield which eliminated the use of arsenic (Singbal *et al.,* 1976; Zingde *et al.,* 1979).

Mandovi Estuary receives about 1300 million litres of urban domestic sewage waste annually through a drain which opens at a discharge point in the city of Panaji (Panjim). Meiofaunal abundance and distribution in the sediment were used as indices of pollution at the discharge point and at the other two sites nearby because many meiofaunal species have a short life and could be used for pollution monitoring. Major groups constituting the meiofauna were nematodes, harpacticoids, oligochaetes, polychaetes and archiannelids. At the sewage discharge point, faunal density was largely confined to topmost (5 cm) layer whereas at the other sites they were uniformly distributed up to 19 cm depth. Major effect of sewage is that it reduces the oxygen supply in the sediment and stimulates the formation of H_2S. A layer of black sulphide was seen below 5-6 cm which was not found at the other two sites. A decline in meiofaunal abundance was found at the discharge point in all the seasons (Ansari *et al.,* 1984).

Mining plays an important role in the economy of Goa and nearly 10 million tonnes of iron and manganese ores are exported from the Marmugao Harbour. Much of the mining activities are carried out along the banks of the two river system (Mandovi and Zuari) and the Cumbarjua Canal. The ores are transported to the port for shipment by specially-built mechanized barges through the inland waterways. Extraction of 1 tonne of export-quality ore generates about 1.5 tonnes of mining rejects. Over the years, nearly 300 million tonnes of mining rejects seem to have accumulated along the mining belts of Goa. During the heavy monsoon rains in the hilly regions and in the catchment areas, where the rainfall is 3750 mm/y (3000 mm in the coastal belt), there is an erosion of accumulated rejects due to flooding and they settle in the estuarine benthic sediments. A survey of the clam beds and bottom fauna in the estuaries conducted in 1972-73 and another in 1982-83 has given very painful results. In less than 10 years, there has been a reduction of more than 70% clam production and nearly disappearance of the resident fauna. The entry of enormous quantities of mining rejects has caused reduction in dissolved oxygen, high load of inert material in suspension leading to total opacity of water and layers of blanketing of bottom deposits by mining rejects. These features have reduced the healthy and productive estuarine environment of 1972-73 into an impoverished ecosystem in 1982-83. It had been suggested that unless some measures are taken fairly soon, the estuarine life along the mining belt shall dwindle completely (Parulekar *et al.,* 1986).

References

1. Achuthankutty, C.T., 1987. Commercially important penaeid shrimp larvae in the estuaries of Goa. *Mahasagar — Bulletin of National Institute of Oceanography*, Vol. 20, pp. 217-224.
2. Achuthankutty, C.T., 1988. Nursery life of marine prawn, *Metapenaeus dobsoni* (miers) in the Mandovi Estuary, along Goa coast, India. *Indian Journal of Marine Sciences*, Vol. 17, pp. 313-316.
3. Achuthankutty, C.T., Geroge, M.J., & Goswami, S.C. 1977. Larval ingression of penaeid prawns in the estuaries of Goa. *Proceedings of Symposium on Warm Water Zooplankton,* National Institute of Oceanography, pp. 412-426.
4. Achuthankutty, C.T., Stirling, A., Nair, S., Lokabharati, P.A. & Menezes, M.R., 1978. Sandy beach at Baina, Goa; The ecology and production. *Indian Journal of Marine Sciences*, Vol. 7, pp. 23-29.
5. Achuthankutty, C.T., & Selvakumar, R.A., 1979. Larval distribution of sergestid shrimp *Acetes* in the estuarine system of Goa. *Mahasagar — Bulletin of National Institute of Oceanography*, Vol. 12, pp. 169-174.
6. Achuthankutty, C.T. & Nair, S.R.S., 1983. Larval migration and growth of marine prawns in the estuarine habitat. *Mahasagar — Bulletin of National Institute of Oceanography*, Vol. 16, pp. 243-250.
7. Achuthankutty, C.T., Ramaiah, N. & Padmavati, G., 1995. Zooplankton variability and copepod assemblage in the coastal and estuarine waters of Goa along the central west coast of India. *Intergovernmental Oceanographic Commission*, I. *Workshop Report No.* 142 (ed.) A.C. Pierrot-Bults & S. Vander Spoel, UNESCO, Paris, pp. 1-11.
8. Ansari, Z.A., 1978. Fishery and cultural possibilities of molluscs in Goa. *Seafood Export Journal*, Vol. 10, pp. 14-17.
9. Ansari, Z.A., Chatterji, A. & Parulekar, A.H., 1984. Effect of domestic sewage on sand beach meiofauna at Goa. *Hydorbiologia*, Vol. 111, pp. 129-233.
10. Ansari, Z.A., Ingole, B.S., Banerjee, G. & Parulekar, A.H., 1986. Spatial and temporal changes in benthic macrofauna from Mandovi and Zuari estuaries of Goa, west coast of India. *Indian Journal of Marine Sciences*, Vol. 15, pp. 223-229.
11. Ansari, Z.A., Sreepada, R.A., Kanti, A. & Gracias, E.S., 1994. Macrobenthic assemblage in the soft sediment of Mormugao harbour, Goa (central west coast of India). *Indian Journal of Marine Sciences*, Vol. 23, pp. 225-231.
12. Ansari, Z.A. & Parulekar, A.H., 1993. Distribution, abundance and ecology of the meiofauna in a tropical estuary along the west cost of India. *Hydrobiologia*. Vol. 262, pp. 115-126.
13. Bhargava, R.M.S., 1973. Diurnal variation in phytoplankton pigments of Mandovi Estuary, Goa. *Indian Journal of Marine Sciences*, Vol. 2, pp. 27-31.

14. Bhargava, R.M.S., Bhattathiri, P.M.A. & Devassy, V.P., 1977. Relative contribution of nannoplankton to the primary production of two estuaries of Goa. *Mahasagar — Bulletin of National Institute of Oceanography*, Vol. 10, pp. 61-66.
15. Bhattathiri, P.M.A., Devassy, V.P. & Bhargava, R.M.S., 1976. Production at different trophic levels in the estuarine system of Goa. *Indian Journal of Marine Sciences*, Vol. 5, pp. 83-86.
16. Bois Penrose, 1960. Goa — Queen of the east (Eredias, M.G., de 1610) Commenmoracoes Do.V Centenario De Morte De Infante De Henrique. Commissao Ultramarina, Lisboa.
17. Cherian, T., Rao, L.V.G. & Varma, K.K., 1974. Hydrography and suspended sediment load of oceanic and estuarine waters adjoining Marmugao harbour during early summer. *Indian Journal of Marine Sciences*, Vol. 3, pp. 99-104.
18. Cherian, T., Rao, L.V.G. & Varma, K.K., 1975. Variations in physical characteristics of the waters of Zuari Estuary. *Indian Journal of Marine Sciences*, Vol. 4, pp. 5-10.
19. Das. P.K., Murty, C.S. & Varadachari, V.V.R., 1972. Flow characteristics of Cumbarjua canal connecting Mandovi and Zuari estuaries. *Indian Journal of Marine Sciences*, Vol. 1, pp. 95-102.
20. Dehadrai, P.V., 1970. Changes in the environmental features of the Zuari and Mandovi estuaries in relation to tides. *Proceedings of Indian Academy of Sciences*, Vol. 72 (B), pp. 68-80.
21. Dehadrai. P.V. & Bhargava, R.M.S., 1972. Seasonal organic production in relation to environmental features in Mandovi and Zuari estuaries, Goa. *Indian Journal of Marine Sciences*, Vol. 1, pp. 52-56.
22. DeSousa, S.N. & Sen Gupta, R., Sanzgiri, S. & Rajagopal, M.P., 1981. Studies on nutrients of Mandovi and Zuari river system. *Indian Journal of Marine Sciences*, Vol. 10, pp. 314-321.
23. DeSousa, S.N., & Sen Gupta, R., 1988. Variations of dissolved oxygen in Mandovi and Zuari estuaries. *Indian Journal of Marine Sciences*, Vol. 17, pp. 67-71.
24. DeSousa, S.N., 1983. Studies on the behaviour of nutrients in the Mandovi Estuary during premonsoon. *Estuarine, Coastal and Shelf Science*, Vol. 16, pp. 299-308.
25. DeSousa, S.N. & Sen Gupta, R., 1988. Distribution and behaviour of fluoride in Mandovi and Zuari estuaries, central west coast of India. *Indian Journal of Marine Sciences*, Vol. 17, pp. 195-201.
26. Devassy, V.P. & Bhargava, R.M.S., 1978. Diel changes in phytoplankton population in the Mandovi and Zuari estuaries of Goa. *Mahasagar — Bulletin of National Institute of Oceanography*, Vol. 11, pp. 195-199.
27. Devassy, V.P., Bhattathiri, P.M.A. & Qasim, S.Z., 1978. *Trichodesmiun* phenomenon. *Indian Journal of Marine Sciences*, Vol. 7, pp. 168-186.
28. Devassy, V.P. & Goes, J.I., 1988. Phytoplankton community structure and succession in a tropical estuaries complex (central west coast of India) *Estuarine, Coastal and Shelf Science*, Vol. 27, pp. 671-685.
29. D'Silva, C. & Bhosle, N.B., 1990. Phosphorus availability and phosphatase activity in the sediments of Mandovi Estuary, Goa. *Indian Journal of Marine Sciences*, Vol. 19, pp. 143-144.

30. Goswami, S.C. & Singbal Y.S., 1974. Ecology of Mandovi and Zuari estuaries: plankton community in relation to hydrographic conditions during monsoon months. *Indian Journal of Marine Sciences*, Vol. 3, pp. 51-57.
31. Goswami, S.C. & Selvakumar, R.A.,. 1977. Plankton studies in the estuarine system of Goa. *Proceedings of the Symposium on Warm Water Zooplankton*, National Institute of Oceanography, pp. 226-241.
32. Goswami, S.C. & Selvakumar, R.A. & Goswami, U., 1979. Diel and tidal variations in zooplanktonic populations in the Zuari Estuary, Goa. *Mahasagar — Bulletin of National Institute of Oceanography*, Vol. 12, pp. 247-258.
33. Goswami, S.C., 1982. Distribution and diversity of copepods in the Mandovi-Zuari estuarine system, Goa. *Indian Journal of Marine Sciences*, Vol. 11, pp. 292-295.
34. Goswami, S.C., 1983. Coexistence and succession of copepod species in the Mandovi and Zuari estuaries. *Mahasagar — Bulletin of National Institute of Oceanography*, Vol. 16, pp. 251-258.
35. Goswami, S.C. & Devassy, V.P., 1991. Seasonal fluctuations in the occurrence of Cladocera in the Mandovi-Zuari estuarine waters of Goa. *Indian Journal of Marine Sciences*, Vol. 20, pp. 138-142.
36. Harkantra, S.N. & Parulekar, A.H., 1985. Community structure of sand-dwelling macrofauna of an estuarine beach in Goa, India. *Marine Ecology — Progress Series*, Vol. 30, pp. 291-294.
37. Ingole B.S. & Parulekar, A.H., 1998. Role of salinity in structuring the intertidal meiofauna of a tropical estuarine beach: Field evidence. *Indian Journal of Marine Sciences*, Vol. 27, pp. 356-361.
38. Jagtap, T.G. & Untawale, A.G., 1980. Some ecological and biochemical observation on *Caloglossa lepreiurii* (Harvey) from Zuari Estuary, Goa. *Seaweed Research Utilization*, Vol. 4, pp. 17-24.
39. Jagtap, T.G., 1985. Structure and composition of the mangrove forest along the Goa coast. In: *The Mangroves*. Proceedings National Symposium on Biological Utilization and Conservation of Mangroves, pp. 188-195.
40. Jagtap, T.G., 1987. Seasonal distribution of organic matter in mangrove environment of Goa. *Indian Journal of Marine Sciences*, Vol. 16, pp. 103-106.
41. Karanth, N.G.K., Lokabharathi, P.A. & Nair, S., 1975. Distribution of phenolic acids in soils from two mangrove areas of Goa. *Indian Journal of Marine Sciences*, Vol. 4, pp. 215-217.
42. Karanth, N.G.K., Nair, S. & Lokabharathi, P.A., 1977. Studies on photosynthetic bacteria isolated from an estuarine beach of Goa. *Indian Journal of Marine Sciences*, Vol. 6, pp. 94-96.
43. Kumari, L.K., Sumitra-Vijayaraghavan, Wafar, M.V.M., Royan J.P. & Rajendran, A., 1978. Studies on detritus in a tropical estuary. *Indian Journal of Marine Sciences*, Vol. 7, pp. 263-266.
44. Lokabharathi, P.A., Nair, S. & Karanth, N.G.K., 1977. Microbial flora and dehydrogenase activity of beaches. *Indian Journal of Marine Sciences*, Vol. 6, pp. 91-94.
45. Lokabharathi, P.A., & Chandramohan, D., 1985. Sulphate reducing potential in an estuarine beach. *Indian Journal of Marine Sciences*, Vol. 14, pp. 187-191.

46. Lokabharathi, P.A. & Chandramohan, D., 1990. Bacterial flora of Dona Paula, India, using numerical profiles. *Nippon Suisan Gokkaishi*, Vol. 53, pp. 463-476.
47. Lokabharathi, P.A.,Oak, S. & Chandramohan, D., 1991. Sulphate-reducing bacteria from mangrove swamp, II: Their ecology and physiology. *Oceanologica Acta*, Vol. 14, pp. 163-171.
48. Matondkar, S.G.P., 1978. Some aspects of culture of mullet (*Mugil cephalus*) and pearl spot (*Etroplus suratensis*) in Siridao fish farm. *Indian Journal of Marine Sciences*, Vol. 7, pp. 191-201.
49. McLusky, D.S., Nair, S.A., Stirling, A. & Bhargava, R.M.S., 1975. The ecology of central west coast Indian beach with particular reference to *Donax incarnatus. Marine Biology*, Vol. 30, pp. 267-276.
50. Murty, C.S. & Das, P.K., 1972. Premonsoon tidal flow characteristics of Mandovi Estuary. *Indian Journal of Marine Sciences*, Vol. 1, pp. 148-151.
51. Nair, S.R.S., Achuthankutty, C.T. & Parulekar, A.H., 1993. Maturation of the penaeid prawn, *Metapenaeus moyebi* in Mandovi Estuary, Goa. *Indian Journal of Marine Sciences*, Vol. 22, pp. 151-152.
52. Nair, S. & Lokabharathi, P.A., 1977. Degradation of hydrocarbons by fungus, *Fusarium* sp. *Indian Journal of Marine Sciences*, Vol. 6, pp. 173-175.
53. Nair, V.R. & Selvakumar, R.A., 1979. The ecology of chaetognaths in the estuarine system of Goa. *Mahasagar — Bulletin of National Institute of Oceanography*, Vol. 12, pp. 17-24.
54. Nair, V.R. 1980a. Organic carbon content of tropical zooplankton. *Indian Journal of Marine Sciences*, Vol. 9, pp. 114-116.
55. Nair, V.R., 1980b. Production and association of zooplankton in estuarine and nearshore waters of Goa. *Indian Journal of Marine Sciences*, Vol. 9, pp. 116-119.
56. Nair, V.R., Achuthankutty, C.T. & Nair, S.R.S., 1983. Zooplankton variability in the Zuari Estuary, Goa. *Mahasagar — Bulletin of National Institute of Oceanography*, Vol. 16, pp. 235-242.
57. Padmavati, G. & Goswami, S.C., 1996. Zooplankton ecology in the Mandovi-Zuari estuarine system of Goa, west coast of India. *Indian Journal of Marine Sciences*, Vol. 25, pp. 268-273.
58. Pant, A., Bhargava, R.M.S. & Goswami, S.C., 1976. Nannoplankton, total phytoplankton and zooplankton standing stock measurements in Goa waters. *Indian Journal of Marine Sciences*, Vol. 5, pp. 103-106.
59. Pant, A. Balasubramanian, T., Rajagopal, M.D., Wafar, M.V.M. & Sumitra-Vijaryaraghavan, 1977. Contribution of extracellular production by nannoplankton to CO_2 fixation in a tropical estuary. *Indian Journal of Marine Sciences*, Vol. 6, pp. 147-150.
60. Parulekar, A.H., Dwivedi, S.N. & Dhargalkar, V.K., 1973. Ecology of clam beds in Mandovi, Cumbarjua Canal and Zuari estuarine system of Goa. *Indian Journal of Marine Sciences*, Vol. 2, pp. 122-126.
61. Parulekar, A.H., Rajamanickam, G.V. & Dwivedi, S.N., 1975. Benthic studies in Goa estuaries: Biomass and faunal composition in the Zuari Estuary. *Indian Journal of Marine Sciences*, Vol. 4, pp. 202-205.

62. Parulekar, A.H., Dhargalkar, V.K. & Singbal, S.Y.S., 1980. Benthic studies of Goa estuaries. Part 3. Annual cycle of macrofaunal distribution, production and trophic relation. *Indian Journal of Marine Sciences*, Vol. 9, pp. 189-200.
63. Parulekar, A.H., Dalal, S.G. & Harkantra, S.N., 1982. Environmental physiology of raft-grown mussels in Goa. *Aquaculture*, Vol. 29, pp. 83-93.
64. Parulekar, A.H., Ansari, Z.A. & Ingole, B.S., 1986. Effect of mining activities on the clam fisheries and bottom fauna of Goa estuaries. *Proceedings of the Indian Academy of Sciences*, Vol.. 95 B, pp. 325-339.
65. Parulekar, A.H. & Dwivedi, S.N., 1974. Benthic studies in Goa estuaries: Part I - Standing crop and faunal composition in relation to bottom salinity distribution and substratum characteristics in the estuary of Mandovi river. *Indian Journal of Marine Sciences*, Vol. 3, pp. 41-45.
66. Parulekar, A.H., Nair, S.A., Ansari, Z.A., Chatterjee, A., Ingole, B.S. & Roy, J.M., 1984. Ecology and culturing of edible bivalves in Goa. *Indian Journal of Marine Sciences*, Vol. 13, pp. 190-192.
67. Parulekar, A.H. & Verlencar, X.N., 1984. Status and prospectus of fish farming in India. *Proceedings of the Symposium on Coastal Aquaculture*, Published by National Institute of Oceanography, Goa. Vol. 3, pp. 732-737.
68. Qasim, S. Z., Parulekar, A.H., Harkantra, S.N., Ansari, Z.A. & Nair, A. 1977. Aquaculture of green mussel, *Mytilus viridis* L.: Cultivation on ropes from floating rafts. *Indian Journal of Marine Sciences*, Vol. 6, pp. 15-21.
69. Qasim, S. Z. & SenGupta, R., 1981. Environmental characteristics of the Mandovi Zuari estuarine system in Goa. *Estuarine, Coastal and Shelf Science*, Vol. 13, pp. 557-578.
70. Raghukumar, C., 1986. Thraustochytrid fungi associated with marine algae. *Indian Journal of Marine Sciences*, Vol. 15, pp. 159-167.
71. Raghukumar, C. & Lande, V., 1988. Shell diseases of rock oyster, *Crassostrea cucullata*. *Diseases of Aquatic Organisma,* Vol. 4, pp. 77-81.
72. Raghukumar, C., Pathak, S. & Chandramohan, D., 1988. Biodegradtion of calcareous shells of the windowpane oyster by shell-boring cyanobacteria. In: *Marine Biodeterioration* (eds.) M.F. Thompson, R. Sarojini and R. Nagabhushanam, pp. 693-701. Oxford and IBH Publishing Co. Pvt. Ltd., New Delhi.
73. Rajagopal, M.D. & Reddy, C.V.G., 1984. Phosphorus retention capacity of sediments in Mandovi Estuary (Goa). *Indian Journal of Marine Sciences*, Vol. 13, pp. 1-4.
74. Rajendran, A., Sumitra-Vijayaraghavan & Wafar, M.V.M., 1978. Effect of some metal ions on the photosynthesis of microplankton and nannoplankton. *Indian Journal of Marine Sciences*, Vol. 7, pp. 99-102.
75. Rao, K.K., 1974. Ecology of Mandovi and Zuari estuaries, Goa: Distribution of foraminiferal assemblages. *Indian Journal of Marine Sciences*, Vol. 3, pp. 61-66.
76. Rao, D.G., & Rao, T.C.S., 1974. Textual characteristics of sediments of Marmugao Bay, central west coast of India. *Indian Journal of Marine Sciences*, Vol. 3, pp. 99-104.
77. Rivonkar, C.U., Sreepada, R.A. & Parulekar, A.H., 1993. Growth parameters in the cultured green mussel, *Perna viridis* L. from the Zuari Estuary, Goa. *Indian Journal of Marine Sciences*, Vol. 22, pp. 72-74.

78. Rivonkar, C.U. & Parulekar, A.H., 1998. Seasonal variation of major elements (Ca, Mg) and trace metals (Fe, Cu, Zn, Mn) in cultured mussel *Perna viridis* L. and seawater in the Dona Paula Bay. *Indian Journal of Marine Sciences*, Vol. 27, pp. 411-415.
79. Sathe-Pathak, V., Raghukumar, C. & Sharma, S., 1993. Thraustochytrid fungi associated with marine algae. *Indian Journal of Marine Sciences*, Vol. 22, pp. 159-167.
80. Saxena, D., Lokabharathi, P.A. & Chandramohan, D., 1988. Sulphate reducing bacteria from mangrove swamps of Goa, central west coast of India. *Indian Journal of Marine Sciences*, Vol. 17, pp. 153-157.
81. Selvakumar, R.A., Nair, V.R. & Madhupratap, M., 1980. Seasonal variations in secondary production of the Mandovi-Zuari estuarine system of Goa. *Indian Journal of Marine Sciences*, Vol. 9, pp. 7-9.
82. Shailaja, M.S., & Pant, A. 1986. Relationship between particulate and extracellular carbon compounds of phytoplankton photosynthesis in a tropical estuary. *Marine Ecology — Progress Series*, Vol. 32, pp. 161-167.
83. Shetye, S.R., Gouveia, A.D., Singbal, S.Y.S., Naik, C.G., Sundar, D., Michael, G.S. & Nampoothiri, G., 1995. Propagation of tides in the Mandovi-Zuari estuarine network. *Proceedings of the Indian Academy of Sciences*, Vol. 104, pp. 667-682.
84. Shetye, S.R. & Murty, C.S., 1987. Seasonal variation of the salinity in the Zuari Estuary, Goa, India. *Proceedings of the Indian Academy of Sciences*, Vol. 96, pp. 249-257.
85. Shetye, S.R. 1999. Propagation of tides in the Mandovi and Zuari estuaries. *Sadhana*, Vol. 24, pp. 5-16.
86. Singbal, S.Y.S., 1973. Diurnal variations of some physico-chemical factors in the Zuari estuary of Goa. *Indian Journal of Marine Sciences*, Vol. 2, pp. 90-93.
87. Singbal, S.Y.S., Fondekar, S.P. & Reddy, C.V.G., 1976. Chemical characteristics of the inshore waters in Velsao Bay (Goa, India). *Mahasagar — Bulletin of National Institute of Oceanography*, Vol. 9, pp. 35-40.
88. Thomas, P.A., 1975. A note on the occurrence of the spiny lobster *Panulirus polyphagus* (Herbst) in Zuari Estuary in Goa. *Indian Journal of Fisheries*, Vol. 22, pp. 299-300.
89. Unnikrishnan, A.S., Shetye, S.R. & Gouveia, A.D., 1997. Tidal propagation in the Mandovi-Zuari Estuarine network, west coast of India: Impact of freshwater influx. *Estuarine, Coastal and Shelf Science*, Vol. 45, pp. 737-744..
90. Untawale, A.G., Dwivedi, S.N. & Singbal, S.Y.S., 1973. Ecology of mangroves in the Mandovi, Zuari estuaries and the interconnecting Cumbarjua Canal of Goa. *Indian Journal of Marine Sciences*, Vol. 2, pp. 47-53.
91. Untawale, A.G. & Parulekar, A.H., 1976. Some observations on the ecology of an estuarine mangrove of Goa. *Mahasagar — Bulletin of National Institute of Oceanography*, Vol. 9, pp. 57-62.
92. Untawale, A.G., Bhosle, N.B., Dhargalkar, V.K., Matondkar, S.G.P. & Bukhari, S., 1977. Biochemical changes in mangrove foliage during growth and development. *Indian Journal of Marine Sciences*, Vol. 6, pp. 104-106.
93. Untawale, A.G., Wafar, S. & Jagtap, T.G., 1982. Application of remote sensing techniques to study the distribution of mangroves along the estuaries of Goa. In: *Wetlands :*

Ecology and Management. (eds.) B. Gopal & R.E. Turner: I. International Wetlands Conference, New Delhi, 10-17 Sept. 1980. National Institute of Ecology, Jaipur, India. pp. 51-67.

94. Varma, K.K., Rao, L.V.G. & Cherian, T., 1975. Temporal and spatial variations in hydrographic conditions of Mandovi Estuary. *Indian Journal of Marine Sciences*, Vol. 4, pp. 11-17.
95. Verlencar, X.N., 1985. Urea as nitrogen source for phytoplankton production in coastal water of Goa. *Indian Journal of Marine Sciences*, Vol. 14, pp. 93-97.
96. Verlencar, X.N., & Qasim, S.Z., 1985. Particulate organic carbon in the coastal and estuarine waters of Goa and its relationship with phytoplankton production. *Estuarine, Coastal and Shelf Science*, Vol. 21, pp. 235-243.
97. Wafar, S., Untawale, A.G. & Wafar, M.V.M., 1997. Litter fall and energy flux in a mangrove ecosystem. *Estuarine, Coastal and Shelf Science*, Vol. 44, pp. 111-124.
98. Wagle, B.G., Gujar, A.R., Subramanyam, V. & Mislankar, P.G., 1988. Seabed survey of of Marmugao harbour, central west coast of India. *Indian Journal of Marine Sciences*, Vol. 17, pp. 59-62.
99. Zingde, M.D., Singbal, S.Y.S. & Reddy, C.V.G., 1979. Some observations on pollutants of Velsao Bay (Goa). *Mahasagar — Bulletin of National Institute of Oceanography*, Vol. 12, pp. 69-74.

Chapter 13

Estuaries of Mumbai (Bombay) Region

The city of Greater Bombay (recently renamed Mumbai) is largely built on reclaimed wetlands, low-lying areas and mangrove swamps. Originally, about 100 years ago, Bombay, one of the largest cities of India, included a few islands only. The extensive growth of Mumbai Metropolitan City in terms of area, population and industrial development, along Lat. 18°55′ N and Long. 72°49′ E (Fig. 13.1), has outstripped the demands of living space, freshwater supply and waste disposal. Along the coastal waters of the Arabian Sea, on the west, is located the famous Bombay Harbour (Fig. 13.1). The inner land of the city is permeated with a number of islands, rivers, creeks, bays and estuaries. Northward extension of the Bombay Harbour leads to a shallow estuary known as the Thane Creek which is fed by a number of small rivulets. Further north, the prominent Ulhas River connects the Thane Creek with the Bassein Creek on the west, which opens into the Arabian Sea. The towns of New Bombay and Kalyan are located along the banks of the Thane Creek and Ulhas River respectively. South of the Bassein Creek lies the Manori Creek and further down south, the famous fishing harbour "Versova" is located. About 10 km south of Versova, lies the shallow Mahim Bay

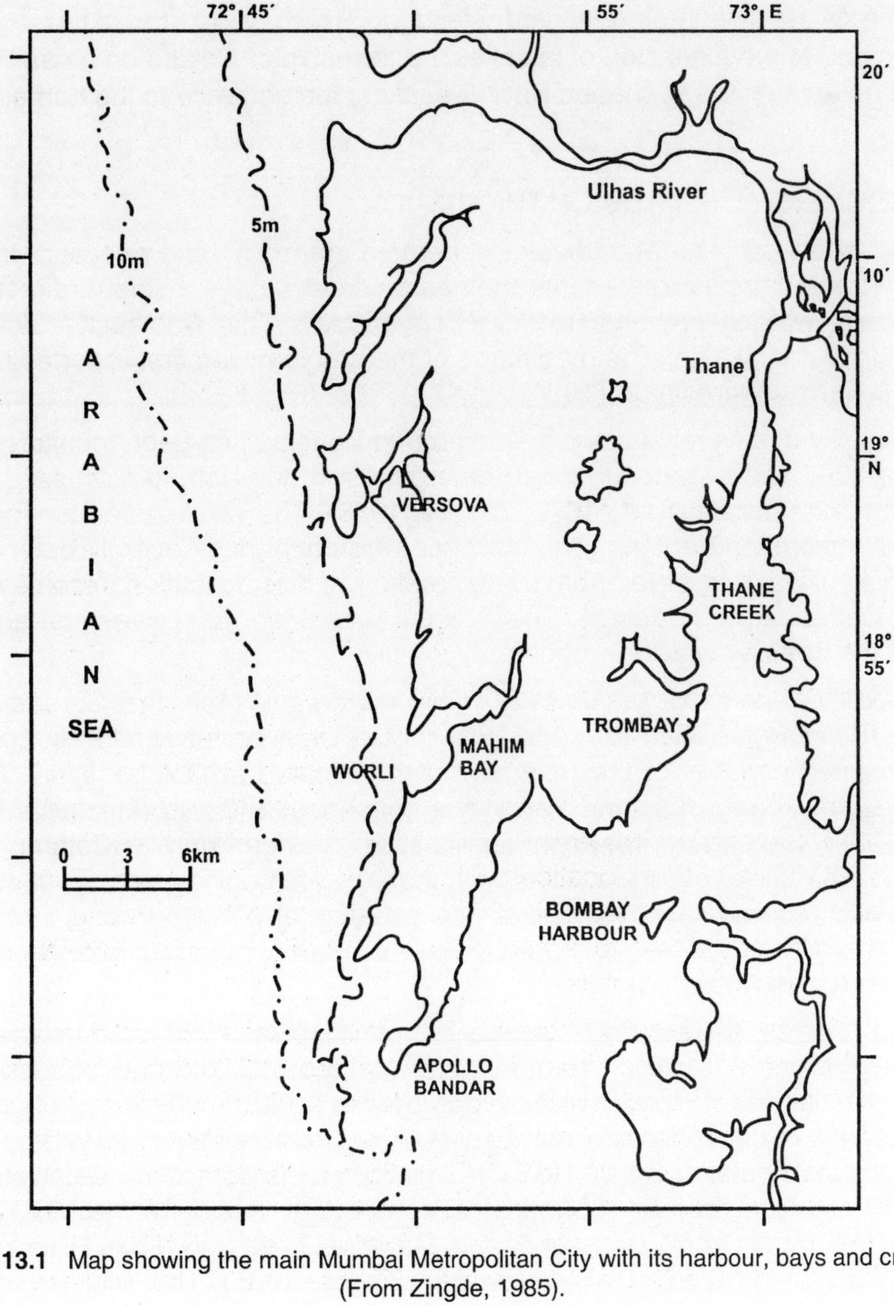

Fig. 13.1 Map showing the main Mumbai Metropolitan City with its harbour, bays and creeks (From Zingde, 1985).

fed by the river Mahim. The Mahim Bay on the west and the Thane Creek on the east demarcate the interconnected island of Trombay. At the extreme south-western end of the extension of land lies the township of Colaba on a narrow strip which demarcates the U-shaped Back Bay along the entrance to the harbour (Fig. 13.1).

ENVIRONMENTAL STATUS OF THE REGION

The estimated domestic wastewater generated in the city and released, treated, partially-treated and untreated into the nearby creeks, bays, rivers or directly into the coastal waters, amounts to 2.0×10^6 m^3/day. This wastewater does not include industrial waste. The magnitude of the problem was first reported by Sen Gupta & Sankaranarayanan (1974).

Water quality at several stations in and around Bombay has been monitored from 1976 to 1987 and a general picture emerging from the data is discussed in the following text (Zingde *et al.,* 1979; Zingde, 1985). The wastewater coming from different regions and entering the marine environment has severely deteriorated the quality of water in several bays and creeks which is described in some details later under separate headings. The account presented here gives just an overview of the Bombay waters in general.

The quantity of domestic wastewater within the area of Municipal Corporation of Greater Bombay (MCGB) exceeds 1200 million litres per day (mld). In contrast, the combined capacity of the treatment plants located at Colaba, Worli, Dadar, Dharavi, Ghatkopar, Khar and Versova is only about 340 mld (Metcalf & Eddy / EEC, 1979). Secondary treatment facilities are provided only at Colaba, Dadar and Dharavi while at other locations only primary treatment is given. Evidently, the wastewater received at these plants and possibly at other pumping stations is released untreated either to a nearby bay or creek or directly into the coastal water through discharge points.

Table 13.1 gives the results of the analysis of wastewater collected from various treatment plants. It is clear from the table that about 300 tonnes of suspended solids, 310 tonnes of biochemical oxygen demand (BOD), 40 tonnes of nitrogen and 7 tonnes of phosphorus enter the marine environment every day through the domestic wastewater (Zingde, 1985). In addition to the domestic wastewater, the nearshore regions receive 180 industrial effluents generated in the MCGB area alone. The Thane Creek, Bassein Creek, Mumbra Creek and Ulhas River receive additional 60 mld of industrial wastewater (Zingde, 1985). The influence of total wastewater on the various environmental parameters is as follows:

Tides

The tides in Mumbai region are of semidiurnal type with a considerable difference in range from one place to the other. For example, at Apollo Bundar the ranges in spring and neap are 4.7 and 1.7 m respectively whereas the corresponding levels at the head of Mahim Creek are 3 and 1.1 m. Currents measured in Thane Creek are entirely due to the flows of tidal ebb and flood water, and the velocity varies depending upon the stage of the tide during the dry season. Maximum ebb velocity of 115 cm/s has been recorded during the spring ebb tide and 70 cm/s during the spring flood tide. Higher velocities of the order of 150 cm/s have been observed on some instances. The currents maintain almost the same direction from surface to bottom and their velocities decrease only slightly. Monsoonal freshwater flow influences the current velocity substantially (Zingde *et al.*, 1979; Zingde & Desai, 1980). A two-dimensional numerical model was applied to study tide-induced currents in the Thane Creek. Calculations of amplitude were in fair agreement with the observations. While there was a good agreement in the high tide phase, it differed in the low tide by about 30 minutes (Naidu & Sarma, 2000).

Table 13.1— Characteristics of domestic wastewater and pollutants entering the marine environment of Mumbai (From Zingde, 1985)

Parameter	µg/l	kg/day
Dissolved solids	1540	17.4×10^5
Suspended solids	245	2.9×10^5
BOD	258	3.1×10^5
Sulphate	75	0.9×10^5
Nitrogen	35	0.4×10^5
Phosphorus	6	7200
Chloride	587	7.0×10^5
Manganese	507	608
Iron	2529	3035
Cobalt	30	36
Nickel	81	97
Copper	110	132
Zinc	251	301
Lead	11	13

Salinity

The salinity is largely influenced by the rainfall and land drainage during the monsoon season (June - September) and largely by the wastewater discharge during the dry season (February - May). Monsoonal influence beyond 10 m depth of the open coast is small and only a marginal decrease is recorded during August while a sharp decline in salinity in inshore regions from 30‰ in June to 5 - 15‰ during August is quite common. After August, the salinity begins to increase and from October there is a sharp rise reaching near seawater value after March.

The salinity in some bays and creeks undergoes considerable change even in the dry season when there is practically no riverine flow. This is largely due to the release of wastewater resulting in incomplete mixing of wastewater with the incoming seawater by the tidal action leading to vertical gradient in salinity. Thus, for example in Mahim Bay and Creek the gradient exceeds 7‰ during the flood tide and during the ebb tide, although there is no freshwater coming through the Mahim River, salinities as low as 15‰ are encountered in the bays and creeks because of the dilution caused by the wastewater (Zingde *et al.,* 1979; Zingde & Desai, 1980).

Suspended solids

The offshore waters of Mumbai are characterized by a high suspended load normally exceeding 30 mg/l during the postmonsoon period. In the harbour region, there is a marked increase (50-300 mg/l) largely due to the suspension of loose bottom sediments into the water column by strong tidal currents. During the monsoon season, there is a sharp increase in suspended matter (150-600 mg/l) in the inshore region because of the suspended load associated with land runoff (Zingde, 1985). About $0.84 \times 10^6 m^3$ of silt flows into the harbour through all the creeks during the monsoon. The average rainfall in the harbour region is about 2000 mm (Naryanaswamy *et al.,* 1980).

Dissolved oxygen (DO)

In the offshore waters, DO of 6 mg/l is recorded in August which attains a maximum of 8-9 mg/l in subsequent months. Thereafter, it records a decrease till May. Vertical distribution of DO is uniform for most of the year except in the dry season when there is marginal decrease with depth. In the inshore regions and bays and creeks, the main impact of wastewater containing sewage (organic matter) is on DO. Substantial reduction in DO and extremely low values generally below 0.5 mg/l and frequently reaching zero are recorded in the Mahim Bay and creek. Higher DO (2-3 mg/l) during July-August is associated with monsoonal freshwater flow (Zingde & Desai, 1980; Zingde, 1985). Diurnal studies in some bays and creeks receiving large volumes of wastewater have revealed that the DO remains practically zero throughout the tidal cycle during neaps after September. However, during the spring tides, DO as high as 3 mg/l is recorded in the water column only for brief periods. Even in some bays, where tidal flushing is appreciable during the spring tides, low DO reaching complete depletion is quite common. Such conditions prevail in Mahim Bay and creek, Thane Creek, Versova Creek and Worli Bay.

Biochemical oxygen demand (BOD)

Coastal waters of Bombay beyond 10 m isoline has BOD within the range of 0.5-4 mg/l. This indicates that about 310 tonnes of BOD entering every day is being effectively dispersed by the tidal currents and gets neutralized every day in the nearshore regions itself. However, Mahim Bay and the adjoining creeks, which are highly polluted, have BOD exceeding 30 mg/l even during the monsoon season. The BOD in most of the bays and creeks is tide-dependent with the values of the order of 30 mg/l at the ebb tide decreasing to 5 mg/l at the flood.

Phosphorus

Highly variable values of PO_4-P are recorded from place to place. In areas associated with domestic and industrial wastewater, values exceeding 10 μg-at/l are quite common. In moderately polluted areas, the values of about 4 μg-at/l have been observed and in offshore waters the values are normally below 2 μg-at/l.

Nitrogen

As noted earlier, about 40 tonnes/day of nitrogen are added from the wastewater to the coastal waters. In areas which are devoid of oxygen, combined nitrogen is present largely as ammonia or as organically-bound nitrogen which breaks down into inorganic nutrients. However, it should be noted that in polluted areas, NO_3-N is either low or completely absent indicating that nitrogen compounds added through the wastewater are not oxidized appreciably in areas like the Mahim Bay. Moreover, the low values of NO_3-N and NO_2-N and high values of NH_4-N indicate that oxidation is only partial because the values of NH_4-N are 3 times higher than those of nitrate and nitrite. During the flood tides, the water entering some creeks records nil NO_3-N probably indicating that the oxygen demand in the creeks is so high that nitrate and nitrite are immediately reduced to ammonia due to extreme oxygen deficiency. At some well-oxygenated areas, nitrate values are found to be abnormally high. This probably indicates that either nitrate is directly added by the industrial waste from fertilizer complexes or ammonia coming from organic matter gets oxidized through nitrite into nitrate (Zingde, 1985).

Sulphide

Sulphate ions form the other source of free energy in seawater and with hydrogen acceptors, sulphate is reduced to sulphide. When this happens, the environment becomes anoxic and most of the marine life except a few types of bacteria, gets exterminated. In Mahim Creek, H_2S-S as high as 37-126 μg-at/l has been observed in the interior. In the areas which are subjected to tidal-flushing, the levels of sulphide are tide-dependent and sulphide is present throughout the tidal cycle except for a brief period of flood slack. This indicates the severity of pollution in the region.

Trace metals in water and sediments

Trace metal concentration measured in particulate matter is given in Table 13.2. Several fold increase in Cr, Mn, Co, Ni, Cu, Zn, Cd and Pb has been found in polluted areas. They are fixed in particulate matter and are ultimately carried to the sediments. Table 13.3 gives the values of 7 trace metals in the top sediment layer. The increase in their concentrations is evident because of the transport of these elements from wastewater to the sediment. It has been estimated that the top 20 cm sediment in Mahim Creek contains 1.3 tonnes of Ni, 37 tonnes of Cu, 106 tonnes of Zn and 4.6 tonnes of Pb in excess of the expected background levels. Likewise, mercury enrichment in the layer of the 10-25 cm sediment in the Thane Creek and 0-8 cm in the harbour area would contain 14 tonnes of mercury extra over the natural background (Zingde & Desai, 1981).

Table 13.2— Average trace metals (ppm) in particulate matter at two stations of Mumbai waters (From Zingde, 1985)

	Station 2		Station 3	
	Low tide	High tide	Low tide	High tide
Chromium	354	192	234	156
Manganese	552	646	375	322
Cobalt	120	25	276	194
Nickel	110	32	348	186
Copper	135	176	489	283
Zinc	538	1077	2964	1284
Cadmium	135	342	427	371
Lead	277	136	374	216

Table 13.3— Trace metals (ppm, dry weight) in surface sediments of Mumbai (From Zingde, 1985)

Station	Mn	Co	Ni	Cu	Zn	Cd	Pb
1	1059	51	89	105	138	1.4	25
2	1036	46	116	128	211	1.6	31
3	660	59	175	198	308	3.3	35
4	980	50	132	132	206	1.8	28
5	960	43	115	115	110	0.5	42

a. Bombay Harbour / Thane Creek

Thane Creek forms the upper reaches of the Bombay Harbour. The two together form a semi-enclosed bay or basin which opens into the Arabian Sea at its south-western end and forms the main entrance to the harbour (Fig. 13.2). At its northern end, it is connected to Ulhas River through a narrow channel. A number of tributaries join the harbour forming tidal inlets and these discharge freshwater within the port area.

Tidal variations in the bay are semidiurnal with an appreciable diurnal element. The flood advances in the northeasterly direction and ebb towards the southwest. At the extreme end of the Thane Creek, the time-lag of the tide is 40 min. with reference to Apollo Bundar and the time-lag for the ebb tide is 1 hr 37 min. On an average, nearly 70% of the water is renewed in the bay per tidal cycle. Current speeds in the bay are tide- induced and show little seasonal variation. Within the harbour, the maximum speed often exceeds 100 cm/s with little variation from surface to bottom. In the Thane Creek, the current speed decreases and ranges between 30 and 60 cm/s. At the junction of the creek with Ulhas River, the speed becomes 10 cm/s. The ebb currents are stronger than the flood almost throughout the bay and velocity increases further during the monsoon months with pronounced freshwater flow from the rivers and tributaries into the bay.

Wastewater discharge

The total amount of wastewater received at the treatment plants and pumping stations located on the western side of the bay is estimated to be 340 mld which is in far excess of the treatment capacity available (MCGB, 1979). Therefore, a lot of untreated wastewater enters the bay. In addition, the Thane Creek receives industrial wastewater from fertilizer, petrochemical, thermal power station, nuclear plant, pharmaceutical and chemical industries with a total wastewater of more than 180 mld. Pollutants released in Ulhas River also enter at the head of Thane Creek.

Table 13.4 shows the result of the analysis of wastewater entering into the harbour and creek termed here as bay (Zingde *et al.*, 1989).

Salinity

As can be expected, there is a seasonal cycle of salinity showing maximum values from Feb. to May (premonsoon) and minimum values from June to Sept.

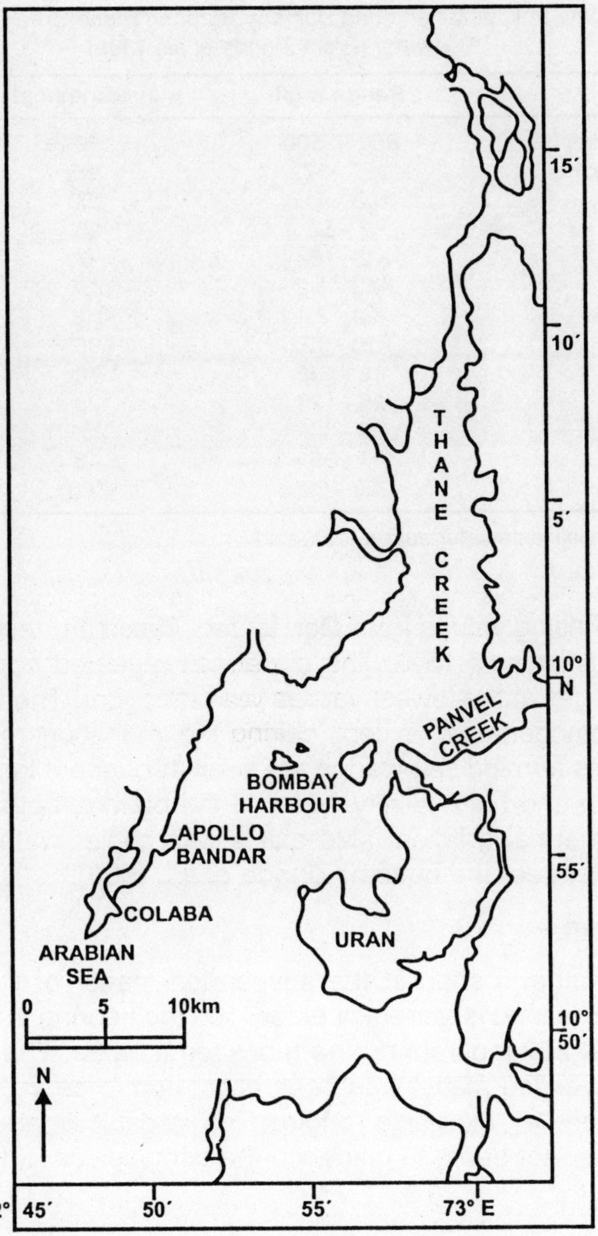

Fig. 13.2 Map showing the Bombay Harbour and Thane Creek (From Zingde *et al.*, 1989).

Table 13.4— Some Pollutants[a] entering Bombay Harbour/Thane Creek through domestic wastewater (From Zingde *et al.*, 1989)

Parameter	Range mg/l	Average mg/l	kg/day
Dissolved solids	980 - 2500	1500	52.5×10^4
Suspended solids	127 - 372	235	8.2×10^4
BOD	109 - 417	250	8.7×10^4
Nitrogen	7 - 62	35	12250
Phosphorus	2 - 10	6	2100
Manganese	0.3 - 1.2	0.7	245
Iron	0.4 - 2.4	1.8	630
Cobalt[b]	10 - 92	35	12
Nickel[b]	12 - 136	78	27
Copper[b]	25 - 126	98	34
Zinc[b]	75 - 331	201	70
Lead[b]	7 - 99	48	17
Boron[b]	220 - 600	360	126

[a] Estimated domestic wastewater output - 350 mld
[b] Value in µg/l

(monsoon) and rising values from Oct. to Jan. Maximum recorded salinity ranged 36-37‰ and minimum 9-15‰. The cycle was repeated from 1976 to 1980 with only small changes in the lowest values year after year. The watermass in the bay is vertically homogeneous except during the monsoon months when marked salinity gradients forming salt-wedge are seen throughout the bay with low-salinity water at the top and high-salinity water at the bottom, both remaining quite distinct. A small thermal gradient also exists with cooler water at the surface and warmer seawater near the bottom (Zingde *et al.*, 1989).

Suspended matter

A seasonal change is seen in the suspended matter of the bay which always remains high. The load is generally below 100 mg/l during the premonsoon period reaching almost 200 mg/l during the monsoon months. The organic carbon content of the suspended matter has been estimated to be < 6% indicating that the matter is largely of inorganic origin. The organic matter coming from the wastewater does not seem to influence the composition of the particulate matter much.

Dissolved oxygen (DO)

Wide and irregular variations in the DO were found in the bay. On most occasions, when the measurements were made, the DO was below 3 mg/l and only the highest value of about 3.7 mg/l was recorded at the high tide. The variation from surface to bottom was not appreciable. However, sudden pulses of high DO were seen during the monsoon months which were short-lived.

Nutrients

The general picture presented earlier about phosphorus and nitrogen was repeated in the bay. The values of PO_4-P ranged between 2 and 9 μg-at/l erratically during the years. Often higher values were recorded near the bottom especially in the harbour region probably indicating its release from the sediment. Nitrogen present was largely in the form of ammonia (5 μg-at/l) particularly in the Thane Creek which subsequently gets converted into nitrite and nitrate. The wastewater released into the bay contributes 12 tonnes of nitrogen/day and 2 tonnes of phosphorus/day.

Trace metals

As indicated in Table 13.4, the bay receives an appreciable load of trace metals through the wastewater. Table 13.5 shows the average values of trace metals recorded in the bay. These values are not very high and fall within the range of those occurring in the coastal waters of Bombay. It appears that the trace metals entering harbour area in a dissolved state are either hydrolysed or are rapidly adsorbed to the particulate matter and removed with the ongoing ebb tides. In the Thane Creek, the values of several dissolved trace metals were found to be higher than in the harbour. As has been noted earlier, the sediment layers of Bombay Harbour and Thane Creek contain 37.6 tonnes of mercury. The details of this are given from the estimated values of mercury in the harbour and Thane Creek which are shown in Table 13.6. Assuming that the background level of mercury in the coastal water of Bombay is 75 ng/l, the excess mercury in the water would be 77 kg. Mercury released through wastewater is approximately 160 g/day. Concentrations of mercury in the grab samples (sediments) varied from 0.17 to 8.21 ppm (average 2.47 ppm). Penetration of mercury in the sediment layer was estimated from the core samples. This is shown in Fig. 13.3. The vertical distribution decreased with depth in the Thane Creek, but in the cores from the harbour area the concentration was relatively small and it appears that because of dredging, the topmost layers of sediments are removed periodically. The average mercury content of 0.73 ppm was recorded in the zooplankton samples (Zingde & Desai, 1981).

Table 13.5— Average trace metals (ppm dry wt) and organic carbon (%) in suspended load of Bombay Harbour / Thane Creek (From Zingde *et al.*, 1989)

Station	Co	Ni	Cu	Zn	Pb	Organic C
1	35	136	157	206	38	5.3
2	37	139	163	229	26	4.7
3	28	85	119	135	32	2.3
4	32	102	137	162	29	2.9
5	27	116	105	159	35	3.8
6	30	159	132	127	29	4.1
7	25	101	98	138	19	1.7
8	–	–	95	121	8	2.2

Table 13.6— Mercury in sediments of Thane Creek (From Zingde & Desai, 1981)

Segment	Approximate area (km^2)	Contamination depth (m)	Sediment mass (Mt)	Hg (wet weight) (mg/kg)	Estimated sediment mercury (t)
I	29	0.20	8.41	2.5	21
II	61	0.16	14.15	1.0	14.1
III	49	0.10	7.10	0.35	2.5

Mt is million tonnes

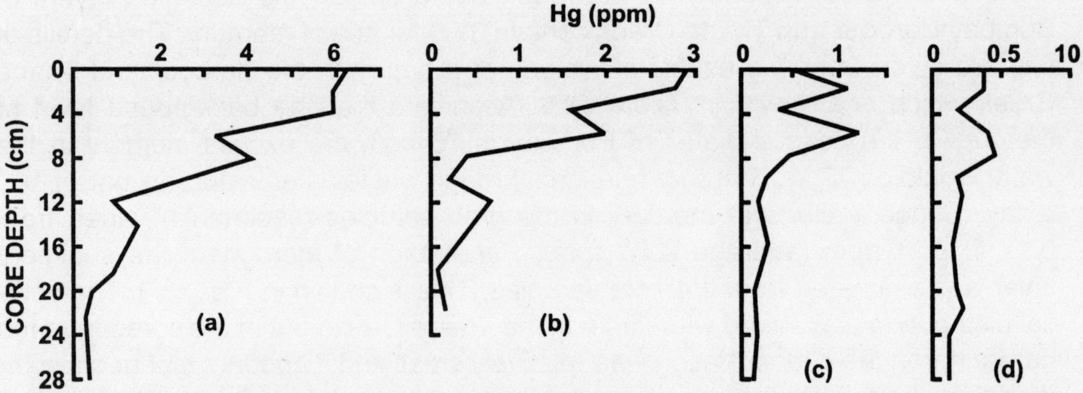

Fig. 13.3 Mercury in the sediment cores in relation to depth. (a), (b), (c) and (d) indicate 4 different locations for the collection of samples in the Bombay Harbour area (From Zingde & Desai, 1981).

The wastewater coming out of the Bhabha Atomic Research Centre seems a major source of low level ratioactive waste into the bay. There are several radionuclides reported from the water, sediment and benthic organisms but these have been found to be within premissible limits (Patel *et al.,* 1985).

Pollution and boron-chlorinity ratio

Boron-chlorinity ratio in polluted waters of Mumbai has been reported to be within the range 0.224-0.230 (average value 0.228). In the Thane Creek, a greater predominance of boron coming from additional sources increased the ratio, and in 45-71% of the samples, the ratios were higher than 0.230 which was the highest limit of unpolluted waters. Evidence was also obtained of the slow removal of externally added boron from the environment (Navekar & Zingde, 1992).

Oil Pollution

The Bombay Harbour is getting increasingly polluted by a variety of petroleum products due to increasing tanker traffic, enhanced activities in the oilfields (Bombay High and Bassein) and by the industrial and refinery wastes.

Investigations on the estimation of hydrocarbons in the waters of Bombay Harbour were conducted because an oil tanker *M.T. Lajpatrai* carrying 29,000 tonnes of crude oil and 800 tonnes of engine oil had caught fire and there was a danger of pollution which fortunately did not occur. However, the area around the oil tanker was surveyed and thin patches of oil present in the water were collected by a skimmer and analysed using proton magnetic resonance spectroscopy (PMR). The result of chromatographic fingerprint pattern showed that the oil on the surface was identical to the Bombay High crude oil and it was not from the oil tanker. This study indicates that there is a lot of oil pollution in the harbour area caused by our own activities (Kadam & Zingde, 1985).

b. Mahim

The shallow semi-enclosed Mahim Estuary is located on the north-east (Fig. 13.4) and harbours extensive growth of mangroves (rather unhealthy due to pollution) which forms a green belt separating north Bombay from south Bombay. The meandering Mahim River passes through several industrial areas, connects the Powai Lake and terminates into the estuary. The mouth of the estuary forms a ring-shaped basin — the Mahim Bay which extends into the Mahim Creek, is one of the worst affected areas in the Mumbai region. A proposal to convert the Mahim Creek, after it is cleaned and restored, into a Birds Sanctuary (Nature Park) is under consideration.

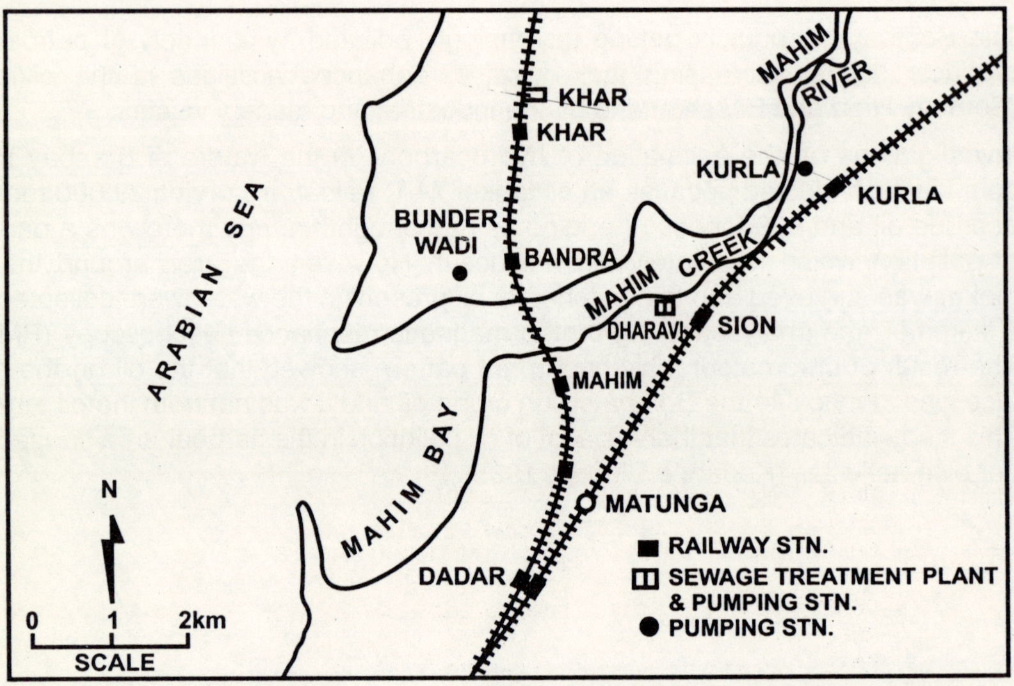

Fig. 13.4 Map showing Mahim Bay and Mahim Creek (From Zingde & Desai, 1980).

Two published accounts on Mahim Estuary are available, based on fairly detailed investigations – one was carried out from July 1976 to December 1977 (Zingde

& Desai, 1980) and the other from 1979 to 1981 (Zingde & Sabnis, 1994). The present overview is largely based on these two studies.

The domestic wastewater flow of 1.6×10^5 m^3/day adds 43 tonnes of suspended solids, 45 tonnes of BOD, 13 tonnes of sulphate, 6 tonnes of nitrogen and 1 tonne of phosphorus into the estuary (Sabnis, 1984; Zingde & Sabnis, 1994). In addition, the estuary receives 0.7 tonnes of suspended solid and 0.7 tonnes of BOD from the industrial wastes (Sabnis, 1984).

Table 13.7 shows the characteristics of the water of the estuary at its mouth. Seasonal salinity cycle shown at Mahim was similar to that described for the Bombay Harbour/Thane Creek. This is shown in Fig. 13.5 along with PO_4-P and NO_3-N. Vertical salinity gradient was observed during August/September in the estuary. This was unlike the coastal region where the water was well-mixed. The gradient was probably due to incomplete mixing of freshwater with the seawater. The monsoonal flow was considerably reduced after September and during October the salinity increased from 8.1‰ to 32.8‰. The difference in salinity between surface and bottom was quite pronounced during the ebb tide and decreased when the tide slacked. At the flood slack, the water was well-mixed and the salinity increased from 31.4‰ to 34.3‰. Diurnal observations conducted during November showed a reduction in salinity to 20‰ at the ebb from 34‰ at the flood because of the influence of wastewater.

Table 13.7— Physicochemical characteristics at the mouth of Mahim Estuary (From Zingde & Sabnis, 1994)

Parameter	May-80			Jan-81		
	Max	Min	Mean	Max	Min	Mean
Sal $\times 10^{3-}$	35.6	34.9	35.2	35.5	34.1	34.9
*p*H	8.1	7.7	7.9	8.2	7.7	7.8
SS (mg/l)	105	38	73	82	30	68
DO (mg/l)	5.0	2.2	3.5	5.3	3.8	4.1
BOD (mg/l)	12.1	2.6	4.9	10.3	3.1	5.2
PO_4^{3-}N (μM)	7.6	2.8	5.2	6.7	2.6	4.8
NO_3-N (μM)	32.9	6.3	14.2	28.3	5.3	15.2
NH_4^+-N (μM)	13.8	4.2	9.1	12.6	2.7	10.9

Suspended matter

Is is evident from Table 13.7 that seasonal changes in suspended material vary within a range of 30 to 105 mg/l which seems to be dependent upon wastewater

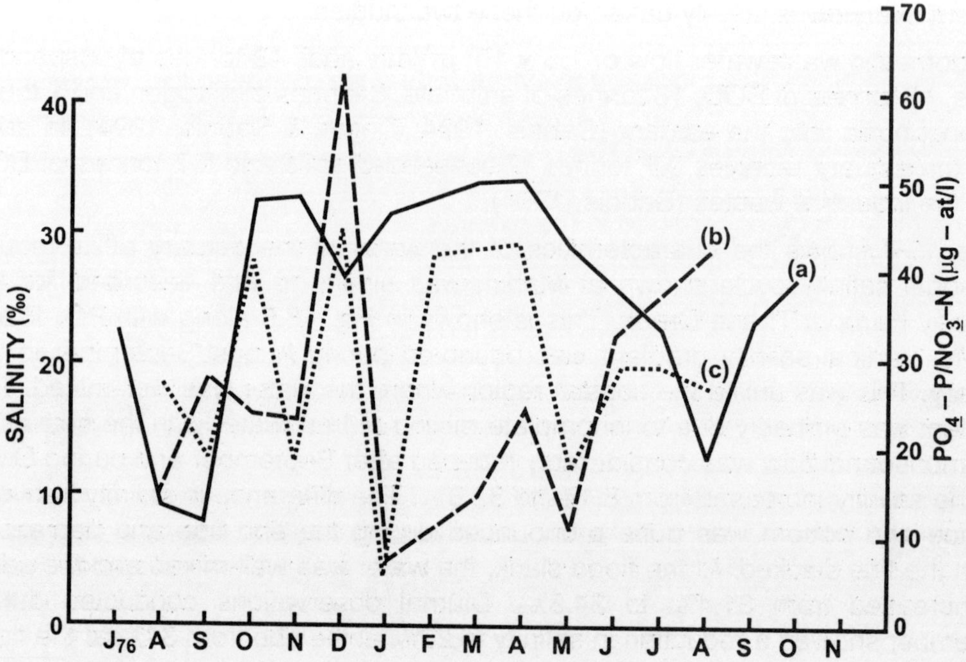

Fig. 13.5 Seasonal variation in (a) salinity, (b) phosphate - phosphorus, (c) nitrate-nitrogen in Mahim Creek at one station (From Zingde & Desai, 1980).

and tidal influxes. About 43 tonnes of suspended material enter the estuary practically every day and a large part of this load appears to be deposited in the estuary (Zingde & Desai, 1980). Therefore, the overall character of the suspended matter changes along the length of the estuary. Inorganic material constitutes about 65% of the suspended matter in the estuary and outside the estuary it increases to more than 80%.

*p*H

The range in *p*H was 7.7 to 8.1 (Table 13.7). It was generally high at the high water and decreased at low water. It was also associated with changes in salinity. No change in *p*H occurred during the neap tide.

Dissolved oxygen (DO)

Maximum and minimum values of DO are given in Table 13.7 for two months.

Nevertheless, several segments in the estuary were totally devoid of DO which was dependent on the tidal cycle. It decreased sharply during the ebb and increased during the flood. The variations, however, were quite irregular and the difference between maximum and minimum was quite pronounced.

Biochemical oxygen demand (BOD)

A water body with a BOD of 8 mg/l is considered to be moderately polluted. The BOD of the estuary, as reported in the two investigations, ranged between 30 and 100 mg/l (Zingde & Desai, 1980, Zingde & Sabnis, 1994). The range indicates the intensity of pollution in the estuary. It was largely tide-dependent and was considerably reduced when the estuary was flushed but still remained high.

Nutrients

Concentrations of PO_4-P varied between 6 and 46 µg-at/l during the year (Fig. 13.5) and the range in NO_3-N was from 8 to 65 µg/l (Zingde & Desai, 1980). Abnormally high concentrations of NH_4-N were usually recorded in the estuary and in such situations, the concentrations of NO_2-N and NO_3-N become very low, often reaching zero at the neap tide. This was due to oxidation of organic matter (Zingde & Sabnis, 1994) — a condition noted earlier in Bombay Harbour/Thane Creek.

Flushing characteristics

Sabnis & Zingde (1989) have studied the flushing features of this estuary from the bathymetry and tidal data obtained from different segments of the estuary and also by releasing neutrally buoyant floats. In addition, the flushing time was also calculated by applying the modified prism method. The load of wastewater entering the estuary works out to be 11 times greater than the load introduced by the tidal cycle. Therefore, the estimated volume of $1.6 \times 10^5 m^3$/day of wastewater can be flushed out by allowing the dilution factor in 19 tidal cycles. This would mean that the Mahim Estuary can not be cleaned by flushing itself because of the continuous flow of wastewater, and hence it will remain intensely polluted unless other management measures are applied to control pollution.

c. Amba

Amba, a minor river in the Western Ghats, opens into the Bombay Harbour area (Fig. 13.6) at Rewas located in Raigad District (Lat. 18° 45′ N, Long. 73° 10′ E). A barrage (Bandhara) at Nagothana impounds the riverine flow which forms the source of water for the water supply scheme of the Maharashtra Irrigation Development Corporation (MIDC). A large establishment of petrochemical complex at Nagothana, about 45 km south of Bombay in Raigad District, releases its wastewater into the Amba Estuary. The quality of treated wastewater is shown in Table 13.8. Maximum discharge was estimated to be 750 m^3/h in the wet season going down to about 600 m^3/h during the dry season (Zingde, 1994).

Table 13.8— Treated wastewater quality and its impact on water quality of Amba Estuary (From Zingde, 1994)

Parameter	Treated wastewater	Water quality above release point	Water quality of the estuary
*p*H	7 to 9	Unaffected	Unaffected
SS (mg/l)	100	Unaffected	Unaffected
BOD (mg/l)	30	9	31
COD (mg/l)	250	50	–
DO (mg/l)	5	Unaffected	Unaffected
Oil & grease (mg/l)	10	4.5	Unaffected
Phenolics (mg/l)	1	–	Unaffected
Sulphide (mg/l)	2	Nil	Nil
TDS (mg/l)	1500	Unaffected	Unaffected
Chloroform extract (mg/l)	0.05	–	–
Temperature (°C)	Ambient	Unaffected	Unaffected

Tides

Tides were of mixed semidiurnal type with two unequal high and low occurring each day. The range of spring tide was 5.08 m at Rewas decreasing to 3.35 m at Nagothana. The neap tidal range, on the other hand, increased from 1.04 m at Rewas to 1.90 m at Nagothana. An increase of 30 cm was recorded from Rewas at Dharamtar probably because of the piling of water at spring due to narrowing of the estuarine channel. The high tide at Rewas preceded that of the Appollo Bundar by 2 to 3 min., while the high tide at Nagothana lagged by 65 to 70 min. (Zingde, 1994).

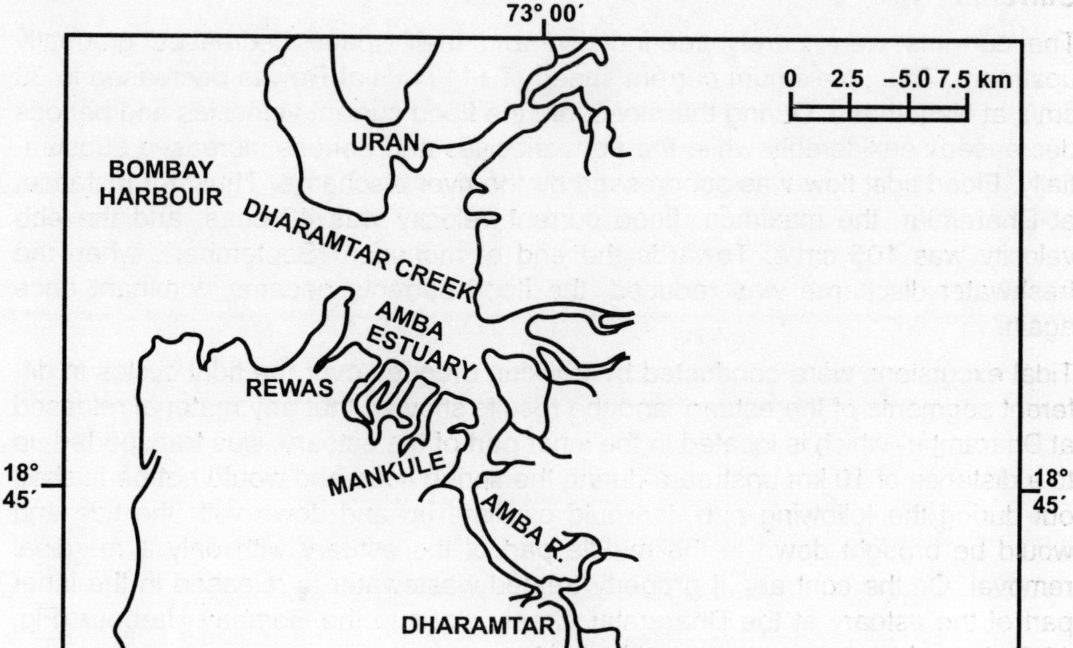

Fig. 13.6 Map showing Amba River and Estuary. The former originates in Western Ghats and opens into Bombay Harbour area (From Zingde, 1994).

Currents

The currents were purely tide-induced and their speed decreased gradually upstream. Thus, maximum current speed of 111 cm/s at Rewas decreased to 38 cm/s at Nagothana. During the monsoon, the flood current velocities and periods decreased considerably while the ebb velocities and periods increased substantially. Flood tidal flow was suppressed by the river discharge. Thus, for instance, at Dharamtar, the maximum flood current velocity was 42 cm/s, and the ebb velocity was 105 cm/s. Towards the end of monsoon (September), when the freshwater discharge was reduced, the flood currents became dominant once again.

Tidal excursions were conducted by tracking drogues over the tidal cycles in different segments of the estuary and the results showed that any material released at Dharamtar, which is located in the inner part of the estuary, was transported up to a distance of 10 km upstream during the spring flood and would not be flushed out during the following ebb. It would oscillate up and down with the tide and would be brought down in the middle part of the estuary with only a marginal removal. On the contrary, if properly treated wastewater is released in the inner part of the estuary at the Dharamtar Creek, close to the Bombay Harbour (Fig. 13.6), it would get dispersed quickly and transported to the sea.

Salinity

In the Bombay Harbour, salinity during the premonsoon period has been noted earlier as 36-37‰. The seawater penetration during the flood tide goes quite deep in the river and at Nagothana, because of some seepage of freshwater from the barrage, the salinity range is 26-27‰ and about 20‰ at Nagothana. During the monsoon period, below Dharamtar, in the lower reaches, the salinity range is 9-27‰ and in the upstream up to Nagothana, largely freshwater is found at low water with increasing surface salinity of 8.7‰ and bottom salinity of 17.9‰ in the vicinity of Dharamtar.

Flushing time

From the river flow data, the average flow during July-August was found to the 4.3 $\times 10^6 m^3$ per tidal cycle. It decreased to about $0.43 \times 10^6 m^3$ per tidal cycle during October-February. Table 13.9 gives the flushing time of the estuary by the modified tidal prism method and also by the riverine flow data. The cumulative flushing time from the riverine flow data would be around 6 to 7 tidal cycles during the spring tide for both the freshwater flow conditions indicating the dominance of the tidal influence over the river discharge. However, during the neaps, when the

Table 13.9— Flushing time of Amba River Estuary (modified tidal prism method) (From Kumar & Sarma, 1991)

Estuary segment (km)	Low tide volume × 10^6 (m^3)	Tidal Prism × 10^6 (m^3)	Exchange ratio	Flushing time (tidal cycles)
Riverine freshwater flow per tidal cycle $4.3 \times 10^6 m^3$*				
0 - 25.7	8.5	4.3	0.336	3.0
25.7 - 33.8	12.8	4.1	0.242	4.1
35.8 - 38.9	16.9	3.2	0.159	6.3
38.9 - 42.8	20.1	5.6	0.218	4.6
	25.7	7.2	0.220	4.5
Riverine freshwater flow per tidal cycle $4.3 \times 10^6 m^3$+				
0 - 15.9	1.2	4.3	0.782	1.3
15.9 - 27.7	5.6	12.7	0.694	1.4
27.7 - 37.2	18.2	35.4	0.660	1.5
37.2 - 44.2	53.7	76.7	0.588	1.7
Riverine freshwater flow per tidal cycle $4.3 \times 10^6 m^3$*				
0 - 8.9	0.53	0.43	0.448	2.2
8.9 - 13.6	0.96	0.67	0.411	2.4
13.6 - 18.0	1.6	0.98	0.38	2.6
18.0 - 21.8	2.6	1.1	0.297	3.4
21.8 - 26.3	3.7	1.4	0.274	3.6
26.3 - 29.5	5.1	1.6	0.239	4.2
29.5 - 33.7	6.7	2.1	0.239	4.2
33.7 - 35.5	8.9	2.5	0.219	4.6
35.5 - 37.2	11.4	3.2	0.219	4.6
37.2 - 39.4	14.6	4.1	0.219	4.6
39.4 - 41.3	18.7	5.2	0.217	4.5
41.3 - 44.9	23.9	6.7	0.219	4.6
Riverine freshwater flow per tidal cycle $4.3 \times 10^6 m^3$+				
0 - 4.9	0.12	0.43	0.782	1.3
4.9 - 13.1	0.55	2.3	0.807	1.2
13.1 - 22.0	2.8	7	0.714	1.4
22.0 - 34.3	9.8	20.4	0.675	1.5
34.3 - 41.8	30.2	57.2	0.654	1.5

* Neap, + spring

seawater incursion gets considerably reduced, the cumulative flushing time of the estuary would be 22 tidal cycles for the riverine flow of $4.3 \times 10^6 m^3$ per tidal cycle and 45 tidal cycles for the flow of $0.43 \times 10^6 m^3$ per tidal cycle (Kumar & Sarma, 1991).

ZOOPLANKTON VARIABILITY IN MAHIM, THANA, BOMBAY HARBOUR AND VERSOVA

Rich collections of zooplankton were obtained in the 4 estuaries noted above (Gajbhiye & Desai, 1981) — the two of which the authors have designated as highly polluted (Mahim and Thane) and the other two or less severely polluted (Bombay Harbour and Versova). The study was extended over a period of 15 months, from October 1977 to December 1978. Seasonal cycle of zooplankton density is shown in Fig. 13.7 in the 4 environments. Copepods formed the most dominant group in each estuary. Other common groups were decapod larvae, chaetognaths, hydromedusae, ctenophores, molluscan larvae and fish larvae.

Table 13.10— Monthly variation of zooplankton biomass (volume ml/ 100 m^3) during high and low tides in four environments (From Gajbhiye & Desai, 1981)

	Versova		Mahim		Harbour		Thane	
Months	High	Low	High	Low	High	Low	High	Low
Oct-77	83.37	17.50	40.60	39.25	63.00	10.68	35.00	42.14
Nov	3.90	4.56	3.56	21.01	2.25	4.01	14.61	238.00
Dec	15.20	8.77	6.86	4.00	10.10	29.00	144.77	87.34
Jan-78	30.58	16.95	14.00	12.18	9.46	33.52	30.72	6.65
Feb	4.14	3.16	8.69	1.80	5.09	4.53	30.72	67.63
Mar	22.20	11.16	11.20	9.46	6.74	42.03	97.14	85.92
Apr	1.94	8.16	9.40	40.16	26.07	20.80	10.28	18.22
May	18.92	1.56	17.36	0.97	11.30	16.00	6.38	66.66
June	6.80	7.64	3.57	0.53	22.48	3.45	0.87	24.26
July	18.30	23.05	11.53	23.00	9.90	19.82	9.48	29.79
Aug	6.95	8.89	14.89	14.89	4.60	5.88	26.44	16.00
Sep	41.27	86.80	15.08	27.38	18.07	18.79	17.91	22.20
Oct	57.73	52.89	29.75	118.73	21.93	129.92	35.90	22.47
Nov	84.10	86.70	14.59	20.05	22.40	28.00	32.87	144.75
Dec	85.00	65.65	31.01	29.56	15.85	19.00	47.00	21.00

Monthly variation of zooplankton biomass is shown in Table 13.10. The interesting feature in the table is the high biomass recorded even from the highly polluted estuaries in some months. This is because of tidal flushing and renewal of water in the estuary which also removed much of the pollution load. However, Bombay

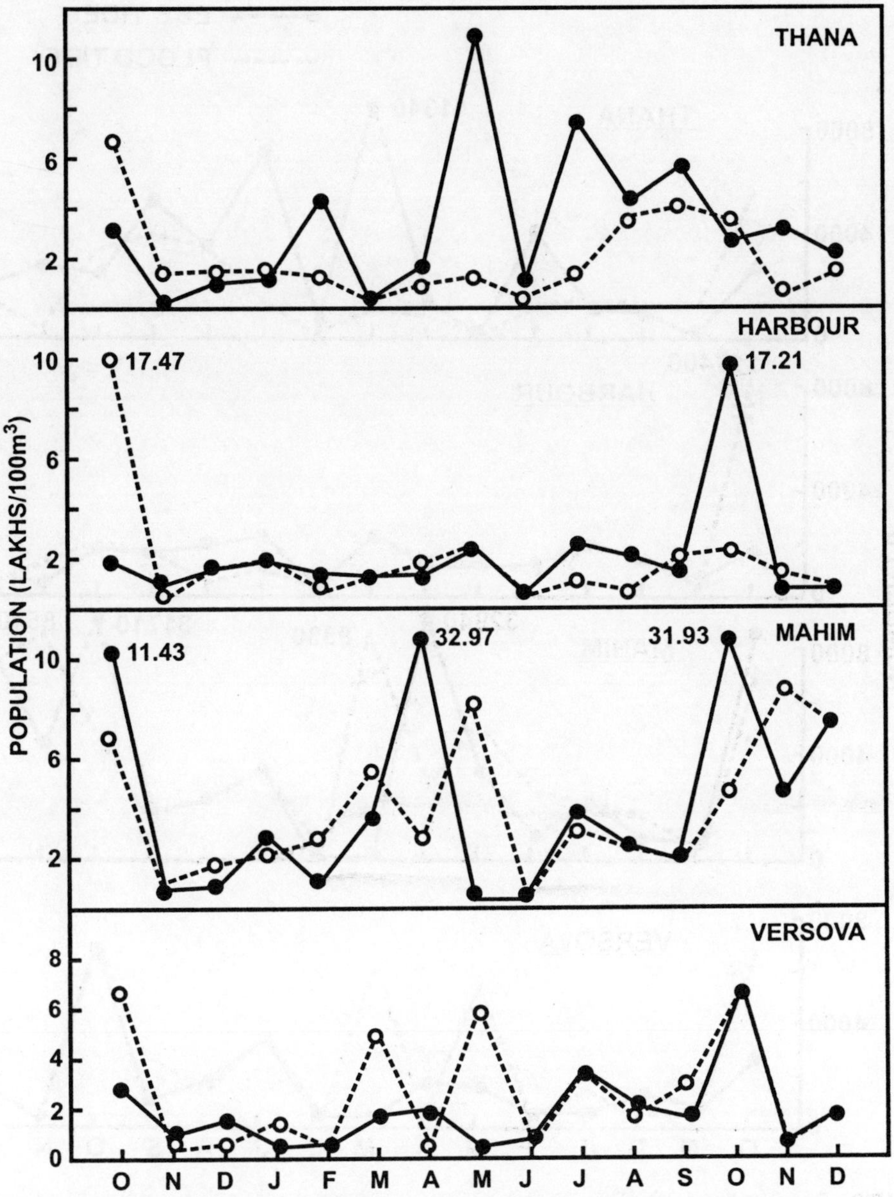

Fig. 13.7 Seasonal variation in zooplankton population density in 4 different environments of Mumbai Region (From Gajbhiye & Desai, 1981). Solid lines, ebb tides; broken lines, flood tides.

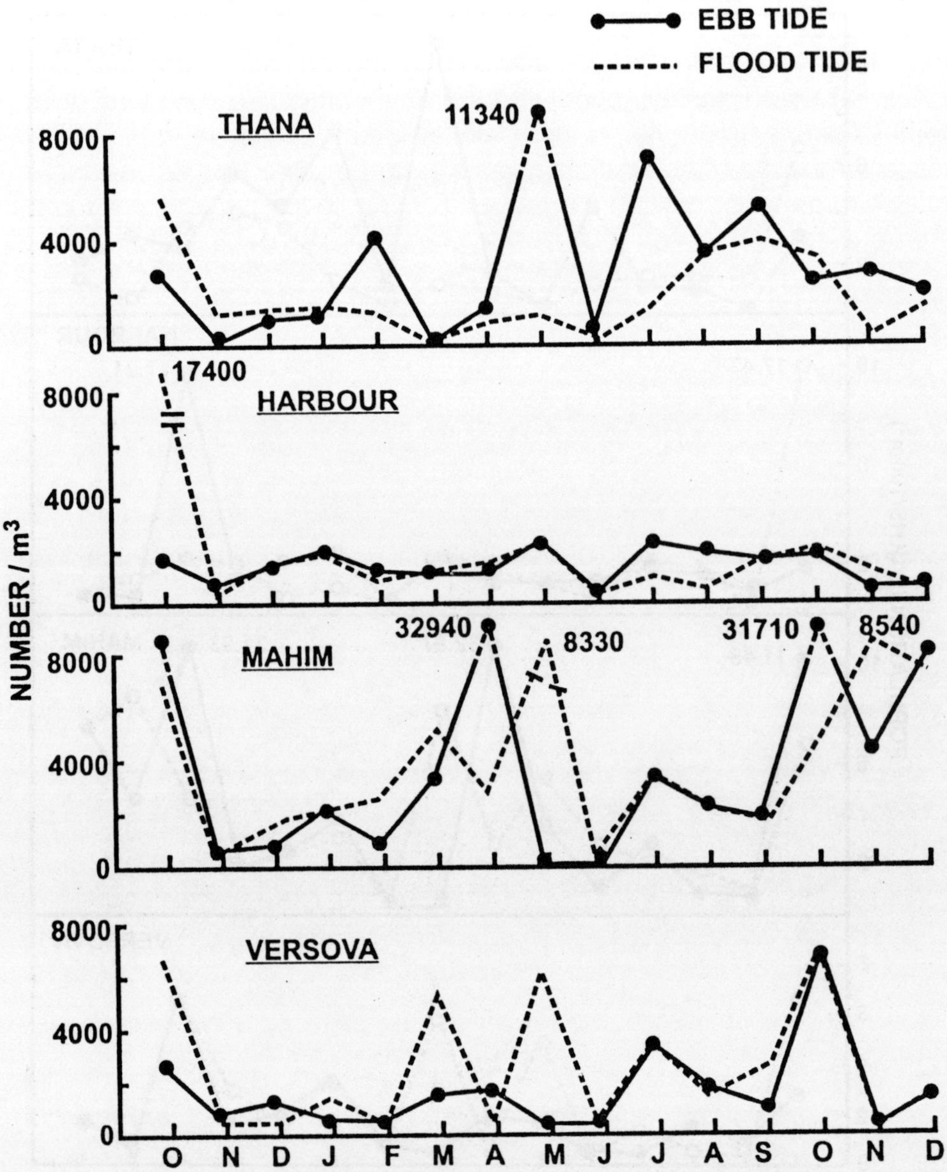

Fig. 13.8 Seasonal variation in copepod numbers during the flood and ebb tides in 4 different environments of Mumbai Region (From Gajbhiye *et al.*, 1981).

Harbour and Versova showed the maximum number of faunal groups and Mahim and Thana had lesser number of faunal groups and this features provided a clear difference between polluted and relatively cleaner environments.

A similar pattern was shown in the abundance of copepods which is given in Fig. 13.8. Maximum population density was observed in Mahim and this was because of the very high predominance of a few species (*Paracalanus, Oithona* and *Acartia*) which densely populated the environment. The generic diversity, on the other hand, was greater in less polluted areas (Gajbhiye *et al.,* 1981). Distribution of chaetognaths and fish eggs and larvae also showed a much greater monthly fluctuations in polluted areas and less diversity as compared to relatively cleaner environments (Nair *et al.,* 1981, Gajbhiye *et al.,* 1982).

References

1. Gajbhiye, S.N. & Desai, B.N., 1981. Zooplankton variability in polluted and unpolluted waters off Bombay. *Mahasagar — Bulletin of National Institute of Oceanography*, Vol. 14, pp. 173-182.
2. Gajbhiye, S.N., Ram. J. & Desai, B.N., 1981. Distribution of copepods from the polluted and unpolluted region of Bombay. *Indian Journal of Marine Sciences*, Vol. 10, pp. 346-349.
3. Gajbhiye, S.N., Govindan, K. & Desai, B.N., 1982. Distribution of planktonic fish eggs and larvae around Bombay waters. *Indian Journal of Marine Sciences*, Vol. 11, pp. 128-131.
4. Kadam, A.N. & Zingde, M.D., 1985. Investigation on oil patches around 'M.T. Lajpatrai', Bombay Harbour. *Mahasagar — Bulletin of National Institute of Oceanography*, Vol. 18, pp. 511-516.
5. Kumar, P.K.D. & Sarma, R.V., 1991. Flushing characteristics of Amba River Estuary. *Indian Journal of Marine Sciences*, Vol. 20, pp. 212-215.
6. Metcalf & Eddy / EEC., 1979. Methods for treatment and disposal of wastewater from Greater Bombay. Vol. 1 (Metcalf and Eddy Inc. and Environmental Engineering Consultant: Joint Venture, Bombay. *NIO*, 1978. *Studies on wastewater disposal and submarine outfall around Bombay. Regional Centre of National Institute of Oceanography, Bombay*, 250 pp.
7. MCGB, 1979. *Report to Municipal Corporation of Greater Bombay upon methods for treatment and disposal of wastewater from Greater Bombay*, Vol. 1, 155 pp. Metcalf and Eddy Inc. and Environmental Engineering Consultants, Joint Venture, Bombay.
8. Naidu, V.S. & Sarma, R.V., 2000. Numerical modelling of tide-induced currents in Thana Creek, west coast of India. *Journal of Waterway, Port, Coastal and Ocean Engineering* (in press).
9. Nair V.R., Gajbhiye, S.N. & Desai, B.N., 1981. Distribution of chaetognaths in the polluted and unpolluted waters around Bombay. *Indian Journal of Marine Sciences*, Vol. 10, pp. 66-69.
10. Narayanaswamy, C., Kolhatkar, V.M. & Fernandes, A.A., 1980. Currents and siltation at Dharamtar Creek, Bombay. *Mahasagar — Bulletin of National Institute of Oceanography*, Vol. 13, pp. 191-203.

11. Narvekar, P.V. & Zingde, M.D., 1992. *Influence on pollution of boron chlorinity ratio.* In: Environment and Biodegradation (eds.) V.P. Agarwal & S.V.S. Rana, pp. 5-68, Society of Biosciences, Muzaffarnagar, India.
12. Patel, B., Muley, C.D. & Ganguly, A.K., 1975. Radioecology of Bombay Harbour tidal estuary. *Estuarine, Coastal and Shelf Science*, Vol. 3, pp. 13-42.
13. Sen Gupta, R. & Sankaranarayanan, V.N., 1974. Pollution studies of Bombay. *Mahasagar — Bulletin of National Institute of Oceanography*, Vol. 7, pp. 73-78.
14. Subnis, M.M. & Zingde. M.D. 1989. Flushing characteristics of Mahim River Estuary. *Advances in Biosciences*, Vol. 8, pp. 1-7.
15. Subnis M.M., 1984. Studies on some major and minor trace elements, in the polluted Mahim Estuary. Ph.D. thesis, University of Bombay, 288 pp.
16. Zingde, M.D. & Desai, B.N., 1980. Wastewater discharge and its effect on the equality of water of Mahim Creek and bay. *Mahasagar — Bulletin of National Institute of Oceanography*, Vol. 13, pp. 205-213.
17. Zingde, M.D. & Desai, B.N., 1981. Mercury in Thana Creek, Bombay Harbour. *Marine Pollution Bulletin*, Vol. 12, pp. 237-241.
18. Zingde, M.D., 1985. Wastewater effluents and coastal marine environment. *Proceedings Seawater Quality Demand*, pp. 20.1-20.23.
19. Zingde, M.D., 1994. Environmental impact assessment of disposal of liquid waste through marine outfall - A case study. In: *Environment and Applied Biology* (eds.) V.P. Agarwal, S.A.H. Abidi, R.K. Sharma and M.D. Zingde, pp. 41-66. Society of Biosciences, Muzaffarnagar, India.
20. Zingde, M.D. & Sabnis, M.M., 1994. Pollution-induced tidal variability in water quality. In: *Environment and Applied Biology* (eds.) V.P. Agarwal, S.A.H. Abidi, R.K. Sharma & M.D. Zingde, pp. 277-288. Society of Biosciences, Muzaffarnagar, India.
21. Zingde, M.D., Bhosle, N.B., Narvekar, P.V. & Desai, B.N., 1989. Hydrography and water quality of Bombay Harbour. In: *Environmental Strategies and Bioscience* (ed.) R. Prakash, pp. 37-58. Society of Biosciences, Muzaffarnagar, India.
22. Zingde, M.D., Trivedi, S.K. & Desai, B.N., 1979. Physiochemical studies of coastal pollution of Bombay. *Indian Journal of Marine Sciences*, Vol. 8, pp. 271-277.

Chapter 14

Estuaries of southern Gujarat

Southern Gujarat has been profusely endowed with perennial rivers. About 16 large, medium and small rivers flow in the eastwest direction in low-lying, marshy land of the state. During the monsoon season, several of these rivers get flooded and inundate a large portion of the adjoining land. All the rivers open into the Arabian Sea. Seven of the northern rivers flow into the Gulf of Cambay (renamed Khambhat) which is the northern extension of the Arabian Sea (Fig. 14.1). Most of the rivers end into shallow, wide estuaries named after the rivers as given below:

(a) Sabarmati	(b) Mahi	(c) Dhabar	(d) Narmada
(e) Kim	(f) Tapti	(g) Mindhola	(h) Purna
(i) Ambika	(j) Kaveri	(k) Karera	(l) Auranga
(m) Par	(n) Kolak	(o) Damanganga	(p) Varoli

Socio-economic development in Gujarat State and rapid industrialisation in southern part have led to the emergence of many industries near rivers utilising freshwater according to their needs and conveniently disposing off the waste-water either into the river or in the estuary depending upon their location. As a

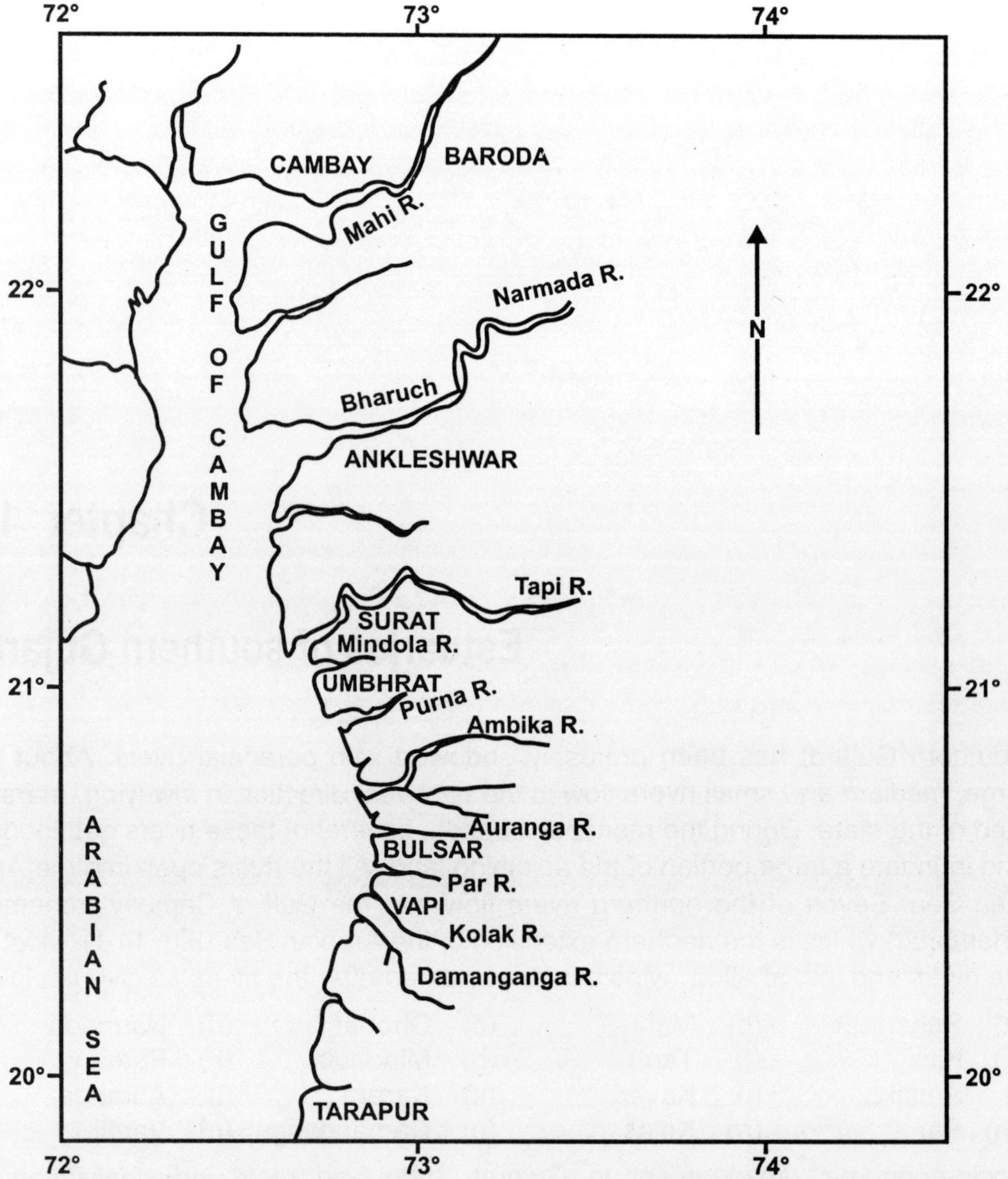

Fig. 14.1 Major rivers and estuaries of southern Gujarat (From Zingde & Desai, 1987).

result, many new towns have come up and some of the older cities which are several kilometres inland (e.g. Vapi, Bulsar, Surat, Navsari, Billimora, Ankleswar, Bharuch, Baroda and Ahmedabad) have flourished at the cost of the quality of river water. It is also to be noted that since ancient times, human habitation in India has grown along the rivers and many villages and small towns located on the banks of the rivers have become dependent on the river water for their domestic needs. Consequently, in many villages there are few wells or hand-pumps and these are largely used for taking potable water for drinking. For all other needs such as washing clothes and utensils, bathing and even for cooking food, the river water is normally used.

Discharge of untreated or partially-treated wastes into the rivers thus provides a health hazard with the result that many environmentalists of the Gujarat State Pollution Control Board, the Gujarat Industrial Development Corporation (GIDC) and several owners of the industries themselves took the initiative for investigating the magnitude of pollutants going into the rivers and estuaries and if proved alarming, measures should be recommended to control the situation. The agency, most of the industries relied upon to conduct investigations was the National Institute of Oceanography (NIO), Goa and its Regional Centre (RC) at Mumbai was entrusted with the responsibility to carry out the desired investigations and submit its report within a time-bound period. The work done was sponsored by various agencies including the industries which were directly involved.

Much of what is known, therefore, about the hydrography, characteristics of the effluents and related aspects of these estuaries is as a result of the work done by Dr. Mahesh D. Zingde, the Scientist-in-Charge and his colleagues at the Regional Centre. Therefore, the account which follows is based on the published information and technical reports prepared by the RC and submitted to the sponsors for implementation. In several cases, the GIDC and the Gujarat State Pollution Control Board acted as guiding force and insisted on a frank and impartial report which may fulfil their mandatory responsibility for the protection and conservation of the environment. Since the work done on each river/estuary was in response to specific terms of reference, enunciated by the sponsors or controlling agency, a uniformity in the results and recommendations in all cases could not be maintained and inevitably the summarised version presented here may not be similar in content for all the estuaries. However, the description leads to an identical objective of delineating the nature and influence of pollutants on the water quality and its relationship with the hydrography, tidal influence, flushing characteristics, etc. The estuaries which have been studied are:

(a) Mahi	(b) Narmada (Narbada)	(c) Tapi (Tapti)
(d) Mindhola	(e) Purna	(f) Ambika
(g) Auranga	(h) Par	(i) Kolak
(j) Damanganga		

Technical reports on most of these estuaries were submitted to the sponsors (NIO, 1980; 1982; 1985).

a. Mahi

The Mahi River is about 600 km long. It joins the northern part of the Gulf of Cambay (Khambhat) near Kamboli forming a broad estuarine stretch extending up to Mohammadpura which is about 50 km inland. The estuary is situated along Lat. 22°17′ N and Long. 72°13′ E. The presence of a rocky sill at Mohammadpura prevents the intrusion of salt water beyond this point except during the spring tide. The sill also forms an effective barrier for the intrusion of freshwater during the dry season (Fig. 14.2). The mouth of the estuary is a wide-stretch of shallow tidal flats with shoals. During the low tide, the estuary becomes almost dry except for a few narrow and meandering channels.

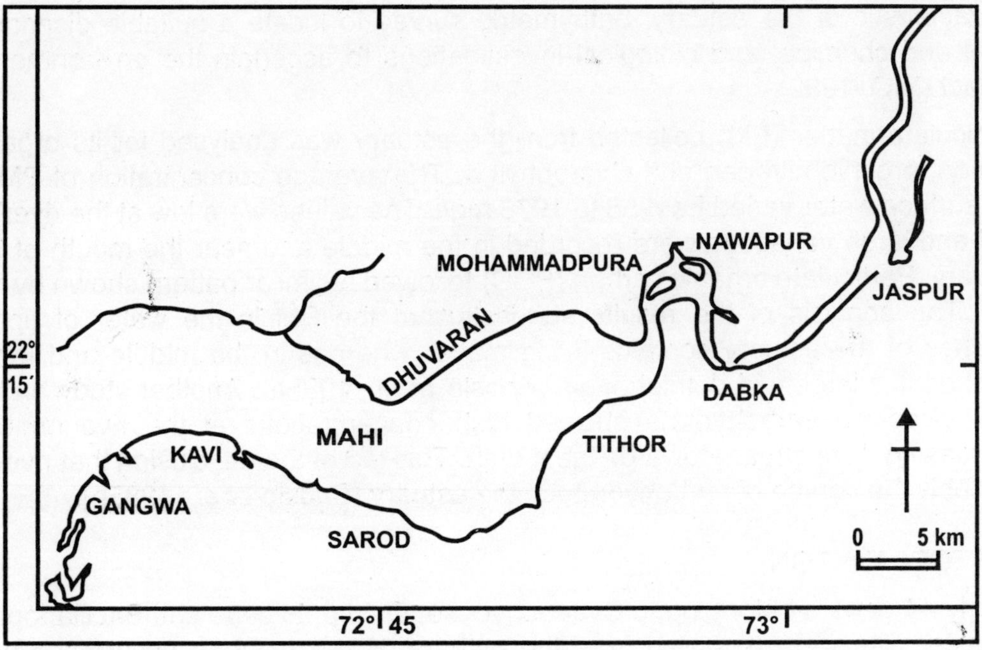

Fig. 14.2 Map showing Mahi River and Estuary (From Ram, 1991).

The estuary receives a large tidal range of 5.5 m (mean spring high water). During the ebb, nearly total drainage of the tidal water occurs leading to complete physical flushing. From July to September, there is a pronounced freshwater discharge from the river resulting in erosion and submergence of the river banks. A small rivulet joins the Mahi River at Jaspur which brings a large amount of wastes from the industries located in and around Baroda and also domestic sewage at Mini point. This rivulet transports a high load of phosphorus and nitrogen into the upper reaches of the estuary which decreases with dilution downstream (Ram, 1991).

With increasing awareness of the dangers of pollution, the Government of Gujarat formulated a scheme for the construction of a 56 km long composite effluent channel to open into the Mahi Estuary. The task of the construction of the channel was entrusted to the GIDC. M/s Environment Engineering Consultant, Bombay, who were the consulting engineers to the GIDC requested the NIO to conduct hydrographic studies needed for the design and execution of the proposed effluent outfall. The work included collection of water samples to assess the water quality of Mahi River, collection of tide and current data to evaluate the flushing characteristic of the estuary, bathymetric survey to locate a suitable discharge point and chemical and biological investigations to ascertain the environmental impact (NIO, 1982).

Particulate matter (PM) collected from the estuary was analysed for its organic carbon, organic nitrogen and chlorophyll *a*. The average concentration of PM in the surface water varied from 56 to 1976 mg/l. The values were low at the riverine end and large variations were recorded in the middle and near the mouth of the estuary. Particulate organic carbon (POC) followed a similar pattern shown by the PM. The analysis of the results suggests that the PM in the water of upper reaches of the estuary contains living matter whereas in the middle and lower reaches it is largely of detrital origin (Bhosle *et al.,* 1985a). Another study on the total dissolved carbohydrate showed high concentrations at the riverine end decreasing downstream towards the mouth. This led to the conclusion that river is probably the source of carbohydrate in the estuary (Bhosle *et al.,* 1985b).

PHYTOPLANKTON

Nearly 44 genera belonging to Cyanophyceae, Chlorophyceae and Bacillariophyceae families were recorded from the estuary. However, their occurrence was observed at a few stations only. Of these, the population density of 22 organisms was studied for 3 months (May, August and October in the year 1981). The results of this study are recorded in Table 14.1. Station 5 (M_5) which is at the riverine end showed the highest phytoplankton density. In the month of October, there was a bloom of *Fragilaria crotonensis*. Probably this is the result of high concentration of nutrients in the region upstream brought by industrial wastes. Figure 14.3 shows the variation in chlorophyll *a*, pheophytin and cell counts for the 3 months. A similar picture emerged from the station 5 in October (Ram, 1991).

Table 14.1— Population density of common species of phytoplankton at different stations (M_1-M_6) in Mahi Estuary during 1981. Values are no × 10^4 cells/l (From Ram, 1991)

Species	M1			M2		M3	M4		M5			M6	
	May	Aug	Oct	Aug	Oct	Oct	May	Oct	May	Aug	Oct	May	Oct
Anabaena sp.	–	0.17	0.17	15.40	8.40	–	–	–	–	–	–	–	–
A. constricta	–	–	–	–	–	1.05	1.20	1.74	–	–	–	–	–
Oscillatoria chlorina	0.65	0.53	1.91	14.50	14.95	–	–	3.68	3.86	2.52	14.20	–	2.41
O. formosa	–	–	2.17	–	1.50	–	1.30	–	3.46	0.96	11.20	–	3.85
O. limosa	0.65	0.95	1.67	10.00	5.00	–	–	1.68	1.73	0.04	12.50	4.55	–
O. tennis	–	–	–	3.20	2.75	54.40	1.65	5.52	23.33	–	14.80	1.32	–
O. lauterbornii	0.85	1.54	0.83	–	–	–	–	–	15.06	1.23	38.50	9.78	–
Oscillatoria sp.	–	–	–	–	–	–	–	–	7.33	–	19.00	–	–
O. putrida	–	–	–	–	–	–	–	–	50.07	3.30	14.80	–	–
Fragilaria crotonensis	–	–	4.13	–	–	1.14	–	1.15	–	–	3453.55	–	–
F. islandica	–	–	1.54	–	–	–	–	–	–	–	86.00	–	–
Nitzschia sp.	0.64	0.25	5.00	6.40	5.72	–	–	–	10.87	1.53	9.90	10.00	–
N. closterium	9.00	1.33	0.42	8.00	2.43	1.36	1.10	1.20	12.55	0.54	9.00	17.66	11.00
N. palea	–	–	–	–	0.84	0.39	5.31	8.52	18.80	2.40	33.80	–	–
N. pungeus	0.10	–	–	–	1.00	0.09	–	–	–	–	–	–	–
N. bilobata	–	–	–	–	–	0.27	–	2.46	–	–	–	–	–
N. sigma	–	–	–	–	–	1.02	1.03	1.30	–	–	–	–	–
Pediastrum sp.	0.83	0.81	0.72	–	1.05	–	–	–	–	–	–	0.61	1.05
P. simplex	–	–	–	–	–	–	–	–	0.83	0.06	0.94	0.30	1.06
Mycrocystis sp.	–	–	–	–	–	–	–	–	–	1.82	427.10	–	–
Scenedesmus sp.	0.75	0.83	0.07	–	1.28	0.05	–	–	0.47	–	1.36	–	–
Stauroneis sp.	0.67	0.33	0.18	–	3.82	0.71	1.15	0.19	14.44	0.84	0.20	0.44	1.04

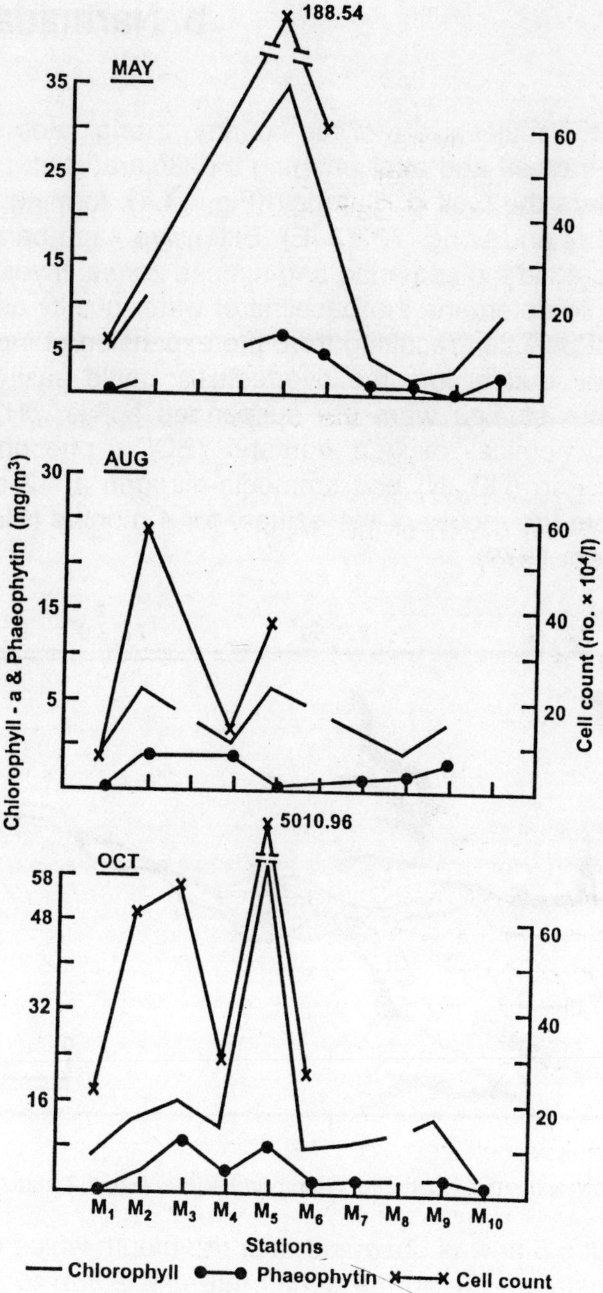

Fig. 14.3 Variation in chlorophyll *a*, phaeophytin and cell counts at 10 stations of Mahi Estuary during 3 months (From Ram, 1991).

b. Narmada (Narbada)

Narmada is one of the major rivers of the country. It originates in the Shahadol District of Madhya Pradesh and after entering the Gujarat State, it takes a westerly course and enters the Gulf of Cambay (Fig. 14.4), forming a large shallow estuary (Lat. 21°39′ N and Long. 72°33′ E). Extensive sand banks get exposed during the low tide both in the estuarine and riverine zones. Investigations on this river began in 1979 to determine the baseline of water quality as a reference so that any subsequent pollution resulting from the expansion of industrial activities at Bharuch and their outlets into the river/estuary could easily be monitored. Environmental factors studied were the suspended solids, *p*H, chlorides, dissolved oxygen, biochemical oxygen demand (BOD), phosphate-phosphorus (PO_4-P), nitrate-nitrogen (NO_3-N) and ammonia-nitrogen at 12 stations along a stretch of 70 km from the mouth of the estuary for 4 months (March, May, June and August in the year 1979).

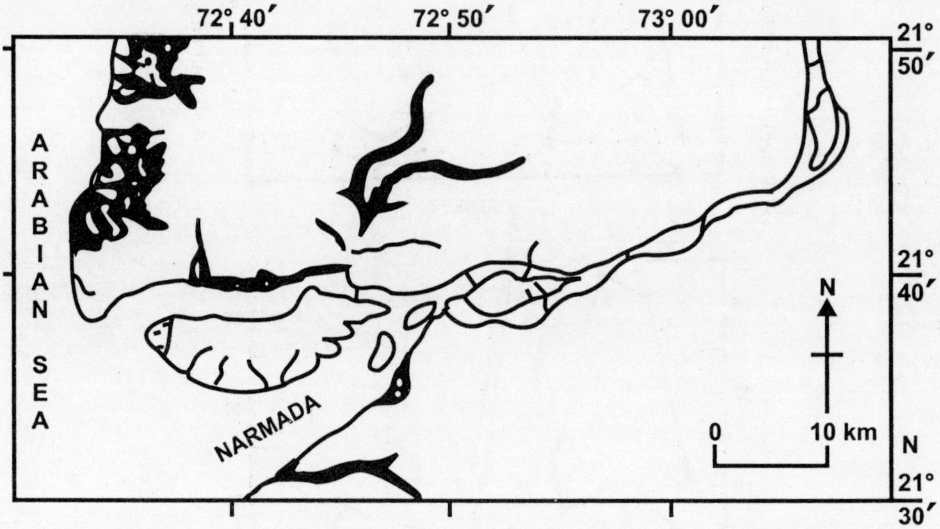

Fig. 14.4 Map showing the location of Narmada Estuary (From Zingde *et al.*, 1981).

Tidal range of about 5.5 m was observed near the mouth which decreased to 1.7 m, about 52 km upstream during the spring tide and 2.6 m to 1.2 m during the neap tide. Intrusion of seawater occurs up to 44 km upstream in early June when the riverine flow is minimum and up to 20 km or more in March. Freshwater flow is maximum in August. Chlorinity of water varied widely between ebb and flood tides. The water was well-mixed vertically with the absence of any significant stratification. The *p*H was high in the riverine region which influenced the estuarine region and an appreciable difference was noticed over the tidal cycle. Suspended load was maximum in the estuarine zone which decreased significantly in the freshwater region. High dissolved oxygen and its increase upstream and low BOD throughout the estuary and in the river indicated the absence of organic pollution in the estuarine and riverine zones. Phosphate-phosphorus showed an increase downstream showing its marine source while nitrate-nitrogen showed a decrease downstream indicating its freshwater origin. There was hardly any change in the ammonia-nitrogen which is indicative of its background level (Zingde *et al.,* 1981).

Phytoplankton were represented by diatoms, green algae and bluegreen algae. Diatoms were dominant. *Cyclotella* sp. and *Synedra* sp. were abundantly seen (Ragothaman & Patil, 1995).

Composition of suspended matter from the Narmada estuarine water and sediment was studied by Borole *et al.* (1982). In the water, the suspended matter varied from 26.7 to 6720 mg/l with the highest values occurring during the monsoon period. Metal to aluminium (Al) ratios, (Al essentially indicate the clay content), remained unchanged from one end of the estuary to the other or in the nearshore sediments. Composition of elements in the suspended particulate matter indicated a higher Al content in the estuarine area as compared to the freshwater zone (Borole *et al.,* 1982).

Chlorophyll *a* and abundance of zooplankton were studied at several stations in the estuary from March to September 1979. Average values of chlorophyll *a* were highest (31.48 mg/m^3) in the premonsoon period at upstream stations where brackishwater prevailed and were lowest (7.8 mg/m^3) during the monsoon period at almost all the stations. Zooplankton abundance was not very high in the river and estuary and average biomass was maximum in September (2.72 ml/100m^3). Lowest biomass value was during the monsoon period. Copepods, decapod larvae, molluscan veligers, fish eggs and larvae were the most common groups in the collection. Species diversity was greater towards the mouth of the estuary than in the riverine portion (Gajbhiye *et al.,* 1981).

c. Tapi (Tapti)

Tapi is another important river of the Gujarat State (Fig. 14.5). It is about 720 km long and its large catchment area measures approximately 1,65,000 km^2. It flows initially through the basaltic terrains of the Deccan traps and then through the alluvial deposits of unconsolidated fine sand, silt and clay before opening

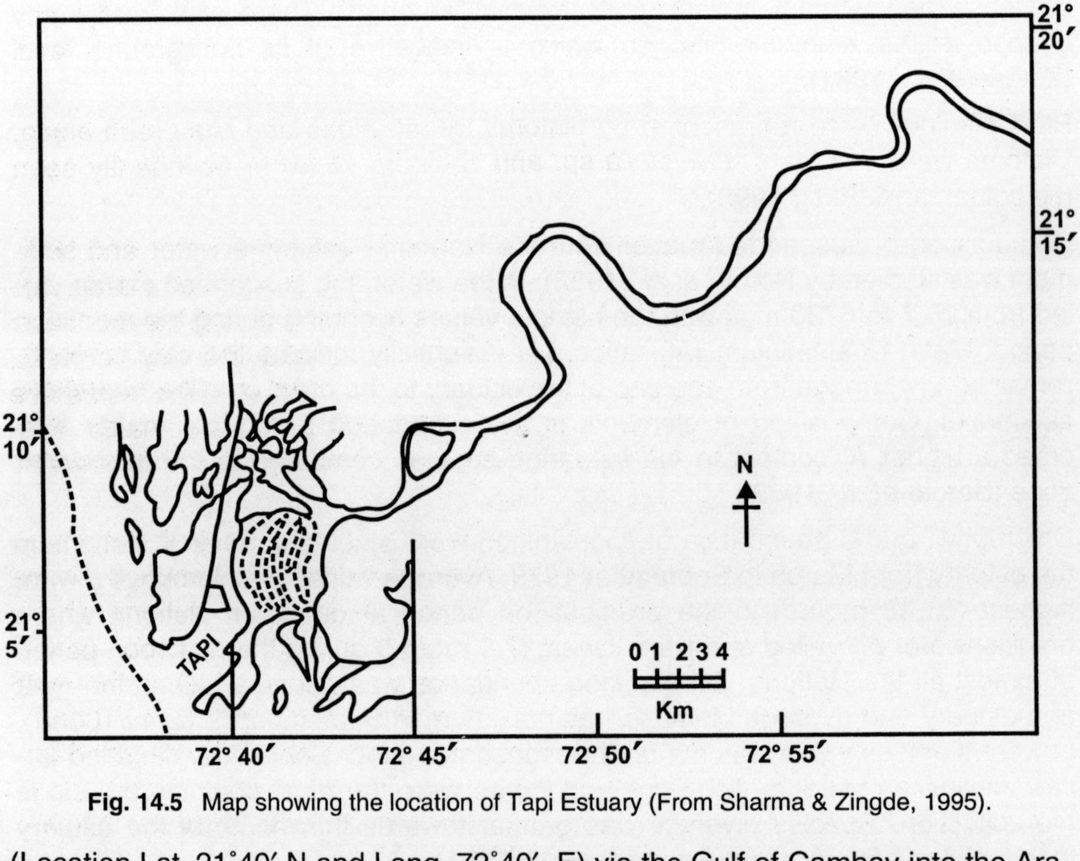

Fig. 14.5 Map showing the location of Tapi Estuary (From Sharma & Zingde, 1995).

(Location Lat. 21°40′ N and Long. 72°40′ E) via the Gulf of Cambay into the Arabian Sea. The annual average rainfall in the coastal plain is about 1,200 mm which largely occurs during the southwest monsoon (June to September) with its peak in July when the discharge of the Tapi River reaches 8,000 m^3/s. During the dry season, the freshwater flow is controlled by two dams located at Ukai and Kakrapar 116 km and 87 km, respectively upstream from Surat City. After September, the freshwater discharge into the estuary decreases considerably.

The estuarine region experiences high, semidiurnal tides with a range of 5.5 m at spring decreasing to 2.3 m, 25 km upstream and 2.3 m at neap going down to 0.4 m at a distance of 25 km in the river. Salinity incursion is largely governed by the tidal phase and is felt 30 km upstream during the dry season when the freshwater discharge is minimum and up to at least 10 km during the monsoon. Strong tidal currents exceeding 1 m/s sweep the shallow estuary making it vertically well-mixed except during short periods of tidal slacks.

Measurements of dissolved aluminium (Al), silicon (Si) and iron (Fe) were made under varying tidal cycle to determine their behaviour under high tidal energy and well-mixed conditions of Tapi Estuary (Sharma & Zingde, 1995). Dissolved Al seems to be released from the suspended particulate material (SPM) and gets dispersed in the estuary by the strong tidal currents. Dissolved Si, on the other hand, gets removed from the water and is adsorbed with the SPM. Removal of dissolved Al seems to occur largely during springs as compared to neap tides because of greater stirring up of sediments. This indicates the clay composition of the sediments. An inverse relationship between dissolved Al and dissolved Si was found. Such a behaviour of Si probably indicates its biogenic removal from the river water. Profiles of *p*H, dissolved oxygen, nitrate-nitrogen and ammonia-nitrogen support the deduction of biogenic removal of Si and partially of Fe. Otherwise dissolved Fe is randomly distributed in the estuary and does not indicate direct correlationship with chlorinity and *p*H (Sharma & Zingde, 1995).

Like Narmada, in the Tapi Estuary also there is a large variation in the concentration of suspended matter (19.7 to 691 mg/l) and the clay component in this estuary also remains unchanged (Borole *et al.*, 1982).

d. Mindhola

Mindhola River Estuary, located along Lat. 21˚8′ N and Long. 72˚43′ E is another important estuary of the Gujarat State (Fig. 14.6). The river experiences a pronounced cycle of freshwater discharge during July-August associated with monsoonal drainage. Its flow decreases considerably during the premonsoon (dry) season reaching its minimum in May-June. Strong tidal action of about 5.5 m in range enters the mouth decreasing to 1.9 m at 32 km inland and strong currents keep the estuary well-mixed. Intrusion of saline water during spring is felt well beyond 35 km inland.

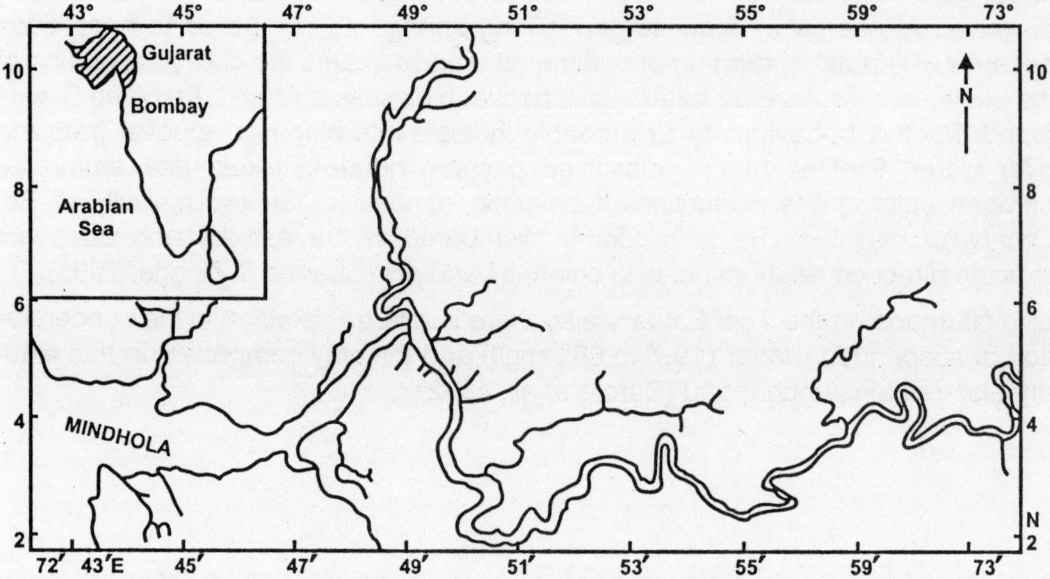

Fig. 14.6 Map showing the location of Mindhola Estuary (From Zingde *et al.*, 1988).

The estuary receives 95 × 10^6 l/day of wastewater from a variety of industries located around Udhna Town through the river via a creek at Udhna. Another group of industries located in the town of Balesar also releases its wastewater at the rate of 33×10^6 l/day through a stormwater drain. In the mid-estuarine region, wastewater from a sugar factory at the rate of 1.2×10^6 l/day is added. These wastewaters carry heavy metals namely Ni, Cu, Zn and Pb at the rate of 10, 12, 31 and 9 kg/day respectively. More than 85% of the total load enters the estuary through the Udhna Creek (NIO, 1980).

Dissolved Cu, Zn and Pb varied considerably throughout the estuary and their concentrations were higher at sites closer to the major sources of pollution. There was a tendency for the metal concentrations to increase with a decrease in salinity because of the reduced volume of seawater during the lean period when the volume of wastewater in the river increases. In the sediments also, there was a marked increase in the values of heavy metals where the sediments were silty sand and clayey silt, and a decrease in sediments containing coarse sand (Zingde *et al.,* 1988).

Besides the heavy metals, flouride is also added into the Mindhola Estuary along with the wastewater. The average fluoride content in the world rivers is about 0.1 mg/l (Burton, 1976). Taking this value as a standard, the average for Mindhola River was 0.24 mg/l. In another estuary (Purna) which is relatively free from pollution, the average values of fluoride were lower than that of Mindhola because there is no externally added flouride in Purna (Zingde & Mandalia, 1988).

Major stations bringing wastewater to the Mindhola Estuary were sampled for the estimation of Cu, Zn and Pb using standard procedures. Several dyeing, printing, fertilizer, rayon, paper, pulp, pharmaceutical, chemical and textile industries release wastewater generally untreated. These streams join the Udhna Creek which passes on its load to its Mindhola River.

Table 14.2 shows the characteristics of the effluents based on the determinations of various parameters. Table 14.3 gives the data on tidal range and current speed for the Mindhola Estuary. High tidal influence generates strong currents which get slightly reduced at the bottom (Table 14.3). The intrusion of seawater in the estuary varied considerably during the state of tide and seasons. Maximum incursion was up to 25 km inland during the spring tide in April when the freshwater flow was leanest in the dry season. It decreased to 15 km in September (during high freshwater runoff). The concentrations of dissolved Cu, Zn and Pb are shown in relation to salinity at 5 stations upstream in Table 14.4.

The tidal prism for the Mindhola Estuary was estimated by the application of Dyer's (1973) prism method. It was approximately 83.9×10^6 m^3 and 23.2×10^6 m^3

during the spring and neap tides, respectively (Zingde *et al.,* 1988). Thus, the flushing volume of the well-mixed water during one tidal cycle was calculated as 90% and 74% during the spring and neap tides, respectively.

Table 14.2— Physicochemical characteristics (mean) of effluents reaching three stations of Mindhola Estuary (From Zingde *et al.*, 1988)

Parameter (mg l^{-1})	Station I	Station II	Station III
Flow (× 10^6 l day^{-1})	95	1.2	33
Suspended solids	323	280	169
Total dissolved solids	338	0.6	0.06
*p*H	6.2	6.7	6.0
BOD	136	130	89
COD	273	409	–
Total phosphorus	2.8	0.4	0.12
Total nitrogen	7.2	0.3	0.1
Phenolics	6	0.1	0.1
Oil & grease	781	0.5	0.2
Copper	0.1	0.03	0.04
Zinc	0.3	0.04	0.08
Lead	0.1	–	–

Table 14.3— Tidal data and current speed data at three stations of Mindhola River Estuary (From Zingde *et al.*, 1988)

Parameter	Stations		
	1	12	14
Spring tidal range (m)	5.5	3	1.9
Neap tidal range (m)	2.5	1	0.5
Average flood period (h)	4 to 5	3 to 4	2 to 3
Average ebb period (h)	7 to 8	8 to 9	9 to 10
High tide time lag (h)	–	1 to 2	2 to 3
Max. Current Speed (ms^{-1})			
Spring (surface)	1.9	0.6	–
(bottom)	1.7	0.6	–
Neap (surface)	1.0	0.4	–
(bottom)	0.8	0.3	–

The distribution of suspended solids in the estuary is largely controlled by the tidal action and the speed of tidal currents. This is a typical feature of the estuaries of southern Gujarat. Combined solids released through wastewater have been estimated to be 36,000 kg/day, of which about 31,000 kg/day is contributed by Udhna

Creek. This appears to be high, but it is not likely to influence much of the movement of total solids due to the tidal action which is considerable, up and down the estuary (Zingde *et al.*, 1988).

The estuarine behaviour of three elements namely boron (B), calcium (Ca) and magnesium (Mg) was studied in the Mindhola Estuary by collecting water samples over a complete tidal cycle from 19 to 21 November 1978 at 2-hourly intervals up to a distance of 10 km from the mouth of the river and analysed for the three constituents. The tides during this period were neap with a range of 3.5 m at the mouth region decreasing to 0.9 m at a point 21 km upstream.

Table 14.4— Dissolved trace metals (µg/l) at five stations in Mindhola River Estuary (From Zingde *et al.*, 1988)

Station	Salinity (‰)	Cu	Zn	Pb
1	33.8	7.8	13	ND*
	17.3	5.2	10	3.5
	6.3	7.5	12	3.2
6	15.6	5.9	16	6.6
	9.2	12.2	28	6.8
	0.3	15.9	48	4.7
12	6.1	8.8	9	ND
	0.8	9.4	7	ND
	0.1	6.9	12	5.7
14	0.06	4.9	6	ND
15	0.05	3.1	10	2.7

* Not detectable

Boron was found to be removed preferentially over the entire tidal cycle and its maximum removal was found to be of the order of 9%. Calcium and magnesium, on the other hand, were found to be added during the observations; their maximum addition was 8% and 5%, respectively. The addition was probably due to the release of calcium from clays and the input of magnesium came from seawater into the riverine water with the tides (Narvekar *et al.*, 1981).

e. Purna

The Purna River is narrow throughout its course. It broadens into a wide shallow estuary located Lat. 21°55′ N and Long. 72°45′ E (Fig. 14.7). During spring tide, the estuary attains a width of 1.5 km which decreases to about 500 m at 20 km inland. The range of spring tide at the mouth is 4.5 m which decrease to 1.5 m at 30 km upstream. The depth of the channel connecting the sea at low tide becomes about 2 m and extensive sand banks get exposed at the mouth region. Several tributaries joining the river Purna get periodically filled with tidal water and these harbour a variety of fauna (mudskippers, crabs, prawns, etc.). The exposed intertidal region is generally muddy or sandy and the bottom in the middle has coarse sand and gravel. The region around the estuary is sparsely populated and only during the fishing season some activity is seen. The water of Purna River is relatively clean except that some of the tributaries in the vicinity of the town Dharagiri carry wastewater from the textile, dyes and chemical industries including domestic sewage and hence there is pollution in this river also although it is not as much as in the Mindhola Estuary which is north of the Purna River close by (Zingde *et al.,* 1987a).

As noted earlier, measurements of fluoride content in this estuary along with Mindhola showed a notable difference based on which it was concluded that the Purna Estuary probably has not externally added fluoride (Zingde & Mandalia, 1988). Further investigations on this estuary were carried out to determine the extent of pollution occurring in this estuary based on its flushing characteristics. Two surveys were conducted along a 40 km stretch during October-November 1978 and April-September 1979 covering 5 stations from the mouth upstream.

Tides in the estuary are of semidiurnal type with two highs and two lows in 24 h varying in range. Table 14.5 shows the tidal data and the time-lag of the high-water reaching the station 6, 40 km away. It varied between 1.5 and 3 h. High tidal influx generated strong currents with speed exceeding 120 cm/s during spring with no appreciable difference between surface and bottom. Off south Gujarat, the current regime is generally parallel to the coast reversing in direction with the ebb from the flood, and hence fall more or less perpendicular to the direction of the estuary. The estuary is generally well-mixed vertically with excellent flushing caused by the tidal action. The flushing time of < 2.5 tidal cycles indicate that the load of pollutants in the estuary will be flushed out and very little will remain per tidal cycle. Suspended load of inert materials increases considerably with the currents in each tidal cycle stirring up the bottom sediments. The wastewater coming to the estuary has an estimated amount of 1,100 kg/day of suspended solids which will not affect appreciably considering the total background of dispersed sediments in the water column by tidal currents.

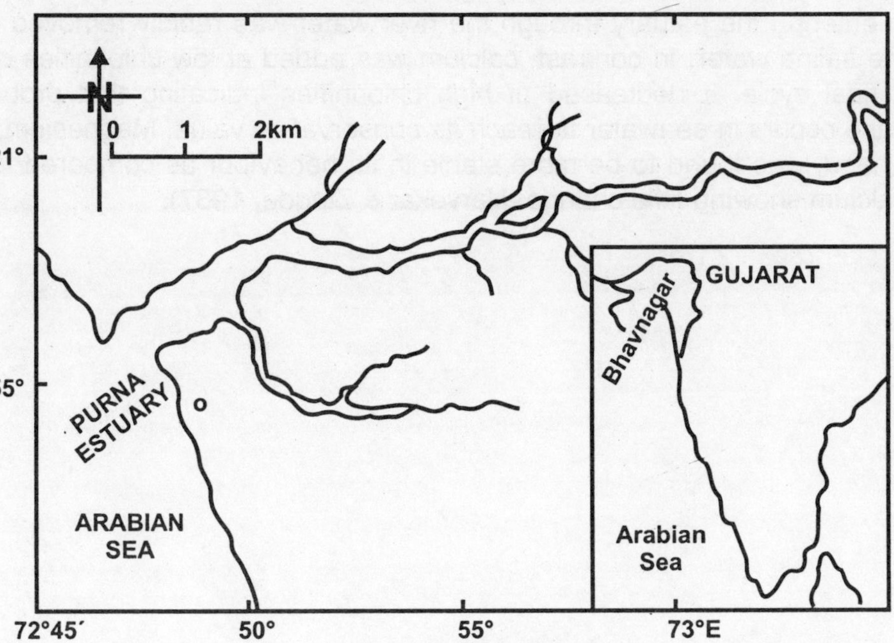

Fig. 14.7 Map showing the location of Purna River Estuary (From Zingde *et al.*, 1987).

Table 14.5— Tidal data at three stations in Purna River Estuary (From Zingde *et al.*, 1987b)

	Stations		
	1	2	3
Tidal range (spring) (m)	4.6	3.4	1.5
Tidal range (neap) (m)	3.1	3	0.5
Av. flood period (h)	4 to 4.5	3 to 4	2 to 2.5
Av. ebb period (h)	7.5 to 8	8 to 9	9.5 to 10

A comparison of the physicochemical features of the wastewater with those of the estuarine waters led to the conclusion that the volume of wastewater discharged till 1979 had not grossly influenced the quality of estuarine water except that it has created some decrease in dissolved oxygen because of high BOD of the wastewater. Some of the pollutants such as phenolics, oil and grease, total phosphorus, total nitrogen and trace metals present in the wastewater would not affect the quality of water of the estuary. However, the collected data should serve as a reference for any pollutant entering the estuary in the future. The flushing time of the estuary is about 5 tidal cycles (Zingde *et al.,* 1987b).

Behaviour of boron, calcium and magnesium was also studied in this estuary. Boron entering the estuary through the river water was rapidly removed when it met the saline water. In contrast, calcium was added at low chlorinities over the entire tidal cycle. It decreased at high chlorinities indicating that probably its decrease occurs in seawater to reach its conservative value. Magnesium, on the other hand, was found to be more stable in its behaviour as compared to boron and calcium showing little change (Narvekar & Zingde, 1987).

f. Ambika

The shallow Ambika Estuary is located along Lat. 20°45′ N and Long. 73°52′ E (Fig. 14.8). It is barely navigable during the low tide but at the high tide, medium-sized crafts can sail up and down up to the town of Billimora. Extensive sand banks get exposed in the estuarine region during the low tide and these are prone to shifting from season to season. The riverine zone has mud banks with narrow and intricate channels between them. Two other rivers, Kaveri and Kaveira, join

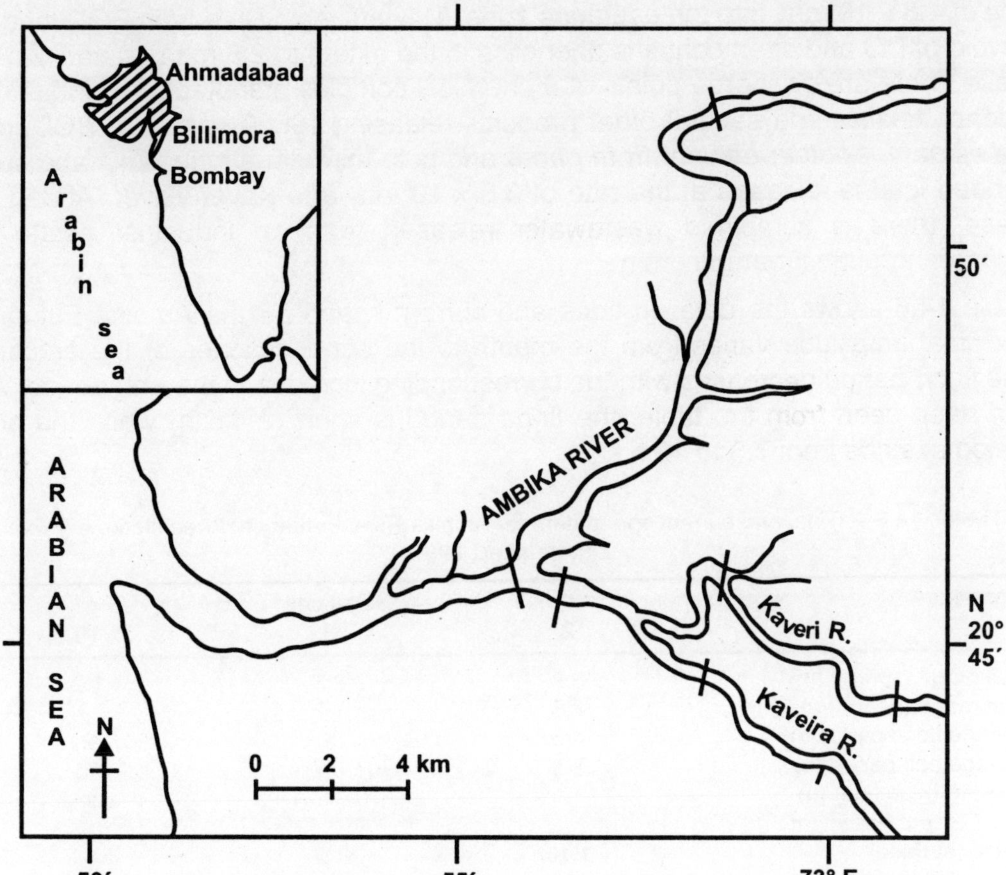

Fig. 14.8 Map showing the location of Ambika Estuary (From Zingde *et al.*, 1986).

the river Ambika. The three rivers have a pronounced seasonal cycle of freshwater discharge and get flooded during the SW monsoon (July to September). Their flow gets considerably reduced after October and becomes minimal in May-June.

The water of the three rivers is clean until it reaches Billimora town (population 35,000) where domestic sewage at the rate of 0.5×10^6/day is released through natural stormwater drains at 4 points. A textile mill manufacturing cotton and polyester fabrics releases combined industrial and domestic wastewater at the rate of 4.8×10^6/day into the estuarine zone. This effluent with a high BOD load is devoid of DO and often contains phenolics to the extent to 2.8 mg/l. In addition to these, there are discharge points of a chemical complex manufacturing industrial alcohol, textiles and several other products releasing 19600 kg/day of BOD into the estuary. Another effluent from paper and pulp mill with a high BOD and suspended load is released at the rate of 3.8×10^6/day into Kaveri River. Added to these, there is combined wastewater released from an industrial estate in Billimora through a natural drain.

Table 14.6 shows the data on tides and current speed for the Ambika Estuary. The tidal amplitude varies from the mouth to the upper reaches of the estuary. The flood period decreases with the corresponding increase in the ebb period. As can been seen from the table, the flood period is short (2-4.5 h) while the ebb period extends from 7.5 to 10 h.

Table 14.6— Tidal and current speed data for Ambika River Estuary at three stations (From Zingde *et al.*, 1986)

Parameter	Stations		
	2	8	10
Tidal range (spring) (m)	3.4	2.3	1.2
Tidal range (neap) (m)	2.6	1.7	0.5
Average flood period (h)	4.5	3	2
Average ebb period (h)	7.5	9	10
Time lag (high tide) (h)	–	0.5 to 1	1 to 2
Max. Current Speed (ms^{-1})			
Spring (surface)	1.15	1.2	–
(bottom)	0.82	0.98	–
Neap (surface)	0.82	0.79	–
(bottom)	0.63	0.6	–

The tidal range in the Ambika Estuary is relatively lower than the expected figures because from Mumbai as one goes northward towards Bhavnagar, the tidal range increases. The tidal range at the mouth of Damanganga River, which is 40 km south of Ambika is 5.6 m (spring) and 3.6 m (neap), has been reported by Zingde *et al.* (1980a). The lower tidal range in Ambika is largely due to the presence of prominent sand bars around the mouth of the estuary which act as a barrier to the tidal ingress (Zingde *et al.,* 1986).

The seawater intrusion into the estuary and river is controlled by the speed and volume of freshwater flow from the river. In May, when the riverine flow is small, the average salinity at 15 km inland is 15.2‰ at high water and 2.3‰ at low water but in October when the flow is relatively large, the salinity at the same points is 0.9‰ and 0.3‰ at high and low water, respectively. The tidal prism of the estuary has been estimated to be 26.8 × $10^6 m^3$ and 20.39 × $10^6 m^3$ during spring and neap tides respectively. The average low tide volume was found to be 5.72 × 10^6 m^3 (Zingde *et al.,* 1986). This allows the flushing time of one tidal cycle and indicates excellent flushing of the estuary. This would also indicate that 80% of the well-mixed added wastewater will be removed from the estuary at every tidal cycle. The *p*H of water ranged from 7.2 to 9.2 with a tendency to increase during the low tide probably due to alkaline wastewater coming through the river. High organic load coming into the estuary influenced the oxygen balance considerably and at some stations the DO varied from 2.5 to 7.8 mg/l over one tidal cycle in October. In May, when the riverine flow was weak, there was a complete depletion of DO at some points. The total BOD load has been estimated to be 24600 kg/day. Measurements of NO_3-N, NO_2-N, NH_4-N and PO_4-P did not show any regular variation over the tidal cycle. There was no clear evidence of variation of nutrients with salinity also. Similarly, the levels of trace metals (Fe, Cu, Zn and As) did not reveal any regular trend of variation (Zingde *et al.,* 1986).

Behaviour of boron added through industrial wastes in the polluted Ambika Estuary was studied along with calcium and magnesium. The concentrations of calcium and magnesium decreased with decreasing chlorinity and the ratios of Ca:Cl and Mg:Cl at varying chlorinities were always within the normal range found in the river water at one upstream end and in the seawater downstream at the other end. The ratios of B:Cl, on the other hand, exceeded the river water end-limit at the ebb tide at the upstream end. The external input of boron probably coming from the wastewater raised the boron concentration in water by 263% in the vicinity of the industrial discharge. An inverse relationship was found between the levels of boron and suspended solids suggesting that boron is probably removed by the suspended clay particles in the mixing zone of the estuary. A similar situation may probably exist with the additional input of calcium and magnesium as their removal by clay particles is also established in estuaries of other geogrphical regions (NIO, 1980; Narvekar *et al.,* 1983).

g. Auranga

The shallow river Auranga, like Ambika, becomes non-navigable during the low tides as extensive sand banks and mudflats get exposed during the ebb. However, medium-size craft can plough through up to the town Lilapur during the flood tide. The Auranga Estuary is located along Lat. 20°36′ N and Long. 73°52′ E (Fig. 14.9). The intertidal region of the estuary is generally muddy while the bottom at the mouth is sandy. A weir (river dam) has been constructed about 12 km upstream for the supply of freshwater to Bulsar City. Domestic wastewater from Bulsar City amounting to 3.2 million litres per day (mld) is released into the river outside the weir through a natural drain opening into the estuary. An industry manufacturing nitrocellulose also releases 0.6 mld of acidic wastewater with low BOD into the estuary.

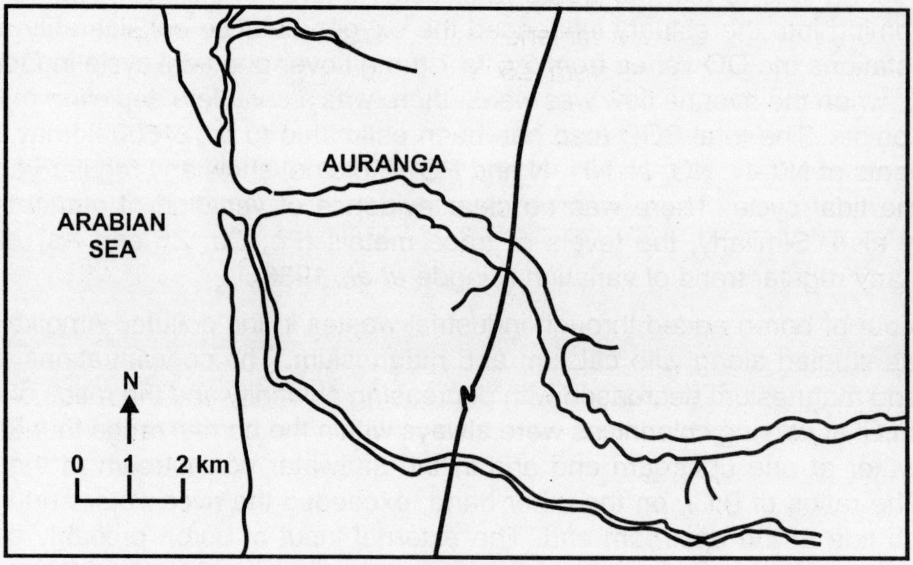

Fig. 14.9 Map showing Auranga Estuary (From Zingde *et al.*, 1985).

The estuary experiences semidiurnal tides with two highs and two lows each day of unequal amplitudes. Table 14.7 gives the data on tides and current speeds at the surface and bottom. Investigations on the estuary were carried out along a 12 km stretch at fortnightly intervals in October 1978 and in January, May, October and December 1979 (Zingde *et al.,* 1985).

Table 14.7— Tidal and current speed data at three stations of Auranga River Estuary (From Zingde *et al.*, 1985)

Parameter	Stations		
	1	4	6
Spring tidal range (m)	4.5	3	1.1
Neap tidal range (m)	3.3	1.9	0.5
Average flood period (h)	3.5 to 4.5	3 to 4	1.5 to 2
Average ebb period (h)	7.5 to 8.5	8 to 9	10 to 10.5
High tide time lag (h)	–	0.5 to 1	1 to 1.5
Max. Current Speed (cm/s)	–	–	–
Spring (surface)	120	110	–
Spring (bottom)	115	84	–
Neap (surface)	76	52	–
Neap (bottom)	64	34	–

As can be seen from Table 14.7, the range of the spring tide at the mouth (station 1) is 4.5 m, about 1.5 m higher than the neap. About 12 km upstream it decreases to 1.2 m. The flood at the mouth had a duration of 3.5 to 4.5 h and the ebb extended over a period of 7.5 to 8.5 h (Table 14.7). High tidal influence generated strong currents (~120 cm/s) during spring with almost of equal intensity at the surface and bottom. Maximum ebb speed of the flow was observed from 3-4 h after the commencement of the ebb with east-west direction of the flow. Float studies showed that it takes about 2-3 h for the float to travel a distance of 12 km, depending upon the nature of the tide. Seawater penetration into the estuary extends upstream up to the weir. Flushing time calculated using tidal prism indicates excellent flushing and just about one tidal cycle seems enough to remove 72% and 83% of well-mixed water from the estuary during neap and spring, respectively.

Under continuous flow of pollutants, the load retained in the estuary after a number of tidal cycles would be less than 3 times the load introduced at each tidal cycle. The suspended load in the estuary was related to the current speed which dispersed the bottom sediments into the water column. In October, when the freshwater flow was high, the upper reaches of the estuary were freshwater dominated, whereas in May when the freshwater flow gets restricted, the seawater influence prevails throughout the estuary. High dissolved oxygen and low BOD were observed throughout the study. These features indicate good oxidizing conditions in the estuary (Zingde *et al.,* 1985).

As noted earlier, the behaviour of boron, calcium and magnesium in this estuary was studied along with Purna Estuary and percentage addition or removal in this estuary followed a similar pattern as observed in Purna (Narvekar & Zingde, 1987).

h. Par

The river Par has its origin in Satpura Mountains. It runs into the plains of Gujarat before opening into the Arabian Sea. It is located along Lat. 20°27′ N and Long. 72°54′ E (Fig. 14.10). The width of the river in the freshwater zone is 100-200 m but it becomes 1500 m near the mouth of estuary. The estuary is shallow and its

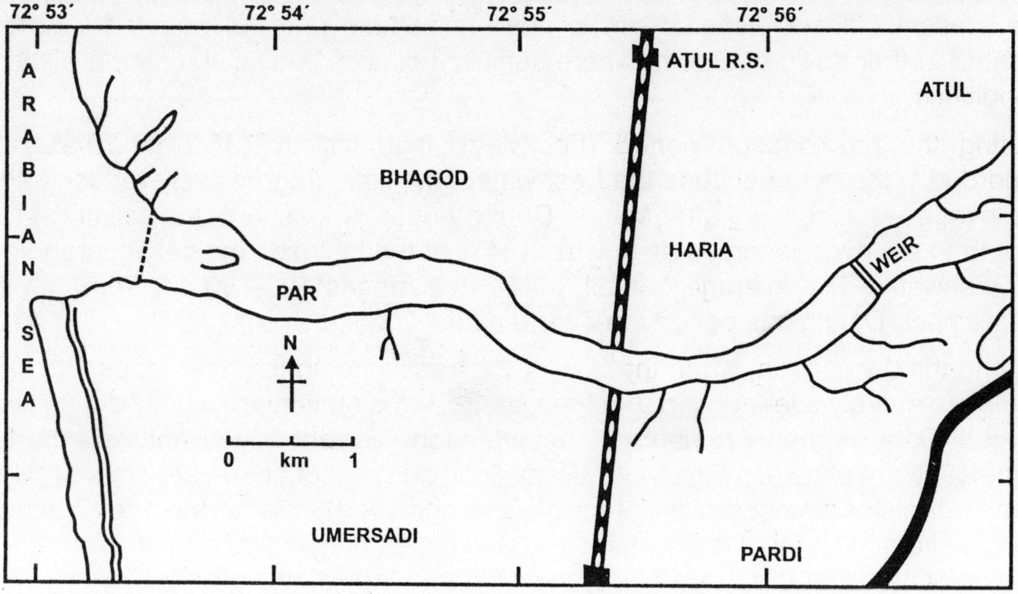

Fig. 14.10 Map showing location of Par River Estuary (From Zingde *et al.*, 1979).

stretch during the postmonsoon season extends to about 6 km. Neither the estuary nor the river is navigable at the low tide due to heavy siltation. At a distance of 6 km upstream, a weir has been constructed in the river (Fig. 14.10) to store freshwater for its supply to a large chemical complex located on its northern side. The chemical complex discharges 25,000 m^3/day of wastewater into a natural drain which opens into the estuarine region just below the weir. A survey was conducted between June and September 1977 to determine the feasibility of discharging the effluent at the existing point into the estuarine region and to evaluate the extent of treatment required to control pollution in the river and the estuary (Zingde *et al.,* 1979).

Like the other estuaries, tides in this estuary are also of mixed semidiurnal type with a range of 5.5 m at spring decreasing to 2.5 m near the weir. At the ebb tide, the entire river-bed gets exposed and the depth at the mouth of the estuary becomes 0.3 m. The effluent is then seen flowing as a narrow midstream channel mixed with seawater. Measurements of the tides have shown that during the spring tides, the seawater for the dilution of effluents will be available for nearly 5 h in a tidal cycle at the disposal site but during the neap tide, the quantity of water gets considerably reduced and it is available only for 3 h. It is, therefore, clear that the present effluent disposal site is quite unsuitable and the outfall should be located further down at a point where sufficient dilution is available under all tidal conditions.

During the premonsoon period (Feb-May), high salinity (35.2 to 20.9‰) is recorded in the river because the freshwater flow gets progressively reduced and the river goes almost dry after March. During August (monsoon), the salinity at the mouth of the river becomes as low as 4.34‰ at the high tide indicating large flow of freshwater. The average rainfall in the area ranges 120-180 cm from July to September. During this period the river remains flooded.

During the dry season, when the flow of the freshwater in the river stops, the currents are entirely tide-induced and their speed and direction are wholly due to tidal sweep. Data on measurements of instantaneous current speed against time for June 1977 are shown in Fig. 14.11. Peak flood currents of about 120 cm/s and the ebb currents of almost similar intensity were observed 3 h after the tide. The currents were maximum at the surface and decreased only marginally at the bottom. This indicates that the estuary is well-mixed and the wastewater if discharged at the right place would facilitate better dispersion.

Flushing time calculated by applying prism method was found to be 1.4 tidal cycles (Zingde *et al.,* 1979). This indicates that about 70% of the well-mixed water will be removed after one tidal cycle. To evaluate the extent of mixing during the neap tide dilution, studies were conducted using fluorescein dye. The dye patch moved with an average speed of about 26 cm/s. The absorbance of the dye colour was measured on a spectrophotometer and the results showed that the dilution factor is quite high. Thus, it can be concluded that if the effluent is released at a proper place it can easily be carried after dilution into the sea during the ebb tide.

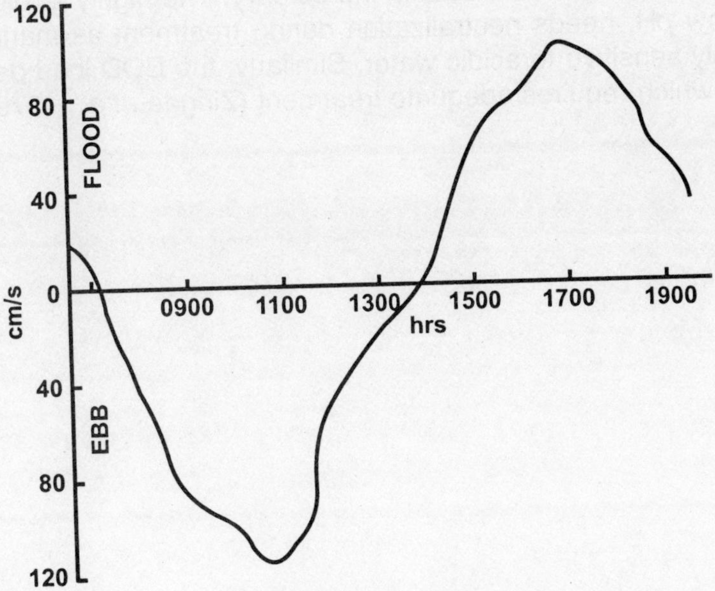

Fig. 14.11 Variation of current speed with time on 7 June 1977 in Par Estuary (From Zingde *et al.*, 1979).

Table 14.8— Characteristics of the wastewater at the effluent discharge point in river Par (From Zingde *et al.*, 1979)

Parameter	Maximum	Minimum	Mean	Mean during monsoon
Flow (mld)	3.88	3.44	3.66	–
Suspended solids (mg/l)	214	39	106	567
Chlorides (mg/l)	419	320	360	150
*p*H	8.5	6.8	–	7.5
Dissolved oxygen (mg/l)	0.8	0	0.1	1.1
BOD (mg/l)	372	98	226	11
Total phosphorus (mg/l)	742	203	548	137
Sulphate (mg/l)	1.29	0.13	0.72	0.8
Phenolics (mg/l)	5.5	2	3.6	0.2
Oil & grease (mg/l)	770	13	197	49

The existing outfall of the wastewater creates incomplete mixing of the effluent with seawater and this affects the quality of water. Table 14.8 shows the physico-chemical characteristics of the effluent at the discharge point. Taking the average suspended load as 200 ppm, about 5 tonnes/day of suspended load would be added to the estuary. This amount seems negligible considering the high suspended load the tidal currents create in the estuary. The highly acidic effluent, as indicated by low *p*H, needs neutralization during treatment as marine flora and fauna are highly sensitive to acidic water. Similarly, the BOD load decreases the DO drastically which requires adequate treatment (Zingde *et al.*, 1979).

i. Kolak

The river Kolak is close to the river Par and runs also parallel to it in the eastwest direction before joining the Arabian Sea near Kolak Village. It has a rocky bed which gets exposed during the low tide and the water flows through the rocky channels. During the monsoon period, it has a large flow which causes floods to the adjacent areas. From October onwards, its flow decreases progressively and after February it becomes negligible. Fears were expressed in the late seventies that because of pollution caused by industrial wastes, the quality of river water has been declining constantly and hence the present work was undertaken to evaluate the extent of pollution in the river and suggest remedial measures (Zingde *et al.,* 1980a). The work was undertaken from January to August 1977 along a 35 km stretch at 6 stations in the river. Figure 14.12 shows the course of the river which is located along Lat. 20°24′ N and Long. 72°53′ E.

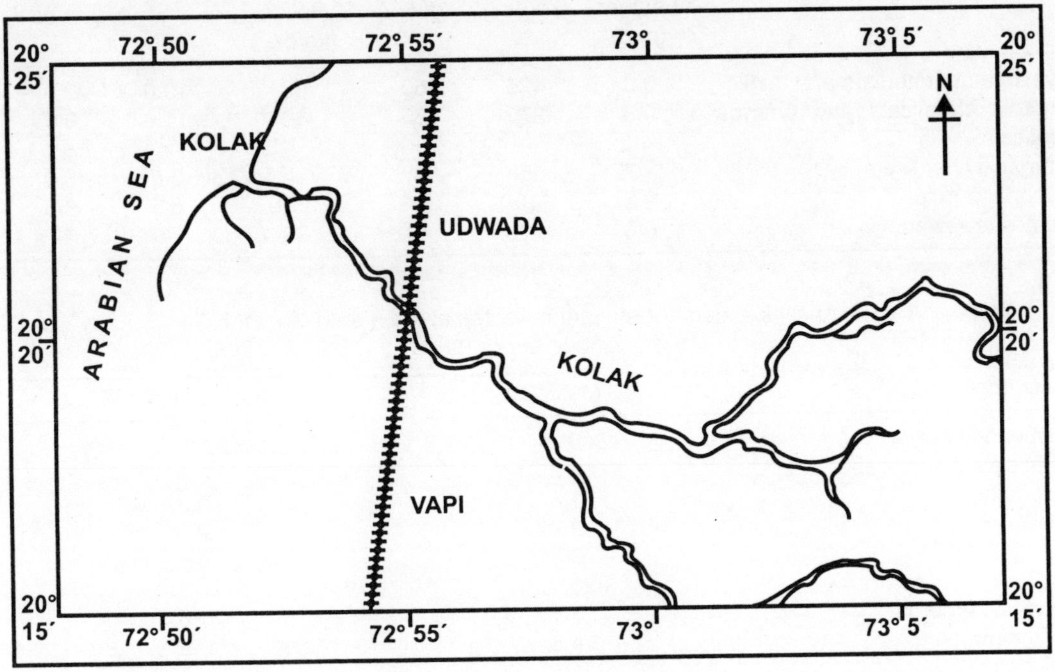

Fig. 14.12 Map showing the location of Kolak Estuary (From Zingde *et al.*, 1980).

Major discharge of wastewater into the river comes from an industrial complex at Vapi established by the GIDC. The complex has an area of about 830 hectares which gets divided into north and south sectors by a highway almost in the middle. The freshwater consumption of the industrial complex is about 9 mld, of this about 7 mld is released as waste. From the northern sector, 4.3 mld of waste is brought to the Kolak River by a narrow channel which has a natural slope towards the river. The remaining 3.4 mld of waste produced by the southern sector is discharged into another nearby river Damanganga which will be described later. Details of the wastewater coming into the river Kolak from different factories located in the northern sector is given in Table 14.9 and the physicochemical analysis of the wastewater is shown in Table 14.10. The analysis of the wastewater was done at the mouth of the estuary.

Table 14.9— Characteristics of wastewater coming from some industries of northern sector (From Zingde *et al.*, 1980a)

Type of Industries	Quantity of effluent (mld)	BOD (kg/day)	COD (kg/day)	Suspended Solids (kg/day)	*p*H Max.	*p*H Min.
Dye, dye-intermediate and textile	0.3	125	350	80	10.0	2.5
Organic chemicals and pharmaceuticals	0.3	275	630	80	11.6	6.5
Inorganic chemicals	0.05	5	–	4	8.0	6.0
Paper and pulp	2.5	1100	–	1200	6.5	8.5
Domestic sewage	0.8	100	–	70	–	–

Table 14.10— Analytical data for effluent collected at the mouth of river Kolak Estuary (From Zingde *et al.*, 1980a)

Conc. (ppm)	Maximum	Minimum
Suspended solids	300	102
Total dissolved solids	10.2	3.6
Chlorides	1.2	0.32
*p*H	3.2	2
DO	0.3	0
BOD	323	100
Total phosphorus	3.1	1.6
Total nitrogen	4.6	0.9
Sulphate	1.5	0.5
Phenolics	8.3	1
Oil & grease	65	22

Although the tidal range during the spring flood is about 5.5 m, its influence varies considerably from monsoon to premonsoon periods. During the neap tide, the range decreases to 3.5 m. Large rock outcrops in the rocky bed of the river, a few kilometres above the mouth, weaken the tidal influence upstream and it appears that the existing outfall of the wastewater comes outside the tidal zone because significant tidal influence is observed only upto 3.5 km upstream from the mouth. Thus, it is clear that very little water will be available for the dilution of effluent at the present discharge site during the dry season when the river flow is minimum. Currents in the estuarine zone vary considerably with the state of tides. At the peak spring flood, the current velocity was 1.1 m/s decreasing to 0.6 m/s during the neap. The corresponding ebb currents were of the same order. Flushing time of the estuary works out to be 1.2 tidal cycles which means that about 85% of the water will be removed after one tidal cycle. Therefore, if the wastewater is discharged in the main tidal zone, a major portion of the effluent will be taken into the sea with every ebb. The flow of the river during the dry season becomes very weak and the water available for diluting the effluent is very inadequate as compared to the wastewater discharged, and worst conditions of pollution occur during the dry season. Salt water intrusion into the river, as indicated by the salinity values, varies seasonally but because of the slope in the river bed the intrusion does not go very far. Nevertheless, the water remains well-mixed throughout the estuary.

In the river, above the discharge point of the effluent, the water was clear and its transparency was upto the bottom. The dark colour of the wastewater decreased the transparency beyond the outfall considerably. From the suspended solids in the river, the total suspended load coming from the industries was estimated to be 900 kg/day. In the month of May, severe conditions of pollution were observed as the environment of the river becomes anaerobic with the emission of hydrogen sulphide. Reduction in DO and a general increase in BOD made the survival of any fauna and flora almost impossible.

Measurements of nutrients (phosphorus and nitrogen) showed low values such as found in estuarine waters without any additional inputs from the effluents. Similarly, boron, sulphate, phenolics and trace metals were all within limited ranges which indicate baseline concentrations for any deterioration in water quality in the future (Zingde *et al.,* 1980a).

j. Damanganga

The river Damanganga runs close by, almost parallel to the river Kolak along Lat. 20°19′ N and Long. 72°50′ E (Fig. 14.13). The general features of this river are similar to those of Kolak as the intrusion of seawater into the estuary and the river varies greatly from season to season depending upon the riverine flow. The river joins the Arabian Sea near Daman and hence it derives its names as Damanganga. The mouth of the estuary is shallow due to heavy siltation.

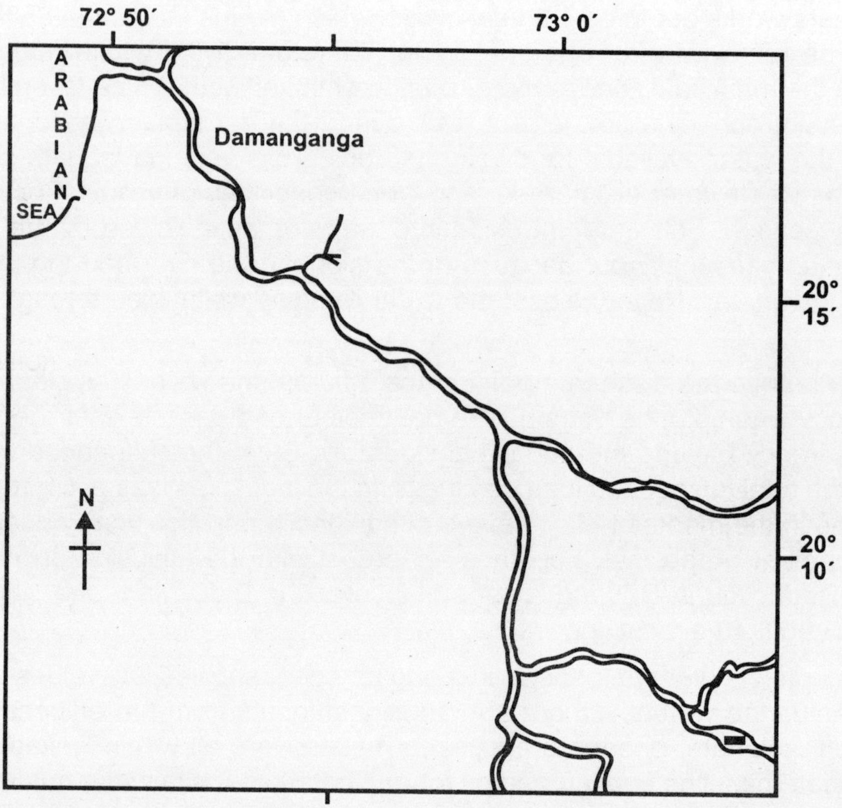

Fig. 14.13 Map showing the location of Damanganga River and estuary (From Zingde *et al.*, 1980).

The river receives wastewater of the order of 3.9 mld from an industrial estate at Vapi (southern sector as noted earlier) and Selvasa. Another industrial estate at Selvasa discharges about 0.2 mld of liquid wastes into Pimpara River — a tributary of Damanganga which drains into the latter. Thus, the river Pimpara dilutes the wastewater considerably before it reaches Damanganga.

Observations on the water quality of this river were made for 7 months from January to July 1977 at 10 stations along a 35 km stretch (Zingde *et al.,* 1980b). The semidiurnal tides, like in other rivers described earlier, have a range of 5.6 m during spring flood which declines to 3.6 m during the neap. Measurements near the discharge point of the effluent released by GIDC, indicated some tidal influence during the spring only and hence it is in the region of weak tidal action and will have little water for dilution during the dry season. Peak flood and ebb were strong (~150 cm/s) and did not vary from surface to bottom. The strength of the currents, however, decreased considerably during the neap period. Thus, any effluent discharged within the main part of the estuary will get well-mixed. Flow characteristics indicate progressively weaker flows during the dry season (April-June) when little water is available for dilution in the riverine zone. From July, the monsoonal flow begins. The site at which the industrial effluent is presently discharged, will have an appreciable tidal influence only during the spring tide. Flushing time calculated for the estuary was found to be nearly 3 days in February for the wastewater to reach large scale dilution and to pass through the mouth of the estuary. The wastewater, therefore, is not carried to the sea completely by each ebbing tide.

In the riverine region upstream, where the tidal action and salinity intrusion were minimal, the water was clear and transparent. Quality of water, where the effluent is discharged, deteriorates considerably after March as the DO decreases to about 1 mg/l. High acid content of the effluent lowers the *p*H of water. However, the wastewater discharged from the Selvas industrial estate does not affect the water quality adversely. Any further expansion would require careful examination against the background information presented here because the wastes will remain accumulated at the Vapi weir of the river. The effluent is presently discharged in the region of weak tidal zone and it deteriorates the water quality considerably during the dry season. It is, therefore, suggested that the effluent should be discharged in the estuarine zone nearer to the mouth of the estuary so that it is easily washed into the sea during the ebb tide (Zingde *et al.,* 1980b).

References

1. Bhosle, N.B., Rokade, M.A. & Zingde, M.D., 1985a. Short term variations in particulate matter in Mahi River Estuary. *Mahasagar — Bulletin of National Institute of Oceanography*, Vol. 18, pp. 449-455.
2. Bhosle, N.B., Rokade, M.A. & Zingde, M.D., 1985b. Total dissolved carbohydrate in Mahi River Estuary. *Mahasagar — Bulletin of National Institute of Oceanography*, Vol. 18, pp. 507-509.
3. Borole, D.V., Sarin, M.M. & Somayajulu, B.L.K., 1982. Composition of Narbada and Tapti estuarine particles and adjacent Arabian Sea sediments. *Indian Journal of Marine Sciences*, Vol. 11, pp. 51-62.
4. Burton, J.D., 1976. Basic properties and processes in estuarine chemistry. In: *Estuarine Chemistry* (eds.) J.D. Burton & P.S. Liss, Academic Press, London, pp. 1-31.
5. Dyer, K.R., 1973. *Estuaries: a physical introduction*. John Wiley, London, 140 pp.
6. Gajbhiye, S.N., Ram, J., Nair, V.R. & Desai, B.N. 1981. Plankton of the Narmada Estuary and adjacent creeks. *Mahasagar — Bulletin of National Institute of Oceanography*, Vol. 14, pp. 23-31.
7. Narvekar, P.V., Zingde, M.D. & Dalal, V.N.K., 1981. Behaviour of boron, calcium and magnesium in Mindhola River Estuary (Gujarat). *Indian Journal of Marine Sciences*, Vol. 10, pp. 90-92.
8. Narvekar, P.V., Zingde, M.D. & Dalal, V.N.K., 1983. Behaviour of boron, calcium and magnesium in polluted estuary. *Estuarine, Coastal and Shelf Sciences*, Vol. 16, pp. 9-16.
9. Narvekar, P.V. & Zingde, M.D., 1987. Behaviour of boron, calcium and magnesium in Purna and Auranga Estuaries (Gujarat) west coast of India. *Indian Journal of Marine Sciences*, Vol. 16, pp. 46-50.
10. NIO, 1980. *Pollution and hydrographic survey of Auranga, Ambika, Purna and Mindhola Rivers (south Gujarat)*. Technical Report, National Institute of Oceanography, Goa.
11. NIO, 1982. *Studies on wastewater disposal in Mahi Estuary*. Technical Report, National Institute of Oceanography, Goa.
12. NIO, 1985. *Oceanographic studies of Tapi Estuary for wastewater disposal from a fertilizer plant*. Technical Report, National Institute of Oceanography, Goa.
13. Ragothaman, G. & Patil, T.S., 1995. Studies on the physico-chemical parameters and phytoplankton of Narmada Estuary. *Pollution Research*, Vol. 14, pp. 221-226.
14. Ram, M.J., 1991. Algae and water pollution in Mahi Estuary. *Journal of Indian Fisheries Association*, Vol. 21, pp. 31-37.
15. Sharma, P. & Zingde, M.D., 1995. Behaviour of aluminium, silicon and iron in Tapi Estuary. In: *Complex Carbohydrate and Advances in Biosciences*, (eds.) V.P. Agarwal, C.B. Sharma, S.A.H. Abidi & M.D. Zingde, Society of Biosciences, Muzaffarnagar, India, pp. 581-606.
16. Zingde, M.D., Sarma, R.V. & Desai, B.N., 1979. Pollution in river Par and its abatement. *Indian Journal of Marine Sciences*, Vol. 8, pp. 266-270.
17. Zingde, M.D. Sabnis, M.M., Mandalia, A.V. & Desai, B.N., 1980a. Effects of industrial waste disposal on the water quality of river Kolak. *Mahasagar — Bulletin of National Institute of Oceanography*, Vol. 13, pp. 99-110.

18. Zingde, M.D., Narvekar, P.V., Sarma, R.V. & Desai, B.N., 1980b. Water quality of the river Damanganga (Gujarat). *Indian Journal of Marine Sciences*, Vol. 9, pp. 94-99.
19. Zingde, M.D., Chander, S., Rokade, M.A. & Desai, B.N., 1981. Base-line water quality of the river Narmada (Gujarat). *Indian Journal of Marine Sciences*, Vol. 10, pp. 161-164.
20. Zingde, M.D., Sharma P. & Sabnis, M.M. 1985. Physico-chemical investigations in Auranga River Estuary. *Mahasagar — Bulletin of National Institute of Oceanography*, Vol. 18, pp. 307-321.
21. Zingde, M.D., Narvekar, P.V., Sharma, P. & Sabnis, M.M., 1986. Environmental studies of the Ambika and associated river estuaries. *Marine Pollution Bulletin*, Vol. 17. pp. 267-274.
22. Zingde, M.D. & Desai, B.N., 1987. Pollution of estuaries of Gujarat — an overview. In: Contribution in Marine Science. Sastyabdaporthi Felicitation Volume on 60th Birthday of Dr. S. Z. Qasim. Published by National Institute of Oceanography, Goa, pp. 245-267.
23. Zingde, M.D. Mandalia, A.V. & Rokade, M.A., 1987a. Estuarine characteristics and pollution assessment of Purna River Estuary. *Indian Journal of Marine Sciences*, Vol. 16, pp. 94-98.
24. Zingde, M.D. Mandalia, A.V. & Rokade, M.A., 1987b. Flushing characteristics and pollution assessment of Purna River Estuary. *Indian Journal of Marine Sciences*, Vol. 16, pp. 94-98.
25. Zingde, M.D. Rokade, A.V. & Mandalia, M.A., 1988. Heavy metals in Mindhola River Estuary, India. *Marine Pollution Bulletin*, Vol. 19, pp. 538-540.
26. Zingde, M.D. & Mandalia, A.V., 1988. Study of fluroide in polluted and unpolluted estuarine environments. *Estuarine, Coastal and Shelf Sciences*, Vol. 27, pp. 707-712.
27. Zingde, M.D., Rokade, M.A., Sharma, P., Mandalia, A.V. & Desai, B.N., 1988. Pollution assessment and flushing characteristics of Mindhola River Estuary. In: *Threatened Habitats* (eds.) V.P. Agarwal & L. D. Chaturvedi, Published by Society of Biosciences, Muzaffarnagar, pp. 225-239.

Conclusion

The foregoing account on Indian Estuaries in this book indicates that there is hardly an estuary in the country which can be said to be free from man-made activities and changes such as being receptacle for domestic and organic wastes, industrial effluents (largely non-organic) including mining wastes, from reclamation, coastal structures, harbour development, fisheries and recreation. In shallow backwaters, natural deposition of sediments is creating new areas of land for the cultivation of rice and other agricultural products and thus enlarging the land acreage. Attempts have also been made to stop salinity incursion in silted lakes by putting barrages at shortest spans to convert the saline areas into freshwater wetlands to be used for paddy cultivation. Some such efforts have been successful while in others ecological changes have brought about unforeseen damages. Whatever may be the subsequent use of the reclaimed land, one cannot deny that a great deal of estuarine areas is lost in this manner every year.

In recent years, there has been a movement in the country to protect and conserve all types of wetlands, and despite the various attempts to control pollution, there has hardly been any improvement in the quality of estuarine environment. On the other hand, in many cases, as time passes, these are deteriorating further.

In the industrial areas, one of the most important variables affecting the fauna and flora is the levels of dissolved oxygen. In the dry season, when the freshwater flow decreases and the temperature of water increases, and if the volume of effluent discharged into the estuary remains unchanged, with a low flushing rate, even small quantities of organic matter increase the microbial load leading to the consumption of whatever oxygen remains in the water.

The most important factor leading to the degradation of coastal and estuarine areas in India has been the rapid growth of human population and increased human settlement around the estuaries. This alone has modified the natural habitats including the mangrove forests, salt marshes, coral reefs and mudflats to a considerable degree. Lack of proper waste disposal facilities and dependence of the population on resources of the environment such as timber, corals and their associated animals (wherever they occur) as curios and exploitation of fish, crustaceans and molluscs as food, impose considerable stress on the environment. The Mumbai city alone, with a human population density of $25000/km^2$ generates about $2.2 \times 10^6 m^3$/day of domestic waste. Much of this waste enters the bays and creeks including the harbour area. Depletion of mangroves in the country, at the rate of several thousand hectares per year, for their use as firewood and for the woodchip industry and their conversion as aquaculture farms is shrinking the estuarine environment rapidly. Mangroves of the Gangetic Sunderbans, estuarine areas of Cauvery, Godavari and of the Gujarat regions have degraded considerably during the last few decades. Similarly, the fringing coral reefs with patches of live corals in the Gulf of Kachchh (Kutch), which mark the northernmost limit of the distribution of corals in the Indian Ocean, have been destroyed by the mining of coralline sand and by siltation coming from the denuded mangrove swamps (Zingde, 1999).

Besides some of the destructive human activities noted above, industries, for example, located in the Mumbai city alone, release effluents of the volume of about $2.3 \times 10^5 m^3$/day, which largely go into the various estuarine bays and creeks of Mumbai. Table C1 shows the collective load of contaminants entering the coastal waters of Mumbai. The estuarine areas from where the contaminants flow frequently, record abnormally high and tide-dependent values of PO_4-P, NO_3-N and NH_4-N, in fluctuating dissolved oxygen, often going down to zero at low tides with abnormally high microbial density. Fortunately, with a tidal range of about 4-5 m, good flushing occurs in the estuaries of Mumbai and Gujarat regions.

Table C1— Selected contaminants entering coastal waters of Mumbai through domestic wastewater (From Zingde, 1999)

Contaminant	Average concentration (mg/l)	Load kg/day
Dissolved solids	1800	3.6×10^6
SPM	235	4.7×10^5
BOD	280	5.6×10^5
Nitrogen	35	7×10^4
Phosphorus	6	1.2×10^4
Manganese	0.7	1400
Iron	2.1	4100
Cobalt	0.03	20
Nickel	0.08	160
Copper	0.10	200
Zinc	2.3	4600
Lead	0.05	100

Environmental degradation of varying degrees is found from severe, as in Mumbai estuaries, to less severe as in Bombay Harbour, Mahi, Mindhola, Narmada, Tapi, Purna, Par, Ambika, Auranga, Kolak, Damanganga estuaries. Other regions of the west coast such as Cochin Backwaters and Ashtamudi estuaries are just as much affected by the industrial wastes. Perhaps the Kali and the Mandovi-Zuari estuarine system are the least affected water bodies in this respect on the west coast, because of the lack of industrialization at Karwar and in Goa, except for the Zuari Agro Chemicals Ltd., in Goa producing urea and which releases substantial quantities of nitrogenous wastes directly into the sea. However, both the Goa estuaries are seriously affected by the mining waste which is destroying the once-flourishing clam and oyster fisheries.

On the east coast of India, almost all the estuaries get some kinds of contamination with considerable load of solid and liquid wastes going from the Chennai city into the Adyar, Cooum and Ennore estuaries. Godavari and Cauvery estuaries are moderately polluted with sewage and industrial wastes. Hooghly gets a heavy load of both types of waste. Of all the estuaries described in this book, probably the Vellar Estuary is the least polluted along the east coast.

Several measures for the protection of coastal waters and conservation of their resources have been taken up by the Government of India from time to time. The important ones are:

(a) Coastal Regulation Zone (CRZ) notified by the Government of India in 1991 and amended in 1997: Under this notification, development activities in the intertidal areas up to a specified distance inland from the highest tide level are not permitted and development of any kind, including tourism, in ecologically sensitive areas such as mangroves and coral reefs, is strictly regulated.

In a nutshell, it suggests that any grant of relaxation in delineating the CRZ categories in the backwaters, creeks, estuaries or other sensitive ecosystems, should not be permitted. Moreover, any fish processing plant, which adds fish wastes to the marine ecosystem, should not be sanctioned within the CRZ. In fact, this zone should be treated as a public-trust area, allowing only customary rights of coastal communities such as taking up of natural fishing. The CRZ also regulates all developmental activities in areas that are ecologically sensitive such as national parks, sanctuaries, mangroves, coral reefs, etc.

(b) Similarly, the Environment Protection Act of 1986 prohibits and restricts the location of industries and defines the maximum allowable limits of the concentration of various environmental pollutants including noise in an area. Taking into consideration the topographic and climatic features, the Act says that the biological diversity of an area must be preserved.

(c) Another notification on Environment Impact Assessment of Development Projects of 1994 lays down the following procedure and conditions for the submission and clearance of the projects:

Any person who desires to undertake any new project or the expansion or modernisation of any existing industry or project shall submit to the Secretary, Ministry of Environment and Forests, New Delhi an application on a proforma specified for the purpose. The project report which shall *inter alia* include an Environment Management Plan and details of public hearing as specified in the schedule should be prepared in accordance with the guidelines issued by the Central Government. The reports submitted with the application shall be evaluated and assessed by the Impact Assessment Agency, and if deemed necessary, it may consult a Committee of Experts. The Committee shall have full right of entry and inspection of the sites or as the case may be, factory premises at any time prior to, during or after the commencement of operations relating to the project.

(d) Another notification of the Ministry of Environment and Forests issued in 1991 and amended in 1999, is specific to Dahanu Taluka, District Thane of

Mumbai which has been declared as an ecologically fragile area. It says that the Central Government, in consultation with the Government of Maharashtra, after considering the need for protecting the ecologically fragile area has imposed restriction on the setting up of industries which have detrimental effects on the environment.

The seriousness of the issues involved in implementing these notifications, and particularly the CRZ, varies from region to region in the country. Some state governments and union territories have begun to address them cautiously while others have paid little attention to them. The result is that the notifications have arrested the trends to pollution going into the estuaries, only marginally.

Estuaries practically throughout the world, despite the various rules and regulations enunciated from time to time for their protection and conservation, have been degrading progressively. The question often asked is "Whether their restoration is possible" For giving an answer, one has to find an example where an estuary after a great deal of degradation over a period of a century or more has been restored almost to its original quality. The answer lies in the Thames Estuary with the city of London along its shores. Its revival from a severely deteriorated condition, almost devoid of fish life in the mid 1950s to its conditions in the mid 1970s with the return of more than 80 species of fish including salmon to the river is one of the success stories of man in estuarine restoration. A brief history of this undertaking is worth noting.

In 1858, the odours emanating from the river Thames in the hot wheather of June, when the flow of the river became low, were so strong that the proceedings in the committee rooms of the British Parliament in London had to be adjourned and it has come to be known as "Great Stink of 1858". Soon afterwards, construction of London's sewers began which was completed in 1865 at a cost of 4.1 million pounds (probably equivalent to several billion dollars of today's cost). Treatment of sewage began in 1989. Sewage treatment and sludge digestion processes were upgraded and regional facilities during the first half of the 20th century were created and constructed. Even then there was no improvement in the water quality of the river Thames. With the increase in population of London City and more sewage discharge, there was a further deterioration near the outfall locations. Use of widespread synthetic detergents in the mid-fifties created more problems. A tidal mixing model was developed which gave a prediction to the water quality with different volumes of pollutants. Many other control measures improved the water quality in the mid-sixties with complete freedom from odour. Dissolved oxygen was increased to 10 per cent saturation or even higher throughout the river (see Gross, 1976).

To achieve the above results, the following four factors were considered important:

(a) An understanding of the behaviour of the estuary which permitted predictions about future conditions with increasing load of pollution.
(b) Accomplishments of well-defined goals of at least 10 per cent saturation of dissolved oxygen throughout the river.
(c) A large outlay of financial investment and its progressive utilisation to achieve the goals.
(d) A political will of the country to overcome difficulties.

In a recent paper of Zingde (1999), the magnitude of pollution problems in the coastal zone including estuaries and open ocean have been highlighted in various zones. Wastes coming from different sources resulting in an increase of nutrients and pathogens, industrial contaminations including heavy metals, chloroinated hydrocarbons [DDT and its metabolites, HCH, aldrin, polychlorinated biphenyls (PCB) and polynuclear aromatic hydrocarbons (PAH_s), etc.] have been described. It also indicates the amount of oil pollution that exists in the Arabian Sea and Bay of Bengal annually. It is of the order of 5×10^6 and 4×10^5 tonnes per annum in the two seas respectively. This is due to routine discharge of ballast waters, bilge and tank washings from the oil tankers coming from Gulf countries and carrying cargoes of hydrocarbons to different parts of the world. Shipping lanes in the Arabian Sea are the only routes for large tankers to ply carrying oil through the Indian Ocean. This often has resulted in accidents and oil spills in different parts of the two seas.

We have not yet decided what levels of environmental degradation in estuaries are inevitable and to what extent deforestation of mangroves should be allowed because in the latter case people inhabiting the estuarine fringes will have to obtain their basic needs for energy from the forest. We must also strike a balance between the benefits of a new harbour or the expansion of the existing one against a potential threat to estuarine fisheries or tourism. Similar judgements are required in building an industrial complex and the destruction of an unique natural ecosystem and the energy and food demands of people living in that area. These are complex issues stretching our wisdom and decision-making processes to the maximum. In the case of an industrial complex, a decision to go ahead with the project, based on our economic needs, must pay for additional cost of pollution control.

Today, the harvest of fish from the estuaries of India amounts to several thousand tonnes per annum and estuarine fishery is the mainstay during monsoon season when fishing in the sea, because of turbulent conditions and stormy weather, gets suspended. Therefore, the cumulative economic gains by preserving a natural ecosystem are just as important as the technological advancement which may spell out its destruction.

The risk to the society as a whole due to destruction of an environment from development project is an exceedingly complex issue. A wide range of possible deleterious consequences of man, animals, plants, microorganisms and even to historical buildings and monuments are to be studied and resolved. One has to look for any probability of immediate and long-term consequences from man-made changes in air, land and water quality. One must foresee the long term changes as a result of imperceptible, insidious leaching of harzardous substances and their cumulative effect on the environment. These are usually associated with ill-health and birth abnormalities. Therefore, to make an objective assessment of the future risks, we need a lot more information, than what we have at present. When adequate direct or indirect information is available from the past or from related experiences elsewhere, risk assessment cannot always be precise, but it rather involves a value judgement.

At this juncture, researches in socio-psychology become important. Social psych-logists believe that the reaction to risk is normally multifarious in which magnitude of seriousness is only one factor, and this need not necessarily be the predominant one. For instance, in order to produce more food for the people, society must ignore the long-term environmental risks associated with the use of pesticides, agrochemicals, monoculture, hybrid vigour and irradiation. Owing to our guilt complexes, we are more worried about the risk to the community than to the individuals or to a very small section of the society. Consequently, public furore about the environmental impact of nuclear power plants, large dams, industrial complexes and so on is very strong. Risk assessment, when scientifically made and understood, can give to the society a choice and an opportunity to save the environment (see Qasim & Ramanathan, 1981).

References

1. Gross, M.G., 1986. Estuarine cleanup – can it work? In: *Estuarine Processes*, Vol. 1, (ed.) M. Wiley, pp. 3-14, Academic Press, New York, 541 pp.
2. Qasim, S.Z., & Ramanathan, N. L., 1981. Science, society and the environment. *Society and Science*, Vol. 4, pp. 86-90.
3. Zingde, M.D., 1999. Marine pollution – what are we heading for? In: *Ocean Science – Trends and Future Directions* (ed.) B.L. Somayajulu, pp. 229-245. Indian National Science Academy & Akademia Books International, New Delhi.

Subject Index

A

Aanderaa current meters, 74
Abyssal plain, 75
Acanthus ilicifolius, 42, 70
Acartia bilobata, 236
Acartia bowmani, 236, 298
Acartia centrura, 236, 298
Acartia erythraca, 79, 298
Acartia gravelyi, 231
Acartia pacifica, 236, 298
Acartia plumosa, 236
Acartia southwelli, 23, 298
Acartia sp., 159, 230, 299
Acartia spinicauda, 235, 298
Acartia tropics, 298
Acarticidae, 232
Acartiella gravelyi, 236
Acartiella keralensis, 236, 296
Acetes indicus, 46
Achankoil, 203
Achnanthes stomii, 115
Acrocalanus monachus, 231
Acrocalanus sp., 195
Acrophialophora, 40
Actinarians, 38
Adyar Estuary, 11, 100, 101, 104, 114-121
Adyar River, 105
Aegiceras corniculatum, 70
Aegiceras majus, 42
African Payal, 208-209, 238
Agrochemicals
Aguada Bay, 279, 286, 287
Alangankulam, 3
Alderina arabianesis, 235
Aldrin, 387
Alepes djeddaba, 150
Algae, 198, 224, 250, 289-293, 295, 304-305
Alkaline phosphatase activity, 301
Alkaline wastewater, 50, 244
Alkalinity, 30, 106, 244
Alleppey, 201, 250
Allodiaptomus sp., 236

Alpheus malabaricus, 153, 159
Aluminium, 357
Amadi, 44
Amba Estuary, 336-343
Ambassis gymnocephalus, 244
Ambassis sp., 150, 151, 240
Ambika, 345, 348, 365-367
Ammonia, 98, 137, 138, 160, 162, 310
Ammonia-nitrogen, 35, 109, 111
Amphioxus sp., 295
Amphipods, 36, 62, 81, 82, 86, 155, 194, 195, 197, 230-232, 234, 237, 238, 242, 251, 270, 295, 296
Amphiprora gigantea, 108
Amphora coffeaeformis, 115
Amphora lineolata, 139
Amphora proteus, 108
Anabaena, 144, 352
Anabaenopsis, 144
Anadara grenosa, 153
Anadara rhombea, 157
Anadontostoma chacunda, 150
Anchovilla commersonii, 86
Ancistrosyllis constricta, 153
Anemones, 153
Animals, 6
Anoxic conditions, 73
Anthron hispidus, 152
Aphanocapsa, 144
Apollo Bundar, 319, 321, 326, 336
Appendicularians, 62
Apseudes killaiyenesis, 153
Apseudes chilkensis, 242
Apseudes gymnophobia, 153, 242
Apseudes sp., 231
Arathron hispidus, 150
Arca granosa, 160
Arca inaequivalvis, 160
Archidiaptomus sp., 236
Arikamedu, 3
Arius, 157
Arothron hispidus, 151
Aryyankuppam, 3
Ashtamudi Estuary, 11, 189-199
Aspergillus, 40, 76
Asphyxiation, 244
Asterionella glacialis, 61
Asterionella japonica, 76, 98, 108, 109, 115, 139, 224, 267
Auranga, 345, 348, 368-370
Avicennia alba, 42, 304
Avicennia marina, 41
Avicennia officinalis, 70
Axiotella sp., 153
Azhikode, 201, 244

B

Babylon, 3
Bacillaria paradoxa, 76, 139
Bacillarophyceae, 31, 75, 267
Back Bay, 320
Backwaters, 6, 144, 154, 201-204
Backwaters of Kerala, 201-247
Bacterial decomposition of the organic matter, 160-162
Bacteriastrum hyalinum, 139
Bacteriastrum varians, 139
Bagirathi, 27
Balanus amphitrite, 85
Balanus amphitrite communis, 155, 198
Balanus pallidus, 155
Balanus variegatus, 155
Bagnet fishery, 46
Balusutippa, 68, 69
Bar-built estuaries, 3, 5, 7, 126, 204
Barnacles, 85-86, 198, 230

Basalt, 356
Bassein Creek, 318
Bellerochea malleus, 139
Benthic animals, 8
Benthic biomass, 237-239, 302-303
Benthic fauna, 49, 82, 84-85, 152-155, 156, 195-197, 245, 268-270
Benthic macrofauna, 38
Benthos, 237-239
Bestiola similis, 236
Bhabha Atomic Research Centre, 331
Bhogava, 1
Bicarbonate (HOC_3), 72, 174
Biddulphia mobiliensis, 98, 108
Biddulphia sinensis, 139, 229
Bioassay tests, 112, 121
Biochemical oxygen demand (BOD), 47-49, 243, 244, 320, 323, 333, 335, 354, 363, 366, 367, 377
Biofouling, 85-86, 198
Biomass, 8, 82, 268-269, 295, 304
Biomass density, 8, 268-269
Biotope, 144, 197
Birds sanctuary, 332
Bivalves, 38, 49, 82, 153, 155, 160, 195, 197, 235, 237, 238, 251, 267, 269, 301-302, 306
Bivalve-species (clams)
Bivalvia, 270
Black clam, 253, 255-256
Black sand, 75
Blackfordia virginica, 236
Bluegreen algae, 31, 61, 129, 138, 144, 145-148, 223, 250, 290, 355
Boat sienes, 272
Bombay (recently renamed Mumbai), 206, 318
Bombay duck, 46
Bombay Harbour, 318, 319, 326-330, 337, 338, 340-342
Boron, 74, 361, 364, 367
Boron-chloronity ratio, 331
Bosminopsis sp., 251
Bothus myriaster, 151
Bottom fauna, 152, 251-253, 302-304
Bottom sediments, 64-65, 75, 129
Bottom salinity, 131
Bottom temperatures, 130, 132
Bottom water, 130, 132, 144
Brachyuran crabs, 40, 302
Brackishwater, 6, 10, 35, 62, 306
Brahmaputra, 27
Branchionus plicatilis, 116
Branchionus rubens, 116
Bruguiera gymnorhiza, 42, 70
Bryozoans, 85, 86, 198, 232, 235, 303
Buckingham Canal, 103, 105, 107, 112-113, 120
Bullia melanoides, 235

C

Cadmium, 97
Calanoida, 36, 62, 233, 297
Calcium carbide, 361
Calcium value, 60, 72, 364, 367
Calibanarius longitarsus, 159
Callionymus sp., 150
Caloglossa leprieurii, 304
Campylodiscus iyengarii, 139
Candida tropicalis, 160
Canthocalanus pauper, 231
Capitella capitala, 246
Capitellid, 153
Carangoides malabaricus, 150

Carbohydrate, 129, 293
Carbon assimilation, 73, 215, 219, 293
Carbon assimilation to chlorophyll *a* ratio, 215, 216
Carnivores, 8, 232-234
^{14}C assimilation, 213, 226, 293, 294
Catfishes, 10, 305
Cauvery (Kaveri) Estuary, 11, 168-178
Cauvery Estuarine Delta, 168-170
Cauvery River, 3, 123, 177
Cauvery River water dispute, 177-178
Cell counts, 32, 223-224, 227
Centre of Advanced Study, 123
Centropages alcocki, 236
Centropages dorsispinatus, 79
Centropages sp., 195, 231
Cephalochordata, 295
Cephalosporium, 40
Ceratium, 224
Ceratium furca, 61, 98, 223, 229, 267, 290, 293
Ceratium fusus, 76, 267
Ceratium lineatum, 61
Ceratium tripos, 138
Ceratoneries costae, 153
Ceriodaphnia sp., 251
Ceriops decandra, 70
Ceriops roxburghiana, 42
Cerithidea (Cerithideopsilla) fluviatilis, 153
Cerithidea cingulata, 38
Chactoceros lorenziamus, 76
Chaetoceros, 138-140, 223
Chaetoceros didymum, 139, 140
Chaetoceros lauderi, 76, 139, 140
Chaetoceros affinis, 139, 140
Chaetoceros crinitum, 76
Chaetoceros gracile, 76
Chaetoceros laciniosus, 76
Chaetoceros perpusilla, 108
Chaetoceros wighami, 108, 109
Chaetoessus chaneda, 103
Chaetognaths, 8, 36, 62, 77-79, 194, 231, 232, 234, 236, 267, 295, 296, 300
Chanos chanos, 64, 151
Chanos fry, 64
Chermaguri Creek, 42
Cherrapunji, 19
Chinese dipnet, 240
Chiramenu fluviatilis, 87
Chloride (Cl), 72
Chlorinity, 33, 35, 74
Chlorite, 111, 137, 171, 174, 175, 177
Chlorosity concentration, 137
Chlorophyceae, 31, 75, 223
Chlorophyll, 33, 73, 99-100, 138, 143, 212, 215, 223, 226, 227, 250, 268, 293, 309, 355
Chrysophris suba, 103
Chuksar Island, 38
Churni, 27
Ciralonidae, 303
Cirripede larvae, 232, 295, 303
Cladocerans, 36, 62, 108, 116, 194, 231, 232, 295, 296, 298
Cladosporium, 40
Clam bed, 255
Clams, 10, 157, 158, 197, 209, 251, 255-256, 269, 302-303
Clay minerals, 74, 171, 195
Clayey sand, 40-41, 248-249
Clayey silt, 75, 248-249
Clerodendron inerme, 70
Clibanarius carpes, 156
Clibanarius olivaceus, 153, 156
Clibanarius padavensus, 156
Clibanarius longitarsus, 153, 156

Clorophyll, 129
Clupeidae
Clupeoids, 10, 240
Coarse sand, 170, 171, 192
Coastal plain estuaries, 3, 5, 6
Coastal Regulation Zone (CRZ), 384-386
Coastal waters, 73
Cochin Backwaters, 11, 189, 190, 201-247
Cochin Harbour, 201, 202, 206, 210
Cochin Port, 205-296
Coconut palms, 203
Coelenterates, 38, 77,78, 79, 80, 85, 270
Coelophaerium, 250
Coenobila cavipes, 156
Coilia borneenis, 44
Colaba, 320
Cold waves, 20
Coleoptera, 38
Coleroon Estuary, 123, 124, 168
Community respiration, 33
Continental Shelves, 75
Cool season (winter), 19-20, 183
Cooum Estuary, 11, 104-113
Copelata, 296
Copepods, 36-38, 62, 77-79, 81, 108, 116, 194-195, 230-232, 234, 236, 250-251, 267, 295-298, 340, 342
Copper, 97, 159
Corals, 383
Corethron hystrix, 139
Coringa, 67-69
Coriolis Effect, 183
Corophium trienonyx, 230, 234
Coscinodiscus, 138-139, 142, 223
Coscinodiscus concinnus, 139, 142
Coscinodiscus centralis, 76
Coscinodiscus excentricus, 33, 139, 142
Coscinodiscus llineatus, 108, 109
Coscinodiscus marginatus, 76, 139, 142
Coscinodiscus radiatus, 33
Coscinodiscus wighami, 108
Cossura delta, 153
Crabs, 10, 40, 43, 102, 116, 154-158, 197, 238, 268, 270, 364
Crassostrea gryphoides, 306
Crassostrea madrasensis, 86, 157, 198
Crassostrea sp., 211
Creseis acicula, 79
Cretaceous Period, 170
Cruantus dealmeida, 86
Cruantus smithi, 86, 87
Crustaceans, 10, 36, 62, 77-79, 81, 84, 108, 116, 153, 194, 195, 197, 235, 238, 250-251, 267, 295, 296, 298, 302-303
Ctenophores, 8, 62, 79, 80, 231, 234, 295, 296
Culicoides oxystoma, 38
Culicoides pelilioensis, 38
Cumaceans, 36, 62, 82, 155, 195, 231, 232, 270, 295
Cumbarjua Canal, 278, 279, 282, 285, 290, 293, 297, 298, 304-310
Cumulative flushing, 244
Currents, 338, 366, 368, 369, 372, 373, 379
Curvularia, 40
Cyanophyceae, 31
Cyclones, 20, 21, 131, 184-185
Cylones/severe cyclones, 21
Cyclopoid copepods, 36, 62
Cyclopoids, 36, 62, 79, 232

Cyclops, 195
Cyclotella meneghiniana, 76, 115
Cyclotella striata, 139
Cymbella marina, 139
Cynobacteria, 309
Cynoglossidae, 240
Cynoglossus brevis, 240
Cynoglossus cynoglossus, 240
Cynoglossus lida, 240
Cynoglossus puncticeps, 150, 151, 158, 240
Cyprids, 230

D

Dadar, 320
Dalbergia spinosa, 70
Damanganga, 345, 348, 376, 378-379
Damanganga River, 366, 378-379
Dayella malabaricus, 240, 255
Daysciaena albida, 256
DDT, 97, 159, 387
Decapod larvae, 77-79, 194, 232, 295
Decapods, 38, 82, 86, 155, 195, 230-231
Decapterus russelli, 150
Demersal fishes, 305
Dendronereis arborifera, 81
Deposit feeders, 40
Derris trifoliata, 70
Desmids, 223, 224
Destephamis micans, 223
Destephamis speculum, 223
Detritus, 8-9, 222-223, 301
Development Corporation (MIDC)
Dhabar, 345
Dharamtar, 336, 338
Dharamtar Creek, 338
Dharavi, 320
Diamond Harbour, 27-32
Diaphanosama sp., 195
Diaptomus sp., 195
Diatoms, 31, 32, 60, 107-109, 115, 129, 138, 139, 143, 194, 212, 223, 290-293, 355
Dictyocha fibula, 108, 223
Diffusion coefficient, 72
Dinobryon sp., 76
Dinoflagellates, 31, 61, 138, 142, 143, 194, 212, 223, 290-293
Dinophyceae, 31, 75, 143, 267
Dinophysis miles, 228
Diogenes avarus, 156, 268
Diopatra, 195
Diopatra neapolitana, 237, 251
Diploneis smithii, 139
Dissolved organic carbon, 74
Dissolved Organic Nitrogen (DON), 137, 138
Dissolved oxygen, 57, 58, 72-73, 74, 97, 101, 106, 114, 116, 129, 132, 192, 286-287, 322-323, 328-329, 334-335, 354, 363, 366, 367, 369, 377, 379, 383, 387
Dissolved silicon, 137, 174, 177
Distephanus speculus, 76
Ditylum brightwellii, 76, 139
Diurnal fluctuations, 61, 71-72, 139, 333
Diversity index, 32, 50
Dolliloides, 62
Domestic wastewater, 10, 114, 320, 321, 333, 366, 384
Donax cuneatus, 160
Donax sp., 197
Donax faba, 302
Donax incarnatus, 235, 306
Donax spiculum, 65, 235

Dotilla Beach, 155
Dotilla myctiroides, 155, 302
Dreschslera, 76, 77
Drowned river valleys, 7
Dust storms, 20

E

Ebb tide, 61, 72, 79, 102, 103, 125, 129, 279, 285, 321, 369, 377
Ebb velocity, 102, 321
Echinoderms, 267
Echiuroids, 82, 303
Eels, 38
Effluents, 244, 245, 347, 371-372, 377
Ehirava fluviatilis, 240, 255, 256
Eirene ceylonensis, 236
Elamenopsis demeloi, 268
Electra bengalensis, 235
Electra crustulenta, 235
Eleutheronema tetradactylum, 43
Elops sp., 151
Emakulam channel, 210-211
Embankment, 1-2
Emerita holthuisi, 235
Endosulfan, 97, 159
Engineering works, 209-211
Engraulis purava, 103
Ennore Estuary, 11, 95-104
Ennore River, 95, 114
Ennore Spout, 96
Enteromorpha compressa, 61
Environment Protection Act, 385
Environment Protection Measures, 384-386
Environmental degradation, 382-388
Environmental notifications, 384-386
Eocuma sp., 231
Epistrate feeders, 40
Equnea sp., 103
Eriopisa chilkensis, 153, 242
Escherichia coli, 239
Esculosa, thoracata, 151
Estuarine beaches, 155
Estuarine ecosystems, 7, 229, 230
Estuarine fisheries, 5, 388
Estuarine phytoplankton, 229
Estuarine sediments, 40-42
Etroplus maculatus, 256
Etroplus suratensis, 256, 307
Etroplus sp., 208
Euastrum, 223
Eucalanus crassus, 231
Eucalanus elongatus, 79
Eucampia zodiacus, 139
Euchaeta sp., 195
Euglena sp., 76, 77
Euglenoids, 31
Euglenophyceae, 31, 75
Eunicidae, 194
Euphausiaceae, 82
Euphausids, 62, 82
Euphotic zone, 212
Eurydice sp., 235
Euryhaline forms, 38, 115, 254
Euterpina sp., 195
Eutima commensalis, 236
Evadne sp., 195
Evadne tergestina, 231, 298
Excoecaria agallocha, 42, 70

F

Farakka Barrage, 35
Faunal group, 82
Fiddler crab, 155
Fish eggs and larvae, 150-152, 158, 194, 232, 240, 296

Fish mortality, 244
Fishery, 10, 38, 43-46, 64, 86-89, 102, 103, 157-160, 197, 198, 205-207, 209, 239-243, 255, 256, 270-273, 305-307, 388
Fishing crafts, 197, 198, 255, 271-273, 306
Fishing gears, 46, 47, 87-89, 158, 197, 198, 255, 271-273, 306
Fjords, 3, 5
Flagellates, 31
Flood tides, 125, 129, 285, 338, 369, 372
Fluorescein dye, 102, 103
Fluoride concentrations, 289, 359, 362
Fluoride-chlorinity relationship, 74, 289
Flushing time, 335, 336, 338-340, 362, 364, 369, 372, 377
Foam, 129
Food chain, 8, 9, 221, 222, 242, 243
Foraminiferan fauna, 79, 80, 194, 197, 235, 237, 253-255, 269, 270, 301
Formation of shoals (sand bars), 7
Fouling intensity, 198, 199
Fouling organisms, 85, 86, 158, 198
Fragilaria crotonensis, 351, 352
Fragilaria oceanica, 139, 290, 293
Freshwater discharge, 6, 7, 29, 72, 201, 244
Freshwater influx, 5, 280, 367
Freshwater runoff, 5, 30, 72
Freshwater zone, 7, 8, 31, 35, 125, 249
Fulvic acid, 41
Fumago, 76
Fungal parasites, 309
Fusarium, 40, 308

G

Gaderu, 67
Gammaridea, 82
Gammarids, 36, 234
Ganga River, 27, 35, 44
Ganges Estuary, 174
Ganges-Brahamputra Delta, 8
Gangetic-Basin, 27
Gangetic Sunderbans, 383
Garnet, 75
Gastropods, 38, 116, 153-156, 195, 237, 238, 270, 295
Gastrotrichs, 84, 195
Gautami-Godavari Estuary, 67, 68, 74, 81, 84
Geochemical studies, 74
Geochemistry, 171-178
Geological History, 170
Gerres filamentosus, 103
Gerres sp., 151
Ghatkopar, 320
Ghost crab, 155
Gill nets, 272
Gills, 102, 119, 120, 272
Glycera alba, 153, 235, 302
Glycinde sp., 153
Glycolic acid, 293, 294
Gobiod-fishes, 38
Gobius giuris, 65
Gobolds, 151
Godavari Basin, 69
Godavari Delta, 69, 70, 89
Godavari Estuary, 11, 67-89, 174
Godavari River, 67, 71, 75-77
Gonyaulax polyedra, 61
Grandidievella sp., 153, 231
Grassostrea cuculata, 49

Grease, 363
Great Stink of 1858, 386
Green algae, 37, 61, 355
Grey mullets, 120, 158, 307
Guinardia flaccida, 139
Gujarat Industrial Development Corporation (GIDC), 347, 350, 376
Gulf of Cambay, 1, 2, 11, 184, 345, 349, 354, 356
Gulf of Kachchh (Kutch), 184, 383
Gymnodinium, 224
Gyrosigma balticum, 139

H

Halacarida, 81
Haldia Channel, 27, 29, 50
Halicarnicus sp., 238
Halobates sp., 295
Hamicola, 40
Harappans, 1, 2, 13
Harmbari, 38
Harpacticoid copepod, 81, 297
Harpacticoida, 62, 81, 83, 84, 155, 197, 269, 270, 302, 304
Heavy metals, 97, 101, 102, 109-112, 117, 119, 120, 174, 198, 246, 247, 253, 359
Heliodiaptomus sinctua, 236
Hemiaulus sinensis, 139
Hemidiscus hardmannianus, 139
Hemirhamphus sp., 103
Heptachlor, 97
Herbivores, 219, 220, 221, 232, 233
Herpacticoids, 36
Hesionid, 153
Heteromastus similis, 153
Heterotrophic bacteria, 106, 162, 253
High tide, 129, 152
Hilsa, 255
Hilsa ilisha, 43, 44, 240, 255
Hilsa kelee, 150, 151
Holocene, 2
Holoplankters, 231, 232
Hooghly (Hugli), 11, 12, 27, 82-84
Hooghly Estuary, 27-50
Hooghly River Estuary, 8
Hooghly-Matlah Estuarine, 27, 38, 43
Horizontal halocline
Hot dry season, 183
Human wastes, 243, 383
Humic acid, 41
Hydrocarbons, 49, 89
Hydrogen sulphide (H_2S), 9, 74, 243
Hydrographic conditions, 7, 8, 114
Hydrographical features, 7, 125-155
Hydrography, 7, 8, 29, 30, 56-60, 71-75, 191, 192, 212, 213, 249, 250, 265, 266, 279-286, 347
Hydrography before the changes, 399
Hydroids, 198
Hydromedusae, 8, 36, 62, 79, 80, 194, 231, 234, 236, 295, 296
Hydrozoans, 82
Hyperia sp., 231
Hyporhamphus limbatus, 151

I

Idunella chilkensis, 153
Illite, 171, 195
Ilmenite, 75
Incra muiltsquamatus, 87
Indian Peninsular Shield, 67
Industrial alcohol, 206
Industrial wastewater, 10, 47-50, 73, 120, 238, 320, 323, 326, 333, 358, 359, 366, 367, 375, 379, 384

Inert material, 74
Influence of salinity
Inorganic nutrients, 73
Inorganic phosphate, 73, 216, 217
Insecticides, 10
Intertidal fauna, 38, 40, 80, 81, 155-157, 235-237, 301, 302, 362
Invertebrate larvae, 148, 149, 152, 296
Ipomoea tuba, 70
Iron (Fe), 109, 110
Isopod, 86, 153, 155, 195, 231, 232, 235, 236, 270
Ittupuzha, 249

J

Jalangi, 27
Jetty construction, 209

K

Kakinada, 67, 89
Kakinada Bay, 67, 69, 81, 85
Kakinada Lock, 89
Kal Baishakhi, 20
Kali Estuary, 11, 264-275
Kallada River, 189, 190, 191
Kalyan, 318
Kamboli, 349
Kaolinite, 171, 195
Karera, 345
Karwar, 270, 271, 273
Karwar Bay, 264
Katelysia opima, 153, 155, 158, 268
Katelysia sp., 197
Kaveri, 3, 168-178
Kaveri River, 168, 345, 365
Kaveripattinam, 3
Kerala Sastra Sahitya Parishat, 209
Keratella sp., 251
Khar, 320
Killai Backwater, 144
Kim, 345
Kinorhyncha, 81, 83-85
Kochi, 201
Kolak, 345, 348, 375-378
Korkai, 3
Krishna Estuary, 73, 74, 79, 81, 82-84, 174
Krishna River, 75-77
Krishna-Godavari Basin, 75, 89
Kuchchh region, 184
Kuttanad, 207-209, 255
Kynorhynchs, 155

L

Labidocera kroyere var gallensis, 231
Labidocera pectinata, 231, 236
Lamellibranchs, 83, 84, 116, 232
Land reclamation, 116
Land-runoff, 115, 133, 136, 322
Laoneme indica, 153
Lates calcarifer, 43, 103
Lead, 97, 110
Leaves, 268
Leiognathus, 157
Lepturacanthus savala, 150, 151
Leydgia sp., 195
Lieognathus, 240
Lime shell deposits, 251-253
Limestone, 251
Limnetic species, 251
Lindane, 97, 159
Liza macrolepis, 65, 102, 111, 112, 120, 121

Longitudinal eddy diffusion, 72
Lothal, 1, 2
Lucifers, 36, 62, 159, 231, 296
Lumbriconeries sp., 153
Luminous bacteria, 162
Lumnitzera racemosa, 70
Lyngbya, 144

M

Mackerel, 240
Macroalgae, 8
Macrobenthic fauna, 82-84, 152, 153, 238, 269, 270, 302, 303
Macrobrachium idella, 256
Macrobrachium sp., 208
Macrofauna, 82-85, 155, 235, 237, 238, 301
Macrones vittatus, 103
Macropthalmus (Venitus) latreilli, 155, 156
Macrosetella gracilis, 79
Macrozoobenthic fauna, 40
Madras Harbour, 95
Maera othonides, 242
Magnesium (Mg), 60, 72, 361, 364, 367
Mahanadi, 82-84
Mahi, 11, 345, 348, 349-353
Mahi River, 345, 349, 350
Mahim Bay, 318-320, 322, 323, 332
Mahim Creek, 321-324, 332, 334
Mahim Estuary, 320, 332-343
Mahim River, 320, 322, 332
Mandirtala, 38
Mandovi Estuary, 11, 277-311
Mandovi-Zuari System, 277-311
Mangifera indica, 85
Mangroves, 8, 9, 28, 40, 42, 69-71, 144-147, 154, 156, 170, 171, 203, 268, 304, 305, 383
Manimala, 203
Manori Creek, 318
Marine *Thiobacilli*, 160
Matlah, 27
Mattanchery Channel, 210, 211
Matuta victor, 153
Mawsynram, 19
Mean high water mark, 81
Mean low tide mark, 80, 81
Mean mid water mark, 80, 81
Mechanised fishing, 272, 273
Meenachil, 201, 203
Megalona cinta, 80
Megelona sp., 153
Meiobenthos, 82, 237, 269, 270, 304
Meiofauna, 40, 81, 83, 84, 155-157, 197, 251, 301, 304
Melosira granulata, 139
Melosira sp., 108, 109
Melosira sulcata, 98, 139, 160
Mercury content 64, 65, 199, 329, 330
Meresmopodia, 223
Meretrix casta, 153, 154, 197, 255, 269, 302, 305, 306
Meretrix meretrix, 153-155, 255
Meretrix sp., 209, 238
Meretrix ovum, 237
Meroplankters, 232-235
Merozooplankton, 295
Mesocyclops, 195
Mesopodopsis orientalis, 230
Mesozoic Era, 170
Metapenaeus affinis, 87, 89, 274, 301
Metapenaeus brevicornis, 45, 46, 87, 88

Metapenaeus dobsoni, 62, 87-89, 207, 231, 240-242, 256, 274, 307
Metapenaeus monoceros, 62, 65, 87-89, 230, 231, 240, 241, 274
Metapenaeus moyebi, 307
Metetix sp., 251
Microbes, 239, 309
Microbiology, 40, 160-162, 308
Micrococus sp., 160
Microplankton, 224, 226
Milk fish, 10, 45, 64
Mindhola, 345, 348, 358-362
Miramar Beach, 301
Modiolus metcalfei, 306
Modiolus sp., 197, 238
Mohammadpura, 349
Molluscan fishery, 79, 158, 255
Molluscan forms, 10
Molluscan larvae, 232
Molluscs, 10, 246
Monilia, 76
Monsoon depression, 20
Monsoonal flow, 8
Montmorillonite, 195
Moovattupuzha, 203
Mormugao Bay, 280
Mougetia, 250
Mudflat algae, 38, 116
Mudskippers, 362
Mudsnail, 81
Mugil cephalus, 46, 65, 103, 112, 121, 150, 307
Mugil dussumieri, 103
Mugil occur, 103
Mugil parsia, 45
Mugil tade, 45
Mullets, 10, 45, 46, 81, 102, 103, 151, 157, 158, 197, 198, 221, 307
Mumbra Creek, 320
Muraenesox cinerous, 151
Musculista sp., 197
Mussel seeds, 306
Mussels, 10, 198, 221, 306
Muvattupuzha, 201, 203, 204, 206, 249
Myriostychya wightiana, 70
Mysids, 36, 62, 194, 195, 230, 232, 270, 296
Mystus gulio, 65
Mytilis virdis, 306
Myxophyceae, 267

N

Nagothana, 336, 338
Namatode worm (unidentified), 153, 304
Nannoplankton production, 33, 139, 144, 224, 226, 290
Narmada (Narbada), 345, 348, 354, 355
Narmada Estuary, 174, 345
Nassa sp., 153
Natica macrochinensis, 153
National Institute of Oceanography (NIO), 347, 350
Nauplii, 155, 230
Navicula, 98
Navicula clavata, 139
Navicula cancellate, 108
Navicula halophila, 115
Navicula longa, 76, 139
Navigation, 210,286, 371
Neap tidal range, 336
Neelarevu, 67
Neendakara, 189, 198
Nematoda, 9,40, 81, 83, 84, 155, 194, 197, 237, 251, 269, 270

Nemertines, 38, 195, 303
Nephthys oligobranchia, 80
Nephthys polybranchia, 153
Nereidae, 194, 303
Nereis, 195
Nerine cirratulus, 302
Neritic organisms, 77
Neritic penetration, 127
Neritic pteropod, 79
Neritic waters, 80
Neritina Oualaniensis, 155
Nickel, 97, 110
Nitrate concentrations, 31, 134, 135, 137, 160, 162
Nitrate values, 50, 59-61, 97, 106-108, 288, 289
Nitrate-nitrogen (NO_3-N), 35, 59, 106, 107, 111, 136, 192, 193, 217, 218, 354
Nitrogen-phosphorus ratio, 136, 137, 147, 213, 218, 323, 329, 363, 364, 377
Nitzschia closterium, 115, 139, 152, 224, 293
Nitzschia longissima, 76, 77, 98
Nitzschia palea, 108, 152
Nitzschia seriata, 76, 77, 139, 267
Noctiluca miliaris, 138, 267
Nodularia, 144
Northeast monsoon, 20, 21, 30
Norwesters, 20
Nuculana sp., 238
Nudibranch, 153
Nutrients, 31, 33, 35, 41, 57, 61, 73, 114, 115, 129, 132-138, 174, 192, 194, 215-221, 229, 288, 289, 329, 335, 377

O

Ocypode ceratophthalma, 235
Ocypoda macrocera, 155
Ogyrides striaticauda, 231
Oikopleura, 77-79
Oil industry wastes, 10
Oil pollution, 331, 363, 387
Oil sardine, 240
Oithona sp., 195
Oligochaetes, 81
Oligohaline, 38
Omnivores, 40, 232, 233
Omobranchus bhattacharyae, 86
Omobranchus bipunctatus, 86
Omobranchus japonicus, 86, 87
Ophichthid, 151
Ophiuroids, 82
Opisthopterus tardoore, 150
Organic carbon, 138, 153, 195, 299, 300, 329, 330
Organic detritus, 8
Organic phosphorus, 301
Organic pollution, 35, 48, 49, 109, 198, 206, 239, 243, 244, 382
Oscillatoria, 61, 144, 152, 223
Ostracoblabe implexa, 308
Ostracods, 36, 62, 81, 83, 84, 153, 155, 195, 231, 232, 295, 304
Oxygen, 57, 58, 72-74, 97, 101, 106, 112, 266, 286, 288, 383
Oysters, 10, 86, 154, 155, 157, 198, 209, 221, 231

P

Paddy, 241
Palaemon sp., 231

Palaemon styliferus, 46
Palaemon tenuipes, 46
Palynological analysis, 170
Pama pama, 43
Pamba River, 201, 203
Pandi, 68, 69
Panulirus polyphagus, 307
Paphia malabarica, 269, 306
Par Estuary, 345, 348, 371-374
Paracalanus aculeatus, 231, ,236
Paracalanus sp., 79, 195
Paradiastylis culicoides, 231
Paraheteromastus tunuis, 244
Paralia sulcata 108
Parangipettai, 131, 143, 154, 159
Parapenaeopsis sculptilis, 46
Partially mixed estuaries, 7
Particulate matter (PM), 350
Particulate organic carbon (POC), 74, 129, 177, 350
Particulate organic matter, 74
Particulate organic nitrogen (PON), 137, 138, 177
Parvocalanus crassirostris, 236
PCHO, 129
Peak flood, 372
Pearl spots, 10, 197, 198, 208, 307
Pectinaria crassa, 153
Pediastrum, 224, 250, 352
Pelagic and demersal fishes, 245
Pelagic fauna, 245
Pelegic tunicate, 79, 232
Penaeid, 64, 240, 307
Penaeidea, 82
Penaeus carinatus, 231
Penaeus indicus 46, 62, 87-89, 103, 158, 207, 231, 240-242, 256
Penaeus japonicus, 44, 88
Penaeus marguiensis, 88, 89, 274
Penaeus monodon, 45, 46, 62, 65, 87-89
Penaeus semisulcatus, 88
Penicillium, 40
Penilia avirostris, 298
Periclimenes sp., 231
Periclimenes indicus, 231, 240
Peridinium, 224
Peridinium depressum, 138, 267
Peridinium ovatum, 76
Perioculodes longimanus, 231
Periyar River, 201, 203, 206, 244-246
Perna viridis, 158, 302
Pestalotia, 40
Pesticides, 10, 97, 98, 159, 209
Peterson grab, 237
Phasa, 43, 44
Phenolics, 363
Phoenix paludosa, 42
Phormidium, 144
Phoronids, 153
Phoronis architecta, 153
Phosphate values, 59, 60, 97, 106, 114, 216, 217, 288, 289, 363
Phosphate-phosphorus(PO_4-P), 31, 33, 59, 192, 193, 248, 249, 323, 329, 333, 354
Photis longicaudata, 230
Photosynthesis, 194, 213, 219, 226, 227, 293
Physical features 125-132
Physico-chemical features, 100, 101
Phytoplankters, 59, 97
Phytoplankton, 8, 31-35, 48, 49, 57, 61, 75-77, 97-100, 107, 108, 138-147, 192, 194, 250, 289-295, 350, 351, 355
Phytoplankton biomass, 31, 143, 212, 219, 220

Phytoplankton bloom, 61, 115, 129, 221
Phytoplankton composition, 223-229
Pichavaram mangrove, 123, 143, 144
Pimpara River, 379
Pinnotheres gracilis, 268
Pinnularia alpina, 139
Pinnularia viridis, 115
Pisces, 38, 270
Placer deposits, 75, 89
Planarians, 153
Plankton biomass, 266-268
Plankton density, 212, 266, 267
Platycephalus sp., 103, 151
Pledorina, 224
Pleurobrachia globosa, 62, 231
Pleurosigma, 223
Pleurosigma aestuarii, 76, 108
Pleurosigma delicatula, 76
Pleurosigma elongatum, 98, 139
Pleurosigma normanii, 98, 115
POC, 74, 129
Poecilochaetus johnsoni, 80
Poecilochaetus serpens, 153
Pollutants, 9, 10, 100, 103, 107-109, 112,197, 320, 321, 326, 328, 364, 365, 369, 382, 386, 387
Pollution, 47-50, 64, 65, 73, 98, 100, 102, 103, 109, 117-121, 159, 160, 197, 198, 238, 243, 244, 246, 247, 274, 275, 309-311, 324, 331, 350, 359, 362, 372, 375, 377, 382, 383, 386-388
Pollution index, 33
Polychaete larvae, 62, 80, 232
Polychaetes 9, 38, 80-85, 116, 153, 154, 194, 195, 197, 231, 237, 238, 246, 251, 267, 269, 270, 301, 302
Polychlorinated biphenyls (PCB), 387
Polyclad, 153
Polydora, 195
Polyester fabrics
Polynemus, 157
Polynemus paradiseus, 43
Polynuclear aromatic hydrocarbons (PAH_s), 387
Pomadasys, 157
PON, 129
Pondichery, 168
POP, 129
Porteresia coarctata, 41
Powai lake, 332
Potomides cingulatus, 155
Pranasus pinguis, 150, 151
Prawn farming, 10, 11, 274, 306, 307
Prawn fishery, 10, 87-89
Prawn seeds, 88, 89, 273, 274
Prawns, 10, 43, 45, 46, 64, 87-89, 102, 103, 157, 158, 205, 207, 209, 221, 238, 240-242, 256, 306-309, 362
Prentice Island, 40, 197
Primary production, 35, 77, 194, 213-215, 279, 293
Primary production with depth, 215, 216
Prionospio cirrobranchiata, 153
Prionospio malmgreni, 153
Prionospio pinnata, 153
Prionospio polybranchiata, 244
Prionospio sp., 238
Production of bricks
Prorocentrum micans, 76, 223
Protochordata, 267
Protozoans, 36, 108, 116, 267
Pseudodiaptomous binghami, 79
Pseudodiaptomus annandalei, 236
Pseudodiaptomus aurivilli, 236

Pseudodiaptomus jonesi, 236
Pseudodiaptomus serricaudatus, 236
Pseudodoptomus binghami malayalus, 236
Pseudodoptomus tollingarae, 230, 236
Pseudopolydora kempi, 153
Pseudorhombus sp, 151, 160, 195
Pseudosciaena axillaris, 87
Pteropoda, 267, 296
Pterosagitta draco, 300
Puffer fish, 152
Purna, 345, 362-364
Purna River, 362, 370
Purse-seining, 272, 273

R

Radioactive waste, 331
Radionuclides
Rainfall, 19-22, 29, 71, 114, 118, 131, 184, 190, 191, 202, 213, 235, 277, 322
Rampani, 271, 272
Rastelliger kanagurta, 240
Rays, 157
Reis Magos Bars, 279
Research Vessal Gaveshani, 41, 73-75, 79, 82
Rewas, 336, 338
Rhaphoneis amphiceros, 108
Rhizophora apiculata, 70
Rhizophora mucronata, 304, 305
Rhizosolenia, 138, 139, 141
Rhizosolenia robusta, 139, 141
Rhizosolenia alata, 76, 139, 141
Rhizosolenia styliformis, 228
Richardson's number (R_1), 285
Risk assessment, 388
River Auranga, 345, 348
River Cooum, 105, 106, 108, 114
River currents, 338
River Kali, 11, 264-275
River Kolak 345, 348, 375-377
River Mahim, 320, 322, 332
River Meenachil, 201, 203
River Muvattupuzha, 201, 203
River Pamba, 201, 203
River Par, 371-374
River Periyar, 201, 203
Riverine environment
Riverine flow data, 338, 339
Rock oysters, 308
Rotifers, 36, 84, 108, 116
Rupnarain, 27
Rushikulya Estuary, 11, 56-65
Rushikulya river mouth, 57
Rutile, 75

S

Sabarmati Estuary, 1, 2, 345
Saccobranchus sp., 103
Saccostrea cucullata, 154, 155
Sagar Island, 29, 30, 38, 40, 42
Sagitta bedoti, 62, 231, 236, 300
Sagitta enflata, 62, 236, 300
Sagitta ferox
Sagitta plulchra, 194, 300
Sagitta robusta, 231, 300
Sagitta bipunctata, 194
Sagitta enflata, 231
Sagitta oceania, 236
Sagitta sp, 159
Saline species, 79
Saline- wedge, 7, 72
Salinity zonations, 7
Salt creek, 89
Salt wedge estuaries, 7

Salt creek, 89
Salt wedge estuaries, 7
Salt-wedge, 192, 282-285, 328, 377
Salvinia detritus, 239
Salvinia sp., 208, 209, 238, 239, 253
Sand, 7, 40, 41, 71, 248, 249, 300
Sand bars, 7, 95, 286, 287, 367
Sand-silt clay, 40, 41, 248, 249
Sandy silt, 75, 248, 249
Sanguinolaria diphos, 154
Santhome, 96
Sardinella, 157, 240
Sardinella longicep, 150, 151, 240
Sargassum cinereum, 309
Sarotherodon mossambicus, 256
Scaphopoda, 82
Scatophagus argus, 151, 157
Schizoporella cochinensis, 235
Schmackeria tollingeri
Sciaena sp., 103, 240
Sciaenids, 10, 157, 305
Scomberoides tol, 151
Scottolana sp., 302
Scylla serrata, 65, 103, 256
Scyphiphora hydrophyllacea, 69
Sea anemone, 153, 238
Seabed morphlogy, 75
Seasonal salinity cycle, 8, 29, 30, 212, 219
Seawater incursion, 72, 338, 367
Secchi Disk readings, 128, 192, 212
Secutor reconius, 150, 151
Sediment and Vegetation, 41, 42
Sediment characteristics, 248, 249
Sediment movement, 3
Sedimentological studies, 75
Sediments, 64, 65, 75, 152, 169, 170, 171, 192, 195, 197, 246, 300, 301, 324, 325, 357
Selaroides leptolepis, 150
Selvasa discharge, 379
Semidiurnal tides, 29, 71, 280, 379
Sensible heat, 184
Sergestid shrimp, 295, 307
Serpulids, 198
Serranus, 157
Sesarma brockii, 156
Setipinna godavariensis, 86
Setipinna phasa, 43, 44
Setipinna taty, 44, 86, 150, 151
Settled detritus, 8, 222
Sewage treatment, 9, 10, 112, 243
Shrimps, 64, 270
Shoals, 7, 286, 287
Silago sihama, 65, 157
Silicates, 31, 61
Silicate-silicon, 73, 107, 192, 193, 289
Silicoflagellate sp., 107, 108, 223
Sillago sihama, 103, 151
Silty clay, 75, 81, 152, 248, 249, 254
Silty sand, 75, 248, 274
Siphonophores, 62, 79, 80, 231, 295, 296
Sipunculida, 62, 82, 195, 303
Siridao Beach, 301
Skeletonema, 223
Skeletonema costatum, 76, 77, 98, 115, 139, 223, 224
Sludge digestion
Smaller brachyuran, 155
Smectite
Sodium(Na), 72
Solea heinii, 240
Soleidae, 240
Solen sp., 153
Soles ovata, 150
Sonneratia apetala, 42, 70

Southwest monsoon, 20, 21, 23, 29, 30, 71, 183, 184, 203, 280, 366
Spheroma annandelei, 237
Spheroma sp., 231
Spheroma terebrans, 237
Sphyraena jello, 151
Spillway at Thottapally, 207
Spinipalma, 155
Spiochaetopterus costatum, 153
Spirogyra, 223, 250
Spirulina, 144
Sponges, 198
Spring tides, 350, 362, 369, 372, 379
Staphylinid beetles, 38
Staphylinidae, 38
Stenohaline, 38, 254
Stigonema, 144
Stolephorus macropa, 150, 151
Stolephorus sp, 103, 158
Storms, 20
Streptococcus faecalis, 239
Suaeda maritima, 70
Suaeda monoica, 70
Submergence of the river banks
Sulphate (SO_4), 72, 174
Sulphate-chlorinity ratio, 288
Sulphide, 324
Summer Season, 20
Sunderbans, 8, 10, 28, 40, 41, 43, 44, 46, 47
Surface water, 60, 75, 130-132
Surirella eximia, 139
Suspended detritus, 8
Suspended matter, 3, 73, 74, 244, 328, 333, 334, 355, 357
Suspended solids, 322, 357, 360, 361, 367, 377
Syndera tabulata, 108
Syngathus spicifer, 76, 151

T

Tabellaria fenestrata, 98
Tachysurus arius, 65
Tachysurus maculatus, 256
Talorchestia, 155
Tambraparani, 3
Tanaidacea, 82, 270
Tanaidaceans, 195, 232
Tanaids, 86
Tanella indica, 79
Tapi (Tapti), 356, 357
Tapi Estuary, 345, 348, 356, 357
Tapti Estuary, 174, 345, 356, 357
Tardigrades, 81, 84
Taxa, 295
Teleosts, 240
Tellina sp., 153
Terebralia palustus, 81
Thalamiter danae, 156
Thalassiosira cormandeliana, 139
Thalassiothrix longissima, 76, 77, 139
Thaleaceans, 62
Thallasionema nitzschioides, 76, 77, 98
Thallasiothrix frauenfeldii, 76, 77, 98, 139
Thallassiosira gravida, 267
Thames Estuary, 386
Thane Creek, 318, 320, 321, 324, 326-330, 340-342
Thanneermukkam Bund, 204, 207, 208, 238, 249, 250, 253
Thar Desert, 19
Thattapally spillway, 207
The African Payal, 208-209, 238
Therapon jarbua, 64, 65, 103, 150, 151
Thiobacilli, 160, 239
Thraustochytrids

Threadfins, 10
Thrissocles, 157, 240
Thryssa sp., 150, 151
Thunder-storms, 20
Tidal creek, 38, 41
Tidal currents, 80, 249, 280, 338, 357
Tidal cycle, 72, 129, 212, 244, 279, 295, 335, 338, 362-364, 367, 369, 372
Tidal flushing, 362, 363
Tidal influx, 206
Tidal mixing model, 126, 127
Tidal prism method, 338, 359, 360, 367, 369
Tidal propagation, 280-282
Tidal rhythm, 212, 265
Tidal water, 243
Tides, 29, 71, 72, 75, 125, 133-135, 153, 154, 264, 265, 321, 336, 361-363, 366-369, 372, 377, 379
Tilapia mossambica, 103
Tintinnids, 62
Tool maach, 44
Tortanus forcipatus, 79
Total dissolved solids (TDS), 175-177
Total suspended matter (TSM), 73, 74, 175-177
Toxic and Non-toxic metals, 73
Trace elements, 172-174, 249
Trace metals, 173, 246, 306, 310, 324, 325, 329, 330, 363, 364
Trawling, 46, 47, 273
Triacanthus brevirostris, 151
Triceratium dubium, 108
Triceratium favus, 108
Triceratium reticulatum, 108, 139
Triceratium scuptum, 108
Trichiurus pantulii, 44
Trichocera sp., 251
Trichodesmium, 142-144, 223
Trichodesmium bloom, 61, 300
Trichodesmium erythraeum, 138, 139, 267, 290
Trichodesmium theibauti, 76
Trombay, 320
Tropical cyclones, 20, 21
Tropical phytoplankton, 226-229
Tunicates, 194
Turbellarians, 81, 83, 84, 304
Turbidity, 30, 59, 72, 77, 111, 128, 132, 212,215, 228, 300
Turtle eggs, 64
Tuthis sp., 103
Two-layered flow estuaries, 7
Tylosurus strongylurus, 151

U

Uca sp., 155
Udhna Creek, 358, 359, 361
Ulberia, 35
Ulhas River, 318, 320, 326
Ulothrix, 144
Undinula sp., 195
Upper reaches, 6, 30, 37

V

Vaigal, 3
Vaikom, 248
Vainateyam, 67
Van Veen grab, 237
Vanishing mangroves, 69
Vapi, 375, 376, 379
Varoli, 345
Vasishta branch, 72
Vasista-Godavari Estuary, 67, 72, 73, 80
Vegetation, 69-71
Vellar Estuary, 11, 123-162

Vellorita cyprinoids, 255
Vembanad Lake, 11, 202-204, 208, 209, 248-256
Versova, 318-320, 340-342
Versova Creek, 318
Viaderiana sp., 238
Vibrio, 162
Villorita cyprinoides, 302, 306
Villorita sp., 153, 197, 209, 238, 251
Volvox, 224
Vrudha, 67

W

Waltair Coast, 86
Water Characteristics, 111, 113
Wastewater discharge, 9, 10, 47-50, 206, 326, 363, 364, 373-376, 379
Water-soluble phosphorus, 110, 111
West coast, 183-199
Western disturbances, 20
Western Ghats, 67, 189, 264, 277, 337
Wetlands, 307, 318, 382, 383
White prawn, 158
Whitebait, 86, 103
Willingdon Island, 248
Wood-boring community, 236, 237
Worli, 320
Worli Bay, 319, 323

X

Xylocarpus mollucensis, 42

Z

Zinc, 97, 110
Zircon, 75
Zooplankton, 8, 31-38, 48, 57, 62, 63, 77-80, 100, 108–110, 116, 147-155, 194, 195, 230-235, 250, 251, 267, 268, 295-300, 340-343, 355
Zooplankton and phytoplankton, 219-221
Zooplankton biomass, 8, 31, 195, 196, 219, 250, 251, 295-297, 340-343
Zooplankton organisms, 35, 36, 48, 49, 195, 196, 221
Zuari Agrochemicals Ltd., 309, 384.
Zuari basins, 277
Zuari Estuary, 11, 277-311

Author Index

A

Abidi, S.A.H. 262
Abraham, M. 165
Abraham, S. 232, 263
Achuthankutty, C.T. 298, 299, 302, 307, 311, 314
Ajmalkhan, S. 166
Anantharaj, B. 106, 108, 110, 111, 113
Annapurna, C. 79, 90
Ansari, Z. A. 83, 84, 90, 209, 237–238, 256–257, 302–305, 310, 311, 315
Ansell, A.D. 235, 256
Anthony, A. 253-255, 256, 257
Aravindakshan, P.N. 239, 257
Arunachalam, M. 200
Arvindakshan, P.N.R. 260
Azariah, J. 117, 121
Azis, P.K.A. 190, 191, 192-199, 200

B

Babu, P.V.L. 170, 178
Bagchi, M.M.
Bagyalakshmi, V. 113
Baidya, A.
Balachand, A.N. 246, 260
Balachandran, K.K. 259, 260
Balachandran, V.K. 262
Balaji, M. 86, 92
Balakrishnan, K.P. 207, 212, 257, 263
Balasubrahmanyn, K. 154, 162, 166
Balasubramanian, N.K. 200
Balasubramanian, T. 235, 242, 243, 257, 260, 262, 314
Bandyopadhyay, A. 75, 90
Banerjee, G. 311
Banerjee, M.K. 46, 51
Barnes, R.S.K. 6, 14

Bhargava, R.M.S. 279, 290, 293, 311, 312, 314
Bhat, U.G. 265, 269, 270, 271
Bhatnagar, G.P. 128, 162
Bhattathiri, P.M.A. 262, 293, 312
Bhosle, N.B. 301, 312, 316, 344, 380
Bhunia, A.
Bhushan, G.P
Bikshan, G. 179
Bois Penrose, 286, 312
Borole, D.V. 93, 357, 380
Bose, B.B. 29, 30, 31, 51
Bowden, K.F. 7, 14
Bristow, R.C, 205, 211, 257
Bukhari, S. 316
Burton, J.D. 162, 380

C

Cameron, W.M. 5, 14
Caspers, H. 6, 14
Chakarbarty, R.D. 46, 51
Chakrabarty, C.
Chakraborti, R.K.
Chakrborty, C.
Chakraborty, S. K. 40, 51
Chamarthi, S. 91
Chander, S. 381
Chandra, R 43, 51
Chandramohan, D. 163, 165, 308, 313-316
Chandramohan, P. 72, 73, 78-80, 90, 92, 93
Chandran, R. 129-137, 138, 152, 153, 161-163
Chatterjee, A. 256, 315
Chatterjee, A.K.,29, 51
Chatterjee, N.
Chatterjee, P
Chatterji, A. 90, 257, 311
Chattopadhyay, S.
Chavan, J.B. 164
Cherian, T. 280, 300, 312, 317
Chetty, P.M. 80, 90
Choudhury, A. 38, 39–40, 50–51, 53–55
Chowdhery, H.J. 40, 51

D

Dalal, V.N.K. 315, 380
Damodaran, K,T. 195, 200
Daniel, A. 116, 121
Das, B.K. 178
Das, P.K. 279, 285, 312, 314
Das, R.L.
Das, S. 90
Das, T.M.
Dasgupta, D.
Datta, N.C.
Day, J.H.. 6, 14
De, D.K.
De, T.K. 32, 33, 35, 44, 51
Dehadrai, P.V. 279, 312
Derbyshire, M. 212, 257
Desai, B.N. 209, 237, 257, 259, 321–322, 324, 329–330, 332–335, 340– 341, 343–344, 380, 381
Desousa, S.N. 91, 288, 289, 312
Devadoss, P. 165
Devassy, V.P. 250–251, 257, 262, 290–293, 299, 312–313
Devendran, K. 160, 163
Devi, C.B.L. 207, 212, 240, 242, 257, 260– 261
Devi, K.S. 238, 244-246, 258, 262
Devi, S.L. 88, 90
Dhargalkar, V.K., 314, 315, 316

Dharmaraj, K. 200
Divakaran, O. 200
Dora, Y.L. 249, 261
D'Silva, C. 301, 312
Dube, S.K. 90
Dutt, S. 86, 90
Dwivedi, S.N. 302, 314-316
Dyer, K.R. 3, 125-128, 163, 359, 380

E

Easo, S. 241, 258
Eisma, D. 93
Emery, K.O. 6, 14
ENVIS(Environmental Information System), 3, 14

F

Fernandes, A.A. 343
Fernando, O.J. 155-157, 163
Fondekar, S.P. 316

G

Gajbhiye, S.N. 340-343, 380
Ganpati, P.N. 67, 68, 88, 93
Ganguly, A.K. 344
Garg, K.L. 40, 51
George, K.C. 240, 258
George, M.J. 212, 230, 240, 241, 311
Ghosh, A. 44, 52
Ghosh, A.N.
Ghosh, B.B. 47, 52
Ghosh, P.B. 35, 52
Ghosh, P.K.
Ghosh, S.K. 36, 41, 42, 52
Goes, J.I. 290-293, 312
Gopalakrishnan, T.C. 257, 260
Gopalakrishnan, V. 43, 46, 52
Gopalan, U.K. 238, 253, 258
Gopinathan C.K. 210, 211, 212, 250, 251, 257, 258, 261
Gopinathan, C.P. 215, 223, 224, 258
Gore, P.S. 239, 258, 262
Goswami, S.C. 295-297, 299, 311, 313, 314
Goswami, U. 313
Gouda, R. 57–61, 63–66
Gouveia, A.D. 316
Govindan, K. 343
Gracias, E.S. 311
Gross, M.G. 387, 389
Gujar, A.R. 317
Gunaga, V. 264, 266, 273–276
Gupta, M.D.

H

Halder, D.D.
Hameed, P.S. 163
Haridas, P. 233, 259, 262
Harkantra, S.N. 269, 275, 301–302, 313, 315
Hedgpeth, J.W. 6, 14,

I

Ilangovan, G. 163
Ingole, B.S. 302, 311, 313, 315
Iwata, H. 166
Iyer, H.K. 257, 259, 260, 261
Iyer, K.M. 160, 163

J

Jagtap, T.G. 305, 313, 316
Jain, C.K. 92
Jaitly, A.K.
Jana, T.K.

Jayabal, R. 154, 155, 158, 163
Jayabalan, N. 162, 163
Jayalakshmy, K.V. 224, 246, 257–260
Jayaraman, R. 212, 262
Jena T.K.
Jhingran, V.G., 43, 44, 52
Joglekar, A. 86, 92
Johns, B. 71, 90
Joseph, K.J. 224, 225, 259, 262
Joseph, K.O. 100, 101, 104, 117, 120, 121
Joseph, P.S. 138–143, 163, 164
Joseph, T. 205, 211, 259, 260

K

Kadam, A.N. 331, 343
Kakati, V.S. 268, 275
Kalyanasundaram, M. 155, 158, 164
Kalyani, M. 154, 155, 163
Kannan, L. 162, 164
Kannupandi, T. 154, 156, 164, 166
Kanti, A. 311
Karande, A.A. 157, 164
Karanth, N.G.K., 308, 313
Kartha, ,K.N.K. 212, 258
Kasinathan, R. 158, 164, 166
Kawabata, Z. 144, 164
Ketchum, C.H. 7, 14, 15
Khan, A.S.
Khan, R. A. 47, 48, 49, 52
Khan, S.A. 156, 164-166
Knox, G.A. 7, 14,
Kolhatkar, V.M. 343
Kondalarao, B. 81, 85, 90
Konnur, R.
Konnur, R.G. 117, 126, 276
Krishnakumar, K., 200
Krishnamurthy, K. 128, 137, 139, 143, 164
Krishnamurthy, S. 160, 164
Krishnamurthy, V. 274, 276
Krishnan, T. 156, 164
Krishnankutty, M. 257
Krishnayya, C.G. 44, 52
Kshirasagar, T.V.S.R. 75, 91
KSSP(Kerala Sastra Sahitya Parishat), 259
Kumar, P.K.D. 207, 259, 339, 340, 343
Kumaran, V.S. 258
Kumari, L.K. 9, 14, 301, 313
Kundu, S.K. 36, 50, 52
Kurian, C.V. 164, 165, 167, 209, 238, 259
Kurup, B. 259
Kurup, B.M. 255, 256
Kurup, B.N. 259
Kurup, M.B.
Kusuma, M.S. 266-267, 276
Kutty, M.K. 209, 237, 257, 259–261
Kuttyamma, V.J. 241, 259

L

Lakshmanaperumalswamy, P. 253, 263
Lakshmi, R. 113
Lal, B, 35, 52
Lalitha, S. 258
Lande, V. 308, 315
Lauff, G.H. 5, 14, 15, 261
Lokabharati, P.A. 308, 311, 313, 314, 316
Lyla, P.S. 165

M

Madhupratap, M. 204, 209, 232, 233, 236, 259–262, 316
Magendran, A. 164
Mahapatra, B
Majumdar, S.K.
Mallik, T.K. 260
Mandalia, A.V. 359, 380, 381
Margalef, R. 260
Martin, J.M. 93
Mathew, K.J. 241, 258
Mathew, T. 200
Matilal, S. 41, 42, 53
Matondkar, S.G. P. 307, 314, 316
MCGB(Municipal Corporation of Greater Bombay), 320, 326, 343
McIntyre, A.D. 155, 165
McLusky, D.S. 302, 314
Meenakshikunjamma, P.P, 258
Menezes, M.R. 311
Menon, C.A. 204, 260
Menon, G.G. 268, 276
Menon, N.R. 235, 260
Menon, P.G. 257
Menzel, D.W. 221, 260
Metcalf & Eddy/EEC. 320, 343
Michael, G.S. 316
Miranda, P.I. 192, 200
Mislankar, P.G. 317
Misra, P. M. 64, 66
Misra, S. 42, 53
Mitra, A. 50, 53
Mitra, P.M. 44, 51
Mohan, D. 166
Mukherjee, B.B. 41, 53
Muley, C. D. 344
Muniyandi, K. 165
Murty, C.R.
Murty, C.S. 279, 282, 283, 285, 312, 314, 316
Murty, K.V.R. 81, 85, 90
Murty, M.R. 75, 90
Murty, P.S. 75, 90
Murty, P.S.N. 249, 260, 263
Murty, V.S. 92

N

Naidu, A.S. 74, 90
Naidu, V.S. 321, 343
Naik, C.G. 316
Naik, U.G. 276
Nair, P.V.R.
Nair, A. 315
Nair, A.K.K. 258, 261
Nair, C.K. 260
Nair, G.S. 260
Nair, G.B. 165
Nair, K.K.C. 231, 234, 241, 257, 260
Nair, M. 246, 247, 259, 260
Nair, N.B. 104, 113, 165, 189–200, 235–237, 258, 260, 261
Nair, P.S.R. 157, 162, 165
Nair, P.V.R 258
Nair, S. 308, 311, 313, 314
Nair, S.A. 314, 315
Nair, S.R.S. 242, 261, 307, 311, 314
Nair, V.R. 296, 299, 300, 314, 316, 343, 380
Nammalwar, P. 102, 104, 111–113, 119–121
Nampoothiri, G. 316
Nandi, N.C
Nandi, S. 38, 44, 53
Nandy, A.C. 35, 53
Narappa, K.V. 79, 90
Narasimham, K.A. 92

Narayanan, B. 256
Narayanaswamy, C. 322, 343
Narvekar, P.V. 331, 344, 361, 364, 367, 370, 380, 381
Natarajan, P. 158, 165
Natarajan, R. 154, 156, 162–166
Nath, D.
Nayak, G.N. 274, 276
Nayak, L. 66
Neelakantan, B. 264–266, 268–271, 274–276
Neelakantan, K. 275
Nigam, R. 1, 14
NIO (National Institute of- Oceanography, Goa), 359, 367, 380

O

Oak, S. 314
Ouseph, P.P. 246, 261

P

Padmavati, G. 295, 311, 314
Pal, A.K. 50, 53
Pal, R.
Pal, U.C. 31, 54
Palanichamy, S. 164
Panda, D. 66
Panda, D.K.
Pandian, A.P. 129, 165
Panigrahy, R.C. 57–61, 63–66
Panikkar, N.K. 1, 14
Pant, A. 293, 294, 314, 316
Parameswaran, U.S. 251, 261
Parulekar, A.H. 90, 257, 301–304, 306, 307, 311, 313–316
Patel, B. 331, 344
Pathak, S. 315
Patil, T. S. 380
Patnaik, K.C. 64, 66
Paulinose, V.T. 90, 257
Paulpandian, A.L. 154, 163, 164
Perumal, P. 159, 165
Peter, K.J. 90
Peter, M.G. 260
Pillai, P.P. 231–233, 261, 263
Pillai, S.M. 46, 53
Pillai, V. K. 160, 163, 224, 225, 259
Pillay, T.V.R. 5, 10, 14, 43, 46, 53, 240, 255, 261
Poddar, T.K. 38, 53
Prasad, B.V. 91
Prasad, N.V.B.S.S. 93
Prasad, P.N. 276
Prasad, P.R. 93
Premswarup, T.V. 77, 91
Pritchard, D.W. 3, 5, 7, 14, 15, 204, 261
Purandra, B.K. 249, 261
Purkayastha, R.P.
Purushan, K.S. 209, 261
Purushothaman, A. 128, 137, 139, 160, 162, 164–166
Pylee, A. 244, 262

Q

Qasim, S. Z. 15, 152, 155, 165, 204, 209–223, 226–230, 258, 261–263, 278, 279, 283, 284, 286–289, 304, 306, 312, 315, 317, 388, 389

R

Rabindranath, P. 259
Radhakrishnan, E.V. 239, 262, 263
Raghukumar, C. 308, 309, 315, 316

Ragothaman, G. 115, 121, 122, 380
Raha, B.N. 90
Rahaman, A.A. 168, 178
Rajagopal, M.D. 289, 314, 315
Rajagopal, M.P. 312
Rajamanickam, G.V. 314
Rajamanickam, S. 166
Rajan, J.P. 14
Rajan, K. 3, 15
Rajendran, A. 14, 73, 91, 129, 137, 159, 160, 162, 165–167, 295, 313, 315
Rajendran, N.
Rajyalakshmi, T. 45, 53, 77, 91
Ram, J. 343, 380
Ram, M.J. 380
Ramachandran, S. 145–147, 165
Ramadhas, V. 144, 159, 166, 167
Ramaiah, N. 311
Ramaiyan, V. 166
Ramakrishna, A. 93
Ramamirtham, C.P. 212, 262
Ramamoorthi, K. 125–137, 152, 155, 161–164, 166–167
Ramamurthy, V.D. 164
Ramana, Y.U. 72, 91
Ramanathan, A.L. 168, 170, 175, 177–179
Ramanathan, N.L. 388, 389
Rambabu, A.V.S. 81, 91
Ramdhas, V. 166
Ramesh, A. 160, 166
Ramesh, R. 179
Rangarajan, K. 125, 166
Rao, A.D. 90, 91
Rao, A.V.P. 30, 46, 54
Rao, B.K. 89, 91, 92
Rao, B.N. 75, 91
Rao, B.V.S. 90
Rao, C.B, 74, 90
Rao, Ch.M. 74, 91, 94
Rao, D.G. 300, 315
Rao, D.S. 80, 81, 91–93
Rao, G.M.N. 69, 70, 73, 91, 92
Rao, G.N. 72, 89, 91
Rao, G.S. 47, 54, 88, 89, 91, 92
Rao, K.K. 235, 262, 315
Rao, K.S. 86, 92, 93
Rao, L.V.
Rao, L.V.G. 75, 93, 312, 317
Rao, M.B. 86, 91, 92
Rao, M.P. 90
Rao, M.S. 90
Rao, M.U. 69, 70, 73, 76, 77, 91, 92
Rao, P.S. 91
Rao, P.V. 241, 262
Rao, S.R. 1, 13–15
Rao, T.S.S. 78–90, 232, 234, 259, 260, 262
Rao, T.C.S. 300, 315
Rao, V.B. 71, 92
Rao, V.N.R. 105–109, 113, 115, 121, 122
Rao, V.R. 71, 72, 91, 92
Rao, V.V. 72, 86, 87, 90, 92
Rao, Y.R. 71,
Rao, Y.R.S. 89, 92
Rasalam, E.J. 251–253, 262
Raveendran, O. 258, 262
Ravichandran, C. 244, 262
Ray, P.
Ray, S. 38, 54
Ray, Y.R.
Reddy, B.S.R. 71, 72, 91, 92
Reddy, C.R. 276
Reddy, C.V.G. 91, 114, 116–118, 122, 212, 261, 289, 315–317
Reghu, R. 240, 262

Remani, K.N. 244, 246, 258, 262, 263
Rivonkar, C.U. 306, 307, 315, 316
Rodrigues, C.L. 90
Rokade, M.A. 380, 381
Roy, A.K.
Roy, J.M.
Roy, S.
Royan, J.P. 313
Russell, R.J. 6,15,
Ryther, J.H. 221, 260

S

Sabnis, M.M. 333, 335,344, 380, 381
Saha, A.
Saha, S.B. 31, 54
Sahu, B.K.
Sahu, K.C. 66
Sai-Sastry, A.G.R. 72, 73, 92, 93
Sajan, K. 195, 200
Samuel, C.T. 255, 259
Sankaran, T.M. 259
Sankaranarayanan, V.N. 15, 215, 217–219, 221, 246, 256, 260, 261, 263, 320, 344
Sankolli, K.N. 268, 275, 276
Santhakumari, V. 233, 263
Santhakumary, N. 239, 263
Santra, S.C. 31, 54
Sanzgiri, S. 312
Sardessai, S. 41, 54
Sarin, M.M. 380
Sarkar, S. 36, 54
Sarkar, S.K. 36–38, 54
Sarladevi, K. 263
Sarma, D.V.R. 67–81, 90–93
Sarma, G.V.S. 92
Sarma, M.S.S. 75, 93
Sarma, R.V. 321, 339, 340, 343, 380, 381
Sarma, V.V. 74, 93
Sarma, V.V.J. 72, 93
Sarojini, Y. 76, 77, 92
Sasamal, S.K. 41, 55
Sastry, A.G.R.S. 93
Sastry, Y.A. 87, 93
Sathe-Pathak, V. 309, 316
Sathiyamurthy, K. 162, 166
Saxena, D. 308, 316
Sebastian, M.J. 251–253, 259, 262
Seetaramaswamy. A. 169, 171, 172, 178, 179
Seethapathi. P.V. 92
Selvakumar, R.A. 297, 300, 307, 311, 313, 314, 316
Selvakumar, S. 156, 166
Sen Gupta, R. 278, 279, 283, 284, 286–289, 312, 315, 320, 344
Sen, P.R.
Seralathan, P. 169, 171, 172, 178, 179
Seshadri, R. 164
Seshaiya, R.V. 125, 166
Shailaja, M.S. 294, 316
Shanmugam, A. 158, 166
Sharma, P. 357, 380
Sharma, S. 316
Sharma, V.S. 93
Shenoy, S. 268, 276
Shetty, D.C. 271–273, 276
Sheety, H.P.C. 30, 31, 34, 36, 55
Shetye, S.R. 280–283, 285, 316
Shoba, V. 192, 200
Shynamma, C.S. 212, 260, 263
Sikka, S.N. 93
Silas, E.G. 231–233, 263

Singbal, S.Y.S. 279, 310, 315–317
Singbal, Y.S. 295, 313
Singh, B.N.
Sinha, B. 39, 40, 55
Sinha, P.C. 50, 55, 90, 91
Sircar, A.K.
Sivadas, P. 256
Sivakumar, V. 162, 163
Sivaswamy, S.N. 95–100, 104
Smayda, T.J. 8, 15
Somaseker, M. 157, 166
Somayajulu, B.L.K. 74, 93, 380
Sreekumari, K.R. 253, 263
Sreepada, R.A. 311, 315
Sridhar, M.K.C. 95, 98, 102–105, 109, 111, 113
Srikrishnadhas, B. 148, 149, 152, 154, 162, 166
Srinivasan, T.M. 1, 14
Sripathi, K. 156, 166
Sriraman, K. 166
Steele, J. H. 221, 261, 263
Stevenson R. E. 6, 14
Stirling, A. 311, 314
Subnis, M.M. 344
Subrahmanyam, M. 87, 88, 93
Subramanian, A.N. 166
Subramanian, B. R. 139, 144, 166, 167
Subramanian, P. 158, 159, 163, 165
Subramanian, V. 174, 177–179
Subramanayam, V. 317
Subramanyam, R. 115, 122
Suchindran, G. K. 260
Sudhakar, U. 93
Sujansingani, K. H. 44, 55
Sumitra-Vijayaraghavan 262, 313–315
Sundar, D. 316
Sundararaj, V. 128, 137, 164, 166
Swamy, A. S. R. 74, 89, 91, 94

T

Tanabe, S. 166
Tatsukawa, R. 164, 166
Thakur, N. K. 45, 55
Thangaraj, G. S. 162
Thangaraja, M. 150–152, 158, 166, 167
Thirupad, P. U. V. 114, 116–118, 122
Thomas, A. J. 93
Thomas, M. 164
Thomas, P. A. 307, 316
Tissot, C. 170, 179
Tranter, D. J. 231, 232, 260, 263
Trevellion, A. 256
Tripathy, S. K. 60, 66
Trivedi, S. K. 344

U

Udhayakumar, M. 164
Unnikrishnan, A. S. 280, 316
Unnithan, R. V. 239, 244, 258, 262, 263
Untawale, A. G. 15, 301, 304, 305, 313, 316, 317

V

Vaithiyanathan, P. 178
Valsaraj, C. P. 105–109, 113, 115, 121
Vannucci, M. 234, 263
Varadachari, V. V. R. 312
Varaprasad, S. J. D. 93
Varghese, T. J. 44, 55
Varma, K. K. 280, 312, 317
Vasantha, K. 162, 164
Veerayya, M. 249, 260, 263
Vengayil, D. T. 258

Venkanna, P. 69, 94
Venkataramanujam, K. 152, 167
Venugopal, P. 128, 244, 257–260, 262, 263
Venugopalan, V. K. 129, 137–139, 145–147, 159, 160, 162, 164–167
Verghese, P. U.
Verlencar, X. N. 289, 304, 307, 315, 317
Vijay, T. 92
Vijayalakshmi, G. S. 129, 167
Vijayan, M. 243, 258, 263
Viswakumar, M. 257

W

Wafar, M. V. M. 9, 14, 15, 154, 167, 313–315, 317
Wafar, S. 15, 301, 316, 317
Wagle, B. G. 300, 317
Wallershaus, S. 262
Wyatt, T. 230, 263

Z

Zachariah, T. 243, 263
Zingde, M. D. 287, 310, 317, 319–337, 343, 344, 357–381, 383, 384